WHERE CHEFS EAT

—

A GUIDE TO CHEFS' FAVOURITE RESTAURANTS

WHERE CHEFS EAT

—

A GUIDE TO CHEFS' FAVOURITE RESTAURANTS

Chef selection and reviews
by Joe Warwick

CONTENTS

Key
Preface
Chefs Biographies

KEY

Breakfast
Whether it's a lazy or a snatched one, the chef couldn't start the day without breakfast here.

Late night
Service is over but the night is still young, this is where the chef satisfies any late-night hunger pangs.

Regular neighbourhood
Around the corner from the chef's work or home, this restaurant serves up food good enough to eat regularly.

Local favourite
This is the restaurant that best expresses the cuisine of the chef's home town.

Bargain
When money is limited but their appetite for good food isn't, this is where the chef goes when they're on a budget.

High end
For a special occasion or when money is no object, this is where the chef goes to splash out.

Wish I'd opened
Professional respect and admiration make this the restaurant that the chef wishes they'd opened.

Worth the travel
Across the country or on the other side of the world, there's no distance the chef wouldn't travel to eat at this restaurant.

PREFACE

Where *do* chefs eat? The answer to that question used to be simple: in their kitchens or restaurants' dining rooms when there were no customers around. But the days of chefs being chained to their stoves have long gone. Chefs today neither operate in a vacuum nor do they pretend to. They trawl the world for inspiration and eat around as much as they can closer to home because food is their passion and they love eating out.

The idea for this book was to find out exactly where they do that. We didn't want a list of the 'world's best restaurants'; we wanted the best places to eat, around the world, for specific occasions. So we sent questionnaires to an international line-up of leading chefs, asking them to tell us where they go for breakfast, where they eat late at night, where they think is a bargain, and which high-end restaurants they like to go to for a treat.

The primary objective was to tap into their local knowledge, to discover their favourite places in their part of the world. But we also wanted to know which places had impressed them on their travels, so we asked them about that too. They told us about fried herrings in Stockholm, wet burgers in Istanbul; where to breakfast on congee in Hong Kong and grab a very late bite in Barcelona; about Tokyo sushi bars, 100-year-old San Francisco oyster bars and seafood shacks on the Lebanese coast.

And that's just for starters.

I'd like to thank all the chefs that kindly took the time to take part. This book really wouldn't have been possible without their help. — Joe Warwick

THE CHEFS

Participating chefs and their restaurant recommendations

ADAM AAMANN
Aamanns
Øster Farimagsgade 12, Copenhagen
Copenhagen based re-inventor of the smørrebrød who has since taken the idea to New York.

1.th 158...High end
Damindra 159...........Regular neighbourhood
Krummen & Kagen 163...................Breakfast
Noma 160..............................Wish I'd opened

CARLES ABELLAN
Bravo 24
Plaça de la Rosa del Vents 1, Barcelona
elBulli graduate with multiple tapas bars to his name his most recent being Bravo 24 in the W Hotel.

Can Jubany 327....................Worth the travel
Chicoa 348.............................Local favourite
Garde Manger 477................Worth the travel
Granja Elena 347..........................Bargain
Luz de Gas Port Vell 340.................Late night
El Quim de la Boqueria 343............Breakfast
Tickets 353.............................Worth the travel
Els Tres Porquets 346......................High end

MATTHEW ACCARRINO
SPQR
1911 Fillmore Street, San Francisco
New Jersey born, Culinary Institute of America educated head chef of Italian inspired SPQR.

Aziza 514...................Regular neighbourhood
Benu 515...................................High end
Brenda's French Soul Food 516.......Breakfast
The French Laundry 484........Wish I'd opened
Gary Danko 508...........................High end
Knead Patisserie 510......................Bargain
Lers Ros Thai 516........Regular neighbourhood
Moto 555.............................Worth the travel
Nopa 513....................................Late night
Outerlands 514.............................Breakfast
The Purple Pig 560...............Worth the travel
Saigon Sandwich 504......................Bargain
Sepia 561.............................Worth the travel
Swan Oyster Depot 513...........Local favourite
Tartine Bakery 511........................Breakfast
Uliassi 406...........................Worth the travel
Urban Belly 554.........Regular neighbourhood

HUGH ACHESON
5 & 10
1653 South Lumpkin Street, Athens
Born in Ottawa, resident of Georgia where his trio of restaurants are leading lights in the new South's rising restaurant scene.

Il Buco 595.................Regular neighbourhood
Holeman & Finch Public House 529......Worth the travel
Husk 539...............................Worth the travel
La Lobera di Martin 314........Worth the travel
Nha Trang 590.............................Bargain
Peaches Fine Foods 529..........Local favourite
Thoroughbred Club 540....................High end
Umaido 530..............Regular neighbourhood

GASTÓN ACURIO
Astrid & Gastón
Calle Cantuarias 175, Lima
Founder of an impressive Lima-based restaurant empire that began with Astrid & Gastón in 1994.

Azurmendi 325...................Worth the travel
Blue Ribbon Brasserie 597.............Late night
Brooklyn Fare 600................Wish I'd opened
Fiesta 620...........................Worth the travel
Maido 620.................Regular neighbourhood
Maras 622............................Worth the travel
La Red 620......................Local favourite
Salón de la Felicidad 619................Breakfast

TOM ADAMS
Pitt Cue Co.
1 Newburgh Street, London
From a meat-peddling truck on London's Southbank Adams has gone on to open his first bricks 'n' mortar BBQ outpost in 2012.

19 Numara Bos Cirrik I 210.................Regular neighbourhood
The Black Rat Restaurant 176..........High end
Canton Arms 194........Regular neighbourhood
Koya 225...................Regular neighbourhood
Quo Vadis 228.....................Wish I'd opened
St. John Bread & Wine 209......Local favourite
Testi 210......................................Bargain

ALBERT ADRIÀ
Tickets
Avinguda Parallel 164, Barcelona
Younger brother of Ferran who's recently branched out from pastry to open Tickets and 41 Grados.

ABaC 347..................................High end
Alkimia 345................................High end
Alta Taberna Paco Meralgo 350..............Local favourite
Bar Cañete 342....................Local favourite
Bar Pinotxo 342.........................Breakfast
Ca l'Isidre 342.....................Local favourite
Café Viena 341............................Bargain
Cal Campaner 328..............Wish I'd opened
Can Fabes 327.....................Wish I'd opened
Can Jubany 327....................Worth the travel
La Cañota 351.......................Local favourite
Els Casals 327............................High end
Les Cols 329........................Local favourite
Coure 345..................Regular neighbourhood
Dos Cielos 346.............................High end
Gaig 349.............................Local favourite
Hispania 326........................Local favourite
Miramar 347..............................High end
Pizzeria Du de Cope 414.......Worth the travel
El Quim de la Boqueria 343............Breakfast
Quimet i Quimet 351....................Late night
Rafa's 330.......................Wish I'd opened
Rias de Galicia 352......................High end
Tapas 24 350..............................Bargain
Els Tres Porquets 346......................High end
Umi 111.............................Worth the travel
Vivanda 348.........................Local favourite
El Xampanyet 340..................Local favourite

FERRAN ADRIÀ
elBulli Foundation
Cala Montjoi, Roses, Girona
From 1984 to 2011 he changed the course of haute cuisine with elBulli. He plans to continue that work with his foundation.

Bar Pinotxo 342.........................Breakfast
Bras 282.............................Wish I'd opened
Dos Palillos Barcelona 342.................Regular neighbourhood
Rias de Galicia 352......................High end

THE CHEFS

ANDONI LUIS ADURIZ
Mugaritz
Otazulueta Baserria Aludura Aldea 20,
Errenteria
With credentials that read like a checklist
of Spanish haute cuisine it's not surprising
Aduriz opened award-winning Mugaritz at
just 26.
Asador Etxebarri **324**............Worth the travel
La Bodega Donostiarra **322**.....Local favourite
Bras **282**................................Wish I'd opened
El Celler de Can Roca **329**.....Worth the travel
Elkano **318**......................Regular neighbourhood
The Fat Duck **172**..................Worth the travel
The French Laundry **484**........Wish I'd opened
La Mañueta **335**..............................Breakfast
Momofuku Seiobo **20**............Worth the travel
Quique Dacosta Restaurante **336**.........Worth the travel
Restaurant Yalde **319**......................Bargain
Va Bene Disco Burger **324**..............Late night
wd~50 **594**................Regular neighbourhood

TOM AIKENS
Tom Aikens
43 Elystan Street, London
Koffmann and Robuchon trained, he made
his name as head chef at Pied à Terre before
opening his own restaurants in 2003 and 2006.
L'Arpège **301**..............................High end
Bincho **222**....................................Bargain
Hegia **275**......................Worth the travel
Hélène Darroze **218**.....................Breakfast
The Hoste Arms **178**..............Worth the travel
Polpo **227**......................................Bargain
The Wolseley **221**..........................Breakfast
Zuma **190**..........................Local favourite

FAUSTO LUIGI AIROLDI
Casino Lisboa
Alameda dos Oceanos, Lisbon
Mozambique born but proudly Portuguese his
current portfolio includes overseeing the culi-
nary outlets within Lisbon's Casino Lisboa.
Belcanto **370**..................Wish I'd opened
Bica Do Sapato **365**..............Wish I'd opened
Galeto **366**....................................Late night
Martín Berasategui **318**........Worth the travel
Pastelaria Bénard **370**....................Breakfast
Restaurante Tascardoso **365**..............Bargain
Riso - Risottoria del Mundo **358**............Worth the travel

RAHUL AKERKAR
Indigo
4 Mandlik Road, Mumbai
In 1999 he opened Indigo in Mumbai, a res-
taurant with a European meets Indian menu.
Branches followed and a new grill restaurant.
L'Arpège **301**................................High end
Bade Miya **66**..............................Late night
Imàgo **398**......................Worth the travel
Royal China India **66**..Regular neighbourhood
Shree Thakker Bhojanalay **68**...Local favourite
Wasabi by Marimoto **62**..................High end

MASSIMILIANO ALAJMO
Le Calandre
Via Liguria 1, Sarmeola di Rubano
After training in France under Veyrat and
Guérard he returned home to Italy and his
family's esteemed restaurant, Le Calandre
in 1983.
Bras **282**..............................Wish I'd opened
Caffè Sicilia **409**.............................Breakfast
La Madia **408**......................Worth the travel
La Mascareta **414**..........................Late night
Trattoria al Sasso **413**..Regular neighbourhood

JOSEAN ALIJA
Nerua
Guggenheim, Avenida Abandoibarra 2, Bilbao
Following spells at hotels, elBulli and Martín
Berasategui he opened Neura and a more
casual bistro in the Guggenheim in 2011.
L'Arpège **301**................................High end
Arzak **320**......................Worth the travel
Asador Etxebarri **324**............Worth the travel
Asador Indusi **317**.....Regular neighbourhood
Baita Gaminiz **317**......Regular neighbourhood
Bras **282**............................Wish I'd opened
El Celler de Can Roca **329**.....Worth the travel
La Grande Cuisine Etoilée **275**..............Wish I'd opened
Masa **573**....................................High end
Mugaritz **319**..................Wish I'd opened
Mugi Ardo Txoko **317**......................Breakfast
Quique Dacosta Restaurante **336**.........Worth the travel

OMAR ALLIBHOY
Tapas Revolution
Westfield, Ariel Way, London
With elBulli and Maze on his resume Allibhoy
joined El Pirata de Tapas in 2008 launching
the popular Tapas Revolution shortly after.
Bistrot de Luxe **191**....Regular neighbourhood
Busaba Eathai **223**..........................Bargain
Dinner by Heston **190**..........Worth the travel
La Fromagerie **192**........................Breakfast
Ibu Oka **129**....................Worth the travel
Khans **185**....................Wish I'd opened
Locale **188**....................................Late night
Taberna de la Daniela **335**......Local favourite
Tickets **353**....................Worth the travel

TED ANDERSON
Campagnola
1020 Main Street, Vancouver
Oversees Vancouver's Campagnola res-
taurant group including a rustic Italian and
Asia-American South offering.
L'Abbatoir **462**........................Local favourite
Ba Le Deli & Bakery **463**................Bargain
Big Lou's Butcher Shop **461**................Bargain
Fol Epi **455**......................Worth the travel
Kirin Restaurant **463**..Regular neighbourhood
Locanda Verde **598**.......................Breakfast
Maenam **462**......................Regular neighbourhood
Nine Dishes **463**............................Late night
Pizzeria Prima Strada **455**....Worth the travel
Q Go Ramen **462**............................Bargain
The Red Wagon **462**.......................Breakfast
Soba ni Umazake Yoshimura **111**..........Worth the travel
Suika Snackbar **461**........................Late night
Sun Sui Wah **463**.........................High end
Sushi Kanesaka **105**............Worth the travel

MICHAEL ANTHONY
Gramercy Tavern
42 East 20th Street, New York
Moved from Cincinnati to Paris where he
worked at L'Aperge and L'Astrance. After
a stint at Blue Hill Stone Barns he joined
Gramercy Tavern.
Kikunoi **97**......................Worth the travel
Maialino **592**..............Regular neighbourhood
McCrady's **540**.................Worth the travel
Momofuku Ssäm Bar **579**.......Wish I'd opened
Per Se **574**......................Worth the travel
Yakitori Totto **570**..........................Late night

AKMAL ANUAR
Iggy's
Hilton Hotel, 581 Orchard Road, Singapore
The head chef of Iggy's in Singapore and a
graduate of the Singapore Hotel Association
Training and Education Centre.
Aoki **126**......................Worth the travel
Arzak **320**......................Worth the travel
Edition Koji Shimomura **108**.................Worth the travel
Koh Nangkam **124**.........................Bargain
Tetsuya's **26**....................Worth the travel
Warung Nasi Pariaman **124**.....Local favourite

CLAUDIO APRILE
Colborne Lane
45 Colborne Street, Toronto
Uruguay born Aprile opened his first
Toronto restaurant Coldborne Lane in 2007
and followed that in 2010 with Origin.
Chantecler **470**............................High end
Gramercy Tavern **591**............Wish I'd opened
Khao San Road **469**........................Bargain
Nobu **219**......................................High end
Swatow **469**..................................Late night
Terroni **470**................Regular neighbourhood
Torito **469**..........................Local favourite

II

VÍCTOR ARGUINZÓNIZ

Asador Etxebarri
Plaza San Juan 1, Atxondo
Owner and chef of Asador Etxebarri, a
Basque Country farmhouse he took over
in 1989 and turned into a gastronomic
destination.
Akelare 320............................Wish I'd opened
Arzak 320...............................Worth the travel
Ibai 323...................................Local favourite
Mugaritz 319.........................Wish I'd opened
Nerua 318..............................Worth the travel
Nihonryori Ryugin 108..........Worth the travel
Zuberoa 320..........................Wish I'd opened

GOVIND ARMSTRONG

Post & Beam
3767 Santa Rosalia Drive, Los Angeles
Started in professional kitchens at 13, at
Wolfgang Puck's Spago, worked at Arzak,
he is the co-owner of Table 8 and 8oz Burger
in LA, and Table 8 in Miami.
Blue Plate 496.......................Wish I'd opened
Bouchon 490....................................High end
Campanile 490........................Local favourite
Minetta Tavern 581................Worth the travel
Osteria Mozza 493...........................High end
Tomato Pie Pizza Joint 500.................Bargain

ARMAND ARNAL

La Chassagnette
Le Sambuc, Arles
After working with Alain Ducasse for seven
years Montpellier born Arnal took the head
chef's position at La Chassagnette.
Binh Tay Market 121.........................Breakfast
Blue Ribbon Brasserie 597.................Late night
La Grenouillère 282................Local favourite
Le Gibolin 284............Regular neighbourhood
Kamiya Bar 106....................Worth the travel
Maison Troisgros 290.............Worth the travel
Marie Rosé 279   Regular neighbourhood
Oustau de Baumanière 284...............High end
Il Ridotto 414.........................Worth the travel
Schwartz's 475.................................Bargain

JUAN MARI & ELENA ARZAK

Arzak
Avenida Alcalde José Elósegui 273,
San Sebastián
Father and daughter behind the three-
Michelin-starred Arzak, owned and run
by the family since 1897.
Akelare 320............................Wish I'd opened
Asador Etxebarri 324.............Worth the travel
Astrid & Gaston 621...............Worth the travel
Bernadina Vinoteca 321.........Wish I'd opened
Biko 610.................................Worth the travel
El Celler de Can Roca 329......Worth the travel
Ganbara jatetxea 322.Regular neighbourhood
Mugaritz 319.........................Wish I'd opened
Tamboril 324.....................................Bargain
Zuberoa 320..........................Wish I'd opened

CORRADO ASSENZA

Caffè Sicilia
Corso Vittorio Emanuele III 125, Noto
A champion pastry chef and owner of Caffè
Sicilia, a pastry-coffee-ice cream bar in Noto,
southeastern Sicily.
La Gazza Ladra 409...........................High end
Il Luogo di Aimo e Nadia 403 Worth the travel
L'Osteria Francescana 395...Worth the travel
Ristorante Maria Fidone 409..............Bargain

ALEX ATALA

D.O.M. Restaurante
Rua Barão de Capanema 549, São Paulo
Chef-proprietor of D.O.M in São Paulo, Atala
is famous for combining unusual indigenous
ingredients with European technique.
Epice 637................................Worth the travel
Estadão 638....................................Late night
Le Chateaubriand 307...........Worth the travel
Jun Sakamoto 636.............................High end
Mani 636...High end
Mocotó 638............................Worth the travel
Nihonryori Ryugin 108.........Worth the travel

JASON ATHERTON

Pollen Street Social
8-10 Pollen Street, London
Created the hugely successful Maze for
Gordon Ramsay before going it alone with
Pollen Street Social, Waterhouse and Esquina.
Baozi Inn 213...................................Bargain
Barrafina 222............Regular neighbourhood
The French Laundry 484........Wish I'd opened
Goodman 218...................................Late night
The Ledbury 194....................Worth the travel
Quintessence 109.................Worth the travel
Restaurant Sat Bains 179......Worth the travel
Roganic 193............................Worth the travel
The Wolseley 221.............................Breakfast

PASCAL AUSSIGNAC

Club Gascon
57 West Smithfield, London
Born in Toulouse, trained across France, he
has founded a London empire based around
gutsy foie gras-loving Gascon cooking.
L'Arpège 301....................................High end
The Breakfast Club 204...................Breakfast
Busaba Eathai 223...........................Bargain
Fox and Anchor 200.................Local favourite
The Gallery 217.................................Late night
J Sheekey 214...........Regular neighbourhood
The Restaurant 59..................Worth the travel
La Tupina 274..........................Worth the travel
The Wolseley 221.............................Breakfast

JOSÉ AVILLEZ

Belcanto
Largo de São Carlos 10, Lisbon
Worked for Adrià, Ducasse and Frechon
before returning home to Portugal and
launching Cantinho do Avillez and Belcanto.
Cantinho do Avillez 370...................Late night
El Celler de Can Roca 329.....Worth the travel
Cervejaria Ramiro 366.............Local favourite
Fortaleza do Guincho 357.................High end
Grande Palácio Hong Kong 370..........Bargain
Ocean 357...............................Worth the travel
Pastelaria Bénard 370.......................Breakfast
Quique Dacosta Restaurante 336....Worth the
travel
Salsa & Coentros 367..............Local favourite

LUIS BAENA

Tivoli Hotels and Resorts
Portugal and Brazil
Legendary Portuguese chef with a career
spanning three decades and several conti-
nents. Currently working with Tivoli Hotels.
El Celler de Can Roca 329.....Worth the travel
Cervejaria Ramiro 366.............Local favourite
O Cortiço 360.....................................Bargain
D.O.M. Restaurante 636.........Worth the travel
Feitoria Restaurante 368....................Regular
neighbourhood
The Gallery 217.................................Late night
Hakkasan 218.........................Worth the travel
Marítima de Xabregas 366......Local favourite
Martín Berasategui 318.........Worth the travel
Midori 357..............................Wish I'd opened
New York Grill 113............................Breakfast
Noélia e Jerónimo 356...Regular neighbourhood
Pastelaria Versailles 367...................Breakfast
Pérgula 627..Breakfast
Restaurante XL 371..........................Late night
São Rosas 356............Regular neighbourhood
Tasca da Esquina 369.Regular neighbourhood
Tsuji Sun 110...........................Worth the travel

SAT BAINS

Restaurant Sat Bains
Lenton Lane, Nottingham
Chef-proprietor of a cutting edge culinary
destination in the unlikely setting of
Nottingham, England.
Casamia 173..........................Worth the travel
The Fat Duck 172....................Worth the travel
The Hand & Flowers 173........Worth the travel
Maroush 185......................................Late night

STEFANO BAIOCCO
Villa Feltrinelli
Via Rimembranza 38, Gargnano
Following spells with Ducasse, Gagnaire and Adrià he worked at Florence's Enoteca Pinchiorri before joining Villa Feltrinelli.
Bras 282..............................Wish I'd opened
Le Louis XV 291................................High end
La Madia 408.....................Worth the travel
Nihonryori Ryugin 108..........Worth the travel
Osteria Teatro Strabacco 405.........Late night
Ristorante Emilia 405..............Local favourite

PASCAL BARBOT
L'Astrance
4 Rue Beethoven, Paris
A protégé of Alain Passard, who he worked under for five years prior to opening the celebrated L'Astrance in 2000.
Asador Etxebarri 324............Worth the travel
L'Atelier de Joël Robuchon 301........High end
Azurmendi 325.....................Worth the travel
Bras 282.........................Wish I'd opened
La Pâtisserie des Rêves 310.....Local favourite
Maison Décoret 276...Regular neighbourhood
Restaurant André 128..........Worth the travel
SaQuaNa 282......................Worth the travel

BRETT BARNES
Ducksoup
41 Dean Street, London
Barnes worked as head chef of the Cross Keys in Leeds before moving to London to work first at Arbutus, then at Ducksoup.
Brawn 197.................Regular neighbourhood
Mangal Ocakbasi 203.........................Bargain
Milkbar 226...................................Breakfast
Mooli's 226.....................................Late night
Moro 200...................Regular neighbourhood
Onyx Restaurant 420.............Worth the travel
The Seafood Restaurant 175.Wish I'd opened
Soif Wine Bar 484.......Regular neighbourhood
The Square 221..............................High end
St. John Bar and Restaurant 201...Local favourite
The Towpath Café 208....................Breakfast

DARIO BASSA
Dassa Bassa
Calle de Villalar 7, Madrid
Madrilenian who cut his teeth in kitchens in Las Palmas, London, Bordeaux, Zurich and Madrid before opening Dassa Bassa.
Corral de la Moreria 332.........Local favourite
El Fogon de Trifon 333.......................Bargain
Moulin Chocolat 333.......................Breakfast
O'Clock Pub & Garden 333..............Late night
Ramon Freixa Madrid 334.....Worth the travel
Tertulia 586........................Worth the travel
Vuelve Carolina 337..............Worth the travel

ITALO BASSI
Enoteca Pinchiorri
Via Ghibellina 87, Santa Croce, Florence
Runs the kitchen at Enoteca Pinchiorri in partnership with Riccardo Monco whom he has worked alongside for close to 20 years.
Celadon 118.......................Wish I'd opened
Château Restaurant 111..................High end
Locanda 4 Cuochi 415.............Local favourite
Il Palagio 410..................................High end
Rossellinis 393......................Worth the travel
Trattoria Fratelli Briganti 411...Local favourite
Tsukiji Market 106................Worth the travel

EMMANUEL BASSOLEIL
Skye
Avenida Brigadeiro Luis Antonio 4700, São Paulo
Born in Burgundy and trained under Troisgros, Bassoleil moved to Brazil in 1987 and currently oversees Skye restaurant.
Alluci Alluci 636.........Regular neighbourhood
Bar do Giba 638....................Local favourite
Blés D'Or 637...................................Breakfast
La Brasserie Erick Jacquin 634.........High end
Clos de Tapas 637................Worth the travel
Daniel 571..High end
Estadão 638....................................Late night
KAA 635.............................Wish I'd opened
Momotaro 638...................................Bargain

BEN BATTERBURY
True South
377 Frankton Road, Queenstown
Born in England but as executive chef at True South Batterbury is now New Zealand based.
@Thai 43..Bargain
Atlas Beer Café 40................Worth the travel
The Cow 41.................Regular neighbourhood
The Fat Duck 172..................Worth the travel
Fergburger 41..................................Late night
Fishbone Bar And Grill 42........Local favourite
Fleurs Place 40....................Local favourite
Hikari Izakaya 42...............................Bargain
Hopgoods 39.........................Worth the travel
Kappa Sushi 42...........Regular neighbourhood
Merediths 50.....................................High end
Pescatore 38........................Worth the travel
Solera Vino 42..................................High end
Vudu Café and Larder 43................Breakfast
wd~50 594.................Regular neighbourhood
Yakitori Daruma 42.........................Late night

JEAN MARIE BAUDIC
Youpala Bistrot
5 Rue Palasne de Champeaux, Saint-Brieuc
A proud Breton who credits Jeffroy and Gagnaire as his two culinary fathers, Baudic cooks market-driven food at Youpala Bistrot.
Bras 282..............................Wish I'd opened
Casa Marcelo 332.................Worth the travel
Le Crapaud Rouge 278..........Local favourite
Crêperie des Promenades 277..........Regular neighbourhood
Restaurant Patrick Jeffroy 277.........High end
Victor'Inn 277...................................Bargain

BENJAMIN BAYLY
The Grove
Saint Patrick's Square, 43 Wyndham Street, Auckland
Stints at London's The Square and The Ledbury laid the ground for Bayley's Auckland home-coming and his position at The Grove.
Depot Eatery 48....................Worth the travel
Ile de France 50.........Regular neighbourhood
The Grill by Sean Connolly 48................Worth the travel
The Ledbury 194....................Worth the travel
Sal's 49..Bargain
Sidart 51...............................Worth the travel
Spicy House 50................................Late night
La Voie Francaise 50........................Breakfast

HEINZ BECK
La Pergola
Rome Cavalieri Hotel, Via Roberto Cadlolo 101, Rome
Born in Germany he worked under Winkler before moving to La Pergola in 1994. Since 2009 he's also overseen the menu at Apsleys.
Antico Forno Roscioli 398................Breakfast
L'Atelier de Joël Robuchon 222........High end
The Botanist 185...............................Breakfast
Brò Porta Portese 398.......................Bargain
Charleston 408......................Wish I'd opened
Residenz Heinz Winkler 374.....Local favourite
Il Restorante Bulgari 105.....Worth the travel
Santa Rosa Ristorante 393....Worth the travel
Sora Lella 399............Regular neighbourhood
Zuma 190..............................Local favourite

JEAN BEDDINGTON
Beddington's
Utrechtsedwarsstraat 141, Amsterdam
English-born, Beddington worked in various Amsterdam restaurants before opening her own French-Japanese-English restaurant.
Conservatorium Brasserie 255.........Breakfast
Eetsalon Van Dobben 252........Local favourite
Restaurant Beyrouth 254....................Regular neighbourhood
Restaurant La Rive 253.........Worth the travel
Restaurant Mi Ka 257.........................Bargain
Tetsuya's 26..........................Worth the travel
Uliassi 406...........................Worth the travel
Yamazato 256.................................High end

MARTIN BENN
Sepia
201 Sussex Street, Sydney
Began his career in London before relocating to Sydney in 1996. After time with Tetsuya he opened the Japanese-inspired Sepia.

Billy Kwong 21	Local favourite
Cumulus Inc. 31	Wish I'd opened
Fish Face 17	Regular neighbourhood
Fratelli Fresh 27	Regular neighbourhood
Narisawa 108	Worth the travel
Rosso Pomodoro Pizzeria 16	Late night
Vue de Monde 34	High end

MARTÍN BERASATEGUI
Martín Berasategui
Loidi Kalea 4, Lasarte-Oria
At only 20 he became head chef of el Bodegón Alejandro, which cemented his reputation as a Basque culinary heavyweight.

Elkano 318	Regular neighbourhood
Kaia Kaipe 318	High end
Lera 325	Worth the travel
Va Bene Disco Burger 324	Late night
Zuberoa 320	Wish I'd opened
Zuma 190	Local favourite

DANIEL BERLIN
Daniel Berlin Krog i Skåne Tranås
Diligensvägen 21, Skåne Tranås
Left the Swedish city of Malmö behind to open a restaurant in the heart of the Österlen countryside, where uber local produce is king.

Bastard 144	Worth the travel
Fäviken Magasinet 143	Worth the travel
Geist 159	Regular neighbourhood
Jalla Jalla 144	Late night
Noma 160	Wish I'd opened
Relæ 162	Worth the travel
Spoonery 145	Bargain
Systrar och Bröder 145	Breakfast

ANDREA BERTON
A protégé of Gualtiero Marchesi who was until recently the head chef of Trussardi Alla Scala in the fashionable heart of Milan.

D.O.M. Restaurante 636	Worth the travel
D'O 403	Wish I'd opened
Greenhouse 125	Breakfast
Hakkasan 218	Worth the travel
Locanda Margon 410	Worth the travel
Le Louis XV 291	High end
Osteria Altran 397	Local favourite
Trattoria del Nuovo Macello 404	Regular neighbourhood

JOHN BESH
August
301 Tchoupitoulas Street, New Orleans
This busy executive chef at August in New Orleans has eight other restaurants in the city, and another in San Antonio, Texas.

Abraxas 57	Worth the travel
Ba Mien 550	Regular neighbourhood
Bon Ton Café 547	Local favourite
Camellia Grill 549	Late night
Galatoire's Restaurant 547	High end
Momofuku Ssäm Bar 579	Wish I'd opened
RedFarm 586	Worth the travel
Satsuma 546	Breakfast

ANTON BJUHR
Gastrologik
Artillerigatan 14, Stockholm
Runs the up and coming Gastrologik in Stockholm where the focus is pastry and baking.

Bras 282	Wish I'd opened
Fabrique 152	Breakfast
Matbaren 148	High end
Max Vasagatan 149	Late night
Mugaritz 319	Wish I'd opened
Operabaren 149	Local favourite
Restaurang Ho's 152	Regular neighbourhood

APRIL BLOOMFIELD
The Spotted Pig
314 West 11th Street, New York
From Birmingham to New York via London, she made her name at The Spotted Pig before opening The Breslin and The John Dory Oyster Bar.

Eleven Madison Park 591	Worth the travel
Kunjip 569	Late night
Maialino 592	Regular neighbourhood
Noma 160	Wish I'd opened

HESTON BLUMENTHAL
The Fat Duck
High Street, Bray
Opened The Fat Duck, famed for its cutting edge cooking, in Berkshire, in 1995. Also owns The Hinds Head, The Crown and Dinner.

Beigel Bake 207	Late night
Maliks Tandoori 172	Late night
Restaurant Sat Bains 179	Worth the travel
Riva 184	Regular neighbourhood
The River Café 188	High end
Tsukiji Market 106	Worth the travel
The Wolseley 221	Breakfast
Zuma 190	Local favourite

JONNIE BOER
Restaurant De Librije
Broerenkerkplein 13-15, Zwolle
Acclaimed Dutch chef with a collection of restaurants and related businesses in the Netherlands, built around his flagship, De Librije.

A-Fusion 252	Bargain
Bai Yok 246	Regular neighbourhood
El Celler de Can Roca 329	Worth the travel
De Kas 256	Wish I'd opened
De Lindenhof 247	High end
Dinner by Heston 190	Worth the travel
Febo 255	Late night
't Nonnetje 246	Worth the travel

SAUL G. BOLTON
Saul
140 Smith Street, New York
Opened the produce-championing Saul in Brooklyn in 1999, which has since been joined by The Vanderbilt, Botanica and Red Gravy.

Al di Là Trattoria 600	Wish I'd opened
Gorilla Coffee 599	Breakfast
Lucali 599	Bargain
Pantagruele 408	Worth the travel
SriPraPhai 604	Regular neighbourhood
Stinky Bklyn 600	High end

UMBERTO BOMBANA
8½ Otto e Mezzo Bombana
18 Chater Road, Hong Kong Island
Arguably Asia's most famous Italian chef who operates 8½ Otto e Mezzo Bombana in Hong Kong and Shanghai.

Le Calandre 412	Worth the travel
Café Causette 84	Breakfast
Celebrity Cuisine 84	Worth the travel
Island Tang 85	Local favourite
Mak's Noodle 86	Bargain
Robuchon au Dôme 79	Wish I'd opened
Wagyu Kaiseki Den 88	Wish I'd opened

CLAUDE BOSI
Hibiscus
29 Maddox Street, London
Has not looked back since transplanting Hibiscus, his intimate haute dining room, from rural England to metropolitan London, in 2007.

Arbutus 222	High end
Burger & Lobster 216	Wish I'd opened
Gail's 184	Breakfast
Le Louis XV 291	High end
Mien Tay 184	Bargain

MARTIN BOSLEY

Martin Bosley's
103 Oriental Parade, Wellington
A fixture on Wellington's restaurant scene since 1991, Bosley opened his current seafood focused dining room in 2006.

Ancestral 44	Late night
Cumulus Inc. 31	Wish I'd opened
Floriditas 44	Regular neighbourhood
Hong Kong Barbeque 43	Bargain
Merediths 50	High end
Nikau Café 45	Local favourite
St Peter's 33	Worth the travel
The Engine Room 51	Worth the travel

ETTORE BOTRINI

Botrini's
Vasileos Georgiou B'24b, Athens
At the reins of his family's long-running restaurant in Corfu and also oversees Botrini's in Athens, and Art O2 in Thessaloniki.

Bodegon Alejandro 322	Bargain
Le Chateaubriand 307	Worth the travel
The Gallery 217	Late night
Klimataria 430	Local favourite
Martín Berasategui 318	Worth the travel
Zanettos 432	Worth the travel

MASSIMO BOTTURA

L'Osteria Francescana
Via Stella 22, Modena
Culinary traditions are not easily challenged in Italy but Bottura has succeeded with Modena's avant guarde L'Osteria Francescana.

Attica 34	Worth the travel
Bar Fragola Corta 394	Breakfast
Brasserie Francechetta 58 394	Late night
La Chersenta 394	Bargain
Le Chateaubriand 307	Worth the travel
Cracco 403	Worth the travel
Dal Pescatore 402	Local favourite
The Ledbury 194	Worth the travel
Il Luogo di Aimo e Nadia 403	Worth the travel
Mugaritz 319	Wish I'd opened
Nuovo Gambero Rosso 395	Regular neighbourhood
Ristorante Piazza Duomo 407	Worth the travel
Roscioli 399	Worth the travel

MEYJITTE BOUGHENOUT

Absynthe
Surfers Paradise Boulevard, Gold Coast
Worked in France for Pic, Blanc and Gagnaire, before arriving in Australia in 1995 and opening Absynthe in 2005.

Duo Deli Café 12	Breakfast
MoVida Bar De Tapas Y Vino 32	Worth the travel
Ocean Seafood 12	Late night
Quay 25	Wish I'd opened
Verve 12	Regular neighbourhood
Vie Bar & Restaurant 12	Local favourite

DANIEL BOULUD

Daniel
60 East 65th Street, New York
After training in France he moved to New York in the 1980s, founding his own Manhattan-based empire with the opening of Daniel in 1993.

15 East 598	High end
540 Park 572	Breakfast
Balthazar 596	Breakfast
The Barn 541	Worth the travel
Le Bernardin 571	High end
Blue Ribbon Brasserie 597	Late night
Casa Mono 592	Late night
La Esquina 593	Late night
The French Laundry 484	Wish I'd opened
Grand Central Oyster Bar 567	Local favourite
La Grande Cuisine Etoilée 275	Wish I'd opened
La Grenouillère 282	Local favourite
Jean Georges 573	Worth the travel
Katz's Deli 593	Local favourite
El Malecón 574	Bargain
Marea 569	High end
Mission Chinese Food 510	Regular neighbourhood
Pastis 594	Late night
Per Se 574	Worth the travel
Peter Luger Steakhouse 602	Local favourite
El Quinto Pino 588	Late night
Thelewala 581	Bargain

SEAN BROCK

Husk
76 Queen Street, Charleston
Since opening McCrady's in 2006 and Husk in 2010 he's led the farm-table charge to reinvent Southern cooking.

Aldea 591	Worth the travel
Blue Hill at Stone Barns 536	Worth the travel
Butcher & Bee 538	Late night
Coi 513	Wish I'd opened
Corton 598	High end
The Glass Onion 539	Regular neighbourhood
Holeman & Finch Public House 529	Worth the travel
Hominy Grill 539	Breakfast
Martha Lou's Kitchen 539	Bargain
Momofuku Ssäm Bar 579	Wish I'd opened
Noma 160	Wish I'd opened
wd~50 594	Regular neighbourhood

BRUCE BROMBERG

Blue Ribbon Brasserie
97 Sullivan Street, New York
Along with his brother Eric, founded the Blue Ribbon group, which takes in everything from high-end sushi to late night comfort food.

L'Atelier de Joël Robuchon 485	High end
Barbuto 582	Local favourite
Camellia Grill 549	Late night
Congee Village 593	Bargain
Keens Steakhouse 569	Wish I'd opened
Sage 485	Worth the travel
Sushi Sho 114	Worth the travel
Wo Hop 590	Late night

FELIPE BRONZE

Oro
Rua Frei Leandro 20, Rio de Janeiro
Began working in Rio de Janeiro restaurants at 16, before leaving to study in the US. In 2011 he opened his latest restaurant Oro.

BB Lanches 629	Bargain
D.O.M. Restaurante 636	Worth the travel
Eñe 629	Regular neighbourhood
Escola do Pao 628	Breakfast
Esplanada Grill 627	Local favourite
Olympe 629	High end
Pizzeria Bráz 628	Late night
Quique Dacosta Restaurante 336	Worth the travel
Sushi Leblon 629	Late night
Ten Kai 627	Regular neighbourhood
Tickets 353	Worth the travel

AL BROWN

Logan Brown
192 Cuba Street, Wellington
A familiar face across New Zealand thanks to TV, he has been the co-owner of Wellington's heavily garlanded Logan Brown since 1996.

Barilla Dumpling House 49	Late night
Coco's Cantina 48	Bargain
The French Café 49	High end
Floriditas 44	Regular neighbourhood
The Grill by Sean Connolly 48	Worth the travel
Hellenic Republic 30	Wish I'd opened
Maranui Café 45	Breakfast
Nikau Café 45	Local favourite
Porteño 22	Worth the travel

PIER BUSSETTI

Restaurante Pier Bussetti
Piazza Vittorio Emanuele II, Govone
A baker's son Bussetti opened Locando Mongreno in Turin in 1997 before relocating it to Castello di Govone in 2010.

Bar Pinotxo 342	Breakfast
Open Baladin 406	Late night
Pizzeria Libery & Artigianial Birra 407	Regular neighbourhood
Tickets 353	Worth the travel
Tim Ho Wan 91	Bargain

JORDI BUTRÓN MELERO

Espai Sucre
Carrer de Sant Pere Més Alt 72, Barcelona
A graduate of elBulli, who worked with pastry for Gagnaire and Bras, Melero opened the dessert-only Espai Sucre in 2000.

El Celler de Can Roca 329	Worth the travel
Chez Cocó 345	Worth the travel
Coure 345	Regular neighbourhood
Federal Café 352	Breakfast
Gresca 349	Bargain
La Guarida 611	Worth the travel
Koy Shunka 341	Late night
Pierre Gagnaire 306	High end
Tickets 353	Worth the travel

ADAM BYATT

Trinity
4 The Polygon, London
Formerly at The Square, Byatt now has three London restaurants of his own: Thyme, Trinity and Bistro Union.

Brew Café **187**	Breakfast
Café Creole **446**	Worth the travel
Canton Arms **194**	Regular neighbourhood
Honest Burger **198**	Bargain
Noma **160**	Wish I'd opened
Spuntino **228**	Wish I'd opened
The Square **221**	High end
St. John Bar and Restaurant **201**	Local favourite

YVES CAMDEBORDE

Le Comptoir du Relais
9 Carrefour de l'Odéon, Paris
A Paris veteran at the helm of Relais Saint-Germain and bistro Le Comptoir since 2005.

L'Ami Jean **301**	Wish I'd opened
L'Ami Louis **297**	High end
Le Baratin **311**	Regular neighbourhood
Café Constant **302**	Bargain
La Cantine du Troquet **308**	Regular neighbourhood
Chez Casimir **307**	Bargain
Epicure **306**	High end
L'Express Bar **294**	Late night
The Fat Duck **172**	Worth the travel
La Grenouillère **282**	Local favourite
Les Papilles **298**	Bargain
Maison Troisgros **290**	Worth the travel
Noma **160**	Wish I'd opened
Que du bon **311**	Bargain
Thoumieux **303**	Local favourite

ANDREAS CAMINADA

Schauenstein
Schauenstein Schloss Hotel, Fürstenau
The new star of Swiss gastronomy who plies his trade in a Schauenstein castle in the heart of the Alps.

Alain Ducasse **305**	High end
L'Arnsbourg **281**	Worth the travel
Bras **282**	Wish I'd opened
Hiltl **388**	Regular neighbourhood
Tibits **388**	Regular neighbourhood
Waldheim **388**	Local favourite

HOMARO CANTU

Moto
945 West Fulton Market, Chicago
Divides his time between cooking at cutting edge Moto and Cantu Designs, his food technology company.

Burt's Place **558**	Regular neighbourhood
Freddy's Pizzeria **555**	Local favourite
Kitsch'n on Roscoe **562**	Breakfast
Piccolo Sogno **562**	Worth the travel
Smoque BBQ **556**	Wish I'd opened
Le Taillevent **307**	Worth the travel
Yusho **554**	Regular neighbourhood

MARIO CARBONE

Torrisi Italian Specialties
250 Mulberry Street, New York
With fellow chef Rich Torrisi, opened the acclaimed Torrisi Italian Specialities in 2009. Retro-styled sandwich shop, Parm, followed.

Attica **34**	Worth the travel
Balthazar **596**	Breakfast
Café Mogador **576**	Breakfast
Daddy-O **582**	Late night
Del Posto **588**	High end
Katz's Deli **593**	Local favourite
Lucali **599**	Bargain
Minetta Tavern **581**	Worth the travel

FRANCIS CARDENAU

Le Sommelier
Bredgade 63, Copenhagen
Cooking since 1975, Cardenau arrived in Copenhagen in 1988 and is now chef-owner of Le Sommelier.

AOC **158**	Worth the travel
Formel B **153**	Regular neighbourhood
Geist **159**	Regular neighbourhood
Geranium **163**	Worth the travel
Ilakkasan **218**	Worth the travel
Kadeau **163**	Worth the travel
Manfreds & Vin **162**	Bargain
Noma **160**	Wish I'd opened
Ovsa **154**	Breakfast
Sukiyabashi Jiro **105**	Worth the travel

ANDREW CARMELLINI

Locanda Verde
377 Greenwich Street, New York
Born in Ohio, Carmellini made his name in New York as head chef at Café Boulud. Currently chef-partner at Locanda Verde and The Dutch.

L'Arpège **301**	High end
Le Bernardin **571**	High end
Daniel **571**	High end
Gahm Mi Oak **568**	Late night
Great NY Noodletown **589**	Late night
Ippudo NY **577**	Bargain
Motorino **579**	Bargain
The Willows Inn **485**	Worth the travel

MIGUEL CASTRO E SILVA

Largo
Rua Serpa Pinto 10a, Lisbon
Respected Portuguese culinary authority whose latest restaurant Largo is housed in a former convent.

Aqui Há Peixe **369**	Regular neighbourhood
Belcanto **370**	Wish I'd opened
Bica Do Sapato **365**	Wish I'd opened
Café de São Bento **368**	Late night
Gigi's Beach Restaurant **356**	Worth the travel
Panorama Restaurante **367**	High end
Pastelaria Versailles **367**	Breakfast
St. John Bar and Restaurant **201**	Local favourite
Taberna Ideal **371**	Bargain
Vale do Gaio **360**	Local favourite

MORENO CEDRONI

La Madonnina del Pescatore
Via Lungomare 11, Senigallia
Owns La Madonnina del Pescatore, opened in 1984, and, since 2000, on the beach in Portonovo.

L'Atelier de Joel Robuchon **107**	Wish I'd opened
Alice Ristorante **402**	Worth the travel
Bistrò 2 **404**	Late night
The Fat Duck **172**	Worth the travel
The Modern Pantry **200**	Breakfast
Osteria del Teatro **405**	Regular neighbourhood
Osteria Sara **405**	Local favourite
Quique Dacosta Restaurante **336**	Worth the travel
Ristorante Da Giacchetti **405**	Regular neighbourhood
Saffi Caffè **405**	Breakfast

JOSEF CENTENO

Bäco Mercat
408 South Main Street, Los Angeles
Former executive chef of LA's Lazy Ox Canteen, Centeno is owner of wildly popular flatbread sandwich outlet Bäco Mercat.

L'Ami Jean **301**	Wish I'd opened
Asanebo **497**	High end
Cactus Tacos **491**	Late night
Château Marmont **492**	Breakfast
Le Comptoir du Relais **299**	Worth the travel
Cotogna **507**	Worth the travel
Din Tai Fung **24**	Bargain
Cicling **490**	Regular neighbourhood
Nishimura **500**	High end
Pizzeria Mozza **500**	Regular neighbourhood

ENRICO & ROBERTO CEREA

Da Vittorio
Via Cantalupa 17, Brusaporto
Lombardian brothers who run the kitchen of Da Vittorio, their family's luxurious restaurant that's been on the culinary map since 1966.

L'Agapé Substance **298**	Worth the travel
Don Alfonso 1890 **392**	Wish I'd opened
Mc Maier's **401**	Late night
Pasticceria Cavour **402**	Breakfast
Ristorante Quattro Passi **393**	Worth the travel
Taverna del Capitano **393**	Worth the travel

CHAKALL
Quinta dos Frades
Rua Luís de Freitas Branco 5, Lisbon
Born in Buenos Aires, he's made turban-wearing his trademark while running multiple restaurants in Portugal.

Le Coq d'Or 380...................................Bargain
Ming Dynastie 383....................Local favourite
O Poleiro Restaurante 366.................Regular neighbourhood
Restaurant Carré des Feuillants 294.....Worth the travel
Restaurant Xavier Mathieu 284.........High end
Il Ritrovo 380.........................Worth the travel
The River Café 188...........................High end
Saporito 381..Late night
Table Fifty-Two 560................Worth the travel
Tauro 385.......................................Breakfast
VAU 384.....................Regular neighbourhood

DAVID CHANG
Momofuku Noodle Bar
171 1st Avenue, New York
Since opening the Momofuku Noodle Bar in 2004, he now has five very different Manhattan outposts, plus restaurants in Sydney and Toronto.

Benu 515...High end
Golden Century Seafood 24.............Late night
Great NY Noodletown 589................Late night
Kajitsu 578.........................Wish I'd opened
Locanda Verde 598.....................Breakfast
Sushi Sawada 105.................Worth the travel
Torrisi Italian Specialties 596..Local favourite
wd~50 594......................Regular neighbourhood

DOMINIC CHAPMAN
The Royal Oak
Paley Street, Maidenhead
Head chef at the Royal Oak he previously ran the kitchen at Heston Blumenthal's Hinds Head.

Agnadio 430............................Worth the travel
The Hardwick 233......Regular neighbourhood
The Ivy 225............................Wish I'd opened
The Pot Kiln 172......................Local favourite
The Sportsman 177................Worth the travel
Viceroy of Windsor 173...................Late night
The Waterside Inn 173.......................High end
The Wolseley 221.............................Breakfast

JEREMY CHARLES
Raymonds
95 Water Street, St. John's
Co-owner of Raymonds in St John's, New-foundland, which was recently voted the best new restaurant in Canada.

Atlantica Restaurant 457...................High end
Basho Restaurant and Lounge 456.....Regular neighbourhood
Blue on Water 456............................Breakfast
Bonavista Social Club 455........Local favourite
Le Club Chasse et Pêche 477 Worth the travel
Duke of Duckworth 456......................Bargain
Haisai 457..............................Wish I'd opened
Maison Lameloise 278...........Worth the travel
Next Restaurant 555.............Wish I'd opened
Venice Pizzeria 456............................Late night

SVEN CHARTIER
Saturne
17 Rue Notre-Dame-des-Victoires, Paris
French with some Swedish roots Chartier creates clean Nordic-like flavours at Saturne, in the Bourse in Paris.

Le Baratin 311...........Regular neighbourhood
In De Wulf 270.......................Worth the travel
Noma 160.............................Wish I'd opened
Relæ 162.............................Worth the travel
Septime 308........................Wish I'd opened

ANDRÉ CHIANG
Restaurant André
41 Bukit Pasoh Road, Singapore
Taiwan-born Chiang cooked at Jaan par An-dre in Singapore's Swissotel, before opening Restaurant Andre in a 1920s townhouse.

L'Astrance 309......................Worth the travel
Da Dong 124.................................Breakfast
Hachi 126...................Regular neighbourhood
Pierre Gagnaire 306.........................High end
Le Pré Catelan 310............................High end

ALBERTO CHICOTE
Nodo
Calle de Velázquez 150, Madrid
Madrilenian born and bred, his restaurants, Nodo and Pan de Lujo in the Spanish capital, fuse Asian and Mediterranean flavours.

Alinea 556............................Worth the travel
Asador Etxebarri 324............Worth the travel
El Celler de Can Roca 329.....Worth the travel
Hakkasan 218.......................Worth the travel
El Horreo 315.........................Wish I'd opened
Momofuku Ko 579..................Worth the travel
L'Orangerie 640................................Breakfast
Per Se 574.............................Worth the travel
Sacha 334..................Regular neighbourhood
La Terraza del Casino 335.................High end

FILIP CLAEYS
De Jonkman
Maalse Steenweg 438, Sint Kruis, Bruges
Following five years at De Karmeliet and four years with Sergio Herman at Oud Sluis, he opened De Jonkman on the outskirts of Bruges.

41 Grados Experience 352.....Worth the travel
Bistro Christophe 268.......................Late night
Bistro de Kruiden Molen 268..............Regular neighbourhood
De Siphon 269.........................Local favourite
The Fat Duck 172...................Worth the travel
Frituur Rakontiki 269.........................Bargain
Het Gebaar 260....................Worth the travel
Oud Sluis 248.....................................High end
Pizzeria Ristorante Romagna 248........Bargain
Restaurant Es Torrent 315.....Wish I'd opened
The Sportsman 177................Worth the travel
Victor's Gourmet 376...........Worth the travel

SAMANTHA AND SAMUEL CLARK
Moro
34-36 Exmouth Market, London
The husband and wife team who opened the Moorish influenced Moro in 1997. Morito, a bijou tapas bar next door, followed.

El Campero 314.....................Worth the travel
Dock Kitchen 191.......Regular neighbourhood
Ducksoup 224.............Regular neighbourhood
Koya 225....................Regular neighbourhood
The Ledbury 194...................Worth the travel
The River Café 188...........................High end
Sömine 201..Late night
The Sportsman 177................Worth the travel
St. John Bread & Wine 209......Local favourite
The Towpath Café 208.....................Breakfast

DERRY CLARKE
L'Ecrivain
109a Lower Baggot Street, Dublin
Worked in Dublin under John Howard at Le Coq Hardi and with Patsy McGuirk at Le Bon Appetit before opening L'Ecrivain.

Arzak 320..............................Worth the travel
Brownes 240..................................Breakfast
Chapter One 238.............................High end
Harvest Room 243.................Worth the travel
Jo-Burger 241.....................................Bargain
Pichet 238.............................Wish I'd opened
Roly's 240..............................Local favourite
Seapoint 237...............Regular neighbourhood
The Trocadero 239...........................Late night

SHAUN CLOUSTON
Logan Brown
192 Cuba Street, Wellington
Executive chef of Wellington's Logan Brown where he began his career and returned in 2006, after years spent working in Sydney.
Attica **34**................................Worth the travel
Depot Eatery **48**.....................Worth the travel
Dragonfly **44**..................................Late night
Huxtable **31**...........................Wish I'd opened
Scopa **45**..................Regular neighbourhood
Ti Kouka Café **45**...........................Breakfast
Yoshii **26**......................................High end

MAURO COLAGRECO
Mirazur
30 Avenue Aristide Briand, Menton
The Argentine born protégé of Passard and the late Loiseau, opened the handsome Côte d'Azur based Mirazur in 2006.
Alain Ducasse **305**..........................High end
L'Astrance **309**.....................Worth the travel
Eleven Madison Park **591**.......Worth the travel
Kunitoraya **295**................................Bargain
Manresa **482**.......................Wish I'd opened
La Merenda **285**....................Local favourite
La Spiaggetta **400**.........................Breakfast
La Vecchia Ostaia **400** Regular neighbourhood

TYSON COLE
Uchi
801 South Lamar Boulevard, Austin
Cole made his name in Austin, training under Takehiko Fuse before opening his own Japanese inspired restaurants Uchi and Uchiko.
Baguette et Chocolat **542**...............Breakfast
Bartlett's **541**...........Regular neighbourhood
Contigo **541**.........................Local favourite
Hopdoddy Burger Bar **541**.....Wish I'd opened
Soto **585**...................Regular neighbourhood

SCOTT CONANT
Scarpetta
355 West 14th Street, New York
Made his way with modern Italian food when he started out in New York in the 1990s. He now runs Scott Conant in Miami and Scarpetta in New York.
Aldea **591**...........................Worth the travel
Blue Hill at Stone Barns **536**..Worth the travel
Blue Ribbon Brasserie **597**..............Late night
Daniel **571**.....................................High end
Estia's Little Kitchen **536**................Breakfast
Jean Georges **573**................Worth the travel
Legend Bar & Restaurant **588**............Bargain
Mamoun's **580**................................Bargain
NoMad **592**...............Regular neighbourhood
Per Se **574**..........................Worth the travel
Ristorante all'Enoteca **407**....Worth the travel
The Saint Austere **603**......................Bargain
Street **493**..........................Worth the travel

LEE COOPER
L'Abbatoir
217 Carrall Street, Vancouver
After 13 years and a resume that includes spells with Blumenthal and Vongerichten, he opened his first restaurant, L'Abattoir in 2010.
Chambar **460**........................Wish I'd opened
DNA **476**.............................Worth the travel
Gyoza King **464**..............................Late night
Hachi Hana **463**...............................Bargain
Hawksworth Restaurant **464** Worth the travel
The Ledbury **194**...................Worth the travel
Nicli Antica Pizzeria **462**......................Regular
  neighbourhood
The Pear Tree **460**.................Worth the travel
Tomahawk Barbeque **464**................Breakfast
Waterfront Restaurant **454**..Worth the travel

KRISTOF COPPENS
Apriori
Sint-Goriksplein 19, Haalter
Since opening the forward-thinking Apriori in 1996, he has, with the University of Louvain, developed 'Crycotuv', a preservation technique.
Arnolfo **411**..........................Worth the travel
De Jonkman **269**...................Worth the travel
De Kuiper **266**................................Bargain
Hostellerie St. Nicolas **270**..............High end
Oud Sluis **248**................................High end
't Overhamme **265**......Regular neighbourhood

JOSÉ CORDEIRO
Feitoria Restaurante
Doca do Bom Sucesso, Lisbon
Born in Angola, his creative interpretations of traditional Portuguese dishes have won him recognition at Feitoria.
Alma **371**.............................Worth the travel
Arzak **320**...........................Worth the travel
Assinatura **365**.....................Worth the travel
Café de São Bento **368**....................Late night
Espaço Lisboa **364**........................Late night
Fortaleza do Guincho **357**.................High end
Maçã Verde **364**..............................Bargain
Restaurante DOC **360**...........Wish I'd opened
Restaurante Geadas **356**........Local favourite
Restaurante Inês do Aleixo **358**.........Regular
  neighbourhood
Shis **359**.............................Wish I'd opened
Spazio Buondi **367**..............Local favourite
Vila Joya **357**.................................High end
The Yeatman **359**...........................High end

OLLIE COUILLAUD
The Lawn Bistro
67 High Street, London
A French man who made his name at London's La Trompette before taking the stove at The Lawn Bistro in Wimbledon.
Fuego Negro **320**..................Worth the travel
Arzak **320**...........................Worth the travel
El Celler de Can Roca **329**.....Worth the travel
Chez Bruce **195**..........Regular neighbourhood
Hakkasan **218**......................Worth the travel
Maki Yaki **195**............Regular neighbourhood
Michel Trama **276**................Worth the travel
Salt Yard **203**......................Wish I'd opened
Santceloni **334**....................Worth the travel
The Square **221**...............................High end
Wong Kei **214**................................Late night

MATTHEW CRABBE
Two Rooms Grill & Bar
3-11-7 Kita-Aoyama, Tokyo
Worked at Sydney's Tetsuya's, then in London, the US and Mexico before arriving in Tokyo to oversee the New York Grill and Two Rooms.
Akanoren **106**................................Late night
Chisoan **99**.........................Worth the travel
Les Enfants Gates **112**.....................Late night
Gion Yata **97**......................Local favourite
Hyotei **98**....................................Breakfast
Komatsu Yasuke **96**.............Worth the travel
Kyubey **104**....................................High end
Maru **112**............................Local favourite
Nihonryori Ryugin **108**.........Worth the travel
Sepia **26**...........................Worth the travel
Shiba Tofuya Ukai **109** Regular neighbourhood
Tensei **110**...........................Local favourite
Toriyoshi **111**.................................Bargain
Waku Ghin **125**....................Wish I'd opened

ENRICO CRIPPA
Ristorante Piazza Duomo
Piazza Risorgimento 4, Alba
Began his career with Marchesi, famously opening Marchesi's in Kobe. Returned to Italy to open Piazza Duomo in 2005.
Bras **282**.............................Wish I'd opened
La Piola **406**...................................Bargain
L'Osteria Francescana **395**....Worth the travel

JORDI CRUZ
ABaC
Avinguda del Tibidabo 1, Barcelona
Worked at Cercs Estany Clar where he became the youngest ever Spaniard to win a Michelin star. He's now ABaC's head chef.
Alinea **556**..........................Worth the travel
Bar Mut **345**..................................Late night
Can Roca **328**......................Local favourite
Fonda Gaig **348**..........Regular neighbourhood
Gaig **349**............................Local favourite
Koy Shunka **341**..............................Late night
Miramar (Llanca) **331**..........Worth the travel
The Mirror **349**...........Regular neighbourhood
Sagàs Pagesos **340**........................Bargain
El Vaso de Oro **340**.........................Late night

TIM CUSHMAN
O Ya
9 East Street, Boston
After travelling the world with US restaurant group Lettuce Entertain You, he now owns O Ya where modern Japanese meets New England.

Kyoto Kitcho 98	High end
La Taqueria 511	Bargain
Oleana 535	Worth the travel
Parish Café 534	Late night
Red Wing Diner 535	Local favourite
The Restaurant 483	High end
Urasawa 490	High end

OLIVIER DA COSTA
Olivier Restaurante
Rua do Alecrim 23, Lisbon
Runs four Lisbon restaurants spanning Mediterranean, Comfort and Japanese food.

Café de São Bento 368	Late night
Cervejaria Ramiro 366	Local favourite
Monte Mar 358	Regular neighbourhood
Pastelaria Versailles 367	Breakfast
Restaurante Praia da Riviera 359	Local favourite
Restaurante Praia do Castelo 359	Local favourite
Varanda Restaurant 365	Breakfast

OLLIE DABBOUS
Dabbous
39 Whitfield Street, London
Trained at Le Manoir aux Quat'Saisons, staged heavily, then became head chef of Texture in London, before opening Dabbous in 2012.

Hereford Road 195	Regular neighbourhood
The Modern Pantry 200	Breakfast
Le Relais de Venise 193	Regular neighbourhood
Tayyabs 211	Local favourite
Trattoria Cammillo 411	Worth the travel
Umu 221	High end

QUIQUE DACOSTA
Quique Dacosta Restaurante
Carreterra de Las Marinas, Denia
Began working at el Poblet in 1989, a decade later having worked his way to head chef, he took over and renamed it.

L'Air du Temps 266	Worth the travel
Aponiente 314	Worth the travel
Asador Etxebarri 324	Worth the travel
Atrio 332	Worth the travel
Azurmendi 325	Worth the travel
Casa Federico 335	Bargain
Casa Gerardo 314	Worth the travel
De Pastorale 260	Worth the travel
Joël Restaurant Bistronomic 335	Local favourite
Le Louis XV 291	High end
Masa 573	High end
Nerua 318	Worth the travel
Pastelería Totel Elda 336	Breakfast
Peix and Brases 336	Local favourite
Per Se 574	Worth the travel
Restaurante La Cuina 336	Local favourite

ANDREAS DAHLBERG
Bastard
Mäster Johansgatan 11, Malmö
The head chef and owner of Bastard in Malmö, who also goes by the rock 'n' roll moniker of Andy Bastard.

Le Comptoir du Relais 299	Worth the travel
La Gazzetta 308	Bargain
Momofuku Ssäm Bar 579	Wish I'd opened
Relæ 162	Worth the travel
The River Café 188	High end
Roberta's 603	Wish I'd opened
Solde Kafferosteri 144	Breakfast
St. John Bar and Restaurant 201	Local favourite

MATHIAS DAHLGREN
Mathias Dahlgren
Södra Blasieholmshamnen 6, Stockholm
Multiple winner of Swedish chef of the year he opened in the Grand Hotel in 2007 where he also has Matbaren.

Amida Kolgrill 152	Bargain
Asador Etxebarri 324	Worth the travel
Frantzén/Lindeberg 148	High end
The French Laundry 484	Wish I'd opened
Noma 160	Wish I'd opened
Strömmingsvagnen 153	Local favourite

LUKE DALE-ROBERTS
The Test Kitchen
The Old Biscuit Mill, 375 Albert Road, Cape Town
British born Dale-Roberts worked in Asia before arriving in South Africa where he now owns The Test Kitchen and The Pot Luck Club.

Bihari 448	Bargain
Carne 446	Wish I'd opened
Col'Cacchio Pizzeria 447	Regular neighbourhood
The Greenhouse 446	High end
Melissa's, The Food Shop 447	Breakfast
Porteño 22	Worth the travel

DAVE DE BELDER
De Godevaart
Sint Katelijnevest 23, Antwerp
Rising Flemish star of the forward-thinking De Godevaart who recently created the menu for the Sydney branch of Cara&Co.

Gastro Park 18	Worth the travel
Jam 261	Breakfast
The Glorious Inn 260	Local favourite
Lam en Yin 261	Regular neighbourhood
La Paix 261	Worth the travel
Pazzo 261	Bargain
Pure C 248	Wish I'd opened
Restaurant De Librije 247	High end

GERT DE MANGELEER
Hertog Jan
Torhoutsesteenweg 479, Bruges
Runs Hertog Jan with sommelier Joachim Boudens who he met while working at Molentje in the Netherlands.

L'Atelier de Joël Robuchon 222	High end
Bistro Christophe 268	Late night
Bistro de Kruiden Molen 268	Regular neighbourhood
Frituur Bosrand 269	Bargain
The Ledbury 194	Worth the travel
Le Pain Quotidien 263	Breakfast
Pure C 248	Wish I'd opened
Restaurant De Librije 247	High end
Rock Fort 270	Regular neighbourhood

MICHAEL DEANE
Deanes
36-40 Howard Street, Belfast
Belfast chef-restaurateur who aside from his flagship Deanes, now runs six other outposts across the city.

All Seasons 234	Regular neighbourhood
The Greenhouse Dublin 239	Worth the travel
The Raj 276	Regular neighbourhood
Vila Joya 357	High end

SANG-HOON DEGEIMBRE
L'Air du Temps
Chaussée de Louvain 181, Noville-sur-Mehaigne
Korean-Belgian, who opened L'Air du Temps in Namur, Wallonia, where he grew up, in 1997. Praised for using super local produce.

L'Astrance 309	Worth the travel
Bras 282	Wish I'd opened
Brasserie François 266	Regular neighbourhood
El Celler de Can Roca 329	Worth the travel
Chez Chen 266	Bargain
De Pastorale 260	Worth the travel
Fäviken Magasinet 143	Worth the travel
Fruits de la Passion 267	Local favourite
Lam Zhou Handmade Noodle 590	Bargain
Le Scaldia 'Chez Pippo' 267	Late night
Per Se 574	Worth the travel

ANTHONY DEMETRE
Arbutus
63-64 Frith Street, London
Runs London's Arbutus restaurant group in partnership with Will Smith.

Bocca di Lupo 223	Regular neighbourhood
Ceviche 223	Late night
Dinner by Heston 190	Worth the travel
L'Enclume 175	Worth the travel
Hibiscus 219	High end
Nahm Bangkok 120	Worth the travel
St. John Bar and Restaurant 201	Local favourite
The Wolseley 221	Breakfast

SEMSA DENIZSEL

Kantin

Akkavak Sokagi 30, Istanbul

Opened Kantin, an outfit that focuses on serving healthy, seasonal Turkish soul food, in Istanbul in 2000.

L'Arcangelo 398....................Worth the travel
Bay Nihat - Lale Restaurant 432...........Worth the travel
Kaymakci Pando 436.......................Breakfast
Kizilkayalar 437................................Late night
Lale Iskembecisi 438..........................Late night
Lokanta Maya 440......Regular neighbourhood
Meshur Filibe Köftecisi 439.............Bargain
Metanet Lokantasi 432.........Worth the travel
Mikla 438......................................High end
Roscioli 399......................Worth the travel
St. John Bar and Restaurant 201............Local favourite

KOBE DESRAMAULTS

In De Wulf

Wulvestraat 1, Heuvelland, Dranouter

In the countryside close to the French-Belgium border, Desramaults runs In De Wulf in the area which was his childhood home.

L'Auberge In De Zon 268.........Local favourite
Bon Bon 262..................................High end
De Lieve 264....................................Bargain
La Grenouillère 282................Local favourite
J.E.F. 264................Regular neighbourhood
Martino 264..................................Late night
Roberta's 603..................Wish I'd opened
Simon Says 265...........................Breakfast
The Sportsman 177...............worth the travel
Volta 265..................Regular neighbourhood

HAROLD DIETERLE

Perilla

9 Jones Street, New York

Graduate of the Culinary Institute of America, he opened his first restaurant, Perilla, in 2007 and followed with the Thai Kin Shop.

15 East 598..................................High end
The Breslin Bar & Dining Room 594.Breakfast
Café Steinhof 601.......Regular neighbourhood
Chao Thai 603.................................Bargain
Char No. 4 599............Regular neighbourhood
Daddy-O 582..................................Late night
Dovetail 572....................Wish I'd opened
Egg 602..Breakfast
Grand Sichuan 583...........................Late night
Kanoyama 578...........Regular neighbourhood
The Little Owl 584......Regular neighbourhood
Lupa 584.........................Wish I'd opened
Miller Union 529.................Worth the travel
Minetta Tavern 581................Worth the travel
Peking Duck House 590.....................Regular neighbourhood
Poonsin Restaurant 119........Worth the travel
Spicy & Tasty 604.......Regular neighbourhood

MATTHEW DILLON

Sitka & Spruce

1531 Melrose Avenue, Seattle

Runs four restaurants one of which, The Old Chaser Farm, outside Seattle, is his home, where he farms and forages.

Abou Hassan 56..................Worth the travel
Asador Etxebarri 324...........Worth the travel
Café Gitane 595.............................Breakfast
Fäviken Magasinet 143.........Worth the travel
Goodies Market 487..........................Bargain
Maneki 486................Regular neighbourhood
Moro 200....................Regular neighbourhood
Noma 160........................Wish I'd opened
Ottolenghi 205...............................Breakfast
Una Pizza Napoletana 516.....Worth the travel

ELOI DION

Van Horne

1268 Avenue Van Horne, Montreal

In charge of the kitchen at Montreal's Van Horne. Prior to that cooked at 357C, Daniel Langlois's private club.

Les 400 Coups 477...............Wish I'd opened
Café Sardine 474...............................Late night
Le Comptoir 474........Regular neighbourhood
Dépanneur le Pick Up 476....................Bargain
Eleven Madison Park 591.......Worth the travel
Patisserie Rhubarbe 475....................Breakfast
Le St-Urbain 474....................Local favourite
Toqué! 478......................................High end

VLADISLAV DJATSUK

Tchaikovsky

Telegraaf Hotel Vene 9, Tallinn

Executive chef at Tallinn's Hotel Telegraaf, Djatsuk has represented Estonia at the Bocuse d'Or.

La Bottega 424................................Late night
Chedi 424.................Regular neighbourhood
Chez Dominique 165...................High end
Geranium 163.....................Worth the travel
Kohvik Moon 424................................Bargain
Leib Resto ja Aed 424...........Worth the travel
Olo 165...............................Worth the travel

CHRISTIAN DOMSCHITZ

Vestibül

Doktor-Karl-Lueger-Ring 2, Vienna

A veteran of Vienna's restaurant scene he's currently behind the stove at Vestibül in the Burgtheater.

Amarantis 418...............................Late night
Balthazar 596...............................Breakfast
Can Fabes 327....................Wish I'd opened
The French Laundry 484........Wish I'd opened
Holy Moly 418.......................Local favourite
Meixner 418..............Regular neighbourhood
Restaurant Mraz & Sohn 418 Worth the travel
Steirereck 419.....................Worth the travel

PETER DOYLE

Est.

Level 1, Establishment 252, George Street, Sydney

With a career spanning three decades, the owner of Est. could be described as a founding father of modern Australian cooking.

Eveleigh 499........................Worth the travel
In Situ 18..Breakfast
Manresa 482....................Wish I'd opened
Mille Vini 21....................................Bargain
Ormeggio 18..............Regular neighbourhood
Pilu at Freshwater 17.............Local favourite
Royal Mail 13.....................Worth the travel
Tetsuya's 26.......................Worth the travel

JULIEN DUBOUÉ

Afaria

15 Rue Desnouettes, Paris

Duboué trained with Dutournier in Paris and Boulud in New York and has gone on to open two Paris bistros inspired by Southwest France.

Le 114 Faubourg 305...............Worth the travel
A Fuego Negro 320.................Worth the travel
Alain Ducasse 305.........................High end
L'Ami Jean 301..................Wish I'd opened
Art Macaron 298............................Breakfast
Au Bon Coin les Pieds de Cochon 275......Local favourite
L'Auberge du Pas de Vent 275.Local favourite
L'Avant Comptoir 299.Regular neighbourhood
Daniel 571......................................High end
Les Fables de la Fontaine 302............Regular neighbourhood
La Forme d'Urffe 276...............Bargain
Le Relais de la Poste 275..............High end
Marismo 639........................Worth the travel
Mercado Municipal 635.....................Bargain
Mocotó 638.........................Worth the travel
La Régalade 309................................Bargain
La Nóoorve Nimbaud 290......Worth the travel
Square One 121.....................Worth the travel

WYLIE DUFRESNE

wd~50

50 Clinton Street, New York

Owner of wd-50, the envelope-pushing Manhattan restaurant he opened with the backing of former boss Jean-Georges Vongerichten.

Asador Portuetxe 321...........Worth the travel
Bar Veloce 576................................Late night
Empellón Cocina 577.............Worth the travel
Katz's Deli 593....................Local favourite
Momofuku Ssäm Bar 579.......Wish I'd opened
Mugaritz 319.......................Wish I'd opened

RAPHAEL DWORAK
Le Loft
Sofitel Hotel Praterstrasse 1, Vienna
Head chef at Le Loft, where the menu is inspired by the French-Austrian style of Antoine Westermann, Dworak's mentor.
décor 419..Breakfast
Le Coq Rico 311....................Wish I'd opened
Drouant 296................Regular neighbourhood
The French Laundry 484........Wish I'd opened
Schnitzelwirt 419.............................Bargain
Silvio Nickol 418..................Worth the travel
Weinbau Österreicher 418......Local favourite

MARCUS EAVES
Pied à Terre
34 Charlotte Street, London
Cooks at Pied à Terre in London. Eaves is a protégé of its previous chef Shane Osborn.
Bras 282........................Wish I'd opened
The Gallery 217...............................Late night
The Hand & Flowers 173.......Worth the travel
Hereford Road 195.....Regular neighbourhood
Polpo 227...Bargain
Restaurant Andrew Fairlie 230.........High end
The Wolseley 221...........................Breakfast

CHRISTIAN EBBE
Søllerød Kro
Søllerødvej 35, Holte
Took over as head chef at the historic Søllerød Kro in 2011, a restaurant that is housed in a building dated 1677.
Le Chateaubriand 307...........Worth the travel
Dragsholm Slot 155..........................High end
Fäviken Magasinet 143..........Worth the travel
Formel B 153..............Regular neighbourhood
Mash 159.......................................Late night
Noma 160..............................Wish I'd opened
Le Pain Quotidien 295.....................Breakfast
Relæ 162.............................Worth the travel
Restaurant Sletten 154.........Worth the travel

MIKAEL EINARSSON
Leijontornet
Lilla Nygatan 5, Stockholm
Oversees the menu at Djuret and Leijontornet in Stockholm having previously worked across Sweden and at London's The Square.
Blue Hill at Stone Barns 536..Worth the travel
Chez Betty 150...........Regular neighbourhood
Fäviken Magasinet 143..........Worth the travel
Frantzén/Lindeberg 148...................High end
Petite France 148............................Breakfast
Råkultur 153.....................................Bargain
Sturehof 151...................................Late night

RICHARD EKKEBUS
Amber
The Landmark, 15 Queens's Road, Hong Kong Island
Gagnaire, Passard and Savoy trained Dutchman who is Culinary Director at Hong Kong's Landmark Mandarin Oriental.
The Chairman 85..................Worth the travel
Dimdim Sum Dimsum 90.....................Bargain
Luk Yu Tea House 85.............Local favourite
Man Wah 86....................................High end
Oud Sluis 248..................................High end
Sang Kee Congee Shop 88...............Breakfast
St. John Hotel 215............................Breakfast
Under Bridge Spicy Crab 82............Late night
Yardbird 88................Regular neighbourhood

EDINHO ENGEL
Amado
Avenida Lafayete Coutinho 660, Salvador
Modern Brazilian food with a regional accent is Engle's raison d'etre, an approach he pioneered at Manaca before opening Amado.
Chez Bernard 626......Regular neighbourhood
Marietta Sanduiches Leves 626..........Bargain
Mercearia Bresser Batel 626..............Regular neighbourhood

SUMITO ESTÉVEZ
Mondeque
Avenida Jovito Villalba, Margarita Island
Born in Caracas and raised in India where he developed a taste for exotic flavours. Founded the Culinary Institute of Caracas.
Alto 618............................Worth the travel
Astrid & Gaston 621..............Worth the travel
Mokambo 618.................................Breakfast

ROB EVANS
Duckfat
43 Middle Street, Portland
A Californian based in Maine. His restaurant Duckfat, is named after the not-so-secret ingredient in its Belgian-style fries.
Acme 595...........................Worth the travel
Boda 531...Late night
Bresca 531.......................................High end
Fore Street 531.......................Local favourite
Gorgeous Gelato 531...........Wish I'd opened
Hot Suppa! 531...............................Breakfast
Otto Pizza 531...................................Bargain
Pai Men Miyake 532...Regular neighbourhood

ANDREW FAIRLIE
Restaurant Andrew Fairlie
The Gleneagles Hotel, Auchterarder
The most highly rated chef in Scotland who trained with Guerard at Les Pres d'Eugenie.
21212 230.........................Worth the travel
Brooklyn Fare 600.................Wish I'd opened
The Burger Joint 568.............Wish I'd opened
Café Gandolfi 232..............................Bargain
Le Caprice 217.......................Wish I'd opened
Crabshakk 232........................Local favourite
Pierre Gagnaire 306..........................High end
The Wolseley 221............................Breakfast

BRAD FARMERIE
Public
210 Elizabeth Street, New York
Pittsburgher, worked in London with Peter Gordon, opened New York's Public in 2003, where he now also oversees Madam Geneva.
Animal 499...........................Worth the travel
Au Pied de Cochon 475...........Local favourite
Blue Hill at Stone Barns 536..Worth the travel
Blue Ribbon Brasserie 597..............Late night
Dabbous 202.......................Worth the travel
Depot Eatery 48....................Worth the travel
Esquina 124.........................Worth the travel
Pok Pok NY 601.........Regular neighbourhood
Primanti Bros 538.............................Bargain
The Providores 192..........................Breakfast

MICHAEL FERRARO
Delicatessen
54 Prince Street, New York
Helped turn around New York's Delicatessen when he arrived in 2008, with credentials that included the Mercer Kitchen and the Biltmore Room.
Balthazar 596..................................Breakfast
Le Bernardin 571.............................High end
Blue Ribbon Brasserie 597..............Late night
DB Bistro Moderne 568....................High end
Great NY Noodletown 589.............Late night
Grimaldi's Pizzeria 600............Local favourite
Maialino 592...............Regular neighbourhood
Marinus 483.........................Worth the travel
Minetta Tavern 581...............Worth the travel
Peter Luger Steakhouse 602....Local favourite
Tapas 24 350....................................Bargain

PAUL FLYNN
The Tannery Restaurant
10 Quay Street, Dungarvan
Opened The Tannery in 1997, following a distinguished London career that included running Chez Nico.
Chapter One 238..............................High end
The Fatted Calf 243...............Worth the travel
Fishy Fishy Café 237..............Wish I'd opened
Genoa Takeaway 242.........................Bargain
The Hand & Flowers 173.......Worth the travel
Nude Food 242.................................Breakfast
O'Brien Chop House 242.....................Regular neighbourhood

MARC FOSH
Simply Fosh
Carrer de la Missió 7, Palma
Began his career at the Greenhouse in London, Fosh now lives in Spain where he's owned Simply Fosh since 2009.

Akelare 320	Wish I'd opened
Aquagrill 596	Worth the travel
Ca Na Toneta 316	Local favourite
El Bungalow 316	Regular neighbourhood
Fibonacci 316	Breakfast
Jacob's & Co. Steakhouse 470	Worth the travel
Katz's Deli 593	Local favourite
Mesón Ca'n Pedro I 316	Wish I'd opened
Sushi Yasuda 567	Worth the travel
Trattoria da Romano 415	Worth the travel
Zaranda 316	High end

PAUL FOSTER
Tuddenham Mill
High Street, Tuddenham
English talent who trained at Le Manoir aux Quat'Saisons and Sat Bains ahead of taking over Tuddenham Mill.

Alimentum 173	Regular neighbourhood
Ducksoup 224	Regular neighbourhood
The Fat Duck 172	Worth the travel
The French Laundry 484	Wish I'd opened
Hawksmoor 197	Breakfast
Pea Porridge 179	Local favourite
Per Se 574	Worth the travel
Red Lodge Café 179	Late night
Viajante 198	High end

JASON FOX
Commonwealth
2224 Mission Street, San Francisco
Co-owner of Commonwealth, opened San Francisco's Mission Street in 2010, Fox has a resume that includes Bar Tartine, and Scott Howard.

Atelier Crenn 505	High end
Aziza 514	Regular neighbourhood
Bar Agricole 515	Local favourite
Benu 515	High end
Bouche 512	Late night
Boulevard 506	Local favourite
Cal Pep 340	Late night
Coi 513	Wish I'd opened
Commis 518	High end
Comstock Saloon 507	Late night
Duc Loi Kitchen 509	Bargain
El Quim de la Boqueria 343	Breakfast
Flour + Water 510	Local favourite
Hisop 345	Worth the travel
Kajitsu 578	Wish I'd opened
Mission Chinese Food 510	Regular neighbourhood
Nojo 504	Worth the travel
Quince 507	High end
The Restaurant 483	High end
S & T Hong Kong 514	Bargain
SPQR 509	Local favourite
State Bird Provisions 514	Bargain
The Willows Inn 485	Worth the travel
Yamo 511	Bargain

BJÖRN FRANTZÉN
Frantzén/Lindeberg
Lilla Nygatan 21, Stockholm
Frantzén met Daniel Lindeberg in 1998 while they were working at Edsbacka Krog. A decade later they opened their Stockholm outpost.

L'Arpège 301	High end
Fäviken Magasinet 143	Worth the travel
Ishikawa 113	Worth the travel
Råkultur 153	Bargain
Rolfs Kök 149	Regular neighbourhood
Sturehof 151	Late night

NEAL FRASER
BLD
7450 Beverly Boulevard, West Hollywood
Worked in Los Angeles for Splichal, Puck and Rockenwagner; ran Rix and his own restaurants, Grace and BLD, before launching Fritzi Dog in 2012.

Brooklyn Fare 600	Wish I'd opened
Fearing's 542	Worth the travel
Loteria Grill 492	Regular neighbourhood
Pho 10 121	Worth the travel
Picca 501	Local favourite
Robata Jinya 494	Bargain
Urasawa 490	High end
Yai 493	Late night

ERIC FRECHON
Epicure, Bristol Hotel
112 Rue du Faubourg Saint-Honoré, Paris
Born in Normandy, first worked at Paris's Hotel Bristol in 1981, cooked his way around the city before returning to the Bristol in 1999.

L'Ambroisie 297	Worth the travel
L'Ami Louis 297	High end
L'Atelier de Joël Robuchon 301	High end
Au Petit Tonneau 302	Bargain
Flocons de Sel 289	Worth the travel
La Maison de l'Aubrac 306	Late night

PIERRE GAGNAIRE
Pierre Gagnaire
6 Rue Balzac, Paris
French toque star whose restaurant empire spans the globe from his eponymous Paris flagship all the way to South Korea and beyond.

8½ Otto e Mezzo Bombana 83	High end
Bras 282	Wish I'd opened
Carette 309	Breakfast
Casa Bini 299	Bargain
Le Contre Quai 277	Local favourite
Le Dôme 309	Late night
Kifune 310	Regular neighbourhood
La Tour d'Argent 298	Wish I'd opened

ANDRÉ GARRETT
Galvin at Windows
22 Park Lane, London
Classically trained in London's finest kitchens, including spells with Ladenis and Loubet, he runs the pass at Galvin at Windows.

The French Laundry 484	Wish I'd opened
Noma 160	Wish I'd opened
Princi 227	Bargain
Restaurant Sat Bains 179	Worth the travel
Roast 198	Breakfast
The Square 221	High end
St. John Bar and Restaurant 201	Local favourite
Terroirs 210	Regular neighbourhood

ALEXANDRE GAUTHIER
La Grenouillère
Rue de la Grenouillère, Madeleine-sous-Montreuil
Discovered by Ducasse, rising star Gauthier took over his family's century-old restaurant La Grenouillère in 2003.

L'Avant Comptoir 299	Regular neighbourhood
La Cour de Rémi 282	Regular neighbourhood
Le Chatillon 282	Local favourite
Les Cimaises 283	Breakfast
In De Wulf 270	Worth the travel
Mugaritz 319	Wish I'd opened
Noma 160	Wish I'd opened
Pierre Gagnaire 306	High end
Roberta's 603	Wish I'd opened

ALEXIS GAUTHIER
Gauthier Soho
21 Romilly Street, London
French born chef-patron at London's Michelin starred Gauthier Soho, where the menu is distinctly un-French with its emphasis on vegetables.

Bob Bob Ricard 223	Local favourite
Ledoyen 306	High end
Little Italy 225	Breakfast
Sukho 188	Regular neighbourhood
La Table de Tee 120	Worth the travel
La Tour d'Argent 298	Wish I'd opened
Voyageur Nissart 286	Bargain
Whitstable Oyster Company 178	Worth the travel

PETER GILMORE

Quay
Overseas Passenger Terminal, 5 Hickson Road, Sydney
Executive chef of Quay since 2001, Gilmore describes his market-driven style as 'a celebration of being a cook in Australia'.

Armchair Collective 18	Breakfast
Attica 34	Worth the travel
Blue Hill at Stone Barns 536	Worth the travel
Bras 282	Wish I'd opened
Golden Century Seafood 24	Late night
Mamak 25	Late night
Marque 21	High end
Mugaritz 319	Wish I'd opened
Rockpool Bar & Grill 25	High end
Sailors Thai Canteen 26	Bargain
Tastebuds 27	Breakfast

GUNNAR KARL GÍSLASON

Dill Restaurant
Norræna húsinu Sturlugötu 5, Reykjavík
Opened Dill in 2009 his Modern (New) Nordic approach is influenced by his time with Lauterbach, Redzepi and Henriksen.

Bæjarins Beztu 134	Late night
Dragsholm Slot 155	High end
Fljótt og Gott 134	Local favourite
Formel B 153	Regular neighbourhood
Grái Kötturinn 134	Breakfast
Noma 160	Wish I'd opened

PETER GOOSSENS

Hof Van Cleve
Riemegemstraat 1, Kruishoutem
Has run his rustic yet refined restaurant since 1987. Combines Belgian traditions and French haute technique and Asian influences.

Louise 164	Worth the travel
Nieuw Stadion 265	Bargain
't Fornuis 261	Regular neighbourhood

PETER GORDON

The Providores
109 Marylebone High Street, London
Ex Sugar Club, Kiwi-born fusion pioneer Gordon now runs restaurants in Auckland, Istanbul and London.

Alibaba Restaurant 439	Worth the travel
Balikçi Sabahattin 439	Worth the travel
Bambi 437	Late night
Caravan 200	Breakfast
Çinaralti Mangalbasi 438	Worth the travel
Depot Eatery 48	Worth the travel
Mangerie Bebek 440	Breakfast
Meze by Lemon Tree 438	Worth the travel
Mikla 438	High end
Nopi 226	Local favourite
The River Café 188	High end
Spuntino 228	Wish I'd opened
Tre Viet 203	Bargain

PATRICK GOUBIER

Chez Patrick
2f Garden East, 222 Queens Road East, Hong Kong Island
Lyonnaise globetrotter who has worked in London, the Caribbean, Vietnam and Rome, Goubier is now settled in Hong Kong.

Amber 83	Worth the travel
L'Atelier de Joël Robuchon 83	Regular neighbourhood
Caprice 84	High end
Cecconi's Italian 84	Regular neighbourhood
Georges Blanc 291	Worth the travel

LORI GRANITO

Magnolia
17 Po Yan Street, Hong Kong Island
Her unconventional career has seen the New Orleans native's small Cajun-Creole private catering business flourish in Hong Kong.

208 Duecento Otto 83	Regular neighbourhood
Al's Diner 83	Late night
L'Auberge de L'Ill 274	Worth the travel
August 546	Worth the travel
Caprice 84	High end
Wagyu Kaiseki Den 88	Wish I'd opened
Yung Kee 87	Local favourite

BENJAMIN GREENO

Momofuku Seiobo
The Star, 80 Pyrmont Street, Sydney
Runs the kitchen for David Chang in Sydney. Born in England, he's worked with Sat Bains and Rene Redzepi.

Attica 34	Worth the travel
Chat Thai 23	Bargain
Golden Century Seafood 24	Late night
Marque 21	High end
Momofuku Ssäm Bar 579	Wish I'd opened
Ms G's 19	Regular neighbourhood
Relæ 162	Worth the travel
Third Village 17	Breakfast

MICHAEL GUERRIERI

City Sandwich
649 9th Avenue, New York
Italian-American who relocated to Portugal to open Mezzaluna. Back in New York now, he runs the Portuguese-inspired City Sandwich.

A Pescaria 369	Worth the travel
Caféteria 588	Late night
Indochine 577	High end
Olieng 570	Regular neighbourhood
Pastis 594	Late night
The Supper Club 254	Wish I'd opened
The Waverly Inn 586	Local favourite

MARIA HELENA GUIMARAES

Spot
Avenida Paulista 1842, São Paulo
In partnership with Lygia Lopes, she runs the lively kitchen at São Paulo's Spot, which opened in 1994 just off the major city artery that is Paulista Avenue.

D.O.M. Restaurante 636	Worth the travel
Fasano 636	High end
Mercado Municipal 635	Bargain
Per Se 574	Worth the travel
The River Café 188	High end
The Wolseley 221	Breakfast

MEHMET GÜRS

Mikla
Marmara Pera Hotel, Mesrutiyet Caddesi 15, Istanbul
Turkish toque star that, thanks to his Finnish-Swedish mother and a childhood partially spent in Stockholm, works some Nordic influences into his cooking at his Istanbul restaurant Mikla, opened in 2005.

Asmali Canim Cigerim 437	Bargain
Kantin 440	Local favourite
Kardesler Et Lokantasi 432	Worth the travel
Kiyi 441	Regular neighbourhood
Mugaritz 319	Wish I'd opened

PACO GUZMÁN

Santa
Avinguda Meridiana 47, Barcelona
Trained at elBulli, he did a stint cooking in Japan ahead of opening Santa Maria in Barcelona's El Born in 2000, following that with Santa, on Avinguda Meridiana in 2008.

Alt Heidelberg 343	Bargain
Arzak 320	Worth the travel
Buen Bocado 341	Late night
Morro Fi 349	Regular neighbourhood
El Raco de la Ciutadella 340	Regular neighbourhood
La Panxa del Bisbe 346	Regular neighbourhood
Teresa Carles 343	Regular neighbourhood
Tucco 342	Regular neighbourhood
Xiringuito Escribà 347	Regular neighbourhood

RODOLFO GUZMÁN

Boragó
Avenida Nueva Costanera 3467, Vitacura
The Owner of Boragó in Santiago, opened in the Chilean capital in 2007, inspired by his time at Mugaritz with Andoni Aduriz and his own study of chemical engineering and bioprocesses.

Altiplánico Hotel - Easter Island 641	Breakfast
Aquí Está Coco 642	Wish I'd opened
Aquí Jaime 643	Regular neighbourhood
La Cocina de la Nana 640	Local favourite
Fuente Chilena 642	Late night
Malabar 621	Worth the travel
Mugaritz 319	Wish I'd opened
Per Se 574	Worth the travel

GABRIELLE HAMILTON

Prune
54 East 1st Street, New York
Owner of Prune in Manhattan, which gained cult status for its gutsy approach as outlined in the memoir 'Blood, Bones and Butter.'

Balthazar **596**	Breakfast
Barbuto **582**	Local favourite
Cotogna **507**	Worth the travel
Daniel **571**	High end
Del Posto **588**	High end
Kafana **578**	Bargain
Marea **569**	High end
Otto Enoteca Pizzeria **581**	Regular neighbourhood
The River Café **188**	High end
Rochelle Canteen **208**	Regular neighbourhood
Two Boroughs Larder **540**	Worth the travel

ANNA HANSEN

The Modern Pantry
47-48 St. John's Square, London
Opened The Providores and Tapa Room with Peter Gordon in London's Marylebone in 2001. She launched her own restaurant, The Modern Pantry, in Clerkenwell in 2008.

Café Habana **595**	Breakfast
The Company Shed **176**	Worth the travel
Koya **225**	Regular neighbourhood
La Chapelle **209**	High end
Ottolenghi **205**	Breakfast
The Providores **192**	Breakfast
Su Furriadroxu **408**	Worth the travel
Tayyabs **211**	Local favourite
The Wolseley **221**	Breakfast

STEFFEN HANSEN

Grefsenkollen
Grefsenkollveien 100, Oslo
In 2008 he took over running the kitchen at Grefsenkollen, a timber ski lodge originally opened in 1927.

Alex Sushi **139**	Regular neighbourhood
Gastrologik **150**	Worth the travel
Hakkasan **218**	Worth the travel
Marcus Wareing **190**	Worth the travel
The Nighthawk Diner **140**	Wish I'd opened
Onda Mezzanine **138**	Wish I'd opened
Oscarsgate **142**	High end
Restaurang Jonas **148**	Worth the travel
Saigon Lille Café **141**	Bargain
Solsiden **142**	Wish I'd opened

HENRY HARRIS

Racine
239 Brompton Road, London
Eldest of the two Harris brothers, he owns Racine in London's Knightsbridge which celebrated a decade in business in 2012.

Asador Etxebarri **324**	Worth the travel
Balthazar **596**	Breakfast
Le Bistrot du Paradou **286**	Worth the travel
Café des Fédérations **283**	Bargain
Cal Pep **340**	Late night
Santa Maria **187**	Regular neighbourhood
The Seahorse **175**	Regular neighbourhood

MATTHEW HARRIS

Bibendum
Michelin House, 81 Fulham Road, London
Has carved out a career at Terence Conran's Bibendum, in Michelin's former London HQ, where he began cooking in 1987.

Au Pied de Cochon **475**	Local favourite
Le Gavroche **218**	High end
The Ivy **225**	Wish I'd opened
The River Café **188**	High end
Royal China **185**	Bargain
St. John Bar and Restaurant **201**	Local favourite
Tamnag Thai **201**	Bargain
The Wolseley **221**	Breakfast

SAM HARRIS

Zucca
184 Bermondsey Street, London
The River Café trained force behind Zucca, a Modern Italian opened in Southeast London's Bermondsey Street in 2010. He's also run the nearby Maltings Café since 2007.

L'Anima **198**	Regular neighbourhood
Cecconi's Mayfair **217**	Late night
The Company Shed **176**	Worth the travel
José **208**	Bargain
Locanda Locatelli **192**	High end
Relæ **162**	Worth the travel
St. John Bar and Restaurant **201**	Local favourite
St. John Bread & Wine **209**	Local favourite

STEPHEN HARRIS

The Sportsman
Faversham Road, Seasalter, Whitstable
Took over a rundown pub in Seasalter, on a remote part of the Kentish coast in 1999, and built it up into one of the England's most exciting destination restaurants.

Fäviken Magasinet **143**	Worth the travel
The Hand & Flowers **173**	Worth the travel
In De Wulf **270**	Worth the travel
Tea & Times **177**	Breakfast
Whitstable Oyster Company **178**	Worth the travel
Williams & Brown Tapas **178**	Regular neighbourhood

ANGELA HARTNETT

Murano
20 Queen Street, London
Began her career with Gordon Ramsay, going solo with her Mayfair Italian, Murano, (opened with Ramsay in 2008) in 2010. Also oversees the menu at the Whitechapel Gallery Dining Room.

Barrafina **222**	Regular neighbourhood
Brawn **197**	Regular neighbourhood
The Delaunay **214**	Breakfast
Hix **225**	Late night
The Modern Pantry **200**	Breakfast
Momofuku Ko **579**	Worth the travel
The Pig **176**	Worth the travel
The Sportsman **177**	Worth the travel
St. John Bread & Wine **209**	Local favourite
The Waterside Inn **173**	High end

DAVID HAWKSWORTH

Hawksworth Restaurant
801 West Georgia Street, Vancouver
Opened his eponymous Hawksworth Restaurant in Vancouver in 2011, made his name at the city's West Restaurant having worked in the UK at Le Manoir aux Qaut'Saisons, L'Escargot and The Square.

Le Caprice **217**	Wish I'd opened
Gjelina **498**	Regular neighbourhood
Gyoza King **464**	Late night
Kirin Restaurant **463**	Regular neighbourhood
Le Louis XV **291**	High end
Masa **573**	High end
Motomachi Shokudo **464**	Bargain
Red Card Sports Bar **461**	Late night

NIGEL HAWORTH

Northcote
Northcote Road, Langho, Blackburn
Has run Northcote in Lancashire, with Craig Bancroft, since 1984. They also operate four food-led pubs across the North of England, including The Three Fishes at Milton, and The Highwayman at Burrow.

Bentley's Oyster Bar & Grill **216**	Wish I'd opened
The Fat Duck **172**	Worth the travel
Clayton Street Chippy **178**	Bargain
The Inn at Whitewell **178**	Local favourite
Ocean **357**	Worth the travel
The Wolseley **221**	Breakfast

SAM HAYWARD

Fore Street
288 Fore Street, Portland
Partner in Portland, Maine's Fore Street, opened in 1996 in the city's Old Port District, and a former winner of the Best Chef in the Northeast for his unembellished style and championing of New England's larder.

Boda **531**	Late night
Boynton-McKay **530**	Breakfast
El Camino **530**	Bargain
Hamersley's Bistro **533**	Wish I'd opened
Hot Suppa! **531**	Breakfast
The Lost Kitchen **530**	Worth the travel
Le Pain Quotidien **597**	Breakfast
Petite Jacqueline **532**	Regular neighbourhood
Prune **580**	Regular neighbourhood
The Slipway **532**	Local favourite

FERGUS HENDERSON

St. John Bar and Restaurant
26 St John Street, London
Champion of using the bits of beast that British chefs tended to leave behind before St. John arrived in 1994. Opened St. John Bread & Wine in 2003, and the St. John Hotel in 2011.

Bar Italia **222**	Late night
Chez Georges **296**	Worth the travel
Jade Garden **213**	Bargain
Sweetings **199**	Local favourite
The Walnut Tree **233**	Worth the travel

MARGOT HENDERSON
Rochelle Canteen
Rochelle School, Arnold Circus, London
Wife of Fergus 'Nose-to-Tail' Henderson, a culinary force in her own right running the Rochelle Canteen in London's East End and Arnold & Henderson with her business partner Melanie Arnold.

Bar Italia 222.................................Late night
Barrafina 222.............Regular neighbourhood
Brawn 197.................Regular neighbourhood
Ducksoup 224.............Regular neighbourhood
Hix Oyster & Fish House 175...Worth the travel
Ikeda 219.....................................High end
Red Rooster 566.................Worth the travel
Royal China 185.................................Bargain
St. John Bar and Restaurant 201...Local favourite

CLAUS MØLLER HENRIKSEN
Dragsholm Slot
Dragsholm Alle 3, Hørve
Danish Noma graduate who oversees dining rooms, one formal / one casual at the striking Dragsholm Slot, a restored 13th century castle 75Km south of Copenhagen that operates as hotel.

Bras 282...........................Wish I'd opened
Brdr. Price 158.................Worth the travel
Dos Palillos Barcelona 342.................Regular
   neighbourhood
Dos Palillos Berlin 382..........Worth the travel
Geist 159...................Regular neighbourhood
Relæ 162...........................Worth the travel
Retour 160...Bargain

SERGIO HERMAN
Oud Sluis
Beestenmarkt 2, Sluis
In 1991 he took over Oud Sluis in the southwest of the Netherlands, a mussel house run by his father for 20 years, and turned it into one of the world's best restaurants.

Bar Pinotxo 342...........................Breakfast
Croissant Show 315.......................Breakfast
De Siphon 269.....................Local favourite
Eleven Madison Park 591......Worth the travel
Juan y Andrea 315............Wish I'd opened
Restaurant Es Torrent 315.....Wish I'd opened
Toscanini 253.............Regular neighbourhood
Zuma 190..............................Local favourite

THOMAS HERMAN
Recently left Nimb in Copenhagen's Tivoli, where he cooked from 2008 to 2012. He is now pursuing other projects.

Bistro Boheme 158.....Regular neighbourhood
Bras 282..........................Wish I'd opened
Meyers Deli 154............................Breakfast
Noma 160.........................Wish I'd opened
Per Se 574.........................Worth the travel
Retour 160...Bargain
Schønnemann 160.................Local favourite

AGUS HERMAWAN
Restaurant Blauw
Amstelveenseweg 158, Amsterdam
Has been overseeing the Indonesian-inspired kitchen at Amsterdam's Blauw since it opened in 2008.

Anne&Max 256.............................Breakfast
Chang-i 255...................................Late night
Grand Restaurant Karel V 247........Worth the
   travel
Lastage 252.....................................High end
Mama San 129...................Worth the travel
Ron Blaauw 256...................Wish I'd opened
Sarong 128.........................Worth the travel
Sie-Joe 253.................Regular neighbourhood
Toscanini 253.............Regular neighbourhood

SHAUN HILL
The Walnut Tree
Llanddewi Skirrid, Abergavenny
British restaurant legend that put Gidleigh Park in Devon and the Merchant House in Ludlow on the map. Now runs the Walnut Tree in Abergavenny in South Wales.

The Butcher's Arms 180.......Worth the travel
The Hardwick 233......Regular neighbourhood
Hibiscus 219.....................................High end
Maison Bertaux 226.......................Breakfast
Opera Tavern 215.............................Bargain
St. John Bar and Restaurant 201...Local favourite

GERALD HIRIGOYEN
Piperade
1015 Battery Street, San Francisco
A resident of the Bay area for over 30 years, Hirigoyen is the French-Basque owner of Piperade, which he opened in 2002 following his earlier San Franciscan success with the bistro Pastis.

Asador Etxebarri 324.............Worth the travel
Bar Agricole 515.......................Local favourite
Le Bernardin 571.............................High end
Café de la Presse 505.....................Breakfast
Cotogna 507........................Worth the travel
The French Laundry 484........Wish I'd opened
Hon's Wun Tun House 504...................Bargain
The House of Prime Rib 512....Local favourite
Yuet Lee 512...................................Late night

MARK HIX
Hix
66-70 Brewer Street, London
Left Caprice Holdings in 2007 to build his own London-based empire of stylish restaurants, built on straightforward modern British cooking. These include Hix Oyster Chophouse, Hix Soho and The Tramshed.

Cay Tre 223.......................................Bargain
Hung 213..Bargain
Locanda Locatelli 192......................High end
Momofuku Noodle Bar 579.....Wish I'd opened
Trishna 193........................Worth the travel
The Wolseley 221...........................Breakfast

REON HOBSON
Pescatore
The George Hotel, 50 Park Terrace, Christchurch
The Kiwi-born chef has returned home and is now at Pescatore in Christchurch, after cheffing worldwide from Level 41, Sydney to Restaurant Gordon Ramsay and Marco-Pierre White's L'Escargot in London.

Beach Café 39................................Breakfast
Burger and Beers Inc. 38.....................Bargain
The Fat Duck 172.................Worth the travel
JC Place 38..Late night
North & South 38.......Regular neighbourhood
Pegasus Bay 39...........Regular neighbourhood
Riverstone Kitchen 40............Worth the travel

PETER HOFFMAN
Back Forty
190 Avenue B, New York
Best-known for his farm-to-table ethics, the outspoken New York chef-restaurateur owns East Village's organic, environmentally responsible burger joint Back Forty plus Back Forty West, on the former Savoy site in Soho.

EN 583...High end
Fore Street 531.....................Local favourite
Morandi 585..................................Breakfast
Pho Bang 593.....................................Bargain
Roberta's 603.....................Wish I'd opened
Tommaso 600.......................Local favourite

ESBEN HOLMBOE BANG
Maaemo
Schweigaards Gate 15, Oslo
Danish chef and partner in Maaemo in Oslo, who took inspiration from Copenhagen, notably Noma, before opening his successful take on Modern (New) Nordic in 2011.

Le Benjamin 140......Regular neighbourhood
Delicatessen 140............................Late night
Fäviken Magasinet 143..........Worth the travel
Fenaknoken 141.....................Local favourite
Fiskeriet Youngstorget 141..................Bargain
Frantzén/Lindeberg 148................High end
Kolonihagen 139............................Breakfast
Pierre Gagnaire 306.........................High end
The Fat Duck 172.................Worth the travel

BRAD HOLMES
Ulla
509 Fisgard Street, Victoria
Owner of Ulla in Victoria, Vancouver, he previously worked at Vancouver hotspots Feenies, West, Chow, Lumière and, lastly, Cibo before setting up with partner and front of house manager Sahara Tamarin.

Brasserie L'Ecole 454......................Late night
El Celler de Can Roca 329.....Worth the travel
Fol Epi 455.........................Worth the travel
Hawksworth Restaurant 464.Worth the travel
Meat & Bread 461................Wish I'd opened
Pizzeria Prima Strada 455....Worth the travel
Point-No-Point Resort 454.................High end
Relish 455..Bargain
Sooke Harbour House 454.......Local favourite

JACOB HOLMSTRÖM
Gastrologik
Artillerigatan 14, Stockholm
The Swedish chef and co-founder of Nordic newcomer Gastrologik in Stockholm (opened in autumn 2011) comes from a family of restaurateurs and honed his skills at Mathias Dahlgren's Matbaren and Matsalen.

Asador Etxebarri **324**	Worth the travel
Blue Hill at Stone Barns **536**	Worth the travel
Fäviken Magasinet **143**	Worth the travel
Gateau **148**	Breakfast
Matbaren **148**	High end
Matsalen **149**	High end
Östermalms Korvspecialist **151**	Bargain
Råkultur **153**	Bargain
Restaurang Prinsen **149**	Local favourite
Sturehof **151**	Late night

LINTON HOPKINS
Restaurant Eugene
2277 Peachtree Road, Atlanta
Native to Atlanta, where he owns Restaurant Eugene (2004) and the pub Holeman & Finch (2008). Worked at Washington's DC Coast, and Mr B's Bistro and Windsor Court in New Orleans.

Animal **499**	Worth the travel
Au Pied de Cochon **475**	Local favourite
Bacchanalia **529**	High end
Carver's Country Kitchen **529**	Local favourite
Per Se **574**	Worth the travel
Trattoria Lucca **540**	Worth the travel
The Varsity **530**	Bargain
White House **530**	Breakfast

ADAM HORTON
Raphael
11616 Ventura Boulevard, Los Angeles
Cooks what he terms 'progressive American' food at Raphael, having previously spent nine years at the more traditional Saddle Peak Lodge, also in Los Angeles.

L'Atelier de Joël Robuchon **485**	High end
The Aviary **563**	Worth the travel
Fatburger **497**	Late night
Fäviken Magasinet **143**	Worth the travel
Krua Thai **496**	Late night
Momofuku Noodle Bar **579**	Wish I'd opened
Noma **160**	Wish I'd opened
Pho 999 **498**	Bargain
Providence **495**	High end
Sanamluang Café **492**	Regular neighbourhood
Scarpetta **490**	Breakfast

PHILIP HOWARD
The Square
6-10 Bruton Street, London
Chef and co-owner of The Square in London since it opened in 1991, he's more recently teamed up with restaurateur Rebecca Mascarenhas at Kitchen W8 (2009) and Sonny's Kitchen (2012).

L'Arpège **301**	High end
Baker & Spice **186**	Breakfast
Eleven Madison Park **591**	Worth the travel
L'Enclume **175**	Worth the travel
Hakkasan **218**	Worth the travel
Meat Liquor **192**	Bargain
The River Café **188**	High end
Rockpool Bar & Grill **35**	Wish I'd opened
Scott's **220**	Local favourite

ALFREDO HOZ
La Oliva
Egelantiersstraat 122, Amsterdam
Spaniard who cooks Basque pintxos at La Oliva, which he opened in 2008 with his Dutch wife Yvette Barents who looks after front of house.

Arzak **320**	Worth the travel
Bodega del Riojano **325**	Local favourite
Burgermeester **254**	Bargain
Elmar **255**	Regular neighbourhood
Graffiti **577**	Worth the travel
Restaurant Marius **257**	Local favourite
El Serbal **325**	High end

CHRISTOFFER HRUSKOVA
North Road
69-72 St John Street, London
Opened North Road in Clerkenwell, London in 2010, before which came Fig in Islington in 2006. Born in Denmark, he earnt his cheffing spurs in Hong Kong, Sydney, San Francisco and New York.

Busaba Eathai **223**	Bargain
Caravan **200**	Breakfast
Ducksoup **224**	Regular neighbourhood
Hibiscus **219**	High end
The Modern Pantry **200**	Breakfast
Mugaritz **319**	Wish I'd opened
Noma **160**	Wish I'd opened
Roganic **193**	Worth the travel
Sông Quê **204**	Bargain
Viajante **198**	High end

DANIEL HUMM
Eleven Madison Park
11 Madison Avenue, New York
Swiss-born chef at Eleven Madison Park in New York, whose resume includes Restaurant Le Pont de Brent near Montreux, Gasthaus zum Gupf in the Swiss Alps and Campton Place in San Francisco.

Alinea **556**	Worth the travel
L'Ambroisie **297**	Worth the travel
Blue Ribbon Brasserie **597**	Late night
Bras **282**	Wish I'd opened
Coi **513**	Wish I'd opened
Daniel **571**	High end
Franny's **601**	Regular neighbourhood
Mandoo Bar **567**	Bargain
Sake Bar Hagi **566**	Late night
Torrisi Italian Specialties **596**	Local favourite

DAN HUNTER
Royal Mail
Royal Mail Hotel 98 Parker Street, Dunkeld
Aussie chef at the Royal Mail Hotel in Victoria, previously cooked at Langton's Restaurant and Verge (both in Melbourne) and then gained more experience in Spain at Caelis and at Mugaritz.

Attica **34**	Worth the travel
Bar Lourinhã **31**	Regular neighbourhood
Commis **518**	High end
The European **31**	Breakfast
Hutong Dumpling Bar **32**	Bargain
Izakaya Den **32**	Late night
Manresa **482**	Wish I'd opened
Mugaritz **319**	Wish I'd opened
Sepia **36**	Worth the travel

ALFONSO & ERNESTO IACCARINO
Don Alfonso 1890
Corso Sant'Agata 11-13, Sant'Agata Sui Due Golfi
Champions of tradition and innovation, they run their family restaurant and hotel on an organic farm and restaurants in Macau and Marrakech.

La Conca del Sogno **392**	Regular neighbourhood
Enoteca Pinchiorri **410**	Worth the travel
Pizzeria Gino Sorbillo **392**	Bargain
Ristorante Teatro alla Scala **404**	Late night
Robuchon au Dôme **79**	Wish I'd opened
Lo Scoglio da Tommaso **392**	Local favourite
Sukiyabashi Jiro **105**	Worth the travel

TAKASHI INOUE

Takashi
456 Hudson Street, New York
A third-generation Korean immigrant born in Japan, he's made his name in New York with Takashi, his take on 'yakiniku' (table-grilling).
15 East 598.................................High end
La Bonbonniere 582..........................Breakfast
Clinton Street Baking Co. 593...........Breakfast
Congee Village 593..............................Bargain
Han Joo 603.........................Local favourite
Kunjip 569.................................Late night
Kyo Ya 578.............Regular neighbourhood
Tetsuya's 26.....................Worth the travel
Tong Sam Gyup Goo Ee 604.....Local favourite
Tori Shin 572.............Regular neighbourhood
Umi 111...........................Worth the travel

JUSTIN IP

The Arts Club
40 Dover Street, London
Previously of Morton's Club, he took over at The Arts Club in 2012, the now fashionable London private members' enclave that was reborn in 2011.
Albion Café 206..............................Late night
Balthazar 596...............................Breakfast
Hawksmoor 197.............................Breakfast
Pollen Street Social 220........Wish I'd opened
Tapas Brindisa 228.................Worth the travel
The Wolseley 221...........................Breakfast
Yauatcha 229...............................Late night

KATSUMI ISHIDA

En mets fais ce qu'il te plait
43 Rue Chevreuil, Lyon
After a decade in French restaurants in Japan, in 1993 he began working in Lyon, opening his own bistro there in 1999.
L'Arpège 301..................................High end
Asador Etxebarri 324............Worth the travel
Le Baratin 311...........Regular neighbourhood
Bras 282.........................Wish I'd opened
Le Chateaubriand 307...........Worth the travel
Le Louis XV 291..............................High end
Pierre Gagnaire 306........................High end

YOSHINORI ISHII

Umu
14-16 Bruton Place, London
Arrived at Umu in 2010, his time at Kyoto Kitcho and Morimoto, equipping him to oversee the London kaiseki destination.
Mizai 97...........................Wish I'd opened

JULIUS JASPERS

Ran the cook shop Studio Bazar, which has two branches in Amsterdam, until 2010. He is currently a judge on Dutch TV's Top Chef.
Amber 83...............................Worth the travel
Beluga 246..........................Worth the travel
Café Restaurant Dauphine 256...........Bargain
De Kas 256.........................Wish I'd opened
De Kromme Watergang 248..Worth the travel
Geranium 163.....................Worth the travel
Hertog Jan 269....................Worth the travel
New King 253....................................Bargain
Pure C 248.........................Wish I'd opened
Restaurant Le Garage 255...............Late night
Ron Blaauw 256..................Wish I'd opened
Thoumieux 303.......................Local favourite
Toscanini 253.............Regular neighbourhood
Visaandeschelde 257..Regular neighbourhood
Vlaamsch Broodhuys 254................Breakfast
wd~50 594.................Regular neighbourhood

MARC-ANDRÉ JETTÉ

Les 400 Coups
400 Rue Notre-Dame Est, Montreal
Opened Les 400 Coups, in Montreal, in 2010, staged in France and earned his stripes in various Quebec kitchens.
Café Sardine 474..............................Late night
Campagnolo 461.........Regular neighbourhood
Le Comptoir 474..........Regular neighbourhood
Corton 598......................................High end
Dominion Square Tavern 474...............Regular neighbourhood
Grumman 78 478............................Bargain
Lawrence Restaurant 475................Breakfast
Roberta's 603....................Wish I'd opened
SaQuaNa 282.......................Worth the travel

TIMOTHY JOHNSON

Apicius
23 Stone Street, Cranbrook
Nico Ladenis protégé, he opened Apicius in 2004, winning acclaim for his imaginative French-influenced cooking.
Alinea 556...........................Worth the travel
Bouchon 484......................Wish I'd opened
Bras 282.........................Wish I'd opened
Dinner by Heston 190...........Worth the travel
Gary Danko 508................................High end
The Landgate Bistro 176.....................Regular neighbourhood
The Pleasant Café 177....................Breakfast

JEAN JOHO

Everest
440 South LaSalle Street, Chicago
Born in Alsace, oversees the restaurant at Las Vegas' Eiffel Tower, Boston's Brasserie Jo and Chicago's Everest and Paris Club.
L'Assiette Champenoise 279..Worth the travel
L'Auberge de L'Ill 274...........Worth the travel
Big Bowl 558.............Regular neighbourhood
Le Bouchon Bordelais 187....Worth the travel
Jean Georges 573................Worth the travel
M Burger 563....................................Bargain
NoMI Kitchen 559..........................Breakfast
Phoenix 555.........................Local favourite
Pierrot 560......................................Breakfast

HYWEL JONES

The Park Restaurant
Lucknam Park Hotel, Colerne, Chippenham
Trained with Nico Ladenis and Marco Pierre White, he's been at Lucknam Park near Bath since 2004.
The Bertinet Bakery + Café 179.....Breakfast
The Facil 385.........................Worth the travel
The Fig Tree 233........Regular neighbourhood
Moksh Indian Restaurant 234.........Late night
The Shed 233.........................Local favourite
The Square 221..............................High end
The Walnut Tree 233.............Worth the travel

JONATHAN JONES

The Anchor & Hope
36 The Cut, London
Co-owner of London's The Anchor and Hope and Great Queen Street, Jones is a graduate of Fergus Henderson's St. John.
The Abbeville Kitchen 187..................Regular neighbourhood
Le Café Anglais 184..................Local favourite
Ducksoup 224............Regular neighbourhood
Lahore Karahi 195...........................Bargain
Osteria del Boccondivino 406.............Worth the travel
Quo Vadis 228...................Wish I'd opened
Restaurant Martin Wishart 232.........High end
St. John Bar and Restaurant 201....Local favourite
St. John Hotel 215...........................Breakfast

DYLAN JONES AND BO (DUANGPORN) SONGVISAVA

Bo.lan
Sukhumvit 26, Klongteoy, Bangkok
A husband and wife team who are Slow Food champions combining ethical ingredients with traditional Thai recipes.
Bras 282.........................Wish I'd opened
Eat Me 120.................Regular neighbourhood
Gastro 1/6 118.................................Breakfast
The Ledbury 194....................Worth the travel
La Monita Taqueria 119......................Bargain
MoVida Bar De Tapas Y Vino 32...Worth the travel
Nahm Bangkok 120...............Worth the travel
Soul Food Mahanakorn 118................Regular neighbourhood
Summer Palace 119.........................Breakfast
Yardbird 88...............Regular neighbourhood

TOMOYASU KAMO

Kamo
Avenue des Saisons 123, Brussels
Young Brussels-based Japanese sushi master, who previously worked at Tagawa Avenue Louise. He opened Kamo in 2007.

Bissoh 278.............................Wish I'd opened
Bon Bon 262...................................High end
Le Chalet De La Forêt 262.....Worth the travel
Het Kriekske 262.......Regular neighbourhood
Makimura 112......................Worth the travel
Nihonryori Ryugin 108..........Worth the travel
Orientalia 262............Regular neighbourhood
Restaurant Le Chat Noir 263...........Late night

TOMAŽ KAVCIC

Gostilna pri Lojzetu
Pri Lojzetu, Dvorec Zemono, Vipava
Slovenian, who cooks at Pri Lojzetu near Ajdovščina, built in 1683 and run as a restaurant by his family since 1897.

Agli Amici 396............Regular neighbourhood
Don Alfonso 1890 392...........Wish I'd opened
Gostilna Rajh 420................Worth the travel
Gostilna Žeja 421.................Worth the travel
La Pergola 398......................Wish I'd opened
Vipavski hram 421..............................Bargain

MICHAEL KEMPF

Facil
Mandala Hotel, Potsdamer Strasse 3, Berlin
Has been running the kitchen at Facil since 2003, prior to that he worked at Dieter Müller and Restaurant Fischerzunft in Switzerland.

AOC 158.............................Worth the travel
La Bastide de Moustiers 285..Worth the travel
Burgermeister 381..........................Late night
Chipps 382.....................................Breakfast
Gourmet Restaurant Lerbach 375.........Worth
  the travel
Lavanderia Vecchia 384.....................Bargain
Restaurant Margaux Berlin 383........High end
Sissi 385...................Regular neighbourhood
Vendôme 376.....................Wish I'd opened

JACOB KENEDY

Bocca di Lupo
12 Archer Street, London
After a decade at Moro he opened Bocca di Lupo in 2008, following that with Gelupo, his gelateria and coffee bar that sits opposite.

Bright Courtyard 191..Regular neighbourhood
Cal Pep 340....................................Late night
Da Dora 392.........................Wish I'd opened
Defune 191..High end
Empress of Sichuan 213.....................Regular
  neighbourhood
Gelatauro 393.....................Worth the travel
Hot Stuff 206.....................................Bargain
Koya 225...................Regular neighbourhood
Moro 200...................Regular neighbourhood
Pitt Cue Co. 227..................Worth the travel
Quimet i Quimet 351......................Late night
Roux at the Landau 202...................High end
St. John Hotel 215...........................Breakfast
Sweetings 199........................Local favourite
Taverna Can Margarit 351................Late night
The Waterside Inn 173........................High end
Tickets 353.........................Worth the travel
La Tomaquera 352...........................Late night
Trattoria da Marcello 400.......Wish I'd opened

TOM KERRIDGE

The Hand & Flowers
126 West Street, Marlow
Owner of the Hand & Flowers, the rundown pub, in Marlow, South East England, he took over in 2005 and turned into a destination.

Le Chateaubriand 307...........Worth the travel
The Fat Duck 172....................Worth the travel
Hibiscus 219.....................................High end
The Hinds Head 172................Local favourite
Hix 225..Late night
Polpo 227...Bargain
Roka 202...High end
The Royal Oak 173..................Local favourite

DAVID KINCH

Manresa
320 Village Lane, Los Gatos
Opened Northern California's Manresa in 2002 having studied cooking in France, Spain, Germany, Japan and the U.S.

L'Arpège 301......................................High end
Benu 515...High end
Brooklyn Fare 600................Wish I'd opened
Coi 513................................Wish I'd opened
Commis 518......................................High end
Ginza Kojyu 104..................Worth the travel
Ishikawa 113.......................Worth the travel
Restaurante Los Pinos 483................Regular
  neighbourhood
Soif Wine Bar 484......Regular neighbourhood
The Sportsman 177...............Worth the travel

MUSTAFA CIHAN KIPÇAK

La Mouette
Tomtom Kaptan Sokak 18, Istanbul
In partnership with Üryan Doğmuş, he overseas the menu at La Mouette, located in a boutique hotel in a 19th century building.

Beyti 436.............................Wish I'd opened
El Celler de Can Roca 329.....Worth the travel
Çinar Restaurant 433.......................Breakfast
Faros Dine & Wine 437......................Regular
  neighbourhood
Mimolett 438.....................................High end
Moo 346.............................Worth the travel
Van Kahvalti Evi 438.........................Breakfast

MILES KIRBY

Caravan
11-13 Exmouth Market, London
Formerly ran the kitchen at The Providores, opened Caravan with fellow Kiwi, Chris Ammermann in 2010.

Afghan Kitchen 204...........................Bargain
Bar Jules 508.......................Worth the travel
Blue Ribbon Sushi 597.....................Late night
The Company Shed 176.........Worth the travel
Ducksoup 224............Regular neighbourhood
Logan Brown 44....................Wish I'd opened
Moro 200...................Regular neighbourhood
Noma 160.............................Wish I'd opened
Palmera Oasis 205..........................Late night
PUBLIC 596.........................Worth the travel
Rochelle Canteen 208 Regular neighbourhood
Roka 202...High end
The Slanted Door 506.............Worth the travel
St John Bar and Restaurant 201.........Local
  favourite
The Towpath Café 208.....................Breakfast
Trullo 206..................Regular neighbourhood

SCOT KIRTON

La Colombe
Spaanschemat River Road, Constantia, Cape Town
South African who took over at La Colombe in 2010. Previously cooked at Constantia Uitsig's River Café.

Beleza 448..Bargain
Borruso's 448....................................Bargain
The Greenhouse 446..........................High end
Ile de Pain 449.....................Worth the travel
Massimo's 447..........Regular neighbourhood
Mzoli's 447...........................Local favourite
Olympia Café 447.............................Breakfast
Pirates Steakhouse 448...................Late night
The Test Kitchen 449.............Wish I'd opened

TOM KITCHIN

The Kitchin
78 Commercial Quay, Edinburgh
Trained with Koffmann, Ducasse and Savoy, owner of The Kitchin, opened in his hometown of Edinburgh in 2006.
Colonnade 118......................Worth the travel
The Dogs 231.................................Bargain
Koffmann's 190...........Regular neighbourhood
Leo's Beanery 231............................Breakfast
Ondine Restaurant 232............Local favourite
The Peat Inn 230...............................High end
La Petite Maison 220.............Wish I'd opened
Porto & Fi 232.................................Breakfast

PAUL KITCHING

21212
3 Royal Terrace, Edinburgh
Kitching's resume includes time at Gidleigh Park and Nunsmere Hall Hotel. 21212, his restaurant with rooms, opened in 2009.
Betty's 180..............................Worth the travel
Forth Floor Restaurant 231................Regular
neighbourhood
Hibiscus 219....................................High end
The Kitchin 231.................Worth the travel
Restaurant Andrew Fairlie 230.........High end
The Starving Man 174.....................Late night
The Strathearn 230.........................Breakfast

ATUL KOCHHAR

Benares
12a Berkeley Square House, Berkeley Square, London
Indian-born British-based chef and owner of Benares (2007) widely accepted as the pioneer of modern Indian cuisine.
Busaba Eathai 223...........................Bargain
Canteen 191...............Regular neighbourhood
Dinner by Heston 190...........Worth the travel
Hakkasan 218.......................Worth the travel
Hélène Darroze 218........................Breakfast
Iggy's 126.........................Worth the travel
Le Manoir aux Quat'Saisons 179.............Wish
I'd opened
Marcus Wareing 190.............Worth the travel
Nobu 219...High end
Patara 226............Regular neighbourhood
Pollen Street Social 220........Wish I'd opened
Restaurant Sat Bains 179......Worth the travel
Seasoning 188...........Regular neighbourhood
The Wolseley 221............................Breakfast

PIERRE KOFFMANN

Koffmann's
The Berkeley Hotel, Wilton Place, London
Gascon-born, he became a legend in London at La Tante Claire, opened in 1977. Made his comeback in 2010 with Koffmann's at The Berkeley.
L'Absinthe 186...................................Bargain
L'Auberge du Pont de Collonges 286.......Wish
I'd opened
Bistro Bruno Loubet 199.....................Regular
neighbourhood
Le Gavroche 218.............................High end
Hélène Darroze 218........................Breakfast
Hereford Road 195....Regular neighbourhood
The Kitchin 231.................Worth the travel
The Ledbury 194....................Worth the travel
La Petite Maison 220.............Wish I'd opened
Opera Tavern 215...............................Bargain
Raoul's 191....................................Breakfast
Texture 193.......................................High end
Thoumieux 303....................Local favourite

RASMUS KOFOED

Geranium
Per Henrik Lings Allé 4, Copenhagen
Danish gold medal winner at the 2011 Bocuse d'Or, the co-owner of Geranium, he trained at Hotel d'Angleterre and at Scholteshof.
Ahaaa 161...Late night
Attica 34...........................Worth the travel
The Coffee Collective 161.................Breakfast
Dragsholm Slot 155.............................High end
Manfreds & Vin 162...........................Bargain
Meyers Bageri 162...........................Breakfast
Selfish 163...................Regular neighbourhood

ONNO KOKMEIJER

Ciel Bleu Restaurant
Ferdinand Bolstraat 333, Amsterdam
Dutch born and trained, he has established Ciel Bleu, as one of the city's best restaurants since his arrival there in 2003.
@7 Breakfast Lunch Tea 257...........Breakfast
L'Atelier de Joël Robuchon 222.........High end
The French Laundry 484........Wish I'd opened
Nam Kee 253......................................Bargain
The Red Sun 246........Regular neighbourhood
Thoumieux 303........................Local favourite
't Amsterdammertje 247.......Worth the travel

ANATOLY KOMM

Varvary
8a Strastnoy Boulevard, Moscow
Russian who trained as a geophysicist before taking up cooking in 2000. He's won acclaim by reinventing traditional Russian dishes.
L'Astrance 309.....................Worth the travel
Cassia 128........................Worth the travel
L'Osteria Francescana 395....Worth the travel
Mugaritz 319.........................Wish I'd opened
Zuma 87................................Wish I'd opened

ROBERT J. K. KRANENBORG

The former executive chef of the Intercontinental Hotels Group, he currently consultants for clients including Hotel De L'Europe.
Bakken met Passie 254....................Breakfast
Bolenius Restaurant 257......................Regular
neighbourhood
Bord'Eau 252.....................................High end
De Kas 256......................Wish I'd opened
De Kromme Watergang 248..................Worth
the travel
Fatty Crab 583....................Worth the travel
La Gazzetta 308..................................Bargain
Restaurant Le Garage 255..............Late night
Restaurant Marius 257............Local favourite
Yam Yam Trattoria Pizzeria 254...........Bargain

MATTHEW KUHN

DC Coast
1401 K Street Northwest, Washington
Raised in South Carolina, worked at Fig, he took over running the kitchen at DC Coast, where he'd been sous chef for two years, in 2011.
2Amys 522...........................Worth the travel
The American Ice Co. 524.....Wish I'd opened
Fiskfélagið 134....................Worth the travel
Obelisk 523.......................................High end
Old Ebbitt Grill 523..........................Late night
Pho DC 522..Bargain
Pizzeria Paradiso 523.Regular neighbourhood
Rustik Tavern 522.............................Breakfast

FILIPPO LA MANTIA

Filippo La Mantia
Via Liguria 1, Rome
Describes himself as 'Innkeeper and chef' of the eponymous Filippo La Mantia, his grand dining room with a Sicilian-inspired menu.
D'O 403................................Wish I'd opened
Somo 399...................Regular neighbourhood
Torre del Saracino 393.....................High end
Trattoria Biondo 409................Local favourite

TIM LAI

Tim's Kitchen
84-90 Bonham Strand, Hong Kong
Born in Hong Kong in 1949, started cooking at 17, worked under Cantonese cooking legend Choi Lee, he opened Tim's Kitchen in 2000.
Gaya 302.............................Wish I'd opened
Lin Heung Tea House 85..........Local favourite
Paradise of King Asia 82.....................Regular
neighbourhood
Sang Kee Congee Shop 88................Breakfast
Sing Heung Yuen 86............................Bargain
Yuet Wah Hui 90..............................Late night

YVONNICK LALLE
Marc
14–16 Bruton Place, London
French expat who's been with Marc, Marlon Abela's London and US based group, since 2004, overseeing openings both sides of the Atlantic.

L'Assiette Champenoise 279...Worth the travel
Dal Pescatore 402....................Local favourite
The Delauney 214............................Breakfast
Le Louis XV 291...................................High end
Nikita's 188.............................Local favourite
Pizzeria Oregano 205...Regular neighbourhood
Sangria 205...Bargain

ALBERTO LANDGRAF
Epice
Rua Haddock Lobo 1002, São Paulo
Runs Sao Paulo's Epice, opened in 2011, trained in London, where he worked with Gordon Ramsay and Tom Aikens.

Arbutus 222..High end
Clos de Tapas 637................Worth the travel
D.O.M. Restaurante 636........Worth the travel
Mocotó 638............................Worth the travel
Pierre Gagnaire 306.........................High end
Shin Zushi 638.......................Worth the travel
Sujinho 635...Late night
Tom Aikens 186.....................Worth the travel

FILIP LANGHOFF
Restaurant ask
Vironkatu 8, 00170 Helsinki
Former head chef at Chez Dominique, he currently is chef and partner in Restaurant ask, opened in 2012.

A21 Dining 165.........................Local favourite
Alex Sushi 139...........Regular neighbourhood
Alexander 424.......................Worth the travel
Café Gran Delicato 166...................Breakfast
Maaemo 140 .... Wish I'd opened
Olo 165...................................Worth the travel
Putte's Bar & Pizza 167.....................Bargain

NORMAND LAPRISE
Restaurant Toqué!
900 Place Jean Paul Riopelle, Montreal
A former accountant turned chef he trained at Hotel de la Cloche near Dijon before returning home to Canada and opening his flagship Toqué!

Au Pied de Cochon 475...........Local favourite
Big in Japan 477...................................Bargain
Bistro Isakaya 476.............................Bargain
Le Chique 611.......................Worth the travel
Joe Beef 478.........................Local favourite
Maison Pic 291....................................High end
Noma 160............................Wish I'd opened
Vila Joya 357......................................High end

DAVID LARIS
Laris
Three on the Bund, Shanghai
A Greek Australian, he's the most well known chef-restaurateur in Shanghai, opening Laris in 2004 and umpteen similar fine dining concepts since.

El Cóctel 77..Late night
Da Dong Roast Duck 79........Worth the travel
Fook Lam Moon 77.............................Breakfast
Ho Hung Kee 82.......................Local favourite
Kappo Yu 78...............Regular neighbourhood
Morton's The Steakhouse 77.............High end
Mr & Mrs Bund 75...............................Late night
Noodle Bull 78.....................................Bargain
Quay 25...............................Wish I'd opened
Tetsuya's 26..........................Worth the travel
Yardbird 88...............Regular neighbourhood

SASU LAUKKONEN
Chef & Sommelier
Huvilakatu 28, Helsinki
Having earned his stripes as head chef of La Petite Maison and Loft Restaurant & Lounge in Helsinki, in 2010 Laukkonen took the helm at his own restaurant.

Café Ekberg 166....................................Breakfast
Café Engel 167......................................Breakfast
Café Gran Delicato 166....................Breakfast
Café Tin Tin Tango 168......................Breakfast
Chez Dominique 165..........................High end
Demo 168.................Regular neighbourhood
Four Seasons 168................................Bargain
Gaijin 166.............................Wish I'd opened
Luomo 168...............Regular neighbourhood
Maaemo 140.......................Wish I'd opened
Le Mirazur 285.....................Worth the travel
Muru 167.....................Regular neighbourhood
Noma 160.............................Wish I'd opened
Putte's Bar & Pizza 167.....................Bargain
Savoy 165...High end

GWENDAL LE RUYET
Brittany-born chef who trained under Ducasse and earned substantial recognition at Prague's Céleste, for his lighter, pared-down versions of French classics.

Bras 282..............................Wish I'd opened
Café de Paris 419.................................Late night
Crêperie du Puits 276....Regular neighbourhood
Cukr Kava Limonada 419.................Breakfast
Filetstück 384.......................Worth the travel
Ichnusa Botega & Bistro 420.............Regular neighbourhood
Louis Allard Patisserie 281...............High end
Paul 420..Bargain
Sushi Seki 572......................Worth the travel

COREY LEE
Benu
22 Hawthorne Street, San Francisco
A James Beard Award-winning chef who trained at seven 3-star Michelin restaurants in England, France and the U.S before opening Benu in 2010.

Attica 34.................................Worth the travel
Che's Cantonese Restaurant 89......Worth the travel
Commis 518..High end
Fook Lam Moon 89................Worth the travel
The French Laundry 484....Wish I'd opened
Gahm Mi Oak 568................................Late night
The Harwood Arms 188........Worth the travel
Hog Island Oyster Bar 506......Local favourite
Momofuku Ko 579.................Worth the travel
Peter Luger Steakhouse 602....Local favourite
R&G Lounge 504........Regular neighbourhood
San Tung 509..Bargain
Sightglass 515.....................................Breakfast
Urasawa 490..High end

JEREMY LEE
Quo Vadis
26–29 Dean Street, London
Scottish-born chef who left the Blueprint Café in 2011 to take the reigns at Quo Vadis, bringing his award-winning combination of French technique and British seasonality.

Chez Georges 296................Worth the travel
St. John Bar and Restaurant 201...........Local favourite
St. John Bread & Wine 209......Local favourite
St. John Hotel 215.............................Breakfast

MAN-SING LEE
Man Wah
5 Connaught Road, Hong Kong Island
Behind the stove at the Man Wah, in the last few years Lee has won the Cantonese restaurant a Michelin star with his careful attention to sourcing the finest ingredients.

Budaoweng Hot Pot Cuisine 90.......Late night
Da Dong Roast Duck 79........Worth the travel
Dragon Inn Seafood 92.........Wish I'd opened
Mandarin Grill & Bar 86....................High end
Sushi Kuu 87...High end
Tsui Wah 91...............Regular neighbourhood

ROWLEY LEIGH
Le Café Anglais
8 Porchester Gardens, London
The Cambridge-educated chef has a resume that includes Le Gavroche and Kensington Place. Opened Le Café Anglais in 2007.

Bellamy's 216............Regular neighbourhood
Four Seasons 185................................Bargain
Joe Allen 214...Late night
The Kitchin 231....................Worth the travel
Le Gavroche 218..................................High end
Quo Vadis 228.....................Wish I'd opened
The River Café 188.............................High end
Trattoria da Teo 400..............Worth the travel
The Wolseley 221..............................Breakfast

ARMIN LEITGEB

Austrian-born chef who spent his early years at Jardin des Sens, Auberge de L'ill, Restaurant Tantris and The French Laundry. Head chef at Singapore's Les Amis until 2012.

Les Amis 126....................................High end
Aoki 126.................................Worth the travel
Canelé 127.......................................Breakfast
DB Bistro Moderne 568....................High end
Imperial Treasure 127...........Wish I'd opened
Long Beach 127...............................Late night
Newton Food Centre 127................Late night
Restaurant Tantris 374............Local favourite
Waku Ghin 125....................Wish I'd opened
Zaffron Kitchen 125..............................Bargain

SÉGUÉ LEPAGE

Le Comptoir
4807 Boulevard Saint-Laurent, Montreal
After immersing himself in charcuterie in France, Lepage opened Le Comptoir – a temple to meat and natural wines – in 2010.

Les 400 Coups 477................Wish I'd opened
Animal 499...........................Worth the travel
Dépanneur le Pick Up 476...................Bargain
Lawrence Restaurant 475...............Breakfast
Momofuku Ko 579...................Worth the travel
New Dynasty 475...............................Breakfast
Les Trois Petits Bouchons 476............Regular
neighbourhood
The Whalesbone 457............Worth the travel

JEREME LEUNG

Made his name with the Whampoa Club, before creating a culinary consultancy specializing in his 'new Chinese' style of cooking.

Ah Yat Shabu Shabu 126..................Late night
Bo Innovation 88................Worth the travel
Da-Wan Yakiniku 92.............Worth the travel
Di Shui Dong 74.........Regular neighbourhood
Goga 78......................Regular neighbourhood
Hai Ji 79......................Worth the travel
Hui Ge 76...........................Late night
Jesse 78.............................Local favourite
The Stage 75..........................Breakfast
Tables 75.............................Breakfast
Tetsuya's 26......................Worth the travel
Yi Café 77................................Breakfast

ROSS LEWIS

Chapter One
18-19 Parnell Square, Dublin
Son of a farmer, Irish-born Lewis found cooking while at university. He opened Chapter One in 1992.

Ananda 241.....................................Late night
Ballymaloe House 236...................Breakfast
Campagne 241.....................Worth the travel
El Celler de Can Roca 329.....Worth the travel
Farmgate Café 237................Local favourite
M & L Szechuan Chinese 238..............Bargain
L'Osteria Francescana 395....Worth the travel
Restaurant Forty One 240.................Regular
neighbourhood

DANIEL LINDEBERG

Frantzén/Lindeberg
Lilla Nygatan 21, Stockholm
A Swede who began cooking at 16 but did not find his true calling – pastry – until staging at Charlie Palmer's Aureole in New York. Now owns Frantzén/Lindeberg with Björn Frantzén.

Albert & Jack's 150........................Breakfast
Fäviken Magasinet 143.........Worth the travel
Hedone 187..........................Worth the travel
Masa 573..............................High end
Råkultur 153..........................Bargain
Riddarbageriet 151......................Breakfast
Rolfs Kök 149.............Regular neighbourhood
Sturehof 151..............................Late night

ANITA LO

Annisa
13 Barrow Street, New York
A second generation Chinese-American, trained in Paris at L'Ecole Ritz-Escoffier, she opened Annisa in New York's Greenwich Village in 2000.

L'Artusi 582.................Regular neighbourhood
Çiya Sofrasi 439...................Worth the travel
Dell'Anima 583..............................Late night
Fig 538.............................Worth the travel
Ippudo NY 577.............................Bargain
Jewel Bako 583..............................High end
Joe 584...............................Breakfast
Moustache 585..............................Bargain
Pearl Oyster Bar 585............Wish I'd opened
The Spotted Pig 585....................Late night
Taïm 586..........................Bargain
Tertulia 586..........................Worth the travel

PAOLO LOPRIORE

Il Canto
Strada di Certosa 82-86, Siena
Born in Como, trained at Sole di Ranco under Gualtiero Marchesi and at Baggatelle in Olso, he arrived at Il Canto in 2002.

Da Caino 411...........................Local favourite
Enoteca I Terzi 412.......................Late night
Mugaritz 319...................Wish I'd opened
Osteria da Trombicche 412.................Bargain
Osteria del Rossi 412.Regular neighbourhood

JEROME LORVELLEC

Matsuhisa
Astir Palace Resort, 40 Apollonos Street, Athens
Returned to Nobu to oversee Matsuhisa in 2010, having launched Pershing Hall and Black Calvados in Paris.

L'Espadon 294.................................High end
Le Grand Restaurant 284........Local favourite
New Hotel 431..............................Breakfast
Nobu 219..............................High end

BRUNO LOUBET

Bistro Bruno Loubet
86-88 Clerkenwell Road, London
Born in Bordeaux, arrived in London in 1982, opened Bistrot Bruno in 1993, L'Odeon in 1995 and Bistrot Bruno Loubet in 2010.

Bar Boulud 189..............................Late night
Brawn 197.................Regular neighbourhood
Caravan 200...................................Breakfast
The Ledbury 194..................Worth the travel
Quay 25......................Wish I'd opened
The River Café 188........................High end
The Wolseley 221........................Breakfast
Yalla Yalla 229............................Bargain

JAMES LOWE

Ran proceedings at Fergus Henderson's St. John Bread & Wine, worked at The Fat Duck and Noma, before forming The Young Turks.

The Anchor & Hope 211.......................Regular
neighbourhood
The Fat Duck 172..................Worth the travel
Kêu Bánh Mì Deli 207....................Bargain
Koya 225.................Regular neighbourhood
Quo Vadis 228..................Wish I'd opened
Relæ 162...........................Worth the travel
The River Café 188........................High end
St. John Bread & Wine 209......Local favourite
Tayyabs 211............................Local favourite

ANTHONY LUI

Flower Drum
17 Market Lane, Melbourne
Partner in Melbourne's legendary Cantonese, Flower Drum, since 2003, where owner Gilbert Lau first enticed him to cook in 1981.

tomica Caffé 30.............................Breakfast
Dragon Seal 90.....................Worth the travel
Lupino 32......................................Bargain
MoVida Next Door 33............Wish I'd opened
Rockpool Bar & Grill 35.........Wish I'd opened
Supper Inn 33.............................Late night
T's Chinese Restaurant 13.....Worth the travel
Vue de Monde 34.........................High end

FRANCIS MALLMANN

1884 Restaurante Francis Mallmann
Belgrano 1188, Godoy Cruz
Born in Buenos Aires, he oversees a South American restaurant group that includes: 1884 Restaurante Francis Mallmann, Patagonia Sur and Garzon.

L'Ami Louis 297.................................High end
Il Buco 595.................Regular neighbourhood
Carlitos LNG 640.............................Bargain
Hélène Darroze 218........................Breakfast
Prune 580.................Regular neighbourhood
Ristorante Cesare 399....Regular neighbourhood
The River Café 188........................High end
The Spotted Pig 585.......................Late night

LUKE MANGAN
Salt Grill
Hilton Hotel 488 Orchid Avenue, Gold Coast
Australian, trained in Melbourne under
Herman Schneider and in the UK with Michel
Roux, he owns and operates branches of his
Salt Grill brand.

Balthazar **596**.............................Breakfast
Bernasconi's **20**...........................Breakfast
Catalina **21**..........................Local favourite
China Doll **27**.............Regular neighbourhood
Esquina **124**.....................Worth the travel
Est. **24**...High end
Golden Century Seafood **24**............Late night
Happy Chef **24**.................................Bargain

WALTER MANZKE
République
1330 Factory Place, Los Angeles
Made his name at Los Angeles bistro Church
& State, which he left in 2010 to open Répub-
lique and the Factory Baking Co.

Angelini Osteria **494**...Regular neighbourhood
L'Atelier de Joel Robuchon **107**.........Wish I'd
opened
El Celler de Can Roca **329**.....Worth the travel
In-N-Out **482**...................................Late night
Pink's Hot Dogs **500**................Local favourite
Plow **514**.......................................Breakfast
Restaurant Le Meurice **295**...Worth the travel
Saison **511**......................................High end

GUALTIERO MARCHESI
Il Marchesino
Via Filodrammatici 2, Milan
Legendary Italian, widely credited as the
father of modern Italian cooking, his current
businesses include Il Marchesino, his flagship restaurant in Milan.

L'Arpège **301**..................................High end
Dispensa Pani e Vini **401**.................Bargain
Octoria dolla Villotta **401**.............Late night
Trattoria ai Due Platani **395**.............Regular
neighbourhood
Trattoria al Carretto **403**.........Local favourite

ROBERT MARCHETTI
Formerly a partner in Sydney's most suc-
cessful restaurant group which included the
Icebergs Dining Room and Bar and North
Bondi Italian Food.

Baxter Inn **23**.................................Late night
Chiswick Restaurant **27**........Wish I'd opened
Din Tai Fung **24**...................................Bargain
Fratelli Fresh **27**........Regular neighbourhood
Fratelli Paradiso **19**....Regular neighbourhood
O Magazin **400**..................Worth the travel
Rockpool Bar & Grill **25**....................High end
Sonoma Bakery Café **16**.................Breakfast
Wasabi **13**.............................Worth the travel

JACQUES MARCON
Régis et Jacques Marcon
Place de l'Eglise, St Bonnet-Le-Froid
Works alongside his father at Restaurant
Regis et Jacques Marcon, which they
launched together in 2008, as the successor
to Auberge de Clos des Cimes.

Flocons de Sel **289**................Worth the travel
Gilles Goujon **280**.......Regular neighbourhood
Maison Décoret **276**..Regular neighbourhood
Le Neuvième Art **290**............Worth the travel
La Remise **286**......................Wish I'd opened
Le Table du Terroir **290**.......................Bargain

DAVID MARTIN
La Paix
Rue Ropsy-Chaudron 49, Brussels
One time disciple of Passard, bought the
Brussels brasserie, La Paix, in 2004, where
butchers who visited the abattoir opposite
began meeting in 1892.

Asador Etxebarri **324**............Worth the travel
Bras **282**............................Wish I'd opened
De Zogeraa **266**.........Regular neighbourhood
Friture René **261**........Regular neighbourhood
Hof Van Cleve **264**............................High end
In De Wulf **270**....................Worth the travel
Wataro **268**.......................................Bargain

VIRGILIO MARTINEZ
Central Restaurante
Calle Santa Isabel 376, Lima
Ran the kitchen at Gastón Acurio's seminal
haute Peruvian Astrid y Gaston, before
opening his own celebrated Lima restaurant,
Central, in 2010.

L'Astrance **309**...................Worth the travel
Canta Rana **619**.................Wish I'd opened
La Gran Fruta **621**...........................Breakfast
Maido **620**.................Regular neighbourhood
Sankuay **622**......................Local favourite
Viajanto **198**....................................High end

THIERRY MARX
Sur Mesure
**Mandarin Oriental Hotel 25 Rue Saint-
Honoré, Paris**
The culinary director of the Mandarin Orien-
tal in Paris, where he has two restaurants,
Sur Mesure and Camélia.

L'Atelier de Joel Robuchon **107**.........Wish I'd
opened
L'Atelier de Joël Robuchon **301**........High end
Carette **309**....................................Breakfast
Le Comptoir du Relais **299**....Worth the travel
Le Monteverdi **300**....Regular neighbourhood
Le Nemrod **300**....................Local favourite
Le Sourire de Saigon **311**....................Regular
neighbourhood
Noma **160**..........................Wish I'd opened
Schwartz's Deli **297**..........................Bargain

TONY MAWS
Craigie on Main
853 Main Street, Cambridge
The owner of Craigie on Main, which he originally ran in a different Cambridge location as
the Craigie Street Bistrot (2003).

The Bite **535**.............................Local favourite
Le Chateaubriand **307**...........Worth the travel
Eleven Madison Park **591**.......Worth the travel
Grill 23 **533**......................................High end
Highland Kitchen **535**.Regular neighbourhood
Jumbo Seafood **533**...Regular neighbourhood
Kupel's Bakery **533**..........................Breakfast
Neptune Oyster **533**..........................High end
Pho Viet **534**.....................................Bargain
Roberta's **603**.....................Wish I'd opened
Super Dog **534**...................Wish I'd opened

FRANCESCO MAZZEI
L'Anima
1 Snowden Street, London
Opened L'Anima in London in 2008, born in
Calabria, he first arrived in the UK in 1996,
working for restaurateurs Corbin and King
and Alan Yau.

Bar Boulud **189**................................Late night
Busaba Eathai **223**............................Bargain
Cipriani **58**.........................Worth the travel
Cut at 45 Park Lane **217**.....................High end
The Duke of Cambridge **205**.....Local favourite
Hakkasan **218**....................Worth the travel
Ristorante L'Approdo **392**.....Worth the travel
The Wolseley **221**............................Breakfast
Zuma **190**.........................Local favourite

ANDREW McCONNELL
Cutler & Co.
55-57 Gertrude Street, Melbourne
Melbourne-born, he worked his way through
the city's restaurant scene before opening
Cutler & Co. in 2009.

Attica **34**.............................Worth the travel
Le Chateaubriand **307**...........Worth the travel
Duchess of Spotswood **35**...............Breakfast
Embassy Taxi Café **35**.......................Late night
I Love Pho **34**.....................................Bargain
Momofuku Seiobo **20**............Worth the travel
Noma **160**..........................Wish I'd opened

BRENDAN MCGILL
Hitchcock
133 Winslow Way East 100, Bainbridge Island
Owner of Seattle's Hitchcock, opened in
2010, and its little sister next door, the
Hitchcock Deli & Charcuterie, launched in
2011, McGill started cooking at 14.

La Bête **486**........................Wish I'd opened
Café Presse **486**..............................Breakfast
Ezell's Famous Chicken **487**................Bargain
Green Leaf **487**.........Regular neighbourhood
Haizea Bar **323**....................Worth the travel
Maekawa Bar **486**.............................Late night
Minetta Tavern **581**.............Worth the travel
Quinn's Pub **487**...............................Late night

ISAAC MCHALE

Co-founder of The Young Turks in 2010,
McHale has worked at The Ledbury and
staged at Noma and Momofuku.

Brunswick House Café 211..............Breakfast
Koya 225.....................Regular neighbourhood
The Ledbury 194....................Worth the travel
Pitt Cue Co. 227......................Worth the travel
Quo Vadis 228.......................Wish I'd opened
Relæ 162................................Worth the travel
Rino 308..Bargain
Roganic 193...........................Worth the travel
Septime 308.......................Wish I'd opened

NIALL MCKENNA

James Street South Restaurant
21 James Street, South Belfast

The owner of Belfast's James Street South,
opened in 2003, and the Bar + Grill,
launched in 2001, both located in a converted
linen mill in the city centre.

The Boat House 234...............Worth the travel
Boojum 234.........................Wish I'd opened
Café Conor 235...........................Breakfast
Cayenne 235...............Regular neighbourhood
Chapter One 238...........................High end
L'Ecrivain 239..............................High end
LeWinters 234.....................Local favourite
Mourne Seafood Bar 235.....................Regular
    neighbourhood
Il Pirata 236...............................Late night
Shu 236.....................Regular neighbourhood

TORY MCPHAIL

Commander's Palace
1403 Washington Avenue, New Orleans

Originally hailing from Washington State, he's
been calling the shots in the kitchen of New
Orleans' Commanders Palace since 2002.

Bouligny Tavern 547.........................Late night
Café Adelaide 546....................Local favourite
Coulis 549..................................Breakfast
Gautreau's 549..............................High end
Mondo 548.................Regular neighbourhood
Oak 550.............................Wish I'd opened
Per Se 574............................Worth the travel
Reginelli's 550................................Bargain
The Square 221.............................High end

ARABELLE MEIRLAEN

Li Cwerneu
Grand Place 2, Huy

Trained at Belgium's Libramont hotel school,
she owns Li Cwerneu and is the only female
chef in Belgium to hold a Michelin star.

Bras 282...............................Wish I'd opened
El Celler de Can Roca 329.....Worth the travel
Hof Van Cleve 264............................High end
La Grenouillère 282.................Local favourite
In De Wulf 270.......................Worth the travel
Martín Berasategui 318........Worth the travel
Oud Sluis 248...................................High end
Pierre Marcolini 263..................High end

NUNO MENDES

Viajante
Town Hall Hotel, Patriot Square, London

Portuguese, trained at the California Culinary
Academy, worked at elBulli, Jean Georges
and the Coyote Café before opening Viajante.

Kikuchi 202...................................High end
Leila's Café 209.............................Breakfast
Mugaritz 319.........................Wish I'd opened
Polpo 227.....................................Bargain
Rochelle Canteen 208 Regular neighbourhood
Spuntino 228.........................Wish I'd opened
St. John Bread & Wine 209......Local favourite
Yum Bun 204..................................Bargain

MICHAEL MEREDITH

Merediths
365 Dominion Road, Auckland

Born in Samoa, moved to New Zealand at
13, made his name at Auckland's The Grove
before opening Meredith's in 2007.

Attica 34..............................Worth the travel
Banzai 49......................................Bargain
Celestial Garden Café 51..................Breakfast
Clooney 49..................................High end
Cocoro 51...........................Wish I'd opened
Depot Eatery 48....................Worth the travel
Frantzén/Lindeberg 148...................High end
New Flavour 50.............................Late night
Noma 160............................Wish I'd opened
Rata 43................................Worth the travel
Royal Mail 13........................Worth the travel
The French Café 49..........................High end
The Grove Restaurant 49..................High end

MORGAN MEUNIER

Morgan M
50 Long Lane, London

Grew up in Champagne, began his career at
Patrick Guenon's L'Eau Sauvage, he opened
Morgan M in 2003, relocating it in 2012.

Almeida 205.................................Late night
Gauthier Soho 224....................Local favourite
La Côte Saint Jacques 279.....Worth the travel
Midsummer House 174.........Worth the travel
Rasa N16 210.............Regular neighbourhood
Viajante 198..................................High end

CLAUS MEYER

Meyer's Bakery
Jaegersborggade 9, Copenhagen

Shareholder in Noma, he has interests in
other Copenhagen restaurants and owns a
group of branded delis and bakeries.

AOC 158................................Worth the travel
Blue Hill at Stone Barns 536..Worth the travel
Les Cols 329.............................Local favourite
Den Rode Cottage 153..............Local favourite
Le Fou est Belge 267.................Local favourite
Geist 159...................Regular neighbourhood
La Nouvelle Maison de Marc Veyrat 291...........
    High end
Maison Pic 291..............................High end
Maison Troisgros 290.............Worth the travel
Manfreds & Vin 162............................Bargain
Red Medicine 490............................Bargain
Relæ 162................................Worth the travel
Restaurant Mêlée 154......................Late night
Saigon Quan 154.........Regular neighbourhood
Sin Huat Eating House 125....Worth the travel
Wee Nam Kee 128.....................Worth the travel

CHRISTOPHE MICHALAK

Alain Ducasse au Plaza Athénée
25 Avenue Montaigne, Paris

Picardy-born pastry chef who has overseen
the dessert menu at Alain Ducasse au Plaza
Athénée since 2000.

L'Atelier de Jean Luc Rabanel 283........Worth
    the travel
Au Pied de Cochon 475............Local favourite
Carette 309..................................Breakfast
Maison Troisgros 290.............Worth the travel
Market 306.................Regular neighbourhood
Pierre Hermé - Bonaparte 300.........High end
Thoumieux 303........................Local favourite
Le Verre Bouteille 311......................Late night

JAKOB MIELCKE

Mielcke & Hurtigkarl
Frederiksberg Runddel 1, Frederiksberg

Born in Aarhus, he left Denmark to work
with Pierre Gagnaire, then opened Mielcke &
Hurtigkarl, with Jan Hurtigkarl, in 2008.

Banzai 163......................................Bargain
Café Zeze 159................................Breakfast
Geist 159....................Regular neighbourhood
Geranium 163........................Worth the travel
Relæ 162................................Worth the travel

THOMASINA MIERS
Wahaca
66 Chandos Place, London
On the back of her 2005 success in BBC's Masterchef, she opened Wahaca in 2008. She now has seven branches across London.

Bentley's Oyster Bar & Grill **216**..............Wish I'd opened
Bocca di Lupo **223**......Regular neighbourhood
Le Café Anglais **184**................Local favourite
Le Caprice **217**......................Wish I'd opened
Dock Kitchen **191**.......Regular neighbourhood
Foxtrot Oscar **186**........................Breakfast
Hereford Road **195**....Regular neighbourhood
Hix **225**................................Late night
J Sheekey **214**............Regular neighbourhood
The Ledbury **194**.................Worth the travel
Lucky 7 **185**................................Bargain
MeroToro **609**......................Worth the travel
Origen **610**......................Worth the travel
The River Café **188**.....................High end
Royal China **185**............................Bargain

MICHAEL MINA
Michael Mina
252 California Street, San Francisco
Born in Egypt, Mina presides over an extensive coast-to-coast empire of American restaurants.

Brooklyn Fare **600**.................Wish I'd opened
Hana **483**.........................Regular neighbourhood
Joan Gatell **332**...................Worth the travel
Petrossian **570**...............................High end
R&G Lounge **504**........Regular neighbourhood
Roli Roti **506**...............................Bargain
Swan Oyster Depot **513**.........Local favourite
Two Bird Café **483**......................Breakfast

CARLO MIRARCHI
Roberta's
261 Moore Street, Brooklyn, New York
Co-owner of the runaway Brooklyn hit, Roberta's, opened in 2008 as a no-nonsense, no-reservations, rock 'n' roll bar and pizza joint.

Bernu **515**....................................High end
The Brooklyn Star **601**...................Late night
Le Comptoir du Relais **299**.....Worth the travel
La Grenouillère **282**................Local favourite
Gus's Fried Chicken **540**........Worth the travel
Hakata Tonton **583**.......................Late night
Katz's Deli **593**...................Local favourite
Mission Chinese Food **510**..................Regular neighbourhood
Peking Duck House **590**...Regular neighbourhood
Pok Pok NY **601**.........Regular neighbourhood
St. John Bar and Restaurant **201**............Local favourite
St. John Bread & Wine **209**......Local favourite
Sushi Mizutani **105**................Worth the travel
Tehuitzingo Mexican Deli **570**.............Bargain
Ushiwakamaru **586**.....Regular neighbourhood

RIKI MIZUKAMI
Pasticceria Ikkouan
5-3-15 Koishikawa, Tokyo
Born into a family of confectioners, following his apprenticeship he opened his own shop that produces Kyoto-style tea sweets.

AsabAsaba Ryokan **100**........Worth the travel
La Beccata **104**...........Regular neighbourhood
The Crescent **107**.............................High end
Écurer **107**..........................Local favourite
Iroha Sushi **97**................................Bargain
Sant Pau **327**....................Worth the travel
Umia **290**.....................Wish I'd opened

KHALID MOHAMMED
Chaud
2 Queen's Park West, Port of Spain
Trained at New York's French Culinary Institute before opening Chaud in the Port of Spain, in 2008.

Blue Hill at Stone Barns **536**..Worth the travel
The Breakfast Shed **613**..................Breakfast
Me Asia **613**................................Late night
Sugarcane Raw Bar Grill **527** Worth the travel
Wings Restaurant & Bar **613**....Local favourite

MATT MOLINA
Osteria Mozza
6602 Melrose Avenue, Los Angeles
Trained at the Los Angeles Culinary Institute, headed east to work at Del Posto, returning to oversee Pizzeria Mozza and Osteria Mozza.

Astro Burger **494**........Regular neighbourhood
Bäco Mercat **491**...................Worth the travel
Esquina **124**...................Worth the travel
Ink. **499**.......................Wish I'd opened
Mélisse **494**...............................High end
Peet's Coffee & Tea **495**.................Breakfast
Pho Café **497**......................Local favourite
Pollo a la Brasa **495**......................Bargain
Vincenti **490**..............Regular neighbourhood

GUILLAUME MONJURÉ
Palégrié
8 Rue Palais Grillet, Lyon
Trained with Olivier Roellinger in Brittany and Jean-Pierre Vigato at Apicius in Paris, ahead of opening Palégrié in 2012.

Apicius **305**.................................High end
Le Bois Fleuri **286**.......Regular neighbourhood
Fäviken Magasinet **143**.........Worth the travel
Flocons de Sel **289**.................Worth the travel
Georges Five **287**...................Local favourite
Grain de Vanille **277**.........................Breakfast
La Maison de l'Aubrac **306**..............Late night
L'Ourson qui Boit **287**...........Worth the travel
La Pause **446**...................Worth the travel
La Régalade **309**............................Bargain

RUSSELL MOORE
Camino
3917 Grand Avenue, Oakland
Worked for Alice Waters at Chez Panisse for 21 years, leaving in 2008 to open Camino where he cooks over a coal-fired grill.

Bar Agricole **515**.....................Local favourite
Cà del Re **406**......................Wish I'd opened
Commis **518**.................................High end
Ippuku **516**.................Regular neighbourhood
Isa **602**............................Worth the travel
Itanoni **611**........................Worth the travel
Kobawoo House **495**.............Worth the travel
Lucques **500**................................Late night
Mission Chinese Food **594**.................Bargain
Namu Gaji **510**...............................Late night
El Paisa **518**................................Bargain
Pizzeria Bianco **482**.............Wish I'd opened
Prune **580**...................Regular neighbourhood
Pyeong Chang Tofu House **518**...........Bargain
Vik's Chaat & Market **517**..................Bargain

MARTIN MORALES
Ceviche
17 Frith Street, London
Left Lima at 12, worked as a Disney Media executive and helped launched iTunes in Europe before opening Ceviche in 2012.

Andres Carne de Res **619**......Wish I'd opened
Arbutus **222**.................................High end
Barrafina **222**.............Regular neighbourhood
Gifto's Lahore Karahi **194**.....Worth the travel
José **208**................................Bargain
Kate's Joint **161**..................Worth the travel
Koya **225**...........Regular neighbourhood
Pho **227**.................................Bargain
Riva **184**.......................Regular neighbourhood
Wright Brothers **228**.....................Late night

PACO MORALES
Ferrero by Paco Morales
Carretera de Villena-Ontinyent 16, Bocairent
Made his name at Sezone in Madrid, following his time as sous chef at Mugaritz, he now runs Ferrero by Paco Morales.

Aponiente **314**......................Worth the travel
El Asador de Nati **314**.........................Bargain
Caféteria La Gela **337**....................Breakfast
Calima **314**........................Worth the travel
El Celler de Can Roca **329**......Worth the travel
Mugaritz **319**.................Wish I'd opened
Paco Gandía **335**.................Local favourite
Portal Fosc **337**............................Late night
La Sirena **330**............Regular neighbourhood

EDUARDO MORENO
La Isabela
Los Churros, Caracas
Quirky Venezuelan cook, who operates his
arty Caracas restaurant, La Isabela, like a
private club, with reservations by introduc-
tion only.
L'Agapé Substance 298.........Worth the travel
Casa Marcelo 332..................Worth the travel
Chez Le Libanais 299........................Late night
Chino de Los Palos Grandes 618.........Bargain
Dos Cielos 346..................................High end
Fugu 618....................Regular neighbourhood
Le Gourmet 618.................................High end
Jacques Genin 297.............Worth the travel
Katz's Deli 593......................Local favourite
Mugaritz 319.......................Wish I'd opened
Pho 67 298..........................Worth the travel
La Régalade 309.....................................Bargain
Shunka 341..................Regular neighbourhood
La Terraza del Casino 335.................High end
Trolly 618...Late night
Yam'Tcha 296....................Wish I'd opened

WILLY TRULLAS MORENO
El Willy
5f 22 Shongshan Dong Er Lu, Shanghai
Left Barcelona behind to open tapas bar,
El Willy, in Shanghai, he followed that with
ElEfante, and Bikini, in 2012.
Bar Pinotxo 342...........................Breakfast
El Celler de Can Roca 329.....Worth the travel
Din Tai Fung 76....................................Bargain
Franck 77...................Regular neighbourhood
Goga 78.....................Regular neighbourhood
Narisawa 108........................Worth the travel
Quimet i Quimet 351.......................Late night
Sushi Oyama 78................................High end
Tenya Twenty Two 75.......................Late night
Ultraviolet 74.....................Worth the travel

KAMAL MOUZAWAK
Tawlet
Naher Street, Mar Mikhael, Beirut
The founder of Beirut's first farmers' market,
Souk el Tayeb, operates Tawlet, a farmers'
kitchen that serves regional Lebanese dishes.
Aux Lyonnais 296................Worth the travel
Boubouffe 56....................................Late night
Chez Maguy 56..........Regular neighbourhood
Dannoun 57.......................Local favourite
Falafel Sahyoun 56.............................Bargain
Momo at the Souks 57..........Wish I'd opened
Naranj 56.............................Worth the travel
Rafic Al Rashidi 57............................Breakfast

MARCO MÜLLER
Rutz
Chausseestrasse 8, Berlin
Arrived at Weinbar Rutz in Berlin in 2004,
where he's won praise for cooking that takes
in German, Austrian and Swiss influences.
Aqua 375.................................Worth the travel
Bandol sur Mer 382..................Local favourite
Bieberbau 385....................................High end
The Bird 384..Bargain
Bloom in the Park 144...........Worth the travel
The Facil 385........................Worth the travel
Hasir 382...Late night
Kuchi 380...................Regular neighbourhood
Pauly Saal 383.....................Wish I'd opened
Restaurantschiff Patio 381..............Breakfast

LISA MUNCAN
Lisa M
3 Place de la Madonne, Vers-Pont-du-Gard
The Francophile Danish owner of Lisa M,
where there's no menu, only a short market-
driven selection of off-the-cuff dishes.
Alain Ducasse 305.............................High end
Le Fumoir 294......................Worth the travel
Les Deux Salons 214..............Wish I'd opened
The Gallery 217...................................Late night
Hertog Jan 269.......................Worth the travel
L'Huître et la Vigne 281.......................Regular
   neighbourhood
Maison Pic 291...................................High end
Maison Troisgros 290............Worth the travel
Pierre Gagnaire 306............................High end
Le Renaissance 281..........................Breakfast
Restaurant Kei 295...............Wish I'd opened
Wasabi Sushi Bar 281.........................Bargain
Ze Kitchen Galerie 300.........Worth the travel

DHARSHAN MUNIDASA
Nihonbashi Honten
11 Galle Face Terrace, Colombo
Sri Lankan-Japanese founder of Nihonbashi,
the original opened in Colombo in 1995, he
opened the Ministry of Crab in 2012.
Indigo 66..............................Worth the travel
Inoue Ramen 104..................................Bargain
Ithaa Undersea Restaurant 69................Wish
   I'd opened
Jubako 108..........................Worth the travel
Kinchan 106.....................................Late night

CARRIE NAHABEDIAN
Naha
500 North Clark Street, Chicago
A Chicagoan of Armenian extraction, began
cooking at the city's Ritz Carlton at 17,
Nahabedian opened Naha in 2000.
Alinea 556...........................Worth the travel
Bottega Ristorante 484..........Worth the travel
Can Fabes 327.......................Wish I'd opened
El Celler de Can Roca 329......Worth the travel
Cheesecake Factory 558....................Bargain
Coq d'Or 558..............Regular neighbourhood
Deca 559...Breakfast
Franks 'n' Dawgs 557............................Bargain
The French Laundry 484.......Wish I'd opened
Frontera Grill 559......Regular neighbourhood
Ina's 561..Breakfast
La Madia 559..............Regular neighbourhood
Matsalen 149.....................................High end
Noma 160.............................Wish I'd opened
Les Nomades 559.................Wish I'd opened
The Purple Pig 560................Worth the travel
Portillo's 562...Bargain
Prairie Grass Café 561............Local favourite
Quince 507...High end
R L 560...................................Wish I'd opened
Spiaggia 560.......................................High end
Sunda 560..Late night

YOSHIHIRO NARISAWA
Narisawa
2-6-15 Minami Aoyama, Tokyo
Trained in Switzerland with Girardet, in
France with Robuchon and in Italy at Antica
Osteria del Ponte, he opened Les Créations
de Narisawa (now called Narisawa) in 2003.
Au Bon Accueil 302...............Worth the travel
Bingo 107..Late night
Chinese Tapas Renge 113...................Bargain
Masuda 99...High end
Meimon 113...............Regular neighbourhood
Shokuninkan 99....................Worth the travel
Tosaka 110..............................Local favourite

PAUL NEWMAN
Coyaba
Caribbean Paradise Inn, Grace Bay,
Providenciales
Opened Coyaba, in 1999, he's worked in
five-star resorts across the Caribbean,
from Jamaica to Bermuda, and Anguilla to
the British Virgin Islands.
5A5 Steak Lounge 506...........Worth the travel
Las Brisas Restaurant 612...............Breakfast
Buccan 528..........................Worth the travel
Da Conch Shack 612.................Local favourite
DBGB Kitchen & Bar 576.......Wish I'd opened
Garam Masala 612............................Late night
George Restaurant 469.........Worth the travel
Starfish Oyster Bed & Grill 469...Worth the travel
The Restaurant 612............................High end
Yoshi's Sushi Bar 612.Regular neighbourhood

MAGNUS NILSSON
Fäviken Magasinet
Fäviken 216, Järpen
Swedish chef, trained in Paris at L'Astrance and L'Arpège, he returned to Sweden in 2008, to open the tiny 12-seat, Fäviken Magasinet.

Attica **34**	Worth the travel
Bras **282**	Wish I'd opened
Le Chateaubriand **307**	Worth the travel
Gastrologik **150**	Worth the travel
Natur Café at Kretsloppshuset **143**	Local favourite
Östermalms Korvspecialist **151**	Bargain

PETTER NILSSON
La Gazzetta
29 Rue de Cotte, Paris
Swede, trained at le Saint-James with Michel Portos, who went on to cook at Les Trois Salons in Uzes before, in 2006, he took over the La Gazzetta.

L'Arpège **301**	High end
L'As de Falafel **297**	Bargain
Le Chateaubriand **307**	Worth the travel
Khachapuri **426**	Worth the travel
Mugaritz **319**	Wish I'd opened
Relæ **162**	Worth the travel
Restaurang Gandhi **152**	Regular neighbourhood
Restaurang Pelikan **152**	Local favourite
Solde Kafferosteri **144**	Breakfast

JUSTIN NORTH
Kiwi who left home at 15 to pursue a career in cooking, worked for Raymond Blanc in the UK, and ran Bécasse up until 2012.

The Bathers' Pavilion Café **18**	Local favourite
The Byron at Byron **12**	Worth the travel
Danks Street Depot **27**	Wish I'd opened
Ginger & Spice **19**	Regular neighbourhood
Golden Century Seafood **24**	Late night
Ishikawa **113**	Worth the travel
Public Dining Room **19**	Breakfast
Spice I Am **22**	Bargain
Spice Temple **26**	Late night
Sushiso Masa **110**	Worth the travel

PATRICK O'CONNELL
The Inn at Little Washington
309 Middle Street, Washington
Owner of The Inn at Little Washington in Virginia, a self-taught cook, he began a catering business Blue Ridge Mountains in 1972, opening the Inn, in 1978.

L'Ambroisie **297**	Worth the travel
Eleven Madison Park **591**	Worth the travel
Johnny's Half Shell **522**	Local favourite
Maison Troisgros **290**	Worth the travel
Le Pré Catelan **310**	High end
Ris **524**	Regular neighbourhood
Sushi Rock Café **525**	Bargain

DAVIDE OLDANI
D'O
Via Magenta 18, San Pietro all'Olmo
Born in Cornaredo, near Milan, he trained with Marchesi, at Le Gavroche in London, and at Louis XV in Monte Carlo, opening D'O in 2003.

Alain Ducasse **305**	High end
Antica Osteria Magenes **402**	Bargain
Biffi **402**	Breakfast
California Bakery **403**	Breakfast
Cracco **403**	Worth the travel
L'Osteria Francescana **395**	Worth the travel
Trussardi alla Scala **404**	Regular neighbourhood
Zero **404**	Late night

TOM OLDROYD
Polpo
41 Beak Street, London
Oversees all of the restaurants in Russell Norman's rapidly expanding, London-based, Polpo group.

Alle Testiere **413**	Worth the travel
Bar Italia **222**	Late night
Big Apple Hot Dogs **207**	Bargain
La Cantina **413**	High end
Corte Sconta **413**	High end
Dean Street Townhouse **224**	Breakfast
Hawksmoor **197**	Breakfast
Koya **225**	Regular neighbourhood
Minetta Tavern **581**	Worth the travel
Pitt Cue Co. **227**	Worth the travel
Sophie's Steakhouse **215**	Late night
St. John Bar and Restaurant **201**	Local favourite

RODRIGO OLIVEIRA
Mocotó
Avenida Nossa Senhora do Loreto 1100, São Paulo
Originally opened by his father, José Oliveira de Almeida, São Paulo's Mocotó serves authentic Amazonian cuisine.

As Veia **629**	Local favourite
Bar Numero **635**	Late night
Corlinhos Restaurante **634**	Bargain
Casa Garabed **631**	Regular neighbourhood
Jun Sakamoto **636**	High end
Il Luogo di Aimo e Nadia **403**	Worth the travel
Padaria Jardim Brasil **635**	Breakfast
Roberta Sudbrack **628**	Worth the travel
Sushi Hiroshi **635**	Regular neighbourhood

ENRIQUE OLVERA
Pujol
Francisco Petrarca 254, Mexico City
Mexico-born Olvera is one of a new wave of Mexican chefs re-imagining indigenous cuisine by marrying it with a fine dining setting.

Bras **282**	Wish I'd opened
La Estación **608**	Regular neighbourhood
El Farolito **610**	Late night
Itanoni **611**	Worth the travel
MeroToro **609**	Worth the travel

UWE OPOCENSKY
Mandarin Grill & Bar
5 Connaught Road, Hong Kong Island
German, worked for Anton Mosimann in London, did a stint with the Shangri-La Hotel group, before joining The Mandarin Oriental, Hong Kong.

The French Laundry **484**	Wish I'd opened
Him Kee Hot Pot **82**	Late night
Kau Kee Restaurant **87**	Bargain
Mugaritz **319**	Wish I'd opened
Noma **160**	Wish I'd opened
Sukiyabashi Jiro **105**	Worth the travel
Tim Ho Wan **91**	Bargain
Vendôme **376**	Wish I'd opened
Yardbird **88**	Regular neighbourhood
Zuma **87**	Wish I'd opened

KEN ORINGER
Clio
370a Commonwealth Avenue, Boston
Boston born, worked across the US before returning home to open Clio in 1997, adding sushi bar Uni to its lounge in 2002 and Italian, Coppa, in 2009.

East Coast Grill **534**	Local favourite
Gourmet Dumpling House **532**	Regular neighbourhood
Morimoto **589**	High end
Oishii Boston **534**	Worth the travel
Sapporo Ramen **535**	Bargain
Taller de Tapas **341**	Wish I'd opened

REFAIE OTHMAN
Zuma
Gate Village 6, Sheikh Zayed Road, Dubai
Took over the kitchen at the Dubai branch of Zuma in 2010, where he arrived in 2009, before which he was with the One Porchester Group in the Far East.

Bakar & Spice **58**	Breakfast
Kozue **113**	Worth the travel
Noodle Bowl **58**	Bargain
Ravi **58**	Late night
Restaurant André **128**	Worth the travel
Stay **58**	High end
Table 9 **59**	Regular neighbourhood
Vapiano Dubai 2 **59**	Regular neighbourhood

HENDRIK OTTO
Vitrum
Potsdamer Platz 3, Berlin
Has overseen Vitrum, in Berlin's Ritz Carlton, since 2008, trained under Harald Wohlfahrt, prior to that he ran the kitchen at La Vision, Cologne.

Anna Blume **384**	Breakfast
Bocca di Bacco **382**	High end
Curry 36 **381**	Late night
Henne **382**	Worth the travel
Strandhalle Binz **375**	Worth the travel
Trattoria Toscana **375**	Regular neighbourhood
Vendôme **376**	Wish I'd opened

NATHAN OUTLAW
Restaurant Nathan Outlaw
St. Enodoc Hotel, Rock, Cornwall
Cornish-based seafood specialist, runs Restaurant Nathan Outlaw and Seafood & Grill, a variation on the latter opened in London at The Capital hotel in 2012.

Fresh from the Sea **174**	Bargain
Le Louis XV **291**	High end
Porthminster Café **174**	Bargain
The Seafood Restaurant **175**	Wish I'd opened
The Seahorse **175**	Regular neighbourhood

IRFAN PABANEY
Hakkasan Mumbai
Krystal, Waterfield Road Bandra Mumbai
Oversaw the kitchen at Mumbai's Indigo until 2010, when he became the chef for Hakkasan brand in India.

Bade Miya **66**	Late night
Bharat Excellensea **68**	Regular neighbourhood
Café Britannia **68**	Regular neighbourhood
Dakshinayan **69**	Bargain
Indigo Delicatessen **67**	Wish I'd opened
Neel **68**	High end
Shree Thakker Bhojanalay **68**	Local favourite
Thai Pavilion **67**	High end
Woodside Inn **67**	Breakfast

CHRISTIAN PAGE
Short Order
6333 West 3rd Street, Los Angeles
Keeps an eye on proceedings at superior Los Angeles's burger joint, Short Order, where he arrived when it opened in late 2011.

Canelé **491**	Worth the travel
Daikokuya **493**	Bargain
Gramercy Tavern **591**	Wish I'd opened
Isa **602**	Worth the travel
Milo and Olive **497**	Regular neighbourhood
Osteria Mozza **493**	High end
Short Cake **494**	Breakfas

PAUL PAIRET
Mr & Mrs Bund
6f 18 Zhongshan Dong Yi Lu, Shanghai
Having worked across Asia, he arrived in Shanghai to open Jade on 36, in 2005, following that up with Mr & Mrs Bund, in 2009, and Ultraviolet in 2012.

Ajisen Ramen **74**	Bargain
Crystal Jade **74**	Local favourite
Franck **77**	Regular neighbourhood
Hotel Costes **295**	Worth the travel
Jean Georges **74**	Breakfast
Nahm Bangkok **120**	Worth the travel
Table No. 1 **75**	Regular neighbourhood
Tippling Club **127**	Worth the travel

MATIAS PALOMO REYES
Sukalde
Nueva Costanera 3451, Vitacura, Santiago
Born in Mexico, trained at Costa Vasca, Arzak, and Daniel, he staged at elBulli, before opening Sukalde in Santiago, Chile, in 2006.

Alto **618**	Worth the travel
Arzak **320**	Worth the travel
Astrid & Gaston **621**	Worth the travel
La Bamba **642**	Late night
Biko **610**	Worth the travel
Café Melba **641**	Breakfast
Casa Cruz **639**	Worth the travel
CasaMar **643**	High end
El Celler de Can Roca **329**	Worth the travel
Coquinaria **642**	Breakfast
D.O.M. Restaurante **636**	Worth the travel
Donde el Guatón **642**	Late night
Fuente Alemana **642**	Bargain
El Hoyo **641**	Local favourite
Kinoshita **631**	Worth the travel
Kiosko Roca **641**	Breakfast
Liguria Manuel Montt **643**	Late night
Malabar **621**	Worth the travel
Mocotó **638**	Worth the travel
Osadía **643**	High end
La Piojera **641**	Local favourite
Pujol **610**	Worth the travel
Restaurant Paco Morales **337**	Worth the travel
Rodrigo **621**	Worth the travel
Tegui **640**	Worth the travel
Unik **640**	Worth the travel

STEVIE PARLE
Dock Kitchen
Portobello Docks 344/342 London
Worked at Moro and the River Café, before opening his own dining room, with a globetrotting menu, in designer Tom Dixon's showroom, in 2009.

Dock Kitchen **191**	Regular neighbourhood
Fäviken Magasinet **143**	Worth the travel
Koya **225**	Regular neighbourhood
Railroad **203**	Breakfast
The River Café **188**	High end
St. John Hotel **215**	Breakfast
Sweetings **199**	Local favourite
The Walnut Tree **233**	Worth the travel

DAVID PASTERNACK
ESCA
402 West 43rd Street, New York
The owner of Esca, opened in partnership with Mario Batali, in 2005. Once described by The New York Times as a 'fish whisperer'.

Astrid & Gaston **621**	Worth the travel
Balthazar **596**	Breakfast
Daniel **571**	High end
Peasant **596**	Wish I'd opened
Sake Bar Hagi **566**	Late night
Super Tacos **574**	Late night
Tertulia **586**	Worth the travel

DANIEL PATTERSON
Coi
373 Broadway, San Francisco
Born in Massachusetts, moved to California in 1989, the self-taught cook and brains behind San Francisco's Coi (2006), he's since opened Plum (2010) and Haven (2012).

4505 Meats **505**	Bargain
Benu **515**	High end
Boot and Shoe Service **517**	Regular neighbourhood
Commis **518**	High end
McCrady's **540**	Worth the travel
Nopa **513**	Late night
Pizzaiolo **518**	Late night
Pujol **610**	Worth the travel
Relæ **162**	Worth the travel

ZAKARY PELACCIO
Fatty Crab
643 Hudson Street, New York
Indiana-born, opened the Asian-tinged Fatty Crabs in 2005, following this up with two additional branches and the offshoot, Fatty 'Cue.

A&A Bake & Doubles Shop **599**	Breakfast
Baanrai Yarmyen **121**	Wish I'd opened
Il Buco **595**	Regular neighbourhood
Il Buco Alimentari e Vineria **577**	Regular neighbourhood
East Corner Wonton **589**	Bargain
Fruit N Spice **121**	Worth the travel
Great NY Noodletown **589**	Late night
Isa **602**	Worth the travel
Vinegar Hill House **601**	Local favourite

TOM PEMBERTON
Hereford Road
3 Hereford Road, London
Driving force behind Hereford Road, which he opened in West London in 2007 following his time running St. John Bread & Wine.

The Anchor & Hope **211**	Regular neighbourhood
Giaconda Dining Room **224**	Bargain
Granger & Co **194**	Breakfast
Halliday's of Funtington **180**	Worth the travel
Le Bernardin **571**	High end
Moro **200**	Regular neighbourhood
Pied à Terre **202**	High end
St. John Bread & Wine **209**	Local favourite
St. John Hotel **215**	Breakfast

ÍÑIGO PEÑA
Narru
Calle Zubieta 56, San Sebastián
Rising young star, who trained with Basque
Country's best at Arzak, Martin Berasategi
and Mugaritz, before, in 2011, he opened
Narru.

El Celler de Can Roca **329**	Worth the travel
Le Chateaubriand **307**	Worth the travel
La Espiga **322**	Late night
Ibai **323**	Local favourite
Kaia Kaipe **318**	High end
Martín Berasategui **318**	Worth the travel
Marugame Café Bar **324**	Breakfast
Va Bene Disco Burger **324**	Late night
Zuberoa **320**	Wish I'd opened

NEIL PERRY
Rockpool
107 George Street, Sydney
Left hairdressing to cook, opened Rockpool in
Sydney (1989), the more casual Rockpool Bar
& Grill launched in Melbourne (2007), and
Sydney (2009), where he also opened Spice
Temple the same year.

Asador Etxebarri **324**	Worth the travel
Azuma **22**	Regular neighbourhood
The Bridge Room **23**	Worth the travel
Chairman Mao **17**	Regular neighbourhood
Chinatown Noodle King **23**	Bargain
Flower Drum **32**	Wish I'd opened
Golden Century Seafood **24**	Late night
Kiroran Silk Road Uighur **24**	Bargain
Madang **25**	Regular neighbourhood
Mugaritz **319**	Wish I'd opened
Noma **160**	Wish I'd opened
Per Se **574**	Worth the travel
Reuben Hills **22**	Wish I'd opened
Room 10 **20**	Breakfast

BJÖRN PERSSON
Kock & Vin
Viktoriagatan 12, Gothenburg
Owner of the French meets west coast
Swedish brasserie, Familjen, the modern
Scandinavian, Kock & Vin (2000); and his
small hours bolthole, Björns Bar (2006).

AOC **158**	Worth the travel
Esperanto **150**	Worth the travel
Frantzén/Lindeberg **148**	High end
Noma **160**	Wish I'd opened

CAL PETERNELL
Chez Panisse
1517 Shattuck Avenue, Berkeley
Raised in New Jersey, he's been at Alice
Water's Chez Panisse since 1995, before
that he cooked at Biba, the Blue Room, Bix
and Bizou.

Bar Pinotxo **342**	Breakfast
Cal Pep **342**	Late night
Camino **517**	Local favourite
Franny's **601**	Regular neighbourhood
Little Saigon **517**	Bargain
Turtle Tower **509**	Bargain
Vik's Chaat & Market **517**	Bargain

JOCKEY PETRIE
The Fat Duck
High Street, Bray
Resident Scot at The Fat Duck, since 2002,
started as pastry chef, he became head of
creative development in 2009.

Alain Ducasse **305**	High end
L'Atelier de Joël Robuchon **222**	High end
Barrafina **222**	Regular neighbourhood
Beigel Bake **207**	Late night
Çiya Sofrasi **439**	Worth the travel
Craft **491**	Worth the travel
De Jonkman **269**	Worth the travel
The French Laundry **484**	Wish I'd opened
Golden Century Seafood **24**	Late night
The Hinds Head **172**	Local favourite
Kiraku **184**	Regular neighbourhood
Lahore Kebab House **197**	Regular neighbourhood
Nopi **226**	Local favourite
Roka **202**	High end

JEAN-FRANÇOIS PIÈGE
Thoumieux
79 Rue Saint-Dominique, Paris
Worked with Cirino, Constant and Ducasse
before taking charge at Les Ambassadeurs,
in Paris' Hôtel de Crillon. Left to launch Brasserie Thoumieux (2009), Jean-Francois Piège
(2010), and Hotel Thoumieux (2011).

L'Auberge du Pont de Collonges **286**	Wish I'd opened
Le Bernardin **571**	
Le Chardenoux des Prés **299**	Local favourite
Château Marmont **492**	Breakfast
Le Comptoir du Relais **299**	Worth the travel
Dinner by Heston **190**	Worth the travel
L'Espadon **294**	High end
Hélène Darroze **218**	Breakfast
Rino **308**	Bargain
Street **493**	Worth the travel

PEETER PIHEL
Alexander
Padaste Manor, Muhu Island
Estonian who oversees the kitchen at Alexan-
der, in the Padaste hotel and spa and the more
casual Neh, in the Estonian capital, Tallinn.

Albert & Jack's **150**	Breakfast
L'Arpège **301**	High end
Bras **282**	Wish I'd opened
Fäviken Magasinet **143**	Worth the travel
Frantzén/Lindeberg **148**	High end
Maaemo **140**	Wish I'd opened
NOP **424**	Breakfast
Relæ **162**	Worth the travel

JOSÉ PIZARRO
José
104 Bermondsey Street, London
Spaniard who's made London his home,
worked with Spanish food purveyors Brindisa
before, in 2011, opening José and Pizarro.

Atrio **332**	Worth the travel
The Azure **446**	Worth the travel
Ceviche **223**	Late night
Dinner by Heston **190**	Worth the travel
Elliot's Café **198**	Late night
El Figon de Eustaquio **332**	Bargain
Ibérica **199**	Late night
Murano **219**	High end
The Wolseley **221**	Breakfast
Zucca **208**	Regular neighbourhood

ZACH POLLACK
Sotto
9575 West Pico Boulevard, Los Angeles
Formerly of Pizzeria Ortica (2009) and now
at Sotto (2010), he was studying architecture
in Florence when he first fell in love with
Italian food.

Animal **499**	Worth the travel
BLD **499**	Breakfast
El Chato Taco Truck **496**	Late night
Cochon **546**	Worth the travel
Jitlada **492**	Regular neighbourhood
Maso Cantanghel **410**	Worth the travel
Torihei **498**	Bargain

BEN POLLINGER
Oceana
120 West 49th Street, New York
New Jersey native, resident at Oceana in
New York since 2006, his resume includes a
stage at Alain Ducasse's Louis XV in Monaco.

ABC Kitchen **599**	Regular neighbourhood
Charles' Pan Fried Chicken **566**	Bargain
Craigie on Main **534**	Worth the travel
Dovetail **572**	Wish I'd opened
Gramercy Tavern **591**	Wish I'd opened
Jean Georges **573**	Worth the travel
Michael's Restaurant **569**	Breakfast
Nedalny Vostok **426**	Worth the travel
Sushi Seki **572**	Worth the trave

BRUCE POOLE
Chez Bruce
2 Bellevue Road, London
Co-owner of Chez Bruce in suburban South-
West London, since 1995, he's also a partner
in The Glasshouse and La Trompette.

The Anchor & Hope **211**	Regular neighbourhood
The Delauney **214**	Breakfast
The Ledbury **194**	Worth the travel
Maison Lameloise **278**	Worth the travel
Tapas Brindisa **228**	Worth the travel
The Wolseley **221**	Breakfast
Zucca **208**	Regular neighbourhood

MICHEL PORTOS
Le Saint James
3 Place Camille Hostein, Bouliac
Based in Bordeaux at Le Saint-James since 2003, he previously ran his own restaurant in Perpignan, having trained at Les Jardins de l'Opéra and Troisgros.

La Cape 274	Regular neighbourhood
Chez Sauveur 284	Regular neighbourhood
Le Cinq 305	Breakfast
Le Cochon Volant 274	Late night
Maison Troisgros 290	Worth the travel
L'Osteria Francescana 395	Worth the travel
Le Petit Nice Passédat 285	Wish I'd opened
Pierre Gagnaire 306	High end
Restaurant Chartier 307	Bargain

NIKOS POULIASIS
Koukoumavlos
Fira, Santorini
Born in Corfu, has lived and worked in Santorini for over 25 years where he owns Koukoumavlos, located in an 18th century ship captain's house.

Botrini's 431	Worth the travel
Caffè Poliziano e Il Grifon D'Oro 411	Wish I'd opened
Kritikos 431	Bargain
La Madonnina del Pescatore 404	Worth the travel
Spondi Restaurant 431	High end
Sunset Taverna 430	Local favourite
Ta Dichtia 430	Regular neighbourhood

JACQUES AND LAURENT POURCEL
Le Jardin des Sens
11 Avenue Saint-Lazare, Montpellier
Identical twin Montpellier-based brothers who run Les Jardins des Sens (1980), with Laurent in the kitchen and Jacques overseeing their international outposts.

L'Ami Jean 301	Wish I'd opened
El Celler de Can Roca 329	Worth the travel
Ku De Ta 129	Worth the travel
La Gazzetta 308	Bargain
Le Georges 297	Late night
Les Templiers 280	Regular neighbourhood

ALFRED PRASAD
Tamarind
20 Queen Street, London
From the south of India, trained at the ITC Maurya Sheraton's Bukhara and Dum-Pukh, he arrived at Tamarind, in London, in 2001.

L'Anima 198	Regular neighbourhood
The Bangala Hotel 62	Worth the travel
Bar Italia 222	Late night
Cay Tre 223	Bargain
One-O-One 190	High end
Osteria del Vicario 410	Wish I'd opened
Pearl 215	High end
Saravanaa Bhavan 201	Breakfast
Sirocco 118	Worth the travel
The Spice Route 62	Worth the travel

CHRISTIAN PUGLISI
Relæ
Jægersborggade 41, Copenhagen
Born in Sicily, moved to Denmark at seven, he worked at elBulli and at Taillevant before becoming sous chef at Noma, leaving to open Relæ in 2010.

Attica 34	Worth the travel
Bastard 144	Worth the travel
The Coffee Collective 161	Breakfast
Golden Fields 35	Regular neighbourhood
Kebabistan 163	Late night
Meyers Bageri 162	Breakfast
Noma 160	Wish I'd opened
Ranee's 162	Bargain
Rumi 30	Worth the travel
Selfish 163	Regular neighbourhood
Søllerød Kro 155	High end

FLÁVIA QUARESMA
Carême
Rua Visconde de Caravelas 113, Rio de Janeiro
Brazilian, studied medicine and journalism before training at Le Cordon Bleu in Paris, back in Brazil, in 1999, she opened Carême Bistrô.

Astrid & Gaston 621	Worth the travel
Bar do Mineiro 630	Bargain
Bar Urca 630	Bargain
BB Lanches 629	Bargain
Cervantes 627	Late night
Chico e Alaíde 628	Local favourite
Filé de Ouro 628	Regular neighbourhood
Mani 636	High end
Olympe 629	High end
Roberta Sudbrack 628	Worth the travel
Talho Capixaba 629	Breakfast
Toyo 300	Worth the travel

PAUL QUI
Uchiko
4200 North Lamar, Austin
Moved from the Philippines to Virginia at ten, first came across Tyson Cole's Uchiko, where he now works, as a customer in 2003.

Benu 515	High end
Comptoir de la Gastronomie 294	Worth the travel
Dinner by Heston 190	Worth the travel
Franklin Barbecue 541	Local favourite
Lily's Sandwich 541	Regular neighbourhood
Musashino 542	High end
Sukiyabashi Jiro 105	Worth the travel
Tam Deli & Café 542	Breakfast
Thai Kitchen 542	Late night
Underbelly 542	Worth the travel

ALEXANDRA RAIJ
El Quinto Pino
401 West 24th Street, New York
Jewish-American with Argentine roots who runs a trio of Iberian-focussed New York outposts; El Quinto Pino, Txikito and La Vara.

Buvette 582	Breakfast
Cong Ly Restaurant 589	Bargain
Franny's 601	Regular neighbourhood
Great NY Noodletown 589	Late night
Mugaritz 319	Wish I'd opened
Poole's Diner 537	Worth the travel
Restaurante Arbolagaña 317	Worth the travel
Roberta's 603	Wish I'd opened
Soto 585	Regular neighbourhood
The Bowery Diner 593	Breakfast

THEO RANDALL
Theo Randall
The InterContinental, 1 Hamilton Place, London
English cook with an Italian bent, he ran the kitchen at the River Café for over a decade, leaving in 2007 to open Theo Randall at the InterContinental.

Aquasale 408	Worth the travel
Cachao 206	Breakfast
Lemonia 206	Bargain
Maison Troisgros 290	Worth the travel
Momo 219	Late night
La Petite Maison 220	Wish I'd opened
Princess Garden of Mayfair 220	Regular neighbourhood
St. John Bar and Restaurant 201	Local favourite
Zuma 190	Local favourite

VICKY RATNANI
Born and bred in Mumbai, he travelled the world cooking on ocean liners before pursuing a career as TV cook and consultant.

Aswad 68	Breakfast
L'Atelier de Joël Robuchon 301	High end
Bade Miya 66	Late night
Bukhara 62	Wish I'd opened
Celini 69	Wish I'd opened
Daniel 571	High end
Gajalee 62	Regular neighbourhood
Gunpowder 62	Worth the travel
Jean Georges 573	Worth the travel
Jimmy Boy 68	Local favourite
Momofuku Ko 579	Worth the travel
Noor Mohammadi 67	Bargain
Olympia Coffee House 67	Breakfast
Peter Luger Steakhouse 602	Local favourite
Sardar Refreshment 69	Bargain
Sergi Arola Gastro 334	Worth the travel
Tetsuya's 26	Worth the travel
Wasabi by Marimoto 62	High end
wd~50 594	Regular neighbourhood

TIM RAUE

Tim Raue
Rudi-Dutschke Strasse 26, Berlin
Berliner, who owns Restaurant Tim Raue, Uma and Shochu Bar having previously won acclaim for Ma Tim Raue.

Amber **83**	Worth the travel
La Belle Epoque **376**	Worth the travel
Curry 36 **381**	Late night
Good Friends **380**	Regular neighbourhood
Lutter & Wegner **383**	Local favourite
Moon Thai **380**	Bargain
Margaux Berlin **383**	High end

ALBERT RAURICH

Dos Palillos
Calle de Elisabets 9, Barcelona
Ferran Adria's righthand man at elBulli for seven years, he left in 2007 to open the Asian tapas bar, Dos Palillos.

41 Grados Experience **352**	Worth the travel
El Celler de Can Roca **329**	Worth the travel
Da Vittorio **401**	High end
Kikunoi **97**	Worth the travel
Kodaiji Wakuden **97**	Worth the travel
Lolita Taperia **353**	Bargain
Mugaritz **319**	Wish I'd opened
Nodaiwa **109**	Worth the travel
Pasteleria Escribà **350**	Breakfast
Sukiyabashi Jiro **105**	Worth the travel
Suppon Sakuma **110**	Worth the travel
Tickets **353**	Worth the travel
Xiringuito Escribà **347**	Regular neighbourhood

RENÉ REDZEPI

Noma
Strandgade 93, Copenhagen
Albanian-Dane behind Noma, opened in 2004, the Nordic-sourced agenda of which has changed haute cuisine in Scandinavia and beyond forever.

Le Châteaubriand **307**	Worth the travel
The Coffee Collective **161**	Breakfast
Manfreds & Vin **162**	Bargain
Relæ **162**	Worth the travel
Schønnemann **160**	Local favourite
Sweet Treat **161**	Breakfast

EMMANUEL RENAUT

Flocons de Sel
1775 Route de Leutaz, Megève
Born in Soisy-sous-Montmorency, trained at London's Claridge's and worked for Marc Veyrat, before, in 1998, he opened Le Flacons de Sel.

La Butte Boisée **111**	Worth the travel
Le Comptoir du Relais **299**	Worth the travel
L'Espadon **294**	High end
Le Jules Verne **303**	Wish I'd opened
Gilles Goujon **280**	Regular neighbourhood
Le Refuge **289**	Bargain
La Sauvageonne **289**	Late night

ANDREA REUSING

Lantern
423 West Franklin Street, Chapel Hill
Opened Lantern, in North Carolina, with her brother in 2002, where she combines Asian flavours with sustainable local ingredients.

Crook's Corner **536**	Regular neighbourhood
Holeman & Finch Public House **529**	Worth the travel
Neal's Deli **536**	Breakfast
Panciuto **537**	High end
Poole's Diner **537**	Worth the travel
Scratch **537**	Local favourite
St. John Hotel **215**	Breakfast
Toast **537**	Bargain

ANDY RICKER

Pok Pok
Southeast Division Street, Portland
Began the Thai-inspired Pok Pok, in Oregon, in 2006, where he now also has the Whiskey Soda Lounge and Pok Pok Noi.

Del Posto **588**	High end
Franklin Barbecue **541**	Local favourite
Nahm Bangkok **120**	Worth the travel
Tertulia **586**	Worth the travel

CRISTIANO RIENZNER

Maremoto
Grolmanstrasse 56, Berlin
Venetian, grew up in Berlin, inspired by two seasons at elBulli, he opened Maremoto in 2008. Relocated his 'Metaphoric cuisine' from Friedrichshain to Charlottenburg, in 2012.

Da Dong Roast Duck **79**	Worth the travel
Harry's Bar **414**	Breakfast
Le Louis XV **291**	High end
Pamfilya **385**	Regular neighbourhood

LIONEL RIGOLET

Comme Chez Soi
Place Rouppe 23, Brussels
Cooks at Brussels' Comme Chez Soi. He took over running its kitchen from his father-in-law, Pierre Wynants, who retired in 2006.

La Brasserie de Bruxelles **262**	Regular neighbourhood
Hof Van Cleve **264**	High end
Martín Berasategui **318**	Worth the travel
Le Perroquet **263**	Bargain
Le Si Bémol **263**	Late night
Silberberg **374**	Breakfast

ERIC RIPERT

Le Bernardin
155 West 51st Street, New York
Antibes-born, trained in Perpignan, he's been in charge of the kitchen at Le Bernadin, his New York flagship, since 1994.

L'Atelier de Joel Robuchon **107**	Wish I'd opened
Balthazar **596**	Breakfast
La Bonne Soupe **568**	Bargain
Daniel **571**	High end
Eleven Madison Park **591**	Worth the travel
Jean Georges **573**	Worth the travel
Masa **573**	High end
Le Pain Quotidien **597**	Breakfast
Per Se **574**	Worth the travel
Serafina Fabulous Pizza **571**	Regular neighbourhood
Sukiyabashi Jiro **105**	Worth the travel
Yakitori Totto **570**	Late night

MARTINS RITINS

Restaurant Vincents
Kārla Ulmana gatve 114a, Riga
Latvian, born in a British refugee camp, grew up in Corby in the English Midlands, worked in Toronto, opened Vincents, in Riga, in 1994.

Alinea **556**	Worth the travel
Foodbox **425**	Bargain
Kukši Manor House **425**	Wish I'd opened
Restaurant Eiropa **425**	Regular neighbourhood
Rosengrals **425**	Local favourite
Rumene Manor House **425**	Worth the travel
Vina Studija **425**	Late night

HELENA RIZZO

Mani
Rua Joaquim Antunes 210, São Paulo
Brazilian, who gave up modelling to cook, training at Fasano, Emmanuel Bassoleil and at El Cellar de Can Roca. She opened Maní in 2006.

Bar da Dona Onça **630**	Local favourite
Brasserie Le Jazz **637**	Regular neighbourhood
Chou **637**	Wish I'd opened
D.O.M. Restaurante **636**	Worth the travel
Malabar **621**	Worth the travel
Mocotó **638**	Worth the travel
Remanso do Bosque **626**	Worth the travel

JOAN, JORDI & JOSEP ROCA
El Celler de Can Roca
Can Sunyer 48, Girona
The band of talented Catalan brothers behind El Cellar de Can Roca; Joan, the eldest of the trio, runs the kitchen; middle brother Josep, is sommelier; and Jordi is pastry chef.

Roca, Joan
Cal Tet 328.................Regular neighbourhood
Can Marques 328............................Breakfast
Can Roca 328............................Local favourite
Es Xarcu 315.............................Local favourite
Koy Shunka 341...............................Late night
La Mar 620............................Worth the travel
Masa 573..High end
Pierre Gagnaire 306............................High end
Tapas 24 350..Bargain
La Taverna del Mar 331.....................Late night

Roca, Jordi
L'Arpège 301......................................High end
Bo Innovation 88.................Worth the travel
Can Roca 328............................Local favourite
Occi 330...Late night
Restaurant Can Xifra 330.........Local favourite
Restaurante Taj 331...........................Bargain
Tickets 353............................Worth the travel

Roca, Josep
Le Baratin 311...............Regular neighbourhood
Can Marques 328............................Breakfast
Can Roca 328............................Local favourite
Els Casals 327....................................High end
Caves Madeleine 278..........Wish I'd opened
Maison Troisgros 290............Worth the travel
Moovida 346.....................................Late night
El Motel 329............................Local favourite
Restaurant Villa Mas 331......Worth the travel

PHILIPPE ROCHAT
Ran Restaurant de L'Hôtel de Ville, Switzerland, until 2012, when he sold it.
Alain Ducasse 305............................High end
L'Astrance 309.....................Worth the travel
L'Atelier de Joël Robuchon 222........High end
Au Chat Noir 388........Regular neighbourhood
Coutanceau 283....................Worth the travel
Le Lexique 388............Regular neighbourhood
Waku Ghin 125.....................Wish I'd opened

BEN ROCHE
Moto
945 West Fulton Market, Chicago
Born in South Carolina, envelope-pushing pastry chef at Moto, he trained at the College of Culinary Arts, in Rhode Island, Providence.
Alkimia 345.......................................High end
The Aviary 563....................Worth the travel
The Barrelhouse Flat 556.................Late night
Big Star 554.......................................Late night
The Bristol 555..........Regular neighbourhood
Chickpea 563..Bargain
Del Posto 588.....................................High end
Jam 261..Breakfast
Level 532.............................Worth the travel
Lula 558..Breakfast
Nightwood 562.................................Breakfast
Les Nomades 559................Wish I'd opened
The Publican 556..................Wish I'd opened
The Wieners Circle 557....................Late night
Tinto 482.............................Worth the travel
Urban Belly 554.........Regular neighbourhood
Yusho 554....................Regular neighbourhood

PERFECTO ROCHER
Lazy Ox Canteen
241 South San Pedro Street, Los Angeles
Took over at Los Angeles' Lazy Ox Canteen in 2012, he's from Valencia, staged at elBulli, and worked at the Beverly Wilshire hotel's Blvd restaurant.
La Cabaña 496..................................Late night
Casa Mono 592.................................Late night
Cecconi's 499.....................................Breakfast
Mario's 495................Regular neighbourhood
Mariscos Guillen La Playita 496.........Bargain
Mélisse 497.......................................High end
Mugaritz 319.....................Wish I'd opened
Providence 495..................................High end
Tickets 353..........................Worth the travel

THOMAS RODE ANDERSON
Kong Hans Kaelder
Vingårdstræde 6, Copenhagen
At Kong Hans Kælder since 1996, he's also the poster boy for the Palaeolithic movement, launching Palæo — healthy fast food, in 2012.
Bras 282.............................Wish I'd opened
Fresh in the Garden 69..........Worth the travel
Mash 159...Late night
Mugaritz 319.....................Wish I'd opened
Noma 160..........................Wish I'd opened
Restaurant Sletten 154..........Worth the travel
Saigon Quan 154........Regular neighbourhood
Umami 161..................Regular neighbourhood
Yan's Wok 164......................................Bargain

DOUGLAS RODRIGUEZ
Alma de Cuba
1623 Walnut Street, Philadelphia
Self-proclaimed 'Godfather of Nuevo Latino', Cuban-American, born in NYC, moved to Miami at 13, he runs Alma de Cuba and De Rodriguez Cuba.
Blue Ribbon Brasserie 597.............Late night
La Guarida 611.....................Worth the travel
Joe's Stone Crab 528.............Local favourite
Oyster House 538......Regular neighbourhood
El Palacios de los Jugos 528..............Bargain
Parc 538...Breakfast

RUTH ROGERS
The River Café
Thames Wharf, Rainville Road, London
Upstate New York-born, co-founder of the River Café, which she opened, in West London with the now sadly deceased Rose Gray, in 1987.
L'Ami Louis 297...................................High end
Maroush 185.......................................Late night
Shake Shack 592.................................Bargain
St. John Bar and Restaurant 201...Local favourite
Trattoria Da Laura 400..........Wish I'd opened
Trattoria Gianni Franzi 401....Worth the travel
The Wolseley 221............................Breakfast

MITCHELL ROSENTHAL
Town Hall
342 Howard Street, San Francisco
Co-owner of San Francisco's Town Hall, Salt House and Anchor & Hope, and Portland's Irving Street Kitchen. He's worked at New York's Four Seasons, San Francisco's Postrio, and Malibu's Granita.
L'Ami Jean 301.....................Wish I'd opened
Boulette's Larder 506.......................Breakfast
In-N-Out 482.....................................Late night
Moro 200......................Regular neighbourhood
Oleana 535...........................Worth the travel
R&G Lounge 504........Regular neighbourhood
Redd 484..............................Wish I'd opened
Saison 511..High end
Shalimar 512..Bargain
Swan Oyster Depot 513..........Local favourite
Tartine Bakery 511...........................Breakfast

MATHIEU ROSTAING-TAYARD
Trained in Lyon, with Nicolas Le Bec, in Paris, with Eric Briffard, and in London, with Pierre Gagnaire. Ran Le 126, in Lyon, which he sold in 2012.

L'Auberge du Pont de Collonges 286.......Wish I'd opened
La Brasserie Georges 287...............Late night
Flocons de Sel 289.................Worth the travel
Noma 160...............................Wish I'd opened
L'Osteria Francescana 395...Worth the travel
Le Palégrié 288...............................Bargain
Le Potager des Halles 288..................Regular neighbourhood
Restaurant Daniel et Denise 288........Regular neighbourhood
Rue Le Bec 288...............................Breakfast

GABRIEL RUCKER
Le Pigeon
738 East Burnside Street, Portland
Grew up in Napa, moved to Oregon in 2003, worked at Paley's Place and the Gotham Building Tavern. He opened Le Pigeon in 2006 and Little Bird in 2010.

Babbo 580.............................Worth the travel
The French Laundry 404........Wish I'd opened
Joe Beef 478.............................Local favourite

CARME RUSCALLEDA
Sant Pau
Carrer Nou 10, Sant Pol de Mar, Barcelona
Owner of Sant Pau in Sant Pol de Mar, which she opened in 1988, she also overseas Sant Pau de Tòquio in Japan and Moments in Bangkok.

Bar del Puerto 326.............................Bargain
El Celler de Can Roca 329.....Worth the travel
Collsacreu 326...............................Bargain
Les Cols 329..............................Local favourite
Diverxo 33.............................Worth the travel
L'Indret de Semon 348...Wish I'd opened
Moments 351.............Regular neighbourhood
La Quadra 326.............................Late night
Ramon Freixa Madrid 334.....Worth the travel
Zurriola 111...........................Worth the travel

ALFREDO RUSSO
Dolce Stil Novo
Piazza della Repubblica 4, Venaria Reale
Born in Turin, he opened Dolce Stil Novo, in the Venaria Palace in 1990, having worked in many of Piedmont's best kitchens.

L'Atelier de Joel Robuchon 107...Wish I'd opened
Piadineria Al Passatore 407................Bargain
Puntarena 609.......................Worth the travel

HENRIQUE SÁ PESSOA
Alma
Calçada Marquês de Abrantes 92, Lisbon
Owner of Alma, gained experience in London and Sydney before returning to Portugal, to work at Bairro Alto and Sheraton hotels.

1300 Taberna 364...................Wish I'd opened
Cervejaria Ramiro 366.............Local favourite
Fortaleza do Guincho 357..............High end
Pastelaria Restelo Careca 369..........Breakfast
Ramon Freixa Madrid 334.....Worth the travel
Restaurante DOP 359...........Worth the travel
Tasca da Esquina 369.Regular neighbourhood

MARA SALLES
Tordesilhas
Rua Bela Cintra 465, São Paulo
Partner in Tordesilhas, her restaurant in São Paulo, she's been researching Brazilian food for over 20 years.

Ame 516...............................Worth the travel
O Bule 630...............................Worth the travel
Estadão 638.............................Late night
Jiyuu Sushi 634.........Regular neighbourhood
Kitanda Brasil 626...............Wish I'd opened
Mani 636.................................High end
Mercado Central 626.............Local favourite
Le Pain Quotidien 597................Breakfast
Sujinho 635.............................Late night

STEVE SAMSON
Sotto
9575 West Pico Boulevard, Los Angeles
Son of a Bolognese mother and American father, runs Southern Italian inspired Sotto (2010) in partnership with fellow chef Zach Pollack.

Hosteria Giusti 395...............Worth the travel
Manhattan Beach Post 493.....Local favourite
Manresa 482..........................Wish I'd opened
Providence 495.........................High end
Red Medicine 490..............................Bargain
Shin-Sen-Gumi 491....Regular neighbourhood
Square One Dining 492................Breakfast
Tsujita 501.............................Bargain
Urasawa 490.............................High end

MARCUS SAMUELSSON
Red Rooster
310 Lenox Avenue, New York
Ethiopian-born, Swedish-raised, Samuelsson made his name at New York's Aquavit. He opened Red Rooster in Harlem in 2011.

Le Bernardin 571.............................High end
Charles' Pan Fried Chicken 566..........Bargain
Daniel 571.................................High end
The Highliner 588.........................Late night
Jean Georges 573.................Worth the travel
Matsalen 149.............................High end
Minetta Tavern 581............Worth the travel
Momofuku Noodle Bar 579.....Wish I'd opened
Patisserie des Ambassades 566......Breakfast
Roberta's 603.......................Wish I'd opened
Shopsin's 594..........................Local favourite
Son of a Gun 494...................Worth the travel
La Taza de Oro 589.........................Bargain

GUY SAVOY
Restaurant Guy Savoy
18 Rue Troyon, Paris
Bourgogne-born, trained with the Troisgros brothers, Savoy opened his eponymous Paris flagship in 1980. Today he has five international outposts.

L'Ami Louis 297.............................High end
L'Arpège 301.............................High end
Atelier Crenn 505.........................High end
Hostellerie du port de Groslée 287.....Bargain
Relais Bernard Loiseau 279...Worth the travel
Roberta's 603.......................Wish I'd opened

EMANUELE SCARELLO
Agli Amici
Via Liguria 252, Godia
The fifth generation of his family to run Ristorante Agli Amici in Udine, which the Scarello's first opened back in 1887.

Ai Bintars 396.............................Bargain
Caffè Ottello 396.........................Late night
Combal.Zero 407..................Worth the travel
Cracco 403..........................Worth the travel
Da Vittorio 401.............................High end
Dal Pescatore 402.................Local favourite
Don Alfonso 1890 392.......Wish I'd opened
Eleven Madison Park 591......Worth the travel
Grosmi Caffè 396........................Breakfast
Il Luogo di Aimo e Nadia 403 Worth the travel
Niù 397.................................Late night
L'Osteria Francescana 395...Worth the travel
Pasticceria Simenoni 397................Breakfast
La Primula 396..........Regular neighbourhood
Trattoria Ai Ciodi 396...............Local favourite

JESSE SCHENKER
Recette
328 West 12th Street, New York
Floridian native, he opened Recette in New York's Greenwich Village in 2010, following his success with his Recette Private Dining.

Blue Ribbon Brasserie 597..............Late night
Emilia Romagna Restaurante 619...Worth the travel
Lupa 584...............................Wish I'd opened
Murray's Bagels 581.......................Breakfast
Per Se 574.............................Worth the travel
Rogue 24 524.......................Worth the travel
Sake Bar Hagi 566.........................Late night
Shake Shack 592...............................Bargain
Soto 585...................Regular neighbourhood
Vanessa's Dumplings 580................Bargain

THORSTEN SCHMIDT
Malling & Schmidt
Grenåvej 127, Risskov
Opened Malling & Schmidt, in central Denmark, in 2005, Schmidt is described by René Redzepi as 'one of the pioneers within Nordic regional cuisine.'

Geist 159...................Regular neighbourhood
Geranium 163.......................Worth the travel
Longrain 21.............................Worth the travel
Noma 160...............................Wish I'd opened

MICHAEL SCHWARTZ
Michael's Genuine Food & Drink
130 Northeast 40th Street, Miami
Owns Michael's Genuine Food & Drink, a Grand Cayman outpost and Harry's Pizzeria, in Miami's Buena Vista.

Cecconi's 527	Breakfast
Enriqueta's Sandwich Shop 525	Breakfast
Gigi 525	Late night
Hakkasan 527	High end
Mandolin 526	Regular neighbourhood
Mindy's Hot Chocolate 563	Worth the travel
El Palacios de los Jugos 528	Bargain
Sapore di Mare 399	Worth the travel
Shake Shack 528	Wish I'd opened

MINDY SEGAL
Mindy's Hot Chocolate
1747 North Damen Avenue, Chicago
Trained in Chicago, where she worked with Charlie Trotter, ahead of opening her dessert bar, Hot Chocolate, in 2005.

Arturo's Tacos 554	Late night
Hot Doug's 554	Local favourite
Longman & Eagle 557	Breakfast
Olive & Gourmando 478	Worth the travel
Potbelly Sandwich Works 557	Bargain
The Bento Box 554	Regular neighbourhood
The Publican 556	Wish I'd opened
Yardbird 528	Worth the travel

DIDEM SENOL
Lokanta Maya
Kemankes Caddesi 35a, Karaköy, Istanbul
Trained in New York at the French Culinary Institute, she returned home in 2010 to open Lokanta Maya, a bistro with a line in modern Turkish cooking.

Asador Etxebarri 324	Worth the travel
Asmali Cavit 437	Regular neighbourhood
Beyti 436	Wish I'd opened
Kaplan Dag Restoran 433	Worth the travel
Karaköy Lokantasi 440	Local favourite
Kiyi 441	Regular neighbourhood
Mikla 438	High end
Müze de Changa 441	Breakfast
Orfoz Bozburun 433	Worth the travel
Sampiyon Kokoreç 440	Late night
Sushi Yasuda 567	Worth the travel
Zuma 190	Local favourite

KARAM SETHI
Trishna
15-17 Blandford Street, London
Runs the British branch of the legendary Mumbai seafood specialist Trishna, worked at the original outpost, New Delhi's Bukhara and at London's Zuma.

Cecconi's Mayfair 217	Late night
Colbeh 184	Bargain
Mary's Fish Camp 584	Worth the travel
Meat Liquor 192	Bargain
La Petite Maison 220	Wish I'd opened
Pitt Cue Co. 227	Worth the travel
The Wolseley 221	Breakfast
Zuma 190	Local favourite

ESTHER SHAM
Ta Pantry
2d Star Street, Hong Kong Island
Raised in LA, staged in restaurants across France, she returned to Hong Kong, where she was born, to open Ta Pantry in 2008.

L'Atelier de Joël Robuchon 222	High end
Cheong Kee 87	Breakfast
Chiu Yuen Chiu Chow Noodle 89	Bargain
Island Tang 85	Local favourite
Le Parc 279	Wish I'd opened
Mandarin Grill & Bar 86	High end
Nihonryori Ryugin 108	Worth the travel
Restaurant Le Meurice 295	Worth the travel

BRUCE SHERMAN
North Pond
2610 North Cannon Drive, Chicago
Chicagoan who has run North Pond, since 1999, formally trained in Paris, he spent four years in India where he consulted for regional palace hotels.

Il Buco 595	Regular neighbourhood
El Chorrito 562	Late night
Coalfire Pizza 561	Bargain
Furama 563	Breakfast
Spoon Thai 557	Bargain
The Wieners Circle 557	Late night

BEN SHEWRY
Attica
74 Glen Eira Road, Ripponlea
Grew up on a farm in New Zealand, apprenticed under Michael Lambie, Andrew McConnell and David Thompson, he arrived at Attica in 2008.

Coi 513	Wish I'd opened
Flower Drum 32	Wish I'd opened
Golden Fields 35	Regular neighbourhood
Jacques Reymond 34	Worth the travel
Marque 21	High end
Momofuku Seiobo 20	Worth the travel
Nahm Bangkok 120	Worth the travel
Noma 160	Wish I'd opened
Quay 25	Wish I'd opened
Royal Mail 13	Worth the travel
Shanghai Village 33	Bargain
Vue de Monde 34	High end

MASATO SHIMIZU
15 East
15 East 15th Street, New York
Following a seven-year apprenticeship at Sukeroku in Tokyo, he moved to New York where, after four years at Jewel Bako, he opened 15 East.

ABC Kitchen 599	Regular neighbourhood
Blue Hill at Stone Barns 536	Worth the travel
Il Buco 595	Regular neighbourhood
Congee Village 593	Bargain
Kunjip 569	Late night
Panya 580	Breakfast
Per Se 574	Worth the travel

TIM SIADATAN
Trullo
300-302 St Paul's Road, London
Star graduate of the 2002 first year intake of Jamie Oliver's Fifteen, he trained further at Moro and St. John, before opening Trullo in 2010.

The Company Shed 176	Worth the travel
Moro 200	Regular neighbourhood
The River Café 188	High end
St. John Bar and Restaurant 201	Local favourite
St. John Bread & Wine 209	Local favourite
Terroirs 210	Regular neighbourhood
Testi 210	Bargain
Trattoria Il Pompiere 415	Worth the travel

ALEXANDRE SILVA
Bocca
Rua Rodrigo da Fonseca 87d, Lisbon
Has been cooking at Lisbon's Bocca, where he reinterprets regional Portuguese dishes, since it opened in 2008.

Aguas Livres 364	Regular neighbourhood
Alinea 556	Worth the travel
Bica Do Sapato 365	Wish I'd opened
El Celler de Can Roca 329	Worth the travel
Confeitaria Colonial 356	Breakfast
Ocean 357	Worth the travel
Panorama Restaurante 367	High end
Viajante 198	High end
Zé da Mouraria 368	Local favourite

KEITH SILVERTON
Mess Hall
4500 Los Feliz Boulevard, Los Angeles
Worked at Berkeley's Chez Panisse, and LA's Water Grill and Dominick's before taking the reins at Nonna of Italy and more recently, Mess Hall.

Blue Ribbon Brasserie 597	Late night
In-N-Out 585	Late night
Norma's 570	Breakfast
The Penthouse 497	Local favourite
Son of a Gun 494	Worth the travel

GEIR SKEIE
Midtåsen
Brygga 11, Sandefjord
Norwegian winner of the 2008 Bocuse d'Or and the 2009 Bocuse d'Or world final, he oversees the kitchen at Mathuset Midtåsen Solvold.

Bekkjarvik Gjestgiveri 138	Worth the travel
The French Café 49	High end
Perfect Pizza 142	Late night
Pollen Street Social 220	Wish I'd opened
Solsiden 142	Wish I'd opened
Villa Provence 142	Regular neighbourhood

BEVAN SMITH

Riverstone Kitchen
1431 State Highway 1, Road 5h, Oamaru
New Zealander who in 2006 opened
Riverstone Kitchen, on his parents' North
Otago farm, following spells in Brisbane and
London.

Amisfield Bistro 41................Worth the travel
Clooney 49.................................High end
Coda 35....................................Late night
Depot Eatery 48....................Worth the travel
Federal Diner 43..........................Breakfast
Marios Café 31............................Breakfast
MoVida Bar De Tapas Y Vino 32.......Worth the travel
No 7 Balmac 40..........Regular neighbourhood
Pegasus Bay 39.........Regular neighbourhood
Sean's Panorama 16..............Wish I'd opened

CLARE SMYTH

Restaurant Gordon Ramsay
68 Royal Hospital Road, London
Northern Irish, she worked at The Fat Duck,
The Waterside Inn, Gidleigh Park and
The French Laundry, before joining Gordon
Ramsay in 2002.

Alain Ducasse 194........................High end
Bar Boulud 189...........................Late night
El Celler de Can Roca 329.....Worth the travel
Le Gavroche 218...........................High end
Hibiscus 219..............................High end
Scott's 220.........................Local favourite
Tom's Kitchen 186.........................Breakfast
Zucca 208.................Regular neighbourhood

ADAM SOBEL

Bourbon Steak
2800 Pennsylvania Avenue, Washington
Overseas the Washington DC branch of
Bourbon Steak, where he arrived in 2011.
Has worked for Bradley Ogden, Guy Savoy
and Rick Moonen.

Bandolero 523............................Late night
Bibiana 522...............................High end
Graffiato 524.............................Late night
Grillmarkaðurinn 134............Worth the travel
The Purple Pig 560...............Worth the travel
Rasika 524.........................Local favourite
Seasons 523..............................Breakfast
The Source 523..........Regular neighbourhood
Standard 524..............................Bargain
Toki Underground 522...........Wish I'd opened

VÍTOR SOBRAL

Tasca da Esquina
Rua Domingos Sequeira 41C, Lisbon
Portuguese cook who made his name at
1990's Lisbon hotspot Alcantara, relaunched
Terreiro do Paço in 2004, and opened Tasca
Da Esquina, in 2009.

Kinoshita 631......................Worth the travel
Panorama Restaurante 367..............High end
Pastéis de Belém 368.....................Breakfast
Porto Santa Maria 358....................High end
Solar dos Presuntos 367.........Local favourite

HIRO SONE

Terra
1345 Railroad Avenue, Napa Valley
His big break came at Wolfgang Puck's Spago
in Tokyo, which eventually brought him to
the Hollywood original. Subsequently opened
Terra and Ame.

Aladdin 112...........................Local favourite
L'Ami Jean 301....................Wish I'd opened
Asador Etxebarri 324...........Worth the travel
Atami Kai 100......................Wish I'd opened
Hagakure 112..............................Bargain
Inoue Ramen 104..........................Bargain
Kyoto Kitcho 98............................High end
Miyagino 99..............................Breakfast
n/naka 496.........................Worth the travel
Nojo 504...........................Worth the travel
Nopa 513..................................Late night
Ristorante Marconi 394..........Worth the travel
Sangouan 109............Regular neighbourhood

BEN SPALDING

Roganic
19 Blandford Street, London
Launched Simon Rogan's two year London
pop-up Roganic in 2011, left after a year to
pursue a solo venture.

L'Enclume 175......................Worth the travel
Escondido 177............Regular neighbourhood
Kock & Vin 142....................Worth the travel
The Ledbury 194...................Worth the travel
Per Se 574..........................Worth the travel
Yauatcha 229.............................Late night

SUSAN SPICER

Bayona
430 Dauphine Street, New Orleans
The grande dame of the New Orleans'
restaurant scene Spicer began her career
with Daniel Bonnot at Louis XVI in 1979.

ABC Kitchen 599.........Regular neighbourhood
Boulud Sud 572...........................High end
Butcher 546........................Wish I'd opened
Crabby Jack's 548..................Local favourite
Domenica 547.............................Late night
Herbsaint 547............Regular neighbourhood
High Hat Café 549........Regular neighbourhood
Jean Georges 573.................Worth the travel
Mandina's 548......................Local favourite
Parkway Bakery & Tavern 548............Bargain
Russells Marina Grill 548................Breakfast

LJUBOMIR STANISIC

100 Maneiras
Rua do Teixeira 35, Lisbon-
Born in Bosnia, he moved Portuguese
food into avant-garde territory with his
100 Maneiras restaurants in Cascais.

Bica Do Sapato 365................Wish I'd opened
O Cadete 368..............................Bargain
Café de São Bento 368...................Late night
Martín Berasategui 318........Worth the travel
Panorama Restaurante 367..............High end
O Pitéu da Graça 371...............Local favourite
Tasca da Esquina 369.Regular neighbourhood
Varanda Restaurant 365..................Breakfast
The Yeatman 359..........................High end

DIRK STARK

Amisfield Bistro
10 Lake Hayes Road, Queenstown
German, who cooks at the Amisfield Wine
Company's Bistro, ran the kitchen ahead
of the arrival in 2012 of new head chef,
Jay Sherwood.

The Bunker 41............................Late night
Cutler & Co 30............................High end
Euro 48.............................Worth the travel
Kappa Sushi 42.........Regular neighbourhood
Vudu Café and Larder 43..................Breakfast

MICHAEL STEH

Reds Bistro
77 Adelaide Street, Toronto
Resident at Red Bistro and Wine Bar in
Toronto since 2006, Steh's a Slow Food
champion known for his charcuterie.

Au Pied de Cochon 475...........Local favourite
Cava 469.................................High end
Corner Café & Bistro 468..............Breakfast
Khmer Thai 468...........................Bargain
King's Noodle House 468...Regular neighbourhood
Nota Bene 468.....................Wish I'd opened
Pizza Gigi 470............................Late night
Red Cabbage Café 608..........Worth the travel

CRAIG STOLL

Delfina Restaurant
3621 18th Street, San Francisco
A native New Yorker with a quartet of neig-
bourhood Italians in San Francisco; Delfina,
two Pizzeria Delfinas and Locanda.

00100 Pizza 397...................Worth the travel
Foreign Cinema 510..Regular neighbourhood
Nopa 513..................................Late night
Swan Oyster Depot 513...........Local favourite
Tartine Bakery 511........................Breakfast
The Walrus and the Carpenter 487.......Worth
the travel
Wing Lee Bakery 508......................Bargain
Yuet Lee 512..............................Late night
Zuni Café 505.....................Local favourite

STEPHEN STRYJEWSKI

Cochon
930 Tchoupitoulas Street, New Orleans
Launched Cochon in partnership with Donald
Link in 2006, followed by a Butcher (2009)
and Cochon Lafayette (2011).

La Boca 546..............................Late night
Commander's Palace 548................Breakfast
The Company Burger 549....Regular neighbourhood
Momofuku Noodle Bar 579....Wish I'd opened
Parador La Huella 639...........Worth the travel
Root 547..................................Late night
Torrisi Italian Specialties 596..Local favourite

PEDRO SUBIJANA
Akelare
Paseo Padre Orcoloaga 56 Gipuzkoa,
San Sebastián
One of the founding fathers of New Basque cooking. After training in Madrid, he opened Akelare in his native San Sebastian in 1975.

Arzak 320...............................Worth the travel
Barkaiztegi 321............................Local favourite
Bernardo Etxea 321............................High end
Calonge Sagardotegia 322......Local favourite
The Fat Duck 172...................Worth the travel
Gandarias 323................................Late night
Kaia Kaipe 318...................................High end
Martín Berasategui 318........Worth the travel
Mugaritz 319......................Wish I'd opened
Quique Dacosta Restaurante 336.........Worth the travel
Restaurante Combarro 334...............High end
Rias de Galicia 352.........................High end
Zuberoa 320.....................Wish I'd opened

ROBERTA SUDBRACK
Roberta Sudbrack
Rua Lineu Paula Machado 916, Rio de Janeiro
Self-taught, she stood behind the stove at Brazil's presidential palace before opening her Rio restaurant in 2005. In 2012, she designed menus for Brazil's Olympic team.

L'Atelier de Joël Robuchon 301...........High end
Casa da Li 634.......................Worth the travel
Gepetto 630..................................Bargain
Juana La Loca 333.................Worth the travel
Olympe 629.......................................High end
L'Ourson qui Boit 287............Worth the travel
Padaria Rio Lisboa 629....................Breakfast
Pousada da Alcobaça 627.......Local favourite
Toyo 300.............................Worth the travel
Zubebi Restaurant 409..........Wish I'd opened

MARK SULLIVAN
Spruce
3640 Sacramento Street, San Francisco
A New Yorker Sullivan made his name at 42 Degrees and PlumpJack Squaw Valley. Now chef-partner at Spruce and The Village Pub where the agenda is 'field-to-fork'.

Bar Boulud 572......................Worth the travel
Le Bernardin 571...............................High end
Boulette's Larder 506....................Breakfast
Locanda 510...............Regular neighbourhood
Pizzaiolo 518...................................Late night
Restaurant Guy Savoy 310.....Worth the travel
State Bird Provisions 514..................Bargain

BJORN SVENSSON
Oscarsgate
Inngang Pilestredet 63, Oslo
Started out making pizzas in his Swedish hometown before training at elBulli, Gordon Ramsay and Bagatelle. At the pocket-sized Oscarsgate he's won plaudits.

Åpent Bakeri 139.......Regular neighbourhood
Blings 138..Breakfast
The Fat Duck 172...................Worth the travel
Hai Café 141....................................Bargain
Noma 160.........................Wish I'd opened
Onda Sea 138..................................Late night
Palace Grill 139...................Wish I'd opened
Relæ 162...............................Worth the travel

AGNAR SVERRISSON
Texture
34 Portman Street, London
Born in Iceland, worked under Marcus Wareing and Raymond Blanc before launching Texture in 2007.

Bar Boulud 189...............................Late night
El Celler de Can Roca 329.....Worth the travel
Dabbous 202.........................Worth the travel
Le Manoir aux Quat'Saisons 179...Wish I'd opened
Pho 227...Bargain
The Wolseley 221............................Breakfast
Zuma 190................................Local favourite

TAKUJI TAKAHASHI
Kinobu
416 Iwatoyamacho, Bukkouji-sagaru, Kyoto
Declared one of Japan's best chefs Takahashi is the third generation chef-owner at Kinobu, a Kyoto kaiseki fixture since 1935.

Côte d'Or 107.......................Worth the travel
Inoda Coffee 98.............................Breakfast
Kyoto Kitcho 98................................High end
Maison Troisgros 290........Worth the travel
Nakamura-Rou 98...............Wish I'd opened
Old Hong Kong Restaurant 99............Regular neighbourhood
Tominokoji Harutaka 98..................Late night

JUN TANAKA
Pearl
252 High Holborn, London
Trained in London by the brothers Roux and Marco Pierre White, he wears two toques; chef of Pearl since 2004 and co-founder of Street Kitchen.

40 Maltby Street 208............Worth the travel
Albion Café 206.............................Late night
Bistro Bruno Loubet 199...Regular neighbourhood
Great Queen Street 224..........Local favourite
HK Diner 213....................................Late night
Koya 225....................Regular neighbourhood
Locanda Verde 598.........................Breakfast
La Petite Maison 220............Wish I'd opened
Sushi Of Gari 571..................Worth the travel

JÉRÔME TAUVRON
L'Etranger
36 Gloucester Road, London
Has worked for a 'who's who' of French gastronomy including Gagnaire and Ducasse. Runs L'Etranger and Meursault in London.

Antepliler 204.............Regular neighbourhood
Aubaine 216.....................................Breakfast
Can Marcel 280....................Worth the travel
China Tang 194...........Regular neighbourhood
Dinings 192.................Regular neighbourhood
Goodman 218...................................Late night
Hakkasan 218......................Worth the travel
Hibiscus 219......................................High end
Massimo 210.............Regular neighbourhood
Min Jiang 189.............Regular neighbourhood
Sucre Salé 114.....................Worth the travel
Umu 221..High end
Zuma 190................................Local favourite

DANIEL TAYLOR
Karpo
23 Euston Road, London
Arrived in London from North Carolina to work with Rowley Leigh at Le Café Anglais and Jeremy Lee at the Blue Print Café. Launched Karpo in 2012.

Le Café Anglais 184..................Local favourite
Dos Taquitos 537.........Regular neighbourhood
The Greenhouse 218........................High end
The Hand & Flowers 173.......Worth the travel
Nick Tahou Hots 536......................Late night
Porter's 538....................................Breakfast
The River Café 188.............................High end
Vin Rouge 537.......................Worth the travel

DAVID TAYLOR
The Brooklyn-born chef's varied career encompasses country clubs, a Naples pizzeria and running a four star in Prague. Left A16 in 2012 to pursue other opportunities.

Crepevine 509..................................Bargain
Diner 602.............................Worth the travel
Nopa 513...Late night
Perbacco 507.....................Wish I'd opened
Quince 507.......................................High end
Ryoko's 512......................................Late night
Zazie 505..Breakfast

JAIR TELLEZ
Laja
Carretera Tecate-Ensenada, Valle de Guadalupe
Grew up in Mexico, moved to New York to study cooking. Opened Laja in 1999 and MeroToro in 2010.

Asian Bay 608............Regular neighbourhood
Biko 610.............................Worth the travel
Fonda Margarita 609.......................Breakfast
La Guerrerense 608........................Breakfast
Kødbyens Fiskebar 164.........Worth the travel
Muelle 3 608........................Local favourite
Néctar 611.........................Worth the travel
The Publican 556...............Wish I'd opened
Taqueria Los Parados 610...............Late night
Tortas al Fuego 610...........................Bargain

PETER TEMPELHOFF
The Greenhouse
93 Brommersvlei Road, Cape Town
Launched fashionable London diner Automat in 2005, his 'progressive South African' cuisine is served at five restaurants within Cape Province luxury hotel group.
Le Bernardin 571..............................High end
Borruso's 448......................................Bargain
Nobu at One&Only 448..................High end
Overture 449..............Regular neighbourhood
The Pot Luck Club 449...........Wish I'd opened
Sunrise Chip and Ranch 449..............Late night
Suzunari 114.........................Worth the travel
The Test Kitchen 449.............Wish I'd opened

PEKKA TERÄVÄ
Olo
Kasarmikatu 44, Helsinki
Finn who cooked at Stockholm's Edsbacka Krog and the Helsinki institution that is G.W. Sundmans. Champions Modern Nordic cooking at Olo.
Bras 282............................Wish I'd opened
Ilmatar Restaurant 166................Breakfast
Sergio's Ravintola 169........................Regular neighbourhood
Trattoria Rivoletto 167.........................Regular neighbourhood

CHRISTOPHER THOMPSON
A16
2355 Chestnut Street, San Francisco
Took charge of the kitchen at San Francisco's A16 in 2012, where previously he was sous chef, prior to that he was working at Spruce in Pacific Heights for three years.
Brenda's French Soul Food 516.......Breakfast
Brothers BBQ 515.......Regular neighbourhood
King of Thai Noodle House 508........Late night
La Ciccia 508....................Wish I'd opened
Nopa 513...............................Late night
Pancho Villa Taqueria 511..............Late night
Ryoko's 512..............................Late night
Shanghai Dumpling King 513..............Bargain
SPQR 509...........................Local favourite

KEVIN THORNTON
Thornton's Restaurant
128 St Stephen's Green, Dublin
From County Tipperary, described as 'the great philosopher of Irish food', opened Thornton's in 1995, before moving to the Fitzwilliam Hotel in 2002.
Café Hans 242....................Worth the travel
The Gallery 217...............................Late night
Lobby Lounge 240.......Regular neighbourhood
Pierre Gagnaire 306..........................High end
Vila Joya 357....................................High end

BEN TISH
Salt Yard
54 Goodge Street, London
Launched London tapas concern Salt Yard in 2006. In 2008 he became responsible for overseeing the growing Salt Yard Group.
Akelare 320.........................Wish I'd opened
Brunswick House Café 211.............Breakfast
Dabbous 202....................Worth the travel
Meat Liquor 192.................................Bargain
Quo Vadis 228...................Wish I'd opened
Spuntino 228......................Wish I'd opened
Tayyabs 211.......................Local favourite
Yildiz 201...Bargain

NEIL ANTHONY TOMES
Alfie's by Kee
10 Chater Road, Hong Kong Island
17 years cooking across Asia and the Caribbean put Tomes in a great position to oversee Alfie's by Kee.
8½ Otto e Mezzo Bombana 83..........High end
Can.teen 84...............Regular neighbourhood
Great Café 87........................Worth the travel
Lei Garden 89......................Local favourite
Maranui Café 45...........................Breakfast
Sushi Toku 91.....................................High end
Yardbird 88.................Regular neighbourhood

MITCHELL TONKS
RockFish
128-130 Whiteladies Road, Bristol
Fishmonger-turned-restaurateur who runs the RockFish Grill & Seafood Market, The Seahorse and RockFish Seafood.
Al Gatto Nero da Ruggero 413....... Worth the travel
L'Ami Louis 297....................................High end
The Delauney 214...........................Breakfast
Harry's Bar 414.................................Breakfast
Mangal Ockabasi 203.........................Bargain
La Petite Maison 220............Wish I'd opened
Rasa Sayang 214...............................Bargain
The Wolseley 221..............................Breakfast
Zuma 190............................Local favourite

CHRISTINA TOSI
Momofuku Milk Bar
163 1st Avenue, New York
Her collaboration with David Chang began in 2009. There are now five branches.
Angar 58............................Worth the travel
Balthazar 596....................................Breakfast
The Bowery Diner 593....................Breakfast
The Brooklyn Star 601......................Late night
Caracas Arepa Bar 576.......................Bargain
Crif Dogs 576.....................................Late night
Del Posto 588....................................High end
Fonuts 494........................Wish I'd opened
The Meatball Shop 584....................Late night
Mission Chinese Food 510.................Regular neighbourhood
Peking Duck House 590...Regular neighbourhood
Pies 'n' Thighs 602................Wish I'd opened
Roberta's 603....................Wish I'd opened
Son of a Gun 494..................Worth the travel
Veselka 580...Late night

FERNANDO TROCCA
Sucre
Sucre 676, Buenos Aires
Owns and cooks at Sucre in northern Buenos Aires, Trocca also overseas the menu for the London based Argentinean restaurant group, Gaucho Grill.
Blue Ribbon Brasserie 597.............Late night
Camino 517....................................Local favourite
El Celler de Can Roca 329.....Worth the travel
Harry Sasson 619..................Worth the travel
La Lucha 620.....................................Bargain
Petite Abeille 592.............................Breakfast
El Pobre Luis 639...............Local favourite
St. John Bar and Restaurant 201............Local favourite

MICHEL TROISGROS
Maison Troisgros
Place Jean Troisgros, Roanne
In 1983 he restored Maison Troisgros, the legendary restaurant made famous by his father and uncle. Has since opened in Paris, Moscow and Tokyo.
L'Astrance 309....................Worth the travel
Aux Anges 289..........Regular neighbourhood
Le Coquillage 277.................Wish I'd opened
Gravelier 274......................................Bargain
La Grenouillère 282...............Local favourite
La Maison de l'Aubrac 306.............Late night
Momofuku Noodle Bar 579....Wish I'd opened
Zuni Café 505...................Local favourite

BRADLEY TURLEY
Goga
1 Yueyang Lu Xuhui Shanghai
Californian who in 2010 opened Goga, his compact 2-seat Cali-Asian concern. Previously worked with Roy Yamaguchi and Floyd Cardoz at New York's Tabla.
The Grumpy Pig 76.............Worth the travel
Jean Georges 74................................Breakfast
Michael Mina 507...............................High end
Mr & Mrs Bund 75...............................Late night
Nougatine at Jean Georges 570.........Regular neighbourhood
La Régalade 309...............................Bargain
Roy's 485..........................Wish I'd opened
Sage 485............................Worth the travel
Tsui Wah 91..............Regular neighbourhood

MICHAEL TUSK
Quince
470 Pacific Avenue, San Francisco
Opened Quince in 2003, which takes an Italian approach to Northern California's larder.
4505 Meats 505.................................Bargain
Bar Agricole 515........................Local favourite
Blue Hill at Stone Barns 536........Worth the travel
The French Laundry 484........Wish I'd opened
Husk 539............................Worth the travel
Koi Palace 517....................................Bargain
Steirereck 419....................Worth the travel

GENÇAY ÜÇOK

Meze by Lemon Tree
Mesrutiyet Caddesi 83b, Istanbul
Owns and cooks at Istanbul's Meze by Lemon Tree, a colourful and accomplished modern meyhane, opened in 2010.

Aynen Dürüm 439......................Bargain
Beyti 436.........................Wish I'd opened
Café Pouchkine 305............Worth the travel
Kale Café 441..............................Breakfast
Kanaat Lokantasi 441..............Local favourite
Meshur Tavaci Recep Usta 436............Regular neighbourhood
Selçuk Köftecisi 433..............Worth the travel
Sunset Grill & Bar 436.....................High end

NAOYA UENO

Gensai
7-5-15 Nakayamate-dori, Kobe
Born in Osaka, he grew up watching his father, Suzo Ueno, cook at Naniwa Kappou Kigawa. Trained further at Kyoto's Kikunoi. Opened Gensai in 2004.

Anonyme 96..............Regular neighbourhood
Ca Sento 96......................Local favourite
Dozeu Iseki 106...............................Bargain
Geumgang San 92..............Worth the travel
Hirasansou 100............................Breakfast
Ittetsu Ramen 96..............................Bargain
Kikusuizushi Nishimise 96...............High end
Sushidokoro Kazuya 100.................Late night
Wasabi 100.....................................Bargain
Xingxing 96..................................Breakfast

HANS VÄLIMÄKI

Chez Dominique
Richardinkatu 4, Helsinki
Owner of Chez Dominque since 1998. Became a household name in Finland as judge on the TV show 'Top Chef Suomi'.

Balthazar 596................................Breakfast
Brooklyn Fare 600.................Wish I'd opened
Café Ekberg 166..............................Breakfast
Eleven Madison Park 591......Worth the travel
Fäviken Magasinet 143.........Worth the travel
Frantzén/Lindeberg 148.................High end
Gaijin 166........................Wish I'd opened
Noma 160.........................Wish I'd opened
Savoy 165.......................................High end
Sea Horse 168.................................Bargain
Sho Shaun Hergatt 591.........Worth the travel
Tertti 165.............................Local favourite
Trattoria Rivoletto 167...Regular neighbourhood

ROGER VAN DAMME

Het Gebaar
Leopoldstraat 24, Antwerp
Dutch cook who opened Het Gebaar in 1994, a luxury tea room only open during the day that's won particular praise for its desserts.

L'Atelier de Joël Robuchon 301........High end
Finjan 260......................................Late night
Hof Van Cleve 264...........................High end
Lam en Yin 261..........Regular neighbourhood
Lung Wah 261........................Local favourite
Zuma 87........................Wish I'd opened
't Fornuis 261..............Regular neighbourhood

MANOJ VASAIKAR

Indian Zing
236 King Street, London
Owner of Indian Zing, Indian Zilla and Indian Zest, Vasaikar was born in Mumbai and moved to London to work at Chutney Mary and Veeraswamy.

Amaya 189.......................................High end
Bukhara 62........................Wish I'd opened
Highway Gomantak 66...........Worth the travel
Konkan Café 67....................Worth the travel
Peshawri 66.........................Worth the travel
La Trompette 187.......Regular neighbourhood
Yas 189..Late night

JARROD VERBIAK

Maison Boulud
Ch'ianmen 23, Beijing
Has worked with Boulud for over a decade, he launched the Miami branch of db Bistro Moderne in 2010, leaving there in 2012 to return Maison Boulud in Beijing.

Barceloneta 527...................Worth the travel
Bouchon 484.........................Wish I'd opened
Café Pushkin 426..................Worth the travel
El Palacios de los Jugos 528.............Bargain
Eternity Coffee Roasters 525...........Breakfast
La Moon 526...................................Late night
Pubbelly 526........................Local favourite
Pubbelly Sushi 526................Local favourite
Sakaya Kitchen 526....Regular neighbourhood
Scarpetta 528....................................High end

THRAINN FREYR VIGFUSSON

Kolabrautin
Harpa Ingólfsgarður Austurbakki 2, Reykjavík
Oversees Kolabrautin, Vigfusson represented Iceland at the Bocuse d'Or in 2011 and is a silver medal winner at the Scandi and Icelandic chef of the year competitions.

ABaC 347...High end
Alinea 556.............................Worth the travel
Bakari Sandholt 135.........................Breakfast
Bæjarins Beztu 134..........................Late night
Dill Restaurant 135...............Worth the travel
Grillið 135.......................................High end
Nauthóll 135..............Regular neighbourhood
Svarta Kaffið 135..............................Bargain

VIKRAM VIJ

Vij's
1480 West 11th Avenue, Vancouver
Born in India, he trained in Austria before arriving in Canada in 1989. Currently owns Vancouver's Vij's and Rangoli.

Bao Bei Chinese Brasserie 460.......Late night
Campagnolo 461........Regular neighbourhood
DNA 476............................Worth the travel
Hawksworth Restaurant 464...Worth the travel
Medina 460....................................Breakfast
The Pear Tree 460.................Worth the travel
Restaurant 18 457.................Worth the travel
Tamarind 598......................Wish I'd opened

EBBE VOLLMER

Vollmers
Tegelgårdsgatan 5, Malmö
Returned to his Swedish hometown of Malmö to open Vollmers in 2011. He's worked in Asia and in the UK with Gordon Ramsay.

L'Atelier de Joël Robuchon 222.........High end
Daniel 571.......................................High end
Gaddi's 91............................Worth the travel
Le Manoir aux Quat'Saisons 179...Wish I'd opened
Östarps Gästgivaregård 143....Local favourite
Radio 164...........................Worth the travel
Retour 160.......................................Bargain

TETSUYA WAKUDA

Tetsuya's
529 Kent Street, Sydney
Arrived in Sydney from Japan in 1982, opening his eponymous restaurant there in 1989, relocating it to larger premises in 2000. Launched in Singapore in 2011.

Azuma 22.....................Regular neighbourhood
Café Morso 20..............................Breakfast
Flower Drum 32.....................Wish I'd opened
Icebergs Dining Room and Bar 16...Local favourite
Kikunoi 97...........................Worth the travel
Kodaiji Wakuden 97..............Worth the travel
Kyoto Kitcho 98................................High end
Marigold 25.....................................Bargain
Miyamasou 98.....................Worth the travel
Ogata 99.............................Worth the travel
Palate 13............................Worth the travel
Pilu at Freshwater 17..............Local favourite
Ristorante Buon Ricordo 19...............High end
Rockpool Bar & Grill 25.....................High end

MARCUS WAREING

Marcus Wareing
The Berkeley Hotel, Wilton Place, London
Re-branded the Gordon Ramsay operated Petrus as Marcus Wareing at The Berkeley in 2008. The Gilbert Scott at London's St. Pancras Renaissance followed in 2011.

Alinea 556.............................Worth the travel
Bar Boulud 189...............................Late night
Le Caprice 21.......................Wish I'd opened
Chez Bruce 195..........Regular neighbourhood
Hélène Darroze 218.........................Breakfast
The Ledbury 194...................Worth the travel
Medlar 186...........................Local favourite
Scott's 220...........................Local favourite

BLAINE WETZEL
The Willows Inn
2579 West Shore Drive, Lummi Island
A Washington State native, he's been cooking at Willows Inn on Lummi Island since 2010. His resume includes time at L'Auberge in California and Copenhagen's Noma.

L'Arpège 301.................................High end
Belltown Pizza 486........................Late night
Canlis 486...........................Worth the travel
Next Restaurant 555............Wish I'd opened

ALYN WILLIAMS
Alyn Williams at the Westbury
Bond Street, London
Londoner Williams spent 6 years as a ski instructor before training with Marcus Wareing at the Berkeley. His hotel dining room at the Westbury opened in 2011.

Burger & Lobster 216...........Wish I'd opened
Epicure 306.................................High end
Goodman 218...............................Late night
Hawksmoor 197............................Breakfast
Hélène Darroze 218......................Breakfast
The Ivy 225........................Wish I'd opened
The Ledbury 194...................Worth the travel
Pollen Street Social 220........Wish I'd opened
Robin's Pie & Mash 176...........Local favourite
Roganic 193........................Worth the travel
St. John Bar and Restaurant 201...Local favourite
Texture 193...................................High end

BRYN WILLIAMS
Odette's
130 Regents Park Road, London
From north Wales, made a name for himself in 2006 with BBC television's Great British Menu. He's since revived the long-running Odette's in London's Primrose Hill.

Benares 216..................................High end
Bentley's Oyster Bar & Grill 216...Wish I'd opened
Camden Bar & Kitchen 199..............Breakfast
Casa Tua 527.......................Worth the travel
Le Gavroche 218.............................High end
Polpo 227..Bargain
The Wolseley 221...........................Breakfast

MICHAEL WILSON
Jing'An
1 Changde Road, Shanghai
Australian who arrived in China in 2012, fresh from Melbourne's Cutler & Co., to take charge at Jing'An, the signature restaurant in the 5-Star PuLi Hotel.

Attica 34............................Worth the travel
Baker & Spice 77...........................Breakfast
Le Bistro du Dr. Wine 76.................Late night
Cumulus Inc. 31....................Wish I'd opened
Cutler & Co 30...............................High end
Longrain 21.........................Worth the travel
Sepia 26.............................Worth the travel

HEINZ WINKLER
Residenz Heinz Winkler
Kirchplatz 1, Aschau im Chiemgau
The youngest of 11 siblings, Winkler grew up on a farm in Tyrol and is the self-proclaimed inventor of "cuisine vitale", combining culinary excellence with health.

Gasthof Messerschmitt 374................Bargain
Maison Lameloise 278...........Worth the travel
La Pergola 398....................Wish I'd opened
Restaurant Tantris 374..........Local favourite
Steirereck 419.....................Worth the travel

MARTIN WISHART
Martin Wishart
54 The Shore, Edinburgh
Trained in starry kitchens in London and New York, his own restaurant, opened in the Port of Leith in his native Edinburgh in 1990.

Daniel 571......................................High end
Khushi's 231..................................Late night
Pujol 610............................Worth the travel
Restaurant De Librije 247.................High end
Restaurant Guy Savoy 310....Worth the travel
The Scottish Café 232.....................Breakfast
The Three Chimneys 230........Worth the travel
The Wee Restaurant 230....................Regular
  neighbourhood

JOACHIM WISSLER
Vendôme
Kadettenstrasse, Bergisch Gladbach
Cooking since 1980, his food is provocative, precise and internationally lauded. His restaurant Vendôme is credited with reinventing modern German cuisine.

Asador Etxebarri 324............Worth the travel
Le Moissonnier 375...Regular neighbourhood

HARALD WOHLFAHRT
Schwarzwaldstube
Tonbachstrasse 237 Baiersbronn-Tonbach
One of Germany's best Wohlfahrt has trained countless chefs since arriving at Die Schwarzwaldstube in 1978. In 2005 he was awarded a German order of merit.

L'Arnsbourg 281...................Worth the travel
Anitastube 374................................Bargain
El Celler de Can Roca 329.....Worth the travel
Maison Pic 291...............................High end
Silvio Nickol 418..................Worth the travel

MICHAEL WOLF
Envy
Prinsengracht 381, Binnenstad
Cooks at Envy, a quirky modern brasserie, opened in Amsterdam in 2009 by IQ Creative of Supperclub fame.

Can Fabes 327.....................Wish I'd opened
Caniço Restaurant and Bar 356...Worth the travel
D.O.M. Restaurante 636........Worth the travel
Jasmijn & Ik 248........Regular neighbourhood
Mazzo 252...........................Worth the travel
Oud Sluis 248.................................High end
Pure C 248..........................Wish I'd opened
Silvio Nickol 418..................Worth the travel
Vlaamsch Broodhuys 254..............Breakfast

SEIJI YAMAMOTO
Nihonryori Ryugin
7-17-24 Roppongi, Tokyo
After 11 years of intense study of kaiseki, he opened Nihonryori Ryugin in Tokyo in 2003, where his attention to detail saw him once send an eel for a CT scan.

Au goût du jour Nouvelle Ère 104...Local favourite
Celebrity Cuisine 84..............Worth the travel
Château Restaurant 111....................High end
Chugoku Hanten Roppongi 107.......Late night
Gaigai 108.......................................Bargain
Hajime 100..........................Worth the travel
Mikawa Zezankyo 106 Regular neighbourhood

ALEX YOUNG
Zingerman's Roadhouse
2501 Jackson Avenue, Ann Arbor
Born in London, he moved to California with his family when he was 17. Currently serving up his particular style of Southern Comfort food at Zingerman's.

53rd and 6th Halal Cart 567...........Late night
Primo 532............................Wish I'd opened

RICARDO ZARATE
Mo-Chica
514 West 7th Street, Los Angeles
Born in Lima, he worked in London at Zuma and at Pengelly's before moving to Los Angeles where he opened the Peruvian-inspired Mo-Chica in 2009, and Pica in 2012.

Akasha 491.....................................Breakfast
El Mercado 620.....................Worth the travel
Mariscos Ruben 608..............Worth the travel
Nobu 219...High end
Park's BBQ 495..............................Late night
Providence 495...............................High end
Ramen Yamadaya 498......................Bargain
Sushi Gen 493...........Regular neighbourhood
Urasawa 490...................................High end
Zuma 190............................Local favourite

SUE ZEMANICK
Gautreau's
1728 Soniat Street, New Orleans
A Pennsylvania native, Zemanick moved to New Orleans in 2003, where she quickly rose up the culinary ranks to take charge of Gautreau's in 2005.

Cochon 546..........................Worth the travel
Dat Dog 549........................Wish I'd opened
Magasin 550.....................................Bargain
Root 547...Late night
Satsuma 546...................................Breakfast
Tertulia 586.........................Worth the travel
Toscanini 253...........Regular neighbourhood

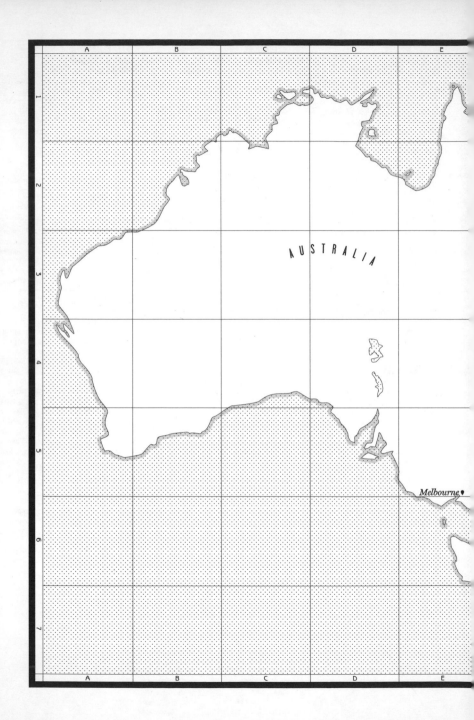

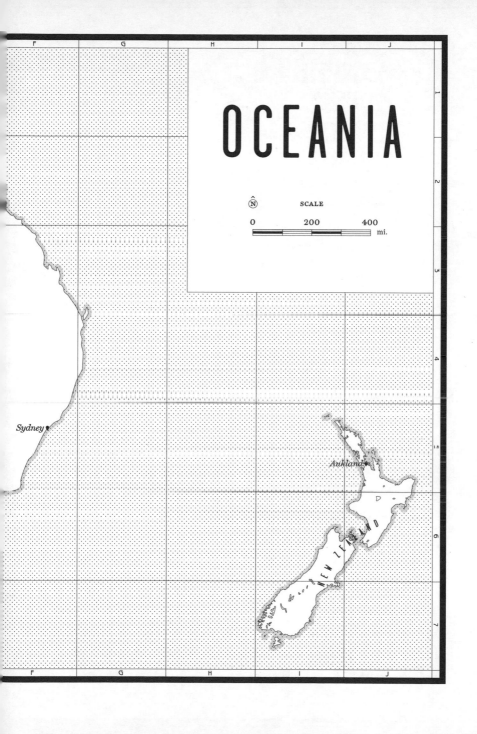

OCEANIA

Sydney

Aukland

NEW ZEALAND

'It's Australia's and possibly the world's best Cantonese restaurant.'

NEIL PERRY P32

'The Chef is inspired by his natural surroundings - the Grampians National Park.'

BEN SHEWRY P13

'MIND BLOWING, ESPECIALLY THE DUMPLINGS. I FEEL VERY FORTUNATE TO HAVE COME ACROSS SUCH A HUMBLE RESTAURANT DOING SUCH SPECTACULAR FOOD.'

ANTHONY LUI P13

AUSTRALIA

'FIVE-STAR SERVICE AND A LUXURIOUS ATMOSPHERE, WHICH IS VERY GOLD COAST.'

MEYJITTE BOUGHENOUT P 35

'The restaurant sits on the waters edge and provides a beautiful view.'

MEYJITTE BOUGHHENOUT P12

'THE BEST JAPANESE FOOD IN THE COUNTRY — ASK ANYONE.'

ROBERT MARCHETTI P13

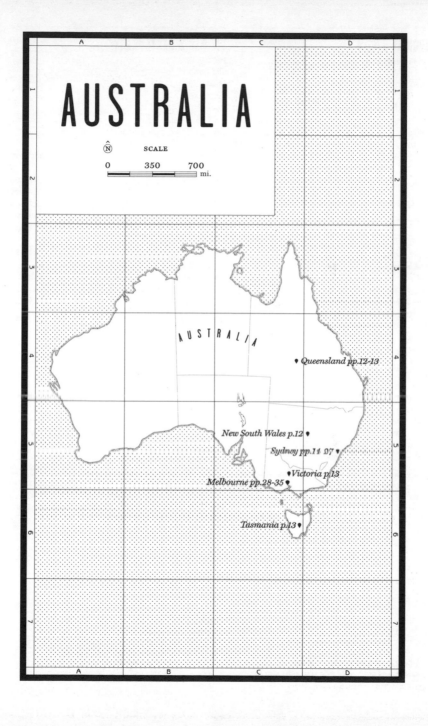

AUSTRALIA

N   SCALE

0   350   700
mi.

AUSTRALIA

♦ Queensland pp.12-13

New South Wales p.12 ♦

Sydney pp.14-27 ♦

♦ Victoria p.13

Melbourne pp.28-35 ♦

Tasmania p.13 ♦

THE BYRON AT BYRON

Recommended by
Justin North

77-97 Broken Head Road
Byron Bay
New South Wales 2481
+61 266392111
www.thebyronatbyron.com.au

Opening hours	7 days for breakfast, lunch and dinner
Reservation policy	Yes
Credit cards	Accepted
Price range	Affordable
Style	Smart casual
Cuisine	Modern Australian
Recommended for	Worth the travel

VERVE

Recommended by
Meyjitte Boughenout

3-1 Sunshine Boulevard
Broadbeach Waters
Gold Coast
Queensland 4218
+61 755267364
www.ververestaurant.com

Opening hours	6 days for lunch and dinner
Reservation policy	Yes
Credit cards	Accepted
Price range	Affordable
Style	Smart casual
Cuisine	Modern Australian
Recommended for	Regular neighbourhood

'Choose their crisp pressed pork belly, and to start, their sticky pork and water chestnut goyza dumplings.'—Meyjitte Boughenout

DUO DELI CAFE

Recommended by
Meyjitte Boughenout

58 Thomas Drive
Chevron Island
Gold Coast
Queensland 4217

Opening hours	7 days for breakfast and lunch
Reservation policy	No
Credit cards	Accepted
Price range	Budget
Style	Casual
Cuisine	Café
Recommended for	Breakfast

'Great seasonal produce in their breakfast specials and unique items to buy such as truffle oils, different grains and types of salt.'—Meyjitte Boughenout

VIE BAR & RESTAURANT

Recommended by
Meyjitte Boughenout

Palazzo Versace
94 Seaworld Drive
Main Beach
Gold Coast
Queensland 4217
+61 755098000
www.palazzoversace.com.au

Opening hours	7 days for lunch and dinner
Reservation policy	Yes
Credit cards	Accepted
Price range	Affordable
Style	Smart casual
Cuisine	Modern Australian
Recommended for	Local favourite

'The restaurant sits on the waters edge and provides a beautiful view. Five-star service and a luxurious atmosphere. Pretension and glamour at its best.'
—Meyjitte Boughenout

OCEAN SEAFOOD

Recommended by
Meyjitte Boughenout

3110 Gold Coast Highway
Surfers Paradise
Gold Coast
Queensland 4217

Opening hours	6 days for lunch and 7 days for dinner
Reservation policy	No
Credit cards	Accepted
Price range	Budget
Style	Casual
Cuisine	Chinese-Malaysian
Recommended for	Late night

'Order the beautiful steamed fish with fresh ginger and shallots and the Chinese vegetables to accompany.'—Meyjitte Boughenout

WASABI

Recommended by
Robert Marchetti

2 Quamby Place
Noosa Sound
Sunshine Coast
Queensland 4567
+61 754492443
www.wasabisb.com

Opening hours.............2 days for lunch and 5 days for dinner
Reservation policy...Yes
Credit cards...Accepted
Price range..Expensive
Style..Smart casual
Cuisine..Japanese
Recommended for..Worth the travel

'When they send someone fishing for your lunch three hours before you arrive it's got to be the best Japanese food in the country. The sashimi doesn't get any more perfect and they have Wagyu steak – to cry for – with traditional condiments and not so traditional onion rings.'—Robert Marchetti

PALATE

Recommended by
Tetsuya Wakuda

Saffire Freycinet
2352 Coles Bay Road
Coles Bay
Tasmania 7215
+61 362567888
www.saffire-freycinet.com.au

Opening hours.............7 days for breakfast, lunch and dinner
Reservation policy...Yes
Reservation email.......................ea@saffire-freycinet.com.au
Credit cards...Accepted
Price range..Expensive
Style..Smart casual
Cuisine...Modern Australian
Recommended for..Worth the travel

T'S CHINESE RESTAURANT

Recommended by
Anthony Lui

83 Main Street
Sheffield
Tasmania 7306

Opening hours...7 days for dinner
Reservation policy...Yes
Credit cards...Not accepted
Price range..Budget
Style...Casual
Cuisine..Chinese
Recommended for..Worth the travel

'This unassuming little place had its own stock of lamb and cattle. The cooking skills and restraint shown with the food is mind blowing, especially the dumplings. I feel very fortunate to have come accross such a humble restaurant doing such spectacular food.'
—Anthony Lui

ROYAL MAIL

Recommended by
Peter Doyle, Michael
Meredith, Ben Shewry

Royal Mail Hotel
98 Parker Street
Dunkeld
Victoria 3294
www.royalmail.com.au

Opening hours...5 days for dinner
Reservation policy...Yes
Credit cards...Accepted
Price range..Expensive
Style...Casual
Cuisine...Modern Australian
Recommended for..Worth the travel

'Chef Dan Hunter is inspired by his natural surrounds (the Grampians National Park) and the huge garden, which provides many of the raw materials that his focused team of cooks turn into some of the most interesting and beautiful dishes around.'—Ben Shewry

This boutique inn in rural Victoria, a three-hour drive from Melbourne, its Art Deco facade set against the Southern Grampians, has rapidly achieved a reputation as a culinary destination. Its two restaurants – a bistro and an ambitious restaurant, the latter considered one of Australia's best – have been run by Melbourne-born Dan Hunter since 2007. Formerly head chef at San Sebastián's Mugaritz, the talents he honed in the Basque Country are applied to the finest local produce he can find, much of it harvested daily from the hotel's own gardens, and expressed through two – one vegetarian, one omnivore – ten-course tasting menus.

'A RELAXED BISTRO WITH AN ENORMOUS VEGETABLE GARDEN.'
ROBERT MARCHETTI P27

'Simple produce, well executed and some of the best coffee in town – a wonderful Sydney experience.'
NEIL PERRY P20

SYDNEY

'Southeast Asian cuisine in Sydney is amazing!'
BEN GREENO

'The ultimate steakhouse with a wine list bigger than the bible. Amazing.'
ROBERT MARCHETTI P25

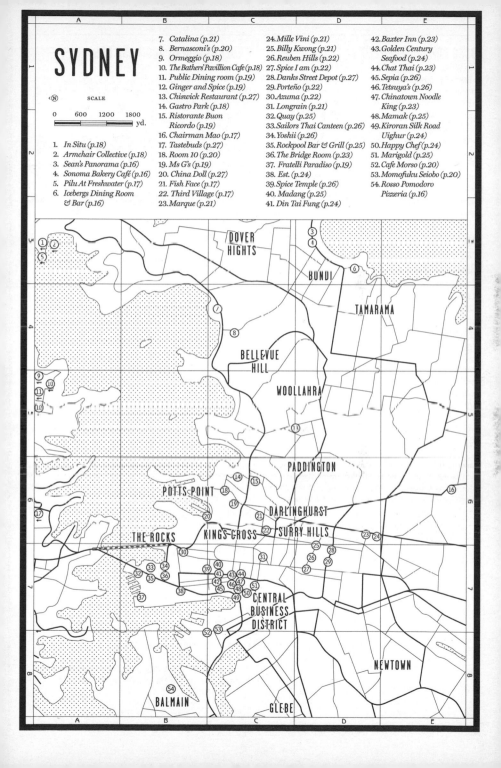

SYDNEY

‹N›   SCALE

0   600   1200   1800
                        yd.

ROSSO POMODORO PIZZERIA
Recommended by
Martin Benn

Shop 90-91
24 Buchanan Street
Balmain
Sydney
New South Wales 2041
+61 295555924
www.rossopomodoro.com.au

Opening hours	6 days for dinner
Reservation policy	Yes
Credit cards	Accepted
Price range	Budget
Style	Casual
Cuisine	Pizza
Recommended for	Late night

SONOMA BAKERY CAFÉ
Recommended by
Robert Marchetti

r10-178 Campbell Parade
Bondi
Sydney
New South Wales 2026
+61 291301124
www.sonoma.com.au

Opening hours	7 days for breakfast and lunch
Reservation policy	No
Credit cards	Accepted
Price range	Budget
Style	Casual
Cuisine	Bakery-Café
Recommended for	Breakfast

'Baker Andrew Connole makes the best bread in the country, hands down. He's got over fifteen styles of naturally leavened bread to choose from. There's also amazing quinoa porridge with seasonal fruits and cappuccino – yum.'—Robert Marchetti

ICEBERGS DINING ROOM AND BAR
Recommended by
Tetsuya Wakuda

1 Notts Avenue
Bondi Beach
Sydney
New South Wales 2026
+61 293659000
www.idrb.com

Opening hours	6 days for lunch and dinner
Reservation policy	Yes
Reservation email	idrb@idrb.com
Credit cards	Accepted
Price range	Affordable
Style	Smart casual
Cuisine	Modern Italian
Recommended for	Local favourite

'Love all the Italian dishes but they have the best steak.'—Tetsuya Wakuda

SEAN'S PANORAMA
Recommended by
Bevan Smith

270 Campbell Parade
Bondi Beach
Sydney
New South Wales 2026
+61 293654924
www.seanspanaroma.com.au

Opening hours	2 days for lunch and 4 days for dinner
Reservation policy	Yes
Reservation email	panaroma@bigpond.net.au
Credit cards	Accepted
Price range	Affordable
Style	Casual
Cuisine	Modern Australian
Recommended for	Wish I'd opened

Serving modern cuisine to local residents, surfers and travellers to Sydney's North Bondi Beach, Sean Moran's restaurant is now in its tenth year of operation. It has a cosy and familial atmosphere with chequered tablecloths and charmingly scribbled chalkboard walls detailing their modern menu and range of boutique Australian wines. The unpretentious atmosphere befits the well-thought-out and eco-conscious menu. Ingredients are seasonal, predominantly grown on Moran's Blue Mountain Farm, thus leaving little by way of a carbon footprint. The prices may sometimes reflect this philosophical approach to cooking but when presented with silk aubergine (eggplant), ocean trout and organic beef of this quality, you tend not to mind.

FISH FACE

Recommended by
Martin Benn

132 Darlinghurst Road
Darlinghurst
Sydney
New South Wales 2010
+61 293324803
www.fishfaceaustralia.com.au

Opening hours	1 day for lunch and 6 days for dinner
Reservation policy	Yes
Credit cards	Accepted
Price range	Affordable
Style	Casual
Cuisine	Seafood
Recommended for	Regular neighbourhood

Fish Face is a tiny, humming restaurant serving top-quality fish and chips. It has just thirty-four covers split between a few tables, some window benches, a sushi counter and three outdoor tables. Stephen Hodges and Zachary Sykes's menu has some regular items and a fish of the day, which could be kingfish. Fish Face is particularly famous for its blue-eye travalla with potato scales, roast beetroot (beet) and horseradish cream, but they also do a lovely Petuna ocean trout with mushrooms and leeks in filo (phyllo) pastry, which comes with a sorrel sauce. When it's full – which is often – customers tend to take away.

THIRD VILLAGE

Recommended by
Benjamin Greeno

80 Stanley Street
Darlinghurst
Sydney
New South Wales 2010
www.thirdvillage.com.au

Opening hours	7 days for breakfast and lunch
Reservation policy	No
Credit cards	Accepted
Price range	Budget
Style	Casual
Cuisine	Café
Recommended for	Breakfast

'Good coffee, nice staff and really good breakfast.'—Benjamin Greeno

PILU AT FRESHWATER

Recommended by
Peter Doyle, Tetsuya Wakuda

Moore Road
Freshwater
Sydney
New South Wales 2096
+61 299383331
www.piluatfreshwater.com.au

Opening hours	6 days for lunch and 5 days for dinner
Reservation policy	Yes
Reservation email	dining@piluatfreshwater.com.au
Credit cards	Accepted
Price range	Affordable
Style	Smart casual
Cuisine	Italian
Recommended for	Local favourite

CHAIRMAN MAO

Recommended by
Neil Perry

189 Anzac Parade
Kensington
Sydney
New South Wales 2033
+61 296979189

Opening hours	6 days for dinner
Reservation policy	Yes
Credit cards	Accepted
Price range	Affordable
Style	Casual
Cuisine	Chinese
Recommended for	Regular neighbourhood

'The pork dishes are amazing and the spice levels incendiary, but I love it. Try the cumin lamb – but it's not for the faint hearted.'—Neil Perry

GASTRO PARK

Recommended by
Dave De Belder

5-9 Roslyn Street
Kings Cross
Sydney
New South Wales 2011
+61 280681017
www.gastropark.com.au

Opening hours..............3 days for lunch and 5 days for dinner
Reservation policy..Yes
Reservation email..............................info@gastropark.com.au
Credit cards..Accepted
Price range..Affordable
Style...Casual
Cuisine..Modern Australian
Recommended for...............................Worth the travel

The Kings Cross area is still edgy enough to be a
perfect choice of location for Gastro Park – Grant
King's first solo venture. He was head chef at the
luxurious Pier in Rose Bay, but here it's all about his
cooking. Gastro Park opened in 2011 to immediate
critical acclaim and you can see why – tuna marrow
appears on the menu and their bones are used
as skewers and tiny cups. Dishes – such as liquid
butternut gnocchi, mushroom consommé with sage
and crispy scaled snapper, smoked potato purée,
calamari crackling and ink sauce – served in this
minimalist venue makes for an experience like none
other in the city.

IN SITU

Recommended by
Peter Doyle

1-18 Sydney Road
Manly
Sydney
New South Wales 2095
+61 299770669
www.insitumanly.com.au

Opening hours..............7 days for breakfast, lunch and dinner
Reservation policy..Yes
Credit cards..Accepted
Price range..Affordable
Style...Casual
Cuisine..Modern Australian
Recommended for...Breakfast

ARMCHAIR COLLECTIVE

Recommended by
Peter Gilmore

9a Darley Street East
Mona Vale
Sydney
New South Wales 2103
www.thearmchair.com.au

Opening hours..........................7 days for breakfast and lunch
Reservation policy..No
Credit cards..Accepted
Price range..Budget
Style...Casual
Cuisine...Café
Recommended for...Breakfast

THE BATHERS' PAVILION CAFE

Recommended by
Justin North

4 The Esplanade
Balmoral Beach
Mosman
Sydney
New South Wales 2088
www.batherspavilion.com.au

Opening hours..............7 days for breakfast, lunch and dinner
Reservation policy..No
Credit cards..Accepted
Price range..Affordable
Style...Casual
Cuisine...Mediterranean
Recommended for..................................Local favourite

ORMEGGIO

Recommended by
Peter Doyle

D'Albora Marinas
The Spit
Mosman
Sydney
New South Wales 2088
+61 299694088
www.ormeggio.com.au

Opening hours..............3 days for lunch and 5 days for dinner
Reservation policy..Yes
Reservation email..............................info@ormeggio.com.au
Credit cards..Accepted
Price range..Affordable
Style...Smart casual
Cuisine.......................................Contemporary Italian
Recommended for...................Regular neighbourhood

PUBLIC DINING ROOM

Recommended by
Justin North

2a The Esplanade
Balmoral Beach
Mosman
Sydney
New South Wales 2088
+61 299684880
www.publicdiningroom.com.au

Opening hours..........7 days for brunch and 6 days for dinner
Reservation policy..Yes
Reservation email..................info@publicdiningroom.com.au
Credit cards...Accepted
Price range...Affordable
Style...Casual
Cuisine...Modern Australian
Recommended for...Breakfast

GINGER & SPICE

Recommended by
Justin North

240 Military Road
Neutral Bay
Sydney
New South Wales 2089
+61 299082552

Opening hours.............6 days for lunch and 7 days for dinner
Reservation policy..Yes
Credit cards...Accepted
Price range...Affordable
Style...Smart casual
Cuisine...Singaporean
Recommended for..............................Regular neighbourhood

RISTORANTE BUON RICORDO

Recommended by
Tetsuya Wakuda

108 Boundary Street
Paddington
Sydney
New South Wales 2021
+61 293606729
www.buonricordo.com.au

Opening hours.............2 days for lunch and 5 days for dinner
Reservation policy..Yes
Reservation email...................buonricordo@bigpond.com.au
Credit cards...Accepted
Price range...Affordable
Style...Smart casual
Cuisine...Italian
Recommended for...High end

'How can you pass up their truffle egg pasta?'
—Tetsuya Wakuda

FRATELLI PARADISO

Recommended by
Robert Marchetti

12-16 Challis Avenue
Potts Point
Sydney
New South Wales 2011
www.fratelliparadiso.com

Opening hours..........7 days for brunch and 6 days for dinner
Reservation policy...No
Credit cards...Accepted
Price range...Affordable
Style...Casual
Cuisine...Italian
Recommended for..............................Regular neighbourhood

'The pasta made in-house is always the real deal and
treated with the utmost respect. It's got an amazing list
of boutique Italian wines too.'—Robert Marchetti

MS G'S

Recommended by
Benjamin Greeno

155 Victoria Street
Potts Point
Sydney
New South Wales 2011
+61 283131000

Opening hours.............2 days for lunch and 7 days for dinner
Reservation policy..Yes
Credit cards...Accepted
Price range...Affordable
Style...Casual
Cuisine...Asian
Recommended for..............................Regular neighbourhood

'It's a fun atmosphere and the food is delicious.'
—Benjamin Greeno

ROOM 10

Recommended by
Neil Perry

10 Llankelly Place
Potts Point
Sydney
New South Wales 2011

Opening hours	7 days for breakfast and lunch
Reservation policy	No
Credit cards	Not accepted
Price range	Budget
Style	Casual
Cuisine	Café
Recommended for	Breakfast

'The "two Dans" do fresh juice, great single-origin coffee and I love their toast with avocado and a soft boiled egg on top. Simple produce and well executed – some of the best coffee in town and a wonderful Sydney Laneway experience.'—Neil Perry

This pocket-sized Potts Point café is a short stroll from Kings Cross station and attracts a cool young crowd. Voted the best newcomer in the *Sydney Morning Herald*'s Good Café, shortly after opening in 2011, it's run by a right pair of Dans – Jackson (chef) and Blackman (manager). Freshly squeezed blood orange juice, loose-leaf teas and single-origin coffee courtesy of Mecca, pastries delivered daily by the Black Star patisserie in Newtown, and a short, sharp menu of simple, wholesome dishes. Spread avocado, tomato or ricotta on toast or try their Breakfast Rice made with banana, stewed rhubarb and honey.

CAFE MORSO

Recommended by
Tetsuya Wakuda

Lower Deck (West Side)
Jones Bay Wharf
Pirrama Road
Pyrmont
Sydney
New South Wales 2009
+61 296920111
www.cafemorso.com.au

Opening hours	7 days for breakfast and lunch
Reservation policy	Yes
Credit cards	Accepted
Price range	Budget
Style	Casual
Cuisine	Café
Recommended for	Breakfast

MOMOFUKU SEIOBO

Recommended by
Andoni Luis Aduriz,
Andrew McConnell,
Ben Shewry

The Star
80 Pyrmont Street, Level G
Pyrmont
Sydney
New South Wales 2009
+61 297779000
www.momofuku.com

Opening hours	2 days for lunch and 6 days for dinner
Reservation policy	Yes
Credit cards	Accepted
Price range	Expensive
Style	Smart casual
Cuisine	Korean
Recommended for	Worth the travel

That David Chang chose Sydney for his first venture outside New York surprised some. But it makes perfect sense when you consider the city's stellar standard of Asian cooking, against which he knew he'd be judged. Opened in late 2011 in the Star casino, reservations, as at other Momofuku establishments, are secured via their website. It's built around an open kitchen, with an L-shaped dining counter offering the best view of the action. With a black-and-white picture of AC/DC's Angus Young on the wall, the rock 'n' roll tasting menu of Asian-accented courses is overseen by the very capable Benjamin Greeno.

BERNASCONI'S

Recommended by
Luke Mangan

23 Plumer Road
Rose Bay
Sydney
New South Wales 2029
+61 293275717

Opening hours	7 days for brunch and 4 days for dinner
Reservation policy	No
Credit cards	Accepted
Price range	Budget
Style	Casual
Cuisine	Café
Recommended for	Breakfast

CATALINA

Recommended by
Luke Mangan

Lyne Park
New South Head Road
Rose Bay
Sydney
New South Wales 2029
+61 293710555
www.catalinarosebay.com.au

Opening hours.............7 days for lunch and 6 days for dinner
Reservation policy...Yes
Reservation email.......reservations@catalinarosebay.com.au
Credit cards...Accepted
Price range..Expensive
Style...Smart casual
Cuisine...Modern Australian
Recommended for...Local favourite

'The view, the setting and the cuisine are very
Sydney.'—Luke Mangan

BILLY KWONG

Recommended by
Martin Benn

355 Crown Street
Surry Hills
Sydney
New South Wales 2010
www.kyliekwong.org

Opening hours....................................7 days for dinner
Reservation policy..Yes
Credit cards...Accepted
Price range..Affordable
Style...Casual
Cuisine...Modern Chinese
Recommended for...Local favourite

Celebrity chef Kylie Kwong's re-creation of a
Shanghai teahouse in the fashionable Surry Hills
district gives the locals something else to be smug
about. Opened in 2000 and partially named in tribute
to then business partner Bill Granger, the tiny
restaurant has been organic and biodynamic since
2005. Serving real Chinese eating-house style food
using locally sourced ingredients, Kwong brings both
her heritage and her training under Neil Perry at
Rockpool and Wokpool to bear. The restaurant has
only one bookable table, serving six to eight, but if
you have to wait, there are plenty of great bars on
the same street.

LONGRAIN

Recommended by
Thorsten Schmidt,
Michael Wilson

85 Commonwealth Street
Surry Hills
Sydney
New South Wales 2010
+61 292802888
www.longrain.com.au

Opening hours...............1 day for lunch and 7 days for dinner
Reservation policy..Yes
Credit cards...Accepted
Price range..Affordable
Style...Casual
Cuisine...Modern Asian
Recommended for...Worth the travel

'Good Australian-influenced Thai food. It has a relaxed
atmosphere.'—Michael Wilson

MARQUE

Recommended by
Peter Gilmore, Benjamin
Greeno, Ben Shewry

4-5 355 Crown Street
Surry Hills
Sydney
New South Wales 2010
+61 293322225
www.marquerestaurant.com.au

Opening hours   1 day for lunch and 6 days for dinner
Reservation policy..Yes
Reservation email.................dine@marquerestaurant.com.au
Credit cards...Accepted
Price range..Expensive
Style...Smart casual
Cuisine...Modern Australian
Recommended for...High end

MILLE VINI

Recommended by
Peter Doyle

397 Crown Street
Surry Hills
Sydney
New South Wales 2010
www.millevini.net

Opening hours.............3 days for lunch and 7 days for dinner
Reservation policy..Yes
Credit cards...Accepted
Price range..Affordable
Style...Casual
Cuisine..Italian
Recommended for...Bargain

PORTEÑO

Recommended by
Al Brown, Luke Dale-Roberts

358 Cleveland Street
Surry Hills
Sydney
New South Wales 2010
+61 283991440
www.porteno.com.au

Opening hours	6 days for dinner
Reservation policy	Yes
Credit cards	Accepted
Price range	Affordable
Style	Smart casual
Cuisine	Argentinian
Recommended for	Worth the travel

Ben Milgate and Elvis Abrahanowicz, chef-owners of game-changing tapas joint Bodega, have a uniquely idiosyncratic idea of what constitutes a good night out – namely: loud music, rockabilly fashion and lots of grilled meat. In 2010 they brought that ethos to Porteño, and with the larger space and more powerful sound system have created an even more outlandish experience. Whole lambs and suckling pigs roast slowly over an open asador (fire) while tattooed staff serve draft Estrella and cocktails such as the Palermo Hollywood (tequila, apple juice, vanilla, cinnamon, sage). It's noisy, wilfully alternative and as much fun as you can have with your clothes on.

REUBEN HILLS

Recommended by
Neil Perry

61 Albion Street
Surry Hills
Sydney
New South Wales 2010
www.reubenhills.com.au

Opening hours	7 days for breakfast and lunch
Reservation policy	No
Credit cards	Accepted
Price range	Budget
Style	Casual
Cuisine	Café
Recommended for	Wish I'd opened

'It is such a cool design. The coffee and food is terrific and I think it shows great innovation.'—Neil Perry

SPICE I AM

Recommended by
Justin North

90 Wentworth Avenue
Surry Hills
Sydney
New South Wales 2010
www.spiceiam.com

Opening hours	7 days for lunch and dinner
Reservation policy	No
Credit cards	Not accepted
Price range	Budget
Style	Casual
Cuisine	Thai
Recommended for	Bargain

Opened in 2004, this is the original bistro of four from executive chef Sujet Saenkham, who left a remote village in Central Thailand to work as a Qantas flight attendant before becoming what critics and customers regard as Sydney's most talented Thai chef. Beyond the queues (waiting lines) – no bookings are taken – walls are plastered with reviews, some yellowing, while tables are tightly packed. Service is fast but friendly, and Saenkham's soulful dishes, featuring spice, chillies and locally grown herbs rather than sugar and salt, can – beware – be very hot. These may include aubergine (eggplant) stir-fry with garlic and prawn (shrimp) paste, deep-fried mini spring rolls and red duck curry.

AZUMA

Recommended by
Neil Perry, Tetsuya Wakuda

Level 1, Chifley Plaza
2 Chifley Square
Sydney
New South Wales 2000
www.azuma.com.au

Opening hours	5 days for lunch and 6 days for dinner
Reservation policy	Yes
Reservation email	azuma@azuma.com.au
Credit cards	Accepted
Price range	Affordable
Style	Smart casual
Cuisine	Japanese
Recommended for	Regular neighbourhood

'The sashimi is first rate and I love the sukiyaki of Wagyu beef (for two people).'—Neil Perry

BAXTER INN

Recommended by
Robert Marchetti

152-156 Clarence Street
Sydney
New South Wales 2000
www.thebaxterinn.com

Opening hours	6 days for dinner
Reservation policy	No
Credit cards	Accepted
Price range	Budget
Style	Casual
Cuisine	Bar-Bistro
Recommended for	Late night

'Amazing underground bar that specializes in great old Bogan wines from the past forty years. They have a "ploughman's" plate with great double smoked ham (we make the small meat products so I'm biased) pickle, Cheddar and lots of goodies with great bread. This with a bottle of 1980s Bogan wine and I'm as happy as they come.'—Robert Marchetti

THE BRIDGE ROOM

Recommended by
Neil Perry

Ground Level
44 Bridge Street
Sydney
New South Wales 2000
| 61 292477000
www.thebridgeroom.com.au

Opening hours	5 days for lunch and dinner
Reservation policy	Yes
Reservation email	reservations@thebridgeroom.com.au
Credit cards	Accepted
Price range	Expensive
Style	Smart casual
Cuisine	Modern Australian
Recommended for	Worth the travel

'For elegant, well crafted and cooked food that is a great pleasure to eat.'—Neil Perry

CHAT THAI

Recommended by
Benjamin Greeno

20 Campbell Street
Sydney
New South Wales 2000
+61 292111808
www.chatthai.com.au

Opening hours	7 days for breakfast until late
Reservation policy	Yes
Reservation email	thaitown@chatthai.com.au
Credit cards	Accepted
Price range	Budget
Style	Casual
Cuisine	Modern Thai
Recommended for	Bargain

CHINATOWN NOODLE KING

Recommended by
Neil Perry

357 Sussex Street
Sydney
New South Wales 2000

Opening hours	7 days for lunch and dinner
Reservation policy	No
Credit cards	Accepted
Price range	Budget
Style	Casual
Cuisine	Chinese
Recommended for	Bargain

'With its spicy hot pots, beer duck laden with chilli and coriander (cilantro), the tea mushroom dish, the cooling and spicy cucumber with chilli oil and the gluten salad, Chinatown Noodle King's not only cheap but delicious. It's hard to beat.'—Neil Perry

DIN TAI FUNG

Recommended by
Josef Centeno,
Robert Marchetti

World Square Shopping Centre
Level 1 Shop 11.04
644 George Street
Sydney
New South Wales 2000
+61 292646010
www.dintaifungaustralia.com.au

Opening hours	7 days for lunch and dinner
Reservation policy	Yes
Credit cards	Accepted
Price range	Budget
Style	Casual
Cuisine	Chinese
Recommended for	Bargain

'Wow. Amazing dumplings made by loads of dumpling cooks right in front of you and steamed to order.'
—Robert Marchetti

EST.

Recommended by
Luke Mangan

Level 1 Establishment
252 George Street
Sydney
New South Wales 2000
+61 292403000

Opening hours	5 days for lunch and 6 days for dinner
Reservation policy	Yes
Reservation email	restaurant.reservations@merivale.com
Credit cards	Accepted
Price range	Expensive
Style	Smart casual
Cuisine	Modern Australian
Recommended for	High end

GOLDEN CENTURY SEAFOOD

Recommended by
David Chang, Peter Gilmore,
Benjamin Greeno, Luke
Mangan, Justin North, Neil
Perry, James "Jockey" Petrie

393-399 Sussex Street
Sydney
New South Wales 2000
+61 292123901
www.goldencentury.com.au

Opening hours	7 days for lunch until late
Reservation policy	Yes
Credit cards	Accepted
Price range	Affordable
Style	Casual
Cuisine	Cantonese Seafood
Recommended for	Late night

'Open until 4.00 a.m. for a greenlip alabone steamboat with noodles and tofu – one of the great pleasures on this earth. Amazing live produce. You spend time cooking it yourself and at the end have the world's greatest soup to drink.'—Neil Perry

The Cantonese seafood specialist that locals like to call the Golden C, which Sydney's chefs make a habit of calling into late at night after work, is a clear cut above any other Chinese restaurants on Sussex Street – and arguably anywhere else in the city that does small-hours trade. The menu ranges from very affordable noodle dishes to a fantastic selection of live seafood. Insider tips from some of Sydney's finest include: trying the greenlip abalone steamboat with noodles and tofu (the abalone sliced live) and asking for the Charles Leong menu, named after Momofuku Seibo's sommelier-at-large.

HAPPY CHEF

Recommended by
Luke Mangan

Sussex Centre Food Court
401-403 Sussex Street
Sydney
New South Wales 2000

Opening hours	7 days for lunch
Reservation policy	No
Credit cards	Not accepted
Price range	Budget
Style	Casual
Cuisine	Chinese
Recommended for	Bargain

'For delicious cheap Laksa.'—Luke Mangan

KIRORAN SILK ROAD UIGHUR

Recommended by
Neil Perry

6 Dixon Street
Sydney
New South Wales 2000
+61 292830998

Opening hours	6 days for lunch and dinner
Reservation policy	Yes
Credit cards	Not accepted
Price range	Budget
Style	Casual
Cuisine	Chinese
Recommended for	Bargain

'Head to Kiroran Silk Road for a braise of chicken, tomato, potatoes, noodles and cumin. This is peasant cooking at it's very best and crazily cheap.'—Neil Perry

MADANG

Recommended by
Neil Perry

371a Pitt Street
Sydney
New South Wales 2000
+61 292647010

Opening hours	7 days for lunch and dinner
Reservation policy	Yes
Credit cards	Accepted
Price range	Budget
Style	Casual
Cuisine	Korean
Recommended for	Regular neighbourhood

'Go for it's bbq, hot pots and loads of kimchee.'
—Neil Perry

MAMAK

Recommended by
Peter Gilmore

15 Goulburn Street
Sydney
New South Wales 2000
www.mamak.com.au

Opening hours	7 days for lunch and dinner
Reservation policy	No
Credit cards	Accepted
Price range	Budget
Style	Casual
Cuisine	Malaysian
Recommended for	Late night

MARIGOLD

Recommended by
Tetsuya Wakuda

Levels 4 & 5
683-689 George Street
Sydney
New South Wales 2000
+61 292813388
www.marigold.com.au

Opening hours	7 days for lunch and dinner
Reservation policy	Yes
Reservation email	info@marigold.com.au
Credit cards	Accepted
Price range	Budget
Style	Casual
Cuisine	Chinese
Recommended for	Bargain

QUAY

Recommended by
Meyjitte Boughenout,
David Laris, Bruno Loubet,
Ben Shewry

Overseas Passenger Terminal
5 Hickson Road
Sydney
New South Wales 2000
+61 292515600
www.quay.com.au

Opening hours	4 days for lunch and 7 days for dinner
Reservation policy	Yes
Reservation email	reservations@quay.com.au
Credit cards	Accepted
Price range	Expensive
Style	Smart casual
Cuisine	Modern Australian
Recommended for	Wish I'd opened

'Peter Gilmore's restaurant serves some of the best
desserts I've ever tasted.'—Bruno Loubet

ROCKPOOL BAR & GRILL

Recommended by
Peter Gilmore, Robert
Marchetti, Tetsuya Wakuda

66 Hunter Street
Sydney
New South Wales 2000
+61 280781900
www.rockpool.com

Opening hours	5 days for lunch and 6 days for dinner
Reservation policy	Yes
Reservation email	reservations@rockpool.com
Credit cards	Accepted
Price range	Expensive
Style	Smart casual
Cuisine	Steakhouse
Recommended for	High end

'This is the quintessential steakhouse with a wine list
bigger than the Bible – amazing, world class.'
—Robert Marchetti

SAILORS THAI CANTEEN

Recommended by
Peter Gilmore

106 George Street, Upstairs
Sydney
New South Wales 2000
www.sailorsthai.com.au/canteen.html

Opening hours	7 days for lunch and dinner
Reservation policy	No
Credit cards	Accepted
Price range	Affordable
Style	Casual
Cuisine	Thai
Recommended for	Bargain

'The food is always good, spicy and reliable.'
—Peter Gilmore

SEPIA

Recommended by
Matthew Crabbe, Dan Hunter,
Michael Wilson

201 Sussex Street
Sydney
New South Wales 2000
+61 292831990
www.sepiarestaurant.com.au

Opening hours	2 days for lunch, 5 days for dinner
Reservation policy	Yes
Reservation email	info@sepiarestaurant.com.au
Credit cards	Accepted
Price range	Expensive
Style	Smart casual
Cuisine	Modern Australian
Recommended for	Worth the travel

'Extremely good.'—Michael Wilson

SPICE TEMPLE

Recommended by
Justin North

10 Bligh Street
Sydney
New South Wales 2000
+61 280781888
www.rockpool.com/sydney/spice-temple

Opening hours	5 days for lunch and 6 days for dinner
Reservation policy	Yes
Credit cards	Accepted
Price range	Affordable
Style	Smart casual
Cuisine	Modern Chinese
Recommended for	Late night

TETSUYA'S

Recommended by
Akmal Anuar, Jean Beddington,
Peter Doyle, Takashi Inoue,
David Laris, Jereme Leung,
Vicky Ratnani

529 Kent Street
Sydney
New South Wales 2000
+61 292672900
www.tetsuyas.com

Opening hours	1 day for lunch and 5 days for dinner
Reservation policy	Yes
Reservation email	info@tetsuyas.com
Credit cards	Accepted
Price range	Expensive
Style	Smart casual
Cuisine	Modern Japanese
Recommended for	Worth the travel

'Character, art, precision, natural, taste is how I would
describe Chef Tetsuya's cuisine. He uses simple
techniques but a lot of flavour. He takes subtlety and
marriage of ingredients seriously.'—Akmal Anuar

YOSHII

Recommended by
Shaun Clouston

115 Harrington Street
Sydney
New South Wales 2000
+61 292472566
www.yoshii.com.au

Opening hours	5 days for lunch and 6 days for dinner
Reservation policy	Yes
Reservation email	info@yoshii.com.au
Credit cards	Accepted
Price range	Expensive
Style	Casual
Cuisine	Japanese
Recommended for	High end

'Amazing food. Try the grilled bonito with ponzu and
wilted Wasabi leaves – and if you are lucky to be there
on the right day, wild-caught blue fin Toro.'
—Shaun Clouston

TASTEBUDS

Recommended by
Peter Gilmore

287 Mona Vale Road
Terrey Hills
Sydney
New South Wales 2084
+61 294500873

Opening hours	7 days for breakfast and lunch
Reservation policy	Yes
Credit cards	Accepted
Price range	Budget
Style	Casual
Cuisine	Café
Recommended for	Breakfast

FRATELLI FRESH

Recommended by
Martin Benn, Robert Marchetti

Shop 8
16 Hickson Road
Walsh Bay
Sydney
New South Wales 2000
www.fratellifresh.com.au

Opening hours	7 days for breakfast, lunch and dinner
Reservation policy	No
Credit cards	Accepted
Price range	Budget
Style	Casual
Cuisine	Italian
Recommended for	Breakfast

'This is a produce store and eating house. Barry McDonald is and always will be the king of tomatoes, so you shop, you eat and you shop some more. Always, and I mean always, seasonal.'—Robert Marchetti

Walsh Bay holds the third branch of Café Sopra, after great successes in Waterloo and Potts Point. Its Yorkshire-born chef, Andy Bunn, cooks inventive Italianate food: spicy quail ragù, a warming lasagne, crisp polenta with Gorgonzola sauce, or a whole baked rainbow trout with mint and marjoram. He's particularly good with vegetables and has done a great deal to introduce banoffee pie (banana-caramel pie) to the Australians. Cate Blanchett is a Sopra regular. The menu is on a blackboard and there are high ceilings, a big, shining bar, good-looking staff and plenty of outdoor seating. A huge and deserved success.

DANKS STREET DEPOT

Recommended by
Justin North

1-2 Danks Street
Waterloo
Sydney
New South Wales 2017
+61 296982201
www.danksstreetdepot.com.au

Opening hours	7 days for brunch and 4 days for dinner
Reservation policy	Yes
Credit cards	Accepted
Price range	Affordable
Style	Smart casual
Cuisine	Modern Australian
Recommended for	Wish I'd opened

CHISWICK RESTAURANT

Recommended by
Robert Marchetti

65 Ocean Street
Woollahra
Sydney
New South Wales 2025
+61 283888688
www.chiswickrestaurant.com.au

Opening hours	6 days for lunch and dinner
Reservation policy	Yes
Credit cards	Accepted
Price range	Affordable
Style	Casual
Cuisine	Modern Australian
Recommended for	Wish I'd opened

'A relaxed bistro with an enormous vegetable garden. And chef Matt Moran has no problem playing a bit of Elvis when things quiet down.'—Robert Marchetti

CHINA DOLL

Recommended by
Luke Mangan

Shop 4
6 Cowper Wharf Road
Woolloomooloo
Sydney
New South Wales 2011
+61 293806744
www.chinadoll.com.au

Opening hours	7 days for lunch and dinner
Reservation policy	Yes
Reservation email	mail@chinadoll.com.au
Credit cards	Accepted
Price range	Expensive
Style	Smart casual
Cuisine	Modern Asian
Recommended for	Regular neighbourhood

'THE THEATRICS AND EXPERIENCE OF DINING HERE IS SECOND TO NONE. THE VIEW IS PRETTY GOOD TOO.'
ANTHONY LUI P 34

'Their fried rice is some of the best in Melbourne.'
BEN SHEWRY P33

'THE SINGLE ORIGIN COFFEE THEY ROAST AND BLEND THEMSELVES PROVIDES THAT PERFECT START TO THE DAY.'
ANTHONY LUI P30

MELBOURNE

'I love being able to watch the chefs as they work then to sit out on the street and watch Melbourne go by.'
SHAUN CLOUSTON P31

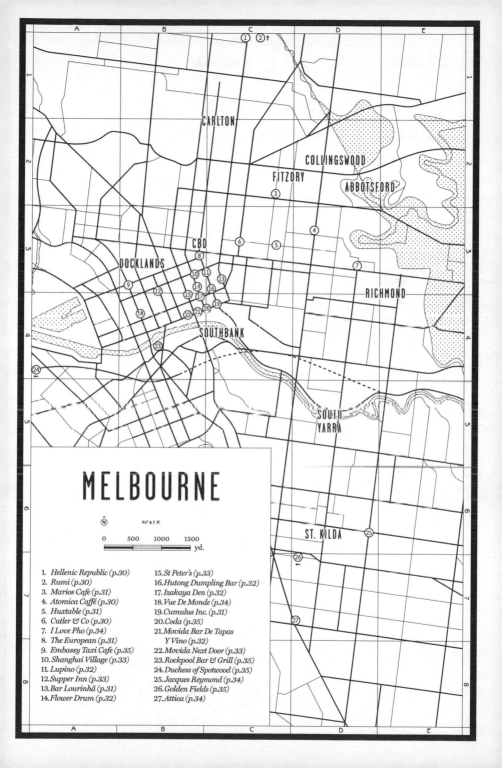

MELBOURNE

HELLENIC REPUBLIC

Recommended by
Al Brown

434 Lygon Street
Brunswick East
Melbourne
Victoria 3057
+61 393811222
www.hellenicrepublic.com.au

Opening hours	3 days for lunch and 7 days for dinner
Reservation policy	Yes
Reservation email	admin@hellenicrepublic.com.au
Credit cards	Accepted
Price range	Affordable
Style	Casual
Cuisine	Greek
Recommended for	Wish I'd opened

Cypriot George Calombaris made his name either as the brains behind the fine-dining restaurant The Press Club, or as a judge on 'MasterChef Australia', depending on your familiarity with popular culture. Hellenic Republic, which opened in 2008, is a less formal affair, and has been an instant hit with tzatziki-loving Melbournites who appreciate the light, bustling room and open kitchen serving small plates of Greek tapas (sorry, mezethakia) at very reasonable prices. This fresh, modern take on a Greek taverna, then, is perhaps more revolutionary than it first appears. Could Calombaris turn out to be the Alan Yau of Greece?

RUMI

Recommended by
Christian Puglisi

116 Lygon Street
Brunswick East
Melbourne
Victoria 3057
+61 393888255
www.rumirestaurant.com.au

Opening hours	7 days for dinner
Reservation policy	Yes
Credit cards	Accepted
Price range	Budget
Style	Casual
Cuisine	Lebanese
Recommended for	Worth the travel

'A very inspiring Lebanese restaurant.'
—Christian Puglisi

ATOMICA CAFFÉ

Recommended by
Anthony Lui

268 Brunswick Street
Fitzroy
Melbourne
Victoria 3065
+61 394863008
www.atomicacoffee.com.au

Opening hours	7 days for breakfast and lunch
Reservation policy	Yes
Credit cards	Not accepted
Price range	Budget
Style	Casual
Cuisine	Café
Recommended for	Breakfast

'The sandwiches are always interesting, whether it be braised lamb, feta and beetroot (beet) or the open pork belly sandwich. Plus the single origin coffee they roast and blend themselves provides that perfect start to the day.'—Anthony Lui

CUTLER & CO

Recommended by
Dirk Stark, Michael Wilson

55-57 Gertrude Street
Fitzroy
Melbourne
Victoria 3065
+61 394194888
www.cutlerandco.com.au

Opening hours	2 days for lunch and 6 days for dinner
Reservation policy	Yes
Credit cards	Accepted
Price range	Affordable
Style	Smart casual
Cuisine	Modern Australia
Recommended for	High end

Chef Andrew McConnell has got about a bit. As well as working for Greg Malouf, Australia's guru of Middle Eastern cuisine, he's run restaurants in Hong Kong and Shanghai. No surprise, then, that the menu of intricate and inventive dishes at this former metal workshop in Melbourne's boho Fitzroy suburb is punctuated with global influences. Start with a sashimi of swordfish with mooli (daikon) and fresh wasabi followed by John Dory with shikake mushrooms, octopus and seaweed butter. The industrial chic surroundings, featuring whitewashed brick walls and sculpted bar, are as cutting-edge as the food.

HUXTABLE

Recommended by
Shaun Clouston

131 Smith Street
Fitzroy
Melbourne
Victoria 3065
+61 394195101
www.huxtablerestaurant.com.au

Opening hours...............................6 days for lunch and dinner
Reservation policy..Yes
Reservation email.......bookings@huxtablerestaurant.com.au
Credit cards...Accepted
Price range...Budget
Style...Casual
Cuisine...Modern Australian
Recommended for...Wish I'd opened

'I love being able to talk to the chefs as they work and you eat. Then sit out on the street and watch Melbourne go by as you enjoy some of the best casual food you can get.'—Shaun Clouston

MARIOS CAFE

Recommended by
Bevan Smith

303 Brunswick Street
Fitzroy
Melbourne
Victoria 3065
www.marioscafe.com.au

Opening hours.............7 days for breakfast, lunch and dinner
Reservation policy..No
Credit cards..Not accepted
Price range...Affordable
Style...Casual
Cuisine..Italian
Recommended for...Breakfast

BAR LOURINHÃ

Recommended by
Dan Hunter

37 Little Collins Street
Melbourne
Victoria 3000
+61 396637890
www.barlourinha.com.au

Opening hours.............5 days for lunch and 6 days for dinner
Reservation policy..Yes
Reservation email.............................info@barlourinha.com.au
Credit cards...Accepted
Price range...Affordable
Style...Casual
Cuisine...Spanish-Portuguese
Recommended for...............................Regular neighbourhood

CUMULUS INC.

Recommended by
Martin Benn, Martin Bosley,
Michael Wilson

45 Flinders Lane
Melbourne
Victoria 3000
+61 396501445
www.cumulusinc.com.au

Opening hours...........................7 days for breakfast until late
Reservation policy..Yes
Reservation email.............................info@cumulusinc.com.au
Credit cards...................................Accepted but not Diners
Price range...Affordable
Style...Casual
Cuisine...Modern Australian
Recommended for...Wish I'd opened

Andrew McConnell's all-day restaurant, a stripped-back rag-trade building in the arty-fashiony Flinders Lane, has given the already well-established chef a place to let his choice of ingredients speak for themselves. The result is an unimaginably perfect variety of food. Breakfast includes a toasted sandwich of wagyu salted (corned) beef on one hand and lemon-curd-filled madeleines on the other. There is a heretofore unimaginably perfect variety of food served here. À la carte, there are nine varieties of oysters, one appetizer is a can of Ortiz anchovies, and there are eleven kinds of charcuterie. This is before even mentioning the cooking… You can never grow tired of Cumulus

THE EUROPEAN

Recommended by
Dan Hunter

161 Spring Street
Melbourne
Victoria 3000.
+61 396504811
www.theeuropean.com.au

Opening hours...........................7 days for breakfast until late
Reservation policy..Yes
Credit cards...Accepted
Price range...Affordable
Style...Casual
Cuisine..European
Recommended for...Breakfast

FLOWER DRUM

17 Market Lane
Melbourne
Victoria 3000
+61 396623655
www.flower-drum.com

Recommended by
Neil Perry, Tetsuya
Wakuda, Ben Shewry

Opening hours............6 days for lunch and 7 days for dinner
Reservation policy..Yes
Credit cards..Accepted
Price range..Affordable
Style..Smart casual
Cuisine..Chinese
Recommended for................................Wish I'd opened

'It is Australia's, and possibly the world's, best Cantonese restaurant. The produce, craft of cooking, service and experience is second to none. I love the drunken pigeon, Peking duck, scallop dumpling, mud crab with noodles, ginger and shallot, pearl meat stir-fry and the lobster with XO. If I'm at the Flower Drum and Jason is looking after us, I'm in heaven.'—Neil Perry

HUTONG DUMPLING BAR

14-16 Market Lane
Melbourne
Victoria 3000
+61 396508128
www.hutong.com.au

Recommended by
Dan Hunter

Opening hours................................7 days for lunch and dinner
Reservation policy..Yes
Credit cards..Accepted
Price range..Budget
Style..Casual
Cuisine..Chinese
Recommended for..Bargain

IZAKAYA DEN

114 Russell Street
Melbourne
Victoria 3000
+61 396542977
www.izakayaden.com.au

Recommended by
Dan Hunter

Opening hours............5 days for lunch and 6 days for dinner
Reservation policy..Yes
Credit cards..Accepted
Price range..Affordable
Style..Casual
Cuisine..Japanese
Recommended for..Late night

LUPINO

41 Little Collins Street
Melbourne
Victoria 3000
+61 396390333
www.lupino.com.au

Recommended by
Anthony Lui

Opening hours................................5 days for lunch and dinner
Reservation policy..Yes
Credit cards..Accepted
Price range..Affordable
Style..Casual
Cuisine..Italian
Recommended for..Bargain

'Simple Italian cuisine done really well. My favourite dish there is the gnocchi – in any sauce – handmade to perfection. Also the braised veal osso bucco with polenta.'—Anthony Lui

MOVIDA BAR DE TAPAS Y VINO

1 Hosier Lane
Melbourne
Victoria 3000
+61 396633038
www.movida.com.au

Recommended by
Meyjitte Boughenout,
Bevan Smith

Opening hours................................7 days for lunch and dinner
Reservation policy..Yes
Credit cards..Accepted
Price range..Budget
Style..Casual
Cuisine..Small Plates
Recommended for................................Worth the travel

'Each dish has impressive powerful flavours. My favourite is the Cecina dish, which has air-dried Wagyu with poached egg and truffle foam.'
—Meyjitte Boughenout

MOVIDA NEXT DOOR

164 Flinders Street
Melbourne
Victoria 3000
+61 396633038
www.movida.com.au

Opening hours..............3 days for lunch and 6 days for dinner
Reservation policy...Yes
Credit cards...Accepted
Price range...Affordable
Style...Casual
Cuisine...Small Plates
Recommended for...Wish I'd opened

'So simple, casual and fun.'—Anthony Lui

SHANGHAI VILLAGE

112 Little Bourke Street
Melbourne
Victoria 3000
+61 396631878

Opening hours................................7 days for lunch and dinner
Reservation policy...Yes
Credit cards...Not accepted
Price range...Affordable
Style...Casual
Cuisine..Chinese
Recommended for...Bargain

'I'm passionate about fried rice and always seek great
versions of it. The fried rice here is some of the best in
Melbourne. Technically perfect, very simple and just the
right balance of texture and flavour.'—Ben Shewry

ST PETER'S

6 Melbourne Place
Melbourne
Victoria 3000
+61 396639882
www.stpetersrestaurantandbar.com

Opening hours..............5 days for lunch and 6 days for dinner
Reservation policy...Yes
Reservation email........dine@stpetersrestaurantandbar.com
Credit cards...Accepted
Price range...Budget
Style..Smart casual
Cuisine..Italian
Recommended for...Worth the travel

Sustainability is a family affair at this stylish trattoria
in Melbourne's busy Central Business District,
where chef Maurice Esposito sources some of his
produce from his own mother's garden. Maria is also
credited on the menu for her 'famous' minestrone
with seasonal local vegetables and basil pesto and
'homely desserts' such as strawberry and almond
tart. Esposito himself is best known for seafood
creations such as chilli and garlic Balmain bugs (a
type of shellfish) with hand-cut lemon tagliatelle and
white wine sauce, but meat dishes, including braised
Maryland chicken in tomato, roasted peppers and
black olives, are equally adept.

SUPPER INN

15 Celestial Avenue
Melbourne
Victoria 3000
+61 396634759

Opening hours.......................................7 days for dinner
Reservation policy...Yes
Credit cards...Accepted
Price range...Affordable
Style...Casual
Cuisine..Chinese
Recommended for...Late night

'I recommend the pork and preserved duck egg congee
with stir-fried vegetables.'—Anthony Lui

VUE DE MONDE

Recommended by
Martin Benn, Anthony
Lui, Ben Shewry

Level 53 Rialto
525 Collins Street
Melbourne
Victoria 3000
+61 396913888
www.vuedemonde.com.au

Opening hours.............5 days for lunch and 6 days for dinner
Reservation policy..Yes
Reservation email..........reservations@vuedemonde.com.au
Credit cards...Accepted
Price range..Expensive
Style..Formal
Cuisine..Modern Australian
Recommended for..High end

'For a complete experience, nothing beats going to
Vue De Monde. The theatrics and experience of dining
there is second to none. And the view is pretty good
too.'—Anthony Lui

On the fifty-fifth floor of Melbourne's iconic Rialto
Building is the third incarnation of Shannon Bennett's
Vue de Monde. With sweeping views across the
city, the pared-back but luxurious space references
Australia's history, as does Bennett's menu. Since
moving here, this devotee of classic French cooking
has focused his offerings on Australia, serving dishes
such as kangaroo, beetroot (beet) and chocolate
and barramundi, herb emulsion, prawn (shrimp) and
smoked bone marrow. Dishes are served on stones,
wood and in kangaroo hide, confirming his reputation
as 'the enfant terrible of Australian haute cuisine'.

JACQUES REYMOND

Recommended by
Ben Shewry

78 Williams Road
Prahran
Melbourne
Victoria 3181
+61 395252178
www.jacquesreymond.com.au

Opening hours.............2 days for lunch and 5 days for dinner
Reservation policy..Yes
Credit cards...Accepted
Price range..Expensive
Style...Smart casual
Cuisine..Modern Australian
Recommended for.....................................Worth the travel

I LOVE PHO

Recommended by
Andrew McConnell

264 Victoria Street
Richmond
Melbourne
Victoria 3121
+61 394277749

Opening hours.............7 days for breakfast, lunch and dinner
Reservation policy...No
Credit cards..Not accepted
Price range...Budget
Style..Casual
Cuisine...Vietnamese
Recommended for...Bargain

ATTICA

Recommended by
Massimo Bottura, Shaun Clouston,
Peter Gilmore, Benjamin Greeno,
Dan Hunter, Rasmus Kofoed,
Corey Lee, Andrew McConnell,
Michael Meredith, Magnus Nilsson,
Christian Puglisi, Michael Wilson

74 Glen Eira Road
Ripponlea
Melbourne
Victoria 3185
+61 395300111
www.attica.com.au

Opening hours...5 days for dinner
Reservation policy..Yes
Reservation email.....................................meet@attica.com.au
Credit cards...Accepted
Price range..Expensive
Style...Smart casual
Cuisine..Modern Australian
Recommended for.....................................Worth the travel

'Ben Shewry is an amazing chef, the service is polished
and the food can only be tried, as a description would
never do it justice.'—Shaun Clouston

Attica's black walls and spotlighting belie the playful
nature of head chef Ben Shewry's renowned
Melbourne place, with dishes much lighter and
vibrant than the stifling decor would have you believe.
What the room lacks in personality is made up for by
the food, with the famously hands-on chef ploughing
his own furrow, often blending Thai and indigenous
ingredients for interesting combos. To catch Attica
at its best, head down on a Tuesday night when the
kitchen is testing and developing new menu ideas
— for a snip of what you'd normally pay, experience
its five-course menu.

ROCKPOOL BAR & GRILL

Recommended by
Philip Howard, Anthony Lui

Crown Complex
8 Whiteman Street
Southbank
Melbourne
Victoria 3006
+61 386481900
www.rockpool.com/melbourne

Opening hours	6 days for lunch and 7 days for dinner
Reservation policy	Yes
Credit cards	Accepted
Price range	Affordable
Style	Smart casual
Cuisine	Steakhouse
Recommended for	Wish I'd opened

DUCHESS OF SPOTSWOOD

Recommended by
Andrew McConnell

87 Hudsons Road
Spotwood
Melbourne Victoria 3015
+61 393916016
www.duchessofspotswood.com.au

Opening hours	7 days for brunch and 3 days for dinner
Reservation policy	Yes
Reservation email	info@duchessofspotswood.com.au
Credit cards	Accepted but not Amex or Diners
Price range	Affordable
Style	Casual
Cuisine	Bar-Bistro
Recommended for	Breakfast

GOLDEN FIELDS

Recommended by
Christian Puglisi,
Ben Shewry

157 Fitzroy Street
St Kilda
Melbourne
Victoria 3182
+61 395254488
www.goldenfields.com.au

Opening hours	7 days for lunch and dinner
Reservation policy	Yes
Reservation email	info@goldenfields.com.au
Credit cards	Accepted
Price range	Expensive
Style	Casual
Cuisine	Asian small plates
Recommended for	Worth the travel

EMBASSY TAXI CAFÉ

Recommended by
Andrew McConnell

547 Spencer Street
West Melbourne
Victoria 3003
+61 393281830

Opening hours	7 days for breakfast, lunch and dinner
Reservation policy	No
Credit cards	Not accepted
Price range	Budget
Style	Casual
Cuisine	Café
Recommended for	Late night

Serving shift workers, ambulance staff, taxi drivers, hungry clubbers and random insomniacs since 1962, this twenty-four-hour stalwart arguably looks its best after midnight. Only then can you truly appreciate its classic interior, seemingly untouched since opening – a combination of lino flooring, plastic chairs, Formica tables and florescent lighting. Then again, at that time of night you're more likely to have called in for one of their rather fine burgers and a milkshake. The Embassy taxi headquarters upstairs, from where the café got its name, might be long gone but there's still no shortage of cabs outside should you need a ride home.

CODA

Recommended by
Bevan Smith

141 Flinders Lane
West Melbourne
Victoria 3003
+61 396503155
www.codarestaurant.com.au

Opening hours	7 days for lunch and dinner
Reservation policy	Yes
Credit cards	Accepted
Price range	Affordable
Style	Smart casual
Cuisine	Asian-European
Recommended for	Late night

'Busy and noisy and serves really good, casual food and a good selection of craft beers to wash it down.'
—Bevan Smith

'Try the Iwi Burger, it's a classic.'

REON HOBSON P38

NEW ZEALAND

'THE FOOD IS COOKED WITH INTELLIGENCE AND HEART.'

AL BROWN P45

'Consistent quality that always satisfies and never lets you down.'

BEN BATTERBURY P42

'The food is always fantastic, the service is great and it's a beautiful place to eat on a hot summer's day.'

BEVAN SMITH P39

Aukland pp.46-51

Nelson p.39   Wellington pp.43-45

Canterbury pp.38-39

Otago pp.40-43

NEW ZEALAND

N   SCALE

0   80   160
                    mi.

PESCATORE

Recommended by
Ben Batterbury

The George Hotel
50 Park Terrace
Christchurch
Canterbury 8013
+64 33710257
www.thegeorge.com/pescatore

Opening hours	5 days for dinner
Reservation policy	Yes
Reservation email	pescatore@thegeorge.com
Credit cards	Accepted
Price range	Expensive
Style	Smart casual
Cuisine	Seafood
Recommended for	Worth the travel

'Interesting modern food, well executed but there is an element of fun in the food too.'—Ben Batterbury

NORTH & SOUTH

Recommended by
Reon Hobson

300 Lincoln Road
Addington
Christchurch
Canterbury 8024
+64 33398887

Opening hours	7 days for lunch and dinner
Reservation policy	Yes
Credit cards	Not accepted
Price range	Budget
Style	Casual
Cuisine	Chinese
Recommended for	Regular neighbourhood

JC PLACE

Recommended by
Reon Hobson

6 Nelson Street
Riccarton
Christchurch
Canterbury 8011

Opening hours	7 days for lunch and dinner
Reservation policy	No
Credit cards	Not accepted
Price range	Budget
Style	Casual
Cuisine	Chinese
Recommended for	Late night

The Riccarton area of Christchurch is known for its student population, its park, its shopping centre and its Asian restaurants, notably this Chinese restaurant in Nelson Street, just off the Riccarton Road. With last orders at 11 p.m. seven nights a week, it's a popular place to come for a late-night, reasonably priced and very tasty feed. Bring your own booze to complement dishes like Lamb stir-fry with VSOP brandy sauce – beautifully tender lamb in a succulent and intensely flavoursome gravy. JC Place isn't just popular with students; it's also well frequented by the local Asian community, which is a better endorsement.

BURGER AND BEERS INC.

Recommended by
Reon Hobson

355 Colombo Street
Sydenham
Christchurch
Canterbury 8023
+64 33663339
www.burgersandbeersinc.co.nz

Opening hours	7 days for lunch and dinner
Reservation policy	Yes
Credit cards	Accepted
Price range	Budget
Style	Casual
Cuisine	Burgers
Recommended for	Bargain

'Try the Iwi burger – it's a classic Kiwi burger combination. '—Reon Hobson

Burger and Beers Inc. does well exactly what you might expect. In pursuit of perfection, a cleverly stylized concept has reborn a gourmet version of the junk-food icon. This confessedly 'rock 'n' roller' joint, with its carefully honed menu, proves that substance can indeed achieve parity with style. Limited variety does not make the offering dull. One hundred per cent Angus patties are served with unusual accompaniments, such as Béarnaise sauce, lemon yogurt and date chutney. If beef isn't to your liking, scan the right side of the menu for Camembert burgers and other more inventive veggie options. Served alongside excellent craft beers.

BEACH CAFÉ

16a Beach Road
Waimairi Beach
Christchurch
Canterbury 8083
+64 33828599
www.beachcafe.co.nz

Opening hours............................7 days for breakfast and lunch
Reservation policy...Yes
Credit cards..Accepted
Price range...Budget
Style...Casual
Cuisine..Café
Recommended for..Breakfast

Antipodeans have been making a meal out of
breakfast for many years. Sourdough and quality
artisanal coffee is yesteryear's news. No surprise
then that the Beach Café is home to perfected and
refined versions of the above. The menu's classic is
The Grill – free-range eggs, streaky bacon, sausages
and hash cakes with homemade tomato-onion jam
on focaccia toast. More health-conscious morning
diners, who might have arrived via a keen run along
the beach, can opt for fruit salad with natural (plain)
yogurt and honeycomb (sponge cake), and rehydrate
with a smoothie from the café's extensive array.

PEGASUS BAY

Pegasus Bay Winery
Stockgrove Road
RD 2, Waipara
Amberley
North Canterbury 7482
+64 33146869
www.pegasusbay.com

Opening hours..7 days for lunch
Reservation policy...Yes
Reservation email.......................restaurant@pegasusbay.com
Credit cards..Accepted
Price range...Expensive
Style...Casual
Cuisine...Modern European
Recommended for...............................Regular neighbourhood

'The food is always fantastic, the service is great
and it's a beautiful place to eat on a hot summer's
day.'—Bevan Smith

Food and wine are in harmony at the restaurant at
Pegasus Bay Winery in the Waipara Valley, one of
New Zealand's best winery restaurants. An Italian-
inspired repast of local ingredients in the restaurant
or garden follows on nicely from a morning's tasting,
though Christchurch foodies see it as destination in
itself and regularly drive the half hour here just for
lunch. All dishes come with a recommended wine
from the family winery's 40-hectare (100-acre)
vineyard. Whole Muscovy duck for two with blood
orange, ricotta and pistachio sounds like a good
excuse to crack open a bottle of Prima Donna Pinot
Noir, the estate's flagship red.

HOPGOODS

284 Trafalgar Street
Nelson
Tasman 7010
+64 35457191
www.hopgoods.co.nz

Opening hours...6 days for dinner
Reservation policy...Yes
Credit cards..Accepted
Price range...Expensive
Style..Smart casual
Cuisine...International
Recommended for..Worth the travel

'Nice, simple, well-cooked fresh food.'—Ben Batterbury

Nelson, on the north coast of South Island, is
something of a cornucopia of great food and wine,
and any restaurateur setting up there would be crazy
not to make the most of it. Suffice it to say, English
chef Kevin Hopgood ain't crazy. Daily deliveries of
fresh, organic produce dictate a short but sweet
menu that usually includes a range of meats, fish,
prawns (shrimp) and duck. As well as the wine list,
which shows off just how lucky they are around
these parts, there's also a beer list, which is always
a good sign, reflecting a level of service that is
casual yet right on the ball.

NO 7 BALMAC

Recommended by
Bevan Smith

7 Balmacewen Road
Maori Hill
Dunedin
Otago 9010
+64 034640064
www.no7balmac.co.nz

Opening hours	7 days for brunch and 6 days for dinner
Reservation policy	Yes
Credit cards	Accepted
Price range	Affordable
Style	Smart casual
Cuisine	Modern New Zealand
Recommended for	Regular neighbourhood

FLEURS PLACE

Recommended by
Ben Batterbury

At the Old Jetty
169 Haven Street
Moeraki
Otago 9482
+64 34394480
www.fleursplace.com

Opening hours	5 days for breakfast, lunch and dinner
Reservation policy	Yes
Credit cards	Accepted
Price range	Affordable
Style	Casual
Cuisine	Seafood
Recommended for	Local favourite

'An iconic Kiwi restaurant with a great personality, in a really unique setting, serving some of the freshest fish you will ever taste.'—Ben Batterbury

Moeraki is an old whaling station in Central Otago and its rich seafaring history is preserved in the setting and cooking of Fleurs Place. Sitting right on the jetty, you couldn't get any closer to the sea without being in it, and the local boats deliver their catch right to Fleur Sullivan's door. Blue cod, dory, blue nose, gurnard, sole, flounder, groper, crayfish... the menu is dictated by what comes in. One non-fish speciality worth trying is mutton-bird, or titi, which is a local seabird. But it's the fish that has earned Fleurs Place its reputation as a must-stop for locals and passing tourists alike.

RIVERSTONE KITCHEN

Recommended by
Reon Hobson

1431 State Highway 1
Road 5H
Oamaru
Otago 9493
+64 34313505
www.riverstonekitchen.co.nz

Opening hours	5 days for brunch and 4 days for dinner
Reservation policy	Yes
Credit cards	Accepted
Price range	Affordable
Style	Casual
Cuisine	Modern New Zealand
Recommended for	Worth the travel

'They do farm to plate with an impressive garden – make a day of it.'—Reon Hobson

Situated 12 km (7 miles) outside Oamaru in North Otago, Riverstone Kitchen is well placed to base its culinary philosophy on local, seasonal ingredients. They grow in abundance here, as a glimpse in the kitchen garden will testify. With its own jams and ice cream on sale, this light, airy establishment is very much the wholesome country café, but the food is on a different level. Chef Bevan Smith learned his trade in London – at Pont de la Tour and Canteen, via a stint at E'cco Bistro in Brisbane – and it shows. From the Mt Cook salmon to the teashop's cakes, every mouthful makes you feel good.

ATLAS BEER CAFÉ

Recommended by
Ben Batterbury

Steamer Wharf
Beach Street
Queenstown
Otago 9300
+64 34425281

Opening hours	7 days for brunch until late
Reservation policy	No
Credit cards	Accepted
Price range	Budget
Style	Casual
Cuisine	Gastropub
Recommended for	Worth the travel

'For its fantastic concept and success I would say Atlas Beer Café. It's just a great place to hang out. '
—Ben Batterbury

'Food and drink and all-round awesomeness' might be a haughty self-description. Shrouded in secrecy, there isn't merely a hint of the smug in the 'Now you've just got to find us' invitation on their website. Despite that — and it may not come as a surprise — they serve an excellent range of craft beers and, with some outside seating, offer stunning views of the mountainous region in which they are situated. The food isn't half bad either — together with their popular tapas menu, steaks and burgers are of a quality that encourages a return visit.

AMISFIELD BISTRO

Recommended by
Bevan Smith

Amisfield Winery
10 Lake Hayes Road
Road 1
Queenstown
Otago 9371
+64 34420556
www.amisfield.co.nz

Opening hours	7 days for lunch and dinner
Reservation policy	Yes
Reservation email	tom@amisfield.co.nz
Credit cards	Accepted
Price range	Affordable
Style	Casual
Cuisine	Modern New Zealand
Recommended for	Worth the travel

THE BUNKER

Recommended by
Dirk Stark

Cow Lane
Queenstown
Otago 9300
+64 034418030
www.thebunker.co.nz

Opening hours	7 days for dinner
Reservation policy	Yes
Reservation email	info@thebunker.co.nz
Credit cards	Accepted
Price range	Affordable
Style	Casual
Cuisine	European
Recommended for	Late night

THE COW

Recommended by
Ben Batterbury

Cow Lane
Queenstown
Otago 9300
+64 34428588
www.thecowrestaurant.co.nz

Opening hours	7 days for lunch and dinner
Reservation policy	No
Credit cards	Accepted
Price range	Budget
Style	Casual
Cuisine	Pizza
Recommended for	Regular neighbourhood

'Just for it's amazing building and great pizzas.' —Ben Batterbury

FERGBURGER

Recommended by
Ben Batterbury

42 Shotover Street
Queenstown
Otago 9300
+64 34411232
www.fergburger.com

Opening hours	7 days for breakfast, lunch and dinner
Reservation policy	No
Credit cards	Accepted
Price range	Budget
Style	Casual
Cuisine	Burgers
Recommended for	Late night

'Who could overlook the legend that is Fergburger... need I say more?'—Ben Batterbury

From backstreet, hole-in-the-wall joint to mainstream Main Street success, Queenstown's Fergburger is an Aotearoa burger legend. Open 21/7, the burgers are made with prime New Zealand cuts, chargrilled and served in a soft white roll, that despite its suspect, pillowy consistency heroically holds together long enough to keep its contents — much like the average Kiwi after a night on the town. They burger up everything from beef in the classic quarter-pound Fergburger, to venison in the Little Bambi, via making an offer that's hard to refuse with The Codfather, the brutally self-explanatory Little Lamby and the vegetarian-friendly falafel-packed Bun Laden.

FISHBONE BAR AND GRILL

Recommended by
Ben Batterbury

7 Beach Street
Queenstown
Otago 9300
+64 34426768
www.fishbonequeenstown.co.nz

Opening hours...7 days for dinner
Reservation policy...Yes
Reservation email................fishbonequeenstown@xtra.co.nz
Credit cards...Accepted
Price range..Affordable
Style...Smart casual
Cuisine..Seafood
Recommended for...Local favourite

'Good quality, honest and consistent food in a good
atmosphere.'—Ben Batterbury

Fishbone is a lively joint in Queenstown where the interior decor – you can sit out on the pavement (sidewalk) too – is as sparklingly fresh as the celebrated seafood they serve. For a restaurant that's been doing it for twenty years, that says something for chef-owner Darren Lovell's energy and commitment to the cause. The fish comes fresh off the boats, the vegetables are locally grown, some on Fishbone's own 'farm', and the cooking just lets them sing. With influences from Britain, America and Asia, the menu ranges from perfectly simple pan-roasted fish fillets with steamed new season potatoes and green salad to Thai-style seafood curry.

HIKARI IZAKAYA

Recommended by
Ben Batterbury

5 Beach Street
Queenstown
Otago 9300
+64 34429030
www.hikariizakaya.co.nz

Opening hours....................7 days for lunch and dinner
Reservation policy...Yes
Credit cards...Accepted
Price range..Affordable
Style..Casual
Cuisine..Japanese
Recommended for...Bargain

KAPPA SUSHI

Recommended by
Ben Batterbury, Dirk Stark

36a The Mall
Queenstown
Otago 9300
+64 34411423

Opening hours.............5 days for lunch and 6 days for dinner
Reservation policy..No
Credit cards...Accepted
Price range..Budget
Style..Casual
Cuisine..Japanese
Recommended for...............................Regular neighbourhood

'I love Japanese food and this is the best in town.'
—Ben Batterbury

SOLERA VINO

Recommended by
Ben Batterbury

25 Beach Street
Queenstown
Otago 9300
+64 34426082

Opening hours.............5 days for lunch and 7 days for dinner
Reservation policy...Yes
Reservation email...................................dine@soleravino.co.nz
Credit cards...Accepted
Price range..Affordable
Style..Casual
Cuisine..French
Recommended for..High end

YAKITORI DARUMA

Recommended by
Ben Batterbury

54 Shotover Street
Queenstown
Otago 9300

Opening hours..7 days for dinner
Reservation policy..No
Credit cards...Accepted
Price range..Budget
Style..Casual
Cuisine..Japanese
Recommended for...Late night

'Great atmosphere and fantastic late night
nibbles.'—Ben Batterbury

RATA

Recommended by
Michael Meredith

Te Nuku
43 Ballarat Street
Queenstown
Otago 9348
+64 34429393
www.ratadining.co.nz

Opening hours	7 days for lunch and dinner
Reservation policy	Yes
Reservation email	bookings@ratadining.co.nz
Credit cards	Accepted
Price range	Affordable
Style	Casual
Cuisine	Modern New Zealand
Recommended for	Worth the travel

@THAI

Recommended by
Ben Batterbury

3f Air New Zealand Building
Church Street
Queenstown
Otago 9300
+64 34423683
www.atthai.co.nz

Opening hours	7 days for lunch and dinner
Reservation policy	Yes
Credit cards	Accepted
Price range	Budget
Style	Casual
Cuisine	Thai
Recommended for	Bargain

VUDU CAFE AND LARDER

Recommended by
Ben Batterbury, Dirk Stark

16 Rees Street
Queenstown
Otago 9300
www.vudu.co.nz

Opening hours	7 days for breakfast and lunch
Reservation policy	No
Credit cards	Accepted
Price range	Budget
Style	Casual
Cuisine	Café
Recommended for	Breakfast

'Good simple food with a display cabinet that makes you want it all! And great coffee too.'—Ben Batterbury

FEDERAL DINER

Recommended by
Bevan Smith

47 Helwick Street
Wanaka
Otago 9305
+64 4435152
www.federaldiner.co.nz

Opening hours	7 days for breakfast and lunch
Reservation policy	Yes
Credit cards	Accepted
Price range	Budget
Style	Casual
Cuisine	Café
Recommended for	Breakfast

HONG KONG BARBEQUE

Recommended by
Martin Bosley

14 Kent Terrace
Mount Victoria
Wellington 6011

Opening hours	7 days for dinner
Reservation policy	No
Credit cards	Not accepted
Price range	Budget
Style	Casual
Cuisine	Chinese
Recommended for	Bargain

ANCESTRAL

Recommended by
Martin Bosley

31-33 Courtenay Place
Te Aro
Wellington 6011
+64 48018867
ancestral.co.nz

Opening hours	4 days for lunch and 6 days for dinner
Reservation policy	Yes
Credit cards	Accepted
Price range	Affordable
Style	Smart casual
Cuisine	Chinese
Recommended for	Late night

With an equal emphasis on modern culinary and cocktail culture, Ancestral promises to 'take customers on a stimulating journey across Eastern Asia'. Their website mission statements seem a little obsessed with a perceived ability to appeal to all senses. However, their commitment to thoughtful and authentic Chinese cuisine makes up for this. A focus on the regions of Szechuan and Guangzhou in their cooking is set against a minimalist, internationally informed design interior in both the Haipai Dining Room and adjacent Garden Bar. This discrete venue manages, with a late-night licence, to create an alluring metropolitan buzz.

DRAGONFLY

Recommended by
Shaun Clouston

70 Courtenay Place
Te Aro
Wellington 6011
+64 48033995
www.dragon-fly.co.nz

Opening hours	6 days for dinner
Reservation policy	Yes
Reservation email	dine@dragon-fly.co.nz
Credit cards	Accepted
Price range	Affordable
Style	Casual
Cuisine	Asian Fusion
Recommended for	Late night

'Mixed Asian flavours using spanking-fresh ingredients. Try the hot and sour southern clams.'—Shaun Clouston

FLORIDITAS

Recommended by
Martin Bosley
Al Brown

161 Cuba Street
Te Aro
Wellington 6011
+64 43812212
www.floriditas.co.nz

Opening hours	7 days for brunch and dinner
Reservation policy	Yes
Reservation email	bookings@floriditas.co.nz
Credit cards	Accepted
Price range	Affordable
Style	Casual
Cuisine	International
Recommended for	Regular neighbourhood

A bustling, perennially popular café in Wellington's Cuba Street (though the Havana connection doesn't really stretch any further than the name), Floriditas has built up a loyal following by doing the basics not just very well, but reliably well. The coffee is excellent, the baked goods as impressive as you'll find anywhere (head baker Emily Keshav's wares are now so popular they supply cafés throughout the area) and the service is efficient enough to slice through the queues (waiting lines) before you have time to finish your Bloody Mary. A top New Zealand wine list and signature dishes like smoked mackerel mash further draw the crowds.

LOGAN BROWN

Recommended by
Miles Kirby

192 Cuba Street
Te Aro
Wellington 6141
www.loganbrown.co.nz

Opening hours	5 days for lunch and 7 days for dinner
Reservation policy	Yes
Credit cards	Accepted
Price range	Expensive
Style	Smart casual
Cuisine	Modern New Zealand
Recommended for	Wish I'd opened

Steve Logan and Al Brown opened this renowned restaurant in a former bank in 1996 with the intention of raising the standard of fine dining in New Zealand to a new level. Job done. The unpretentious style of cooking's been packing them in ever since, even leading to a television show for the pair, where they catch, trap and forage their ingredients. The simple but stylish decor — marble, velvet, dark wood and linen — suits perfectly the extensive, native and international, wine list and dishes such as rabbit and pistachio terrine with truffle toasts, apple and calvados (apple brandy) and venison chops with beetroot (beet) risotto, goat mascarpone and black pudding (blood sausage).

SCOPA

Recommended by
Shaun Clouston

141 Cuba Street
Te Aro
Wellington 6011
www.scopa.co.nz

Opening hours	7 days for breakfast, lunch and dinner
Reservation policy	No
Credit cards	Accepted
Price range	Budget
Style	Casual
Cuisine	Pizza
Recommended for	Regular neighbourhood

'Great pizza and house-made pasta, smart wine list and snappy service. An Emerson's Pilsner is a great start to the meal also. The value for the price you pay is outstanding.'—Shaun Clouston

MARANUI CAFÉ

Recommended by
Al Brown

Maranui Surf Life Saving Club
The Parade
Lyall Bay
Wellington 6022
+64 43874539
www.maranuicafe.co.nz

Opening hours	7 days for breakfast and lunch
Reservation policy	No
Credit cards	Accepted
Price range	Budget
Style	Casual
Cuisine	Café
Recommended for	Breakfast

After nearly being destroyed by a fire in 2009, it looked like the end for the 100-year-old Maranui Surf Lifesaving Club. But a spontaneous outpouring of affection (not to mention money) from politicians and concerned locals meant a refurbished clubroom and café opening a little under a year later. Decorated in quirky 1940s surf style, with stunning views over Lyall Bay, it's not hard to see why so many fought for its survival. There's great coffee ('The fire,' reads the menu, 'only made the coffee stronger'), friendly service and crowd-pleasing dishes like Eggs Benedict and the gut-busting Victory Breakfast (a vegetarian fried breakfast).

NIKAU CAFÉ

Recommended by
Martin Bosley, Al Brown

City Art Gallery, Civic Square
101 Wakefield Street
Wellington 6011
www.nikaucafe.co.nz

Opening hours	6 days for breakfast and lunch
Reservation policy	No
Credit cards	Accepted
Price range	Budget
Style	Casual
Cuisine	Café
Recommended for	Local favourite

'Produce driven menu, where the food is cooked with intelligence and heart.'—Al Brown

Opened in 1998, the Nikau is Wellington's best-kept secret, serving creative food using good (organic, local, you know the score) ingredients in an improbably attractive corner of the Wellington Gallery. Like many of the town's better coffee shops, they offer excellent coffee and baked goods alongside more substantial dishes like the popular kedgeree or crisped spiced lamb on hummus and pitta. The fact that they grow their own vegetables in a courtyard garden, make their own sloe gin and roll their own pasta, perhaps shows the effort and attention to detail that goes into the menu here.

TI KOUKA CAFÉ

Recommended by
Shaun Clouston

3rd Floor
76 Willis Street
Wellington 6011
+64 44727682
www.tikouka-cafe.co.nz

Opening hours	6 days for brunch and 2 days for dinner
Reservation policy	Yes
Reservation email	tikoukacafe@gmail.com
Credit cards	Accepted
Price range	Affordable
Style	Casual
Cuisine	Café
Recommended for	Breakfast

'The house-made crumpets with beech dew honey, strawberry jam and whipped mascarpone, and the smoked paprika and tomato baked organic eggs are a great way to start the day.'—Shaun Clouston

'BUSY, NOISY AND SERVES REALLY GOOD CASUAL FOOD AND CRAFT BEERS TO WASH IT DOWN.'
BEVAN SMITH P35

'*Amazing.*'
BENJAMIN BAYLY P50

'INTERESTING MODERN FOOD THAT'S WELL EXECUTED.'
BEN BATTERBURY P50

AUCKLAND

'THE FOOD IS REGIONAL WITH A TWIST - THINK GRILLED KINGFISH OR CHERMOULA-SPICED MERINO LAMB RIBS WITH YOGURT - ABSOLUTELY DELICIOUS.'
SHAUN CLOUSTON P48

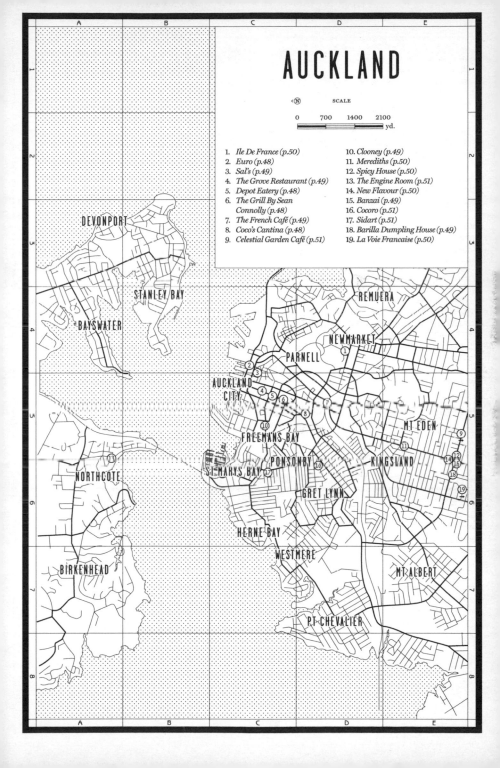

AUCKLAND

N

SCALE

0   700   1400   2100
yd.

1. *Ile De France (p.50)*
2. *Euro (p.48)*
3. *Sal's (p.49)*
4. *The Grove Restaurant (p.49)*
5. *Depot Eatery (p.48)*
6. *The Grill By Sean Connolly (p.48)*
7. *The French Café (p.49)*
8. *Coco's Cantina (p.48)*
9. *Celestial Garden Café (p.51)*
10. *Clooney (p.49)*
11. *Merediths (p.50)*
12. *Spicy House (p.50)*
13. *The Engine Room (p.51)*
14. *New Flavour (p.50)*
15. *Banzai (p.49)*
16. *Cocoro (p.51)*
17. *Sidart (p.51)*
18. *Barilla Dumpling House (p.49)*
19. *La Voie Francaise (p.50)*

DEVONPORT

STANLEY BAY

BAYSWATER

REMUERA

NEWMARKET

PARNELL

AUCKLAND CITY

MT EDEN

FREEMANS BAY

NORTHCOTE

PONSONBY

KINGSLAND

ST MARYS BAY

GREY LYNN

HERNE BAY

BIRKENHEAD

WESTMERE

MT ALBERT

PT CHEVALIER

COCO'S CANTINA

376 Karangahape Road
Auckland 1010
+64 93007582
www.cocoscantina.co.nz

Opening hours	5 days for dinner until late
Reservation policy	No
Credit cards	Accepted
Price range	Budget
Style	Casual
Cuisine	Italian
Recommended for	Bargain

Karangahape Road, much like London's Soho, is shared by the most undesirable elements of Auckland's seedy underbelly and some of its hippest no-reservations bars and restaurants. Coco's Cantina, a tiny, eccentrically decorated space has been wildly popular since it opened its doors in 2010. Its time-worn air, not to mention its mature selection of Italian food and drink – think bruschetti, meatballs and cocktails for NZ$10 (£5; $8) – is all the more impressive considering this is the first shot at being restaurateurs for its two sister owners. Prepare to enjoy a boisterous night out, and remember – all the cool kids are queuing (lining up) these days.

DEPOT EATERY

86 Federal Street
Auckland 1010
+64 93637048

Opening hours	7 days for breakfast, lunch and dinner
Reservation policy	No
Credit cards	Accepted
Price range	Budget
Style	Casual
Cuisine	Seafood
Recommended for	Worth the travel

'A very casual but delicious restaurant/bar. The food is regional with a twist - think grilled kingfish or chermoula-spiced Merino lamb ribs with yogurt - absolutely delicious.'—Shaun Clouston

EURO

Shed 22, Princes Wharf
143 Quay Street
Auckland 1010
+64 93099866
www.eurobar.co.nz

Opening hours	7 days for lunch and dinner
Reservation policy	Yes
Reservation email	reservations@eurobar.co.nz
Credit cards	Accepted
Price range	Expensive
Style	Smart casual
Cuisine	Eclectic
Recommended for	Worth the travel

THE GRILL BY SEAN CONNOLLY

SkyCity Grand Hotel
90 Federal Street
Auckland 1010
+64 93637067
www.skycityauckland.co.nz

Opening hours	5 days for lunch and 7 days for dinner
Reservation policy	Yes
Reservation email	reservations@thegrillnz.co.nz
Credit cards	Accepted
Price range	Affordable
Style	Formal
Cuisine	Steakhouse
Recommended for	Worth the travel

In the TV series 'Under the Grill', a plucky British chef based in Australia was given just 100 days to open a profitable restaurant in a city he'd barely even visited. The city was Auckland, the chef was Sean Connolly and the fruit of his labours was the glitzy The Grill by Sean Connolly, in the Skycity Grand Hotel. Reality TV is rarely a fertile breeding ground for a success story, but The Grill found itself an instant destination restaurant by getting the steakhouse formula absolutely right – stunning surroundings, the best steaks in South Island (grain-fed Wakanui) and pitch-perfect service.

THE GROVE RESTAURANT

Recommended by
Michael Meredith

Saint Patrick's Square
43 Wyndham Street
Auckland 1010
+64 93684129
www.thegroverestaurant.co.nz

Opening hours............5 days for lunch and 6 days for dinner
Reservation policy..Yes
Credit cards..Accepted
Price range..Expensive
Style..Smart casual
Cuisine..Modern New Zealand
Recommended for..High end

SAL'S

Recommended by
Benjamin Bayly

8 Commerce Street
Auckland 1010
www.sals.co.nz

Opening hours................7 days for lunch and dinner
Reservation policy...No
Credit cards...Accepted
Price range...Budget
Style...Casual
Cuisine..Pizza
Recommended for..Bargain

THE FRENCH CAFÉ

Recommended by
Al Brown, Michael Meredith,
Bevan Smith

210 Symonds Street
Eden Terrace
Auckland 1010
+64 93771911
www.thefrenchcafe.co.nz

Opening hours..............1 day for lunch and 5 days for dinner
Reservation policy..Yes
Credit cards..Accepted
Price range..Expensive
Style..Smart casual
Cuisine..French
Recommended for..High end

Lauded by critics and showered with awards in
the over twenty-five years it's been doing its thing,
The French Café is Auckland's own multi-Michelin-
starred restaurant, or at least it would be if Michelin
operated in the Antipodes. Classic French fine dining
with a local twist is the spin, meaning tuna sashimi
rubs shoulders with quail ballotine for appetizers,

and beef with wasabi butter sits alongside pork
fillet (tenderloin) with caramelized belly for the main
course. Prices are, understandably, also starry, but
nobody seems to mind – this husband-and-wife team
provides world-class cuisine (him) framed by effortlessly slick service (her).

CLOONEY

Recommended by
Michael Meredith,
Bevan Smith

33 Sale Street
Freemans Bay
Auckland 1010
+64 93581702
www.clooney.co.nz

Opening hours...............1 day for lunch and 6 days for dinner
Reservation policy..Yes
Credit cards..Accepted
Price range..Expensive
Style..Smart casual
Cuisine..Modern New Zealand
Recommended for..High end

BANZAI

Recommended by
Michael Meredith

583 Dominion Road
Mount Eden
Auckland 1041
+64 96304489

Opening hours............3 days for lunch and 6 days for dinner
Reservation policy..Yes
Credit cards..Accepted
Price range..Budget
Style...Casual
Cuisine..Japanese
Recommended for..Bargain

BARILLA DUMPLING HOUSE

Recommended by
Al Brown

571 Dominion Road
Mount Eden
Auckland 1041
+64 96388032

Opening hours................7 days for lunch and dinner
Reservation policy...No
Credit cards..Not accepted
Price range...Budget
Style...Casual
Cuisine..Asian
Recommended for.......................................Late night

MEREDITHS

Recommended by
Ben Batterbury,
Martin Bosley

365 Dominion Road
Mount Eden
Auckland 1024
+64 96233140
www.merediths.co.nz

Opening hours	1 day for lunch and 5 days for dinner
Reservation policy	Yes
Credit cards	Accepted
Price range	Expensive
Style	Smart casual
Cuisine	International
Recommended for	High end

'Interesting modern food that's well executed.'
—Ben Batterbury

Like New Zealand itself, the flavours you'll encounter at Merediths run the gamut from Northern European to Southeast Asian, yet the transition is seamless. It's tasting menus all the way, so prepare to immerse yourself for a good long stint in the intimate surrounds of dark wood and subdued lighting, as course after course of beautifully crafted food is laid before you by the well-trained staff. The wine list is conveniently compact – probably no more than a hundred wines in all – but the country's own wines are strongly represented and the sommelier will match them to your menu.

NEW FLAVOUR

Recommended by
Michael Meredith

541 Dominion Road
Mount Eden
Auckland 1041
+64 96386880

Opening hours	6 days for dinner
Reservation policy	Yes
Credit cards	Not accepted
Price range	Budget
Style	Casual
Cuisine	Chinese
Recommended for	Late night

SPICY HOUSE

Recommended by
Benjamin Bayly

557 Dominion Road
Mount Eden
Auckland 1041

Opening hours	7 days for lunch and dinner
Reservation policy	Yes
Credit cards	Not accepted
Price range	Budget
Style	Casual
Cuisine	Chinese
Recommended for	Late night

LA VOIE FRANCAISE

Recommended by
Benjamin Bayly

Shop 4, 875 Dominion Road
Mount Roskill
Auckland 1041
+64 96205947

Opening hours	5 days for breakfast, lunch and tea
Reservation policy	No
Credit cards	Accepted
Price range	Budget
Style	Casual
Cuisine	Patisserie
Recommended for	Breakfast

ILE DE FRANCE

Recommended by
Benjamin Bayly

Watercare Building
2 Nuffield Street
Newmarket
Auckland 1023
+64 95230293
www.iledefrance.co.nz

Opening hours	5 days for lunch and 6 days for dinner
Reservation policy	Yes
Credit cards	Accepted
Price range	Affordable
Style	Casual
Cuisine	French Bistro
Recommended for	Regular neighbourhood

'Amazing French brasserie.'—Benjamin Bayly

THE ENGINE ROOM

Recommended by
Martin Bosley

115 Queen Street
Northcote Point
Auckland 0627
+64 94809502
www.engineroom.net.nz

Opening hours................1 day for lunch and 5 days for dinner
Reservation policy..Yes
Credit cards..Accepted
Price range..Affordable
Style..Casual
Cuisine..Modern European
Recommended for..Worth the travel

CELESTIAL GARDEN CAFÉ

Recommended by
Michael Meredith

117 Trafalgar Street
Onehunga
Auckland 1061
+64 96361327
www.aotearaw.co.nz

Opening hours...........................6 days for breakfast and lunch
Reservation policy..Yes
Credit cards..Not accepted
Price range..Budget
Style..Casual
Cuisine..Vegetarian
Recommended for..Breakfast

COCORO

Recommended by
Michael Meredith

56a Brown Street
Ponsonby
Auckland 1021
+64 93600927
www.cocoro.co.nz

Opening hours.................................5 days for lunch and dinner
Reservation policy..Yes
Reservation email..........................bookmytable@coroco.co.nz
Credit cards..Accepted
Price range..Affordable
Style..Casual
Cuisine..Modern Japanese
Recommended for..Wish I'd opened

SIDART

Recommended by
Benjamin Bayly

Three Lamps Plaza
283 Ponsonby Road
Ponsonby
Auckland 1011
+64 93602122
www.sidart.co.nz

Opening hours................1 day for lunch and 5 days for dinner
Reservation policy..Yes
Reservation email..........................reservations@sidart.co.nz
Credit cards..Accepted
Price range..Expensive
Style..Smart casual
Cuisine..Modern New Zealand
Recommended for..Worth the travel

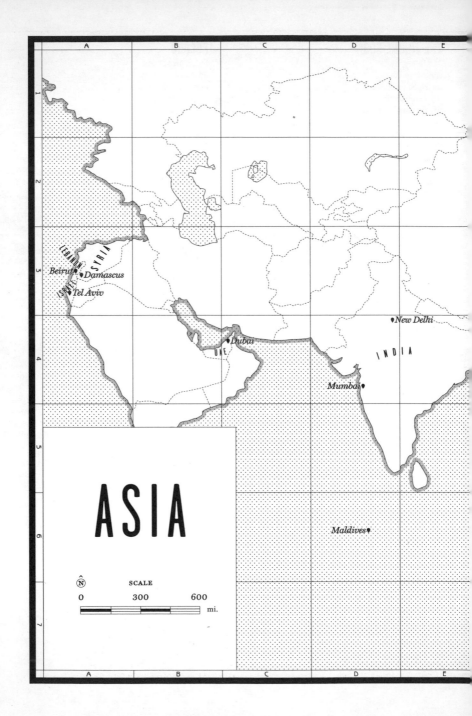

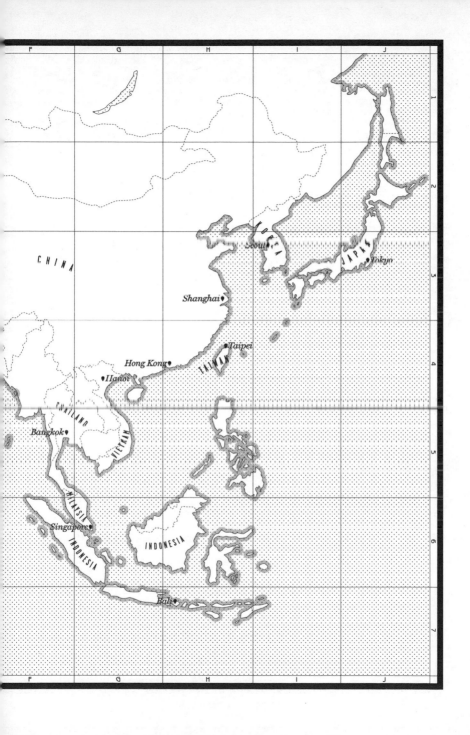

'A SIMPLE HUMMUS AND FOUL PLACE IN TRIPOLI'S SOUK.'

KAMAL MOUZAWAK P57

'IT WAS A PLEASURE FOR ALL MY SENSES.'

PASCAL AUSSIGNAC P59

SOUTHWEST ASIA

'IT BLEW MY MIND SO FAR THAT I ATE THERE THREE NIGHTS IN A ROW!'

CHRISTINA TOSI P58

'The best dishes from all over the world. You can eat four different types of cuisine and mix your dishes as you wish. A must go!'

PASCAL AUSSIGNAC P59

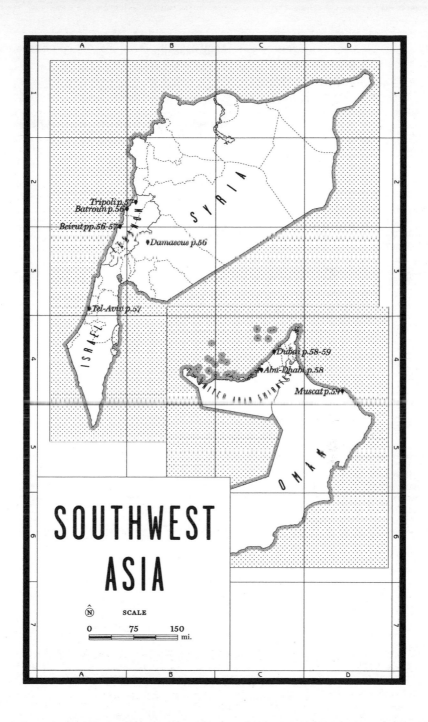

SOUTHWEST ASIA

Tripoli p.57
Batroun p.56
Beirut pp.56-57
Damascus p.56
Tel-Aviv p.57
Dubai p.58-59
Abu-Dhabi p.58
Muscat p.59

SYRIA
LEBANON
ISRAEL
UNITED ARAB EMIRATES
OMAN

N

SCALE

0   75   150
mi.

NARANJ
Recommended by
Kamal Mouzawak

Medhat Basha Street
Bab Sharki
Damascus
Syria
+963 115413444

Opening hours	7 days for breakfast, lunch and dinner
Reservation policy	Yes
Credit cards	Not accepted
Price range	Affordable
Style	Smart casual
Cuisine	Middle Eastern
Recommended for	Worth the travel

'Sophisticated, quality, old style local cuisine.'
—Kamal Mouzawak

CHEZ MAGUY
Recommended by
Kamal Mouzawak

Mak'ad el Mir
Batroun
Lebanon
+961 3439147

Opening hours	7 days for breakfast, lunch and dinner
Reservation policy	Yes
Credit cards	Not accepted
Price range	Affordable
Style	Casual
Cuisine	Seafood
Recommended for	Regular neighbourhood

'A shack over the water in Batroun.'—Kamal Mouzawak

A brightly painted beachfront shack on the coast at Batroun, forty-five minutes north of Beirut, Chez Maguy is run by Maguy, who makes her living selling dishes of beautifully simple seafood. The menu is dictated by whatever comes in that day on the local fishing boats: crab, scallops, prawns (shrimp), snapper, smelts and tuna; sea urchins she dives for herself. All of it cooked on her charcoal grill, with just a touch of lemon, garlic and olive oil. During the winter, guests are served in her dining room, but the rest of the year they eat on her rock-perched terrace, looking out to the Mediterranean.

ABOU HASSAN
Recommended by
Matthew Dillon

Salaheddine El Ayoubi
Beirut
Lebanon
+961 1741725

Opening hours	7 days for breakfast, lunch and dinner
Reservation policy	No
Credit cards	Not accepted
Price range	Budget
Style	Casual
Cuisine	Lebanese
Recommended for	Worth the travel

BOUBOUFFE
Recommended by
Kamal Mouzawak

Alfred Naccash
Mar Mitr, Achrafieh
Beirut
Lebanon
+961 1334040

Opening hours	7 days for breakfast, lunch and dinner
Reservation policy	Yes
Credit cards	Accepted but not AMEX and Diners
Price range	Budget
Style	Casual
Cuisine	Sandwiches
Recommended for	Late night

FALAFEL SAHYOUN
Recommended by
Kamal Mouzawak

Bechara El Khoury
Beirut
Lebanon
+961 1633188

Opening hours	6 days for breakfast, lunch and dinner
Reservation policy	No
Credit cards	Not accepted
Price range	Budget
Style	Casual
Cuisine	Falafel
Recommended for	Bargain

MOMO AT THE SOUKS

Beirut Souks Jewellery 7
Beirut
Lebanon
+961 76700407
www.momobeirut.com

Opening hours	7 days for lunch and dinner
Reservation policy	Yes
Credit cards	Accepted
Price range	Affordable
Style	Smart casual
Cuisine	North African-French
Recommended for	Wish I'd opened

Mourad Mazouz is not a restaurateur who likes repeating himself, so the Beirut outpost of Momo is not simply a retread of the branch he originally opened in London in 1997. Located above the jewellery souk, it overlooks the rest of the market from its garden terrace. The restaurant is a series of different areas that divide drinking, dancing and dining, the interior a frenetic mix of painted patterned walls, psychedelic bathrooms, vintage furniture and custom-made designer pieces. Meanwhile, the menu puts an emphasis on small plates, dropping a few traditional French delicacies like foie gras into the mix, alongside the North African dishes.

RAFIC AL RASHIDI

Monot
Achrafieh
Beirut
Lebanon

Opening hours	7 days for breakfast until late
Reservation policy	No
Credit cards	Not Accepted
Price range	Budget
Style	Casual
Cuisine	Sweets-Pastries
Recommended for	Breakfast

DANNOUN

Beik, Azmi
Tripoli
Lebanon

Opening hours	7 days for breakfast, lunch and dinner
Reservation policy	No
Credit cards	Not accepted
Price range	Budget
Style	Casual
Cuisine	Lebanese
Recommended for	Local favourite

'A simple hummus and foul place.'—Kamal Mouzawak

ABRAXAS

Lilienblum 40
Rothchild Quarter
Tel Aviv
Israel
+972 35104435
www.abraxas.co.il

Opening hours	7 days for dinner
Reservation policy	Yes
Credit cards	Accepted
Price range	Affordable
Style	Casual
Cuisine	Israeli
Recommended for	Worth the travel

ANGAR

Recommended by
Christina Tosi

Yas Hotel
Yas Island
Abu Dhabi
United Arab Emirates
+971 26560600
www.viceroyhotelsandresorts.com

Opening hours..............2 days for lunch and 7 days for dinner
Reservation policy...Yes
Credit cards...Accepted
Price range..Expensive
Style..Smart casual
Cuisine...Indian
Recommended for...Worth the travel

'It blew my mind so far that I ate there three nights in a row!'—Christina Tosi

CIPRIANI

Recommended by
Francesco Mazzei

Yas Yacht Club
Yas Island
Abu Dhabi
United Arab Emirates
+971 026575400
www.cipriani.com

Opening hours..............2 days for lunch and 5 days for dinner
Reservation policy...Yes
Credit cards...Accepted
Price range..Affordable
Style...Formal
Cuisine..Italian
Recommended for...Worth the travel

BAKER & SPICE

Recommended by
Refaie Othman

Souk Al Bahar
Exit 32 Sheik Zayed
Dubai
United Arab Emirates
+971 44252240
www.bakerandspiceme.com

Opening hours.........................7 days from breakfast until late
Reservation policy...No
Credit cards...Accepted
Price range...Budget
Style...Casual
Cuisine...Café
Recommended for..Breakfast

NOODLE BOWL

Recommended by
Refaie Othman

Al Dhiyafah
Al Badaa
Dubai
United Arab Emirates

Opening hours................................7 days for lunch and dinner
Reservation policy...No
Credit cards...Accepted
Price range...Budget
Style...Casual
Cuisine..Chinese
Recommended for..Bargain

RAVI

Recommended by
Refaie Othman

Satwa (Al Dhiyafa)
Dubai
United Arab Emirates

Opening hours..7 days for dinner
Reservation policy...No
Credit cards...Not accepted
Price range...Budget
Style...Casual
Cuisine..Pakistani
Recommended for...Late night

STAY

Recommended by
Refaie Othman

One & Only Resort
West Crescent
The Palm
Dubai
United Arab Emirates
+971 44401030
www.thepalm.oneandonlyresorts.com

Opening hours..6 days for dinner
Reservation policy...Yes
Credit cards...Accepted
Price range..Expensive
Style..Smart casual
Cuisine...Modern European
Recommended for..High end

TABLE 9

Recommended by
Refaie Othman

Hilton Dubai Creek Hotel
17th Street
Deira
Dubai
United Arab Emirates
+971 42127551
www.table9dubai.com

Opening hours	5 days for lunch and 6 days for dinner
Reservation policy	Yes
Reservation email	table9.creek@hilton.com
Credit cards	Accepted
Price range	Expensive
Style	Smart casual
Cuisine	International
Recommended for	Regular neighbourhood

VAPIANO DUBAI 2

Recommended by
Refaie Othman

Dubai Mall
Lower Ground, Shop 92
Dubai
United Arab Emirates
www.vapiano.de

Opening hours	7 days for lunch and dinner
Reservation policy	No
Credit cards	Accepted
Price range	Budget
Style	Casual
Cuisine	Italian
Recommended for	Regular neighbourhood

THE RESTAURANT

Recommended by
Pascal Aussignac

Chedi Hotel
North Ghubra 32, Way 3215
18th November Street
Muscat
Oman
+968 24524343
www.ghmhotels.com

Opening hours	7 days for breakfast, lunch and dinner
Reservation policy	Yes
Reservation email	restaurant@chedimuscat.com
Credit cards	Accepted
Price range	Expensive
Style	Smart casual
Cuisine	International
Recommended for	Worth the travel

'Four open kitchens where you can see top chefs in operation preparing the best dishes from all over the world. You can eat four different types of cuisine and mix your dishes as you wish. The food is top quality with very experienced chefs working in all the kitchens and a perfect front of house. A difficult concept to achieve and rare enough to be mentioned. A must go!'—Pascal Aussignac

'IT'S UNDERWATER AND THE MENU SWIMS AROUND YOU!'

DHARSHAN MUNIDASA P69

'BEHIND THE TAJ IS GREAT FOR LATE NIGHT MUNCHIES.'

RAHUL AKERKAR P66

CENTRAL AND SOUTH ASIA

'There's lots of local Maldivian seafood and chicken from the neighbouring island on the menu all prepared with herbs from the garden underneath the very restaurant. All this in the middle of the Indian Ocean.'

THOMAS RODE ANDERSON P69

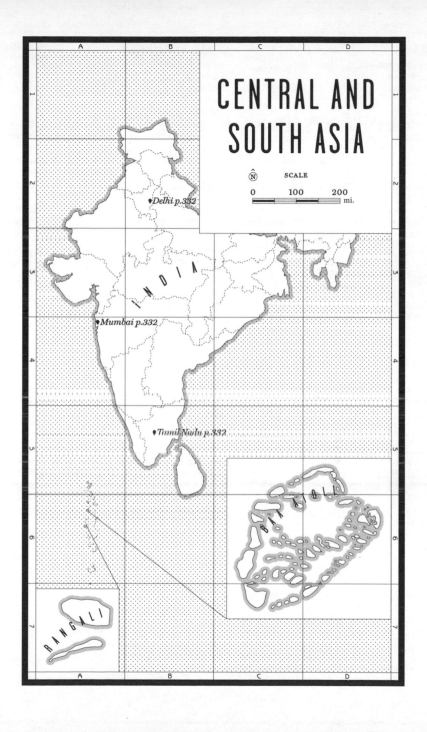

CENTRAL AND
SOUTH ASIA

N̂   SCALE

0   100   200
                  mi.

•Delhi p.332

I N D I A

•Mumbai p.332

•Tamil Nadu p.332

B   A   N   G   A   L   I

R A N G A L I

BUKHARA

ITC Maurya Sheraton Hotel
Diplomatic Enclave
Sardar Patel Lane
New Delhi
Delhi 110 021
+91 1126112233
www.itchotels.in

Opening hours...................................7 days for lunch and dinner
Reservation policy...Yes
Reservation email.........reservations.itcmaurya@itchotels.in
Credit cards...Accepted
Price range...Expensive
Style...Smart casual
Cuisine...Northwest Indian
Recommended for..Wish I'd opened

GUNPOWDER

22 Hauz Khaz Village
New Delhi
Delhi 110 016
+91 1126535700
www.gunpowder.co.in

Opening hours.................................6 days for lunch and dinner
Reservation policy...Yes
Reservation email...................reservations@gunpowder.co.in
Credit cards...Accepted
Price range...Affordable
Style...Casual
Cuisine...South Indian
Recommended for..Worth the travel

THE SPICE ROUTE

Imperial Hotel
Janpath Lane
Connaught Place
New Delhi
Delhi 110 001
+91 1123341234
theimperialindia.com

Opening hours.................................7 days for lunch and dinner
Reservation policy...Yes
Credit cards...Accepted
Price range...Affordable
Style...Formal
Cuisine...Southeast Asian
Recommended for..Worth the travel

WASABI BY MARIMOTO

Taj Mahal Hotel
1 Mansingh Road
New Delhi
Delhi 110 011
www.tajhotels.com

Opening hours.................................7 days for lunch and dinner
Reservation policy...Yes
Reservation email.....................tmhwasabi.del@tajhotels.com
Credit cards...Accepted
Price range...Expensive
Style...Formal
Cuisine...Modern Japanese
Recommended for..High end

THE BANGALA HOTEL

Devakottai Road
Senjai
Karaikudi
Tamil Nadu 630 001
+91 4424934851
www.thebangala.com

Opening hours..............7 days for breakfast, lunch and dinner
Reservation policy...Yes
Reservation email.................................thebangala@gmail.com
Credit cards...Accepted but not AMEX
Price range...Budget
Style...Smart casual
Cuisine...Chettinad
Recommended for..Worth the travel

'The feast I had here was cuisine gastronomy! My most memorable meal in a long time.'—Alfred Prasad

'Go for the biryani and nali nihari.'

VICKY RATNANI P67

'DOES A MEAN BOMBIL FRY.'

VICKY RATNANI P67

MUMBAI

'HERE THEY SERVE CHEAP, HOME-COOKED, VEGETARIAN, GUJARATI FOOD IN A THALI FORMAT.'

RAHUL AKERKAR P68

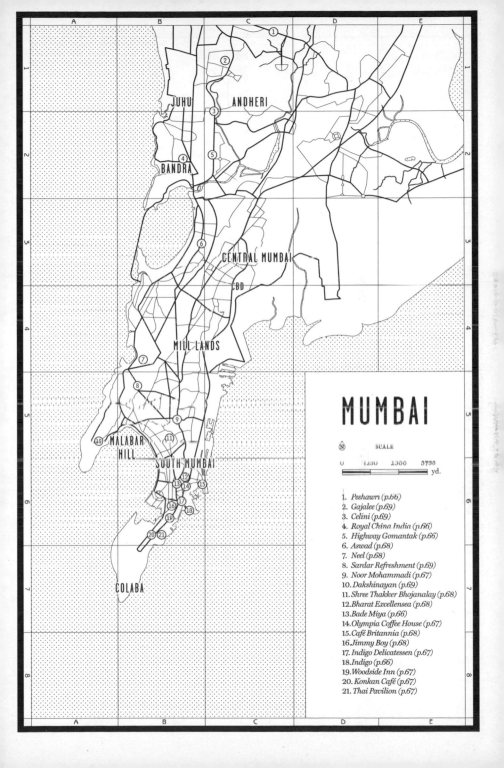

MUMBAI

PESHAWRI

Recommended by
Manoj Vasaikar

ITC Maratha Hotel
Sahar
Andheri East
Mumbai
Maharashtra 400 099
+91 28303030
www.itchotels.in

Opening hours	7 days for lunch and dinner
Reservation policy	Yes
Credit cards	Accepted
Price range	Expensive
Style	Smart casual
Cuisine	Northwest Indian
Recommended for	Worth the travel

HIGHWAY GOMANTAK

Recommended by
Manoj Vasaikar

44-2179 Gandhi Nagar
Highway Service Road
Bandra East
Mumbai
Maharashtra 400 051
www.highwaygomantak.com

Opening hours	6 days for lunch and dinner
Reservation policy	No
Credit cards	Not accepted
Price range	Budget
Style	Casual
Cuisine	Goan
Recommended for	Worth the travel

ROYAL CHINA INDIA

Recommended by
Rahul Akerkar

192 Turner Road
3rd Road
Bandra West
Mumbai
Maharashtra 400 050
+91 2226425533
www.royalchina.in

Opening hours	7 days for lunch and dinner
Reservation policy	Yes
Credit cards	Accepted
Price range	Expensive
Style	Smart casual
Cuisine	Cantonese
Recommended for	Regular neighbourhood

'They have great dim sum.'—Rahul Akerkar

BADE MIYA

Recommended by
Rahul Akerkar, Irfan
Pabaney, Vicky Ratnani

Tulloch Road
Apollo Bandar
Colaba
Mumbai
Maharashtra 400 039

Opening hours	7 days for dinner until late
Reservation policy	No
Credit cards	Not accepted
Price range	Budget
Style	Casual
Cuisine	Street food
Recommended for	Late night

'Bade Miya behind the Taj is great for the late night
munchies if you like kebabs.'—Rahul Akerkar

INDIGO

Recommended by
Dharshan Munidasa

4 Mandlik Road
Colaba
Mumbai
Maharashtra 400 001
+91 2266368981
www.foodindigo.com

Opening hours	7 days for lunch and dinner
Reservation policy	Yes
Reservation email	info@foodindigo.com
Credit cards	Accepted
Price range	Affordable
Style	Smart casual
Cuisine	Modern European
Recommended for	Worth the travel

Bollywood's – and Hollywood's – most glamorous
stars adore Indigo Restaurant in Mumbai's fashionable
Colaba district. This chic stand-alone operation offers
rubbernecking opportunities aplenty, but it hasn't
maintained its status as the city's hottest address
since 1999 thanks to Brad and Angelina alone. New
York-trained chef Rahul Akerkar's innovative global
menus, matched with stellar international wines, put
an exciting local spin on European fine dining. Polenta
gnocchi with Madras chilli butter and asparagus,
fenugreek-spiced tuna with Shiraz and clove, or
chocolate jalapeño fondant are perfect examples.
Lobster risotto with black olive tapenade is never
off the menu. From November to March the best
tables are on the candlelit terrace.

INDIGO DELICATESSEN

Recommended by Irfan Pabaney

50 Ground Floor, Pheroze Building
Chhatrapati Shivaji Maharishi Marg
Apollo Bunder
Colaba
Mumbai
Maharashtra 400 039
+91 2266551010
www.indigodeli.com

Opening hours............7 days for breakfast, lunch and dinner
Reservation policy..Yes
Credit cards..Accepted
Price range..Affordable
Style..Casual
Cuisine..European
Recommended for.............................Wish I'd opened

KONKAN CAFÉ

Recommended by Manoj Vasaikar

President Mumbai Hotel
90 Cuffe Parade
Colaba
Mumbai
Maharashtra 400 005
+91 2266650808
www.vivantabytaj.com

Opening hours........................ 7 days for lunch and dinner
Reservation policy...Yes
Reservation email..............vivanta.president@tajhotels.com
Credit cards...Accepted
Price range..Affordable
Style..Smart casual
Cuisine....................................Southern Indian
Recommended for............................Worth the travel

NOOR MOHAMMADI

Recommended by Vicky Ratnani

Abdul Hakim Noor Mohammadi Chowk
Bhendi Bazaar, Girgaum
Mumbai
Maharashtra 400 003

Opening hours............7 days for breakfast, lunch and dinner
Reservation policy..No
Credit cards..Not accepted
Price range...Budget
Style..Casual
Cuisine..North Indian
Recommended for...Bargain

'Go for the *biryani* and *nali nihari* – classic meat dishes'
—Vicky Ratnani

OLYMPIA COFFEE HOUSE

Recommended by Vicky Ratnani

Rahim Mansion
1 Shahid Bhagat Singh Road
Colaba
Mumbai
Maharashtra 400 039

Opening hours..............7 days for breakfast, lunch and dinner
Reservation policy..No
Credit cards..Not accepted
Price range...Budget
Style..Casual
Cuisine...North West Indian
Recommended for..Breakfast

'Order the *kheema pao* (minced [ground] meat and
soft traditional bread).'—Vicky Ratnani

THAI PAVILION

Recommended by Irfan Pabaney

President Mumbai Hotel
90 Cuffe Parade
Colaba
Mumbai
Maharashtra 400 005
+91 2266650808
www.vivantabytaj.com

Opening hours........................ 7 days for lunch and dinner
Reservation policy...Yes
Reservation email..............vivanta.president@tajhotels.com
Credit cards...Accepted
Price range..Expensive
Style..Smart casual
Cuisine...Thai
Recommended for...High end

WOODSIDE INN

Recommended by Irfan Pabaney

Wodehouse Road
Colaba
Mumbai
Maharashtra 400 039
www.woodsideinn.in

Opening hours............7 days from breakfast until late
Reservation policy..Yes
Credit cards..Accepted
Price range...Budget
Style..Casual
Cuisine..International
Recommended for..Breakfast

ASWAD

Recommended by
Vicky Ratnani

Shivaji Park
Gadkari Chowk
Dadar West
Mumbai
Maharashtra 400 028

Opening hours..........................7 days from breakfast until late
Reservation policy...No
Credit cards..Not accepted
Price range..Budget
Style..Casual
Cuisine..Street Food
Recommended for...Breakfast

'For *kaanda poha.*'—Vicky Ratnani

BHARAT EXCELLENSEA

Recommended by
Irfan Pabaney

317 Bharat House
Shaheed Bhagat Singh Road
Fort
Mumbai
Maharashtra 400 001
+91 222235994
www.excellenseagroup.com

Opening hours................................7 days for lunch and dinner
Reservation policy...Yes
Credit cards..Accepted
Price range...Affordable
Style..Casual
Cuisine...North Indian-Seafood
Recommended for................................Regular neighbourhood

CAFÉ BRITANNIA

Recommended by
Irfan Pabaney

Wakefield House
11 Sprott Road
Ballard Estate
Fort
Mumbai
Maharashtra 400 038

Opening hours...6 days for lunch
Reservation policy...No
Credit cards..Not accepted
Price range...Affordable
Style..Casual
Cuisine..Northwest Indian
Recommended for................................Regular neighbourhood

JIMMY BOY

Recommended by
Vicky Ratnani

Vikas Building,
11 Bank Street
Near Horniman Circle
Fort
Mumbai
Maharashtra 400 023
+91 2222700880

Opening hours................................7 days for lunch and dinner
Reservation policy...Yes
Credit cards..Accepted
Price range...Affordable
Style..Casual
Cuisine..Northwest Indian
Recommended for..Local favourite

**'You must try *akuri* on toast, *salli per idu* and
dhansak.'—Vicky Ratnani**

SHREE THAKKER BHOJANALAY

Recommended by
Rahul Akerkar,
Irfan Pabaney

31 Dadyseth Agiary Marg
Kalbadevi
Mumbai MH 400 002

Opening hours................................7 days for lunch and dinner
Reservation policy...No
Credit cards..Not accepted
Price range..Budget
Style..Casual
Cuisine..Western Indian
Recommended for..Local favourite

**'Here they serve home-cooked, vegetarian, *Gujarati*
food in a *thali* format. The menu changes every day,
and it's all you can eat for about the equivalent of
under £3 ($5)!'—Rahul Akerkar**

NEEL

Recommended by
Irfan Pabaney

Mahalaxmi Racecourse
Keshva Rao Khadye Lane
Mahalaxmi
Mumbai
Maharashtra 400 034
+91 2261577777
www.thetote.in

Opening hours................................7 days for lunch and dinner
Reservation policy...Yes
Credit cards..Accepted
Price range...Expensive
Style...Formal
Cuisine...Modern North Indian
Recommended for...High end

DAKSHINAYAN

Recommended by
Irfan Pabaney

183 Teen Batti Road
Walkeshwar
Malabar Hill
Mumbai
Maharashtra 400 006

Opening hours..................7 days for lunch and dinner
Reservation policy...No
Credit cards...Not accepted
Price range...Budget
Style...Casual
Cuisine...South Indian
Recommended for...Bargain

CELINI

Recommended by
Vicky Ratnani

Grand Hyatt Hotel
Off Western Express Highway
Santacruz East
Mumbai
Maharashtra 400 055
+91 2266761149
www.mumbai.grand.hyatt.com

Opening hours..................7 days for lunch and dinner
Reservation policy...Yes
Reservation email.....................celini.ghmumbai@hyatt.com
Credit cards..Accepted
Price range..Expensive
Style...Smart casual
Cuisine..Italian
Recommended for......................................Wish I'd opened

SARDAR REFRESHMENT

Recommended by
Vicky Ratnani

166a Tardeo Road Junction
Tardeo
Mumbai
Maharashtra 400 034

Opening hours..............7 days for breakfast, lunch and dinner
Reservation policy...No
Credit cards...Not accepted
Price range...Budget
Style...Casual
Cuisine.......................................Indian Street food
Recommended for...Bargain

'Try the *pao bhaji*.'—Vicky Ratnani

GAJALEE

Recommended by
Vicky Ratnani

Kadamgiri Complex
Hanuman Road
Vile Parle East
Mumbai
Maharashtra 400 057
+91 2226114093
www.gajalee.com

Opening hours..................7 days for lunch and dinner
Reservation policy...Yes
Credit cards..Accepted
Price range..Affordable
Style...Casual
Cuisine..Seafood
Recommended for...................Regular neighbourhood

'Does a mean bombil fry.'—Vicky Ratnani

ITHAA UNDERSEA RESTAURANT

Recommended by
Dharshan Munidasa

Conrad Hotel
Rangali Island
Maldives 2034
+960 9606680629
www.conradhotels3.hilton.com

Opening hours..................7 days for lunch and dinner
Reservation policy...Yes
Reservation email........Conrad_Maldives@conradhotels.com
Credit cards..Accepted
Price range..Expensive
Style...Smart casual
Cuisine...Maldivian-European
Recommended for......................................Wish I'd opened

'It's underwater and the menu swims around
you!'—Dharshan Munidasa

FRESH IN THE GARDEN

Recommended by
Thomas Rode Anderson

Soneva Fushi Resort
Kunfunadhoo Island
Baa Atoll
Maldives
+960 6600304
www.sixsenses.com

Opening hours..................6 days for lunch and dinner
Reservation policy...Yes
Reservation email................reservations-fushi@soneva.com
Credit cards..Accepted
Price range..Expensive
Style...Smart casual
Cuisine..Maldivian
Recommended for.................................Worth the travel

'REALLY SUBMERSES YOU IN HONG KONG LIFE: TONS OF PEOPLE, NOISE... AND A BIG CRAZY FISH TANK FULL OF FRESH FISH, CRABS AND LOBSTERS.'
NEIL ANTHONY TOMES P89

'THE BEST BEEF IS GRILLED ON LITTLE INDIVIDUAL CHARCOAL STOVES.'
JEREME LEUNG P92

The finest dim sum in town.
ESTHER SHAM P85

CHINA, MACAU, HONG KONG, TAIWAN & KOREA

'A freshly slaughtered cow is served at every meal.'
JEREME LEUNG P79

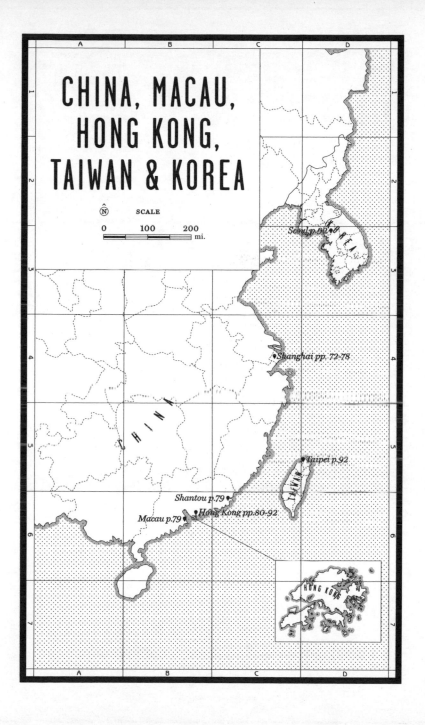

CHINA, MACAU, HONG KONG, TAIWAN & KOREA

N

SCALE

0   100   200
mi.

Seoul p.92

Shanghai pp. 72-78

CHINA

Taipei p.92

TAIWAN

Shantou p.79
Hong Kong pp.80-92
Macau p.79

KOREA

HONG KONG

'The best Hong Kong-style dim sum in town.'
DAVID LARIS P77

'A BRILLIANT TECHNOLOGICAL RESTAURANT WITH A SECRET LOCATION.'
WILLY TRULLAS MOREN P74

SHANGHAI

'A classic example of Shanghainese cuisine.'
JEREME LEUNG P78

'The place is filled with smoke, booze and cheese, perfect after a long week.'
MICHAEL WILSON P76

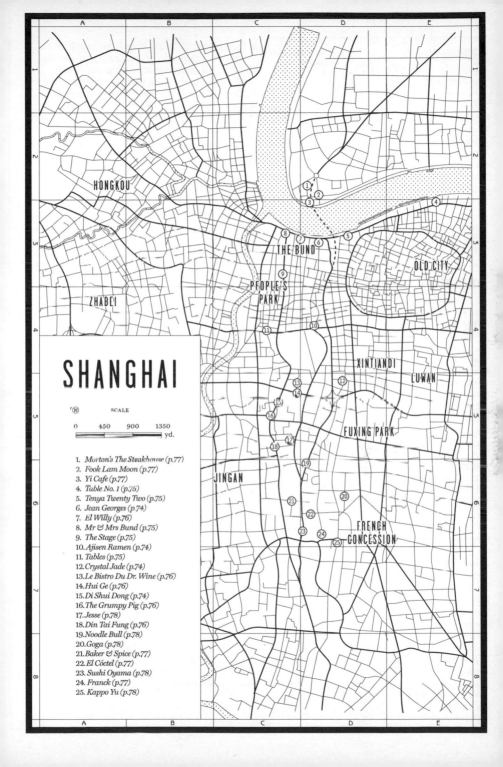

SHANGHAI

HONGKOU

ZHABEI

THE BUND

PEOPLE'S PARK

OLD CITY

XINTIANDI

LUWAN

FUXING PARK

JINGAN

FRENCH CONCESSION

ULTRAVIOLET

Shanghai
+86 2161425198
www.uvbypp.cc

Opening hours	5 days for dinner
Reservation policy	Yes
Reservation email	thehost@uvbypp.cc
Credit cards	Accepted
Price range	Expensive
Style	Smart casual
Cuisine	Modern International
Recommended for	Worth the travel

'A brilliant ten-seat technological restaurant created
by Paul Pairet with a secret location.'
—Willy Trullas Moren

AJISEN RAMEN

318 Xizang Zhong Lu
Huangpu
Shanghai
www.ajisen.com.cn

Opening hours	7 days for breakfast, lunch and dinner
Reservation policy	No
Credit cards	Accepted
Price range	Budget
Style	Casual
Cuisine	Japanese
Recommended for	Bargain

CRYSTAL JADE

South Block Plaza
2f 123 Xingye Lu
Huangpu
Shanghai
+86 2163858752
www.crystaljade.com

Opening hours	7 days for lunch and dinner
Reservation policy	Yes
Credit cards	Accepted
Price range	Affordable
Style	Casual
Cuisine	Cantonese
Recommended for	Local favourite

Crystal Jade is one of the most famous dim sum
restaurants in Shanghai – there are now two
branches in the city. They specialize in great Cantonese and Shanghainese dumplings, but also do

brilliant soups: the double-boiled chicken and the *dan
dan mien* (spicy peanut) are particularly renowned.
Chinese wine can be variable, but bottles of vodka
are relatively cheap and a great match for the handmade noodles here. Crystal Jade is popular among
affluent Chinese, but since there are pictures on the
menu it's great for tourists too. Don't miss the sweet
crispy eel.

DI SHUI DONG

2f 56 Maoming Nan Lu
Huangpu
Shanghai
+86 2162532689

Opening hours	7 days for lunch and dinner
Reservation policy	Yes
Credit cards	Not accepted
Price range	Budget
Style	Casual
Cuisine	Hunanese
Recommended for	Regular neighbourhood

JEAN GEORGES

4f 3 Zhongshan Dong Yi Lu
Huangpu
Shanghai
+86 2163217733
www.jean-georges.com

Opening hours	7 days for brunch and dinner
Reservation policy	Yes
Reservation email	JGreservation@on-the-bund.com
Credit cards	Accepted
Price range	Expensive
Style	Smart casual
Cuisine	French-Asian
Recommended for	Breakfast

This Asian outpost of the jet-setting New York-based
Jean-Georges Vongerichten, opened in 2004, remains one of the most beautiful-looking dining rooms
on the planet. Designed by acclaimed American
architect Michael Grave, it occupies the entire fourth
floor of the redeveloped 1916 Beaux-Arts building
that's now known as 'Three on the Bund'. Its lavish
and sultry-lit interior, inspired by the grandeur of old
Shanghai, has as its backdrop a view across the
Huangpu River to Pudong and the wonders of new
Shanghai. The Asian accented, modern French menu
gives way to Eggs Benedict, French toast and pastries come their weekend brunch.

MR & MRS BUND

6f 18 Zhongshan Dong Yi Lu
Huangpu
Shanghai
+86 2163239898
www.mmbund.com

Recommended by
David Laris, Bradley Turley

Opening hours............5 days for lunch and 7 days for dinner
Reservation policy..Yes
Credit cards...Accepted
Price range...Affordable
Style...Smart casual
Cuisine..French
Recommended for...Late night

'I love the approach to great French-inspired bistro food executed so well and with a simplicity only someone who knows what they are doing can do well – with all the fearless, fun elements that are thrown in.'—David Laris

THE STAGE

Westin Bund Center
88 Henan Zhong Lu
Huangpu
Shanghai
+86 2163350577
www.starwoodhotels.com/westin

Recommended by
Jereme Leung

Opening hours............7 days for breakfast, lunch and dinner
Reservation policy...Yes
Credit cards...Accepted
Price range...Affordable
Style...Casual
Cuisine..International
Recommended for...Breakfast

TABLE NO. 1

Waterhouse Hotel
1-3 Maojiayuan Lu
Huangpu
Shanghai
+86 2160802918
www.tableno-1.com

Recommended by
Paul Pairet

Opening hours....................7 days for lunch and dinner
Reservation policy...Yes
Credit cards...Accepted
Price range...Affordable
Style...Smart casual
Cuisine...Modern European
Recommended for.......................Regular neighbourhood

TABLES

Portman Ritz Carlton
1376 Nanjing Xi Lu
Hunagpu
Shanghai
+86 2162798888
www.ritzcarlton.com

Recommended by
Jereme Leung

Opening hours............7 days for breakfast, lunch and dinner
Reservation policy..Yes
Credit cards...Accepted
Price range...Expensive
Style...Smart casual
Cuisine..International
Recommended for...Breakfast

'For their champagne brunch.'—Jereme Leung

TENYA TWENTY TWO

3f 22 Zhongshan Dong Er Lu
Huangpu
Shanghai
+86 2153025317

Recommended by
Willy Trullas Moreno

Opening hours...............................6 days for dinner
Reservation policy..Yes
Credit cards...Accepted
Price range...Affordable
Style...Smart casual
Cuisine..Japanese
Recommended for...Late night

'High-quality sushi bar where a chef from Hokkaido makes sushi until 2.00 a.m.'—Willy Trullas Moreno

EL WILLY

Recommended by
Bradley Turley

5f 22 Shongshan Dong Er Lu
Huangpu
Shanghai
+86 2154045757
www.el-willy.com

Opening hours	6 days for lunch and dinner
Reservation policy	Yes
Credit cards	Accepted
Price range	Affordable
Style	Casual
Cuisine	Spanish
Recommended for	Regular neighbourhood

LE BISTRO DU DR. WINE

Recommended by
Michael Wilson

177 Fumin Lu
Jingan
Shanghai
+86 2154035717

Opening hours	7 days for dinner
Reservation policy	Yes
Credit cards	Accepted
Price range	Affordable
Style	Smart casual
Cuisine	Bar-Bistro
Recommended for	Late night

'The place is filled with smoke, booze and cheese – perfect after a long week.'—Michael Wilson

THE GRUMPY PIG

Recommended by
Bradley Turley

65-4 Maoming Bei Lu
Jingan
Shanghai

Opening hours	7 days for lunch and dinner
Reservation policy	No
Credit cards	Accepted
Price range	Budget
Style	Casual
Cuisine	Southeast Asian
Recommended for	Worth the travel

HUI GE

Recommended by
Jereme Leung

795 Julu Lu
Jingan
Shanghai
+86 2154038811

Opening hours	7 days for lunch and dinner
Reservation policy	Yes
Credit cards	Accepted
Price range	Affordable
Style	Smart casual
Cuisine	Hot pot
Recommended for	Late night

'They specialize in hot pot which comes with a personal waiter to serve every table. It also has one of the best exclusive wine lists in the city.'
—Jereme Leung

DIN TAI FUNG

Recommended by
Willy Trullas Moreno

GF Shanghai Centre
No. 1376 Nanjing Xi Lu
Jingan
Shanghai
www.dintaifung.com.tw

Opening hours	7 days for breakfast, lunch and dinner
Reservation policy	No
Credit cards	Accepted
Price range	Budget
Style	Casual
Cuisine	Taiwanese
Recommended for	Bargain

'Ding Tai Fung is a Taiwanese Dim Sum chain that's excellent value for money.'—Willy Trullas Moreno

FOOK LAM MOON

Recommended by
David Laris

Shangri-La Hotel
33 Fu Cheng Lu
Pudong
Shanghai
+86 2158773786
www.fooklammoon-grp.com

Opening hours.................................7 days for lunch and dinner
Reservation policy..Yes
Credit cards...Accepted
Price range..Expensive
Style...Smart casual
Cuisine...Cantonese
Recommended for..Breakfast

'The best Hong Kong-style dim sum in town.'
—David Laris

MORTON'S THE STEAKHOUSE

Recommended by
David Laris

8 Shi Ji Da Dao
Pudong
Shanghai
+86 2160758888
www.mortons.com/shanghai

Opening hours.................................7 days for lunch and dinner
Reservation policy..Yes
Credit cards...Accepted
Price range..Expensive
Style...Smart casual
Cuisine...Steakhouse
Recommended for...High end

'A huge, top of the line steak from Morton's – old
school is still cool school!'—David Laris

YI CAFE

Recommended by
Jereme Leung

Shangri-La Hotel
33 Fu Cheng Lu
Pudong
Shanghai
+86 2158775372
www.shangri-la.com

Opening hours..............7 days for breakfast, lunch and dinner
Reservation policy..Yes
Credit cards...Accepted
Price range...Affordable
Style...Casual
Cuisine..International
Recommended for..Breakfast

BAKER & SPICE

Recommended by
Michael Wilson

195 Anfu Lu
Xuhui
Shanghai
www.bakerandspice.com.cn

Opening hours..............7 days for breakfast, lunch and dinner
Reservation policy...No
Credit cards...Accepted
Price range..Budget
Style...Casual
Cuisine...Bakery-Café
Recommended for..Breakfast

EL CÓCTEL

Recommended by
David Laris

47 Yongfu Lu
Xuhui
Shanghai
+86 2164336511
www.el-coctel.com

Opening hours...7 days for dinner
Reservation policy..Yes
Credit cards...Accepted
Price range...Affordable
Style...Smart casual
Cuisine...Tapas
Recommended for...Late night

FRANCK

Recommended by
Willy Trullas Moreno, Paul
Pairet

376 Wukang Lu
Xuhui
Shanghai
+86 2164376465
www.franck.com.cn

Opening hours..............2 days for lunch and 6 days for dinner
Reservation policy..Yes
Reservation email.................................resa@franck.com.cn
Credit cards...Accepted
Price range...Affordable
Style...Smart casual
Cuisine..French
Recommended for.................................Regular neighbourhood

'The chef is Japanese and the owner is French,
it is a beautiful environment and they have
a great product.'—Willy Trullas Moreno

GOGA

Recommended by
Jereme Leung, Willy
Trullas Moreno

1 Yueyang Lu
 Xuhui
Shanghai
+86 2164319700

Opening hours	7 days for dinner
Reservation policy	Yes
Credit cards	Not accepted
Price range	Affordable
Style	Casual
Cuisine	American-Asian
Recommended for	Regular neighbourhood

'Chef Brad Turley serves great California-style
cooking.'—Willy Trullas Moreno

KAPPO YU

Recommended by
David Laris

33 Wuxing Lu
Xuhui
Shanghai
+86 2164667855

Opening hours	6 days for dinner
Reservation policy	Yes
Credit cards	Accepted
Price range	Expensive
Style	Smart casual
Cuisine	Japanese
Recommended for	Regular neighbourhood

'A great little Japanese place where the chef is always
creative using great produce. It's a place I go to sit
back and feel good.'—David Laris

JESSE

Recommended by
Jereme Leung

41 Tianping Lu
Xuhui
Shanghai
+86 2162829260
www.xinjishi.com

Opening hours	7 days for lunch and dinner
Reservation policy	Yes
Credit cards	Accepted
Price range	Affordable
Style	Casual
Cuisine	Shanghaiese
Recommended for	Local favourite

'Many restaurants in China produce little gems −
unique ingredients or regional cooking styles that are
special to the region. Old Jesse is a classic example
of Shanghainese cuisine.'—Jereme Leung

NOODLE BULL

Recommended by
David Laris

3b 291 Fumin Lu
Xuhui
Shanghai

Opening hours	7 days for lunch and dinner
Reservation policy	No
Credit cards	Not accepted
Price range	Budget
Style	Smart casual
Cuisine	Taiwanese
Recommended for	Bargain

'Amazing Taiwan-style beef noodles.'—David Laris

SUSHI OYAMA

Recommended by
Willy Trullas Moreno

2f 20 Donghu Lu
Xuhui
Shanghai
+86 2154047705

Opening hours	6 days for dinner
Reservation policy	Yes
Credit cards	Accepted
Price range	Expensive
Style	Smart casual
Cuisine	Japanese
Recommended for	High end

'I am a big fan of Sushi Oyama. Chef and owner Takeo
Oyama prepares sushi for fifteen guests a night with
premium fish from Nagasaki market.'
—Willy Trullas Moreno

DA DONG ROAST DUCK

Recommended by
David Laris, Man-Sing
Lee, Cristiano Rienzner

Building 3
Tuanjiehu Beikou
Beijing 100007
+86 65822892

Opening hours	7 days for lunch and dinner
Reservation policy	Yes
Credit cards	Accepted
Price range	Affordable
Style	Casual
Cuisine	Modern Chinese
Recommended for	Worth the travel

'Go for its artistic take on Chinese Cuisine.'
—Man-Sing Lee

Should you fancy a duck in the city where the Peking variety gained its name – the rebranding as Beijing duck is not sticking, even in China – Da Dong is the place. The Jinbao branch of chef Dong Zhengxiang's eponymous brand follows the success of the Tuanjiehu original and its Dongsishitiao sequel. Locals argue over which produces the best roast duck, made with a lean bird bred for its lower fat content. Moving far beyond fowl, haute European influences are often detectable in the vast modern Chinese menu. If it's only duck you want, call ahead because they're cooked to order.

HAI JI

Recommended by
Jereme Leung

GF Ping Dong Building 6
Huang Gang Lu
Jin Ping
Shantou Guangdong

Opening hours	7 days for lunch and dinner
Reservation policy	No
Credit cards	Not accepted
Price range	Budget
Style	Casual
Cuisine	Hainanese
Recommended for	Worth the travel

'A freshly slaughtered cow is served at every meal.'
—Jereme Leung

ROBUCHON AU DÔME

Recommended by
Umberto Bombana, Alfonso
& Ernesto Iaccarino

Grand Lisboa Hotel
2-4 Avenida de Lisboa
Macau
+852 88037878
www.grandlisboa.com

Opening hours	7 days for lunch and dinner
Reservation policy	Yes
Reservation email	robuchonaudome@grandlisboa.com
Credit cards	Accepted
Price range	Expensive
Style	Formal
Cuisine	French
Recommended for	Wish I'd opened

'NO ONE DOES CONGEE AND NOODLES LIKE HONG KONG AND THIS IS THE BEST PLACE IN MY OPINION.'
DAVID LARIS P82

'The classic Hong Kong mix of surly waiters that you put up with in exchange for the great food!'
LORI GRANITO P87

HONG KONG

'Very good char sui – luscious, deep-red, sweet and savoury.'
NEIL ANTHONY TOMES P84

'THE DIM SUM, CANTONESE CUISINE AND THE ATMOSPHERE OF OLD HONG KONG TEA HOUSE CULTURE... YOU CAN'T FIND THIS ANYWHERE ELSE IN THE WORLD, ONLY IN HONG KONG.'
TIM LAI P85

'Represents the good old days of Cantonese cooking.'
RICHARD EKKEBUS P85

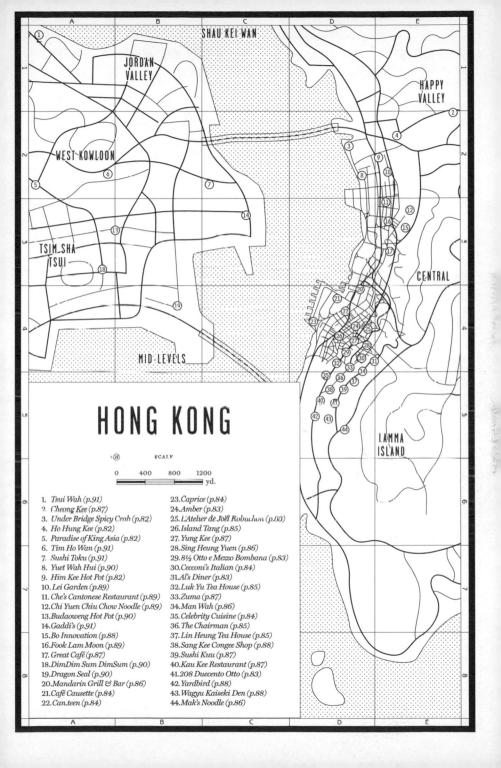

HONG KONG

SCALE

0   400   800   1200
yd.

HIM KEE HOT POT

Recommended by
Uwe Opocensky

Workingfield Commercial Building
408-412 Jaffe Road
Causeway Bay
Hong Kong Island
+852 28386116

Opening hours	7 days for lunch and dinner
Reservation policy	Yes
Credit cards	Accepted
Price range	Affordable
Style	Casual
Cuisine	Hot pot
Recommended for	Late night

Despite the steamy summers, Hong Kong hot pot season is all year round – the city's aficionados prefer to crank up the air con rather than forgo their favourite ritual. So don't expect just to walk straight in to Him Kee Hot Pot, one of the most popular temples to the hallowed dish. Book in advance, as Him Kee's reputation for fresh ingredients in clean-cut surroundings makes for a packed dining room, right through to 2.00 a.m. The Szechuan spiced broth makes a lively starting point, and while seafood, dumplings and meatballs are solid choices for dipping, the goose giblets will reward the more adventurous. A rainbow of condiments and complementary sweet treats are other pluses that keep locals loyal.

HO HUNG KEE

Recommended by
David Laris

2 Sharp Street East
Causeway Bay
Hong Kong Island

Opening hours	7 days for lunch and dinner
Reservation policy	No
Credit cards	Not accepted
Price range	Budget
Style	Casual
Cuisine	Chinese
Recommended for	Local favourite

'I have to eat here one last time before I die. No one does congee and noodles like Hong Kong, and this is the best place in my opinion.'—David Laris

PARADISE OF KING ASIA

Recommended by
Tim Lai

610K San Building
31-35 Tang Lung Street
Causeway Bay
Hong Kong Island
+852 25730552

Opening hours	7 days for dinner
Reservation policy	Yes
Credit cards	Accepted but not AMEX and Diners
Price range	Budget
Style	Casual
Cuisine	Asian
Recommended for	Regular neighbourhood

'All my family love it!'—Tim Lai

UNDER BRIDGE SPICY CRAB

Recommended by
Richard Ekkebus

414-424 Jaffe Road
Causeway Bay
Hong Kong Island
+852 28346268
www.underspicycrab.com

Opening hours	7 days for lunch and dinner
Reservation policy	Yes
Credit cards	Accepted but not AMEX and Diners
Price range	Affordable
Style	Casual
Cuisine	Cantonese-Seafood
Recommended for	Late night

'I go here with colleagues after I've had a beer or two. It's open until 6.00 a.m. and the Typhoon Shelter Crab is the best in Hong Kong.'— Richard Ekkebus

From a humble stall under the Jaffe Road bypass in the late 1980s, Wong Ching Tuen has grown Under Bridge Spicy Crab into a booming business. This, the original branch on the Jaffe Road, is favoured by those in the know for its after-hours 'ambience' over those nearby on the Lockhart Road. They come, as the name would suggest, for the crab. It's deep-fried and then tossed in a generous helping of a secret chilli mix, with garlic, black beans and spring onion (scallion). To go with your crab, the clams in black bean sauce and the deep-fried sliverfish both come highly recommended.

208 DUECENTO OTTO

Recommended by
Lori Granito

208 Hollywood Road
Central
Hong Kong Island
+852 25490208
www.208.com.hk

Opening hours	7 days for lunch and dinner
Reservation policy	Yes
Credit cards	Accepted
Price range	Affordable
Style	Smart casual
Cuisine	Italian
Recommended for	Regular neighbourhood

8½ OTTO E MEZZO BOMBANA

Recommended by
Pierre Gagnaire, Neil
Anthony Tomes

Shop 202, Landmark Alexandra
18 Chater Road
Central
Hong Kong Island
+852 25378859
www.ottoemezzobombana.com

Opening hours	6 days for lunch and dinner
Reservation policy	Yes
Credit cards	Accepted
Price range	Expensive
Style	Smart casual
Cuisine	Modern Italian
Recommended for	High end

AL'S DINER

Recommended by
Lori Granito

27-39 D'Aguilar Street
Lan Kwai Fong
Central
Hong Kong Island
+852 25218714

Opening hours	7 days for lunch and dinner
Reservation policy	Yes
Credit cards	Accepted
Price range	Affordable
Style	Casual
Cuisine	American
Recommended for	Late night

'Juicy burger and fries.'—Lori Granito

AMBER

Recommended by
Patrick Goubier, Julius
Jaspers, Tim Raue

Landmark Oriental Hotel
15 Queen's Road
Central
Hong Kong
+852 21320066
www.amberhongkong.com

Opening hours	7 days for breakfast, lunch and dinner
Reservation policy	Yes
Reservation email	lmhkg-amber@mohg.com
Credit cards	Accepted
Price range	Expensive
Style	Smart casual
Cuisine	French-Asian
Recommended for	Worth the travel

' I like the creativity of Richard Ekkebus.'
—Patrick Goubier

A chandelier made up of thousands of bronze rods covers almost the entire ceiling at this far from subtle destination restaurant at the Landmark Oriental. Here, Dutch-born and French-trained chef Richard Ekkebus fights for the attention of the diner's eye with his cooking, which celebrates Hong Kong's location as a crossroads between East and West. His list of ingredients is better travelled than Michael Palin's passport: produce is plucked from as far afield as France, Japan and Australia, combined with home-grown Hong Kong ingredients and prepared using classical French techniques. The outcome: fine French food with a twist.

L'ATELIER DE JOËL ROBUCHON

Recommended by
Patrick Goubier

Shop 401, 4/F. The Landmark
15 Queen's Road
Central
Hong Kong Island
+852 21669000
www.robuchon.hk

Opening hours	7 days for lunch and dinner
Reservation policy	Yes
Credit cards	Accepted
Price range	Expensive
Style	Smart casual
Cuisine	French
Recommended for	Regular neighbourhood

CAFÉ CAUSETTE

Recommended by
Umberto Bombana

Mandarin Oriental Hotel
5 Connaught Road
Central
Hong Kong Island
+852 28254005
www.mandarinoriental.com/hongkong

Opening hours..............7 days for breakfast, lunch and dinner
Reservation policy...Yes
Reservation email...............................mohkg-cafe@mohg.com
Credit cards..Accepted
Price range...Affordable
Style...Smart casual
Cuisine...International
Recommended for...Breakfast

CAN.TEEN

Recommended by
Neil Anthony Tomes

Prince's Building
10 Chater Road
Central
Hong Kong Island
+852 25246792
www.maxims.com

Opening hours..........7 days for brunch and 5 days for dinner
Reservation policy..No
Credit cards..Accepted
Price range...Budget
Style...Casual
Cuisine...Asian
Recommended for..............................Regular neighbourhood

'Great value, very good *char siu* – luscious, deep-red,
sweet and savoury, honey, biscuity lengths of juicy pork
cooked in what can only be described as a furnace.'
—Neil Anthony Tomes

CAPRICE

Recommended by
Patrick Goubier, Lori Granito

Four Seasons Hotel
8 Finance Street
Central
Hong Kong Island
+852 31968860
www.fourseasons.com/hongkong

Opening hours.................................7 days for lunch and dinner
Reservation policy...Yes
Credit cards..Accepted
Price range..Expensive
Style...Smart casual
Cuisine..Modern French
Recommended for...High end

'The ultimate indulgence.'—Lori Granito

CECCONI'S ITALIAN

Recommended by
Patrick Goubier

43 Elgin Street
Central
Hong Kong Island
+852 21475500
www.diningconcepts.com.hk/cecconis

Opening hours.................................7 days for lunch and dinner
Reservation policy...Yes
Credit cards..Accepted
Price range...Affordable
Style...Smart casual
Cuisine..Modern Italian
Recommended for..............................Regular neighbourhood

CELEBRITY CUISINE

Recommended by
Umberto Bombana, Seiji
Yamamoto

Lan Kwai Fong Hotel
3 Kau U Fong
Central
Hong Kong Island
+852 36500066
www.lankwaifonghotel.com.hk

Opening hours.................................7 days for lunch and dinner
Reservation policy...Yes
Credit cards.......................Accepted but not AMEX and Diners
Price range...Affordable
Style...Smart casual
Cuisine...Cantonese
Recommended for..Worth the travel

THE CHAIRMAN

Kau U Fong No. 18
Central
Hong Kong Island
+852 25552202
www.thechairmangroup.com

Opening hours	7 days for lunch and dinner
Reservation policy	Yes
Reservation email	reservations@thechairmangroup.com
Credit cards	Accepted
Price range	Affordable
Style	Casual
Cuisine	Modern Cantonese
Recommended for	Worth the travel

'Represents the good old days of Cantonese cooking, when everything was made with fresh and honest ingredients.'—Richard Ekkebus

The Chairman sits in the newly fashionable section of the city that Hong Kong's estate agents (real estate brokers) have decided to christen Noho, as in north of Hollywood Road. Steering away from the traditional and increasingly controversial Cantonese culinary bling that is shark's fin (endangered) and abalone (unsustainable), it has still managed to set out its stall as a destination for quality modern Cantonese cooking. From free-range chicken raised in the New Territories to steamed flower crab with chicken oil and Chinese rice wine, the emphasis here is on the quality of the ingredients, keeping things light and presenting them simply.

ISLAND TANG

Shop 222, The Galleria
9 Queen's Road
Central
Hong Kong Island
+852 25268798
www.islandtang.com

Opening hours	7 days for lunch and dinner
Reservation policy	Yes
Credit cards	Accepted
Price range	Affordable
Style	Smart casual
Cuisine	Cantonese
Recommended for	Local favourite

'For the finest Dim Sum in town.'—Esther Sham

The cigar-loving, jet-setting entrepreneur Sir David Tang was so busy establishing spin-offs from his decadent, retro-chic China Club around the world that it was not until 2008 that he finally got around to opening a Hong Kong follow-up to his original members-only outpost, sat at the top of the Old Bank of China building in 1991. Island Tang is styled to evoke the glamour of 1940s Hong Kong, whereas the China Club was always more about Shanghai in the 1930s. Unlike its predecessor, Island Tang's doors are, in theory, open to anyone, although prices for its polished Cantonese staples are anything but plebeian.

LIN HEUNG TEA HOUSE

160-164 Wellington Street
Central
Hong Kong Island
+852 25444556

Opening hours	7 days for breakfast, lunch and dinner
Reservation policy	No
Credit cards	Accepted but not AMEX and Diners
Price range	Budget
Style	Casual
Cuisine	Cantonese
Recommended for	Local favourite

'This is one of the oldest (open in 1926) Cantonese style teahouses in Hong Kong. The dim sum, the old style Cantonese cuisine and the atmosphere of the Hong Kong teahouse you can't find anywhere else in the world.'—Tim Lai

LUK YU TEA HOUSE

24 Stanley Street
Central
Hong Kong Island
+852 25235464

Opening hours	7 days for breakfast until late
Reservation policy	No
Credit cards	Accepted
Price range	Affordable
Style	Casual
Cuisine	Cantonese
Recommended for	Local favourite

'One of the best teahouses in Hong Kong, prepare yourself for tasty and traditionally prepared dim sum.'—Richard Ekkebus

MAK'S NOODLE

Recommended by
Umberto Bombana

77 Wellington Street
Central
Hong Kong Island
+852 28543810

Opening hours	7 days for lunch and dinner
Reservation policy	No
Credit cards	Not accepted
Price range	Budget
Style	Casual
Cuisine	Cantonese
Recommended for	Bargain

There is much local speculation among Hong Kongers as to what sets Mak's wonton noodles apart, but there's something about this particular holy trinity of slow-cooked umami broth – infused with dried fish and pork bones – springy noodles and plump prawn (shrimp)-packed wonton (popped into the mouth whole) that just keeps them coming back. And back. The Wellington Street original – now part of a Mak's mini-chain – is in the hands of the family's third generation, but don't expect an open-armed welcome; hard wooden seating, stark lighting and small portions make lingering almost impossible. Go outside the lunchtime rush unless you want to bolt down your bowl full along with hoards of local businessmen.

MANDARIN GRILL & BAR

Recommended by
Man-Sing Lee, Esther Sham

Mandarin Oriental Hotel
5 Connaught Road
Central
Hong Kong Island
+852 28254004
www.mandarinoriental.com/hongkong

Opening hours	5 days for brunch and 7 days for dinner
Reservation policy	Yes
Reservation email	mohkg-grill@mohg.com
Credit cards	Accepted
Price range	Expensive
Style	Smart casual
Cuisine	Modern French
Recommended for	High end

'Great high quality organic ingredients and seasonally inspired and artistic delicacies, such as wok-fried dishes, noodles and congee.'—Man-Sing Lee

MAN WAH

Recommended by
Richard Ekkebus

Mandarin Oriental Hotel
5 Connaught Road
Central
Hong Kong Island
+852 28254003
www.mandarinoriental.com/hongkong

Opening hours	7 days for lunch and dinner
Reservation policy	Yes
Reservation email	mohkg-manwah@mohg.com
Credit cards	Accepted
Price range	Expensive
Style	Smart casual
Cuisine	Modern Cantonese
Recommended for	High end

'This is Hong Kong's signature Cantonese restaurant and often referred to as Hong Kong's most beautiful dining spaces due to its imperial splendor and panoramic views of Victoria Harbour and the cityscape. The menu by Chef Man-Sing Lee's contains local favourites alongside seasonal specialties with touches of modern flair. No doubt some of the very best Peking duck in town. They also do have some excellent steamed seafood dishes and I truly enjoy their great hot and sour seafood soup.'—Richard Ekkebus

SING HEUNG YUEN

Recommended by
Tim Lai

2 Mei Lun Street
Central
Hong Kong Island
+852 25448368

Opening hours	6 days for breakfast and lunch
Reservation policy	No
Credit cards	Not accepted
Price range	Budget
Style	Casual
Cuisine	Cantonese
Recommended for	Bargain

'Congee and noodles for under HK$40 (£3, $5).'—Tim Lai

SUSHI KUU

1st Floor, Wellington Place
2-8 Wellington Street
Central
Hong Kong Island
+852 29710180

Opening hours	7 days for lunch and dinner
Reservation policy	Yes
Credit cards	Accepted
Price range	Affordable
Style	Casual
Cuisine	Japanese
Recommended for	High end

'Go for its fresh sashimi.'—Man-Sing Lee

YUNG KEE

32 Wellington Street
Central
Hong Kong Island
+852 25221624
www.yungkee.com.hk

Opening hours	7 days for lunch and dinner
Reservation policy	Yes
Credit cards	Accepted
Price range	Affordable
Style	Smart casual
Cuisine	Beijng Duck
Recommended for	Local favourite

'The classic Hong Kong mix of surly waiters that
you put up with in exchange for the great food.'
—Lori Granito

ZUMA

Levels 5 & 6, The Landmark
15 Queen's Road
Central
Hong Kong Island
+852 36576388
www.zumarestaurant.com

Opening hours	7 days for lunch and dinner
Reservation policy	Yes
Credit cards	Accepted
Price range	Expensive
Style	Smart casual
Cuisine	Modern Japanese
Recommended for	Wish I'd opened

CHEONG KEE

Stalls 1 & 5, 2nd Floor
2 Yuk Sau Street
Happy Valley
Hong Kong Island

Opening hours	7 days for breakfast, lunch and dinner
Reservation policy	No
Credit cards	Not accepted
Price range	Budget
Style	Casual
Cuisine	Street food
Recommended for	Breakfast

'Friendly servers and great preserved vegetables, egg
rice vermicelli and 5-cm (2-inch) thick toast.'
—Esther Sham

GREAT CAFÉ

Great Food Hall
2 Pacific Place
Queensway
Hong Kong Island
www.greatfoodhall.com

Opening hours	7 days from breakfast until late
Reservation policy	No
Credit cards	Accepted
Price range	Budget
Style	Casual
Cuisine	International
Recommended for	Worth the travel

'A little café that does real, honest, good food
at reasonable prices.'—Neil Anthony Tomes

KAU KEE RESTAURANT

21 Gough Street
Sheung Wan
Hong Kong Island
+852 28150123

Opening hours	6 days for lunch and dinner
Reservation policy	No
Credit cards	Not accepted
Price range	Budget
Style	Casual
Cuisine	Cantonese
Recommended for	Bargain

SANG KEE CONGEE SHOP

Recommended by
Richard Ekkebus, Tim Lai

26 Hillier Street
Sheung Wan
Hong Kong Island
+852 25411099

Opening hours	6 days for breakfast, lunch and dinner
Reservation policy	No
Credit cards	Not accepted
Price range	Budget
Style	Casual
Cuisine	Congee
Recommended for	Breakfast

'In true Hong Kong style, if you want to go for a great, authentic congee breakfast, here's where you'll find one of the very best.'—Richard Ekkebus

Run by the same family for over forty years, this specialist in Sheung Wan is worth seeking out for the viscous rice porridge that the locals call breakfast. There's no sign in English, so have the name written down in Chinese, and remember you're here for the congee not the interior design. The choice of ingredients changes according to the seasons, as does the consistency of the congee – the colder the weather, the thicker it gets. You're spoiled for choice if you're after pig – tripe, liver, kidney or meatballs – or fish – head, tail, belly or bones. Other choices include various green vegetables, squid and whole fresh crab.

WAGYU KAISEKI DEN

Recommended by
Umberto Bombana,
Lori Granito

Upper Ground Floor
263 Hollywood Road
Sheung Wan
Hong Kong Island
+852 28512820
www.wagyukaisekiden.com.hk

Opening hours	6 days for dinner
Reservation policy	Yes
Credit cards	Accepted
Price range	Expensive
Style	Smart casual
Cuisine	Modern Japanese
Recommended for	Wish I'd opened

'It's a classic example of great value for money. It's nice enough for a business lunch, but casual enough to go in shorts as well. The food is always consistent and the service is good.'—Lori Granito

YARDBIRD

Recommended by
Richard Ekkebus, Dylan
Jones and Bo (Duangporn)
Songvisava, David Laris,
Uwe Opocensky,
Neil Anthony Tomes

33-35 Bridges Street
Sheung Wan
Hong Kong Island
www.yardbirdrestaurant.com

Opening hours	6 days for dinner, until late
Reservation policy	No
Credit cards	Accepted but not AMEX and Diners
Price range	Affordable
Style	Casual
Cuisine	Japanese
Recommended for	Regular neighbourhood

'It's the perfect place for an informal meal.'
—Richard Ekkebus

Smart Soho *izakaya* (bar with restaurant) that's quickly made a name for itself by being an unfussy combination of cocktails and yakitori. The result is the kind of modern casual dining that Hong Kong has never seen before. Opened by Canadian chef Matt Arbegal (ex Masa in New York and the Hong Kong branch of Zuma) whose charcoal grill gets the best out of various parts of bird. The skewers menu reads like a chicken autopsy – liver, heart, gizzard, tail, skin and knee – with each part given a different seasoning, whether that's *yuzu kosho*, pepper (neck) or simply sea salt and lemon (oyster).

BO INNOVATION

Recommended by
Jereme Leung, Jordi Roca

Shop 13, 2nd Floor, J Residence
60 Johnston Road
Wan Chai
Hong Kong Island
+852 28508371
www.boinnovation.com

Opening hours	5 days for lunch and 6 days for dinner
Reservation policy	Yes
Reservation email	dine@boinnovation.com
Credit cards	Accepted
Price range	Expensive
Style	Smart casual
Cuisine	Modern Chinese
Recommended for	Worth the travel

The Wanchai headquarters of the self-styled proponent of 'X-treme Chinese', with its bare-bones industrial aesthetic, doesn't look like the average Chinese restaurant. But then Alvin Leung isn't your average Chinese chef. With hair dyed to match his purple-tinted glasses and a fondness for tattoos, his image is pure chef as rock star. Self-taught, having worked as an acoustic engineer before taking up cooking late in life as a hobby, at Bo Innovation – and the now recently opened Bo London – he deconstructs the traditional Chinese palate to produce tasting menus via modern techniques borrowed from the cutting edge of Western haute cuisine.

CHE'S CANTONESE RESTAURANT

Recommended by
Corey Lee

4th Floor, The Broadway
54-62 Lockhart Road
Wan Chai
Hong Kong Island
+852 25281123

Opening hours.................................7 days for lunch and dinner
Reservation policy...Yes
Credit cards......................Accepted but not AMEX and Diners
Price range..Affordable
Style...Smart casual
Cuisine..Cantonese
Recommended for...Worth the travel

'By far the best pork buns I've ever had.'—Corey Lee

CHIU YUEN CHIU CHOW NOODLE

Recommended by
Esther Sham

37 Spring Garden Lane
Wan Chai
Hong Kong Island
+852 28922322

Opening hours..............7 days for breakfast, lunch and dinner
Reservation policy...No
Credit cards...Not accepted
Price range...Budget
Style..Casual
Cuisine..Cantonese
Recommended for..Bargain

'Fishballs and octopus balls... yum.'—Esther Sham

Chiu Yuen Chiu Chow Noodle is one of Hong Kong's more famous holes in the wall, equally popular among locals, roaming bloggers and tourists who've done a bit of research. It's a small place on a crowded street in Wanchai, its brown frontage covered in handsome gold lettering. The classics here are the beefcakes: deliciously springy balls in a clear and flavoursome soup, with slippery and well-textured noodles. To this can be added fish balls, tripe and pigs' intestines – few concessions are made to unadventurous Western palates.

FOOK LAM MOON

Recommended by
Corey Lee

35-45 Johnston Road
Wan Chai
Hong Kong Island
+852 28660663
www.fooklammoon-grp.com

Opening hours.................................7 days for lunch and dinner
Reservation policy...Yes
Reservation email..............enquiries@fooklammoon-grp.com
Credit cards..Accepted
Price range..Expensive
Style...Smart casual
Cuisine..Cantonese
Recommended for...Worth the travel

'For roast suckling pig.'—Corey Lee

LEI GARDEN

Recommended by
Neil Anthony Tomes

1f CNT Tower
338 Hennessy Road
Wan Chai
Hong Kong Island
+852 28920333
www.leigarden.hk

Opening hours.................................7 days for lunch and dinner
Reservation policy...Yes
Credit cards..Accepted
Price range..Affordable
Style...Smart casual
Cuisine..Chinese
Recommended for...Local favourite

'It really submerges you in Hong Kong life – tons of people at big round tables, noise, controlled chaos, a big crazy fish tank full of, clearly, fresh fish, crabs and lobsters, not to mention abalone. Great, precise dim sum.'—Neil Anthony Tomes

YUET WAH HUI

Recommended by
Tim Lai

Shop B, Ground Floor
Wan Chai
Hong Kong Island
+852 25916803

Opening hours...7 days for dinner
Reservation policy...Yes
Credit cards..Not accepted
Price range...Budget
Style...Casual
Cuisine...Cantonese-Seafood
Recommended for...Late night

'Excellent seafood.'—Tim Lai

BUDAOWENG HOT POT CUISINE

Recommended by
Man-Sing Lee

2nd Floor, Sino Cheer Plaza
23-29 Jordan Road
Jordan
Kowloon
Hong Kong Island
+852 35260918

Opening hours..................7 days from lunch until late
Reservation policy...Yes
Credit cards.......................Accepted but not AMEX and Diners
Price range..Affordable
Style...Casual
Cuisine...Hot pot
Recommended for...Late night

Don't be deterred by Budaoweng being located in a high-rise Tsim Sha Tsui office building – you'll forget all about it when you see the views of Victoria Harbour from the twenty-third floor dining room. A little more upmarket – and less cut and thrust – than other local hot-pot joints, there's still a steady stream of locals slurping their way through a menu of more than twenty types of soup base (from tom yam to spicy edible frog) until 1.00 a.m. Accompanying platters groan with tightly marbled slices of beef, plump prawn (shrimp) dumplings and 'loud bells' (rolled and deep-fried tofu). Ask for a window table when you book.

DIMDIM SUM DIMSUM

Recommended by
Richard Ekkebus

Man Wah Building
21-23 Man Ying Street
Jordan
Kowloon
Hong Kong Island
+852 27717766

Opening hours................................7 days for lunch and dinner
Reservation policy..No
Credit cards..Not accepted
Price range...Budget
Style...Casual
Cuisine...Cantonese
Recommended for...Bargain

'The mirrored walls let you see what the locals are ordering. You'd be really pushed to spend more than HK$100 (£8; $13) per person here.'—Richard Ekkebus

This unremarkable looking little dim sum shop in Kowloon has found fame since winning an award for Hong Kong's best dim sum – no mean feat in a city that's drowning in top-drawer dumpling dispensaries. The menu mixes classics with more unusual house specialities. Go beyond Siu Mai and Har Gow for pan-fried tofu skin with chicken and cumin; fried nine dishes and pig's blood with XO sauce; and steamed tripe with black pepper sauce. For those with a sweet tooth a special mention goes to their pineapple buns – made with chunks of fresh fruit – and their sesame seed balls.

DRAGON SEAL

Recommended by
Anthony Lui

1 Austin Road
Kowloon
Hong Kong Island
+852 25689886

Opening hours................................7 days for lunch and dinner
Reservation policy...Yes
Credit cards..Accepted
Price range..Expensive
Style...Smart casual
Cuisine..Cantonese-European
Recommended for................................Worth the travel

'Really inspiring in terms of the original approach to it's dishes, especially with the hint of Western fusion, with service to match. A truly great experience.'
—Anthony Lui

GADDI'S

Recommended by
Ebbe Vollmer

The Peninsula Hotel
Salisbury Road
Kowloon
Hong Kong Island
+852 26966763
www.peninsula.com

Opening hours...............................7 days for lunch and dinner
Reservation policy...Yes
Reservation email...........................diningphk@peninsula.com
Credit cards...Accepted
Price range...Expensive
Style...Formal
Cuisine...French
Recommended for...Worth the travel

TIM HO WAN

Recommended by
Pier Bussetti,
Uwe Opocensky

2-20 Kwong Wa Street
Mong Kok
Kowloon
Hong Kong Island
+852 23322896

Opening hours.............7 days for breakfast, lunch and dinner
Reservation policy..No
Credit cards..Not accepted
Price range..Budget
Style...Casual
Cuisine...Cantonese
Recommended for...Bargain

'Amazing! Look for baked buns with barbecue pork.
Overwhelming!'—Pier Bussetti

The queues (waiting lines) outside this lovably scruffy,
basket-sized dim sum joint, in the fantastically hectic
Kowloon district of Mong Kok, have not shortened at
all since further branches opened in trendier Sham
Shui Po and, more recently, on the other side of
Victoria Harbour in the International Finance Centre
(IFC) Mall in Central on Hong Kong Island itself.
Opened in 2008 by Mak Pui Gor, former dim sum chef
from Four Seasons' swanky and garlanded Lung King
Heen, Tim Ho Wan means 'add good luck', which it
apparently didn't need to be crowned Hong Kong's —
make that the world's — cheapest Michelin-starred
meal in 2009.

TSUI WAH

Recommended by
Man-Sing Lee, Bradley Turley

81-83 Shung Ling Street
San Po Kong
Kowloon
Hong Kong Island
www.tsuiwahrestaurant.com

Opening hours.............7 days for breakfast, lunch and dinner
Reservation policy..No
Credit cards..Not accepted
Price range..Budget
Style...Casual
Cuisine...Cantonese
Recommended for.............................Regular neighbourhood

'There is a variety of local food for selection and the
food is good value for money. I like its pineapple bun
and milk tea.'—Man-Sing Lee

SUSHI TOKU

Recommended by
Neil Anthony Tomes

Cameron Plaza
23-25a Cameron Road
Tsim Sha Tsui
Kowloon
Hong Kong Island
+852 23013555

Opening hours ....7 days for lunch and dinner
Reservation policy...Yes
Credit cards...Accepted
Price range...Expensive
Style...Casual
Cuisine...Japanese
Recommended for...High end

'Just great Japanese food!'—Neil Anthony Tomes

DRAGON INN SEAFOOD

Recommended by
Man-Sing Lee

Castle Peak Road, Miles 19
New Territories
Hong Kong
+852 24506366
www.dragoninn1939.com

Opening hours	7 days for lunch and dinner
Reservation policy	Yes
Credit cards	Accepted
Price range	Budget
Style	Casual
Cuisine	Seafood
Recommended for	Wish I'd opened

Forty minutes drive from Central, along the Castle Rock Road into the New Territories, the Dragon Inn has been a Hong Kong fixture since 1939. A popular location during the golden age of Cantonese movies in the 1950s and 60s, its setting overlooking Castle Peak, plus its distinctive architecture and mini zoo, were a source of cinematic inspiration. Formerly known as the Dragon Inn Villa, but rebuilt and re-named in 1989, its reputation as one of Hong Kong's best seafood destinations remains. Nearby Sam Shing market provides the fish for trademark dishes such as cheese-baked baby lobster, braised whelks and smoked pomfret.

DA-WAN YAKINIKU

Recommended by
Jereme Leung

22 Dunhua Nan Lu
Daan
Taipei
Taiwan
+886 227110179

Opening hours	7 days for dinner
Reservation policy	Yes
Credit cards	Not accepted
Price range	Affordable
Style	Casual
Cuisine	Japanese
Recommended for	Worth the travel

'The best beef grilled on little individual charcoal stoves.'—Jereme Leung

GEUMGANG SAN

Recommended by
Naoya Ueno

Nonhyun-dong 257-2
Gangnam-gu
Seoul
South Korea

Opening hours	7 days for lunch and dinner
Reservation policy	No
Credit cards	Accepted
Price range	Budget
Style	Casual
Cuisine	Korean
Recommended for	Worth the travel

'BEAUTIFUL JAPANESE HOME-STYLE COOKING WITH GREAT SERVICE.'
MATTHEW CRABB P99

'GO TO KYOTO AND OSAKA AND ENJOY THE BEST QUALITY SASHIMI AND TEMPURA.'
TIM LAI

JAPAN

'Set in a beautiful Japanese garden with a view of Kyoto Forest. You will have a once in a lifetime experience here.'
HIRO SONE P98

'THE FOOD IS AMAZING AND COOKED BY AN 85 YEAR OLD MASTER.'
UWE OPOCENSKY P105

JAPAN

N

SCALE

0   100   200 mi.

Miyagi p.99

Ishikawa p.96

Nagano p.99

Shiga p.100

Kanagawa p.97

Kyoto pp.97-99

Shizuoka p.100

Hyogo p.96

Osaka p.100

Oita p.99

KIKUSUIZUSHI NISHIMISE

1-4-15 Matsunouchi
Akashi
Hyogo 673-0016
+81 789287157
www.akashi-sushi.jp/kikusuinishi

Opening hours	6 days for lunch and dinner
Reservation policy	Yes
Credit cards	Accepted
Price range	Expensive
Style	Smart casual
Cuisine	Sushi
Recommended for	High end

ANONYME

4-13-3 Shimoyamate-dori
Chuo-ku
Kobe
Hyogo 650-0011
+81 787780965
www.kobeanony.exblog.jp

Opening hours	6 days for lunch and dinner
Reservation policy	Yes
Credit cards	Accepted
Price range	Affordable
Style	Casual
Cuisine	Japanese-French
Recommended for	Regular neighbourhood

CA SENTO

4-16-14 Nakayamate-dori
Chuo-ku
Kobe
Hyogo 650-0004
+81 782726882
www.casento.jp

Opening hours	6 days for lunch and dinner
Reservation policy	Yes
Credit cards	Accepted
Price range	Expensive
Style	Smart casual
Cuisine	Spanish
Recommended for	Local favourite

XINGXING

1 - 16 Suwayama Cho
Chuo-ku
Kobe
Hyogo 650-0006
+81 782521107
www.xingxing.jp

Opening hours	7 days for breakfast and lunch
Reservation policy	No
Credit cards	Not accepted
Price range	Affordable
Style	Casual
Cuisine	Chinese
Recommended for	Breakfast

ITTETSU RAMEN

1-8-11 Kitahirano
Himeji
Hyogo 670-0893
+81 792820208

Opening hours	4 days for lunch and dinner
Reservation policy	No
Credit cards	Not accepted
Price range	Budget
Style	Casual
Cuisine	Noodles
Recommended for	Bargain

KOMATSU YASUKE

APA Hotel Kanazawa
2-21-1 Ikeda-cho
Kanazawa
Ishikawa 920-0984
+81 762616809

Opening hours	5 days for lunch and dinner
Reservation policy	Yes
Credit cards	Accepted
Price range	Expensive
Style	Smart casual
Cuisine	Sushi
Recommended for	Worth the travel

IROHA SUSHI

Recommended by
Riki Mizukami

Kawashima Building 1f
4-48 Ootamachi
Naka-ku
Yokohama
Kanagawa 231-0011
+81 456813366

Opening hours	6 days for dinner
Reservation policy	Yes
Credit cards	Accepted
Price range	Affordable
Style	Casual
Cuisine	Sushi
Recommended for	Bargain

GION YATA

Recommended by
Matthew Crabbe

Shinbashi-higashiiru, Yamatoojii
Higashiyama-ku
Kyoto 605-0933
+81 755255511
www.kaland.co.jp/yata_honten

Opening hours	7 days for dinner
Reservation policy	Yes
Reservation email	info.y@kaland.co.jp
Credit cards	Accepted
Price range	Affordable
Style	Smart casual
Cuisine	Modern Japanese
Recommended for	Local favourite

KIKUNOI

Recommended by
Michael Anthony, Albert
Raurich, Tetsuya Wakuda

459 shimokawara-cho
Yasakatoriimae-sagaru
Higashiyama-ku
Kyoto 605-0825
+81 755610015
www.kikunoi.jp

Opening hours	7 days for lunch and dinner
Reservation policy	Yes
Credit cards	Accepted
Price range	Expensive
Style	Smart casual
Cuisine	Kaiseki-Kyotonese
Recommended for	Worth the travel

To experience exquisite Japanese cuisine in a typical Japanese environment, come to Kikunoi. First the environment: ten private rooms of elegant minimalism where you sit, shoeless, on cushions at low tables. Secondly the food: a traditional *kaiseki* or flight of courses of artistic brilliance and seasonal harmony from chef Yoshihiro Murata, probably the foremost expert on Kyoto cooking. Pea soup with prawn (shrimp) balls; sea eel and yuba rolls; steamed tilefish with fresh green tea leaves... all served by kimono-clad hostesses. If you don't speak Japanese, don't worry, just let the food lead you to your goal.

KODAIJI WAKUDEN

Recommended by
Albert Raurich,
Tetsuya Wakuda

512 Washio-cho
Kodaiji-kitamonzen
Higashiyama-ku
Kyoto 605-0072
+81 0755333100
www.wakuden.jp

Opening hours	6 days for lunch and dinner
Reservation policy	Yes
Credit cards	Not accepted
Price range	Expensive
Style	Style
Cuisine	Kaiseki
Recommended for	Worth the travel

The most luxurious and comfortable of four traditional *ryotei* throughout the city, styled as a classical teahouse, amid moss, pine trees and bamboo. Highly rated, refined Japanese cuisine is served over many courses at tatami mats and sunken tables. It is close to the entrance of Kodaiji temple, which dates to 1606. Seasonal dishes may feature delicately textured sansho flowers (added to individual simmering hot pots for example), while large creamy, summer oysters from the Oki islands are served simply with citrus and soy. Supple Junsai water-shield buds are cooled and offered with dashi and vinegar. The shop on the first floor is known for lotus root cakes.

MIZAI

Recommended by
Yoshinori Ishii

Maruyama Park
620-1 Maruyama-cho
Yasakatorii mae-higashiiru
Higashiyama-ku
Kyoto 605-0071
+81 755513310

Opening hours	6 days for dinner
Reservation policy	Yes
Credit cards	Accepted
Price range	Expensive
Style	Formal
Cuisine	Kaiseki
Recommended for	Wish I'd opened

NAKAMURA-ROU

Yasaka Jinjya Toriinai
Gion-cho
Higashiyama-ku
Kyoto 605-0074
+81 755610016
www.nakamurarou.com

Opening hours...................6 days for lunch and dinner
Reservation policy...Yes
Credit cards...Accepted
Price range...Expensive
Style...Formal
Cuisine...Kaiseki
Recommended for.........................Wish I'd opened

INODA COFFEE

140 Douyuucho Sanjyo Sagaru
Sakaimachi-dori
Nakagyou-ku
Kyoto 604-8118
+81 752210507
www.inoda-coffee.co.jp

Opening hours.............7 days for breakfast, lunch and dinner
Reservation policy...No
Credit cards...Accepted
Price range...Budget
Style..Casual
Cuisine..Café
Recommended for..................................Breakfast

TOMINOKOJI HARUTAKA

Sanyou Tachibana Building 1f
633 Tachibana-cho, Oike Aguru
Tomikouji
Nakagyou-ku
Kyoto 604-0944
+81 752114327

Opening hours.............................7 days for dinner
Reservation policy...Yes
Credit cards........................Accepted but not Visa
Price range...Affordable
Style..Casual
Cuisine..Japanese
Recommended for...................................Late night

KYOTO KITCHO

58 Susukinobaba-cho
Saga Tenryuji
Ukyo-ku
Kyoto 616-8385
+81 758811101
www.kitcho.com/kyoto

Opening hours...................6 days for lunch and dinner
Reservation policy...Yes
Credit cards...Accepted
Price range...Expensive
Style...Formal
Cuisine...Kaiseki
Recommended for.....................................High end

'This restaurant is in a beautiful Japanese garden
with a view of Kyoto Forest. Course after course,
every bite is full of surprises. You will have a once-in-
a-lifetime experience here'—Hiro Sone

HYOTEI

35 Kusagawa-cho
Nanzenji
Sakyo-ku
Kyoto 606-8437
+81 757714116
www.hyotei.co.jp

Opening hours.............6 days for breakfast, lunch and dinner
Reservation policy...Yes
Credit cards...Accepted
Price range...Expensive
Style...Formal
Cuisine...Kaiseki
Recommended for..................................Breakfast

MIYAMASOU

375 Daihizan
Hanaseharachi-cho
Sakyo-ku
Kyoto 601-0233
+81 757460231
www.miyamasou.jp

Opening hours...................7 days for lunch and dinner
Reservation policy...Yes
Reservation email......................info@miyamasou.jp
Credit cards...Accepted
Price range...Expensive
Style..Smart casual
Cuisine..Japanese
Recommended for.........................Worth the travel

MASUDA

Recommended by
Yoshihiro Narisawa

682 Ishinofudo-cho
Matubara-dori Gokomachi-nishiiru
Shimogyo-ku
Kyoto 600-8047
+81 753611508

Opening hours...6 days for dinner
Reservation policy...Yes
Credit cards...Accepted but not Visa
Price range...Expensive
Style...Smart casual
Cuisine...Kaiseki
Recommended for..High end

OGATA

Recommended by
Tetsuya Wakuda

726 Shinkamanza-cho
Nishinotoin-higashiiru Ayanokoji
Shimogyo-ku
Kyoto 600-8471
+81 753448000

Opening hours...6 days for dinner
Reservation policy..No
Credit cards...Accepted
Price range...Expensive
Style...Smart casual
Cuisine...Kaiseki
Recommended for..Worth the travel

OLD HONG KONG RESTAURANT

Recommended by
Takuji Takahashi

Cocon Karasuma Building B1f
620 Suiginyachou Shijyo Sagaru
Karasuma-dori
Shimogyou-ku
Kyoto 600-8411
+81 753411800
www.oldhongkong-kyoto.com

Opening hours...................................7 days for lunch and dinner
Reservation policy...Yes
Credit cards...Accepted
Price range...Affordable
Style...Casual
Cuisine...Chinese
Recommended for..................................Regular neighbourhood

MIYAGINO

Recommended by
Hiro Sone

Naruko Hotel
36 Narukonsenyumoto
Osaki
Miyagi 989-6823
+81 229832001
www.narukohotel.co.jp

Opening hours..........................7 days for breakfast and dinner
Reservation policy...Yes
Credit cards...Accepted
Price range...Expensive
Style...Casual
Cuisine...Japanese
Recommended for..Breakfast

'Their breakfast has incredible selections of local
classic dishes and ingredients. I always end up eating
too much breakfast here.'—Hiro Sone

SHOKUNINKAN

Recommended by
Yoshihiro Narisawa

3250-3 Kasuga
Saku
Nagano 384-2205
+81 267522010

Opening hours...................................5 days for lunch and dinner
Reservation policy...Yes
Credit cards...Not accepted
Price range...Affordable
Style...Casual
Cuisine..Soba noodles
Recommended for..Worth the travel

CHISOAN

Recommended by
Matthew Crabbe

Nihon No Ashitaba
918-18 Yufuincho Kawakita
Yufu
Oita 879-5114
+81 977842664
www.2hon-no-ashitaba.co.jp

Opening hours..........................7 days for breakfast and dinner
Reservation policy...Yes
Credit cards...Accepted
Price range...Expensive
Style...Smart casual
Cuisine...Japanese
Recommended for..Worth the travel

'Beautiful Japanese home-style cooking with great
service.'—Matthew Crabbe

SUSHIDOKORO KAZUYA

Recommended by
Naoya Ueno

1-5-18 Dotonbori
Chuo-ku
Osaka 542-0077
+81 662111757
www.kazuya.in

Opening hours...................................6 days for dinner
Reservation policy...Yes
Credit cards.........................Accepted but not Visa
Price range..Expensive
Style..Casual
Cuisine..Sushi
Recommended for...............................Late night

WASABI

Recommended by
Naoya Ueno

1-1-17 Nanba
Chuo-ku
Osaka 542-1176
+81 662126666
www.hozenji-wasabi.jp

Opening hours...................................7 days for dinner
Reservation policy...Yes
Credit cards...Not accepted
Price range..Budget
Style..Casual
Cuisine...Kushiage
Recommended for..................................Bargain

HAJIME

Recommended by
Seiji Yamamoto

1-9-11-1f Edobori
Nishi-ku
Osaka 550-0002
+81 664476688
www.hajime-artistes.com

Opening hours...............1 day for lunch and 2 days for dinner
Reservation policy...Yes
Credit cards...Accepted
Price range..Expensive
Style..Formal
Cuisine..French
Recommended for.......................Worth the travel

HIRASANSOU

Recommended by
Naoya Ueno

94 Katsuragawabomuracho
Otsu
Shiga 520-0475
+81 775992058
www.hirasansou.com

Opening hours...................6 days for lunch and dinner
Reservation policy...Yes
Credit cards...Accepted
Price range..Expensive
Style..Formal
Cuisine..Kaiseki
Recommended for..............................Breakfast

ASABA RYOKAN

Recommended by
Riki Mizukami

3450-1 Syuzenji
Izu
Shizuoka 410-2416
www.ryokancollection.com

Opening hours....................7 days for breakfast and dinner
Reservation policy...Yes
Reservation email............................asaba@izu.co.jp
Credit cards...Accepted
Price range..Expensive
Style..Formal
Cuisine...Japanese
Recommended for.......................Worth the travel

ATAMI KAI

Recommended by
Hiro Sone

750-6 Izuyama
Atami
Shizuoka 413-0002
+81 5037860099
www.kai-atami.jp

Opening hours............7 days for breakfast, lunch and dinner
Reservation policy...Yes
Credit cards...Accepted
Price range..Expensive
Style..Casual
Cuisine...Japanese
Recommended for..........................Wish I'd opened

'Each course is brought to your room, one by one, so you just enjoy the morsels, sake and sound of the waves.'—Hiro Sone

'THEY SERVE TRADITIONAL KUSHIYAKI AND EVERY IMAGINABLE TYPE OF INNARD'

HIRO SONE P112

TOKYO

'It's as old school as it gets – there's nothing in the kitchen except charcoal and a box of rice. People argue about rice it's serious.'

DAVID CHANG P105

'EIGHTEEN SEATS, ONLY TWO CHEFS AND ONE WAITER SERVING TRADITIONAL JAPANESE DISHES.'

PETER TEMPLEHOFF P114

'GET THERE FOR AROUND 4.00 A.M. FOR THE SASHIMI.'

HESTON BLUMENTHAL P106

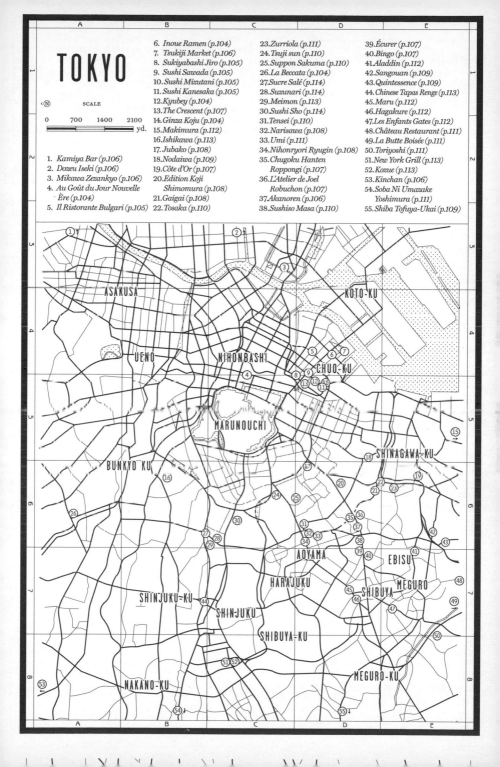

TOKYO

SCALE

0 700 1400 2100 yd.

LA BECCATA

Recommended by
Riki Mizukami

3-34-9 Otsuka
Bunkyo-ku
Tokyo 112-0012
+81 0353193459
www.la-beccata.com

Opening hours	6 days for lunch and dinner
Reservation policy	Yes
Credit cards	Accepted
Price range	Affordable
Style	Casual
Cuisine	Italian
Recommended for	Regular neighbourhood

AU GOÛT DU JOUR NOUVELLE ÈRE

Recommended by
Seiji Yamamoto

Shin-Marunouchi Building 5f
1-5-1 Marunouchi
Chiyoda-ku
Tokyo 100-6505
+81 352248070
www.augoutdujour-group.com

Opening hours	7 days for lunch and dinner
Reservation policy	Yes
Credit cards	Accepted
Price range	Expensive
Style	Smart casual
Cuisine	French
Recommended for	Local favourite

GINZA KOJYU

Recommended by
David Kinch

Carioca Building 4f
5-4-8 Ginza
Chuo-ku
Tokyo 104-0061
+81 362159544
www.kojyu.jp

Opening hours	6 days for dinner
Reservation policy	Yes
Credit cards	Accepted
Price range	Expensive
Style	Formal
Cuisine	Japanese
Recommended for	Worth the travel

Located in Ginza, an upmarket area known for its coffeehouses, department stores and boutiques, Ginza Kojyu takes its name from a master potter whose work includes the restaurant's rather alarmingly valuable sake cups. Always drawing inspiration from the most ephemeral, finest market produce, Shizuoka-born chef and sommelier Tooru Okuda presents his Southern heritage via dishes that have earned him three Michelin stars. These may include seasonal wild blue fin toro from Kyushu, *yakimono* broiled fish and meats, and octopus, pumpkin and winter melon. An intimate, comfortable restaurant, panelled in uplifting light wood.

INOUE RAMEN

Recommended by
Dharshan Munidasa,
Hiro Sone

4-9-16 Tsukiji
Chuo-ku
Tokyo 104-0045
+81 335420620

Opening hours	6 days for breakfast and lunch
Reservation policy	No
Credit cards	Not accepted
Price range	Budget
Style	Casual
Cuisine	Ramen noodles
Recommended for	Bargain

If you find yourself in Tokyo needing to grab a quick lunch, or you just fancy seeing how the locals do it, Inoue Ramen will satisfy your needs. It's cheap (a fiver [$8] should be enough), it's fast (no loitering, they've got jobs to go to and it closes at 1.30 p.m.), it's tasty (tender pork, noodles, bean sprouts and spring onions [scallions] in a bowl of warming broth) and it is all a joyous Japanese jamboree – for the visitor anyway… The locals tuck it away with singular efficiency, but return to their desks sated and energized for the afternoon's shift.

KYUBEY

Recommended by
Matthew Crabbe

7-6 Ginza
Chuo-ku
Tokyo 104-0061
+81 335716523
www.kyubey.jp

Opening hours	6 days for lunch and dinner
Reservation policy	Yes
Credit cards	Accepted
Price range	Expensive
Style	Smart casual
Cuisine	Sushi
Recommended for	High end

IL RESTORANTE BULGARI

Recommended by
Heinz Beck

Ginza Tower
2-7-12 Ginza
Chuo-ku
Tokyo 104-0061
+81 363620555
www.bulgarihotels.com

Opening hours	7 days for lunch and dinner
Reservation policy	Yes
Credit cards	Accepted
Price range	Expensive
Style	Smart casual
Cuisine	Modern Italian
Recommended for	Worth the travel

SUKIYABASHI JIRO

Recommended by
Francis Cardenau, Alfonso
& Ernesto Iaccarino, Uwe
Opocensky, Paul Qui, Albert
Raurich, Eric Ripert

Tsukamoto Sogyo Building b1f
4-2-15 Ginza
Chuo-ku
Tokyo
+81 335353600
www.sushi-jiro.jp

Opening hours	6 days for lunch and dinner
Reservation policy	Yes
Credit cards	Not accepted
Price range	Expensive
Style	Smart casual
Cuisine	Japanese
Recommended for	Worth the travel

'The food is amazing and cooked by an eighty-five year old master.'—Uwe Opocensky

SUSHI KANESAKA

Recommended by
Ted Anderson

Misuzu Building b1f
8-10-3 Ginza
Chuo-ku
Tokyo 104-0061
+81 355684411

Opening hours	7 days for dinner
Reservation policy	Yes
Credit cards	Accepted
Price range	Expensive
Style	Casual
Cuisine	Sushi
Recommended for	Worth the travel

SUSHI MIZUTANI

Recommended by
Carlo Mirarchi

Jundo Building 9f
8-7-7 Ginza
Chuo-ku
Tokyo 104-0061
+81 335735258

Opening hours	6 days for lunch and dinner
Reservation policy	Yes
Credit cards	Not accepted
Price range	Expensive
Style	Casual
Cuisine	Sushi
Recommended for	Worth the travel

SUSHI SAWADA

Recommended by
David Chang

5-9-19 Ginza
Chuo-ku
Tokyo 104-0061
+81 335714711

Opening hours	6 days for lunch and dinner
Reservation policy	Yes
Credit cards	Accepted
Price range	Expensive
Style	Smart casual
Cuisine	Sushi
Recommended for	Worth the travel

'Sushi Sawada serves the best sushi in Tokyo. It's as old school as it gets – there's nothing in the kitchen except charcoal and a box of rice. People argue about rice, it's serious. It's simply one of the best sushi restaurants in the world.'—David Chang

Sushi master Koji Sawada's seven-seater Tokyo *sushi-ya* is hidden down a quiet Ginza alley where its discreetly marked entrance is obvious only to those in the know. That hasn't stopped Sushi Sawada becoming Tokyo's most talked about sushi restaurant, thanks in part to the Michelin Guide anointing it with two stars and the ensuing, breathless, media coverage. The discreet, panelled room is only for the deepest of pockets but it's arguably the definitive, reverential raw fish experience. Expect various types of sea urchin, otoro tuna ever so lightly grilled over charcoal, and miniature sushi masterpieces served directly onto the hinoki wood counter.

TSUKIJI MARKET

Recommended by
Italo Bassi, Heston Blumenthal

5-2-1 Tsukiji
Chuo-ku
Tokyo 104-0055
www.tsukiji-market.or.jp

Opening hours...........................7 days for breakfast and lunch
Reservation policy...No
Credit cards...Not accepted
Price range...Budget
Style..Casual
Cuisine..Seafood
Recommended for...Bargain

'Get there for around 4.00 a.m. for the sashimi.'
—Heston Blumenthal

KAMIYA BAR

Recommended by
Armand Arnal

1-1-1 Asakusa
Daito-ku
Tokyo 111-0032
+81 338415400
www.kamiya-bar.com

Opening hours................................6 days for lunch and dinner
Reservation policy...Yes
Reservation email.............................info@kamiya-bar.com
Credit cards..Accepted
Price range...Affordable
Style..Casual
Cuisine..International
Recommended for...Worth the travel

DOZEU ISEKI

Recommended by
Naoya Ueno

2-5 Takabashi
Koto-ku
Tokyo 135-0005
+81 336310005

Opening hours................................6 days for lunch and dinner
Reservation policy...Yes
Credit cards..Accepted
Price range...Affordable
Style..Casual
Cuisine..Seafood
Recommended for...Bargain

MIKAWA ZEZANKYO

Recommended by
Seiji Yamamoto

1-3-1 Fukuzumi
Koto-ku
Tokyo 135-0032
+81 336649843
www.kayabacho-mikawa.jimdo.com

Opening hours................................6 days for lunch and dinner
Reservation policy...Yes
Credit cards..Accepted
Price range..Expensive
Style..Casual
Cuisine...Tempura
Recommended for...............................Regular neighbourhood

KINCHAN

Recommended by
Dharshan Munidasa

5-16-3 Toyotamakita
Nerima
Tokyo 176-0012
+81 339942507

Opening hours.......................................6 days for dinner
Reservation policy...No
Credit cards...Not accepted
Price range...Budget
Style..Casual
Cuisine...Japanese
Recommended for..Late night

AKANOREN

Recommended by
Matthew Crabbe

3-21-24 Nishi-Azabu
Minato-ku
Tokyo 106-0031
+81 334084775

Opening hours................................6 days for lunch and dinner
Reservation policy...No
Credit cards...Not accepted
Price range...Budget
Style..Casual
Cuisine...Ramen noodles
Recommended for..Late night

L'ATELIER DE JOEL ROBUCHON

Roppongi Hills Hillside 2f
6-10-1 Roppongi
Minato-ku
Tokyo 106-0032
+81 357727500
www.robuchon.jp

Opening hours................................7 days for lunch and dinner
Reservation policy..Yes
Credit cards..Accepted
Price range..Expensive
Style..Smart casual
Cuisine..Modern French
Recommended for.................................Wish I'd opened

'It's convivial but with a tiny bit of formality that I like, and the food is simple but ultra-refined.'—Eric Ripert

BINGO

Wall Nishi-Azabu b1f
4-19-9 Nishi-Azabu
Minato-ku
Tokyo 106-0031
+81 357745721

Opening hours................................6 days for dinner
Reservation policy..Yes
Credit cards..Not accepted
Price range..Expensive
Style..Casual
Cuisine..Italian
Recommended for...Late night

CHUGOKU HANTEN ROPPONGI

Oriental Building 1f
1-1-5 Nishi-Azabu
Minato-ku
Tokyo 106-0031
+81 334783828
www.chuugokuhanten.com

Opening hours................................7 days for lunch and dinner
Reservation policy..Yes
Credit cards..Accepted
Price range..Affordable
Style..Style
Cuisine..Chinese
Recommended for...Late night

CÔTE D'OR

Mita House 1f
5-2-18 Mita
Minato-ku
Tokyo 108-0073
+81 334555145

Opening hours................................6 days for lunch and dinner
Reservation policy..Yes
Credit cards..Accepted
Price range..Affordable
Style..Smart casual
Cuisine..French
Recommended for..............................Worth the travel

THE CRESCENT

1-8-20 Shiba-koen
Minato-ku
Tokyo 105-0011
+81 334363211
www.restaurantcrescent.com

Opening hours................................6 days for dinner
Reservation policy..Yes
Credit cards..Accepted
Price range..Expensive
Style..Formal
Cuisine..French
Recommended for..High end

ÉCURER

2-26-20 Nishi-Azabu
Minato-ku
Tokyo 106-0031
+81 364274670
www.ecurer.co.jp

Opening hours................................7 days for lunch and dinner
Reservation policy..Yes
Credit cards..Accepted
Price range..Expensive
Style..Smart casual
Cuisine..Spanish
Recommended for..............................Local favourite

EDITION KOJI SHIMOMURA

Roppongi T-Cube f1
3-1-1 Roppongi
Minato-ku
Tokyo 106-0032
+81 355494562
www.koji-shimomura.jp

Opening hours..............................6 days for lunch and dinner
Reservation policy...Yes
Credit cards...Accepted
Price range..Expensive
Style...Formal
Cuisine..Japanese-French
Recommended for...Worth the travel

GAIGAI

Aporia Building 1f
1-3-1 Azabu-Juban
Minato-ku
Tokyo 106-0045
+81 335863335

Opening hours...............................7 days for lunch and dinner
Reservation policy...Yes
Credit cards...Accepted
Price range...Budget
Style..Casual
Cuisine...Yakitori
Recommended for...Bargain

JUBAKO

2-17-61 Akasaka
Minato-ku
Tokyo 10-0052
+81 335831319

Opening hours..............................6 days for lunch and dinner
Reservation policy...Yes
Credit cards...Accepted
Price range..Expensive
Style...Smart casual
Cuisine..Eel
Recommended for...Worth the travel

NARISAWA

2-6-15 Minami Aoyama
Minato-ku
Tokyo 107-0062
+81 357850799
www.narisawa-yoshihiro.com

Opening hours..............................6 days for lunch and dinner
Reservation policy...Yes
Credit cards...Accepted
Price range..Expensive
Style...Smart casual
Cuisine..Japanese-French
Recommended for...Worth the travel

Chef Yoshihiro Narisawa trained in Switzerland at Girardet's, in France at Robuchon's and in Italy at Antica Osteria del Ponte. After nine years in Europe, he returned to Japan, first to Odawara, where he opened La Napoule, then to Minato-ku, Tokyo, where he opened Les Créations de Narisawa, the name of which he later changed to 'Narisawa'. While his French training and his molecular gastronomic influences are clear (he has two Michelin stars, after all), the dishes he serves are expressions of the Japanese seasons and the ingredients they provide. This is a fusion worth travelling for.

NIHONRYORI RYUGIN

Side Roppongi Building 1f
7-17-24 Roppongi
Minato-ku
Tokyo 106-0032
+81 334238006
www.nihonryori-ryugin.com

Opening hours.......................................7 days for Dinner
Reservation policy...Yes
Credit cards...Accepted
Price range..Expensive
Style...Smart casual
Cuisine..Modern Japanese
Recommended for...Worth the travel

NODAIWA

Recommended by
Albert Raurich

1-5-4 Higashiazabu
Minato-ku
Tokyo 106-0044
+81 335837852
www.nodaiwa.co.jp

Opening hours	6 days for lunch and dinner
Reservation policy	Yes
Credit cards	Accepted
Price range	Affordable
Style	Casual
Cuisine	Eel
Recommended for	Worth the travel

Nodaiwa, Tokyo's most fashionable freshwater eel restaurant, has specialized in unagi and nothing but since the mid-nineteenth century. Still family run – it's now in the hands of the fifth generation – it now boasts four addresses in Tokyo, plus one more in Paris. But the one to visit is its flagship, a wonderful beamed *kura* (traditional storehouse) transplanted from the sticks to Nishi-Azabu. Nodaiwa uses only wild eel, traditionally filleted, cooked over embers, steamed, then coated in a secret recipe taré sauce before being grilled one last time. Try it served over rice in a lacquer box or as part of a tasting that includes eel liver soup.

QUINTESSENCE

Recommended by
Jason Atherton

Barbizon 25 Building, 1f
5-4-7 Shirokanedai
Minato-ku
Tokyo 108-0071
+81 357913715
www.quintessence.jp

Opening hours	6 days for lunch and dinner
Reservation policy	Yes
Credit cards	Accepted
Price range	Expensive
Style	Smart casual
Cuisine	French
Recommended for	Worth the travel

Beyond its boutique-like entrance on a residential street in Shirokane, Quintessence's interior chicly collages copper tones and rosewood with leather, and, in the private rooms, silk. Chef Shuzo Kishida is a fanatic of slow-roasting meat, a technique learned while at Paris's legendary L'Astrance. Kishida's shonai-sangen pork with onion-herb sauce, for example, is roasted for one minute, allowed to rest

for five more, then roasted for a further minute – a process repeated up to thirty times. There are no written menus for the French-influenced seven-course lunch, nor eleven-course dinner, for which only ingredients sourced on the day appear. The predominantly French wine list is considerable.

SANGOUAN

Recommended by
Hiro Sone

510 1f Shirokane
5-10-10 Shirokane
Minato-ku
Tokyo
+81 334443570

Opening hours	6 days for lunch and dinner
Reservation policy	Yes
Credit cards	Not accepted
Price range	Budget
Style	Casual
Cuisine	Japanese
Recommended for	Regular neighbourhood

'Ask for *omakase* (chef's choice menu), which usually contains a few courses of seasonal Japanese vegetable dishes, sashimi, tempura and their homemade soba. It's reasonable and very satisfying.'—Hiro Sone

SHIBA TOFUYA-UKAI

Recommended by
Matthew Crabbe

4-4-13 Shiba-Koen
Minato-ku
Tokyo 105-0011
+81 334361028
www.ukai.co.jp

Opening hours	7 days for lunch and dinner
Reservation policy	Yes
Credit cards	Accepted
Price range	Affordable
Style	Smart casual
Cuisine	Kaiseki
Recommended for	Regular neighbourhood

Finding any address in Japan can be a bit of a trial, but there's no excuse for missing Shiba Tofuya-Ukai, set right in the shadow of Tokyo Tower. Encompassing a sprawling – and suitably stunning – Japanese garden, this oasis in the heart of the metropolis serves *kaiseki* cuisine specializing in tofu. As with many such restaurants, exquisite surroundings, immaculate service and world-class food (*kaiseki* is arguably the pinnacle of the Japanese chef's craft) doesn't come cheap, but Shiba Tofuya-Ukai is consistent enough in excellence to draw a regular crowd, and to attract the attention of Michelin — it won a star in 2009.

SUPPON SAKUMA

Recommended by
Albert Raurich

4-5-20 Akasaka
Minato-ku
Tokyo 107-0052
+81 335846891
www.suppon-sakuma.com

Opening hours	6 days for dinner
Reservation policy	Yes
Credit cards	Accepted
Price range	Expensive
Style	Smart casual
Cuisine	Suppon
Recommended for	Worth the travel

Suppon is a soft-shelled turtle soup that is a delicacy in Japan and China, and it's fair to say that this Tokyo restaurant that bears its name does one of the best. The soup, which is prepared using the time-honoured method of cooking in clay bowls over burning coals, is served steaming to your table. This is an intensely rich eating experience the likes of which many Westerners have not had before, but which has had locals coming back for years. The setting is tranquil, with soft lighting and neutral colours, providing a rare oasis in Tokyo's bustling metropolis.

SUSHISO MASA

Recommended by
Justin North

Seven Nishi-Azabu b1
4-1-15 Nishi-Azabu
Minato-ku
Tokyo 106-0031
+81 334999178

Opening hours	6 days for dinner
Reservation policy	Yes
Credit cards	Accepted
Price range	Expensive
Style	Smart casual
Cuisine	Sushi
Recommended for	Worth the travel

Amid the international embassies of Nishiazabu, a mysterious doorway leads to a seven-seat basement bar, which requires booking at least two weeks in advance. Here, in the cool, laid-back, music-free setting, Masakatsu Oka authors a story of up to forty courses of impeccable sashimi, delicately seasoned sushi and fleetingly grilled fish – particularly lower fat, white-fleshed fish – with care and friendliness. The result is mesmerizing – an exploration of tastes, textures and lingering aftertastes. Morsels that particularly impress may include smoky pike conger eel, meaty bonito, ultra-rich monkfish liver and raw and charred baby swordfish.

TENSEI

Recommended by
Matthew Crabbe

Central Aoyama Building 1f
1-3 Minami-Aoyama
Minato-ku
Tokyo 107-0062
+81 357862228
www.four-seeds.co.jp

Opening hours	6 days for lunch and dinner
Reservation policy	Yes
Credit cards	Accepted
Price range	Affordable
Style	Casual
Cuisine	Tempura
Recommended for	Local favourite

TOSAKA

Recommended by
Yoshihiro Narisawa

Azabu Takano Building 2f
1-2-8 Azabu-Juban
Minato-ku
Tokyo 106-0045
+81 362344311
www.azabu-tosaka.com

Opening hours	6 days for dinner
Reservation policy	Yes
Credit cards	Accepted
Price range	Affordable
Style	Smart casual
Cuisine	Yakitori
Recommended for	Local favourite

TSUJI SUN

Recommended by
Luis Baena

2 Toraya Building b1
1-5-8 Motoakasaka
Minato-ku
Tokyo 107-0051
+81 334033984
www.tsujitome.co.jp

Opening hours	6 days for lunch and dinner
Reservation policy	Yes
Reservation email	info@tsujitome.co.jp
Credit cards	Accepted
Price range	Expensive
Style	Formal
Cuisine	Kaiseki
Recommended for	Worth the travel

UMI

Recommended by
Albert Adrià, Takashi Inoue

3-2-8 Minami-Aoyama
Minato-ku
Tokyo 107-0062
+81 334013368

Opening hours	6 days for lunch and dinner
Reservation policy	Yes
Credit cards	Accepted
Price range	Affordable
Style	Casual
Cuisine	Sushi
Recommended for	Worth the travel

'I had the best sushi of my life here. Order the *omakase* and it will change your life.'—Takashi Inoue

ZURRIOLA

Recommended by
Carme Ruscalleda

Rhizome Azabu-Juban Building 1f
3-2-7 Azabu-Juban
Minato-ku
Tokyo 106-0045
+81 357300240
www.zurriola.jp

Opening hours	6 days for lunch and dinner
Reservation policy	Yes
Credit cards	Accepted
Price range	Expensive
Style	Smart casual
Cuisine	Spanish
Recommended for	Worth the travel

CHÂTEAU RESTAURANT

Recommended by
Italo Bassi, Seiji Yamamoto

Ebisu Garden Place
1-13-1 Mita
Meguro-ku
Tokyo 153-0062
+81 354241347
www.robuchon.jp

Opening hours	7 days for lunch and dinner
Reservation policy	Yes
Credit cards	Accepted
Price range	Expensive
Style	Formal
Cuisine	French
Recommended for	High end

TORIYOSHI

Recommended by
Matthew Crabbe

Tanizima Building 1f
2-8-6 Kamimeguro
Meguro-ku
Tokyo 153-0051
+81 337167644

Opening hours	7 days for dinner
Reservation policy	No
Credit cards	Not accepted
Price range	Budget
Style	Casual
Cuisine	Yakitori
Recommended for	Bargain

SOBA NI UMAZAKE YOSHIMURA

Recommended by
Ted Anderson

2-29-8 Kichijoji
Minami-cho
Musashino
Tokyo 180-0003

Opening hours	6 days for lunch and dinner
Reservation policy	Yes
Credit cards	Not accepted
Price range	Budget
Style	Casual
Cuisine	Japanese
Recommended for	Worth the travel

LA BUTTE BOISÉE

Recommended by
Emmanuel Renaut

6-19-6 Okusawa
Setagaya-ku
Tokyo 158-0083
+81 337033355
www.shinsei-sha.com

Opening hours	6 days for lunch and dinner
Reservation policy	Yes
Credit cards	Accepted
Price range	Affordable
Style	Smart casual
Cuisine	French
Recommended for	Worth the travel

ALADDIN
Recommended by
Hiro Sone

Hiroo Riverside G
2-22-10 Ebisu
Shibuya-ku
Tokyo 150-0013
+81 354200038
www.restaurant-aladdin.com

Opening hours	6 days for lunch and dinner
Reservation policy	Yes
Credit cards	Accepted but not AMEX
Price range	Affordable
Style	Casual
Cuisine	French
Recommended for	Local favourite

LES ENFANTS GATES
Recommended by
Matthew Crabbe

2-3 Sarugakucho
Shibuya-ku
Tokyo 150-0033
+81 334762929
www.terrine-gates.com

Opening hours	6 days for lunch and dinner
Reservation policy	Yes
Credit cards	Accepted
Price range	Affordable
Style	Smart casual
Cuisine	French
Recommended for	Late night

'The terrines here are out of this world.'
—Matthew Crabbe

HAGAKURE
Recommended by
Hiro Sone

2-8-11 Shibuya
Shibuya-ku
Tokyo 150-0033
+81 334003294

Opening hours	6 days for dinner
Reservation policy	Yes
Credit cards	Not accepted
Price range	Budget
Style	Casual
Cuisine	Japanese
Recommended for	Bargain

'They serve traditional *Kushiyaki* (grilled ingredients on skewers) and every imaginable type of innard – even sashimi of innards.'—Hiro Sone

MARU
Recommended by
Matthew Crabbe

Aoyama KT Building b1f
5-50-8 Jingumae
Shibuya-ku
Tokyo 150-0001
+81 0364185572
www.maru-mayfont.jp

Opening hours	7 days for dinner
Reservation policy	Yes
Credit cards	Accepted
Price range	Affordable
Style	Casual
Cuisine	Kaiseki
Recommended for	Local favourite

Take a seat at the long wooden counter in this simple but chic room, tucked down a side street in Tokyo's central Aoyama district, and prepare for a feast. Based on Kyoto-style *kaiseki*, or multi-course style of dining, owner and chef Keiji Mori offers small sharing dishes made with seasonal ingredients that might include *kamo manjyu*, Kyoto's (a traditional bun made with wild duck and lily bulbs); *sakuramasu to hanazansho* (simmered ocean trout and spring vegetables) and *imo tako nankin takiawase* (simmered octopus, taro and pumpkin, served cold). The list of Japanese sake and *shochu* is impressive, but there are European wines for the less adventurous.

MAKIMURA
Recommended by
Tomoyasu Kamo

6-19-10 Minami-Oi
Shinagawa-ku
Tokyo 140-0013
+81 0337686388

Opening hours	6 days for lunch and dinner
Reservation policy	Yes
Credit cards	Accepted
Price range	Expensive
Style	Smart casual
Cuisine	Kaiseki
Recommended for	Worth the travel

CHINESE TAPAS RENGE

Recommended by
Yoshihiro Narisawa

3-12-1 Shinjuku
Shinjuku-ku
Tokyo 160-0022
+81 333546776

Opening hours..6 days for dinner
Reservation policy..Yes
Credit cards..Accepted
Price range...Affordable
Style..Casual
Cuisine...Chinese small plates
Recommended for..Bargain

ISHIKAWA

Recommended by
Björn Frantzén, David
Kinch, Justin North

Takamura Building 1f
5-37 Kagurazaka
Shinjuku-ku
Tokyo 162-0825
+81 352250173
www.kagurazaka-ishikawa.co.jp

Opening hours..6 days for dinner
Reservation policy..Yes
Credit cards..Accepted
Price range..Expensive
Style...Smart casual
Cuisine...Japanese
Recommended for...Worth the travel

'One of the finest restaurant experiences in
the world.'—David Kinch

Ishikawa, a temple of gastronomy, is located just
behind Kagurazaka's Bishamon temple to Buddha in
the geisha district. Beyond an unpretentious, black
wood exterior unravels an interior of four serene,
private dining rooms and a seven-seat counter
carved from 400-year-old Japanese cypress trees.
Head chef Hideki Ishikawa's dishes, which are more
about flavour than presentation, are delivered by
polite, often English-speaking, waitresses in kimo-
nos. They might include melted white sesame tofu,
tempura turtle with taro, and quail shabu-shabu in
sultry broth with five types of mushrooms. The wine
list is as extensive as the sake menu.

KOZUE

Recommended by
Refaie Othman

Park Hyatt Hotel
3-7-1-2 Nishi-Shinjuku
Shinjuku-ku
Tokyo 163-1055
+81 353233460
www.tokyo.park.hyatt.com

Opening hours...............................7 days for lunch and dinner
Reservation policy..Yes
Credit cards..Accepted
Price range..Expensive
Style...Smart casual
Cuisine..Modern Japanese
Recommended for...Worth the travel

MEIMON

Recommended by
Yoshihiro Narisawa

Matsukawa Building 1f
11 Funamachi
Shinjuku-ku
Tokyo 160-0006
+81 333577748
www.y-meimon.com

Opening hours..6 days for dinner
Reservation policy..Yes
Credit cards..Accepted
Price range...Affordable
Style..Casual
Cuisine...Korean
Recommended for...Late night

NEW YORK GRILL

Recommended by
Luis Baena

Park Hyatt Hotel
3-7-1-2 Nishi Shinjuku
Shinjuku-ku
Tokyo 163-1055
+81 353233458
www.tokyo.park.hyatt.com

Opening hours...............................7 days for lunch and dinner
Reservation policy..Yes
Credit cards..Accepted
Price range..Expensive
Style...Smart casual
Cuisine...American
Recommended for...Breakfast

SUCRE SALÉ

Recommended by
Jérôme Tauvron

Nao Building 1f
9-7 Arakicho
Shinjuku-ku
Tokyo 160-0007
+81 333518741
www.eatpia.com

Opening hours..................................6 days for lunch and dinner
Reservation policy...Yes
Credit cards..Not accepted
Price range...Affordable
Style...Casual
Cuisine..French
Recommended for...Worth the travel

SUSHI SHO

Recommended by
Bruce Bromberg

Yorindo Building 1f
1-11 Yotsuya
Shinjuku-ku
Tokyo 160-0004
+81 333516387

Opening hours..............3 days for lunch and 6 days for dinner
Reservation policy...Yes
Credit cards..Accepted
Price range..Expensive
Style...Casual
Cuisine..Sushi
Recommended for...Worth the travel

SUZUNARI

Recommended by
Peter Tempelhoff

Seiwa House 1f
Araki-cho 7
Shinjyuku-ku
Tokyo 160-0007
+81 333501178

Opening hours..6 days for dinner
Reservation policy...Yes
Credit cards..Accepted
Price range...Affordable
Style...Casual
Cuisine...Japanese
Recommended for...Worth the travel

'Eighteen seats, only two chefs and one waiter serving traditional Japanese dishes.'—Peter Tempelhoff

SOUTHEAST ASIA

SOUTHEAST ASIA

N SCALE

0   250   500 mi.

THAILAND

VIETNAM

MALAYSIA

INDONESIA

INDONESIA

CELADON

Sukhothai Hotel
13/3 Thanon Sathorn Tai
Bangkok 10120
Thailand
+66 23448888
www.sukhothai.com

Opening hours	7 days for lunch and dinner
Reservation policy	Yes
Reservation email	promotions@sukhothai.com
Credit cards	Accepted
Price range	Affordable
Style	Smart casual
Cuisine	Thai
Recommended for	Wish I'd opened

COLONNADE

Sukhothai Hotel
13/3 Thanon Sathorn Tai
Bangkok 10120
Thailand
+66 23448888
www.sukhothai.com

Opening hours	7 days for breakfast and lunch
Reservation policy	Yes
Reservation email	promotions@sukhothai.com
Credit cards	Accepted
Price range	Affordable
Style	Smart casual
Cuisine	International
Recommended for	Worth the travel

GASTRO 1/6

RMA Institute
Soi Sainamthip 2
22 Thanon Sukhumvit
Bangkok 10110
Thailand
+66 806036421

Opening hours	6 days for breakfast and lunch
Reservation policy	No
Credit cards	Not accepted
Price range	Budget
Style	Casual
Cuisine	Cafe
Recommended for	Breakfast

SOUL FOOD MAHANAKORN

Soi 55
56/10 Thanon Sukhumvit
Bangkok 10110
Thailand
+66 27147708
www.soulfoodmahanakorn.com

Opening hours	7 days for dinner
Reservation policy	Yes
Reservation email	eat@soulfoodmahanakorn.com
Credit cards	Not accepted
Price range	Budget
Style	Casual
Cuisine	Thai
Recommended for	Regular neighbourhood

'It's fun, it's funky, the food is solid and the cocktails are always great!'—Dylan Jones and Bo (Duangporn) Songvisava

SIROCCO

The Dome at Lebua
1055 Thanon Silom
Bangkok 10500
Thailand
+66 26249555
www.lebua.com

Opening hours	7 days for dinner
Reservation policy	Yes
Reservation email	reservations@thedomebkk.com
Credit cards	Accepted
Price range	Expensive
Style	Smart casual
Cuisine	Mediterranean
Recommended for	Worth the travel

'For it's stunning views and ambiance.'—Alfred Prasad

LA MONITA TAQUERIA

Recommended by
Dylan Jones,
Bo (Duangporn) Songvisava

888/26 Mahatun Plaza
Ploenchit, Pathum Wan
Bangkok 10330
Thailand
+66 26509581
www.lamonita.com

Opening hours	7 days for lunch and dinner
Reservation policy	Yes
Reservation email	info@lamonita.com
Credit cards	Accepted
Price range	Budget
Style	Casual
Cuisine	Mexican
Recommended for	Bargain

'La Monita does Mexican well and we enjoy a quick bite there from time to time. Their Xtra Spicy Sauce is always a crowd-pleaser.'—Dylan Jones and Bo (Duangporn) Songvisava

SUMMER PALACE

Recommended by
Dylan Jones,
Bo (Duangporn) Songvisava

Intercontinental Hotel
973 Thanon Ploenchit
Pathum Wan
Bangkok 10330
Thailand
| 66 26560111613 |
www.ichotelsgroup.com

Opening hours	7 days for lunch and dinner
Reservation policy	Yes
Credit cards	Accepted
Price range	Expensive
Style	Smart casual
Cuisine	Cantonese
Recommended for	Breakfast

'Try the dim sum. It's worth it just for the xia long bao.'—Dylan Jones and Bo (Duangporn) Songvisava

POONSIN RESTAURANT

Recommended by
Harold Dieterle

460 Thanon Wisut Kasat
Phra Nakhon
Bangkok 10200
Thailand

Opening hours	7 days for breakfast, lunch and dinner
Reservation policy	No
Credit cards	Accepted
Price range	Budget
Style	Casual
Cuisine	Thai-Chinese
Recommended for	Worth the travel

'A favourite of mine.'—Harold Dieterle

They've been serving *ped yang* (homestyle roast duck) and *ped palo* (braised duck with Chinese herbs) for half a century here. The dishes have become almost as famous as the temples and palaces that surround this Thai–Chinese restaurant on Rattanakosin Island in the centre of Bangkok. The cafeteria-like surroundings are unremarkable, but the inexpensive menu of delicious dishes such as crispy catfish with basil, stewed duck and pork, beef in oyster sauce, steamed snapper with soy sauce and the unusual dessert of sweet almond tofu keep the customers coming back.

NAHM BANGKOK

Metropolitan Hotel
27 Thanon Sathorn Tai
Tungmahamek
Sathorn
Bangkok 10120
Thailand
+66 26253388
www.metropolitan.bangkok.como.bz

Opening hours	5 days for lunch and 7 days for dinner
Reservation policy	Yes
Reservation email	res.bkk@nahm.como.bz
Credit cards	Accepted
Price range	Affordable
Style	Smart casual
Cuisine	Thai
Recommended for	Worth the travel

'My favourite meal this year overseas has to be David Thompson's restaurant in Bangkok. I came away with the feeling that my taste buds had had a complete make over. Incredible flavour juxtaposition that if not handled in such a professional way could strike disaster. It has to rank alongside my all time favourites.'—Anthony Demetre

Australian Thai-food scholar David Thompson took Nahm, the modern Thai restaurant he originally opened in London's Halkin hotel in 1991, to Bangkok in 2010. Returning to the source of his inspiration, his second outpost, on the ground floor of the Metropolitan hotel, has arguably eclipsed the widely championed original. The reason? Access to the raw materials, the building blocks for his creative cooking, are now easily available to him – as opposed to sitting wilting while they wait to clear UK customs – freshness being everything in Thai cooking. Skip the à la carte and take on the tasting menu.

EAT ME

Thanon Convent
Soi Pipat 2
Silom
Bangkok 10500
Thailand
+66 22380931
www.eatmerestaurant.com

Opening hours	7 days for dinner
Reservation policy	Yes
Reservation email	reservations@eatmerestaurant.com
Credit cards	Accepted
Price range	Affordable
Style	Casual
Cuisine	International
Recommended for	Regular neighbourhood

'Eat Me is always tasty and interesting. We like their use of ingredients and the casual yet knowledgeable service.'—Dylan Jones and Bo (Duangporn) Songvisava

LA TABLE DE TEE

69/5 Soi
Thanon Saladaeng
Silom
Bangkok 10500
Thailand
+66 26363220
www.latabledetee.com

Opening hours	6 days for dinner
Reservation policy	Yes
Reservation email	info@latabledetee.com
Credit cards	Accepted
Price range	Affordable
Style	Smart casual
Cuisine	Thai-French
Recommended for	Worth the travel

BAANRAI YARMYEN

Recommended by
Zakary Pelaccio

14 Moo 3
Soi Lanka 3
Thanon Jaroenraj
Faham
Chiang Mai 50000
Thailand
+66 53247999

Opening hours	7 days for lunch and dinner
Reservation policy	No
Credit cards	Not accepted
Price range	Budget
Style	Casual
Cuisine	Northern Thai
Recommended for	Wish I'd opened

PHO 10

Recommended by
Neal Fraser

10 Ly Quoc Su
Hang Trong
Hoan Kiem
Hanoi
Vietnam
+84 438257338
www.pho10lyquocsu.com

Opening hours	7 days from breakfast until late
Reservation policy	Yes
Credit cards	Accepted
Price range	Budget
Style	Casual
Cuisine	Pho
Recommended for	Worth the travel

BINH TAY MARKET

Recommended by
Armand Arnal

57 Tháp Muoi, 2
Cholon
Ho Chi Minh
Vietnam
+84 838571512

Opening hours	7 days for breakfast, lunch and dinner
Reservation policy	No
Credit cards	Not accepted
Price range	Budget
Style	Casual
Cuisine	Street food
Recommended for	Breakfast

SQUARE ONE

Recommended by
Julien Duboué

Park Hyatt Hotel
2 Lam Son
Quan 1
Ho Chi Minh
Vietnam
+84 835202359
www.saigon.park.hyattrestaurants.com

Opening hours	7 days for lunch and dinner
Reservation policy	Yes
Credit cards	Accepted
Price range	Expensive
Style	Smart casual
Cuisine	Vietnamese-European
Recommended for	Worth the travel

FRUIT N SPICE

Recommended by
Zakary Pelaccio

Air Putih
202-B Jalan
Penang
Sungai Pinang
Malaysia
+60 124010101

Opening hours	2 days for breakfast, lunch and dinner
Reservation policy	Yes
Reservation email	info@fruitnspice.com
Credit cards	Not accepted
Price range	Budget
Style	Casual
Cuisine	Malaysian
Recommended for	Worth the travel

'AN INFORMAL EATERY WITH STUNNING FOOD.'
CLAUS MEYER P128

'Order the Kaya toast, black coffee and local red tea.'
ANDRÉ CHIANG P124

SINGAPORE

'The hawker stalls in Singapore – my most recent overseas eye opening food moment'
BRAD FARMERIE

'Have the piping hot oxtail at this Southern Thai restaurant.'
AKMAL ANUAR P124

'An authentic Malay restaurant that you couldn't find anywhere outside of Singapore.'
AKMAL ANUAR P124

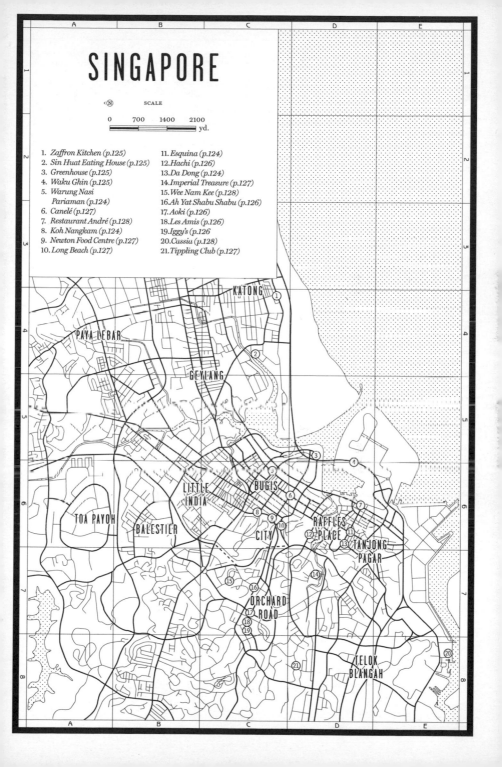

SINGAPORE

‹N› SCALE

0   700   1400   2100
yd.

KOH NANGKAM

Recommended by
Akmal Anuar

743 North Bridge Road
Beach Road
Singapore 198711

Opening hours..............5 days for lunch and 7 days for dinner
Reservation policy...No
Credit cards..Not Accepted
Price range...Budget
Style...Casual
Cuisine...Southern Thai
Recommended for...Bargain

'Go and have the piping hot oxtail with potatoes or rice.
Good portions and very cheap.'—Akmal Anuar

WARUNG NASI PARIAMAN

Recommended by
Akmal Anuar

738 North Bridge Road
Beach Road
Singapore 198706

Opening hours.........................7 days from breakfast until late
Reservation policy...No
Credit cards..Not accepted
Price range...Budget
Style...Casual
Cuisine..Malaysian
Recommended for...Local favourite

'This is an authentic local Malay restaurant handed
down from generation to generation. They serve
amazing rice and dishes done by grinding spices and
herbs on stones and they still carry on the style of
cooking and braising over a charcoal fire. My favourite
dish is a chicken dish called *Ayan masak putih*:
free-range chicken is marinated with various spices,
grilled over charcoal and braised with a coconut-based
stock.'—Akmal Anuar

DA DONG

Recommended by
André Chiang

39 Smith Street
Chinatown
Singapore 058952
+65 62213822
www.dadong.biz

Opening hours..............................7 days for brunch and dinner
Reservation policy..Yes
Credit cards...Accepted
Price range...Budget
Style...Casual
Cuisine...Cantonese
Recommended for...Breakfast

'Order the Kaya toast, black coffee and local red
tea.'—André Chiang

ESQUINA

Recommended by
Luke Mangan

16 Jiak Chuan Road
Chinatown
Singapore 089267
www.esquina.com.sg

Opening hours..............5 days for lunch and 6 days for dinner
Reservation policy...No
Credit cards...Accepted
Price range...Affordable
Style...Casual
Cuisine...Tapas
Recommended for...Worth the travel

Jason Atherton is the chef who set up and launched
the all-conquering Maze for Gordon Ramsay,
before leaving to open his own acclaimed London
restaurant, Pollen Street Social. Esquina, opened in
2011, is his take on a modern Spanish tapas bar, in
the unexpected setting that is a post-war colonial
building in Singapore's Chinatown. The vibe is
no-reservations casual, a classic L-shaped counter
with rather trendy industrial-styled stools, the menu
divided simply into four short sections: *para picar*
(meaning 'for the table'), including croquetas, tomato
bread and olives; meat; fish; dessert. The snappy
menu is supplemented by daily specials. Add to that
an all-Spanish beer list and servings of sangria.

SIN HUAT EATING HOUSE

659-661 Geylang Road
Geylang
Singapore 389589

Recommended by
Claus Meyer

Opening hours	7 days for dinner
Reservation policy	No
Credit cards	Accepted
Price range	Affordable
Style	Casual
Cuisine	Seafood
Recommended for	Worth the travel

ZAFFRON KITCHEN

135-137 East Coast Road
Joo Chiat
Singapore 428820
+65 64406786
www.zaffronkitchen.com

Recommended by
Armin Leitgeb

Opening hours	7 days for lunch and dinner
Reservation policy	Yes
Credit cards	Accepted
Price range	Budget
Style	Casual
Cuisine	Indian
Recommended for	Bargain

Someone obviously had fun kitting out Singapore's Zaffron Kitchen. This East Coast Road newcomer (owned by First Gourmet) is filled with covetable designer furniture (Wishbone chairs, red Tolix chairs and Tom Dixon Beat Lights, etc.), not to mention a vintage popcorn machine and imported playhouse in the kids' play area. In spite of all this loveliness, it's the fresh Indian cuisine — at anything but designer prices — that's got people talking. Excellent renditions of classics such as dum chicken biryani, palak paneer or chicken tikka from the showpiece tandoor compete with newer dishes such as spicy wraps and burgers with chat masala chips (fries).

GREENHOUSE

Ritz Carlton Hotel
7 Raffles Avenue
Singapore 039799
+65 64345288
www.ritzcarlton.com

Recommended by
Andrea Berton

Opening hours	7 days for breakfast, lunch and dinner
Reservation policy	Yes
Reservation email	sinrz.leads@ritzcarlton.com
Credit cards	Accepted
Price range	Affordable
Style	Smart casual
Cuisine	International
Recommended for	Breakfast

WAKU GHIN

Marina Bay Sands Hotel
10 Bayfront Avenue
Marine Bay
Singapore 018956
+65 66888507
www.marinabaysands.com

Recommended by
Matthew Crabbe, Armin
Leitgeb, Philippe Rochat

Opening hours	1 day for lunch and 7 days for dinner
Reservation policy	Yes
Credit cards	Accepted
Price range	Expensive
Style	Smart casual
Cuisine	Modern Japanese
Recommended for	Wish I'd opened

Marina Bay Sands did a smart thing in getting Tetsuya Wakuda to come and open his first venture outside Australia. This is luxury dining at its most exciting. Having cemented his reputation as one of the world's finest exponents of French-influenced Japanese cooking with Tetsuya's in Sydney, he has now created a whole new experience, where you are taken on a multi-course adventure, moving from room to room as you go. Start with aperitifs in the caviar lounge, move into your private dining room for the ten-course *omakase* menu, and wind up in the main dining room for desserts and digestifs, while enjoying fabulous views of Singapore.

AH YAT SHABU SHABU

Recommended by
Jereme Leung

Heeren Shopping Centre
260 Orchard Road
Orchard
Singapore 238855

Opening hours	7 days for lunch and dinner
Reservation policy	No
Credit cards	Not accepted
Price range	Budget
Style	Casual
Cuisine	Hot pot
Recommended for	Late Night

LES AMIS

Recommended by
Armin Leitgeb

2-16 Shaw Centre
1 Scotts Road
Orchard
Singapore 228208
+65 67332225
www.lesamis.com.sg

Opening hours	6 days for lunch and 5 days for dinner
Reservation policy	Yes
Reservation email	lesamis@lesamis.com.sg
Credit cards	Accepted
Price range	Expensive
Style	Smart casual
Cuisine	Modern European
Recommended for	High end

AOKI

Recommended by
André Chiang

2-17 Shaw Centre
1 Scotts Road
Orchard
Singapore 228208
+65 63338015
www.aoki-restaurant.com.sg

Opening hours	6 days for lunch and dinner
Reservation policy	Yes
Credit cards	Accepted
Price range	Expensive
Style	Smart casual
Cuisine	Japanese
Recommended for	Worth the travel

It's name meaning 'blue tree', Aoki is a sushi bar with an inconspicuous and unassuming entrance. Inside it is discrete and unshowy. Dedicated to the purest form of Japanese sushi technique, guests are invited to sit at the bar to observe the masterful preparation of their meal. The decor is puritanically minimalist with sheets of cream cloth hanging soothingly from the ceiling. Tempura vegetables, miso soups bobbing with prawn (shrimp) heads and the freshest, slithers of sashimi abound the bar top. Aoki manages to strike a careful balance between clinical starkness and a deeply conscientious approach to fine ingredients.

HACHI

Recommended by
André Chiang

01-01 6 Mohamed Sultan Road
Orchard
Singapore 238956
www.hachirestaurant.com

Opening hours	5 days for lunch and 7 days for dinner
Reservation policy	Yes
Credit cards	Accepted
Price range	Expensive
Style	Smart casual
Cuisine	Japanese
Recommended for	Regular neighbourhood

An evening in Hachi feels like being a guest at a neighbourhood celebration. Chef Watanabe is the life and soul, cooking his myriad of daily changing dishes before an audience of enthralled diners, with whom he chatters non-stop. The interior is simple but livened up by the shelves of personalized spirit bottles and traditional Japanese tableware that hint at the eclectic mix of dishes to come. Watanabe is both entertainer and artist, pulling out a series of surprises that truly take you into new culinary territory: sea cucumber, horse sashimi, monkfish liver… all prepared with passion, expertise and a smile.

IGGY'S

Recommended by
Atul Kochhar

The Hilton Hotel
581 Orchard Road,
Orchard
Singapore 238883
+65 7322234
www.iggys.com.sg

Opening hours	5 days for lunch and 6 days for dinner
Reservation policy	Yes
Credit cards	Accepted
Price range	Expensive
Style	Smart casual
Cuisine	International
Recommended for	Worth the travel

IMPERIAL TREASURE

Recommended by
Armin Leitgeb

Great World City
1 Kim Seng Promenade
Orchard
Singapore 237994
www.imperialtreasure.com

Opening hours	7 days for lunch and dinner
Reservation policy	Yes
Credit cards	Accepted
Price range	Affordable
Style	Casual
Cuisine	Cantonese
Recommended for	Wish I'd opened

NEWTON FOOD CENTRE

Recommended by
Armin Leitgeb

500 Clemenceau Avenue North
Orchard
Singapore 229495

Opening hours	7 days from lunch until late
Reservation policy	No
Credit cards	Not accepted
Price range	Budget
Style	Casual
Cuisine	Singaporean
Recommended for	Late night

CANELÉ

Recommended by
Armin Leitgeb

b1-46/47 Raffles City Shopping Centre
252 North Bridge Road
River Valley
Singapore 179103
www.canele.com.sg

Opening hours	7 days for brunch until late
Reservation policy	No
Credit cards	Accepted but not AMEX
Price range	Budget
Style	Casual
Cuisine	Cafe
Recommended for	Breakfast

Chocolate brittle, bonbons, macaroons and pastries
aplenty – indulgence is unavoidable at Canelé. Not
for the faint-hearted, nor for the umami-hunters
among you, this fast-breaker involves doing away
with any nutritional conscience you may have. Rows
of sweets (confectionary) are arranged with
Singaporean precision and the range is quite
astounding: praline, salted caramel and hazelnut
creations form orderly queues (waiting lines) on the

counter. The relative tranquillity of the dining area is
a welcome antidote to the lavish bar, so it is probably
here that you will take shelter and fend off your
sugar rush with an Earl Grey tea.

LONG BEACH

Recommended by
Armin Leitgeb

25 Dempsey Road
Tanglin
Singapore 249670
+65 63232222
www.longbeachseafood.com.sg

Opening hours	7 days for lunch and dinner
Reservation policy	Yes
Credit cards	Accepted
Price range	Affordable
Style	Smart casual
Cuisine	Seafood
Recommended for	Late night

Take a seat on the terrace overlooking the beach a
few kilometres (miles) east of Singapore's city centre
for what they claim is the original black pepper crab.
Large, meaty Sri Lankan mud crabs are deep fried
with crushed black pepper and finished with butter.
The dish was first created in the 1960s as a less
spicy and more fragrant alternative to the searingly
hot chilli crab. It's since been imitated and adapted
by many but Long Beach's simple version remains
the most celebrated. Specializing in seafood from all
over the world, the menu also features Canadian
geoduck and Scottish blue lobster.

TIPPLING CLUB

Recommended by
Paul Pairet

8D Dempsey Road
Tanglin
Singapore 249672
+65 64752217
www.tipplingclub.com

Opening hours	1 day for lunch and 6 days for dinner
Reservation policy	Yes
Reservation email	enquiries@tipplingclub.com
Credit cards	Accepted
Price range	Expensive
Style	Smart casual
Cuisine	Modern European
Recommended for	Worth the travel

RESTAURANT ANDRÉ

Recommended by
Refaie Othman

41 Bukit Pasoh Road
Tanjong Pagar
Singapore 089855
+65 65348880
www.restaurantandre.com

Opening hours............4 days for lunch and 6 days for dinner
Reservation policy...Yes
Reservation email...................reserve@restaurantandre.com
Credit cards..Accepted
Price range..Expensive
Style...Smart casual
Cuisine..Modern French
Recommended for.....................................Worth the travel

CASSIA

Recommended by
Anatoly Komm

Capella Hotel
1 The Knolls
Sentosa Island
Singapore 098297
+65 65915045
www.capellahotels.com/singapore

Opening hours.................................7 days for lunch and dinner
Reservation policy...Yes
Reservation email........cassia.singapore@capellahotels.com
Credit cards..Accepted
Price range..Expensive
Style...Smart casual
Cuisine...Modern Chinese
Recommended for.....................................Worth the travel

WEE NAM KEE

Recommended by
Claus Meyer

Novena Ville
275 Thomson Road
Thomson
Singapore 307645
+65 62556396
www.wnk.com.sg

Opening hours............7 days for breakfast, lunch and dinner
Reservation policy...Yes
Reservation email.............wnk_chickenrice@singnet.com.sg
Credit cards..Accepted
Price range...Affordable
Style..Casual
Cuisine..Hainanese
Recommended for.....................................Worth the travel

'An informal eatery with stunning food.'—Claus Meyer

SARONG

Recommended by
Agus Hermawan

19 Jalan Petitenget
Kerobokan
Bali
Indonesia 80361
+62 3614737809
www.sarongbali.com

Opening hours...7 days for dinner
Reservation policy...Yes
Credit cards..Accepted
Price range...Budget
Style...Smart casual
Cuisine...Asian
Recommended for.....................................Worth the travel

'It's more than a restaurant: it's a mission, an experiment and a place to discover what real Asians eat. Authentic Asian street food presented in a very stylish and modern setting.'—Agus Hermawan

KU DE TA

Recommended by
Jacques & Laurent Pourcel

Jalan Kayu Aya 9
Seminyak
Bali
Indonesia 80361
+62 361736969
www.kudeta.net

Opening hours..............7 days for breakfast, lunch and dinner
Reservation policy...Yes
Credit cards..Accepted
Price range...Affordable
Style...Smart casual
Cuisine..International
Recommended for...Worth the travel

MAMA SAN

Recommended by
Agus Hermawan

Jalan Raya Kerobokan 135
Seminyak
Bali
Indonesia 80361
+62 361730436
www.mamasanbali.com

Opening hours..6 days for dinner
Reservation policy...Yes
Credit cards..Accepted
Price range..Budget
Style..Smart casual
Cuisine..Asian
Recommended for...Worth the travel

'Done in over-the-top 1920s style with wild cocktails
and the most wonderful dishes Will Meyrick has come
across during his exploration of the East.'
—Agus Hermawan

IBU OKA

Recommended by
Omar Allibhoy

Jalan Suweta
Tegal Sari 2
Ubud
Bali
Indonesia
+62 361976345

Opening hours..7 days for lunch
Reservation policy...No
Credit cards..Not accepted
Price range..Budget
Style..Casual
Cuisine..Balinese
Recommended for...Worth the travel

'If you ever visit Bali, which by the way you should,
the suckling pig here is one of the world's best
delicacies!'—Omar Allibhoy

EUROPE

N

SCALE

0   250   500
mi.

ICELAND
Reykjavik

NORWAY
Oslo

SCOTLAND

IRELAND
Dublin
WALES
ENGLAND
Amsterdam
London
Antwerp
NETHERLANDS
BELGIUM
GERMANY

Paris

FRANCE
Zurich
SWITZERLAND
Milan

PORTUGAL
SPAIN
Lisbon
Madrid
Barcelona

'FRESHEST
SEAFOOD
IN THE
WORLD.'
MATTHEW KUHN P134

'This is a
world class
restaurant
doing Nordic
comfort food.'
ADAM SOBEL P134

ICELAND

'Iceland is
out of this
world.
Its nature
is obscene!
In the
best way.'
JAKOB MIELCKELE

'Icelandic
hot dogs
— the best!'
THRAINN FREYR VIGFUSSON P134

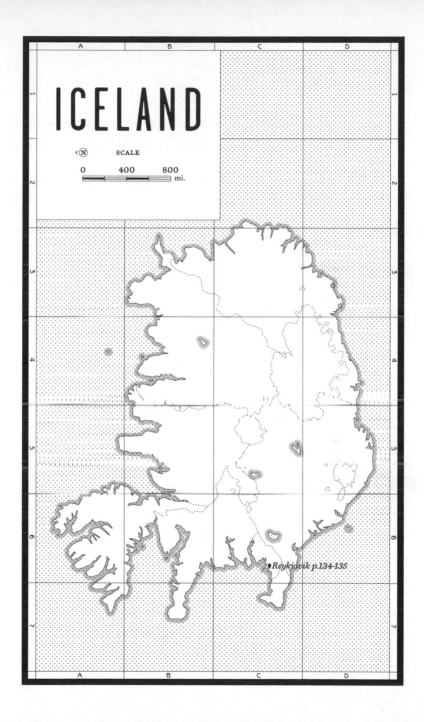

ICELAND

‹N SCALE

0   400   800 mi.

Reykjavik p.134-135

BÆJARINS BEZTU

Recommended by
Gunnar Karl Gíslason,
Thrainn Freyr Vigfusson

Tryggvagata
Downtown
Reykjavík 101
www.bbp.is

Opening hours...................................7 days from lunch until late
Reservation policy..No
Credit cards...Not accepted
Price range...Budget
Style..Casual
Cuisine..Hot dogs
Recommended for...Late night

'Icelandic hot dogs – the best in the world.'
—Thrainn Freyr Vigfusson

FISKFÉLAGIÐ - FISH COmpany

Recommended by
Matthew Kuhn

Vesturgötu 2a
Grófartorg
Downtown
Reykjavik 101
+354 5525300
www.fishcompany.is

Opening hours.............5 days for lunch and 7 days for dinner
Reservation policy...Yes
Credit cards...Accepted
Price range...Affordable
Style..Casual
Cuisine..Modern Icelandic
Recommended for..Worth the travel

'Freshest seafood in the world.'—Matthew Kuhn

FLJÓTT OG GOTT

Recommended by
Gunnar Karl Gíslason

BSÍ bus terminal
Vatnsmýravegi 10
Downtown
Reykjavik 101
www.fljottoggott.is

Opening hours...........................7 days for breakfast until late
Reservation policy..No
Credit cards...Not Accepted
Price range...Budget
Style..Casual
Cuisine..Fast food
Recommended for...Local favourite

GRÁI KÖTTURINN

Recommended by
Gunnar Karl Gíslason

Hverfisgata 16a
Downtown
Reykjavik 101
+354 5511544

Opening hours...7 days for brunch
Reservation policy..Yes
Credit cards...Accepted
Price range...Budget
Style..Casual
Cuisine..Breakfast
Recommended for...Breakfast

Reykjavik's hipsters – sorry, intellectuals, artists
and bohemian types – have their very own breakfast
bolt-hole in the form of Grái Kötturinn (Grey Cat).
Legendary for its early opening hours as well as
its highbrow clientele, the tiny basement room
holds just six tables but could fill many more on the
strength of its excellent food – think bacon and
eggs, American pancakes, bagels and the like –
accompanied by a coffee so strong it'll make your
heart flutter. Owner Hulda Hakon is, naturally, also
an artist, whose works have been displayed in
various galleries around the capital.

GRILLMARKAÐURINN

Recommended by
Adam Sobel

Lækjargata 2a
Downtown
Reykjavik 101
+354 571777
www.grillmarkadurinn.is

Opening hours.............5 days for lunch and 7 days for dinner
Reservation policy...Yes
Credit cards...Accepted
Price range...Affordable
Style..Smart casual
Cuisine..Icelandic
Recommended for..Worth the travel

'This place is so awsome. From the decor, to the music,
to the food. This is a world class restaurant doing
Nordic comfort cuisine.'—Adam Sobel

SVARTA KAFFIÐ

Recommended by
Thrainn Freyr Vigfusson

Laugavegur 54a
Downtown
Reykjavik 101
+354 5512999

Opening hours....................................7 days for lunch until late
Reservation policy..No
Credit cards..Accepted
Price range..Budget
Style..Casual
Cuisine...Café
Recommended for...Bargain

DILL RESTAURANT

Recommended by
Thrainn Freyr Vigfusson

Norræna húsinu
Sturlugötu 5
Háskóli
Reykjavík 101
+354 5521522
www.dillrestaurant.is

Opening hours................................6 days for lunch and dinner
Reservation policy..Yes
Reservation email..................dillrestaurant@dillrestaurant.is
Credit cards..Accepted
Price range..Affordable
Style..Smart casual
Cuisine...Modern Nordic
Recommended for....................................Worth the travel

NAUTHÓLL

Recommended by
Thrainn Freyr Vigfusson

Nauthólsvegur 106
Háskóli
Reykjavik 101
+354 5996660
www.nautholl.is

Opening hours.......................7 days for lunch and dinner
Reservation policy..Yes
Reservation email.................................nautholl@nautholl.is
Credit cards..Accepted
Price range..Affordable
Style..Casual
Cuisine..European
Recommended for...........................Regular neighbourhood

Reykjavik's thermal beach provides the impressive
backdrop for Nauthóll, a contemporary bistro that
has become one of the city's top informal destinations.
Head chef Eyþór Rúnarsson places emphasis on
local ingredients but this manifests itself as simple,
comfort food rather than in the abundance of wild
herbs and vegetables that usually comes with this
approach. In fact, there's very little pretension at all,
with deep-fried Camembert, fish soup, steak sandwiches and roast beef with remoulade tempting
Icelandic youngsters to head to the city's outskirts.
Admittedly, the bright room's uniform white chairs
and wooden tables are straight out of an Ikea
catalogue, but don't let that put you off.

BAKARI SANDHOLT

Recommended by
Thrainn Freyr Vigfusson

Laugavegur 36
Hverafold 1-3
Holt
Reykjavik 101
www.sandholt.is

Opening hours..........................7 days for breakfast and lunch
Reservation policy...No
Credit cards......................Accepted but not AMEX and Diners
Price range..Affordable
Style..Casual
Cuisine...Bakery-Café
Recommended for...Breakfast

Reykjavik's longest running artisan bakery opened
in 1920 and has been family-run ever since. The
award-winning chocolate maker Ásgeir Sandholt,
who studied painting before deciding to join the family business, is the fourth generation of the Icelandic
baking dynasty to run this shop on Laugavegur, the
city's historic central shopping street. Iceland does
not have a long history of baking but much of what's
offered at this coffeehouse would not look out of
place at the best Parisian patisseries. Macaroons,
cakes, croissants, chocolates and generously stuffed
baguettes sit alongside indigenous delicacies such as
the doughnut-like twists that Icelanders call kleinur.

GRILLIÐ

Recommended by
Thrainn Freyr Vigfusson

Hótel Sögu
Við Hagatorg
Vesturbær
Reykjavik 107
+354 5259960
www.grillid.is

Opening hours...5 days for dinner
Reservation policy..Yes
Credit cards..Accepted
Price range..Expensive
Style..Formal
Cuisine...Modern Icelandic
Recommended for...High End

'Good food and service.'—Thrainn Freyr Vigfusson

'UNIQUELY SITUATED IN AN OLD WAREHOUSE ON THE HISTORIC QUAY RIGHT BELOW AKERSHUS CASTLE. GREAT PLACE.'
STEFFEN HANSEN P142

'It has a magic connection to the local land and nature.'
SANG HOON DEGEIMBRE
P143

'Really fresh fish and chips.'
ESBEN HOLMBOE BANG P141

NORWAY, SWEDEN, DENMARK & FINLAND

'PROBABLY ONE OF THE BEST PLACES IN THE WORLD FOR A CREATIVE SUSHI EXPERIENCE.'
STEFFEN HANSEN P139

NORWAY, SWEDEN, DENMARK & FINLAND

N̂ SCALE

0   90   180 mi.

FINLAND

SWEDEN

NORWAY

Jämtland p.143

Etelä Savo p.165

Uusimaa pp.165-168

Hordaland p.136

Varsinais-Suomi p.165

Oslo pp.138-142

Vestfold p.142

Stockholm p.146-153

Gothenburg p.142

Hovedstaden pp.153-155

Copenhagen pp.156-164

Scania pp.143-145

Sjælland p.155

BEKKJARVIK GJESTGIVERI

Recommended by
Geir Skeie

Austevoll
Bekkjarvik
Hordaland 5399
Norway
+47 55084240
www.bekkjarvikgjestgiveri.no

Opening hours	7 days for lunch and 6 days for dinner
Reservation policy	Yes
Credit cards	Accepted
Price range	Affordable
Style	Casual
Cuisine	Nordic
Recommended for	Worth the travel

'They serve very fresh seafood and have a very nice location in the harbour at Bekkjarvik, Austevoll.'
—Gier Skeie

In a secluded harbour on the coastal route between Haugesund and Bergen, Bekkjarvik Gjestgiveri was established by royal decree and built at the end of the seventeenth century as lodgings for sailors and sea traders. It's been open ever since. The white buildings are beautifully maintained, and the community now has a warehouse, bakery and distillery, while its old barrel factory has been restored. Wild sheep skitter outside. Chef and 2011 and 2012 Bocuse d'Or Europe winner Orjan Johannessen serves simple and hearty food that includes such delights as a good club sandwich, grilled asparagus with sherry and toasted almonds, and entrecôte with cheese, tomatoes and salad.

ONDA MEZZANINE

Recommended by
Steffen Hansen

Stranden 30
Aker Brygge
Oslo 0250
Norway
+47 47660700
www.onda.no

Opening hours	5 days for dinner
Reservation policy	Yes
Reservation email	mezzanine@onda.no
Credit cards	Accepted
Price range	Expensive
Style	Smart casual
Cuisine	Modern Nordic
Recommended for	Wish I'd opened

'Beautiful restaurant. Luxury all the way.'
—Steffen Hanson

Terje Ness and Rune Pals, owners of Onda Mezzanine, have made their ambitions for the place very clear — they want nothing less than to jump straight to two stars in their first entry in the Michelin Red Guide. Certainly the ingredients fit all the high-end gastronomy requirements — think sea urchin with butter and dill, wild turbot with morels, Norwegian lobster. What remains to be seen is whether enough people, even in this famously spendy city, can afford 3,000kr (£320; $500) to see if the kitchen knows what to do with them — watch this space.

ONDA SEA

Recommended by
Bjorn Svensson

Stranden 30
Aker Brygge
Oslo 0250
Norway
+47 45502000
www.onda.no

Opening hours	7 days for lunch and dinner
Reservation policy	Yes
Credit cards	Accepted
Price range	Affordable
Style	Smart casual
Cuisine	Seafood
Recommended for	Late night

'A really nice seafood restaurant by the sea.'
—Bjorn Svensson

BLINGS

Recommended by
Bjorn Svensson

St. Olavs Plass 3
Bislett
Oslo 0164
Norway
www.blings.no

Opening hours	6 days for breakfast, lunch and tea
Reservation policy	No
Credit cards	Accepted
Price range	Budget
Style	Casual
Cuisine	Bakery-Café
Recommended for	Breakfast

'They do lovely sandwiches and coffee.'
—Bjorn Svensson

ALEX SUSHI

Cort Adelers Gate 2
Bygdoy-Frogner
Oslo 0254
Norway
+47 22439999
www.alexsushi.no

Opening hours..7 days for dinner
Reservation policy..Yes
Credit cards..Accepted
Price range...Expensive
Style...Smart casual
Cuisine...Japanese
Recommended for................................Regular neighbourhood

'Probably one of the best places in the world for creative sushi.'—Steffen Hansen

Eating out in Norway can be ruinously expensive at the best of times, so it's a brave soul who opts to spend their evening in a sushi restaurant. But Alex Sushi, which only arrived in Oslo in 2011, is already making waves thanks to the quality of the sashimi and sushi, and for offering a flexible tiered omakase menu, allowing big spenders to splash out, while offering a more modest option for those on a budget. Head chef Ernesto Manalo (previously of the Dubai branch of Zuma) insists on fresh wasabi and has created his own secret recipe house soya.

ÅPENT BAKERI

Parkveien 27
Frogner
Oslo 0350
Norway
www.apentbakeri.no

Opening hours...................6 days for breakfast, lunch and tea
Reservation policy..No
Credit cards..Accepted
Price range..Budget
Style...Casual
Cuisine..Bakery-Café
Recommended for................................Regular neighbourhood

KOLONIHAGEN

Frognerveien 33a
Frogner
Oslo 0263
Norway
+47 99316810
www.kolonihagenfrogner.no

Opening hours.............7 days for lunch and 6 days for dinner
Reservation policy..Yes
Reservation email.....................reservasjon@kolonihagen.no
Credit cards..Accepted
Price range...Affordable
Style...Casual
Cuisine...Nordic
Recommended for..Breakfast

'Fantastic brunch.'—Esben Holmboe Bang

The bright outside courtyard of Kolonihagen Frogner, flanked by crisp whitewashed walls on all sides, is the place to be after sunrise in Oslo, although you'll have to jostle with trendy prams (baby carriages) and well-heeled mums to bag a much-coveted parasol table. If you don't succeed, there's plenty of space inside this all-day café-cum-restaurant, where you can sit with an early morning coffee and decide which of the impressive selection of breads and pastries you want to plump for. The on-site bakery means everything is baked freshly on the day, while the friendly staff ensure you start your day on the right note.

PALACE GRILL

Solligata 2
Frogner
Oslo 0254
Norway
+47 23131140
www.palacegrill.no

Opening hours..7 days for dinner
Reservation policy..No
Credit cards..Accepted
Price range...Expensive
Style...Casual
Cuisine...International
Recommended for..Wish I'd opened

'It's gourmet, but very rough and laid back.'
—Bjorn Svensson

MAAEMO

Recommended by
Filip Langhoff, Sasu Laukkonen,
Peeter Pihel

Schweigaards Gate 15
Annette Thommessens Plass
Gamle Oslo
Oslo 0191
Norway
+47 91994805
www.maaemo.no

Opening hours	5 days for dinner
Reservation policy	Yes
Credit cards	Accepted
Price range	Expensive
Style	Smart casual
Cuisine	Modern Nordic
Recommended for	Wish I'd opened

LE BENJAMIN

Recommended by
Esben Holmboe Bang

Søndre Gate 6
Grünerløkka
Oslo 0550
Norway
+47 22357944
www.lebenjamin.no

Opening hours	1 day for lunch and 6 days for dinner
Reservation policy	Yes
Reservation email	post@lebenjamin.no
Credit cards	Accepted
Price range	Affordable
Style	Casual
Cuisine	French
Recommended for	Regular neighbourhood

DELICATESSEN

Recommended by
Esben Holmboe Bang

Søndre Gate 8
Grünerløkka
Oslo 0550
Norway
+47 22714546
www.delicatessen.no

Opening hours	7 days for lunch and dinner
Reservation policy	Yes
Credit cards	Accepted
Price range	Affordable
Style	Casual
Cuisine	Tapas
Recommended for	Late night

'Good for late-night tapas.'—Esben Holmboe Bang

Oslo's Hispanophiles convene daily around the wooden tables at Delicatessen in Grünerløkka to sip sherry and mop up aïoli after a long day's work or before a long night's partying. The popular tapas bar, now fourteen years old and with a second branch in Majorstuen, does the Iberian classics well – tortilla, chorizo, fried artichokes, and chilli and garlic prawns are smart choices from an appealing menu of tapas, sandwiches and salads. Big Spanish red wines – or ice-cold San Miguel – go down nicely too. There's almost always a wait but it's worth it for a table at this vibey, candlelit hang-out.

THE NIGHTHAWK DINER

Recommended by
Steffen Hansen

Seilduksgata 15
Grünerløkka
Oslo 0553
Norway
+47 96627327
www.nighthawkdiner.com

Opening hours	7 days for breakfast, lunch and dinner
Reservation policy	Yes
Credit cards	Accepted
Price range	Affordable
Style	Casual
Cuisine	American
Recommended for	Breakfast

'Egg and bacon sunny side up and bottomless coffee served by smiling waitresses. Great for early birds.'—Steffen Hansen

Despite the Edward Hopper-inspired name, this retro-styled Oslo diner, opened in 2010, doesn't stay open until the small hours and is rarely as sparsely populated as that in Hopper's iconic paining. It's a fine bit of simulacrum, taking in chrome-trimmed booths, apron-wearing waitresses and a jukebox – all of which might look like it's been reclaimed from somewhere stateside were it not so shiny and new. Their burgers, made from organic Norwegian beef, are worthy of investigation but it's the all-day breakfast menu of pancakes, classic egg dishes and the sausage and bacon-laden brunch that catch the eye.

SAIGON LILLE CAFÉ

Recommended by
Steffen Hansen

Møllergata 32
Grünerløkka
Oslo 0179
Norway

Opening hours	7 days for lunch and dinner
Reservation policy	No
Credit cards	Accepted
Price range	Budget
Style	Casual
Cuisine	Vietnamese
Recommended for	Bargain

'Authentic Vietnamese cuisine with big portions and good prices.'—Steffen Hanson

While 'bargain' is a relative term in Norway, the Vietnamese food served at Saigon Lille is certainly tasty, and the portions are generous. A no-frills, family-run place tucked down an anonymous alley near Youngstorget, they're never going to win any awards for interior design but 69kr (£7; $11) for chicken in sweet and sour sauce is about as reasonable as you're going to find in this town, and the soups (sorry, pho) are also worth your hard-earned money. There's no English or Norwegian menu, so either point at the pictures and hope, or ask a member of staff for their favourites.

FENAKNOKEN

Recommended by
Esben Holmboe Bang

Tordenskiolds Gate 12
Sentrum
Oslo 0160
Norway
www.fenaknoken.no

Opening hours	6 days for breakfast and lunch
Reservation policy	No
Credit cards	Accepted
Price range	Budget
Style	Casual
Cuisine	Deli
Recommended for	Local favourite

'It has some of the best Norwegian traditional cured meats and legendary Norwegian specialities.'
—Esben Holmboe Bang

Fancy some cured reindeer heart? Or how about smalahove (salted sheep's head)? Then make a beeline for chef Eirik Bræk's deli, near Oslo City Hall where he's preserving traditional Norwegian food traditions in more ways than one. There are dried moose, lamb ribs and legs, and numerous hams hanging from the ceiling. But it's not just about meat here. There's a range of Norwegian cheeses, including several varieties of brunost ('brown cheese' made from whey), as well as intriguing home-made jams such as rowanberry, and flatbreads and dried fruits too. If you're a food lover, you won't want to miss it.

FISKERIET YOUNGSTORGET

Recommended by
Esben Holmboe Bang

Youngstorget 2b
Sentrum
Oslo 0181
Norway
www.fiskeriet.com

Opening hours	6 days for lunch and 2 days for dinner
Reservation policy	No
Credit cards	Accepted
Price range	Budget
Style	Casual
Cuisine	Seafood
Recommended for	Bargain

'Really fresh fish and chips.'—Esben Holmboe Bang

HAI CAFÉ

Recommended by
Bjorn Svensson

Calmeyers Gate 6
Sentrum
Oslo 0183
Norway

Opening hours	7 days for lunch and dinner
Reservation policy	No
Credit cards	Accepted
Price range	Budget
Style	Casual
Cuisine	Vietnamese
Recommended for	Bargain

'Traditional Vietnamese cooking that's light and fresh.'—Bjorn Svensson

OSCARSGATE

Recommended by
Steffen Hansen

Inngang Pilestredet 63
Sentrum
Oslo 0350
Norway
+47 22465906
www.restaurantoscarsgate.no

Opening hours	5 days for dinner
Reservation policy	Yes
Reservation email	mail@restaurantoscarsgate.no
Credit cards	Accepted
Price range	Expensive
Style	Smart casual
Cuisine	Modern Nordic
Recommended for	High End

SOLSIDEN

Recommended by
Steffen Hansen, Geir Skeie

Søndre Akershuskai 34
Sentrum
Oslo 0150
Norway
+47 22333630
www.solsiden.no

Opening hours	7 days for dinner in summer
Reservation policy	Yes
Credit cards	Accepted
Price range	Affordable
Style	Casual
Cuisine	Seafood
Recommended for	Wish I'd opened

'Uniquely situated in an old warehouse on the historic quay right below Akershus Castle. Great place.' —Steffen Hansan

Open only for the four summer months, Solsiden (The Sunny Side) makes the most of its brief tenure in this fjordside location, with large windows overlooking the water and a menu that resolutely consists of just seafood and fish. Most come for the spectacular seafood platter, a towering sculpture of lobster, langoustine and scallops in their shells to share between two, but just ask for *dagens fisk* (catch of the day) and you can't go far wrong. Savvy locals snap up the tables early, so book in advance for your best chance of joining them.

PERFECT PIZZA

Recommended by
Geir Skeie

Torgatta 4
Sandefjord
Vestfold 3210
Norway
www.perfect-pizza.no

Opening hours	6 days for dinner
Reservation policy	No
Credit cards	Accepted
Price range	Budget
Style	Casual
Cuisine	Pizza
Recommended for	Late night

VILLA PROVENCE

Recommended by
Geir Skeie

Kirkegata 7
Sandefjord
Vestfold 3211
Norway
+47 33450480
www.villaprovence.no

Opening hours	4 days for lunch
Reservation policy	Yes
Reservation email	villaprovence@netcom.no
Credit cards	Accepted
Price range	Expensive
Style	Casual
Cuisine	French
Recommended for	Regular neighbourhood

'Very authentic Provencal cuisine in an old mansion in the middle of the city. In summer they have a nice outside garden to eat in.'—Geir Skeie

KOCK & VIN

Recommended by
Ben Spalding

Viktoriagatan 12
Vastesr
Gothenburg 411 25
Sweden
+46 317017979
www.kockvin.se

Opening hours	6 days for dinner
Reservation policy	Yes
Reservation email	info@kockvin.se
Credit cards	Accepted
Price range	Expensive
Style	Smart casual
Cuisine	Modern Swedish
Recommended for	Worth the travel

Having started life as a French bistro in 2000, Björn Persson's Kock & Vin only started taking shape in 2006 when the restaurateur bought the cellar below, upgraded the kitchen and set his sights on creating a world-class restaurant. Six years later, the modern Swedish cuisine has a Michelin star and is rated third in Sweden by the prestigious White Guide. However, Kock & Vin remains very much a Gothenburg establishment: the menu brims with west-coast produce – salted herring, seaweed, nettles, langoustine, lingonberry, lovage. If you indulge in the nine-course Journey Menu, you'll appreciate the comfort of the confortable, pared-back dining room. Wine is giving equal billing, so make sure you take pairings from Alexander Bäckman, one of Sweden's top sommeliers.

FÄVIKEN MAGASINET

Fäviken 216
Järpen
Jämtland 830 05
Sweden
+46 64740177
www.favikenmagasinet.se

Recommended by
Daniel Berlin, Sang-Hoon
Degeimbre, Matthew Dillon,
Christian Ebbe, Mikael Einarsson,
Björn Frantzén, Stephen Harris,
Esben Holmboe Bang, Jacob
Holmström, Daniel Lindeberg,
Guillaume Monjuré, Stevie Parle,
Peeter Pihel, Hans Välimäki

Opening hours	4 days for dinner
Reservation policy	Yes
Reservation email	bokning@favikenmagasinet.se
Credit cards	Accepted but not Diners
Price range	Expensive
Style	Smart casual
Cuisine	Modern Swedish
Recommended for	Worth the travel

'It has a magical connection to the local land and nature.'—Sang-Hoon Degeimbre

To say that Fäviken is worth the journey is high praise indeed when you consider that your destination is Järpen in the unspoiled northwest of Sweden, 750 km (466 miles) north of Stockholm, well on your way towards the Arctic Circle. It's run by farmer/forager/hunter/chef Magnus Nilsson, who transforms wild ingredients into an haute experience for only a handful of guests. Almost everything served at the strikingly intimate, twelve-seat, wood-panelled restaurant is collected, caught, hunted or grown on the vast estate that surrounds it. Show-stopping dishes include a charcoal-grilled moose thigh bone, sawed in half on a block in the dining room, and its marrow served.

NATUR CAFÉ AT KRETSLOPPSHUSET

Kyrkvägen 5
Mörsil
Jämtland 830 04
Sweden
+46 647665212
www.kretsloppshuset.com

Recommended by
Magnus Nilsson

Opening hours	6 days for lunch
Reservation policy	Yes
Credit cards	Not accepted
Price range	Affordable
Style	Casual
Cuisine	Swedish
Recommended for	Local favourite

Kretsloppshuset, a name that translates as 'The Circle of Life House', is a sustainable, eco-conscious cooperative run by a forty-strong team of volunteers. From growing organic vegetables to raising free-range chickens in a traditional hen house, Kretsloppshuset's aim, via environmentally sensitive small-scale agriculture, is to provide inspiration for a more sustainable lifestyle. They operate a farm shop and a café where everything served is made from raw ingredients, the majority of which are their own home-grown vegetables. The hippy dream is, it seems, still alive and well in rural northern Sweden.

ÖSTARPS GÄSTGIVAREGÅRD

Gamla Lundavägen 2481-79
Blentarp
Scania 270 35
Sweden
+46 4680229
www.ostarpsgastis.se

Recommended by
Ebbe Vollmer

Opening hours	March to December
Reservation policy	Yes
Credit cards	Accepted
Price range	Affordable
Style	Casual
Cuisine	Swedish
Recommended for	Local favourite

BASTARD

Recommended by
Daniel Berlin, Christian Puglisi

Mäster Johansgatan 11
Malmö
Scania 211 21
Sweden
+46 40121318
www.bastardrestaurant.se

Opening hours	5 days for dinner
Reservation policy	Yes
Reservation email	info@bastardrestaurant.se
Credit cards	Accepted
Price range	Affordable
Style	Formal
Cuisine	Modern European
Recommended for	Worth the travel

'Very, very impressive. Innovative, rustic, bistro style. Not to be missed.'—Christian Puglisi

Chef Andreas Dahlberg's illegitimately named Malmö outpost opened in late 2009. A smartly restyled tavern, all dark wood and white butcher's tiles, its doors open each night at 5.00 p.m. and the bar quickly fills up with the city's most fashionable foodies, who drink natural wine and eat charcuterie, sliced by the huge red machine that sits behind the open counter. When the kitchen proper opens at 6.00 p.m., the menu is meat-heavy with a love of offal (variety of meats) and game that would please Fergus 'St. John' Henderson. The kitchen is proud of its eco-credentials – a champion of local, organic and high-welfare farming.

BLOOM IN THE PARK

Recommended by
Marco Müller

Pildammsvägen 17
Malmö
Scania 214 66
Sweden
+46 4079363
www.bloominthepark.se

Opening hours	5 days for lunch and 6 days for dinner
Reservation policy	Yes
Credit cards	Accepted
Price range	Affordable
Style	Smart casual
Cuisine	Modern European
Recommended for	Worth the travel

JALLA JALLA

Recommended by
Daniel Berlin

Bergsgatan 16
Malmö
Scania 211 54
Sweden

Opening hours	7 days for lunch and dinner
Reservation policy	No
Credit cards	Not accepted
Price range	Budget
Style	Casual
Cuisine	Middle Eastern
Recommended for	Late night

SOLDE KAFFEROSTERI

Recommended by
Andreas Dahlberg, Petter Nilsson

Mejselgatan 3
Malmö
Scania 211 24
Sweden
www.soldekafferosteri.se

Opening hours	6 days for breakfast and lunch
Reservation policy	No
Credit cards	Not accepted
Price range	Budget
Style	Casual
Cuisine	Café
Recommended for	Breakfast

Breakfast at Malmö's Solde Kafferosteri (coffee roastery) usually means a swift espresso from the La Marzocco and a baguette stuffed with cured wild boar ham or artisan salami. High counters and stools to perch on don't make for lingering, so grab one of the coveted corner seats if you can. Set up in 2006 by a trio of coffee nuts, among them a former pro tennis player and a latte art world champion, the centrally located café is catnip to local hipsters who know their Ethiopian Yirgacheffe from their Sumatra Blue Batak. While you're there, pick up a bag of beans adorned with Solde's signature off-the-wall graphics.

SPOONERY

Recommended by
Daniel Berlin

Östra Stallmästaregatan 2
Malmö
Scania 217 49
Sweden
www.spoonery.se

Opening hours	7 days for lunch and dinner
Reservation policy	No
Credit cards	Accepted but not AMEX
Price range	Budget
Style	Casual
Cuisine	Swedish
Recommended for	Bargain

SYSTRAR OCH BRÖDER

Recommended by
Daniel Berlin

Östra Rönneholmsvägen 26
Malmö
Scania 211 47
Sweden
www.systrarbroder.se

Opening hours	7 days for breakfast and lunch
Reservation policy	No
Credit cards	Accepted
Price range	Budget
Style	Casual
Cuisine	Café
Recommended for	Bargain

'Seasonal and local produce is the focus here including little known herbs that the chefs have rescued from obscurity.'

MICHAEL MEREDITH

'HAVE THE SKAGEN TOAST.'

JACON HOLMSTROM

STOCKHOLM

'IN A CITY FULL OF BEAUTIFUL DINING ROOMS THIS PLACE TAKES IT ONE STEP FURTHER.'

BJORN PERSSON

'Forget New York. The best hot dogs in the world are found in Stockholm.'

MAGNUS NILSSON

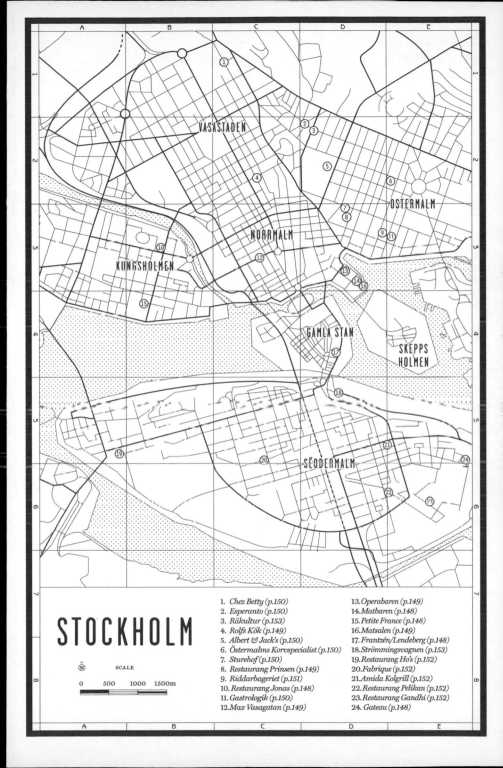

STOCKHOLM

1. *Chez Betty (p.150)*
2. *Esperanto (p.150)*
3. *Räkultur (p.153)*
4. *Rolfs Kök (p.149)*
5. *Albert & Jack's (p.150)*
6. *Östermalms Korvspecialist (p.150)*
7. *Sturehof (p.150)*
8. *Restaurang Prinsen (p.149)*
9. *Riddarbageriet (p.151)*
10. *Restaurang Jonas (p.148)*
11. *Gastrologik (p.150)*
12. *Max Vasagatan (p.149)*
13. *Operabaren (p.149)*
14. *Matbaren (p.148)*
15. *Petite France (p.148)*
16. *Matsalen (p.149)*
17. *Frantzén/Lendeberg (p.148)*
18. *Strömmingsvagnen (p.153)*
19. *Restaurang Ho's (p.152)*
20. *Fabrique (p.152)*
21. *Amida Kolgrill (p.152)*
22. *Restaurang Pelikan (p.152)*
23. *Restaurang Gandhi (p.152)*
24. *Gateau (p.148)*

N̂

SCALE

0   500   1000   1500m

FRANTZÉN/LINDEBERG

Lilla Nygatan 21
Stockholm 111 28
+46 8208580
www.frantzen-lindeberg.com

Recommended by
Mathias Dahlgren, Mikael
Einarsson, Esben Holmboe Bang,
Michael Meredith, Björn Persson,
Peeter Pihel, Hans Välimäki

Opening hours..5 days for dinner
Reservation policy...Yes
Reservation email.........reservation@frantzen-lindeberg.com
Credit cards..Accepted
Price range...Expensive
Style...Smart casual
Cuisine...Modern Swedish
Recommended for...High End

This rapidly rising Stockholm star opened in 2008 in the city's picturesque Old Town. It's a partnership between chef Björn Frantzén and pastry chef Daniel Lindeberg, who divide up the savoury and the sweet, working with raw materials from the restaurant's two gardens and from a list of trusted local producers, farmers and growers that they have carefully cultivated. Menus are made up of whatever they have in each day and presented in a series of bite-sized courses. Try and book a berth at one of the four front-row counter seats that overlook the action at the kitchen's pass.

PETITE FRANCE

John Ericssonsgatan 6
Kungsholmen
Stockholm 112 22
www.petitefrance.se

Recommended by
Mikael Einarsson

Opening hours..........................6 days for breakfast and lunch
Reservation policy..No
Credit cards......................Accepted but not AMEX and Diners
Price range...Budget
Style..Casual
Cuisine..Bakery-Café-Deli
Recommended for..Breakfast

RESTAURANG JONAS

Fleminggatan 39
Kungsholmen
Stockholm 112 32
www.restaurangjonas.se

Recommended by
Steffen Hansen

Opening hours..5 days for dinner
Reservation policy...Yes
Credit cards..Accepted
Price range...Expensive
Style...Smart casual
Cuisine...International
Recommended for...Worth the travel

GATEAU

Ektorpsvägen 4
Nacka
Stockholm 131 47
www.gateau.se

Recommended by
Jacob Holmström

Opening hours..........................7 days for breakfast and lunch
Reservation policy..No
Credit cards..Accepted
Price range..Affordable
Style..Casual
Cuisine..Bakery-Café
Recommended for..Breakfast

'Decent and close to where I live, for when I've just got out of bed and don't feel like a long walk!'
—Jacob Holmström

MATBAREN

The Grand Hôtel
Södra Blasieholmshamnen 8
Norrmalm
Stockholm 103 27
+46 86793584
www.grandhotel.se

Recommended by
Anton Bjuhr
Jacob Holmström

Opening hours..............5 days for lunch and 6 days for dinner
Reservation policy...Yes
Reservation email...........................reservations@mdghs.com
Credit cards..Accepted
Price range..Affordable
Style...Smart casual
Cuisine...Modern Swedish
Recommended for...High End

MATSALEN

Grand Hôtel
Södra Blasieholmshamnen 8
Norrmalm
Stockholm 103 27
+46 86793584
www.grandhotel.se

Opening hours................................5 days for dinner
Reservation policy..Yes
Reservation email.....................reservations@mdghs.com
Credit cards..Accepted
Price range...Affordable
Style..Smart casual
Cuisine...Modern Swedish
Recommended for.......................................High End

MAX VASAGATAN

Vasagatan 7
Norrmalm
Stockholm 111 20
www.max.se

Opening hours.......................7 days from breakfast until late
Reservation policy...No
Credit cards..Accepted
Price range..Budget
Style..Casual
Cuisine..Burgers
Recommended for....................................Late night

OPERABAREN

Operahuset
Karl XII:S Torg
Norrmalm
Stockholm 111 86
+46 86765808
www.operakallaren.se

Opening hours................................7 days for lunch and dinner
Reservation policy..Yes
Reservation email...................operabaren@operakallaren.se
Credit cards..Accepted
Price range...Affordable
Style..Smart casual
Cuisine...Modern Swedish
Recommended for.............................Local favourite

RESTAURANG PRINSEN

Mäster Samuelsgatan 4
Norrmalm
Stockholm 111 44
+46 86111331
www.restaurangprinsen.se

Opening hours................................7 days for lunch and dinner
Reservation policy..Yes
Credit cards..Accepted
Price range...Affordable
Style..Casual
Cuisine...Swedish
Recommended for.............................Local favourite

ROLFS KÖK

Tegnérgatan 41
Norrmalm
Stockholm 111 61
+46 8101696
www.rolfskok.se

Opening hours.............5 days for lunch and 7 days for dinner
Reservation policy..Yes
Reservation email...................................info@rolfskok.se
Credit cards..Accepted
Price range...Affordable
Style..Casual
Cuisine...Swedish French
Recommended for...................Regular neighbourhood

ALBERT & JACK'S

Recommended by
Daniel Lindeberg,
Peeter Pihel

Engelbrektsgatan 3
Östermalm
Stockholm 114 32
www.albertjacks.se

Opening hours	6 days for breakfast and lunch
Reservation policy	No
Credit cards	Accepted
Price range	Budget
Style	Casual
Cuisine	Bakery-Deli
Recommended for	Breakfast

'A nice deli.'—Peter Pihel

This cool, industrial-look bakery and deli nestles in imposing arches overlooking the haven of the Humlegården gardens in elegant Östermalm. Quiet first thing on a Saturday morning, when partygoers, who danced the hours away at nearby Stureplan's exclusive clubs, are still asleep, it makes a pleasant pit stop, particularly if sitting at a pavement (sidewalk) table in summer. Emphasis here is on healthy foods from wraps and salads, to speciality squid crisps. The range of pastries and tarts are as tasty as they are appealing to the eye. As well as aromatic coffees, teas are exotic (e.g. green tea and carrot). And be sure to try the ice cream.

CHEZ BETTY

Recommended by
Mikael Einarsson

Roslagsgatan 43
Östermalm
Stockholm 113 54
+46 8292293
chezbetty.se

Opening hours	5 days for dinner
Reservation policy	Yes
Credit cards	Accepted
Price range	Affordable
Style	Casual
Cuisine	French
Recommended for	Regular neighbourhood

ESPERANTO

Recommended by
Björn Persson

Kungstensgatan 2
Östermalm
Stockholm 114 25
+46 86962323
www.esperantorestaurant.se

Opening hours	4 days for dinner
Reservation policy	Yes
Reservation email	esperanto@sollevi.se
Credit cards	Accepted
Price range	Expensive
Style	Smart casual
Cuisine	International
Recommended for	Worth the travel

Swedish chef Sayan Isaksson won gold at the World Culinary Olympics in 2004, but has since shown he can create art on a plate even when there's no podium place at stake. His grand restaurant Esperanto opened in 2005 in what was the foyer of Stockholm's old Jarla Theatre (John Cale and Blondie played there in the 1970s) and was awarded a Michelin star two years later. Isaksson's cuisine is minimal yet flamboyant 'international gastronomy without boundaries' – hence 'Esperanto' – and shows marked French, Japanese and local influences. Choose from a seasonal or 'dégustation' menu of, say, Swedish wagyu beef, served with fine wines or rare teas.

GASTROLOGIK

Recommended by
Steffen Hansen, Magnus Nilsson

Artillerigatan 14
Östermalm
Stockholm 114 51
+46 86623060
www.gastrologik.se

Opening hours	4 days for lunch and 5 days for dinner
Reservation policy	Yes
Reservation email	info@gastrologik.se
Credit cards	Accepted
Price range	Expensive
Style	Smart casual
Cuisine	Modern Swedish
Recommended for	Worth the travel

Opened in late 2011 in Östermalm, by chefs Jacob Holmström and Anton Bjuhr, Gastrologik has quickly established a reputation as one of Stockholm's freshest, forward-thinking restaurants. The relaxed modern dining room – a beautifully understated combination of oak floors, white walls, copper lampshades, aquamarine glass and sturdy but stylish Scandinavian furniture – is a suitable setting for daily-changing dishes that are exercises in product driven simplicity. At lunch it's a simply dictated choice of two or three courses; at dinner, a tasting menu of six. Next door sits Speceriet, their delicatessen, in which the stone oven bakes their sourdough bread.

ÖSTERMALMS KORVSPECIALIST

Recommended by
Jacob Holmström,
Magnus Nilsson

Nybrogatan 57
Östermalm
Stockholm 114 40
www.ostermalmskorvspecialist.se

Opening hours	7 days for lunch and dinner
Reservation policy	No
Credit cards	Not accepted
Price range	Budget
Style	Casual
Cuisine	Hot dogs
Recommended for	Bargain

Some Swedes would argue that the world's best hot dog stand is in Stockholm. Known to locals as Bruno's, after its German-born owner Bruno Fortkord, it's near the city's famous Östermalms Saluhall indoor food market. Select your sausage from a list that takes in Argentinian chorizo, Tunisian *merguez*, Hungarian *kabonos* and Slovenian *kransky*, before heading to the heartland of the wurst, with Switzerland, Austria and Germany represented. Vegetarians get grilled halloumi. All are cooked to order and stuffed inside a grilled baguette with sauerkraut and your mustard of choice. Forget ketchup – Bruno has his own homemade spicy tomato sauce.

RIDDARBAGERIET

Recommended by
Daniel Lindeberg

Riddargatan 15
Östermalm
Stockholm 114 57

Opening hours	6 days from breakfast until late
Reservation policy	No
Credit cards	Accepted
Price range	Budget
Style	Casual
Cuisine	Bakery-Café
Recommended for	Breakfast

STUREHOF

Recommended by
Mikael Einarsson, Björn
Frantzén, Jacob Holmström,
Daniel Lindeberg

Stureplan 2
Östermalm
Stockholm 114 46
+46 84405730
www.sturehof.com

Opening hours	7 days for lunch and dinner
Reservation policy	Yes
Credit cards	Accepted
Price range	Affordable
Style	Smart casual
Cuisine	Seafood
Recommended for	Late night

'I have the *skagentoast*.'—Jacob Holmström

AMIDA KOLGRILL

Recommended by
Mathias Dahlgren

Folkungagatan 76
Södermalm
Stockholm 116 22
www.amida.se

Opening hours	7 days for lunch and dinner
Reservation policy	No
Credit cards	Accepted
Price range	Budget
Style	Casual
Cuisine	Turkish
Recommended for	Bargain

Serving grilled meats and charred vegetables to hungry Stockholmares in search of a satisfyingly salty hit, this renowned cheap-eat is in its tenth year of operation. Kurdish, Turkish and Persian kebabs and salads dominate the menu in a city not known for its culinary multiculturalism. Think huge plates of mint-specked lamb shish or marinated chicken skewers with mounds of rice, melanges of pickles dusted with sumac. Key to the unique flavour of their meats is the use of a traditional Mesopotamiskt aromatic charcoal bed. Eat in with a view of the open kitchen or order to take away.

FABRIQUE

Recommended by
Anton Bjuhr

Rosenlundsgaten 28
Södermalm
Stockholm 118 53
www.fabrique.se

Opening hours	7 days for breakfast and lunch
Reservation policy	No
Credit cards	Accepted
Price range	Budget
Style	Casual
Cuisine	Bakery-Café
Recommended for	Breakfast

'The perfect place to buy breakfast bread.'
—Anton Bjuhr

RESTAURANG GANDHI

Recommended by
Petter Nilsson

Katarina Bangata 47
Södermalm
Stockholm 116 39
+46 86439788
www.restauranggandhi.se

Opening hours	7 days for lunch and dinner
Reservation policy	Yes
Credit cards	Accepted but not AMEX and Diners
Price range	Budget
Style	Casual
Cuisine	Indian
Recommended for	Regular neighbourhood

RESTAURANG HO'S

Recommended by
Anton Bjuhr

Hornsgatan 151
Södermalm
Stockholm 117 34
www.restauranghos.se

Opening hours	2 days for lunch and 7 days for dinner
Reservation policy	Yes
Credit cards	Accepted
Price range	Affordable
Style	Casual
Cuisine	Chinese
Recommended for	Regular neighbourhood

RESTAURANG PELIKAN

Recommended by
Petter Nilsson

Blekingegatan 40
Södermalm
Stockholm 116 62
+46 855609092
www.pelikan.se

Opening hours	7 days for lunch and dinner
Reservation policy	Yes
Credit cards	Accepted
Price range	Affordable
Style	Casual
Cuisine	Swedish
Recommended for	Local favourite

STRÖMMINGSVAGNEN

Södermalms Torg
Södermalm
Stockholm 1116 45
www.strommingsvagnen.webatu.com

Recommended by
Mathias Dahlgren

Opening hours.......................7 days for lunch and early dinner
Reservation policy...No
Credit cards...Accepted
Price range..Budget
Style...Casual
Cuisine..Seafood
Recommended for..Local favourite

Snow or shine, this Stockholm institution has been plying its fishy trade near the Slussen Tunnelbana for over twenty years. A small green-roofed kiosk with a few wooden picnic tables overlooking the Riddarfjärden, look out for its large yellow fish-shaped sign, which reads 'Nysert Strömming' (fresh fried herring). On the menu – it shouldn't surprise you to hear – are various fortifying servings of freshly fried Baltic herring. Have them on rye bread topped with red onion, fresh dill and mustard, with homemade mashed potato and sour cream, or in a warm burger bun, or on their own, by the kilogram.

RÅKULTUR

Kungstensgatan 2
Vasastaden
Stockholm 114 25
+46 86962325
www.rakultur.se

Recommended by
Mikael Einarsson, Björn Frantzen,
Jacob Holmström, Daniel Lindeberg

Opening hours................................6 days for lunch and dinner
Reservation policy...Yes
Reservation email.................................Rakultur@sollevi.se
Credit cards...Accepted
Price range...Affordable
Style...Smart casual
Cuisine..Japanese
Recommended for..Bargain

'Really good sushi and Japanese food at decent prices.'—Jacob Holmström

DEN RODE COTTAGE

Strandvejen 550
Klampenborg
Hovedstaden 2930
Denmark
+45 39904614
www.dengulecottage.dk

Recommended by
Claus Meyer

Opening hours..7 days for dinner
Reservation policy...Yes
Reservation email.........................info@dengulecottage.dk
Credit cards...Accepted
Price range...Affordable
Style...Casual
Cuisine...Modern Nordic
Recommended for..Local favourite

In an idyllic woodland setting in the countryside north of Copenhagen, Den Rode Cottage occupies a nineteenth-century forestry officer's house that, surrounded by ancient beech trees, looks so sweet it could grace a Danish biscuit (cookie) tin. The kitchen is run by Lars Thomsen, formerly of Dragsholm Slot, the monthly changing Nordic menus – three, five or seven courses – devised in partnership with Anita Klemensen, previously of the quirky Copenhagen apartment-based 1.th. Together with Anders Wulff-Sorensen, another ex-city chef who worked at Sollerod Kro. They also run Den Gule Cottage (The Yellow Cottage) in another picture-perfect dwelling, overlooking the coast slightly further south.

FORMEL B

Vesterbrogade 182
Frederiksberg C
Hovedstaden 1800
Denmark
+45 33251066
www.formel-b.dk

Recommended by
Francis Cardenau, Christian
Ebbe, Gunnar Karl Gíslason

Opening hours..6 days for dinner
Reservation policy...Yes
Credit cards...Accepted
Price range...Affordable
Style...Smart casual
Cuisine..French
Recommended for...............................Regular neighbourhood

MEYERS DELI

Recommended by
Thomas Herman

107 Gammel Kongevej
Frederiksberg
Hovedstaden 1850
Denmark
+45 33243706
www.meyersdeli.dk

Opening hours.............7 days for breakfast, lunch and dinner
Reservation policy...Yes
Credit cards...Accepted
Price range..Budget
Style...Casual
Cuisine...Deli-Café
Recommended for...Breakfast

OVSA

Recommended by
Francis Cardenau

Tuborg Havnevej 4
Hellerup
Hovedstaden 2900
Denmark
+45 39402900
www.ovsa.dk

Opening hours...........7 days for brunch and 5 days for dinner
Reservation policy...Yes
Credit cards...Accepted
Price range..Budget
Style...Casual
Cuisine..Café
Recommended for...Breakfast

RESTAURANT MÊLÉE

Recommended by
Claus Meyer

Martensens Allé 16
Frederiksberg C
Hovedstaden 1828
Denmark
+45 35131134
www.melee.dk

Opening hours...4 days for dinner
Reservation policy...Yes
Credit cards...Accepted
Price range..Affordable
Style...Casual
Cuisine...French
Recommended for..Late night

'Melee is a wonderful place serving French rustic
food until late into the night.'—Claus Meyer

RESTAURANT SLETTEN

Recommended by
Christian Ebbe,
Thomas Rode Anderson

Gammel Strandvej 137
Humlebaek
Hovedstaden 3050
Denmark
+45 49191321
www.sletten.dk

Opening hours.................................5 days for lunch and dinner
Reservation policy...Yes
Credit cards...Accepted
Price range..Affordable
Style...Smart casual
Cuisine..Modern Nordic
Recommended for.............................Worth the travel

'Tasty, well-prepared, original and extremely
interesting meals.'—Thomas Rode Anderson

SAIGON QUAN

Recommended by
Claus Meyer,
Thomas Rode Anderson

Godthåbsvej 48
Frederiksberg
Hovedstaden 2000
Denmark
+45 38101900
www.saigonquan.dk

Opening hours..6 days for dinner
Reservation policy...Yes
Reservation email..................................long@pc.dk
Credit cards...Accepted
Price range..Budget
Style...Casual
Cuisine..Vietnamese
Recommended for.............................Regular neighbourhood

'The food is cheap, skillfully prepared and properly
seasoned.'—Thomas Rode Anderson

SØLLERØD KRO

Søllerødvej 35
Holte
Hovedstaden 2840
Denmark
+45 45802505
www.soelleroed-kro.dk

Recommended by
Christian Puglisi

Opening hours	5 days for lunch and dinner
Reservation policy	Yes
Reservation email	mail@soelleroed-kro.dk
Credit cards	Accepted
Price range	Expensive
Style	Smart casual
Cuisine	European
Recommended for	High End

'Classic food with a fresh and modernaproach.'
—Christian Puglisi

DRAGSHOLM SLOT

Dragsholm Alle 3
Hørve
Sjælland 4534
Denmark
www.dragsholm-slot.dk

Recommended by
Christian Ebbe, Gunnar Karl
Gíslason, Rasmus Kofoed

Opening hours	2-6 days for dinner in season
Reservation policy	Yes
Credit cards	Accepted
Price range	Expensive
Style	Smart casual
Cuisine	Modern Nordic
Recommended for	High End

An hour's drive northwest of Copenhagen, in the
Odsherred countryside, lies Dragsholm Slot, one of
Denmark's oldest castles – the sort of baroque early
thirteenth-century pile that, looking at it from the
outside, you can imagine Hamlet sulking around.
Now a thirty-six-room hotel, it has two restaurants:
the serious Castle and the casual Eatery. Claus M.
Henriksen, yet another talented alumni from Noma's
kitchen, where he was sous-chef, oversees both.
As at Noma, the focus is very much on vegetable
over animal protein, with much of former grown
in the castle's garden and the surrounding island
of Zealand.

'Loud, casual and uncomplicated and the food is creative and daring. A very vibrant place.'
JAKOB MIELCKELE P159

'Great Arabic street food. Try the falafel.'
RASMUS KOFOED P161

COPENHAGEN

'THE FOOD IS WONDERFUL, DELICIOUS AND CREATIVE. THEY MAKE YOU FEEL SO WELCOME FROM THE SECOND YOU ARRIVE. I CAN'T WAIT TO GO BACK!'
SEAN BROCK P160

'IT WAS WAY BEYOND MY EXPECTATIONS.'
BJØRN SVENSSON P162

'Really cool space and sexy atmosphere.'
JAIR TELLEZ P164

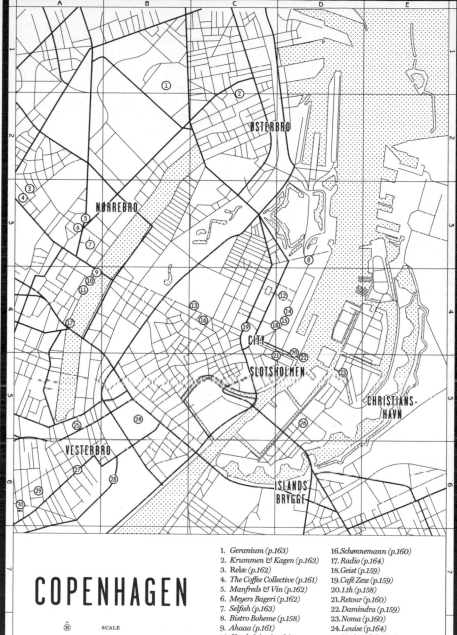

COPENHAGEN

N̂   SCALE

0   75   150   225m

1.TH

Recommended by
Adam Aamann

Herluf Trolle Gade 9
Indre By
Copenhagen 1052
www.1th.dk

Opening hours..................................4 days for dinner
Reservation policy...Yes
Credit cards...Accepted
Price range...Expensive
Style...Casual
Cuisine...Modern Danish
Recommended for...High End

You make a reservation to be invited to the trendy Danish dinner party experience that is the 1.th (its name is an abbreviation of 'first floor to the right'). Hosted in a chic retro-styled apartment in Herluf Trolles Gade behind the Royal Theatre, the ambience is secret society meets old-fashioned Danish hospitality. The creation of Mette Martinussen, who hosted her first dinner party here over a decade ago, you mingle for drinks and canapés in the drawing room, with the twenty or so other diners, before sitting down in an intimate dining room to an innovative ten-course tasting menu.

AOC

Recommended by
Francis Cardenau, Michael
Kempf, Claus Meyer,
Björn Persson

Dronningens Tværgade 2
Indre By
Copenhagen 1302
+45 33111145
www.restaurantaoc.dk

Opening hours..................................5 days for dinner
Reservation policy...Yes
Reservation email........................booking@restaurantaoc.dk
Credit cards...Accepted
Price range...Expensive
Style...Smart casual
Cuisine...Modern Nordic
Recommended for...Worth the travel

The 'Modern/New Nordic Kitchen' trend doesn't begin and end with Noma. Restaurant AOC offers another take on its themes, shifting the focus from obscure Scandinavian ingredients to techniques and combinations designed to thrill all the senses. For an example look no further than ex-elBulli chef Ronny Emborg's edible pastoral tableau of a 'tree' with

leaves of smoked ham or mackerel in hay ash, green tomatoes and buttermilk. For the full AOC experience go for the 'sensory evening' of ten-course tasting menu with wines from one of the best collections in town. The surroundings – the whitewashed cellar of an old mansion – are beautiful.

BISTRO BOHEME

Recommended by
Thomas Herman

Esplanaden 8
Indre By
Copenhagen 1263
+45 70220870
www.bistroboheme.dk

Opening hours..................................7 days for lunch and dinner
Reservation policy...Yes
Credit cards...Accepted
Price range...Affordable
Style...Smart casual
Cuisine...French
Recommended for..................................Regular neighbourhood

BRDR. PRICE

Recommended by
Claus Moller Henriksen

Rosenborggade 15-17
Indre By
Copenhagen 1130
www.brdr-price.dk

Opening hours..................................7 days for lunch and dinner
Reservation policy...Yes
Credit cards...Accepted
Price range...Affordable
Style...Casual
Cuisine...Danish
Recommended for...Worth the travel

CAFÉ ZEZE

Ny Østergade 20
Indre By
Copenhagen 1101
+45 33142390
www.cafe-zeze.dk

Opening hours.............7 days for breakfast, lunch and dinner
Reservation policy...Yes
Credit cards..Accepted
Price range...Affordable
Style..Casual
Cuisine..European
Recommended for...Breakfast

DAMINDRA

Holbergsgade 26
Indre By
Copenhagen 1057
+45 33123375
www.damindra.dk

Opening hours.................................5 days for lunch and dinner
Reservation policy...Yes
Reservation email..hello@damindra.dk
Credit cards....................Accepted but not AMEX and Diners
Price range...Affordable
Style..Casual
Cuisine..Japanese
Recommended for............................Regular neighbourhood

'Great Japanese style food at affordable prices. The chef has served under Nobu and I love his cooking style and taste.'—Adam Aamann

GEIST

Kongens Nytorv 8
Indre By
Copenhagen 1050
+45 33133713
www.restaurantgeist.dk

Opening hours..7 days for dinner
Reservation policy...Yes
Reservation email.............................mail@restaurantgeist.dk
Credit cards..Accepted
Price range...Affordable
Style..Casual
Cuisine...Modern Nordic
Recommended for............................Regular neighbourhood

'Loud, casual and uncomplicated and the food is simple, creative and daring.'—Jakob Mielcke

MASH

Bredgade 20
Indre By
Copenhagen 1260
+45 33139300
www.mashsteak.dk

Opening hours.............5 days for lunch and 7 days for dinner
Reservation policy..Yes
Reservation email..mall@mashsteak.dk
Credit cards..Accepted
Price range...Expensive
Style..Smart casual
Cuisine...Steakhouse
Recommended for...Late night

NOMA

Strandgade 93
Indre By
Copenhagen 1401
+45 32963297
www.noma.dk

Opening hours	5 days for lunch and 6 days for dinner
Reservation policy	Yes
Reservation email	booking@noma.dk
Credit cards	Accepted
Price range	Expensive
Style	Smart casual
Cuisine	Modern Nordic
Recommended for	Wish I'd opened

'The food is wonderful, delicious and creative. But that isn't just it. It is the room, the stories, the beverage pairings, the pace, and what really blows me away is the hospitality. I thought we knew hospitality in the American South, but it's simply over the top at Noma. They make you feel so welcome from the second you arrive. I can't wait to go back!'—Sean Brock

'Probably the best restaurant in the world…' – that's famously been the opinion of an international jury of chefs, restaurateurs and restaurant critics, for three years running since 2010. A 200-year-old harbourside warehouse in Christianshavn, originally built to store goods from Iceland, Greenland and the Faroe Islands, has been the home of René Redzepi's headline-grabbing, agenda-setting dining room since 2004. Given a new look late in the summer of 2012, the waiting list hasn't got any shorter and the kitchen hasn't stopped pushing boundaries with avant-garde and rediscovered techniques applied to products farmed, fished and foraged from the rich Nordic larder (pantry).

RETOUR

Tordenskjoldsgade 11
Indre By
Copenhagen 1055
+45 33338330
www.retour.dk

Opening hours	6 days for dinner
Reservation policy	Yes
Reservation email	info@retour.dk
Credit cards	Accepted
Price range	Affordable
Style	Casual
Cuisine	French
Recommended for	Bargain

SCHØNNEMANN

Hauser Plads 16
Indre By
Copenhagen 1127
+45 33120785
www.restaurantschonnemann.dk

Opening hours	6 days for lunch
Reservation policy	Yes
Reservation email	danishlunch@mail.dk
Credit cards	Accepted
Price range	Affordable
Style	Casual
Cuisine	Danish
Recommended for	Local favourite

Proudly serving traditional smørrebrød (open sandwiches) since 1877, its dark wooden interior with gingham-draped tables is an essential stop for any right-thinking food tourist on a visit to the Danish capital. The organic meat, poultry and dairy used on the menu might be twenty-first century but the sand on the floor is a reminder of the nineteenth century, when it was warmed by charcoal burners and filled with farmers on their way back from delivering to the market. The sandwiches are huge; the aquavit (a favourite Danish alcoholic drink) list long. If in search of 'New Nordic', go elsewhere – this is a taste of old Copenhagen.

SWEET TREAT

Recommended by
René Redzepi

Skt. Annæ Gade 3a
Indre By
Copenhagen 1416
www.sweettreat.dk

Opening hours............................7 days for breakfast and lunch
Reservation policy..No
Credit cards..Accepted
Price range...Budget
Style...Casual
Cuisine...Café
Recommended for..Breakfast

UMAMI

Recommended by
Thomas Rode Anderson

Store Kongensgade 59
Indre By
Copenhagen 1264
+45 33387500
www.restaurantumami.dk

Opening hours..6 days for dinner
Reservation policy...Yes
Credit cards..Accepted
Price range..Affordable
Style..Smart casual
Cuisine..Japanese-French
Recommended for................................Regular neighbourhood

AHAAA

Recommended by
Rasmus Kofoed

Blågårdsgade 21
Nørrebro
Copenhagen 2200

Opening hours.............7 days for breakfast, lunch and dinner
Reservation policy..No
Credit cards..Not accepted
Price range...Budget
Style...Casual
Cuisine...Middle Eastern
Recommended for...Late night

'Try the falafel. Great Arabic street food.'
—Rasmus Kofoed

THE COFFEE COLLECTIVE

Recommended by
Rasmus Kofoed, Christian
Puglisi, René Redzepi

Jægersborggade 10
Nørrebro
Copenhagen N 2200
www.coffeecollective.dk

Opening hours..........7 days for brunch and 5 days for dinner
Reservation policy..No
Credit cards..Accepted
Price range...Budget
Style...Casual
Cuisine...Café
Recommended for..Breakfast

The Dane's take their coffee very seriously and the Coffee Collective in Nørrebro is widely regarded as probably Copenhagen's very best caffeine dispensary, no small compliment in a city where the competition and the coffee is so strong. A microroastery is run by an expert team of award-winning Danes – roasters, buyers and baristas – and the beans are sourced directly from farmers around the world, with sustainability and fair trade, as well as quality, at the top of the agenda. If you are a coffee geek you'll be in heaven here: you'll have to try very hard to find a better crema on your cuppa.

KATE'S JOINT

Recommended by
Martin Morales

Blågårdsgade 12
Nørrebro
Copenhagen 2200
+45 35374496

Opening hours.............4 days for lunch and 7 days for dinner
Reservation policy..No
Credit cards..Accepted
Price range...Budget
Style...Casual
Cuisine...International
Recommended for..Worth the travel

MANFREDS & VIN

Jægersborggade 40
Nørrebro
Copenhagen 2200
+45 36966593
www.manfreds.dk

Recommended by
Francis Cardenau, Rasmus
Kofoed, Claus Meyer,
René Redzepi

Opening hours............2 days for breakfast and 6 days dinner
Reservation policy...Yes
Reservation email........................booking@manfreds.dk
Credit cards...Accepted
Price range...Affordable
Style...Casual
Cuisine........................Nordic-European small plates
Recommended for.......................................Bargain

Run by the team behind Restaurant Relæ, which sits across the street, Manfreds & Vin began life as more of a takeaway (takeout) before morphing into a wine bar and casual dining room. They have a 200-strong list of natural wines, with the dozen or so selections by the glass available displayed on the blackboard behind the bar. Dishes are mostly tapas-sized and designed for sharing, whether you order from the short and snappy à la carte or go with one of their set menus. Come the weekend and brunch, their Eggs Benedict with apple slaw has its own fan club.

MEYERS BAGERI

Jægersborggade 9
Nørrebro
Copenhagen 2200
+45 25101134
www.clausmeyer.dk

Recommended by
Rasmus Kofoed,
Christian Puglisi

Opening hours...........................7 days for breakfast and lunch
Reservation policy..No
Credit cards...Accepted
Price range...Budget
Style...Casual
Cuisine..Bakery
Recommended for.......................................Breakfast

RANEE'S

Blågårds Plads 10
Nørrebro
Copenhagen 2200
+45 35368505
www.ranees.dk

Recommended by
Christian Puglisi

Opening hours....................................6 days for dinner
Reservation policy...Yes
Credit cards...Accepted
Price range...Budget
Style...Casual
Cuisine..Thai
Recommended for.......................................Bargain

'Great Thai kitchen.'—Christian Puglisi

RELÆ

Jægersborggade 41
Nørrebro
Copenhagen 2200
+45 36966609
www.restaurant-relae.dk

Recommended by
Daniel Berlin, Sven Chartier,
Andreas Dahlberg, Christian
Ebbe, Benjamin Greeno,
Sam Harris, Claus Moller
Henriksen, James Lowe, Isaac
McHale, Claus Meyer, Jakob
Mielcke, Petter Nilsson, Daniel
Patterson, Peeter Pihel, René
Redzepi, Bjorn Svensson

Opening hours....................................4 days for dinner
Reservation policy...Yes
Reservation email....................booking@restaurant-relae.dk
Credit cards...Accepted
Price range...Affordable
Style..Smart casual
Cuisine..Modern Nordic
Recommended for...............................Worth the travel

'Christian Puglisi is running an awesome place – it's somewhere you shouldn't miss when you are in town.'—Benjamin Greeno

Opened in 2010 by a pair of graduates from Noma, Copenhagen's seminal culinary kingpin: its former head chef, the Sicilian-born, Danish-raised Christian Puglisi, and Dane Kim Rossen, who worked there as a chef and waiter. Relæ sits in Copenhagen's gentrifying but still colourful Nørrebro district, in the northwest of the city. The vibe is informal, the simply styled dining room with open kitchen, an exercise in clever Danish design, form perfectly meeting function in tables built with neat drawers that hold the table settings and menu. The cooking, expressed via a choice of two four-course options – one meat-free – remains seriously ambitious.

SELFISH

Recommended by
Rasmus Kofoed,
Christian Puglisi

Elmegade 4
Nørrebro
Copenhagen 2200
+45 35359626
www.selfish.dk

Opening hours................................5 days for lunch and dinner
Reservation policy...Yes
Reservation email...selfish@mail.dk
Credit cards...Accepted
Price range...Budget
Style...Casual
Cuisine..Japanese
Recommended for................................Regular neighbourhood

'A great humble sushi place with just four to
six seats.'—Christian Pulisi

GERANIUM

Recommended by
Francis Cardenau, Vladislav
Djatsuk, Julius Jaspers,
Jakob Mielcke, Thorsten Schmidt

Per Henrik Lings Allé 4
Østerbro
Copenhagen 2100
+45 69960020
www.geranium.dk

Opening hours..............3 days for lunch and 4 days for dinner
Reservation policy...Yes
Credit cards...Accepted
Price range..Expensive
Style..Smart casual
Cuisine...Modern Nordic
Recommended for...Worth the travel

KRUMMEN & KAGEN

Recommended by
Adam Aamann

Nordre Frihavnsgade 43
Østerbro
Copenhagen 2100
+45 61270817
www.krummen-kagen.dk

Opening hours.................7 days for breakfast, lunch and tea
Reservation policy...Yes
Reservation email......................kontakt@krummen-kagen.dk
Credit cards...Accepted
Price range..Affordable
Style...Casual
Cuisine..Cafe
Recommended for...Breakfast

BANZAI

Recommended by
Jakob Mielcke

Skydebanegade 16
Vesterbro
Copenhagen 1709
+45 36963331
www.restaurantbanzai.dk

Opening hours..5 days for dinner
Reservation policy...Yes
Credit cards...Accepted
Price range...Budget
Style...Casual
Cuisine..Japanese
Recommended for...Bargain

'Simple but extremely delicious and true to its
Japanese origins.'—Jakob Mielcke

KADEAU

Recommended by
Francis Cardenau

Vesterbrogade 135
Vesterbro
Copenhagen 1620
+45 33252223
www.kadeau.dk

Opening hours...5 days for dinner
Reservation policy...Yes
Credit cards...Accepted
Price range..Affordable
Style..Smart casual
Cuisine...Modern Nordic
Recommended for...Worth the travel

KEBABISTAN

Recommended by
Christian Puglisi

Istedgade 105
Vesterbro
Copenhagen 1650

Opening hours................................7 days for lunch and dinner
Reservation policy...No
Credit cards...Accepted
Price range...Budget
Style...Casual
Cuisine...Fast food
Recommended for...Late night

'Definitely the best kebab in town.'—Christian Puglisi

KØDBYENS FISKEBAR

Recommended by
Jair Tellez

Flæsketorvet 100
Vesterbro
Copenhagen 1711
+45 32155656
www.fiskebaren.dk

Opening hours	2 days for lunch and 5 days for dinner
Reservation policy	Yes
Credit cards	Accepted
Price range	Affordable
Style	Casual
Cuisine	Seafood
Recommended for	Worth the travel

'Really cool space, sexy athmosphere and it is amazing how they manage to serve a relaxed fare of shellfish and oysters alongside complex and extremely well-excecuted dishes made with local produce.' –Jair Tellez

LOUISE

Recommended by
Peter Goossens

Nimb Hotel
Bernstorffsgade 5
Vesterbro
Copenhagen 1577
+45 88700020
www.nimb.dk

Opening hours	5 days for lunch and 6 days for dinner
Reservation policy	Yes
Reservation email	louise@nimb.dk
Credit cards	Accepted
Price range	Expensive
Style	Smart casual
Cuisine	Modern Nordic
Recommended for	Worth the travel

'It was a great adventure for me. I loved it!' —Peter Goosens

Within an astonishing Moorish-palace-style building in the ludicrously pretty Tivoli Gardens, Nimb Louise is anything but an anti-climax. It looks amazing – diaphanous, ceiling-high curtains in muted tones and elegant wooden chairs and white tablecloths. But executive chef Allan Poulsen really makes it worth the visit. He's very much of the modern Nordic school, cooking foraged and unusual ingredients as well as locally sourced seasonal vegetables using

cutting-edge techniques that manage also to evoke Danish tradition – pickled scallops and celery with grilled cucumber, for instance, or *frikadeller* and black lobster, new onions, jus. Usually *frikadeller* are traditional Danish meatballs. Not here they aren't.

RADIO

Recommended by
Ebbe Vollmer

Julius Thomsens Gade 12
Vesterbro
Copenhagen 1632
+45 25102733
www.restaurantradio.dk

Opening hours	2 days for lunch and 5 days for dinner
Reservation policy	Yes
Reservation email	info@restaurantradio.dk
Credit cards	Accepted
Price range	Affordable
Style	Casual
Cuisine	Modern Nordic
Recommended for	Worth the travel

YAN'S WOK

Recommended by
Thomas Rode Anderson

Bagerstræde 9
Vesterbro
Copenhagen 1617
+45 33237333
www.yanswok.dk

Opening hours	6 days for dinner
Reservation policy	Yes
Credit cards	Not accepted
Price range	Budget
Style	Casual
Cuisine	Chinese
Recommended for	Bargain

'A fabulous place with extremely well-balanced and well-seasoned Chinese food.'—Thomas Rode Anderson

TERTTI

Recommended by
Hans Välimäki

Tertin Kartano
Kuopiontie 68
Mikkeli
Etelä Savo 50350
Finland
+358 15176012
www.tertinkartano.fi

Opening hours...............7 days for dinner in summer
Reservation policy..Yes
Reservation email..................tertti@tertinkartano.fi
Credit cards..Accepted
Price range..Affordable
Style..Smart casual
Cuisine..Modern Finnish
Recommended for..........................Local favourite

CHEZ DOMINIQUE

Recommended by
Vladislav Djatsuk,
Sasu Laukkonen

Richardinkatu 4
Kaartinkaupunki
Helsinki
Uusimaa 00130
Finland
+358 096127393
www.chezdominique.fi

Opening hours.............4 days for lunch and 5 days for dinner
Reservation policy..Yes
Credit cards..Accepted
Price range..Expensive
Style..Formal
Cuisine..Nordic-French
Recommended for..................................High End

OLO

Recommended by
Vladislav Djatsuk,
Filip Langhoff

Kasarmikatu 44
Kaartinkaupunki
Helsinki
Uusimaa 00130
Finland
+358 103206250
www.olo-restaurant.com

Opening hours...............5 days for lunch and dinner
Reservation policy..Yes
Reservation email......................info@olo-ravintola.fi
Credit cards..Accepted
Price range..Expensive
Style..Smart casual
Cuisine..Modern Nordic
Recommended for..........................Worth the travel

SAVOY

Recommended by
Sasu Laukkonen,
Hans Välimäki

Royal Ravintolat Hotel
Eteläesplanadi 14
Kaartinkaupunki
Helsinki
Uusimaa 00130
Finland
+358 961285300
www.ravintolasavoy.fi

Opening hours.............5 days for lunch and 6 days for dinner
Reservation policy..Yes
Credit cards..Accepted
Price range..Expensive
Style..Formal
Cuisine..Modern Nordic
Recommended for..................................High End

A21 DINING

Recommended by
Filip Langhoff

Kalevankatu 17
Kamppi
Helsinki
Uusimaa 00100
Finland
+358 9401711117
www.a21.fi

Opening hours..5 days for dinner
Reservation policy..Yes
Reservation email..................................dining@a21.fi
Credit cards..Accepted
Price range..Affordable
Style..Smart casual
Cuisine..Modern Finnish
Recommended for..........................Local favourite

'They do some interesting menus that they combine
with cocktails instead of wine. That is something
I haven't seen before. Their story is very strong with
menus that follow different themes.'—Filip Langhoff

CAFÉ EKBERG

Recommended by
Sasu Laukkonen,
Hans Välimäki

Bulevardi 9
Kamppi
Helsinki
Uusimaa 00120
Finland
+358 968118660
www.cafeekberg.fi

Opening hours..........................7 days for breakfast and lunch
Reservation policy...Yes
Credit cards..Accepted
Price range..Budget
Style...Casual
Cuisine...Bakery-Café
Recommended for...Breakfast

Café Ekberg, its name emboldened in large, custard-yellow capitals above crimped canopies, stands testament to the energetic orphan who founded it after packing in clockmaking to become apprentice to a master baker. Dating to the 1850s, with ninety seats and its own bakery, specialities include the famed, multilayered, creamy Napoleon cake and canelé-like Champagne Cork. Although also serving lunches from 11 a.m., those in the know come for the good-value breakfast buffet, which usually includes porridge, omelettes, cold cuts, marmalades and pastries, alongside some twenty types of fresh breads, from rustic loaves to Basler Brot.

CAFÉ GRAN DELICATO

Recommended by
Filip Langhoff,
Sasu Laukkonen

Kalevankatu 34
Kamppi
Helsinki
Uusimaa 00180
Finland
www.grandelicato.fi

Opening hours..........5 days for brunch and 6 days for dinner
Reservation policy...No
Credit cards..Accepted
Price range..Budget
Style...Casual
Cuisine...Café
Recommended for...Breakfast

'Great continental atmosphere, good coffee and nice sandwiches.'—Filip Langhoff

It's a testament to the popularity of Gran Delicato that since opening as a one-room operation back in 2001 they have expanded into the next-door apartment and opened a new outpost in downtown Helsinki. Its popularity as a breakfast spot is largely thanks to the quality of the Greek coffee, considered to be among the best in town, but freshly squeezed orange juice, fresh salads and sandwiches draw in customers throughout the day. The owner's Greek heritage is reflected in the comfortable, Mediterranean decor and the rather eccentric service – all part of the charm of this quirky neighbourhood deli.

GAIJIN

Recommended by
Sasu Laukkonen,
Hans Välimäki

Bulevardi 6
Kamppi
Helsinki
Uusimaa 00120
Finland
+358 103229386
www.gaijin.fi

Opening hours.............4 days for lunch and 7 days for dinner
Reservation policy...Yes
Reservation email...................................info@gaijin.fi
Credit cards..Accepted
Price range..Affordable
Style..Smart casual
Cuisine...Modern Asian
Recommended for...................................Wish I'd opened

ILMATAR RESTAURANT

Recommended by
Pekka Terävä

Klaus K Hotel
Bulevardi 2-4
Kamppi
Helsinki
Uusimaa 00120
Finland
+358 207704714
www.ravintolailmatar.fi

Opening hours.....................................7 days for brunch
Reservation policy...Yes
Reservation email...............varausilmatar@klauskhotel.com
Credit cards..Accepted
Price range..Affordable
Style..Smart casual
Cuisine...Modern Nordic
Recommended for...Breakfast

MURU

Fredrikinkatu 41
Kamppi
Helsinki
Uusimaa 00120
Finland
+358 942891213
www.murudining.fi

Opening hours................................5 days for dinner
Reservation policy...Yes
Reservation email.....................varaukset@murudining.fi
Credit cards..Accepted
Price range..Affordable
Style..Smart casual
Cuisine..French
Recommended for..............................Regular neighbourhood

PUTTE'S BAR & PIZZA

Kalevankatu 6
Kamppi
Helsinki
Uusimaa 00100
Finland
+358 96981301
www.puttes.fi

Opening hours..........................7 days for lunch and dinner
Reservation policy...Yes
Reservation email....................................info@puttes.fi
Credit cards..Accepted
Price range..Affordable
Style..Casual
Cuisine...Pizza
Recommended for...Bargain

'Fabulous pizza and good beer. You won't find a better cheap meal.'—Filip Langhoff

TRATTORIA RIVOLETTO

Albertinkatu 38
Kamppi
Helsinki
Uusimaa 00180
Finland
+358 9643455
www.rivolirestaurants.fi

Opening hours..........................7 days for lunch and dinner
Reservation policy...Yes
Credit cards..Accepted
Price range..Affordable
Style..Casual
Cuisine...Italian
Recommended for..............................Regular neighbourhood

'The owner (since 1962) is funny and it's a really easy place to go. My kids love it!'—Hans Välimäki

CAFÉ ENGEL

Aleksanterinkatu 26
Kruununhaka
Senaatintori
Helsinki
Uusimaa 00170
Finland
+358 9652776
www.cafeengel.fi

Opening hours...................7 days from breakfast until late
Reservation policy...Yes
Credit cards..Accepted
Price range..Budget
Style..Casual
Cuisine..Café
Recommended for...Breakfast

LUOMO

Pohjoisesplanadi 9
Kruununhaka
Helsinki
Uusimaa 00170
Finland
+358 91357287
www.luomo.fi

Opening hours	5 days for dinner
Reservation policy	Yes
Reservation email	info@luomo.fi
Credit cards	Accepted
Price range	Expensive
Style	Smart casual
Cuisine	Modern Nordic
Recommended for	Regular neighbourhood

DEMO

Uudenmaankatu 9-11
Punavuori
Helsinki
Uusimaa 00120
Finland
+358 922890840
www.restaurantdemo.fi

Opening hours	5 days for dinner
Reservation policy	Yes
Reservation email	demo@restaurantdemo.fi
Credit cards	Accepted
Price range	Expensive
Style	Smart casual
Cuisine	Modern Nordic
Recommended for	Regular neighbourhood

Running off a busy boulevard in lively Punavuori, red chairs boldly contrast with light and dark walls in this small, intensely popular restaurant. It is owned by chefs Tommi Tuominen – who specializes in main courses and 'whipping the whole team into top performance' – and 'dessert artist' and 'bread wizard' Teemu Auru. The duo's dishes may include asparagus flan with roast quail, roast breast of goose with gizzards and kumquat sauce, and praline soufflé. Particularly worth booking for is the unwritten six-course Saturday night dinner with wine pairings. Tuominen and Auru also own Grotesk at Ludviginkatu.

CAFÉ TIN TIN TANGO

Töölöntorinkatu 7
Taka-Töölö
Helsinki
Uusimaa 00260
Finland
+358 927090972
www.tintintango.info

Opening hours	7 days from breakfast until late
Reservation policy	Yes
Credit cards	Accepted
Price range	Budget
Style	Casual
Cuisine	Café
Recommended for	Breakfast

FOUR SEASONS

Kapteeninkatu 24
Ullanlinna
Helsinki
Uusimaa 00140
Finland
www.4s.fi

Opening hours	6 days for lunch and 5 days for dinner
Reservation policy	No
Credit cards	Accepted
Price range	Budget
Style	Casual
Cuisine	Café
Recommended for	Bargain

SEA HORSE

Kapteeninkatu 11
Ullanlinna
Helsinki
Uusimaa 00140
Finland
+358 9628169
www.seahorse.fi

Opening hours	7 days for lunch and dinner
Reservation policy	Yes
Credit cards	Accepted
Price range	Affordable
Style	Casual
Cuisine	Finnish
Recommended for	Bargain

Opened in 1934, the Sea Horse, one of Helsinki's oldest restaurants, has served traditional Finnish specialities to sailors, artists, piss artists and the odd jazz legend. Dizzy Gillespie, when he visited, was supposedly such a fan of their fried herring and mash potatoes that he ran into the kitchen, trumpet in hand, saying 'Please, sir, can I have some more?' Herrings aside, Finnish favourites offered include cabbage rolls and reindeer fillet, served in the sort of portions that not even a hungry trumpeter could complain about. Note the restaurant's nickname, *Sikala*, which means 'animal house', because late at night things, and the Finns, can get quite strange.

SERGIO'S RAVINTOLA

Läntinen Rantakatu 27
Turku
Varsinais-Suomi 20100
Finland
www.sergio.fi

Recommended by
Pekka Terävä

Opening hours	6 days for lunch and dinner
Reservation policy	Yes
Credit cards	Accepted
Price range	Affordable
Style	Casual
Cuisine	Italian
Recommended for	Regular neighbourhood

'Simple Scottish seafood sourced from local fishermen.'

ANDREW FAIRLIE P233

'A BATTERED SAUSAGE TO DIE FOR'

PAUL FLYNN P242

'Overlooks one of the most amazing coastlines in the world.'

HYWEL JONES P233

UNITED KINGDOM & REPUBLIC OF IRELAND

'WORKING HARD TO PROVIDE A DIFFERENT APPROACH TO NORTHERN IRISH CUISINE.'

NIALL MCKENNA P234

'Always Brilliant'

HESTON BLUMENTHAL P172

'Still serving "tripe and drisheen" a very old traditional Cork dish.'

ROSS LEWIS P237

'GREAT LOCATION DEEP IN THE COUNTRYSIDE WITH ITS OWN VEGETABLE GARDEN AND VENISON SHOT ON THE SURROUNDING ESTATES.'

DOMINIC CHAPMAN P172

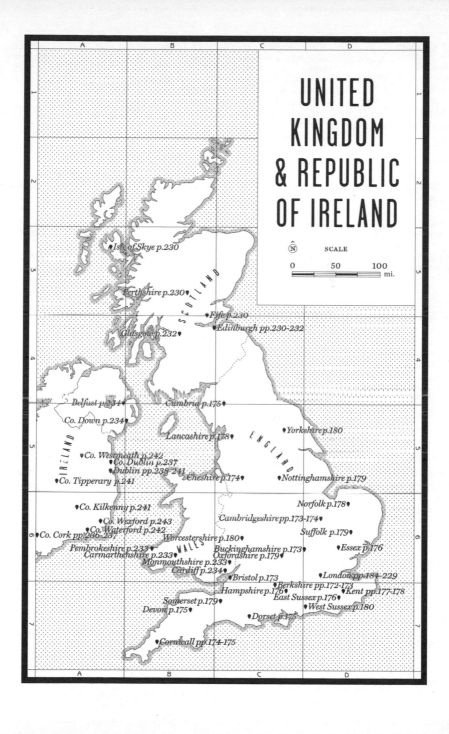

THE FAT DUCK

High Street
Bray
Berkshire
England SL6 2AQ
+44 1628580333
www.thefatduck.co.uk

Opening hours..................................5 days for lunch and dinner
Reservation policy...Yes
Credit cards...Accepted
Price range...Expensive
Style...Formal
Cuisine...Modern British
Recommended for...Worth the travel

'Still pushing the limits of what feelings a meal can provoke.'—Esben Holmboe Bang

Imaginative, innovative and creative restaurants are ten a penny these days, but for people who want their levels of crazy turned up to eleven there's still only one place to go. Few restaurants can boast the creativity and sheer brilliance displayed by Heston Blumenthal and The Fat Duck team – currently headed up by chef Jonny Lake – with a taste experience to match. Nowadays you don't get to choose what to eat, but it doesn't matter: from the golden 'Mad Hatter fob watch' that dissolves into a veal reduction to pour over a Mock Turtle egg, to the iconic snail porridge – it's all food alchemy.

THE HINDS HEAD

High Street
Bray
Berkshire
England SL6 2AB
+44 1628626151
www.hindsheadbray.com

Opening hours..............7 days for lunch and 6 days for dinner
Reservation policy...Yes
Reservation email.............................info@hindsheadbray.com
Credit cards...Accepted
Price range...Affordable
Style...Casual
Cuisine...Bar-Bistro
Recommended for...Local favourite

MALIKS TANDOORI

High Street
Cookham
Maidenhead
Berkshire
England SL6 9SF
+44 1628520085
www.maliks.co.uk

Opening hours..................................7 days for lunch and dinner
Reservation policy...Yes
Credit cards...Accepted
Price range...Affordable
Style...Casual
Cuisine...Indian
Recommended for...Late night

'I think it's the best Indian restaurant in the country – they win award after award every year. I don't even order, I just let them send out stuff and try a bit of everything; it's always brilliant.'—Heston Blumenthal

THE POT KILN

Frilsham
Yattendon
Berkshire
England RG18 0XX
+44 1635201366
www.potkiln.org

Opening hours..................................6 days for lunch and dinner
Reservation policy...Yes
Credit cards...Accepted
Price range...Affordable
Style...Casual
Cuisine...Modern British
Recommended for...Local favourite

'Great location deep in the country with its own vegetable garden and venison shot on the surrounding estates.'—Dominic Chapman

THE ROYAL OAK

Recommended by
Tom Kerridge

Paley Street
Littlefield Green
Maidenhead
Berkshire
England SL6 3JN
+44 1628620541
www.theroyaloakpaleystreet.com

Opening hours.............7 days for lunch and 6 days for dinner
Reservation policy...Yes
Credit cards...Accepted
Price range...Affordable
Style...Casual
Cuisine..Bar-Bistro
Recommended for.................................Local favourite

CASAMIA

Recommended by
Sat Bains

38 High Street
Westbury Village
Westbury-on-Trym
Bristol
England BS9 3DZ
+44 1179592884
www.casamiarestaurant.co.uk

Opening hours...............1 day for lunch and 5 days for dinner
Reservation policy...Yes
Credit cards...Accepted
Price range...Expensive
Style...Smart casual
Cuisine..Modern European
Recommended for..............................Worth the travel

VICEROY OF WINDSOR

Recommended by
Dominic Chapman

49-51 St Leonards Road
Windsor
Berkshire
England SL4 3BP
+44 1753858005
www.viceroyofwindsor.co.uk

Opening hours................................7 days for lunch and dinner
Reservation policy...Yes
Credit cards...Accepted
Price range...Affordable
Style...Casual
Cuisine...Indian
Recommended for.....................................Late night

THE HAND & FLOWERS

Recommended by
Sat Bains, Marcus Eaves,
Paul Flynn, Stephen Harris,
Daniel Taylor

126 West Street
Marlow
Buckinghamshire
England SL7 2BP
+44 1628482277
www.thehandandflowers.co.uk

Opening hours.............7 days for lunch and 6 days for dinner
Reservation policy...Yes
Reservation email....reservations@thehandandflowers.co.uk
Credit cards...Accepted
Price range...Affordable
Style...Smart casual
Cuisine...Modern British
Recommended for..............................Worth the travel

THE WATERSIDE INN

Recommended by
Dominic Chapman, Angela
Hartnett, Jacob Kenedy

Ferry Road
Bray
Berkshire
England SL6 2AT
+44 1628620691
www.waterside-inn.co.uk

Opening hours................................5 days for lunch and dinner
Reservation policy...Yes
Reservation email.............reservations@waterside-inn.co.uk
Credit cards...Accepted
Price range...Expensive
Style...Formal
Cuisine...French
Recommended for.....................................High end

'Pure class in every way.'—Dominic Chapman

ALIMENTUM

Recommended by
Paul Foster

152-154 Hills Road
Cambridge
Cambridgeshire
England CB2 8PB
+44 1223413000
www.restaurantalimentum.co.uk

Opening hours................................6 days for lunch and dinner
Reservation policy...Yes
Credit cards...Accepted
Price range...Affordable
Style...Smart casual
Cuisine..Modern European
Recommended for..........................Regular neighbourhood

MIDSUMMER HOUSE

Recommended by
Morgan Meunier

Midsummer Common
Cambridge
Cambridgeshire
England CB4 1HA
+44 1223369299
www.midsummerhouse.co.uk

Opening hours.............4 days for lunch and 5 days for dinner
Reservation policy...Yes
Reservation email......reservations@midsummerhouse.co.uk
Credit cards..Accepted
Price range..Expensive
Style..Smart casual
Cuisine...Modern British
Recommended for.................................Worth the travel

THE STARVING MAN

Recommended by
Paul Kitching

10 Lloyd Street
Altrincham
Cheshire
England WA14 2DE
www.thestarvingman.co.uk

Opening hours..................7 days for dinner, until late
Reservation policy..No
Credit cards..Accepted
Price range..Budget
Style..Casual
Cuisine..Fast food
Recommended for.................................Late night

FRESH FROM THE SEA

Recommended by
Nathan Outlaw

18 New Road
Port Isaac
Cornwall
England PL29 3SB
+44 1208880849
www.freshfromthesea.co.uk

Opening hours..7 days
Reservation policy..No
Credit cards..Accepted
Price range..Budget
Style..Casual
Cuisine..Seafood
Recommended for...................................Bargain

'Calum's crabs make a fantastic sandwich and they are
fished responsibly too.'—Nathan Outlaw

Perfectly formed little fish shop in the picture-perfect
fishing village of Port Isaac on the Atlantic coast of
North Cornwall. It is run by the husband and wife
team Calum and Tracey Greenhalgh, who catch their
lobster and crab daily from their own boat, the *Mary
D.* They specialize in selling and serving sustainable
Cornish fish: from hand-line caught mackerel and
pollack, to mussels, oysters and clams from the
Camel estuary, and smoked fish from the Tregida
Smokehouse. They serve lobster salads and rolls,
hand-picked crab sandwiches and soup, and their
own smoked mackerel pâté with toast.

PORTHMINSTER CAFÉ

Recommended by
Nathan Outlaw

Porthminster Beach
St Ives
Cornwall
England TR26 2EB
+44 1736795352
www.porthminstercafe.co.uk

Opening hours..............7 days for breakfast, lunch and dinner
Reservation policy..Yes
Reservation email......................info@porthminstercafe.co.uk
Credit cards..Accepted
Price range..Affordable
Style..Smart casual
Cuisine..International
Recommended for...................................Bargain

'Great food, child friendly and literally right on the
beach. What more could you ask for?'—Nathan Outlaw

Sat bang on Porthminster Beach, in the popular
Cornish seaside town of St Ives, getting a table here
in season takes a bit of forward planning. Nevertheless, with a handsome modern terrace that overlooks
the immaculately clean beach, it's invariably packed
throughout the summer due to a menu that
understands its audience. Lunch offers simple
seafood dishes that take in a few Asian influences,
alongside a decent-sized vegetarian section and
simple bowls of pasta for the kids. Things get a little
more elaborate and expensive in the evening – but
not prohibitively so – and the kids will still be alright.

THE SEAFOOD RESTAURANT

Riverside
Padstow
Cornwall
England PL28 8BY
+44 1841532700
www.rickstein.com

Opening hours................................7 days for lunch and dinner
Reservation policy...Yes
Reservation email.......................reservations@rickstein.com
Credit cards...Accepted
Price range...Affordable
Style...Casual
Cuisine..Seafood
Recommended for................................Wish I'd opened

L'ENCLUME

Cavendish Street
Cartmel
Cumbria
England LA11 6PZ
+44 1539536362
www.lenclume.co.uk

Opening hours.............5 days for lunch and 7 days for dinner
Reservation policy...Yes
Reservation email.....................................info@lenclume.co.uk
Credit cards...Accepted
Price range...Expensive
Style...Smart casual
Cuisine..Modern British
Recommended for......................Worth the travel

'They strive to stand out.'—Ben Spalding

Thanks to L'Enclume the Lake District can offer greater culinary highlights than twee tea rooms and tourist traps churning out 'hearty' quiches for tired ramblers. Operating out of a former blacksmith's since 2006, head chef Simon Rogan was in the vanguard of the now ubiquitous approach of using local ingredients and remains one of the most innovative chefs to have graced the UK restaurant scene in the past decade. Rogan's passion for his produce, seeking out a perplexing variety of unusual herbs and vegetables, isn't yawn-inducingly worthy – nor is it PR puff. Rather, it is driven by a desire to serve decent ingredients in an eye-opening manner.

THE SEAHORSE

5 South Embankment
Dartmouth
Devon
England TQ6 9BH
+44 1803835147
www.seahorserestaurant.co.uk

Opening hours................................5 days for lunch and dinner
Reservation policy...Yes
Credit cards...Accepted
Price range...Affordable
Style...Smart casual
Cuisine..Seafood
Recommended for................................Regular neighbourhood

'It showcases the region's finest ingredients. The food is a reflection of the respect and care that is given to those raw materials.'—Nathan Outlaw

The Devon flagship of accountant turned fishmonger turned self taught chef and restaurateur Mitch Tonks is, it shouldn't surprise you to hear, all about fish. While the smart-looking Seahorse on the bank of the River Dart does cater for carnivores with a couple of dishes under the heading 'Today's Meat', the majority, understandably, come here for the kitchen's way with seafood. Tonks's love of Italy comes across in a menu that features Sardinian red mullet soup, *fritto misto* (which includes monkfish, John Dory, red prawns (shrimps), whitebait and cuttlefish) and charcoal-grilled sea bass with peperonata.

HIX OYSTER & FISH HOUSE

Cobb Road
Lyme Regis
Dorset
England DT7 3JP
+44 1297446910
www.hixoysterandfishhouse.co.uk

Opening hours................................7 days for lunch and dinner
Reservation policy...Yes
Credit cards...Accepted
Price range...Affordable
Style...Smart casual
Cuisine..Seafood
Recommended for................................Worth the travel

THE LANDGATE BISTRO

Recommended by
Timothy Johnson

5-6 Landgate
Rye
East Sussex TN31 7LH
+44 1797222829
www.landgatebistro.co.uk

Opening hours	2 days for lunch and 4 days for dinner
Reservation policy	Yes
Credit cards	Accepted
Price range	Affordable
Style	Casual
Cuisine	Modern British
Recommended for	Regular neighbourhood

'Local food cooked simply.'—Timothy Johnson

THE COMPANY SHED

Recommended by
Anna Hansen, Sam Harris,
Miles Kirby, Tim Siadatan

129 Coast Road
West Mersea
Colchester
Essex CO5 8PA
+44 1206382700
www.the-company-shed.co.uk

Opening hours	6 days for breakfast and lunch
Reservation policy	No
Credit cards	Not accepted
Price range	Affordable
Style	Casual
Cuisine	Seafood
Recommended for	Worth the travel

'Awesomely fresh seafood quite simply served in the shed! Bring your own booze and bread. A fantastic day out.'—Anna Hansen

A weather-beaten hut among the boatyards of West Mersea on the Essex coast, The Company Shed is a quirky fishmonger's with a few tables. Opened in the late 1980s by Heather Haward, originally as a weekend-only concern to sell husband Richard's fish and oysters, it's gained a cult following. The combination of setting, BYOB and the honest pleasures of smoked fish, dressed crab and simply grilled shellfish are irresistible to anyone with a love of seafood and salty air. Make the journey September to April to try the local native oysters that get their distinctive green hue and flavour from the salt marshes.

ROBIN'S PIE & MASH

Recommended by
Alyn Williams

17 Chapel Road
Ilford
Essex IG1 2AF
www.robinspieandmash.com

Opening hours	7 days from breakfast until late
Reservation policy	No
Credit cards	Not accepted
Price range	Budget
Style	Casual
Cuisine	English
Recommended for	Local favourite

'This place is so English – pie and mash potatoes with stewed eels and liquor.'—Alyn Williams

THE BLACK RAT RESTAURANT

Recommended by
Tom Adams

88 Chesil Street
Winchester
Hampshire SO23 0HX
+44 1962844465
www.theblackrat.co.uk

Opening hours	2 days for lunch and 7 days for dinner
Reservation policy	Yes
Credit cards	Accepted
Price range	Affordable
Style	Smart casual
Cuisine	Modern British
Recommended for	High end

THE PIG

Recommended by
Angela Hartnett

Beaulieu Road
Brockenhurst
Hampshire SO42 7QL
+44 1590622354
www.thepighotel.co.uk

Opening hours	7 days for lunch and dinner
Reservation policy	Yes
Credit cards	Accepted
Price range	Affordable
Style	Casual
Cuisine	Modern British
Recommended for	Worth the travel

Chef James Golding previously worked for Mark Hix at The Ivy, The Caprice, J Sheekey and Soho House in New York. He's now at The Pig, a beautifully rustic New Forest groom keeper's lodge built in 1602, where his closest co-workers are the forager and the kitchen gardener. In the tastefully muted, forest-hued restaurant the menu is perpetually changing, depending on what's been most recently foraged or what's ready in the garden – eighty per cent of the ingredients are sourced from within 40 km (25 miles). The results include whole roasted Hampshire free-range quail, chanterelle layered potato, cavolo nero and cep (porcini sauce.

ESCONDIDO

28 Sandgate High Street
Folkestone
Kent CT20 3AP
www.escondido.co.uk

Opening hours	7 days for lunch and dinner
Reservation policy	Yes
Credit cards	Accepted
Price range	Budget
Style	Casual
Cuisine	Mexican
Recommended for	Regular neighbourhood

'Very tasty Mexican food served by waiters in baseball caps!'—Ben Spalding

THE PLEASANT CAFÉ

7 Mount Pleasant Road
Tunbridge Wells
Kent TN1 1NT

Opening hours	7 days for breakfast and lunch
Reservation policy	No
Credit cards	Not accepted
Price range	Budget
Style	Casual
Cuisine	Café
Recommended for	Breakfast

THE SPORTSMAN

Faversham Road
Seasalter
Whitstable
Kent CT5 4BP
+44 1227273370
www.thesportsmanseasalter.co.uk

Opening hours	6 days for lunch and 5 days for dinner
Reservation policy	Yes
Credit cards	Accepted
Price range	Affordable
Style	Smart casual
Cuisine	Modern British
Recommended for	Worth the travel

What chef-proprietor Stephen Harris likes to describe as a 'grotty rundown pub by the sea' is exactly what The Sportsman was before he took it over in 1999. Today, despite its somewhat desolate location, 3 km (2 miles) outside Whitstable on the Kent coast, it has become a destination, a place of gastronomic pilgrimage based purely on the quality of its cooking. There are two menus – the daily changing à la carte and a tasting menu that has to be ordered at least forty-eight hours in advance, and for which you'd be advised to put your name down for when you book.

TEA & TIMES

36a High Street
Whitstable
Kent CT5 1BQ

Opening hours	7 days for breakfast and lunch
Reservation policy	No
Credit cards	Not accepted
Price range	Budget
Style	Casual
Cuisine	Café
Recommended for	Breakfast

WILLIAMS & BROWN TAPAS

Recommended by
Stephen Harris

48 Harbour Street
Whitstable
Kent CT5 1AQ
+44 1227273373
www.thetapas.co.uk

Opening hours..................................7 days for lunch and dinner
Reservation policy...Yes
Credit cards.............................Accepted but not AMEX
Price range..Budget
Style...Casual
Cuisine..Tapas
Recommended for....................Regular neighbourhood

WHITSTABLE OYSTER COMPANY

Recommended by
Alexis Gauthier,
Stephen Harris

Royal Native Oyster Stores
Horsebridge
Whitstable
Kent CT5 1BU
+44 1227276856
www.whitstableoystercompany.com

Opening hours..................................7 days for lunch and dinner
Reservation policy...Yes
Credit cards...Accepted
Price range...Affordable
Style...Casual
Cuisine...Seafood
Recommended for.................................Worth the travel

CLAYTON STREET CHIPPY

Recommended by
Nigel Haworth

9 Clayton Street
Great Harwood
Blackburn
Lancashire BB6 7AQ

Opening hours....................................7 days for lunch until late
Reservation policy...No
Credit cards...Not accepted
Price range...Price
Style...Casual
Cuisine...Fast food
Recommended for...Bargain

THE INN AT WHITEWELL

Recommended by
Nigel Haworth

Near Clitheroe
Forest of Bowland
Whitewell
Lancashire BB7 3AT
+44 1200448222
www.innatwhitewell.com

Opening hours................................7 days for lunch and dinner
Reservation policy...Yes
Reservation email...................reception@innatwhitewell.com
Credit cards...Accepted
Price range...Affordable
Style...Smart casual
Cuisine...Bar-Bistro
Recommended for.................................Local favourite

THE HOSTE ARMS

Recommended by
Tom Aikens

The Green
Burnham Market
Norfolk PE31 8HD
+44 1328738777
www.hostearms.co.uk

Opening hours..............7 days for breakfast, lunch and dinner
Reservation policy...Yes
Reservation email......................reception@hostearms.co.uk
Credit cards.......................Accepted but not AMEX and Diners
Price range...Affordable
Style...Smart casual
Cuisine...British
Recommended for.................................Worth the travel

RESTAURANT SAT BAINS

Lenton Lane
Nottingham
Nottinghamshire NG7 2SA
+44 1159866566
www.restaurantsatbains.com

Opening hours......................................5 days for dinner
Reservation policy..Yes
Reservation email......................info@restaurantsatbains.net
Credit cards..Accepted
Price range...Expensive
Style...Formal
Cuisine...Modern British
Recommended for..............................Worth the travel

One of the UK's most gastronomically adventurous
destination restaurants is unconventionally set on
the industrial outskirts of Nottingham. A modern
take on the old-fashioned concept of the husband
and wife run restaurant with rooms, Sat and Amanda
Bains's edgily located, urban oasis is housed in a
collection of renovated Victorian farm buildings that
predate the panorama of pylons. Book a night in one
of the eight rooms plus dinner at either the chef's
or the kitchen table — the former overlooking the
main kitchen, the latter with your own personal
chef — to get closer to the cutting-edge but
playful cooking

LE MANOIR AUX QUAT'SAISONS

Church Road
Great Milton
Oxfordshire OX44 7PD
+44 1844278881
www.manoir.com

Opening hours............7 days for breakfast, lunch and dinner
Reservation policy..Yes
Credit cards..Accepted
Price range...Expensive
Style...Formal
Cuisine..Modern French
Recommended for................................Wish I'd opened

THE BERTINET BAKERY + CAFÉ

6 New Bond Street Place
Bath BA1 1BH
Somerset
www.bertinet.com/bertinetbakery

Opening hours.........................7 days for breakfast and lunch
Reservation policy...No
Credit cards..Accepted
Price range..Budget
Style..Casual
Cuisine..Bakery-Café
Recommended for...Breakfast

PEA PORRIDGE

28-29 Cannon Street
Bury St Edmunds IP33 1JR
Suffolk
+44 1284700200
www.peaporridge.co.uk

Opening hours.................................5 days for lunch and dinner
Reservation policy..Yes
Credit cards..Accepted
Price range..Budget
Style..Casual
Cuisine..European
Recommended for..Local favourite

RED LODGE CAFÉ

70 Turnpike Road
Red Lodge
Bury St Edmunds
Suffolk IP28 8LB

Opening hours............7 days for breakfast, lunch, and dinner
Reservation policy...No
Credit cards...Not accepted
Price range..Budget
Style..Casual
Cuisine...Cafe
Recommended for...Late night

HALLIDAY'S OF FUNTINGTON

Recommended by
Tom Pemberton

Watery Lane
Funtington
Chichester
West Sussex PO18 9LF
+44 1243575331
www.hallidays.info

Opening hours.................................4 days for lunch and dinner
Reservation policy..Yes
Credit cards........................Accepted but not AMEX and Diners
Price range...Affordable
Style...Smart casual
Cuisine...British
Recommended for...Worth the travel

THE BUTCHER'S ARMS

Recommended by
Shaun Hill

Lime Street
Eldersfield
Worcestershire GL19 4NX
+44 1452840381
www.thebutchersarms.net

Opening hours.............6 days for lunch and 5 days for dinner
Reservation policy..Yes
Credit cards..Accepted
Price range...Affordable
Style...Casual
Cuisine...Bar-Bistro
Recommended for...Worth the travel

**'A proper remote country pub with stunning food
and decent beers.'—Shaun Hill**

A superior food-peddling pub run by the young
husband and wife team James and Elizabeth Winter,
who oversee the kitchen and front of house
respectively. It's a pleasingly compact operation,
the pub having only two rooms and the menu offering
only five choices in each section. Word has got
around and reservations are now compulsory for
lunch and advisable for dinner. Despite that, they
don't, as is the inexplicable tendency for many pubs
that go gastro, neglect keeping a decent beer list
and, as a free house, are able to pull a fine selection
of straight-from-the-cask real ales.

BETTYS

Recommended by
Paul Kitching

6-8 St Helen's Square
York
Yorkshire YO1 8QP
+44 1904659142
www.bettys.co.uk

Opening hours........................7 days from breakfast until late
Reservation policy..No
Reservation email......belmont.room@bettysandtaylors.co.uk
Credit cards.......................................Accepted but not AMEX
Price range..Budget
Style...Casual
Cuisine...Café
Recommended for...Worth the travel

Although the original outpost of this proudly
Yorkshire-only group of teahouses was opened in
Harrogate in 1919, this handsome café on York's St
Helen's Square has been their flagship since it was
launched in 1936. Its Art Deco design was inspired
by the RMS *Queen Mary*, which first set sail the same
year. Founded by a Swiss German confectioner who,
having arrived in Bradford in 1907, proceeded to go
native, it is, as the quote on the front of their menu
suggests, 'Where the Dales meet the Alps'. That
translates as properly served tea, and properly
made cakes, pastries and savouries.

'Breakfast buns & devilled kidneys.'
JACOB KENNEDY P215

'It's very old London in its style and location.'
THEO RANDALL P201

'CHEEKY BENGALI RESTAURANTS IN BRICK LANE.'
MICHAEL WILSON

'The food is delicious and the setting on the banks of the Thames is incredible.'
HESTON BLUMENTHAL P188

LONDON

'BACON SANDWICHES & ECCLES CAKES.'
SAMANTHA & SAMUEL CLARK P209

'EXCELLENT SERVICE AND A BUZZY ATMOSPHERE.'
BRUNO LOUBET P189

'A fried egg please with a large pot of tea or a Bloody Mary.'
TOM OLDROYD P224

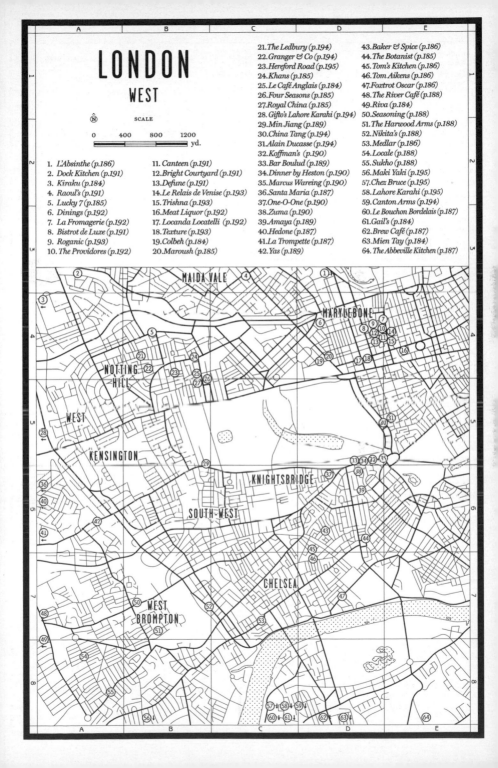

KIRAKU

Recommended by
Jockey Petrie

8 Station Parade
Uxbridge Road
Acton
London W5 3LD
+44 2089922848
www.kiraku.co.uk

Opening hours.............2 days for lunch and 6 days for dinner
Reservation policy...Yes
Credit cards...Accepted
Price range...Affordable
Style..Casual
Cuisine..Japanese
Recommended for..........................Regular neighbourhood
Recommended for...Bargain

RIVA

Recommended by
Martin Morales
Heston Blumenthal

169 Church Road
Barnes
London SW13 9HR

Opening hours.............6 days for lunch and 7 days for dinner
Reservation policy...Yes
Credit cards...Accepted
Price range...Affordable
Style...Smart casual
Cuisine..Italian
Recommended for..High End

'Delivers excellent food and the great natural, relaxed
feeling you want for a local place.'
—Heston Blumenthal

GAIL'S

Recommended by
Claude Bosi

64 Northcote Road
Battersea
London SW11 6QL
www.gailsbread.co.uk

Opening hours.........................7 days from breakfast until late
Reservation policy..No
Credit cards...Accepted
Price range...Budget
Style..Casual
Cuisine...Café
Recommended for..Breakfast

MIEN TAY

Recommended by
Claude Bosi

180 Lavender Hill
Battersea
London SW11 5TQ
+44 2073500721
www.mientay.co.uk/battersea

Opening hours..................................7 days for lunch and dinner
Reservation policy...Yes
Credit cards...Accepted
Price range...Budget
Style..Casual
Cuisine..Vietnamese
Recommended for...Bargain

LE CAFÉ ANGLAIS

Recommended by
Jonathan Jones
Thomasina Miers
Daniel Taylor

8 Porchester Gardens
Bayswater
London W2 4DB
+44 2072211415
www.lecafeanglais.co.uk

Opening hours..................................7 days for lunch and dinner
Reservation policy...Yes
Reservation email...........................info@lecafeanglais.co.uk
Credit cards...Accepted
Price range...Affordable
Style...Smart casual
Cuisine..French
Recommended for...Local favourite

'I haven't found anywhere like Le Cafe Anglais
anywhere else in the world.'—Daniel Taylor

COLBEH

Recommended by
Karam Sethi

6 Porchester Place
Bayswater
London W2 2BS
+44 2077064888
www.colbeh.co.uk

Opening hours..................................7 days for lunch and dinner
Reservation policy...Yes
Reservation email.....................................info@colbeh.co.uk
Credit cards...Accepted
Price range...Budget
Style..Casual
Cuisine...Persian
Recommended for...Bargain

'The best Persian in London. The special naan, paneer
sabzi and chelo kebab koobideh are musts.'
—Karam Sethi

FOUR SEASONS

Recommended by
Rowley Leigh

84 Queensway
Bayswater
London W2 3RL
+44 2072294320
www.fs-restaurants.co.uk

Opening hours..................7 days for lunch and dinner
Reservation policy...Yes
Credit cards...Accepted
Price range..Affordable
Style...Casual
Cuisine...Chinese
Recommended for..Bargain

'Great for Char Siu and Pak Choi.'—Rowley Leigh

KHANS

Recommended by
Omar Allibhoy

13-15 Westbourne Grove
Bayswater
London W2 4UA
+44 2077275420
www.khansrestaurant.com

Opening hours..................7 days for lunch and dinner
Reservation policy...Yes
Reservation email.........................info@khansrestaurant.com
Credit cards...Accepted
Price range..Budget
Style...Casual
Cuisine...Indian
Recommended for.............................Wish I'd opened

'A place my Indian grandfather used to come thirty
years ago and it's still kicking ass with the chillies.'
—Omar Allibhoy

LUCKY 7

Recommended by
Thomasina Miers

127 Westbourne Park Road
Bayswater
London W2 5QL
+44 2077276771
www.lucky7london.co.uk

Opening hours..................7 days for brunch and dinner
Reservation policy...No
Credit cards.......................Accepted but not AMEX and Diners
Price range..Budget
Style...Casual
Cuisine...Diner-Cafe
Recommended for..Bargain

MAROUSH

Recommended by
Sat Bains, Ruth Rogers

21 Edgware Road
Bayswater
London W2 2JE
+44 2077230773
www.maroush.com

Opening hours..................7 days for lunch and dinner
Reservation policy...Yes
Credit cards...Accepted
Price range..Affordable
Style...Casual
Cuisine...Lebanese
Recommended for.....................................Late night

ROYAL CHINA

Recommended by
Matthew Harris, Margot
Henderson, Thomasina Miers

13 Queensway
Bayswater
London W2 4QJ
+44 2072212535
www2.royalchinagroup.biz

Opening hours..................7 days for lunch and dinner
Reservation policy...Yes
Credit cards...Accepted
Price range..Affordable
Style...Casual
Cuisine...Chinese
Recommended for..Bargain

THE BOTANIST

Recommended by
Heinz Beck

7 Sloane Square
Belgravia
London SW1W 8EE
+44 2077300077
www.thebotanistsloanesquare.com

Opening hours............7 days for breakfast, lunch and dinner
Reservation policy...Yes
Reservation email.......info@thebotanistsloanesquare.com
Credit cards...Accepted
Price range..Affordable
Style..Smart casual
Cuisine..European
Recommended for.....................................Breakfast

'Try their freshly squeezed orange juice and plates
of fresh fruit.'—Heinz Beck

L'ABSINTHE

Recommended by
Pierre Koffmann

40 Chalcot Road
Chalk Farm
London NW1 8LS
+44 2074834848
www.labsinthe.co.uk

Opening hours............6 days for lunch and 7 days for dinner
Reservation policy..Yes
Credit cards...Accepted
Price range...Budget
Style..Casual
Cuisine..French
Recommended for...Bargain

BAKER & SPICE

Recommended by
Philip Howard

47 Denyer Street
Chelsea
London SW3 2LX
+44 2072253417
www.bakerandspice.uk.com

Opening hours............................7 days for breakfast and lunch
Reservation policy..Yes
Credit cards.........................Accepted but not AMEX and Diners
Price range...Budget
Style..Casual
Cuisine...Bakery-Cafe
Recommended for...Breakfast

FOXTROT OSCAR

Recommended by
Thomasina Miers

79 Royal Hospital Road
Chelsea
London SW3 4HN
+44 2073524448
www.gordonramsay.com/foxtrotoscar

Opening hours............................7 days for brunch and dinner
Reservation policy..Yes
Reservation email..............foxtrotoscar@gordonramsay.com
Credit cards...Accepted
Price range..Affordable
Style..Style
Cuisine...Modern European
Recommended for...Breakfast

MEDLAR

Recommended by
Marcus Wareing

438 Kings Road
Chelsea
London SW10 0LJ
+44 2073491900
www.medlarrestaurant.co.uk

Opening hours................................7 days for lunch and dinner
Reservation policy..Yes
Reservation email.....................info@medlarrestaurant.co.uk
Credit cards...Accepted
Price range..Affordable
Style...Smart casual
Cuisine..Modern European
Recommended for...Local favourite

'Good food in friendly surroundings.'—Marcus Wareing

TOM AIKENS

Recommended by
Alberto Landgraf

43 Elystan Street
Chelsea
London SW3 3NT
www.tomaikens.co.uk

Opening hours............5 days for lunch and 6 days for dinner
Reservation policy..Yes
Credit cards...Accepted
Price range..Affordable
Style...Smart casual
Cuisine..Modern European
Recommended for...Worth the travel

TOM'S KITCHEN

Recommended by
Clare Smyth

27 Cale Street
Chelsea
London SW3 3QP
+44 2073490202
www.tomskitchen.co.uk

Opening hours............7 days for breakfast, lunch and dinner
Reservation policy..Yes
Credit cards...Accepted
Price range..Affordable
Style..Casual
Cuisine..Modern British
Recommended for...Breakfast

HEDONE

Recommended by
Daniel Lindeberg

301-303 Chiswick High Road
Chiswick
London W4 4HH
+44 2087470377
www.hedonerestaurant.com

Opening hours.............2 days for lunch and 5 days for dinner
Reservation policy...Yes
Reservation email........reservations@hedonerestaurant.com
Credit cards..Accepted
Price range...Expensive
Style...Casual
Cuisine..Modern European
Recommended for....................................Worth the travel

LE BOUCHON BORDELAIS

Recommended by
Jean Joho

5-9 Battersea Rise
Clapham
London SW11 1HG
+44 02031370174
www.lebouchon.co.uk

Opening hours.............6 days for lunch and 7 days for dinner
Reservation policy...Yes
Reservation email.........................enquiries@lebouchon.co.uk
Credit cards..Accepted
Price range...Affordable
Style...Casual
Cuisine..French
Recommended for....................................Worth the travel

LA TROMPETTE

Recommended by
Manoj Vasaikar

5-7 Devonshire Road
Chiswick
London W4 2EU
+44 2087471836
www.latrompette.co.uk

Opening hours..................................7 days for lunch and dinner
Reservation policy...Yes
Reservation email.....................reception@latromplette.co.uk
Credit cards..Accepted
Price range..Affordable
Style..Smart casual
Cuisine..French
Recommended for...............................Regular neighbourhood

BREW CAFÉ

Recommended by
Adam Byatt

45 Northcote Road
Clapham
London SW11 1NJ
+44 2075852198
www.brew-cafe.com

Opening hours.......................7 days from breakfast until late
Reservation policy...Yes
Reservation email.....................45northcote@brew-cafe.com
Credit cards...Not accepted
Price range...Budget
Style...Casual
Cuisine...Café
Recommended for...Breakfast

THE ABBEVILLE KITCHEN

Recommended by
Jonathan Jones

47 Abbeville Road
Clapham
London SW4 9JX
+44 2087721110
www.abbevillekitchen.com

Opening hours.............6 days for lunch and 7 days for dinner
Reservation policy...Yes
Credit cards..Accepted
Price range..Budget
Style...Casual
Cuisine..Modern European
Recommended for...............................Regular neighbourhood

SANTA MARIA

Recommended by
Henry Harris

15 Saint Mary's Road
Ealing
London W5 5RA
+44 2085791462
www.santamariapizzeria.com

Opening hours..................................7 days for lunch and dinner
Reservation policy..No
Credit cards..Accepted
Price range..Budget
Style...Casual
Cuisine...Pizza
Recommended for...............................Regular neighbourhood

'Best Neopolitan pizzeria.'—Henry Harris

THE HARWOOD ARMS

Recommended by
Corey Lee

27 Walham Grove
Fulham
London SW6 1QP
www.harwoodarms.com

Opening hours	6 days for lunch and 7 days for dinner
Reservation policy	Yes
Credit cards	Accepted
Price range	Affordable
Style	Casual
Cuisine	British
Recommended for	Worth the travel

LOCALE

Recommended by
Omar Allibhoy

222 Munster Road
Fulham
London SW6 6AY
+44 2073816137
www.localerestaurants.com

Opening hours	7 days for lunch and dinner
Reservation policy	Yes
Credit cards	Accepted
Price range	Budget
Style	Casual
Cuisine	Italian
Recommended for	Late night

'A great Italian restaurant which serves a proper seafood linguine.'—Omar Allibhoy

NIKITA'S

Recommended by
Yvonnick Lalle

65 Ifield Road
Fulham
London SW10 9AU
+44 2073526326
www.nikitasrestaurant.co.uk

Opening hours	5 days for dinner
Reservation policy	Yes
Reservation email	reservations@nikitasrestaurant.co.uk
Credit cards	Accepted
Price range	Affordable
Style	Smart casual
Cuisine	Russian
Recommended for	Local favourite

SEASONING

Recommended by
Atul Kochhar

84d - 86 Lillie Road
Fulham
London SW6 1TL
+44 2073860303
www.seasoning-restaurant.com

Opening hours	7 days for lunch and dinner
Reservation policy	Yes
Credit cards	Accepted
Price range	Budget
Style	Smart casual
Cuisine	Indian Chinese
Recommended for	Regular neighbourhood

SUKHO

Recommended by
Alexis Gauthier

855 Fulham Road
Fulham
London SW6 5HJ
+44 02073717600
www.sukhogroups.com

Opening hours	7 days for lunch and dinner
Reservation policy	Yes
Credit cards	Accepted
Price range	Affordable
Style	Casual
Cuisine	Thai
Recommended for	Regular neighbourhood

THE RIVER CAFÉ

Recommended by
Heston Blumenthal, Chakall,
Samantha and Samuel Clark,
Andreas Dahlberg, Peter Gordon,
Maria Helena Guimaraes,
Gabrielle Hamilton, Matthew Harris,
Philip Howard, Rowley Leigh
Bruno Loubet, James Lowe, Francis
Mallmann, Thomasina Miers, Stevie
Parle, Tim Siadatan, Daniel Taylor

Thames Wharf
Rainville Road
Hammersmith
London W6 9HA
+44 2073864200
www.rivercafe.co.uk

Opening hours	7 days for lunch and 6 days for dinner
Reservation policy	Yes
Credit cards	Accepted
Price range	Expensive
Style	Smart casual
Cuisine	Italian
Recommended for	High End

'The food is delicious and the setting on the banks of the Thames is incredible.'
—Heston Blumental

Italian food made by Ruth Rogers and her team with the very best produce money can buy, assembled in neo-rustic style, served in a stylish modern glass-fronted canteen (originally an old oil storage facility before architect Richard Rogers got hold of it), down where the old Thames does flow. That's been the River Café's formula for success since it opened in 1988. Co-founder Rose Gray, who sadly passed away in 2010, would be pleased to see nothing has changed in her absence. Perfect setting meets perfect produce, meets educated service and a wine list, aside from the odd Champagne, that is all-Italian and runs from humble bottles to super Tuscans.

YAS

Recommended by
Manoj Vasaikar

7 Hammersmith Road
Hammersmith
London W14 8XJ
+44 2076039148
www.yasrestaurants.com

Opening hours..............................7 days for lunch and dinner
Reservation policy..Yes
Reservation email............reservations@yasrestaurants.com
Credit cards...Accepted
Price range..Affordable
Style...Casual
Cuisine...Persian
Recommended for..Late night

MIN JIANG

Recommended by
Jérôme Tauvron

Royal Garden Hotel
2-24 Kensington High Street
Kensington
London W8 4PT
+44 2073611988
www.minjiang.co.uk

Opening hours..............................7 days for lunch and dinner
Reservation policy..Yes
Reservation email...info@minjiang.co.uk
Credit cards...Accepted
Price range..Affordable
Style..Formal
Cuisine...Chinese
Recommended for.......................Regular neighbourhood

'The best Peking Duck, spring rolls and dim sum in London'—Jérôme Tauvron

AMAYA

Recommended by
Manoj Vasaikar

Halkin Arcade
Motcomb Street
Knightsbridge
London SW1X 8JT
www.amaya.biz

Opening hours..............................7 days for lunch and dinner
Reservation policy..Yes
Credit cards...Accepted
Price range..Expensive
Style...Smart casual
Cuisine...Modern Indian
Recommended for..High End

BAR BOULUD

Recommended by
Bruno Loubet, Francesco Mazzei, Clare Smyth, Agnar Sverrisson, Marcus Wareing

Mandarin Oriental Hyde Park
66 Knightsbridge
London SW1X 7LA
+44 2072013899
www.barboulud.com

Opening hours..............................7 days for lunch and dinner
Reservation policy..Yes
Credit cards...Accepted
Price range..Affordable
Style...Smart casual
Cuisine...French
Recommended for..Late night

'Bar Boulud is great for a late-night table. Excellent service and a buzzy atmosphere.'—Bruno Loubet

A restaurant in a five star hotel in the heart of Knightsbridge might seem an unlikely late-night hang-out for anyone other than the supremely wealthy and unimaginative, but then Bar Boulud isn't your typical operation. Firstly, the French bistro-style food, with all manner of charcuterie and tempting tidbits, is much more accessible than many hotels offer. Secondly, it does a bloody good burger, including the traditional style Yankee, the Frenchie (made with confit pork belly and Morbier) and the Piggie (BBQ pulled pork and green chilli mayonnaise). What's more, you can wash it down with one of their uncommonly large selection of draught (draft) beers.

DINNER BY HESTON

Mandarin Oriental Hyde Park
66 Knightsbridge
London SW1X 7LA
+44 2072013833
www.dinnerbyheston.com

Recommended by
Omar Allibhoy, Jonnie Boer,
Anthony Demetre, Timothy
Johnson, Atul Kochhar,
Jean-François Piège,
José Pizarro

Opening hours...............................7 days for lunch and dinner
Reservation policy...Yes
Credit cards...Accepted
Price range..Expensive
Style..Smart casual
Cuisine...Modern British
Recommended for....................................Worth the travel

Heston Blumenthal's Fat Duck follow-up is a bustling brasserie with a playful menu, much of it surprisingly straightforward despite being inspired by a geeky love of British food history. Overlooking Hyde Park from the handsome rear of Knightsbridge's Mandarin Oriental, its spacious dining room seats 136 at large, luxuriously spaced tables. Inside the vast glass-fronted kitchen, a giant Swiss watch movement turning a series of spits catches the eye. So too the now trademark Meat Fruit — a chicken liver parfait made to resemble a mandarin — and the Tipsy Cake — vanilla-custard-filled brioche served with pineapple roasted on that showcase rotisserie.

KOFFMANN'S

The Berkeley Hotel
Wilton Place
Knightsbridge
London SW1X 7RL
+44 2072351010
www.the-berkeley.co.uk/koffmanns.aspx

Recommended by
Tom Kitchin

Opening hours...............................7 days for lunch and dinner
Reservation policy...Yes
Reservation email....................koffmanns@the-berkeley.co.uk
Credit cards...Accepted
Price range..Expensive
Style..Smart casual
Cuisine..French
Recommended for..........................Regular neighbourhood

MARCUS WAREING

The Berkeley Hotel
Wilton Place
Knightsbridge
London SW1X 7RL
+44 2072351200
www.the-berkeley.co.uk/marcus_wareing.aspx

Recommended by
Steffen Hansen,
Atul Kochhar

Opening hours............5 days for lunch and 6 days for dinner
Reservation policy...Yes
Reservation email..........marcuswareing@the-berkeley.co.uk
Credit cards...Accepted
Price range..Expensive
Style...Formal
Cuisine...Modern European
Recommended for....................................Worth the travel

ONE-O-ONE

101 Knightsbridge
Knightsbridge
London SW1X 7RN
+44 2072907101
www.oneoonerestaurant.com

Recommended by
Alfred Prasad

Opening hours...............................7 days for lunch and dinner
Reservation policy...Yes
Credit cards...Accepted
Price range..Expensive
Style..Smart casual
Cuisine..Seafood
Recommended for..High End

ZUMA

5 Raphael Street
Knightsbridge
London SW7 1DL
+44 2075841010
www.zumarestaurant.com

Recommended by
Tom Aikens, Heinz Beck,
Martín Berasategui,
Sergio Herman, Francesco
Mazzei, Theo Randall, Didem
Şenol, Karam Sethi, Agnar
Sverrisson, Jérôme Tauvron,
Mitchell Tonks

Opening hours...............................7 days for lunch and dinner
Reservation policy...Yes
Credit cards...Accepted
Price range..Expensive
Style...Formal
Cuisine...Modern Japanese
Recommended for................................Wish I'd opened

DOCK KITCHEN

Recommended by
Samantha and Samuel Clark,
Thomasina Miers,
Stevie Parle

Portobello Docks
344-342 Ladbroke Grove
London W10 5BU
+44 2089621610
www.dockkitchen.co.uk

Opening hours............7 days for lunch and 6 days for dinner
Reservation policy...Yes
Reservation email......................bookings@dockkitchen.co.uk
Credit cards...Accepted
Price range...Affordable
Style...Casual
Cuisine...International
Recommended for...............................Regular neighbourhood

'We love the diversity of the menus.'
—Samantha and Samuel Clark

RAOUL'S

Recommended by
Pierre Koffmann

13 Clifton Road
Maida Vale
London W9 1SZ
+44 2072897313
www.raoulsgourmet.com

Opening hours............7 days for breakfast, lunch and dinner
Reservation policy...Yes
Credit cards...Accepted
Price range...Budget
Style...Casual
Cuisine...Bakery-Cafe
Recommended for...Breakfast

BISTROT DE LUXE

Recommended by
Omar Allibhoy

66 Baker Street
Marylebone
London W1U 7DJ
+44 2079354007
www.galvinrestaurants.com

Opening hours.............................7 days for lunch and dinner
Reservation policy...Yes
Credit cards...Accepted
Price range...Affordable
Style..Smart casual
Cuisine...French
Recommended for...............................Regular neighbourhood

'A proper neighbourhood Parisian bistro where the
staff truly care about their clientele and the food and
service is impeccable.'—Omar Allibhoy

BRIGHT COURTYARD

Recommended by
Jacob Kenedy

43-45 Baker Street
Marylebone
London W1U 8EW
+44 2074866998
www.lifefashiongroup.com/home.html

Opening hours.............................7 days for lunch and dinner
Reservation policy...Yes
Credit cards...Accepted
Price range...Affordable
Style..Smart casual
Cuisine...Chinese
Recommended for...............................Regular neighbourhood

'Elegant cuisine.'—Jacob Kenedy

CANTEEN

Recommended by
Atul Kochhar

55 Baker Street
Marylebone
London W1U 8EW
+44 8456861122
www.canteen.co.uk

Opening hours............7 days for breakfast, lunch and dinner
Reservation policy...Yes
Credit cards...Accepted
Price range...Affordable
Style...Casual
Cuisine...British
Recommended for...............................Regular neighbourhood

DEFUNE

Recommended by
Jacob Kenedy

34 George Street
Marylebone
London W1U 7DP
+44 2079358311

Opening hours.............................7 days for lunch and dinner
Reservation policy...Yes
Credit cards...Accepted
Price range...Expensive
Style..Smart casual
Cuisine..Japanese
Recommended for...High End

DININGS

Recommended by
Jérôme Tauvron

22 Harcourt Street
Marylebone
London W1H 4HH
+44 2077230666
www.dinings.co.uk

Opening hours	6 days for lunch and dinner
Reservation policy	Yes
Credit cards	Accepted
Price range	Affordable
Style	Smart casual
Cuisine	Japanese
Recommended for	Regular neighbourhood

'Very casual with no pretentious decor but the food makes me go back again and again and again.'—Jérôme Tauvron

LA FROMAGERIE

Recommended by
Omar Allibhoy

2-6 Moxon Street
Marylebone
London W1U 4EW
www.lafromagerie.co.uk

Opening hours	7 days from breakfast until late
Reservation policy	No
Credit cards	Accepted
Price range	Affordable
Style	Smart casual
Cuisine	Deli-Cafe
Recommended for	Breakfast

LOCANDA LOCATELLI

Recommended by
Sam Harris
Mark Hix

8 Seymour Street
Marylebone
London W1H 7JZ
+44 02079359088
www.locandalocatelli.com

Opening hours	7 days for lunch and dinner
Reservation policy	Yes
Credit cards	Accepted but not Diners
Price range	Expensive
Style	Smart casual
Cuisine	Modern Italian
Recommended for	High End

MEAT LIQUOR

Recommended by
Philip Howard, Karam Sethi,
Ben Tish

74 Welbeck Street
Marylebone
London W1G 0BA
www.meatliquor.com

Opening hours	6 days for lunch and dinner
Reservation policy	No
Credit cards	Accepted
Price range	Budget
Style	Casual
Cuisine	Burgers
Recommended for	Bargain

Meat Liquor – born in late 2011, the child of the rather rock 'n' roll burger van turned pop-up – produces burgers, Philly cheese steaks, chilli dogs, buffalo wings, key lime pie and so on – all of which, unlike many others, aren't a sad, pale imitation of what you find stateside. The bar does a good selection of microbrews and no-nonsense cocktails served in jars that don't skimp on the liquor. Whether the queues (waiting lines) of trendy young tattooed things waiting to sink their teeth into a Dead Hippy will shorten, now that they have a second outpost (Meat Market in Covent Garden), remains to be seen.

THE PROVIDORES

Recommended by
Anna Hansen

109 Marylebone High Street
Marylebone
London W1U 4RX
+44 2079356175
www.theprovidores.co.uk

Opening hours	7 days for lunch and dinner
Reservation policy	Yes
Reservation email	anyone@theprovidores.co.uk
Credit cards	Accepted
Price range	Expensive
Style	Smart casual
Cuisine	International
Recommended for	Breakfast

'Order the Turkish eggs, banana stuffed French toast or brown rice, miso and apple porridge.'—Anna Hansen

This Marylebone High Street establishment has been the darling of London brunchers since 2001. Come any time of day and you'll be welcomed by smiling service and knockout blends of flavour, but breakfasts in the Tapa Room will exceed your wildest dreams. Chef Peter Gordon creates true fusion food without forgetting his Kiwi roots, which is reflected in the wine list that includes Bellinis made with New Zealand sparkling wine. Popular favourites include Turkish (poached) eggs with whipped yogurt and hot chilli butter on sourdough, or Thai basil and lime waffles with jalapeño chutney. A solid Bloody Mary, tamarillo and kiwi fruit smoothies, and excellent coffee provide a memorable morning hit.

LE RELAIS DE VENISE

Recommended by
Ollie Dabbous

120 Marylebone Lane
Marylebone
London W1U 2QG
+44 2074860878
www.relaisdevenise.com

Opening hours...............................7 days for lunch and dinner
Reservation policy...No
Credit cards...Accepted
Price range...Affordable
Style...Casual
Cuisine...French
Recommended for.............................Regular neighbourhood

ROGANIC

Recommended by
Jason Atherton, Christoffer
Hruskova, Isaac McHale,
Alyn Williams

19 Blandford Street
Marylebone
London W1U 3DH
+44 2074860380
www.roganic.co.uk

Opening hours ....5 days for lunch and dinner
Reservation policy..Yes
Reservation email......................................info@roganic.co.uk
Credit cards...Accepted
Price range...Affordable
Style...Casual
Cuisine...Modern British
Recommended for...Worth the travel

TEXTURE

Recommended by
Pierre Koffmann,
Alyn Williams

34 Portman Street
Marylebone
London W1H 7BY
+44 2072240028
texture-restaurant.co.uk

Opening hours................................5 days for lunch and dinner
Reservation policy..Yes
Credit cards...Accepted
Price range...Expensive
Style..Smart casual
Cuisine...Modern European
Recommended for...High End

Agnar Sverrisson and Xavier Rousset absconded from Raymond Blanc's famed Oxford restaurant Le Manoir aux Quat'Saisons, where they were head chef and head sommelier, to open their smart Champagne bar and restaurant in the capital. The menu is modern European, but Sverrisson's Icelandic background brings additional Scandinavian flair to the proceedings, while Rousset pulls out all the stops with a wine list of more than 100 different bottles of bubbly alone. To experience it at its best, ditch the à la carte and opt for the Scandinavian fish-tasting menu. Order a bottle of Pol Roger Sir Winston Churchill '95 to wash down the Icelandic cod.

TRISHNA

Recommended by
Mark Hix

15-17 Blandford Street
Marylebone
London W1U 3DG
+44 2079355624
www.trishnalondon.com

Opening hours................................7 days for lunch and dinner
Reservation policy...Yes
Reservation email..............................info@trishnalondon.com
Credit cards...Accepted
Price range...Affordable
Style..Smart casual
Cuisine..Indian
Recommended for...Worth the travel

GRANGER & CO

Recommended by
Tom Pemberton

175 Westbourne Grove
Notting Hill
London W11 2SB
www.grangerandco.com

Opening hours	7 days for breakfast, lunch and dinner
Reservation policy	No
Credit cards	Accepted
Price range	Affordable
Style	Casual
Cuisine	Modern Australian
Recommended for	Breakfast

THE LEDBURY

Recommended by
Jason Atherton, Benjamin Bayly,
Massimo Bottura, Samantha and
Samuel Clark, Lee Cooper, Gert
de Mangeleer, Dylan Jones and
Bo (Duangporn) Songvisava,
Pierre Koffmann, Bruno Loubet,
Isaac McHale, Thomasina Miers,
Bruce Poole, Ben Spalding,
Marcus Wareing, Alyn Williams

127 Ledbury Road
Notting Hill
London W11 2AQ
+44 2077929090
www.theledbury.com

Opening hours	6 days for lunch and 7 days for dinner
Reservation policy	Yes
Reservation email	info@theledbury.com
Credit cards	Accepted
Price range	Expensive
Style	Smart casual
Cuisine	Modern French
Recommended for	Worth the travel

'The cooking at The Ledbury is quite exceptional.
Flawless technique and pretty to look at but more
importantly it all tastes very, very good.'—Lee Cooper

ALAIN DUCASSE

Recommended by
Clare Smyth

The Dorchester Hotel
Park Lane
London W1K 1QA
+44 2076298866
www.alainducasse-dorchester.com

Opening hours	4 days for lunch and 5 days for dinner
Reservation policy	Yes
Credit cards	Accepted
Price range	Expensive
Style	Smart casual
Cuisine	French
Recommended for	High End

CHINA TANG

Recommended by
Jérôme Tauvron

The Dorchester
Park Lane
London W1K 1QA
+44 2073176500
www.chinatanglondon.co.uk

Opening hours	7 days for lunch and dinner
Reservation policy	Yes
Reservation email	reservations@chinatanglondon.co.uk
Credit cards	Accepted
Price range	Affordable
Style	Smart casual
Cuisine	Chinese
Recommended for	Regular neighbourhood

'A very relaxed atmosphere and great dim sum
and congee.'—Jérôme Tauvron

GIFTO'S LAHORE KARAHI

Recommended by
Martin Morales

Fort Lahore
162-164 The Broadway
Southall
London UB1 1NN
+44 2088138669
www.gifto.com

Opening hours	7 days for lunch and dinner, until late
Reservation policy	No
Credit cards	Accepted
Price range	Budget
Style	Casual
Cuisine	Pakistani-Indian
Recommended for	Worth the travel

CANTON ARMS

Recommended by
Tom Adams, Adam Byatt

177 South Lambeth Road
Stockwell
London SW8 1XP
www.cantonarms.com

Opening hours	6 days for lunch and dinner
Reservation policy	No
Credit cards	Accepted but not AMEX
Price range	Affordable
Style	Casual
Cuisine	Bar-Bistro
Recommended for	Regular neighbourhood

LAHORE KARAHI

Recommended by
Jonathan Jones

1 Tooting High Street
Tooting
London SW17 0SN
+44 2087672477

Opening hours	7 days for lunch and dinner
Reservation policy	No
Credit cards	Accepted
Price range	Budget
Style	Casual
Cuisine	Pakistani
Recommended for	Bargain

'Go for the grilled lamb chops, prawn (shrimps) korma and naans.'—Jonathan Jones

CHEZ BRUCE

Recommended by
Ollie Couillaud,
Marcus Wareing

2 Bellevue Road
Wandsworth
London SW17 7EG
+44 2086720114
www.chezbruce.co.uk

Opening hours	7 days for lunch and dinner
Reservation policy	Yes
Credit cards	Accepted
Price range	Affordable
Style	Smart casual
Cuisine	French
Recommended for	Regular neighbourhood

'The standard of food is always good and there's always friendly faces to look after you.'
—Marcus Wareing

HEREFORD ROAD

Recommended by
Ollie Dabbous, Marcus
Eaves, Pierre Koffmann,
Thomasina Miers

3 Hereford Road
Westbourne Grove
London W2 4AB
+44 2077271144
www.herefordroad.org

Opening hours	7 days for lunch and dinner
Reservation policy	Yes
Reservation email	info@herefordroad.org
Credit cards	Accepted
Price range	Affordable
Style	Casual
Cuisine	British
Recommended for	Regular neighbourhood

The West London chapter of the school of St. John, Hereford Road first brought its gutsy, no-nonsense cooking built around British seasonal ingredients to nearby Notting Hill in 2007. Driven by hardworking chef-proprietor Tom Pemberton, formerly head chef of St. John Bread & Wine, it's housed in a Victorian butcher's shop, open kitchen in the window where the counter would have been, wrought ironwork on the ceiling above the red leather upholstered love-seats. The daily changing menu delivers perfect simplicity, from whole fish and helpings of offal (variety meats) to bowls of ice cream. Their set lunch remains one of London's great bargains.

MAKI YAKI

Recommended by
Ollie Couillaud

149 Merton Road
Wimbledon
London SW19 1ED
+44 2085403113
www.makiyaki.co.uk

Opening hours	2 days for lunch and 6 days for dinner
Reservation policy	Yes
Credit cards	Accepted
Price range	Affordable
Style	Casual
Cuisine	Japanese
Recommended for	Regular neighbourhood

LONDON
EAST

$\hat{N}$ SCALE

0   400   800   1200
yd.

LAHORE KEBAB HOUSE

Recommended by
Jockey Petrie

2-10 Umberston Street
Aldgate
London E1 1PY
+44 2074819737
www.lahore-kebabhouse.com

Opening hours	7 days for lunch and dinner
Reservation policy	Yes
Credit cards	Accepted
Price range	Budget
Style	Casual
Cuisine	Pakistani
Recommended for	Regular neighbourhood

HAWKSMOOR

Recommended by
Paul Foster, Justin Ip, Tom
Oldroyd, Alyn Williams

10 Basinghall Street
Barbican
London EC2V 5BQ
+44 2073978120
www.thehawksmoor.com

Opening hours	5 days for breakfast, lunch and dinner
Reservation policy	Yes
Reservation email	guildhall@thehawksmoor.com
Credit cards	Accepted
Price range	Affordable
Style	Smart casual
Cuisine	Steakhouse
Recommended for	Breakfast

'You'll get a great full English at Hawksmoor including baked beans with pigs trotters.'—Alyn Williams

The weekday breakfast menu offered only at this branch of Hawksmoor is worth a special trip to the City. Not least for the that's-what-I-call-a-power-breakfast excess of their eye-opening platter for two, which includes a smoked bacon chop; their own recipe sausages made with pork, beef and mutton; black pudding (blood sausage); short-rib bubble & squeak (cabbage and mashed potatos); grilled bone marrow; 'Trotter baked beans'; fried eggs; grilled mushrooms; and roast tomatoes. Combine that with several Bloody Marys — you can pimp your own from a buffet of condiments should you wish — and you'll be set up for the day. Or possibly for a lie-down.

BRAWN

Recommended by
Brett Barnes, Angela
Hartnett, Margot Henderson,
Bruno Loubet

49 Columbia Road
Bethnal Green
London E2 7RG
+44 2077295692
www.brawn.co

Opening hours	4 days for lunch and 6 days for dinner
Reservation policy	Yes
Credit cards	Accepted but not AMEX
Price range	Affordable
Style	Casual
Cuisine	Bar-Bistro
Recommended for	Regular neighbourhood

'Brilliant food.'—Angela Hartnett

The likeable follow-up to Terroirs, Brawn sits on Columbia Road, in the hip heart of the East End. Utilitarian furniture meets whitewashed walls, Pop art, amusingly random bric-a-brac and a soundtrack that's big on reggae. It's staffed by a mixture of pretty young things and arty bearded blokes. The gutsy, daily-changing menu, made for sharing, is divided into five fairly self-explanatory sections: 'Taste Tickler', 'Cold', 'Hot', 'Pig' and 'Puddings & Cheese.' All of which is designed to go with a wine list that's big on natural wines — or 'cloudy reds and murky whites' as they like to describe them.

VIAJANTE

Patriot Square
Bethnal Green
London E2 9NF
+44 2078710461
www.viajante.co.uk

Recommended by
Paul Foster, Christoffer
Hruskova, Virgilio Martinez,
Morgan Meunier,
Alexandre Silva

Opening hours.............3 days for lunch and 7 days for dinner
Reservation policy...Yes
Reservation email.....................................info@viajante.co.uk
Credit cards..Accepted
Price range..Expensive
Style...Formal
Cuisine..Modern European
Recommended for...High End

'Spectacular cooking from a very approachable and pleasingly down to earth chef.'—Morgan Meunier

The bold move to open in the as yet ungentrified heart of Bethnal Green has paid off. Located in a striking Edwardian town hall turned boutique hotel, Viajante has successfully carved out a reputation as one of London's most gastronomically innovative destinations. At lunchtime there is a three-course menu, but dinner has six, nine or twelve-course tasting menus. There's definite emphasis put on vegetables over animal protein in dishes that arrive, straight from the open kitchen, carried by chefs who carefully explain each course.

ELLIOT'S CAFÉ

12 Stoney Street
Borough Market
Borough
London SE1 9AD
+44 2074037436
www.elliotscafe.com

Recommended by
José Pizarro

Opening hours.............7 days for lunch and 6 days for dinner
Reservation policy...Yes
Reservation email.....................................info@elliotscafe.com
Credit cards..Accepted
Price range..Affordable
Style...Casual
Cuisine..Cafe
Recommended for...Late night

ROAST

The Floral Hall
Stoney Street
Borough Market
Borough
London SE1 1TL
+44 8450347300
www.roast-restaurant.com

Recommended by
André Garrett

Opening hours.............................7 day for brunch and dinner
Reservation policy...Yes
Credit cards..Accepted
Price range..Affordable
Style..Smart casual
Cuisine..British
Recommended for...Breakfast

HONEST BURGER

Unit 12 Brixton Village
Brixton
London SW9 8PR
+44 2077337963
www.honestburgers.co.uk

Recommended by
Adam Byatt

Opening hours.............7 days for lunch and 3 days for dinner
Reservation policy..No
Credit cards..Not accepted
Price range..Budget
Style...Casual
Cuisine...Burgers
Recommended for...Bargain

L'ANIMA

1 Snowden Street
Broadgate
London EC2A 2DQ
+44 2074227000
www.lanima.co.uk

Recommended by
Sam Harris, Alfred Prasad

Opening hours.............5 days for lunch and 6 days for dinner
Reservation policy...Yes
Reservation email...info@lanima.co.uk
Credit cards..Accepted
Price range..Affordable
Style..Smart casual
Cuisine...Modern Italian
Recommended for...Regular neighbourhood

CAMDEN BAR & KITCHEN

Recommended by
Bryn Williams

102 Camden High Street
Camden
London NW1 0LU
+44 2074852744
www.camdenbarandkitchen.com

Opening hours.............7 days for breakfast, lunch and dinner
Reservation policy...Yes
Credit cards...Accepted
Price range...Budget
Style...Casual
Cuisine..International
Recommended for...Breakfast

'Wide selection of breakfasts and best of all on the
weekends most are available throughout the day.'
—Bryn Williams

IBÉRICA

Recommended by
José Pizarro

12 Cabot Square
Canary Wharf
London E14 4QQ
+44 2076368650
www.ibericalondon.co.uk

Opening hours.............7 days for lunch and 6 days for dinner
Reservation policy...Yes
Reservation email........... reservations@ibericalondon.co.uk
Credit cards...Accepted
Price range...Affordable
Style...Casual
Cuisine...Spanish
Recommended for...Late night

SWEETINGS

Recommended by
Fergus Henderson, Jacob
Kenedy, Stevie Parle

39 Queen Victoria Street
City of London
London EC4N 4SF
www.sweetingsrestaurant.com

Opening hours...5 days for lunch
Reservation policy...No
Credit cards...Accepted
Price range...Affordable
Style...Casual
Cuisine..Seafood
Recommended for.......................................Local favourite

'Fantastic working chaos, it couldn't exist anywhere
else but the City of London.'—Fergus Henderson

Serving simply prepared fish in the City of London
since 1889, without being pompous Sweetings revels
in being fantastically old fashioned, a right earned by
having survived two world wars and more financial
crashes than you can shake a skate wing at. It's the
like of crab bisque, smoked eel, potted shrimps, fried
whitebait and grilled scampi and bacon to start, with
main courses running from extravagant, simply
prepared catches such as turbot and Dover sole, to
their infinitely more affordable fish pie and salmon
cake. Desserts are hefty boarding school classics
such as rhubarb crumble (crisp) and spotted dick

BISTRO BRUNO LOUBET

Recommended by
Pierre Koffmann,
Jun Tanaka

St John's Square
86-88 Clerkenwell Road
Clerkenwell
London EC1M 5RJ
+44 2073244455
www.bistrotbrunoloubet.com

Opening hours.............7 days for breakfast, lunch and dinner
Reservation policy...Yes
Reservation email.....................eat@bistrotbrunoloubet.com
Credit cards...Accepted
Price range...Affordable
Style..Smart casual
Cuisine..Modern French
Recommended for................................Regular neighbourhood

CARAVAN

Recommended by
Peter Gordon, Christoffer
Hruskova, Bruno Loubet

11-13 Exmouth Market
Clerkenwell
London EC1R 4QD
+44 2078338115
www.caravanonexmouth.co.uk

Opening hours...........7 days for brunch and 6 days for dinner
Reservation policy...Yes
Credit cards...Accepted
Price range..Affordable
Style...Smart casual
Cuisine...International
Recommended for...Breakfast

'Great creamy mushrooms on toast.'—Bruno Loubet

Caravan sits at the mouth of Exmouth Market, where
creatives and crusties rub shoulders with Post Office
workers. The all-day menu, a well-travelled selection
of snacks, small plates and grown-up main courses,
is no slouch. But it's perhaps for breakfast or a
relaxed weekend brunch, sat over their take on the
classic fried breakfast or a plate of baked eggs with
chorizo, that its charms are best appreciated. They
roast their own coffee beans in the basement: the
combination of aroma, choice – from Flat Whites to
proper filter – and quality are more than enough to
satisfy even the most discerning of coffee geeks.

FOX AND ANCHOR

Recommended by
Pascal Aussignac

115 Charterhouse Street
Clerkenwell
London EC1M 6AA
+44 2072501300
www.foxandanchor.com

Opening hours..............7 days for breakfast, lunch and dinner
Reservation policy...Yes
Reservation email...............bookingscentral@hotelduvin.com
Credit cards...Accepted
Price range..Affordable
Style..Casual
Cuisine..Bar-Bistro
Recommended for...Local favourite

'Every time I'm in London I go the Fox and Anchor to
feel the London vibe. I love the mix of laid back attitude
and very fine food.'—Pascal Aussignac

THE MODERN PANTRY

Recommended by
Ollie Dabbous, Angela
Hartnett, Christoffer
Hruskova, Moreno Cedroni

47-48 St John's Square
Clerkenwell
London EC1V 4JJ
+44 2075539210
www.themodernpantry.co.uk

Opening hours..............7 days for breakfast, lunch and dinner
Reservation policy...Yes
Credit cards...Accepted
Price range..Affordable
Style..Casual
Cuisine...International
Recommended for...Breakfast

'I love the grilled haloumi breakfast with
spinach.'—Angela Hartnett

The Modern Pantry's bright ground-floor café, with
its all-white tables and chairs that amplify the light
through its large front windows across St John's
Square, is the perfect morning venue. Kiwi-born
chef-proprietor Anna Hansen puts as much care into
breakfast as she does lunch and dinner. Expect the
likes of ricotta pancakes, soft-boiled eggs with
Vegemite soldiers (strips of toast) and grilled chorizo
with plantain fritters. Star of the show is a, rightly
celebrated, Sri Lankan-inspired omelette filled with
sugar-cured prawns (shrimp), green chilli, spring
onions (scallions) and coriander (cilantro), topped
with a smoked chilli sambal. The smoothies also
demand your attention.

MORO

Recommended by
Brett Barnes, Matthew
Dillon, Jacob Kenedy, Miles
Kirby, Tom Pemberton,
Mitchell Rosenthal,
Tim Siadatan

34-36 Exmouth Market
Clerkenwell
London EC1R 4QE
+44 2078338336
www.moro.co.uk

Opening hours..............7 days for lunch and 6 days for dinner
Reservation policy...Yes
Credit cards...Accepted
Price range..Affordable
Style..Casual
Cuisine..North African-Spanish
Recommended for...............................Regular neighbourhood

'The best consistently honest food.'—Miles Kirby

ST. JOHN BAR AND RESTAURANT

Recommended by
Brett Barnes, Adam Byatt, Miguel Castro e Silva, Andreas Dahlberg Anthony Demetre, Şemsa Denizsel, André Garrett, Matthew Harris, Sam Harris, Margot Henderson, Shaun Hill, Jonathan Jones, Miles Kirby, Jeremy Lee, Tom Oldroyd, Theo Randall, Ruth Rogers, Tim Siadatan, Fernando Trocca, Alyn Williams

26 St John Street
Clerkenwell
London EC1M 4AY
+44 2033018069
www.stjohnrestaurant.com

Opening hours................................6 days for lunch and dinner
Reservation policy...Yes
Reservation email........reservations@stjohnhotellondon.com
Credit cards...Accepted
Price range...Affordable
Style...Smart casual
Cuisine...British
Recommended for...Local favourite

'In its style, location and food it's the very best
of old London.'—Theo Randall

Arguably the most seminal London restaurant of the
last twenty years, the original branch of St. John has
barely changed since it opened back in 1994. The
birthplace of Fergus Henderson's famed 'nose-to-tail'
philosophy, the twice-daily changing menu is still
tersely written, strictly seasonal and still likes to
make use of bits of beast that Anglo-Saxon chefs
used to throw away until he made them fashionable.
The other star is the Georgian building, an old
smokehouse, its high ceilings, whitewashed walls
and surfeit of natural light somehow managing to
make it feel like nowhere else in London, and somewhere that couldn't exist anywhere else.

TAMNAG THAI

Recommended by
Matthew Harris

50-54 Westow Hill
Crystal Palace
London SE19 1RX
+44 2087615959
www.tamnagthai.com

Opening hours................................7 days for lunch and dinner
Reservation policy...Yes
Credit cards...Accepted
Price range...Budget
Style...Casual
Cuisine...Thai
Recommended for...Bargain

SÖMINE

Recommended by
Samantha and Samuel Clark

131 Kingsland High Street
Dalston
London E8 2PB

Opening hours................................7 days for 24 hours
Reservation policy...No
Credit cards...Not accepted
Price range...Budget
Style...Casual
Cuisine...Turkish
Recommended for...Late night

'Open twenty-four hours a day for Turkish mezze.
We always have the yogurt soups and delicious
slow-cooked dishes.'—Samantha and Samuel Clark

SARAVANAA BHAVAN

Recommended by
Alfred Prasad

300 High Street North
East Ham
London E12 6SA
www.saravanabhavan.co.uk

Opening hours................................7 days for lunch and dinner
Reservation policy...No
Credit cards...........................Accepted but not AMEX and Diners
Price range...Budget
Style...Casual
Cuisine...Indian-Vegetarian
Recommended for...Breakfast

'I tuck into dosas and chutneys and feel like I'm back
home in India.'—Alfred Prasad

YILDIZ

Recommended by
Ben Tish

163 Blackstock Road
Finsbury Park
London N4 2JS
+44 2073543899
www.yildizocakbasi.co.uk

Opening hours................................7 days for lunch and dinner
Reservation policy...Yes
Credit cards...........................Accepted but not AMEX and Diners
Price range...Budget
Style...Casual
Cuisine...Turkish
Recommended for...Bargain

DABBOUS

Recommended by
Agnar Sverrisson, Ben Tish

39 Whitfield Street
Fitzrovia
London W1T 2SF
+44 2073231544
www.dabbous.co.uk

Opening hours	5 days for lunch and dinner
Reservation policy	Yes
Reservation email	info@dabbous.co.uk
Credit cards	Accepted
Price range	Affordable
Style	Smart casual
Cuisine	Modern European
Recommended for	Worth the travel

Critics' darling on opening in 2012 meant Dabbous's compact thirty-six-cover dining room found itself booked until kingdom come. Believe the hype – the universal praise for the playful French-meets-Nordic-in-London cooking of its well-travelled young chef Ollie Dabbous (ex of Texture and Le Manoir) is more than justified. The gritty, no-frills, industrial aesthetic of the dining room – artfully distressed concrete, meshed metal, exposed ducting – has its detractors. But perhaps it's partially why everything – particularly the set lunch and the tasting menus – seems so reasonably priced and so much fun. The basement bar does classy cocktails and a short menu of bar snacks.

KIKUCHI

Recommended by
Nuno Mendes

14 Hanway Street
Fitzrovia
London W1T 1UD
+44 2076377720

Opening hours	6 days for dinner
Reservation policy	Yes
Credit cards	Accepted
Price range	Affordable
Style	Smart casual
Cuisine	Japanese
Recommended for	High End

'I'm obsessed with Japanese food and the simplicity and delicacy of almost everything on the menu here is show-stopping.'—Nuno Mendes

The first thing you're asked on entering Kikuchi is "Have you been here before?" If you answer in the negative, you're informed that there is "Minimum spend of £25 ($40) per person." While not eye-wateringly expensive compared with London's more feted Japanese establishments, it's still not aimed at the average budget-conscious tourist. Although it's admittedly lost some of its quirky charm following a recent modern refit of its interior, the exceptional standard of the sushi, sashimi, yakitori, tempura and the ever-enticing list of daily specials remains intact. If there's space, opt for a berth at the seven-seat sushi counter.

PIED À TERRE

Recommended by
Tom Pemberton

34 Charlotte Street
Fitzrovia
London W1T 2NH
+44 2076361178
www.pied-a-terre.co.uk

Opening hours	5 days for lunch and 6 days for dinner
Reservation policy	Yes
Reservation email	reservations@pied-a-terre.co.uk
Credit cards	Accepted
Price range	Expensive
Style	Smart casual
Cuisine	Modern French
Recommended for	High End

ROKA

Recommended by
Tom Kerridge, Miles Kirby,
Jockey Petrie

37 Charlotte Street
Fitzrovia
London W1T 1RR
+44 2075806464
www.rokarestaurant.com

Opening hours	7 days for lunch and dinner
Reservation policy	Yes
Credit cards	Accepted
Price range	Expensive
Style	Smart casual
Cuisine	Modern Japanese
Recommended for	High End

ROUX AT THE LANDAU

Recommended by
Jacob Kenedy

Langham Hotel
1c Portland Place
Fitzrovia
London W1B 1JA
+44 2079650165
www.thelandau.com

Opening hours	5 days for lunch and 6 days for dinner
Reservation policy	Yes
Reservation email	reservations@rouxatthelandau.com
Credit cards	Accepted
Price range	Expensive
Style	Smart casual
Cuisine	Modern French
Recommended for	High End

SALT YARD

Recommended by
Ollie Couillaud

54 Goodge Street
Fitzrovia
London W1T 4NA
+44 2076370657
www.saltyard.co.uk

Opening hours	6 days for lunch and dinner
Reservation policy	Yes
Reservation email	info@saltyard.co.uk
Credit cards	Accepted
Price range	Affordable
Style	Smart casual
Cuisine	Small plates
Recommended for	Wish I'd opened

MANGAL OCAKBASI

Recommended by
Brett Barnes, Mitchell Tonks

10 Arcola Street
Hackney
London E8 2DJ
www.mangal1.com

Opening hours	7 days for lunch and dinner
Reservation policy	Yes
Credit cards	Not accepted
Price range	Budget
Style	Casual
Cuisine	Turkish
Recommended for	Bargain

'Great, cheap Turkish BBQ and mezze.'—Brett Barnes

RAILROAD

Recommended by
Stevie Parle

120-122 Morning Lane
Hackney
London E9 6LH
+44 2089852858
www.railroadhackney.co.uk

Opening hours	7 days for brunch and 4 days for dinner
Reservation policy	Yes
Reservation email	mail@railroadhackney.co.uk
Credit cards	Accepted but not AMEX and Diners
Price range	Budget
Style	Casual
Cuisine	International
Recommended for	Breakfast

'Have Moroccan eggs or a bacon sandwich on the best bread in London.'—Stevie Parle

TRE VIET

Recommended by
Peter Gordon

247-251 Mare Street
Hackney
London E8 3NS
+44 2085337390
www.treviet.co.uk

Opening hours	7 days for lunch and dinner
Reservation policy	Yes
Credit cards	Accepted
Price range	Budget
Style	Casual
Cuisine	Vietnamese
Recommended for	Bargain

YUM BUN

Recommended by
Nuno Mendes

Broadway Market School Yard
Westgate Street
Hackney
London E8 4PH
www.yumbun.co.uk

Opening hours	1 day for lunch
Reservation policy	No
Credit cards	Not accepted
Price range	Budget
Style	Casual
Cuisine	Chinese
Recommended for	Bargain

'They serve the most delicious steamed buns filled with high-quality Blytheburgh pork belly, hoi sin, chilli sauce and fresh cucumber.'—Nuno Mendes

Among the series of food stalls that have sprung up in recent years in the schoolyard at the London Fields end of Broadway Market, you'll find Yum Bun every Saturday. As the name would suggest, buns are what they do – 'pillow soft', steamed Chinese-style buns. While they thoughtfully and sensibly cater for vegetarians with their filling of Portobello mushroom and toasted walnuts (finished with a miso glaze), everyone else is here for the variety stuffed with slow-roasted Suffolk belly pork, spring onion (scallion) and shiracha sauce. Asian broths, from hot and sour to sumashi, are available as sides for slurping or dipping.

ANTEPLILER

Recommended by
Jérôme Tauvron

46 Grand Parade
Green Lanes
Haringey
London N4 1AG
+44 2088025588

Opening hours	7 days for lunch and dinner
Reservation policy	Yes
Credit cards	Accepted but not AMEX and Diners
Price range	Budget
Style	Casual
Cuisine	Turkish
Recommended for	Regular neighbourhood

THE BREAKFAST CLUB

Recommended by
Pascal Aussignac

2-4 Rufus Street
Hoxton
London N1 6PE
+44 2077295252
www.thebreakfastclubcafes.com

Opening hours	7 days from breakfast until late
Reservation policy	Yes
Reservation email	sylvester@loveTBC.com
Credit cards	Accepted
Price range	Budget
Style	Casual
Cuisine	Diner-Cafe
Recommended for	Breakfast

'Amazing range of food, great atmosphere, smiley service and cool music.'—Pascal Aussignac

SÔNG QUÊ

Recommended by
Christoffer Hruskova

134 Kingsland Road
Hoxton
London E2 8DY
+44 2076133222
www.songque.co.uk

Opening hours	7 days for lunch and dinner
Reservation policy	Yes
Credit cards	Accepted but not AMEX and Diners
Price range	Budget
Style	Casual
Cuisine	Vietnamese
Recommended for	Bargain

AFGHAN KITCHEN

Recommended by
Miles Kirby

35 Islington Green
Islington
London N1 8DU
+44 2073598019

Opening hours	5 days for lunch and dinner
Reservation policy	Yes
Credit cards	Not accepted
Price range	Budget
Style	Casual
Cuisine	Afghan
Recommended for	Bargain

ALMEIDA

Recommended by
Morgan Meunier

30 Almeida Street
Islington
London N1 1AD
+44 2073544777
www.almeida-restaurant.co.uk

Opening hours................................6 days for lunch and dinner
Reservation policy..Yes
Reservation email. almeida-reservations@danddlondon.com
Credit cards..Accepted
Price range...Affordable
Style...Smart casual
Cuisine...French
Recommended for...Late night

THE DUKE OF CAMBRIDGE

Recommended by
Francesco Mazzei

30 St Peter's Street
Islington
London N1 8JT
+44 2073593066
www.dukeorganic.co.uk

Opening hours................................7 days for lunch and dinner
Reservation policy..Yes
Reservation email..........................duke@dukeorganic.co.uk
Credit cards..Accepted
Price range...Affordable
Style...Casual
Cuisine...Bar-Bistro
Recommended for...Local favourite

OTTOLENGHI

Recommended by
Matthew Dillon,
Anna Hansen

287 Upper Street
Islington
London N1 2TZ
+44 2072881454
www.ottolenghi.co.uk

Opening hours.............7 days for breakfast, lunch and dinner
Reservation policy..Yes
Reservation email..............................upper@ottolenghi.co.uk
Credit cards..Accepted
Price range...Budget
Style...Casual
Cuisine...Mediterranean
Recommended for...Breakfast

'I'm a fan of the rarebit with poached egg and chard.
The coffee is very good and the staff friendly and
helpful.'—Anna Hansen

PALMERA OASIS

Recommended by
Miles Kirby

332 Essex Road
Islington
London N1 3PB
+44 2077046149
www.palmeraoasis.co.uk

Opening hours................................7 days for lunch and dinner
Reservation policy...No
Reservation email......................palmeraoasis@hotmail.co.uk
Credit cards....................Accepted but not AMEX and Diners
Price range...Budget
Style...Casual
Cuisine...Lebanese
Recommended for...Late night

PIZZERIA OREGANO

Recommended by
Yvonnick Lalle

18-19 St Albans Place
Islington
London N1 0NX
+44 2072881123
www.pizzeriaoregano.co.uk

Opening hours.............2 days for lunch and 7 days for dinner
Reservation policy..Yes
Credit cards..Accepted
Price range...Budget
Style...Casual
Cuisine...Italian
Recommended for.............................Regular neighbourhood

SANGRIA

Recommended by
Yvonnick Lalle

88 Upper Street
Islington
London N1 0PN
+44 2077045253

Opening hours................................7 days for lunch and dinner
Reservation policy..Yes
Credit cards....................Accepted but not AMEX and Diners
Price range...Budget
Style...Casual
Cuisine...Spanish
Recommended for...Bargain

TRULLO

Recommended by
Miles Kirby

300-302 St Paul's Road
Islington
London N1 2LH
+44 2072262733
www.trullorestaurant.com

Opening hours.............7 days for lunch and 6 days for dinner
Reservation policy...Yes
Reservation email...............enquiries@trullorestaurant.com
Credit cards......................Accepted but not AMEX and Diners
Price range..Affordable
Style...Casual
Cuisine..Modern Italian
Recommended for..............................Regular neighbourhood

HOT STUFF

Recommended by
Jacob Kenedy

23 Wilcox Road
Lambeth
London SW8 2XA
+44 02076278181
www.eathotstuff.com

Opening hours..................................6 days for dinner
Reservation policy...................................Yes
Credit cards.......................Accepted but not AMEX
Price range...Budget
Style..Casual
Cuisine..Indian
Recommended for.......................................Bargain

CACHAO

Recommended by
Theo Randall

140 Regent's Park Road
Primrose Hill
London NW1 8XL
www.cachaotoycafe.com

Opening hours.........................7 days for breakfast and lunch
Reservation policy...No
Credit cards......................................Accepted
Price range..Budget
Style..Casual
Cuisine...Café
Recommended for................................Breakfast

LEMONIA

Recommended by
Theo Randall

89 Regent's Park Road
Primrose Hill
London NW1 8UY
+44 2075867454
www.lemonia.co.uk

Opening hours................................6 days for lunch and dinner
Reservation policy..Yes
Credit cards.............................Accepted but not AMEX
Price range...Budget
Style..Casual
Cuisine..Greek
Recommended for.....................................Bargain

ALBION CAFE

Recommended by
Justin Ip
Jun Tanaka

2-4 Boundary Street
Shoreditch
London E2 7DD
+44 2077291051
www.albioncaff.co.uk

Opening hours.........................7 days from breakfast until late
Reservation policy..No
Reservation email..............................info@theboundary.co.uk
Credit cards..Accepted
Price range......................................Affordable
Style..Casual
Cuisine...Bakery-Cafe
Recommended for....................................Late night

BEIGEL BAKE

Recommended by
Jockey Petrie

159 Brick Lane
Shoreditch
London E1 6SB

Opening hours	7 days for 24 hours
Reservation policy	No
Credit cards	Not accepted
Price range	Budget
Style	Casual
Cuisine	Bakery
Recommended for	Late night

BIG APPLE HOT DOGS

Recommended by
Tom Oldroyd

239 Old Street
Shoreditch
London EC1V 9EY
www.bigapplehotdogs.com

Opening hours	4 days for lunch and dinner
Reservation policy	No
Credit cards	Not accepted
Price range	Budget
Style	Casual
Cuisine	Hot Dogs
Recommended for	Bargain

'I always feel like I've cheated someone when I get change from £5 (\$8) in return for one of their superbly made hot dogs.'—Tom Oldroyd

New York inspired but proudly made in London, the dogs at this cart stationed at Old Street are pedigree. From their trademark 'Big Dog' via the all-beef 'Pimp Steak' to a classic Frankfurter, these wieners are about high meat content from free-range pork and quality beef in natural casings, stuffed in quality buns from a local bakery. You can top them with 'Desiréed onions' (fried in butter, thyme and black pepper), Polish sauerkraut, pickled cucumbers and various mustards and relishes. Their motto – 'No brains, no bones, no butts. The best dog you've ever had' – doesn't ring hollow this side of the Atlantic.

KÊU BÁNH MÌ DELI

Recommended by
James Lowe

332 Old Street
Shoreditch
London EC1V 9LA
+44 2077396686
www.keudeli.co.uk

Opening hours	6 days from breakfast until late
Reservation policy	No
Credit cards	Accepted
Price range	Budget
Style	Casual
Cuisine	Vietnamese
Recommended for	Bargain

'I love the fact that the best sandwiches in London aren't British. The duck is amazing and it's the best version of a classic *Bánh mì* that I've had.'
—James Lowe

This Vietnamese deli in Shoreditch specializes in *Bánh mì*, the filled baguettes that are the delicious bastard child of Indochina's French colonial era. Kêu, from team behind the nearby Vietnamese stalwarts Viet Grill and Cây Tre, have their baguettes baked for them by the Sally Clarke bakery. They're softer than a traditional French bread stick, as they should be, despite not being made with rice flower as they are back in Vietnam. Fillings include lemongrass infused mackerel with mooli (daikon) and coriander (cilantro); spiced pork belly, ham terrine and chicken liver pâté; and pork meatballs in a spicy gravy.

ROCHELLE CANTEEN

Recommended by
Gabrielle Hamilton, Miles
Kirby, Nuno Mendes

Rochelle School
Arnold Circus
Shoreditch
London E2 7ES
+44 2077295677
www.arnoldandhenderson.com

Opening hours.............................5 days for breakfast and lunch
Reservation policy...Yes
Reservation email............canteen@arnoldandhenderson.com
Credit cards...Accepted
Price range..Budget
Style...Casual
Cuisine..British
Recommended for.................................Regular neighbourhood

'I live nearby in East London and end up here quite often on my days off. Only open until 4.00 p.m., it's a great spot for lunch.'—Nuno Mendes

Occupying the converted bike sheds of a Victorian school, what began as a canteen for the local arty souls has become a Shoreditch institution. Open weekdays only, it's run by Melanie Arnold and Margot Henderson (other half of Fergus of St. John fame) and doubles up as the headquarters for their in demand catering company. Come summertime, they set up tables outside, overlooking the school's grassy playground. The menu changes daily and is very much of the school of St. John – short, British, seasonal, tersely descriptive and delicious.

THE TOWPATH CAFÉ

Recommended by
Brett Barnes, Samantha and
Samuel Clark, Miles Kirby

42 De Beauvoir Crescent
Shoreditch
London N1 5SB

Opening hours..........................6 days from breakfast until late
Reservation policy..No
Credit cards...Not accepted
Price range..Budget
Style...Casual
Cuisine..Mediterranean
Recommended for...Breakfast

40 MALTBY STREET

Recommended by
Jun Tanaka

40 Maltby Street
Southwark
London SE1 3PA
www.40maltbystreet.com

Opening hours................2 days for dinner and 1 day for lunch
Reservation policy..No
Credit cards...Accepted but not AMEX
Price range..Affordable
Style...Casual
Cuisine...Italian
Recommended for..Worth the travel

JOSÉ

Recommended by
Sam Harris, Martin Morales

104 Bermondsey Street
Southwark
London SE1 3UB
www.josepizarro.com/restaurants/jose

Opening hours.............7 days for lunch and 6 days for dinner
Reservation policy..No
Credit cards...Accepted
Price range..Budget
Style...Casual
Cuisine..Tapas
Recommended for...Bargain

ZUCCA

Recommended by
José Pizarro, Bruce Poole,
Clare Smyth

184 Bermondsey Street
Southwark
London SE1 3TQ
+44 2073786809
www.zuccalondon.com

Opening hours.................................6 days for lunch and dinner
Reservation policy...Yes
Reservation email..................reservations@zuccalondon.com
Credit cards...Accepted but not AMEX
Price range..Affordable
Style...Smart casual
Cuisine...Modern Italian
Recommended for.................................Regular neighbourhood

'In my opinion it's the best Italian restaurant in London. It never fails to excite me either: the food and ambiance are stunning.'—José Pizarro

Since opening in 2010 in fashionable Bermondsey Street, not far from the foodie hub of Borough Market, Zucca has become a fixture on the London food scene. Part of the new wave of affordable, rustic Italians in London, plain, excellently executed dishes such as grilled octopus, sprouting (baby) broccoli, rosemary and anchovy, and slow-cooked rabbit, tomato, olives and speck are served up in this plain but cheerful canteen-like space. The simple stylishness keeps prices down — all the better to enjoy the extensive, all-Italian wine list that saw Zucca win Decanter magazine's 'Restaurant of the Year' title in 2011.

LA CHAPELLE

Recommended by
Anna Hansen

35 Spital Square
Spitalfields
London E1 6DY
+44 2072990400
www.galvinrestaurants.com

Opening hours	7 days for lunch and dinner
Reservation policy	Yes
Credit cards	Accepted
Price range	Expensive
Style	Smart casual
Cuisine	Modern French
Recommended for	High End

'Best stuffed pigs trotters (feet) with madeira sauce ever served in a particularly beautiful space.'
—Anna Hansen

LEILA'S CAFÉ

Recommended by
Nuno Mendes

17 Calvert Avenue
Spitalfields
London E2 7JP

Opening hours	6 days for breakfast and lunch
Reservation policy	No
Credit cards	Accepted
Price range	Budget
Style	Casual
Cuisine	Café
Recommended for	Breakfast

'You can't beat the eggs here. Next door is their shop, which has very carefully sourced some of the best produce from around the UK.'—Nuno Mendes

An annexe of Lelia's shop, which sits next door, styled like an old-fashioned grocer's by virtue of the fact that that's exactly what it was until the mid-1960s, its shelves today stocked like that of a lovably eclectic delicatessen. The café has a truly open kitchen, with nothing between those cooking and the communal tables. Depending on your tolerance level, the eccentric service could at times be described as borderline surly or just plain rude. But that doesn't deter its loyal and fashionable following, who come for the atmosphere, the simple home-cooked dishes and the excellent coffee.

ST. JOHN BREAD & WINE

Recommended by
Tom Adams,
Samantha and Samuel Clark,
Sam Harris, Angela Hartnett,
Jeremy Lee, James Lowe,
Nuno Mendes, Tom
Pemberton, Tim Siadatan

94-96 Commercial Street
Spitalfields
London E1 6LZ
+44 2033018069
www.stjohnbreadandwine.com

Opening hours	7 days for breakfast, lunch and dinner
Reservation policy	Yes
Reservation email	reservations@stjohnrestaurant.com
Credit cards	Accepted
Price range	Affordable
Style	Smart casual
Cuisine	British
Recommended for	Local favourite

'I've had one of the best meals of my life here: a late lunch of smoked slow-cooked pork belly simply served with carrots and mustard.'—Nuno Mendes

The middle child of the St. John family lies across from Spitalfields Market and runs a staggered, just shy of all-day, menu from breakfast — via elevenses, lunch and early afternoon nibbles — through to supper. Built around its bakery and wine shop, the cooking naturally reflects the British seasonal nose-to-tail approach that is St. John's trademark but tailors it more to tapas-style sharing. The open kitchen and bakery overlook a no-nonsense dining room, brightly lit with whitewashed walls, tightly packed with simple wooden tables and chairs. If there's one complaint, it's that the latter don't favour bony behinds.

19 NUMARA BOS CIRRIK I

34 Stoke Newington Road
Stoke Newington
London N16 7XJ
+44 2072490400
www.cirrik1.co.uk

Opening hours..............................7 days for lunch and dinner
Reservation policy..Yes
Credit cards............................Accepted but not AMEX
Price range..Budget
Style..Casual
Cuisine..Turkish
Recommended for...............................Regular neighbourhood

RASA N16

55 Stoke Newington Church Street
Stoke Newington
London N16 0AR
+44 2072490344
www.rasarestaurants.com

Opening hours.............2 days for lunch and 6 days for dinner
Reservation policy..Yes
Credit cards..Accepted
Price range..Budget
Style..Casual
Cuisine...Indian-Vegetarian
Recommended for...............................Regular neighbourhood

'Authentic, home-cooked, southern Indian food. I love
the spice and freshness of the food.'—Morgan Meunier

This, the original bijou branch of Rasa in deepest
Stoke Newington, has changed little since it opened a
decade and a half ago with a focus on the distinctive
vegetarian cooking of Keralan Nair. Its hot pink
frontage and incense-burning dining room has since
spawned a mini empire, with a further six restaurants across London and one in Newcastle, which
have branched out and serve meat and seafood.
But here they've stuck to a hugely affordable, colourful, vegetarian menu typified by dishes such as Beet
Cheera Pachadi – beetroot (beet) and spinach blended together with yogurt, roasted coconut, mustard
seeds and curry leaves.

TESTI

38 Stoke Newington High Street
Stoke Newington
London N16 7PL
+44 2072497151

Opening hours......................6 days for lunch and early dinner
Reservation policy..No
Credit cards............................Accepted but not AMEX
Price range..Budget
Style..Casual
Cuisine..Turkish
Recommended for..Bargain

MASSIMO

Corinthia Hotel
10 Northumberland Avenue
Strand
London WC2N 5AE
+44 2079980555
www.massimo-restaurant.co.uk

Opening hours..................................6 days for lunch and dinner
Reservation policy..Yes
Reservation email.............tables@massimo-restaurant.co.uk
Credit cards..Accepted
Price range..Affordable
Style..Formal
Cuisine..Italian
Recommended for...............................Regular neighbourhood

'Every time I eat here it always ends up a feast.'
—Jérôme Tauvron

TERROIRS

5 William IV Street
Strand
London WC2N 4DW
+44 2070360660
www.terroirswinebar.com

Opening hours..................................6 days for lunch and dinner
Reservation policy..Yes
Credit cards..Accepted
Price range..Affordable
Style..Smart casual
Cuisine..French
Recommended for...............................Regular neighbourhood

BRUNSWICK HOUSE CAFÉ

Recommended by
Isaac McHale, Ben Tish

30 Wandsworth Road
Vauxhall
London SW8 2LG
+44 2077202926
www.brunswickhousecafe.com

Opening hours..........7 days for brunch and 5 days for dinner
Reservation policy..Yes
Reservation email.................info@brunswickhousecafe.co.uk
Credit cards..Accepted but not AMEX
Price range...Affordable
Style...Casual
Cuisine...British
Recommended for...Breakfast

By Vauxhall's gyratory system and bleak urban
sprawl lies Brunswick House, a Georgian mansion
rescued from future demolition in 2004, when
LASSCO (London Architectural Salvage and Supply
Company) took it over as a base from which to sell
their reclaimed wares. Full of random bric-a-brac,
its café looks fantastically idiosyncratic. The cooking
at breakfast – and later at lunch and dinner – is of
the simple, gutsy, seasonal, tersely described 'School
of St. John.' In practice that means soft-boiled eggs,
sea salt and soldiers (strips of toast); bacon and
eggs on toast; and granola, yogurt and poached fruit.
Coffee is by boutique London roastery Coleman.

THE ANCHOR & HOPE

Recommended by
James Lowe, Tom
Pemberton, Bruce Poole

36 The Cut
Waterloo
London SE1 8LP
www.charleswells.co.uk/home/pub-guide

Opening hours.............7 days for lunch and 6 days for dinner
Reservation policy...No
Credit cards......................Accepted but not AMEX and Diners
Price range...Affordable
Style...Casual
Cuisine...Bar-Bistro
Recommended for..................................Regular neighbourhood

TAYYABS

Recommended by
Ollie Dabbous, Anna Hansen,
James Lowe, Ben Tish

83-89 Fieldgate Street
Whitechapel
London E1 1JU
+44 2072479543
www.tayyabs.co.uk

Opening hours................................7 days for lunch and dinner
Reservation policy..Yes
Reservation email..info@tayyabs.co.uk
Credit cards...Accepted
Price range...Budget
Style...Casual
Cuisine...Pakistani
Recommended for...Local favourite

'What says London more than a great curry?'
—Anna Hansen

No one comes to Tayyabs for the ambience. Forty
years after opening, E1's worst-kept secret is more
cut and thrust than ever, from the location around the
back of Whitechapel High Street to the hour-plus
queues (waiting lines) – and that's with a reservation
– and the ferocious noise levels. However, the
Punjabi food – specifically the sizzling lamb chops
and groaning mixed grill plate, as well as fresh-from-
the-tandoor naan – makes it all worthwhile,
especially with change from £20 ($32). Don't get
caught out by the BYO policy – bring an extra beer
or two so you can enjoy a pre-dinner drink while you
wait for a table.

LONDON
CENTRAL

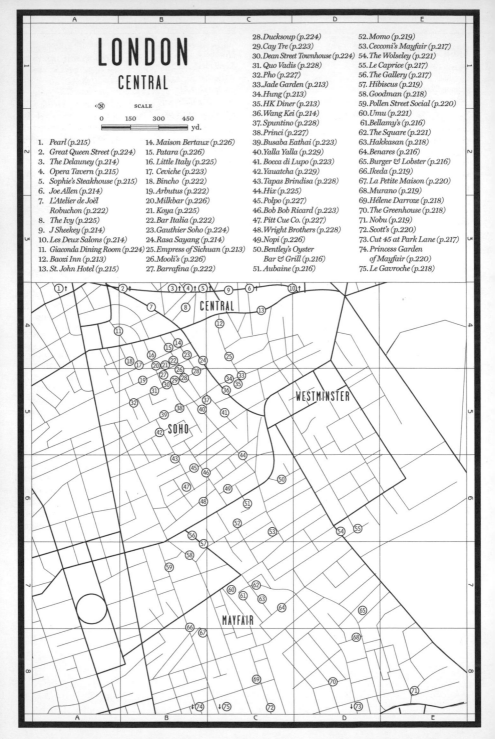

‹N› SCALE

0   150   300   450   yd.

CENTRAL

WESTMINSTER

SOHO

MAYFAIR

BAOZI INN

Recommended by
Jason Atherton

25 Newport Court
Chinatown
London WC2H 7JS

Opening hours	7 days for lunch and dinner
Reservation policy	No
Credit cards	Not accepted
Price range	Budget
Style	Casual
Cuisine	
Recommended for	Bargain

EMPRESS OF SICHUAN

Recommended by
Jacob Kenedy

6 Lisle Street
Chinatown
London WC2H 7BG
+44 2077348128
www.restaurantprivilege.com/empress-of-sichuan

Opening hours	7 days for lunch and dinner
Reservation policy	Yes
Credit cards	Accepted
Price range	Affordable
Style	Smart casual
Cuisine	Szechuanese
Recommended for	Regular neighbourhood

HK DINER

Recommended by
Jun Tanaka

22 Wardour Street
Chinatown
London W1D 6QQ
+44 2074349544
www.hkdiner.com

Opening hours	7 days for lunch and dinner
Reservation policy	No
Credit cards	Accepted but not AMEX and Diners
Price range	Budget
Style	Casual
Cuisine	Chinese
Recommended for	Late night

'I always order from the shorter menu. I can't go there without ordering the minced ground pork poached egg – it's addictive.'—Jun Tanaka

This is as friendly as Chinatown gets in the small hours, open until 4.00 a.m. every morning, the only rather reasonable proviso for entrance being a minimum spend of £6 ($10) a head. Ignore the large menu, offering set meals and a lengthy à la carte, and focus instead on their shorter menu, which includes 'Chicken (on the bone)' and 'Traditional clay hot pot'. Fans of bubble tea are spoiled for choice with various jellies and fruit boba available alongside traditional tapioca pearls. Chances are you might be after the hard stuff, in which case try a Victoria Harbour – vodka with lychee juice.

HUNG

Recommended by
Mark Hix

27 Wardour Street
Chinatown
London W1D 6PR

Opening hours	7 days for lunch and dinner
Reservation policy	No
Credit cards	Accepted
Price range	Budget
Style	Casual
Cuisine	Chinese
Recommended for	Bargain

JADE GARDEN

Recommended by
Fergus Henderson

15 Wardour Street
Chinatown
London W1D 6PH
+44 2074375065

Opening hours	7 days for lunch and dinner
Reservation policy	Yes
Credit cards	Accepted
Price range	Affordable
Style	Casual
Cuisine	Chinese
Recommended for	Bargain

'Order the dumplings.'—Fergus Henderson

RASA SAYANG

Recommended by
Mitchell Tonks

5 Macclesfield Street
Chinatown
London W1D 6AY
+44 2077341382
www.rasasayangfood.com

Opening hours	7 days for lunch and dinner
Reservation policy	Yes
Credit cards	Accepted
Price range	Budget
Style	Casual
Cuisine	Malaysian
Recommended for	Bargain

WONG KEI

Recommended by
Ollie Couillaud

41-43 Wardour Street
Chinatown
London W1D 6PY
+44 2074378408

Opening hours	7 days for lunch and dinner
Reservation policy	No
Credit cards	Not accepted
Price range	Budget
Style	Casual
Cuisine	Chinese
Recommended for	Late night

THE DELAUNEY

Recommended by
Angela Hartnett, Yvonnick
Lalle, Bruce Poole,
Mitchell Tonks

55 Aldwych
Covent Garden
London WC2B 4BB
+44 2074998558
www.thedelaunay.com

Opening hours	7 days for breakfast, lunch and dinner
Reservation policy	Yes
Reservation email	reservations@thedelaunay.com
Credit cards	Accepted
Price range	Affordable
Style	Smart casual
Cuisine	European
Recommended for	Breakfast

LES DEUX SALONS

Recommended by
Lisa Muncan

40-42 William IV Street
Covent Garden
London WC2N 4DD
+44 2074202050
www.lesdeuxsalons.co.uk

Opening hours	7 days for lunch and dinner
Reservation policy	Yes
Reservation email	info@lesdeuxsalons.co.uk
Credit cards	Accepted
Price range	Affordable
Style	Smart casual
Cuisine	French
Recommended for	Wish I'd opened

J SHEEKEY

Recommended by
Pascal Aussignac,
Thomasina Miers

28-34 St Martin's Court
Covent Garden
London WC2N 4AL
+44 2072402565
www.j-sheekey.co.uk

Opening hours	7 days for lunch and dinner
Reservation policy	Yes
Credit cards	Accepted
Price range	Expensive
Style	Smart casual
Cuisine	Seafood
Recommended for	Regular neighbourhood

'Great value for money and excellent, fresh seafood platters.'—Pascal Aussignac

JOE ALLEN

Recommended by
Rowley Leigh

13 Exeter Street
Covent Garden
London WC2E 7DT
+44 2078360651
www.joeallen.co.uk

Opening hours	7 days for brunch and dinner
Reservation policy	Yes
Credit cards	Accepted
Price range	Affordable
Style	Casual
Cuisine	American
Recommended for	Late night

OPERA TAVERN

Recommended by
Shaun Hill, Pierre Koffmann

23 Catherine Street
Covent Garden
London WC2B 5JS
+44 2078363680
www.operatavern.co.uk

Opening hours............7 days for lunch and 6 days for dinner
Reservation policy...Yes
Reservation email...............................info@operatavern.co.uk
Credit cards..Accepted
Price range...Affordable
Style...Smart casual
Cuisine...Small plates
Recommended for...Bargain

The youngest in a trio that includes Salt Yard and
Dehesa, the Opera Tavern specializes in small Span
ish and Italian plates accompanied by a wine list with
a pleasingly extensive by-the-glass selection. If it
paradoxically feels a bit more grown up than its older
siblings, that's probably because what was previously a spacious old Theatreland boozer has taken
extremely well to its repurposing as a smart tapas
operation. The street level bar and grill is laid out
with lots of comfortable counter seating, while the
above houses a notionally more formal dining room
for those who prefer their tables and chairs.

SOPHIE'S STEAKHOUSE

Recommended by
Tom Oldroyd

29-31 Wellington Street
Covent Garden
London WC2E 7DB
www.sophiessteakhouse.co.uk

Opening hours...................................7 days for lunch and dinner
Reservation policy...No
Credit cards...Accepted
Price range..Affordable
Style..Casual
Cuisine...Steakhouse
Recommended for..Late night

'For a substantial late night feed order the baby back
ribs and a lobster roll.'—Tom Oldroyd

PEARL

Recommended by
Alfred Prasad

252 High Holborn
Holborn
London WC1V 7EN
+44 2078297000
www.pearl-restaurant.com

Opening hours............5 days for lunch and 6 days for dinner
Reservation policy...Yes
Reservation email......................info@pearl-restaurant.co.uk
Credit cards..Accepted
Price range...Expensive
Style...Formal
Cuisine..Modern French
Recommended for..High End

ST. JOHN HOTEL

Recommended by
Richard Ekkebus, Jonathan
Jones, Jacob Kenedy,
Jeremy Lee, Stevie Parle,
Tom Pemberton

1 Leicester Street
Leicester Square
London WC2H 7BL
+44 2033018069
www.stjohnhotellondon.com

Opening hours............7 days for breakfast, lunch and dinner
Reservation policy...Yes
Reservation email.......reservations@stjohnhotellondon.com
Credit cards..Accepted
Price range...Affordable
Style...Smart casual
Cuisine..British
Recommended for..Breakfast

'It's heavenly having it around the corner in the West
End where there are few better places to start the
day.'—Jeremy Lee

This, the youngest offspring in the St. John family,
marked Fergus Henderson & Co.'s arrival in the West
End. Sat on the edge of Chinatown, it's housed in
what used to be Manzi's, the triple-decked 'Lan-
gouste, Huîtres, Moules' sign retained as a memorial
to that legendary fish restaurant of the old school
that ran for some sixty years until 2005. Breakfast
here offers a chance to sample Henderson's long-
perfected British take on the croissant, which he
playfully describes as 'warm little buttock-like buns'.
The morning's three-strong selection, plain butter,
cinnamon and raisin, served with marmalade and
golden raspberry jam, are a meal in their own right.

AUBAINE

Recommended by
Jérôme Tauvron

4 Heddon Street
Mayfair
London W1B 4BS
+44 2074402510
www.aubaine.co.uk

Opening hours..........7 days for brunch and 6 days for dinner
Reservation policy..Yes
Credit cards..Accepted
Price range..Affordable
Style..Smart casual
Cuisine..French
Recommended for...Breakfast

'Casual, fresh and simple food.'—Jérôme Tauvron

BELLAMY'S

Recommended by
Rowley Leigh

18 Bruton Place
Mayfair
London W1J 6LY
+44 2074912727
www.bellamysrestaurant.co.uk

Opening hours.............5 days for lunch and 6 days for dinner
Reservation policy..Yes
Credit cards..Accepted
Price range..Affordable
Style..Smart casual
Cuisine..French
Recommended for...................................Regular neighbourhood

BENARES

Recommended by
Bryn Williams

12a Berkeley Square House
Berkeley Square
Mayfair
London W1J 6BS
+44 2076298886
www.benaresrestaurant.com

Opening hours.....................7 days for lunch and dinner
Reservation policy..Yes
Reservation email.....reservations@benaresrestaurant.co.uk
Credit cards..Accepted
Price range..Expensive
Style..Smart casual
Cuisine..Modern Indian
Recommended for...High End

'A very classy restaurant that offers wonderful modern
Indian cuisine.'—Bryn Williams

BENTLEY'S OYSTER BAR & GRILL

Recommended by
Nigel Haworth,
Thomasina Miers,
Bryn Williams

11-15 Swallow Street
Mayfair
London W1B 4DG
+44 2077344756
www.bentleys.org

Opening hours............................7 days for brunch and dinner
Reservation policy..Yes
Reservation email....................reservations@bentleys.org
Credit cards..Accepted
Price range..Affordable
Style..Smart casual
Cuisine..Seafood
Recommended for...Wish I'd opened

'I admire Richard Corrigan's confidence to focus on
a seafood menu and yet somehow make every dish
unique and wonderful every time.'—Bryn Williams

Irish chef Richard Corrigan rebuilt the reputation of
this most English of restaurants when he took it over
and refurbished it in 2005. First opened in 1916, a
classic West End oyster bar and grill, located on a
cut-through between Regent's Street and Piccadilly,
it now consists of a upper floor grill, where meat sits
alongside the fish, and a street level floor oyster bar.
The latter, where marble counter meets red leather
upholstery at bar and booth, and seasoned old oyster
campaigners in white jackets do their shucking,
is a jewel. Outside, a large swathe of Swallow
Street does al fresco dining.

BURGER & LOBSTER

Recommended by
Claude Bosi, Alyn Williams

29 Clarges Street
Mayfair
London W1J 7EF
+44 2074091699
www.burgerandlobster.com

Opening hours.............7 days for lunch and 6 days for dinner
Reservation policy..No
Credit cards..Accepted
Price range..Budget
Style..Casual
Cuisine..Burgers-Seafood
Recommended for...Wish I'd opened

From the people behind Goodman – the butch Mos-
cow-born chain of meat palaces – comes this child-
ishly simple, no-reservations set-up. Guess what?
They serve only burgers and lobsters. The former,

undeniably excellent, are lifted straight from the menu at Goodman; the latter, shipped from Canada and displayed in a tank, are available grilled, steamed or in a roll. All come with chips (fries) and salad, and are priced at a nice round £20 ($31). They've added monstrous 4.5 kg (10 lb) lobsters to their tank, at a more bling-friendly £150 ($240) a pop. A runaway hit since it opened in Mayfair in late 2011, it's spawned branches in Soho and Farringdon.

LE CAPRICE

Arlington House
25 Arlington Street
Mayfair
London SW1A 1RJ
+44 2072692239
www.le-caprice.co.uk

Recommended by
Andrew Fairlie, David Hawksworth, Thomasina Miers, Marcus Wareing

Opening hours.............................7 days for lunch and dinner
Reservation policy...Yes
Reservation email....................reservations@le-caprice.co.uk
Credit cards...Accepted
Price range..Expensive
Style..Smart casual
Cuisine...Modern European
Recommended for..Wish I'd opened

'It's a classic. '—David Hawksworth

CECCONI'S MAYFAIR

5a Burlington Gardens
Mayfair
London W1S 3EP
+44 2074341500
www.cecconis.co.uk

Recommended by
Sam Harris, Karam Sethi

Opening hours.............7 days for breakfast, lunch and dinner
Reservation policy...Yes
Credit cards...Accepted
Price range..Affordable
Style..Smart casual
Cuisine...Italian
Recommended for...Late night

CUT AT 45 PARK LANE

The Dorchester Hotel
45 Park Lane
Mayfair
London W1K 1PN
+44 2074934554
www.45parklane.com/CUTat45ParkLane

Recommended by
Francesco Mazzei

Opening hours.............7 days for breakfast, lunch and dinner
Reservation policy...Yes
Credit cards...Accepted
Price range..Expensive
Style..Smart casual
Cuisine...Steakhouse
Recommended for...High End

THE GALLERY

Sketch
9 Conduit Street
Mayfair
London W1S 2XG
+44 2076594500
www.sketch.uk.com

Recommended by
Pascal Aussignac, Luis Baena, Ettore Botrini, Marcus Eaves, Lisa Muncan, Kevin Thornton

Opening hours..6 days for dinner
Reservation policy...Yes
Credit cards...Accepted
Price range..Affordable
Style..Smart casual
Cuisine..International
Recommended for..Late night

'It's the only place I know that perfectly combines fine cuisine and a trendy nightclub. (Normally when it's trendy the food is never good...)'—Pascal Aussignac

Mourad Mazouz's operation with partner Pierre Gagnaire, opened in 2003, remains the most bizarrely ambitious ever-evolving bar/restaurant/gallery/nightclub that London — perhaps anywhere — has ever seen. For pure fun forget the fine-dining opulence of The Lecture Room and head downstairs to The Gallery instead. Dramatically transformed in mid-2012 to a design courtesy of celebrated Scottish artist Martin Creed, the all-white walls and video projectors retired, replaced with artfully mix-matched furniture, brightly tiled floor and patterned walls. The plan is for a different artist to redesign the room every year or so. Gagnaire's ever-wacky menu continues to mix luxury, comfort and creativity.

LE GAVROCHE

43 Upper Brook Street
Mayfair
London W1K 7QR
+44 2074080881
www.le-gavroche.co.uk

Opening hours..............5 days for lunch and 6 days for dinner
Reservation policy...Yes
Reservation email.........................bookings@le-gavroche.com
Credit cards...Accepted
Price range...Expensive
Style...Smart casual
Cuisine...French
Recommended for...High End

GOODMAN

26 Maddox Street
Mayfair
London W1S 1QT
www.goodmanrestaurants.com

Opening hours..................6 days for lunch and dinner
Reservation policy...Yes
Credit cards...Accepted
Price range...Affordable
Style...Smart casual
Cuisine..American
Recommended for...Late night

THE GREENHOUSE

27a Hay's Mews
Mayfair
London W1J 5NY
+44 2074993331
www.greenhouserestaurant.co.uk

Opening hours..............5 days for lunch and 6 days for dinner
Reservation policy...Yes
Credit cards...Accepted
Price range...Expensive
Style...Smart casual
Cuisine..Modern French
Recommended for...High End

HAKKASAN

17 Bruton Street
Mayfair
London W1J 6QB
+44 2079071888
www.hakkasan.com

Opening hours................................7 days for lunch and dinner
Reservation policy...Yes
Reservation email...........mayfairreservation@hakkasan.com
Credit cards...Accepted
Price range...Expensive
Style...Smart casual
Cuisine...Modern Chinese
Recommended for...Worth the travel

HÉLÈNE DARROZE

The Connaught Hotel
Carlos Place
Mayfair
London W1K 2AL
+44 2071078880
www.the-connaught.co.uk

Opening hours..........4 days for brunch and 5 days for dinner
Reservation policy...Yes
Reservation email........................dining@the-connaught.co.uk
Credit cards...Accepted
Price range...Expensive
Style...Formal
Cuisine...French
Recommended for...Breakfast

The Connaught has seen many fine chefs and
France's culinary queen Hélène Darroze is the latest
to weave her magic in this historic Mayfair hotel. Her
native Landes in southwest France is name-checked
several times on the menu: terrine of duck foie gras
from les Landes; corn-fed chicken from les Landes...
And she cleverly introduces her native cuisine into
her take on the American brunch, served on Saturdays from 11 a.m. Charcuterie, terrines and Périgord
truffles join smoked salmon, York ham and hot dogs,
all in the most stylish and refined of circumstances,
of course.

HIBISCUS

29 Maddox Street
Mayfair
London W1S 2PA
+44 2076292999
www.hibiscusrestaurant.co.uk

Recommended by
Anthony Demetre, Shaun Hill,
Christoffer Hruskova, Tom
Kerridge, Paul Kitching,
Clare Smyth, Jérôme Tauvron

Opening hours	6 days for lunch and dinner
Reservation policy	Yes
Reservation email	info@hibiscusrestaurant.co.uk
Credit cards	Accepted
Price range	Expensive
Style	Smart casual
Cuisine	Modern French
Recommended for	High End

It was a brave decision after seven successful years in rural Shropshire to move Hibiscus to metropolitan Mayfair. But since successfully transplanting Hibiscus from Ludlow to London back in 2007, Lyon-born Claude Bosi's reputation as a purveyor of forward-thinking haute cuisine has soared and he's had no reason to look back. The kitchen is discreetly hidden behind a set of swish sliding doors, which open onto an intimate oak-panelled dining room, where the focus is on polished service and Bosi's ever-evolving modern French menus that trawl the British Isles for raw materials and the globe for inspiration.

IKEDA

30 Brook Street
Mayfair
London W1K 5DJ
+44 2076292730
www.ikedarestaurant.co.uk

Recommended by
Margot Henderson

Opening hours	5 days for lunch and 6 days for dinner
Reservation policy	Yes
Credit cards	Accepted
Price range	Expensive
Style	Smart casual
Cuisine	Japanese
Recommended for	High End

MOMO

25 Heddon Street
Mayfair
London W1B 4BH
+44 2074344040
www.momoresto.com

Recommended by
Theo Randall

Opening hours	6 days for lunch and 7 days for dinner
Reservation policy	Yes
Credit cards	Accepted
Price range	Affordable
Style	Smart casual
Cuisine	North African
Recommended for	Late night

MURANO

20 Queen Street
Mayfair
London W1J 5PP
+44 2074951127
www.muranolondon.com

Recommended by
José Pizarro

Opening hours	6 days for lunch and dinner
Reservation policy	Yes
Reservation email	enquiries@muranolondon.com
Credit cards	Accepted
Price range	Expensive
Style	Formal
Cuisine	Italian
Recommended for	High End

NOBU

Metropolitan Hotel
19 Old Park Lane
Mayfair
London W1K 1LB
+44 2074474747
www.noburestaurants.com/london

Recommended by
Claudio Aprile, Atul Kochhar,
Jerome Lorvellec,
Ricardo Zarate

Opening hours	7 days for lunch and dinner
Reservation policy	Yes
Credit cards	Accepted
Price range	Expensive
Style	Smart casual
Cuisine	Modern Japanese
Recommended for	High End

LA PETITE MAISON

53-54 Brook's Mews
Mayfair
London W1K 4EG
+44 2074954774
www.lpmlondon.co.uk

Recommended by
Tom Kitchin, Pierre
Koffmann, Theo Randall,
Karam Sethi, Jun Tanaka,
Mitchell Tonks

Opening hours	7 days for lunch and dinner
Reservation policy	Yes
Reservation email	info@lpmlondon.co.uk
Credit cards	Accepted
Price range	Affordable
Style	Smart casual
Cuisine	French
Recommended for	Wish I'd opened

'Great location in Brook's Mews and delicious food that comes when it's ready – my idea of heaven.'
—Theo Randall

This offshoot of the famous Nice hotspot of the same name (Sarkozy is said to be a fan) caters for its similarly starry regulars and the Mayfair set by combining a luxuriously bourgeois French menu with suave but informal service. Dishes are designed for sharing and arrive at the table in their own time, from hors d'oeuvres to rich comforting mains such as truffled macaroni and Mediterranean classics such as salt-baked sea bass. If there's a dish that sums up the whole experience, it's probably the whole Black Leg chicken stuffed with foie gras – roasted to order and well worth the hour's wait.

POLLEN STREET SOCIAL

8-10 Pollen Street
Mayfair
London W1S 1NQ
+44 2072907600
www.pollenstreetsocial.com

Recommended by
Justin Ip, Atul Kochhar, Geir
Skeie, Alyn Williams

Opening hours	6 days for lunch and dinner
Reservation policy	Yes
Reservation email	reservations@pollenstreetsocial.com
Credit cards	Accepted
Price range	Affordable
Style	Smart casual
Cuisine	Modern British
Recommended for	Wish I'd opened

PRINCESS GARDEN OF MAYFAIR

8-10 North Audley Street
Mayfair
London W1K 6ZD
+44 2074933223
www.princessgardenofmayfair.com

Recommended by
Theo Randall

Opening hours	7 days for lunch and dinner
Reservation policy	Yes
Reservation email	dine@princessgardenofmayfair.com
Credit cards	Accepted
Price range	Affordable
Style	Formal
Cuisine	Chinese
Recommended for	Regular neighbourhood

'Fantastic dim sum - great for a big Sunday lunch.'—Theo Randall

SCOTT'S

20 Mount Street
Mayfair
London W1K 2HE
+44 2074957309
www.scotts-restaurant.com

Recommended by
Philip Howard, Clare Smyth,
Marcus Wareing

Opening hours	7 days for lunch and dinner
Reservation policy	Yes
Credit cards	Accepted
Price range	Expensive
Style	Smart casual
Cuisine	Seafood
Recommended for	Local favourite

THE SQUARE

6-10 Bruton Street
Mayfair
London W1J 6PU
+44 2074957100
www.squarerestaurant.com

Opening hours	6 days for lunch and 7 days for dinner
Reservation policy	Yes
Reservation email	reception@squarerestaurant.com
Credit cards	Accepted
Price range	Expensive
Style	Smart casual
Cuisine	Modern French
Recommended for	High End

'Go to The Square for the white truffle risotto when it's in season.'—Brett Barnes

Now in its third decade, The Square has earned itself a reputation as a perennial source of high-quality fine dining in the heart of Mayfair. Chef patron Philip Howard and head chef Robert Weston specialize in taking seasonal and predominantly British ingredients such as Dover sole, prawns (shrimp) and pork cheeks, and applying a twist of French flair that transforms them into sophisticated yet refreshingly unfussy dishes that are simply delicious. A menu like this deserves a impressive good wine list and in this respect The Square doesn't disappoint.

THE WOLSELEY

160 Piccadilly
Mayfair
London W1J 9EB
+44 2074996996
www.thewolseley.com

Opening hours	7 days for breakfast, lunch and dinner
Reservation policy	Yes
Reservation email	reservations@thewolseley.com
Credit cards	Accepted
Price range	Expensive
Style	Formal
Cuisine	European
Recommended for	Breakfast

Such is its overwhelming popularity as a breakfast venue, many of its loyal regulars never go to The Wolseley for either lunch or dinner, although it's typically full for both. The lengthy morning menu is packed with comfort: crumpets, Cumberland sausage sandwiches, crispy bacon rolls, Eggs Benedict, fried haggis with duck eggs, Omelette Arnold Bennett and a fine selection of Viennese pastries – to name but a fraction of what's offered. But it's also about the setting and the sumptuous space. Once the Piccadilly showroom for the old marque it's named after, it's now a sweeping grand café in the European style.

UMU

14-16 Bruton Place
Mayfair
London W1J 6LX
+44 2074998881
www.umurestaurant.com

Opening hours	5 days for lunch and 6 days for dinner
Reservation policy	Yes
Reservation email	reception@umurestaurant.com
Credit cards	Accepted
Price range	Expensive
Style	Smart casual
Cuisine	Japanese
Recommended for	High End

L'ATELIER DE JOËL ROBUCHON

13-15 West Street
Soho
London WC2H 9NE
+44 2070108600
www.joelrobuchon.co.uk

Recommended by
Heinz Beck, Gert de
Mangeleer, Onno Kokmeijer,
Jockey Petrie, Philippe
Rochat, Esther Sham,
Ebbe Vollmer

Opening hours.....................................7 days for lunch and dinner
Reservation policy...Yes
Reservation email.............................info@joelrobuchon.co.uk
Credit cards...Accepted but not Diners
Price range..Expensive
Style...Smart casual
Cuisine...Modern French
Recommended for...High End

ARBUTUS

63-64 Frith Street
Soho
London W1D 3JW
+44 2077344545
www.arbutusrestaurant.co.uk

Recommended by
Claude Bosi, Alberto
Landgraf, Martin Morales

Opening hours.................................7 days for lunch and dinner
Reservation policy...Yes
Reservation email.....................info@arbutusrestaurant.co.uk
Credit cards...Accepted
Price range..Affordable
Style...Smart casual
Cuisine..French
Recommended for...High End

BAR ITALIA

22 Frith Street
Soho
London W1D 4RF
www.baritaliasoho.co.uk
+44 2074374520

Recommended by
Fergus Henderson, Margot
Henderson, Tom Oldroyd,
Alfred Prasad

Opening hours..........................7 days from breakfast until late
Reservation policy...No
Credit cards.............................Accepted but not AMEX
Price range..Affordable
Style...Casual
Cuisine..Café
Recommended for..Late night

'A great place for tiramisù, coffee and watching
the Soho crowds.'—Tom Oldroyd

BARRAFINA

54 Frith Street
Soho
London W1D 4SL
www.barrafina.co.uk

Recommended by
Jason Atherton, Angela
Hartnett, Margot Henderson,
Martin Morales,
Jockey Petrie

Opening hours.................................7 days for lunch and dinner
Reservation policy...No
Credit cards...Accepted
Price range..Affordable
Style...Smart casual
Cuisine..Tapas
Recommended for...............................Regular neighbourhood

The Hart brothers' tribute to Barcelona's legendary
Cal Pep consists of only twenty-three stools around a
marble counter. The crammed open kitchen behind it
produces top-class tapas, from grilled meat and
game, to seafood cooked à la plancha. Throw in an
excellent all-Iberian wine list and good-natured
service that deals efficiently and politely with the
inevitable waiting throng come peak times. Relax,
grab a draught of cold Cruzcampo or two and a plate
of jamón while you wait, and watch Soho go by. Those
in the vicinity can check the length of the line via a
live webcam link on Barrafina's website.

BINCHO

16 Old Compton Street
Soho
London W1D 4TL
+44 2072879111
www.bincho.co.uk

Recommended by
Tom Aikens

Opening hours.............6 days for lunch and 7 days for dinner
Reservation policy...Yes
Reservation email...miki@bincho.co.uk
Credit cards...Accepted
Price range..Budget
Style...Casual
Cuisine...Japanese
Recommended for...Bargain

BOB BOB RICARD

Recommended by
Alexis Gauthier

1 Upper James Street
Soho
London W1F 9DF
+44 2031451000
www.bobbobricard.com

Opening hours	5 days for lunch and dinner
Reservation policy	Yes
Reservation email	reservations@bobbobricard.com
Credit cards	Accepted
Price range	Affordable
Style	Smart casual
Cuisine	Russian-British
Recommended for	Local favourite

BOCCA DI LUPO

Recommended by
Anthony Demetre,
Thomasina Miers

12 Archer Street
Soho
London W1D 7BB
+44 2077342223
www.boccadilupo.com

Opening hours	7 days for lunch and dinner
Reservation policy	Yes
Reservation email	info@boccadilupo.com
Credit cards	Accepted
Price range	Affordable
Style	Smart casual
Cuisine	Italian
Recommended for	Regular neighbourhood

BUSABA EATHAI

Recommended by
Umar Allibhoy, Pascal
Aussignac, Christoffer
Hruskova, Atul Kochhar,
Francesco Mazzei

106–110 Wardour Street
Soho
London W1F 0TR
www.busaba.com

Opening hours	7 days for lunch and dinner
Reservation policy	No
Credit cards	Accepted
Price range	Affordable
Style	Casual
Cuisine	Thai
Recommended for	Bargain

CAY TRE

Recommended by
Mark Hix
Alfred Prasad

42-43 Dean Street
Soho
London W1D 4QD
+44 2073179118
www.caytresoho.co.uk

Opening hours	7 days for lunch and dinner
Reservation policy	Yes
Credit cards	Accepted
Price range	Budget
Style	Casual
Cuisine	Vietnamese
Recommended for	Bargain

CEVICHE

Recommended by
Anthony Demetre,
José Pizarro

17 Frith Street
Soho
London W1D 4RG
+44 2072922040
www.cevicheuk.com

Opening hours	7 days for lunch and dinner
Reservation policy	Yes
Reservation email	welcome@cevicheuk.com
Credit cards	Accepted
Price range	Affordable
Style	Casual
Cuisine	Peruvian
Recommended for	Late night

DEAN STREET TOWNHOUSE

Recommended by
Tom Oldroyd

69-71 Dean Street
Soho
London W1D 3SE
+44 2074341775
www.deanstreettownhouse.com

Opening hours	7 days for breakfast, lunch and dinner
Reservation policy	Yes
Credit cards	Accepted
Price range	Affordable
Style	Smart casual
Cuisine	British
Recommended for	Breakfast

'Great service with simple, well-executed dishes. I always have the ham hock and fried egg, with a large pot of tea. And a Bloody Mary on the weekends.'
—Tom Oldroyd

This handsome Georgian townhouse in the heart of Soho has seen some action over the years, notably as the Gargoyle club, a louche drinking den frequented by arty souls such as Francis Bacon and Lucian Freud. Since then its various parts have been a snooker club and a sauna, and most recently it was a branch of a grim pub chain. It suits its latest role as a stylish Soho House operated boutique hotel with an all-day dining room doing simple British food. It's a luxuriously relaxed place to start the day, the menu offering everything from baskets of pastries to Manx kippers.

DUCKSOUP

Recommended by
Samantha and Samuel Clark,
Paul Foster, Margot
Henderson, Christoffer
Hruskova, Jonathan Jones,
Miles Kirby

41 Dean Street
Soho
London W1D 4PY
+44 2072874599
www.ducksoupsoho.co.uk

Opening hours	7 days for lunch and dinner
Reservation policy	No
Credit cards	Accepted
Price range	Affordable
Style	Casual
Cuisine	International
Recommended for	Regular neighbourhood

GAUTHIER SOHO

Recommended by
Morgan Meunier

21 Romilly Street
Soho
London W1D 5AF
+44 2074943111
www.gauthiersoho.co.uk

Opening hours	6 days for lunch and dinner
Reservation policy	Yes
Reservation email	info@gauthiersoho.co.uk
Credit cards	Accepted
Price range	Expensive
Style	Formal
Cuisine	Modern French
Recommended for	Local favourite

GIACONDA DINING ROOM

Recommended by
Tom Pemberton

9 Denmark Street
Soho
London WC2 H8LS
+44 2072403334
www.giacondadining.com.

Opening hours	4 days for lunch and 5 days for dinner
Reservation policy	Yes
Credit cards	Accepted
Price range	Affordable
Style	Casual
Cuisine	European
Recommended for	Bargain

GREAT QUEEN STREET

Recommended by
Jun Tanaka

32 Great Queen Street
Soho
London WC2B 5AA
+44 2072420622

Opening hours	7 days for lunch and 6 days for dinner
Reservation policy	Yes
Credit cards	Accepted but not AMEX and Diners
Price range	Affordable
Style	Casual
Cuisine	British
Recommended for	Local favourite

HIX

66-70 Brewer Street
Soho
London W1F 9UP
+44 2072923518
www.hixsoho.co.uk

Recommended by
Angela Hartnett, Tom
Kerridge, Thomasina Miers

Opening hours	7 days for breakfast, lunch and dinner
Reservation policy	Yes
Credit cards	Accepted
Price range	Affordable
Style	Smart casual
Cuisine	British
Recommended for	Late night

Mark Hix's Soho flagship, like the man himself, is often at its best late at night. The buzz of the street level dining room tends to crescendo until it closes, by which time there is the basement bar and its cocktail menu in which to take refuge. The simple British seasonal approach of the kitchen is applied to everything from shellfish to steaks. The informal ambience is arguably a double-edged sword – while you'll feel comfortable enough to eat a late-night dinner here after a few too many, so does everyone else. But then who comes here for a quiet dinner?

THE IVY

1-5 West Street
Soho
London WC2H 9NQ
+44 2078364751
www.the-ivy.co.uk

Recommended by
Dominic Chapman, Matthew
Harris, Alyn Williams

Opening hours	7 days for lunch and dinner
Reservation policy	Yes
Credit cards	Accepted
Price range	Affordable
Style	Smart casual
Cuisine	European
Recommended for	Wish I'd opened

KOYA

49 Frith Street
Soho
London W1D 4SG
www.koya.co.uk

Recommended by
Tom Adams, Samantha and
Samuel Clark, Anna Hansen,
Jacob Kenedy, James Lowe,
Isaac McHale, Martin Morales,
Tom Oldroyd, Stevie Parle,
Jun Tanaka

Opening hours	7 days for lunch and dinner
Reservation policy	No
Credit cards	Accepted but not AMEX
Price range	Affordable
Style	Casual
Cuisine	Japanese
Recommended for	Regular neighbourhood

'They make the best udon noodles I have ever eaten. Their specials board is always changing and every single dish on it is a winner.'—Tom Oldroyd

It would be damning Koya with faint praise to say it's the best udon noodle shop in London, because in truth there's not really a lot of competition at the moment. Radiating a low-key authenticity, Koya's udon noodles – made on site in the traditional way, served with umami-rich stocks and a range of toppings – would hold their own back in Japan. Similarly, the site that first found fame in the 1980s as Alastair Little's Soho home now feels authentically Japanese, its understated interior a mix of utilitarian tables and chairs, white walls hung with wooden menu boards and a mosaic-tiled floor.

LITTLE ITALY

21 Frith Street
Soho
London W1D 4RN
+44 2077344737
www.littleitalysoho.co.uk

Recommended by
Alexis Gauthier

Opening hours	7 days for lunch and dinner
Reservation policy	Yes
Credit cards	Accepted
Price range	Budget
Style	Smart casual
Cuisine	Italian
Recommended for	Breakfast

MAISON BERTAUX

Recommended by
Shaun Hill

28 Greek Street
Soho
London W1D 5DD
www.maisonbertaux.com

Opening hours	7 days from breakfast until late
Reservation policy	No
Credit cards	Accepted
Price range	Budget
Style	Casual
Cuisine	Bakery-Cafe
Recommended for	Breakfast

This old Soho spot boasts of being London's oldest patisserie, originally opened by Communards who, having fled Paris following the failure of the Fourth French Revolution, took refuge in cake. While it's true that the service can be hit and miss, it never fails to be entertainingly theatrical. The French fancies and cream cakes, still baked daily on the premises, are a reliable source of calories and le café au lait 'c'est bon'. Whether it's from a window table at street level or out on the pavement (sidewalk), there are few better vantage points from which to watch Soho go by.

MILKBAR

Recommended by
Brett Barnes

3 Bateman Street
Soho
London W1D 4AG
www.flatwhitecafe.com

Opening hours	7 days from breakfast until late
Reservation policy	No
Credit cards	Accepted
Price range	Budget
Style	Casual
Cuisine	Café
Recommended for	Breakfast

MOOLI'S

Recommended by
Brett Barnes

50 Frith Street
Soho
London W1D 4SQ
+44 2074949075
www.moolis.com

Opening hours	6 days for breakfast, lunch and dinner
Reservation policy	No
Credit cards	Accepted
Price range	Budget
Style	Casual
Cuisine	Indian
Recommended for	Late night

'A filled roti from Mooli makes a good late night snack.'—Brett Barnes

NOPI

Recommended by
Peter Gordon, Jockey Petrie

21-22 Warwick Street
Soho
London W1B 5NE
+44 2074949584
www.nopi-restaurant.com

Opening hours	7 days from breakfast until late
Reservation policy	Yes
Credit cards	Accepted
Price range	Affordable
Style	Smart casual
Cuisine	Middle Eastern Asian
Recommended for	Local favourite

'A really tasty mix of the world's cuisines.'
—Peter Gordon

PATARA

Recommended by
Atul Kochhar

15 Greek Street
Soho
London W1D 4DP
+44 2074371071
www.pataralondon.com

Opening hours	6 days for lunch and 7 days for dinner
Reservation policy	Yes
Credit cards	Accepted
Price range	Affordable
Style	Smart casual
Cuisine	Modern Thai
Recommended for	Regular neighbourhood

PHO

163-165 Wardour Street
Soho
London W1F 8WN
+44 2074343938
www.phocafe.co.uk

Opening hours	7 days for lunch and dinner
Reservation policy	No
Credit cards	Accepted but not AMEX and Diners
Price range	Budget
Style	Casual
Cuisine	Vietnamese
Recommended for	Bargain

PITT CUE CO.

1 Newburgh Street
Soho
London W1F 7RB
www.pittcue.co.uk

Opening hours	6 days for lunch and dinner
Reservation policy	No
Reservation email	info@pittcue.co.uk
Credit cards	Accepted
Price range	Affordable
Style	Casual
Cuisine	Barbecue
Recommended for	Worth the travel

'Exceptional ribs and pulled pork. Be prepared to wait for a couple of hours at peak times but rest assured it's well worth the wait.'—Tom Oldroyd

Following a successful summer residency operating out of a van on the South Bank, the Pitt Cue Co. made these bijou premises off Carnaby Street their permanent home. Head here for a late lunch early in the week to avoid the queues (waiting lines) for a stool in the pint-sized bar or to bagsy a table in their basement bunker of a dining room. Chef Tom Adams's skill with a smoker, combined with the sourcing of the perfect cuts of pork and beef, make for a carnivores' Shangri-La. A short list of craft beers, ciders and bourbon-based cocktails provide the liquid refreshment.

POLPO

41 Beak Street
Soho
London W1F 9SB
+44 2077344479
polpo.co.uk

Opening hours	6 days for lunch and 7 days for dinner
Reservation policy	Yes
Credit cards	Accepted
Price range	Affordable
Style	Casual
Cuisine	Italian small plates
Recommended for	Bargain

'A really large selection of small plates and all at very reasonable prices.'—Bryn Williams

PRINCI

135 Wardour Street
Soho
London W1F 0UT
+44 2074788888
www.princi.co.uk

Opening hours	7 days from breakfast until late
Reservation policy	No
Credit cards	Accepted
Price range	Budget
Style	Casual
Cuisine	Bakery-Cafe
Recommended for	Bargain

QUO VADIS

Recommended by
Tom Adams, Jonathan Jones,
Rowley Leigh, James Lowe,
Isaac McHale, Ben Tish

26-29 Dean Street
Soho
London W1D 3LL
+44 2074379585
www.quovadissoho.co.uk

Opening hours.................................6 days for lunch and dinner
Reservation policy...Yes
Reservation email...........................info@quovadissoho.co.uk
Credit cards..Accepted
Price range...Budget
Style...Smart casual
Cuisine..British
Recommended for...Wish I'd opened

'Quo Vadis' chef Jeremy Lee sticks to his ethos of treating great ingredients with the minimum of fuss making every meal I've had here simply amazing. A great place.'—Tom Adams

The arrival in 2011 of Jeremy Lee at Quo Vadis, after years at the Blueprint Café, breathed new life into the old Soho landmark that's been running as a restaurant since 1929. He has a smart, seasonal way with British produce and remains one of the best cooks of game in London, if not the country. Trademark dishes include baked salsify wrapped in phyllo pastry and topped with grated Parmesan, a smoked eel and horseradish sandwich and the classic Elizabeth David dessert – although Lee prefers to talk about 'puddings' – St Emilion au chocolat. The 'Theatre Set' menu is a steal.

SPUNTINO

Recommended by
Adam Byatt, Peter Gordon,
Nuno Mendes, Ben Tish

61 Rupert Street
Soho
London W1D 7PW
www.spuntino.co.uk

Opening hours.................................7 days for lunch and dinner
Reservation policy...No
Credit cards..Accepted
Price range...Affordable
Style...Smart casual
Cuisine..Small plates
Recommended for...Wish I'd opened

'I really admire the simple model used by Russell Norman's restaurants Polpo, Polpetto and Spuntino. The food is delicious and the atmosphere is always great.'—Nuno Mendes

Russell Norman's follow-up to Polpo channels the aesthetic of a hip Brooklyn diner meets a fashion forward Lower Eastside speakeasy. It's darkly lit with artfully aged white tiles on the walls, rusty tin on the ceiling, alt-rock soundtrack and a U-shaped zinc-topped counter around which there are twenty-six fixed stools. No telephone, no reservations, and a long wait at peak times for the menu of Italian-American small plates that take in various sliders, meatballs and pizzette. The popcorn machine churns out complimentary cups of the salty snack laced with chilli to make you thirsty for the predominantly Italian and reasonably priced wine list.

TAPAS BRINDISA

Recommended by
Justin Ip, Bruce Poole

46 Broadwick Street
Soho
London W1F 7AF
+44 2075341690
www.brindisa.com

Opening hours.................................7 days for lunch and dinner
Reservation policy...Yes
Credit cards..Accepted
Price range...Affordable
Style...Casual
Cuisine...Tapas
Recommended for...Worth the travel

WRIGHT BROTHERS

Recommended by
Martin Morales

13 Kingly Street
Soho
London W1B 5PW
+44 2074343611
www.thewrightbrothers.co.uk

Opening hours.............7 days for lunch and 6 days for dinner
Reservation policy...Yes
Credit cards..Accepted
Price range...Affordable
Style...Smart casual
Cuisine...Seafood
Recommended for...Late night

YALLA YALLA

1 Green's Court
Soho
London W1F 0HA
+44 2072877663
www.yalla-yalla.co.uk

Recommended by
Bruno Loubet

Opening hours	7 days for breakfast, lunch and dinner
Reservation policy	No
Credit cards	Accepted but not AMEX and Diners
Price range	Budget
Style	Casual
Cuisine	Lebanese
Recommended for	Bargain

'Great Beirut street food.'—Bruno Loubet

YAUATCHA

15-17 Broadwick Street
Soho
London W1F 0DL
www.yauatcha.com

Recommended by
Justin Ip, Ben Spalding

Opening hours	7 days for lunch and dinner
Reservation policy	Yes
Reservation email	reservations@yauatcha.com
Credit cards	Accepted
Price range	Affordable
Style	Smart casual
Cuisine	Chinese
Recommended for	Late night

THE PEAT INN

Recommended by
Tom Kitchin

By Cupar
Fife
Scotland KY15 5LH
+44 1334840206
www.thepeatinn.co.uk

Opening hours...............................5 days for lunch and dinner
Reservation policy...Yes
Reservation email................................stay@thepeatinn.co.uk
Credit cards...Accepted
Price Range...Affordable
Style...Smart casual
Cuisine...Scottish
Recommended for..High End

'The food is always first class.'—Tom Kitchin

THE WEE RESTAURANT

Recommended by
Martin Wishart

17 Main Street
North Queensferry
Fife
Scotland KY11 1JG
+44 1383616263
www.theweerestaurant.co.uk

Opening hours...............................6 days for lunch and dinner
Reservation policy...Yes
Credit cards...Accepted
Price Range...Affordable
Style...Smart casual
Cuisine...Scottish
Recommended for.............................Regular neighbourhood

THE THREE CHIMNEYS

Recommended by
Martin Wishart

Colbost
Dunvegan
Isle of Skye
Scotland IV55 8ZT
+44 1470511258
www.threechimneys.co.uk

Opening hours.............6 days for lunch and 7 days for dinner
Reservation policy...Yes
Reservation email...............eatandstay@threechimneys.co.uk
Credit cards...Accepted
Price Range...Affordable
Style...Smart casual
Cuisine..Modern Scottish
Recommended for..................................Worth the travel

ANDREW FAIRLIE

Recommended by
Marcus Eaves,
Paul Kitching

Gleneagles Hotel
Auchterarder
Perthshire
Scotland PH3 1NF
+44 1764694267
www.andrewfairlie.co.uk

Opening hours...6 days for dinner
Reservation policy...Yes
Reservation email.............reservations@andrewfairlie.co.uk
Credit cards...Accepted
Price Range...Expensive
Style...Formal
Cuisine..Modern French
Recommended for..High End

THE STRATHEARN

Recommended by
Paul Kitching

Gleneagles Hotel
Auchterarder
Perthshire
Scotland PH3 1NF
+44 8003893737
www.gleneagles.com

Opening hours.......................7 days for breakfast and dinner
Reservation policy...Yes
Reservation email.....................Resort.sales@gleneagles.com
Credit cards...Accepted
Price Range...Expensive
Style...Formal
Cuisine..French-Scottish
Recommended for..Breakfast

'Splendid buffet with everything including
champagne.'—Paul Kitching

21212

Recommended by
Andrew Fairlie

3 Royal Terrace
Edinburgh
ScotlandEH7 5AB
+44 1315231030
www.21212restaurant.co.uk

Opening hours...............................5 days for lunch and dinner
Reservation policy...Yes
Reservation email........reservations@21212restaurant.co.uk
Credit cards...Accepted
Price Range...Affordable
Style...Formal
Cuisine...British
Recommended for..................................Worth the travel

'Great cooking, great hospitality.'—Andrew Fairlie

THE DOGS

Recommended by
Tom Kitchin

110 Hanover Street
Edinburgh
Scotland EH2 1DR
+44 1312201208
www.thedogsonline.co.uk

Opening hours................................7 days for lunch and dinner
Reservation policy..Yes
Reservation email..........................info@thedogsonline.co.uk
Credit cards..Accepted
Price Range..Budget
Style..Casual
Cuisine..British
Recommended for...Bargain

'It's a brilliant place and fantastic value
for money.'—Tom Kitchin

In British slang 'The Dogs' has two opposite mean-
ings – destitution, as in 'gone to the dogs', or
something rather spiffing, as in 'the dog's danglies'.
In this case, despite the absence of an apostrophe,
it's very much the latter that applies. Founder David
Ramsden has taken one of Edinburgh's Georgian
masterpieces, given it a modest but chic interior and
used it to champion good but inexpensive British
cooking. Try the braised spale bone of beef with pearl
barley, root vegetables and horseradish. The flavours
are fantastic and, at these prices, no wonder it's
packed out.

FORTH FLOOR RESTAURANT

Recommended by
Paul Kitching

Harvey Nichols
30-34 St Andrew Square
Edinburgh
Scotland EH2 2AD
+44 1315248350
www.harveynichols.com/restaurants

Opening hours.............7 days for breakfast, lunch and dinner
Reservation policy..Yes
Credit cards..Accepted
Price Range...Affordable
Style..Casual
Cuisine..Modern British
Recommended for............................Regular neighbourhood

KHUSHI'S

Recommended by
Martin Wishart

10 Antigua Street
Edinburgh
Scotland EH1 3NH
+44 1315581947
www.khushis.com

Opening hours................................7 days for lunch and dinner
Reservation policy..Yes
Credit cards..Accepted
Price Range..Budget
Style..Casual
Cuisine..Indian
Recommended for...Late night

THE KITCHIN

Recommended by
Paul Kitching, Pierre
Koffmann, Rowley Leigh

78 Commercial Quay
Leith
Edinburgh
Scotland EH6 6LX
+44 1315551755
www.thekitchin.com

Opening hours................................5 days for lunch and dinner
Reservation policy..Yes
Reservation email.......................................info@thekitchin.com
Credit cards..Accepted
Price Range...Expensive
Style...Smart casual
Cuisine..Modern Scottish
Recommended for......................................Worth the travel

LEO'S BEANERY

Recommended by
Tom Kitchin

23a Howe Street
Edinburgh
Scotland EH3 6TF
+44 1315568403
www.leosbeanery.co.uk

Opening hours................................6 days breakfast and lunch
Reservation policy...No
Credit cards..Accepted
Price Range..Budget
Style..Casual
Cuisine..Café
Recommended for..Breakfast

'A little gem.'—Tom Kitchin

ONDINE RESTAURANT

Recommended by
Tom Kitchin

2 George IV Bridge
Edinburgh
Scotland EH1 1AD
+44 1312261888
www.ondinerestaurant.co.uk

Opening hours................................7 days for lunch and dinner
Reservation policy..Yes
Credit cards...Accepted
Price Range...Expensive
Style..Smart casual
Cuisine..Seafood
Recommended for...Local favourite

'The shellfish is of fantastic quality and I especially like
its commitment to sustainable Scottish fish.'
—Tom Kitchin

PORTO & FI

Recommended by
Tom Kitchin

47 Newhaven Main Street
Edinburgh
Scotland EH6 4NQ
+44 1315511900
www.portofi.com

Opening hours...........7 days for brunch and 6 days for dinner
Reservation policy..Yes
Credit cards...Accepted
Price Range...Budget
Style..Casual
Cuisine..Deli-Cafe
Recommended for...Breakfast

'Excellent artisan bread.'—Tom Kitchin

RESTAURANT MARTIN WISHART

Recommended by
Jonathan Jones

54 The Shore
Leith
Edinburgh
Scotland EH6 6RA
+44 1315533557
www.martin-wishart.co.uk

Opening hours................................5 days for lunch and dinner
Reservation policy..Yes
Credit cards...Accepted
Price Range...Expensive
Style..Smart casual
Cuisine...Modern Scottish
Recommended for..High End

THE SCOTTISH CAFÉ

Recommended by
Martin Wishart

The Scottish National Gallery
The Mound
Edinburgh
Scotland EH2 2EL
+44 1312266524
www.centotre.com/thescottishcafe

Opening hours................7 days for breakfast, lunch and tea
Reservation policy..Yes
Credit cards...Accepted
Price Range...Affordable
Style..Casual
Cuisine..Cafe
Recommended for...Breakfast

'Great food and views of Edinburgh castle and Princess
Street Gardens.'—Martin Wishart

CAFÉ GANDOLFI

Recommended by
Andrew Fairlie

64 Albion Street
Glasgow
Scotland G1 1NY
+44 1415526813
www.cafegandolfi.com

Opening hours..............7 days for breakfast, lunch and dinner
Reservation policy..Yes
Credit cards...Accepted
Price Range...Budget
Style..Casual
Cuisine...Scottish
Recommended for..Bargain

'Serves amazing Stornoway black pudding (blood
sausage) on pancakes with poached eggs and great
mince and tatties (ground meat and potatoes).'
—Andrew Fairlie

CRABSHAKK

Recommended by
Andrew Fairlie

1114 Argyle Street
Finnieston
Glasgow
Scotland G3 8TD
+44 1413346127
www.crabshakk.com

Opening hours................................6 days for lunch and dinner
Reservation policy..Yes
Credit cards...Accepted
Price Range...Affordable
Style..Casual
Cuisine..Seafood
Recommended for...Local favourite

'A tiny seafood restaurant in a shabby but up and coming area in Glasgow. It serves very, very, simple Scottish seafood sourced from local fishermen from the Western Isles.'—Andrew Fairlie

THE FIG TREE
The Esplanade
Penarth
Carmarthenshire
Wales CF64 3AU
+44 2920702512
www.thefigtreepenarth.co.uk

Recommended by
Hywel Jones

Opening hours	6 days for lunch and 5 days for dinner
Reservation policy	Yes
Credit cards	Accepted
Price Range	Affordable
Style	Casual
Cuisine	European
Recommended for	Regular neighbourhood

'A great family friendly restaurant serving good food.'—Hywel Jones

THE HARDWICK
Old Raglan Road
Abergavenny
Monmouthshire
Wales NP7 9AA
+44 1873854220
www.thehardwick.co.uk

Recommended by
Dominic Chapman, Shaun Hill

Opening hours	7 days for breakfast, lunch and dinner
Reservation policy	Yes
Credit cards	Accepted
Price Range	Affordable
Style	Smart casual
Cuisine	Bar-Bistro
Recommended for	Regular neighbourhood

A London restaurant scene legend, chef Stephen Terry returned to his native Wales to take ownership of a pub called the Horse & Jockey on the outskirts of Abergavenny, the Monmouthshire market town famous for the Walnut Tree and the annual food festival it hosts each September. Reopened as the Hardwick four weeks after he first took it over in 2005, it has since grown into an award-winning restaurant with rooms. Terry's unfussy menu makes the most of the best local ingredients, combining them with the good taste and technical ability with which he originally made his name.

THE WALNUT TREE
Llanddewi Skirrid
Abergavenny
Monmouthshire
Wales NP7 8AW
+44 1873852797
www.thewalnuttreeinn.com

Recommended by
Fergus Henderson, Hywel
Jones, Stevie Parle

Opening hours	5 days for lunch and dinner
Reservation policy	Yes
Reservation email	mail@thewalnuttreeinn.com
Credit cards	Accepted but not AMEX and Diners
Price Range	Affordable
Style	Casual
Cuisine	International
Recommended for	Worth the travel

One of the Britain's great cooking heroes, Shaun Hill 'retired' to Abergavenny to take over The Walnut Tree in 2007. He formerly ran the fine and tiny Merchant House in Ludlow, where he always cooked alone. He has more help in the kitchen here, a famous dining destination on and off since the 1960s. The cooking, wonderfully straightforward but with the sort of seasoned skill that only years at the stove can bring, makes use of local produce sourced from Monmouthshire's rich larder (pantry). Make a proper meal of it and book a room in one of their two nearby cottages.

THE SHED
Llanrhian Road
Porthgain
Pembrokeshire
Wales SA62 5BN
+44 1348831518
www.theshedporthgain.co.uk

Recommended by
Hywel Jones

Opening hours	7 days for lunch and dinner
Reservation policy	Yes
Reservation email	caroline@theshedporthgain.co.uk
Credit cards	Accepted
Price Range	Budget
Style	Casual
Cuisine	Seafood
Recommended for	Local favourite

'Situated in the old boat shed on the quay with a view of one of the most amazing coastlines in the world. This place serves top quality seafood.'—Hywel Jones

MOKSH INDIAN RESTAURANT

Ocean Building
Bute Crescent
Cardiff
Wales CF10 5AY
+44 2920498120
www.moksh.co.uk

Opening hours	7 days for lunch and dinner
Reservation policy	Yes
Credit cards	Accepted
Price Range	Affordable
Style	Casual
Cuisine	Modern Indian
Recommended for	Late night

'First class Indian cuisine.'—Hywel Jones

THE BOAT HOUSE

1a Seacliff Road
Bangor
County Down
Northern Ireland BT20 5HA
+44 2891469253
www.theboathouseni.co.uk

Opening hours	5 days for lunch and dinner
Reservation policy	Yes
Credit cards	Accepted
Price Range	Affordable
Style	Smart casual
Cuisine	Irish
Recommended for	Worth the travel

'A great spot for lunch and the chefs are working hard to provide a different approach to Northern Irish cuisine.'—Niall McKenna

On the southern side of Belfast Lough, housed in the old harbourmaster's office overlooking Bangor Marina, the Boat House is run by the Dutch chef Joery Castel, who, with brother Jasper, opened it back in 2009. The interior of the boxy Victorian stone building has been given a modern makeover that, like Dr Who's Tardis, means it somehow feels much larger inside that seems possible. Menus take a sophisticated approach to Ulster ingredients, with seafood from the local Loughs – Belfast, Strangford and Neagh – and the Atlantic to the fore. It's all far too good to be left to the have-yachts.

LE WINTERS

Strangford Arms Hotel
92 Church Street
Newtownards
County Down
Northern Ireland BT23 4AL
+44 2891814141
www.lewinters.com

Opening hours	7 days for breakfast, lunch and dinner
Reservation policy	Yes
Credit cards	Accepted
Price Range	Budget
Style	Casual
Cuisine	International
Recommended for	Local favourite

'I have never tasted fresher seafood and enjoyed more simple, relaxed service.'—Niall McKenna

ALL SEASONS

96 Botanic Avenue
Belfast
Northern Ireland BT2 1JR
+44 2890808833

Opening hours	7 days for lunch and dinner
Reservation policy	Yes
Credit cards	Accepted
Price Range	Affordable
Style	Casual
Cuisine	Chinese
Recommended for	Regular neighbourhood

BOOJUM

19-27 Chichester Street
Belfast
Northern Ireland BT1 4JB
+44 2891469253
www.boojummex.com

Opening hours	7 days for lunch and 6 days for dinner
Reservation policy	No
Credit cards	Accepted
Price Range	Budget
Style	Casual
Cuisine	Mexican
Recommended for	Wish I'd opened

'A great little Mexican restaurant that serves burritos and beer. The concept and delivery is so simple it makes me smile every time I walk through the door.'—Niall McKenna

CAFÉ CONOR

11a Stranmillis Road
Belfast
Northern Ireland BT9 5AF
www.cafeconor.com

Recommended by
Niall McKenna

Opening hours	7 days for breakfast, lunch and dinner
Reservation policy	Yes
Reservation email	gic@cafeconor.com
Credit cards	Not accepted
Price Range	Budget
Style	Casual
Cuisine	Café
Recommended for	Breakfast

This café is named after William Conor, the celebrated Belfast artist, who, as the blue plaque on the outside wall will tell you, had his studio here from 1944 to 1954. The surfeit of natural light that drew Conor to this handsome, high-ceilinged, lantern-roofed room makes it a very pleasant place for breakfast on a fair morning or, in fact, all day, as they serve it until 5.00 p.m. Their 'Ulster Fry' comes in two sizes: a five-item 'Wee Breakfast' and the forget-lunch-and-call-it-a-day 'Big Breakfast' – soda and potato bread, two rashers (slices) of bacon, two sausages, egg, black pudding (blood sausage), tomato, mushroom and baked beans.

CAYENNE

7 Ascot House
Shaftesbury Square
Belfast
Northern Ireland BT2 7DB
+44 2890331532
www.cayenne-restaurant.co.uk

Recommended by
Niall McKenna

Opening hours	5 days for lunch and dinner
Reservation policy	Yes
Reservation email	belinda@cayenne-restaurant.co.uk
Credit cards	Accepted
Price Range	Affordable
Style	Smart casual
Cuisine	Modern European
Recommended for	Regular neighbourhood

MOURNE SEAFOOD BAR

34-36 Bank Street
Belfast
Northern Ireland BT1 1HL
+44 2890248544
www.mourneseafood.com

Recommended by
Niall McKenna

Opening hours	7 days for lunch and 5 days for dinner
Reservation policy	Yes
Credit cards	Accepted
Price Range	Affordable
Style	Casual
Cuisine	Seafood
Recommended for	Regular neighbourhood

'Great for something light and fishy.'—Niall McKenna

The flagship branch of Mourne Seafood (there is another at Dundrum, on the County Down coast) is as pleasantly unpretentious as a seafood restaurant gets. Located in the very heart of the city, down a side alley along from the legendary Belfast pub that is Kelly's Cellars, Mourne's menu always includes hugely generously portions of classic beer-battered fish and chips; a whole grilled catch with boiled buttered spuds; and oysters and mussels sourced from Mourne's own beds. If you're after something more elaborate – say a seafood risotto or a ceviche – the daily specials have you covered.

IL PIRATA

Recommended by
Niall McKenna

279-281 Newtownards Road
Belfast
Northern Ireland BT4 3JF

Opening hours	7 days for lunch and dinner
Reservation policy	No
Credit cards	Accepted
Price Range	Affordable
Style	Casual
Cuisine	Italian
Recommended for	Late night

'Really good for sharing plates, relaxed and chilled out.'—Niall McKenna

Indicating where this part of East Belfast seems to be going, the recently arrived Il Pirata occupies what was previously a branch of KFC. A modish casual Italian, of the sort familiar to New York and London, the menu is built around a series of small plates and larger dishes designed for sharing. There's no pizza, as the nearby Little Wings has covered. The white-tiled, stripped back, darkly-lit, industrial space's plain wooden tables are given over to the serving of sliders (made with mini Belfast rolls), fried fish, bruschetti, Italian spiced sausage, salads, pasta dishes and polenta chips (cornmeal crisps).

THE RAJ

Recommended by
Michael Deane

461 Lisburn Road
Belfast
Northern Ireland BT9 7EQ
+44 2890662168
www.therajbelfast.com

Opening hours	7 days for dinner
Reservation policy	Yes
Credit cards	Accepted
Price Range	Budget
Style	Casual
Cuisine	Indian
Recommended for	Regular neighbourhood

SHU

Recommended by
Niall McKenna

253 Lisburn Road
Belfast
Northern Ireland BT9 7EN
+44 2890381655
www.shu-restaurant.com

Opening hours	6 days for lunch and dinner
Reservation policy	Yes
Reservation email	eat@shu-restaurant.com
Credit cards	Accepted
Price Range	Affordable
Style	Smart casual
Cuisine	European
Recommended for	Regular neighbourhood

BALLYMALOE HOUSE

Recommended by
Ross Lewis

Shanagarry
County Cork
Republic of Ireland
+353 214652531
www.ballymaloe.ie

Opening hours	7 days for breakfast, lunch and dinner
Reservation policy	Yes
Reservation email	res@ballymaloe.ie
Credit cards	Accepted
Price Range	Affordable
Style	Smart casual
Cuisine	Irish
Recommended for	Breakfast

'A country house that is the original of the species and where Myrtle Allen still presides over one of the finest locally-sourced artisanal breakfasts around.' —Ross Lewis

Not many people know this: you don't need to be staying at Ballymaloe, the renowned country house of the Allen family, to go for breakfast there – a reservation will do. Most of the produce is from their 160-hectare (400-acre) organic farm and just about everything is homemade. Breakfast includes soda bread and scones, and homemade muesli and yogurt, which can be piled up with seasonal fruit such as rhubarb, gooseberries, pears and apples. Eggs are from their own hens, the sausages are from Woodside, the black and white puddings (blood sausage) are from Rosscarbery, and there's always fresh fish from nearby Ballycotton.

FARMGATE CAFÉ

The English Market
Cork
County Cork
Republic of Ireland
+353 214278134
www.farmgate.ie

Recommended by
Ross Lewis

Opening hours	6 days for breakfast, lunch and tea
Reservation policy	Yes
Credit cards	Accepted
Price Range	Budget
Style	Casual
Cuisine	Irish
Recommended for	Local favourite

'Still serving, among many other specialities of the market, "tripe and drisheen", a very old traditional Cork dish.'—Ross Lewis

The Cork English Market is even more impressive when viewed from a height, which is just one of the reasons to sit down and tuck into lunch at Kay Harte's daytime Farmgate Café. With an enviably short supply chain, oysters are shucked to order, one of the staff popping downstairs to the fishmonger Pat O'Connell as the need arises. Food is local and the cooking is skilfully simple. Traditional dishes – such as corned leg of mutton with caper sauce and drisheen (black pudding/blood sausage) and tripe – can be washed down with craft beer.

FISHY FISHY CAFÉ

Crowley's Quay
Kinsale
County Cork
Republic of Ireland
+353 214700415
www.fishyfishy.ie

Recommended by
Paul Flynn

Opening hours	7 days for lunch and dinner
Reservation policy	Yes
Credit cards	Not accepted
Price Range	Affordable
Style	Casual
Cuisine	Seafood
Recommended for	Wish I'd opened

Having evolved from a small fish shop that serves a limited number of fish dishes at lunchtime, Martin Shanahan's second, larger Fishy Fishy restaurant has an enviable position at the end of the pier in Kinsale, a fashionable fishing village in Cork. On a sunny day there are few better places to be than the courtyard, in the shade of mature trees, with a bottle of crisp white wine and simply cooked fish from local boats. But it's no secret, so at lunchtime you may have to wait at the bar for a table; they do, however, take bookings for dinner.

SEAPOINT

4 The Crescent
Monkstown
County Dublin
Republic of Ireland
+353 16638480
www.seapointrestaurant.com

Recommended by
Derry Clarke

Opening hours	7 days for lunch and dinner
Reservation policy	Yes
Reservation email	info@seapointrestaurant.com
Credit cards	Accepted but not AMEX and Diners
Price Range	Affordable
Style	Smart casual
Cuisine	Seafood-Grill
Recommended for	Regular neighbourhood

'Very popular with the locals' is a phrase much overused but in this case it's true. When your neighbourhood restaurant has a blackboard with fish dishes chalked up daily, you know it's a safe bet. A reputation for good grilled meat helps keep the peace with the carnivores, and a well-selected wine list with fifty per cent off bottles on Tuesdays is a nice touch by owner Shane Kenny, whose former life in the wine business ensures a keen eye for small producers. The rest of the team are equally good, with Nick Clapham in the kitchen and Chad Gugliotta looking after front of house.

CHAPTER ONE

Recommended by
Derry Clarke, Paul Flynn,
Niall McKenna

18-19 Parnell Square
Central North
Dublin 1
County Dublin
Republic of Ireland
+353 18732266
www.chapteronerestaurant.com

Opening hours.............4 days for lunch and 5 days for dinner
Reservation policy...Yes
Reservation email.................info@chapteronerestaurant.com
Credit cards..Accepted
Price Range...Expensive
Style..Smart casual
Cuisine...Irish
Recommended for...High End

Ross Lewis's restaurant beneath the Dublin Writer's Museum is a warm bastion of Irish hospitality at its very best. Housed in the basement of a handsome eighteenth-century townhouse, once the family home of John Jameson of the distilling dynasty, the dining room is a welcoming combination of exposed brickwork and sage-green carpet, its walls hung with work by emerging Irish artists. Lewis's menus champion the very best of Ireland's larder (pantry), with a penchant for pork, game and seafood in cooking that's both refined and generous. As befits the building's history, there's a lengthy list of Irish whiskeys for after dinner.

M & L SZECHUAN CHINESE

Recommended by
Ross Lewis

13 Cathedral Street
Central North
Dublin 1
County Dublin
Republic of Ireland
+353 18748038

Opening hours.................................7 days for lunch and dinner
Reservation policy...Yes
Credit cards..Not accepted
Price Range...Budget
Style...Casual
Cuisine...Szechuan
Recommended for...Bargain

'Offers seriously good Chinese food at great value.'—Ross Lewis

'Unexpected' is probably one of the better words to describe this inexpensive Szechuan restaurant, situated down one of Dublin's side streets, which is frequented by the Chinese community and more adventurous diners. For an authentic experience and the full Szechuan heat, either visit with a Chinese friend and order from the Chinese menu, or refuse vehemently to order from the English menu. Pointing to the more interesting dishes being demolished at other tables is one way of doing this, but if there's resistance, insist on 'original' Chinese food, so that the staff choose the dishes and you enjoy the pay-off of your perseverance.

PICHET

Recommended by
Derry Clarke

14-15 Trinity Street
Central South
Dublin 2
County Dublin
Republic of Ireland
+353 16771060
www.pichetrestaurant.ie

Opening hours..................................7 days for lunch and dinner
Reservation policy..Yes
Reservation email.........................info@pichetrestaurant.com
Credit cards...Accepted
Price Range...Affordable
Style..Smart casual
Cuisine...European
Recommended for...Wish I'd opened

There was nothing quiet about the way this bistro opened back in July 2009. A six-part TV documentary followed co-owners Nick Munier (who worked front of house with the Roux Brothers and Marco Pierre White and is now a judge on Irish Masterchef) and Michelin-trained chef Stephen Gibson. Three years later, it's still at the top of the who's who list. Its continued success can be attributed to well-priced bistro dishes that are packed with flavour — like the crispy hen's egg with Serrano ham — plus Nick's unrelenting charm, great service and a fantastic location in the centre of town.

THE TROCADERO

Recommended by
Derry Clarke

4 Saint Andrew Street
Central South
Dublin 2
County Dublin
Republic of Ireland
+353 16775545
www.trocadero.ie

Opening hours	6 days for dinner
Reservation policy	Yes
Credit cards	Accepted
Price Range	Affordable
Style	Smart casual
Cuisine	European
Recommended for	Late night

Long a haunt of Dublin's literati and thespians, the 'Troc' is probably the most nostalgic restaurant in town, filled with old-time showbiz glamour. Liberty-style lampshades, gilt mirrors, bordello-red upholstery and photo-lined walls create a decadent feel, and with the legendary Robert Doggett running the show front of house, the atmosphere is more clubby than restaurant. As the Olympia Theatre is nearby, the pre-theatre menu is popular, but the real action starts later in the evening with people, who all seem to know each other, dropping into the bar or tucking into unpretentious food such as grilled steak and sole on the bone.

L'ECRIVAIN

Recommended by
Niall McKenna

109a Lower Baggot Street
Georgian Dublin
Dublin 2
County Dublin
Republic of Ireland
+353 16611919
www.lecrivain.com

Opening hours	2 days for lunch and 6 days for dinner
Reservation policy	Yes
Reservation email	enquiries@lecrivain.com
Credit cards	Accepted
Price Range	Affordable
Style	Smart casual
Cuisine	French
Recommended for	High End

Derry Clarke's established canteen to the Dublin establishment occupies a pair of Georgian coach houses in a courtyard mews off Lower Baggot Street. His sensible response to Ireland's economic ructions was to introduce a three-course lunch menu for a rather reasonable €25 (£20; $33). However, you can still indulge yourself like the Celtic Tiger is ever roaring, as opposed to purring apologetically, with a multi-course tasting menu and a wine list that continues to list magnums of vintage Grands Crus. As always, the cooking showcases the kitchen's fine French technique let loose on the best Irish produce.

THE GREENHOUSE DUBLIN

Recommended by
Michael Deane

Dawson Street
Georgian Dublin
Dublin 2
County Dublin
Republic of Ireland
+353 16767015
www.thegreenhouserestaurant.ie

Opening hours	5 days for lunch and dinner
Reservation policy	Yes
Credit cards	Accepted
Price Range	Expensive
Style	Smart casual
Cuisine	Modern Irish
Recommended for	Worth the travel

RESTAURANT FORTY ONE

Recommended by
Ross Lewis

Residence Club
41 Saint Stephen's Green
Georgian Dublin
Dublin 2
County Dublin
Republic of Ireland
www.residence.ie/restaurant-fortyone.html

Opening hours................................5 days for lunch and dinner
Reservation policy..Yes
Credit cards..Accepted
Price Range..Expensive
Style...Smart casual
Cuisine..Modern Irish
Recommended for..............................Regular neighbourhood

'Chef Graham Neville has a sophisticated and light touch with his food in an extremely comfortable, clubby and elegant environment.'—Ross Lewis

A private members' club isn't everyone's glass of port, but Residence bears none of the dust of your typical gentleman's club, with a restaurant that is open to non-members for lunch and dinner. Nevertheless, if you want to be a regular at the white-linen-clad tables in the light-filled dining room of this Georgian townhouse, lunch is considerably more affordable than dinner. In the kitchen is Graham Neville, who has a solid Michelin pedigree anchored in the French classics. There's plenty to amuse your fine dining bouche here, from a veritable line-up of Irish ingredients to stalwarts like foie gras.

LOBBY LOUNGE

Recommended by
Kevin Thornton

Four Seasons Hotel
Simmonscourt Road
Ballsbridge
Dublin 4
County Dublin
Republic of Ireland
+353 16654000
www.fourseasons.com/dublin/dining

Opening hours..........................7 days from breakfast until late
Reservation policy..Yes
Credit cards..Accepted
Price Range..Affordable
Style...Smart casual
Cuisine...Café
Recommended for..............................Regular neighbourhood

ROLY'S

Recommended by
Derry Clarke

7 Ballsbridge Terrace
Ballsbridge
Dublin 4
Republic of Ireland
+353 16682611
www.rolysbistro.ie

Opening hours................................7 days for lunch and dinner
Reservation policy..Yes
Credit cards..Accepted
Price Range..Affordable
Style...Smart casual
Cuisine..International
Recommended for..Local favourite

Few restaurants manage to be all things to all men, but since it opened, in 1992, Roly's, in Dublin's ambassador belt of Ballsbridge, has managed to hold its position as favourite regular haunt for the well-heeled locals. The food steers well clear of any molecular frippery, and has happily continued in bistro mode without a glitch. This is because the cooking here is rock solid, service is slick and a fundamental sense of generosity prevails, with reasonably priced food and a wine list with a res-pectably low mark-up. Lunch upstairs on a Sunday is always a pleasure.

BROWNES

Recommended by
Derry Clarke

18 Sandymount Green
Sandymount
Dublin 4
County Dublin
Republic of Ireland
+353 12697316

Opening hours..............7 days for breakfast, lunch and dinner
Reservation policy..Yes
Credit cards..Accepted
Price Range..Budget
Style..Casual
Cuisine...Cafe
Recommended for...Breakfast

Restaurants that have plenty of newspapers on hand tend to have a better understanding of what a leisurely breakfast should be, but you generally expect there to be a sign over the door. For naviga-tion purposes, look for a restaurant on the village green, which has annexed what was previously a gallery next door. And if you see Colin Farrell or

Jeremy Irons tucking into Eggs Benedict – two poached eggs sitting atop ham that has been hacked off the bone and doused in hollandaise – then you know you're in Peter Bark's café, which morphs into a bistro at night.

JO-BURGER

Recommended by
Derry Clarke

137 Lower Rathmines Road
Rathmines
Dublin 6
County Dublin
Republic of Ireland
www.joburger.ie
+353 14913731

Opening hours	7 days for lunch and dinner
Reservation policy	Yes
Credit cards	Accepted but not AMEX
Price Range	Budget
Style	Casual
Cuisine	Burger
Recommended for	Bargain

Joe Macken has a sixth sense and an admirable sense of humour when it comes to pleasing the hipsters, and Jo-Burger was his first toe in the culinary waters of cool. Keeping things simple with long wooden tables and benches, a tight well-priced menu covers the burger spectrum of beef, lamb and chicken, with plenty of organic leanings. Names like 'mapetla' and 'zondi' do little to communicate the interesting toppings, but you can read all about them in the menu, which is bound in a hardback kids' comic book. Music is loud, in a good way, and different DJs on weekend nights keep things interesting.

ANANDA

Recommended by
Ross Lewis

Sandyford Road
Dundrum
Dublin 14
County Dublin
Republic of Ireland
+353 12960099
www.anandarestaurant.ie

Opening hours	3 days for lunch and 7 days for dinner
Reservation policy	Yes
Credit cards	Accepted
Price Range	Affordable
Style	Smart casual
Cuisine	Modern Indian
Recommended for	Late night

It's hard to believe that Sunil Ghai, executive chef of the Jaipur group of restaurants, only arrived in Dublin in 2001, such has been his impact. His light, modern approach to Indian cooking marries traditional spices with more local aromatics like lavender for an Irish slant. Ananda, which is his joint venture with Atul Kochher of Benares in London, is a tram ride out of town to the Dublin suburb of Dundrum. Monkfish, tandoori prawns (shrimp) and guinea fowl cooked on the robata grill are among the popular dishes he serves. For a long leisurely dinner, try the grazing menu.

CAMPAGNE

Recommended by
Ross Lewis

The Arches
5 Gashouse Lane
Kilkenny
County Kilkenny
Republic of Ireland
+353 567772858
www.campagne.ie

Opening hours	3 days for lunch and 5 days for dinner
Reservation policy	Yes
Credit cards	Accepted
Price Range	Affordable
Style	Smart casual
Cuisine	Modern French
Recommended for	Worth the travel

'Strong regional cooking with fabulous flavours that reflect the land.'—Ross Lewis

As its name indicates, the influence In Garrett Byrne's swish, urban, Kilkenny restaurant is French, but he keeps his dishes solidly connected to the local countryside. Suppliers are listed and locavores will be gratified to see that he even uses local rapeseed (canola) oil. With a Michelin background, there are plenty of prime ingredients taking centre stage and his cooking has remained highly accomplished, even as he has moved towards simpler dishes. Popularity of the Sunday lunch, which has achieved practically cult status, means diners are happy to hop on the train down to Kilkenny for the day, just to eat there.

CAFÉ HANS

Moor Lane
Cashel
County Tipperary
Republic of Ireland
+353 6263660

Opening hours	5 days for lunch and tea
Reservation policy	No
Credit cards	Not accepted
Price Range	Budget
Style	Casual
Cuisine	International
Recommended for	Worth the travel

GENOA TAKEAWAY

30 Grattan Square
Dungarvan
County Waterford
Republic of Ireland
+353 5843539

Opening hours	7 days for lunch until late
Reservation policy	No
Credit cards	Not accepted
Price Range	Budget
Style	Casual
Cuisine	Fast food
Recommended for	Bargain

'Our local chipper. It does a battered sausage to die for.'—Paul Flynn

NUDE FOOD

86 O'Connell Street
Dungarvan
County Waterford
Republic of Ireland
+353 5824594
www.nudefood.ie

Opening hours	6 days for breakfast, lunch and tea
Reservation policy	Yes
Credit cards	Accepted
Price Range	Budget
Style	Casual
Cuisine	Deli-Cafe
Recommended for	Breakfast

'The outside space is lovely on a sunny day.'
—Paul Flynn

Londoner Louise Clarke moved to Dungarvan in County Waterford fifteen years ago, and quickly became part of its vibrant food scene, first with her Naked Lunch market stall and more recently with her café and deli, opened in 2008. It's the sort of place where you immediately feel comfortable, with mismatched chairs and plenty of conversation. Everything is wholesome, starting with breakfast: porridge, made from local Flahavan's oats, is elevated with the addition of double heavy cream, and topped with local honey and seeds; Spanish eggs baked with tomatoes and sweet peppers are mopped up with Clarke's homemade sourdough bread.

O'BRIEN CHOP HOUSE

Main Street
Lismore
County Waterford
Republic of Ireland
+353 5853810
www.obrienchophouse.ie

Opening hours	4 days for lunch and dinner
Reservation policy	Yes
Reservation email	info@obrienchophouse.ie
Credit cards	Accepted
Price Range	Affordable
Style	Smart casual
Cuisine	Irish
Recommended for	Regular neighbourhood

'Simple, local, rustic, seasonal food.'—Paul Flynn

For those lucky enough to live nearby, the long timber bar sets the mood in this unpretentious restaurant, where Justin and Jenny Green's simple menu solidly adheres to the principle of ingredients being the driving force. Chops, cutlets and steaks on the bone come from the local butcher. As they raise their own pigs, the nose to tail eating at the 'piggy feast' is particularly rewarding, especially the crispy pig's tail with sauce gribiche. In-house smoked meats and foraged foods are incorporated into dishes without being too sanctimonious. Altogether very confident cooking that manages to be modern, Irish and devoid of attention-seeking antics.

THE FATTED CALF

Recommended by
Paul Flynn

Glasson
Athlone
County Westmeath
Republic of Ireland
+353 906485208
www.thefattedcalf.ie

Opening hours	6 days for lunch and dinner
Reservation policy	Yes
Credit cards	Accepted
Price Range	Affordable
Style	Casual
Cuisine	Bar-Bistro
Recommended for	Worth the travel

'The perfect gastropub.'—Paul Flynn

The midlands is not renowned as the culinary centre of Ireland, but since taking over the Village Inn pub in 2010, Feargal O'Donnell has given the cross-country driver a reason to stop. With roaring fires and bare wooden tables, The Fatted Calf exudes an authentic, old-world charm, and the hearty food, which has a strong Irish focus, follows in the same vein. Their home-raised Tamworth pigs feature strongly on the menu with traditional dishes like crispy crubeens made from pigs' trotters (feet), pulled pork, pork belly, home-cured ham and Mc-Geogh's black puddings (blood sausages). Plus there's an impressive selection of Irish craft beers.

HARVEST ROOM

Recommended by
Derry Clarke

Dunbrody Country House Hotel
Strand Road
Arthurstown
County Wexford
Republic of Ireland
+353 51389600
www.dunbrodyhouse.com

Opening hours	1 day for lunch and 7 days for dinner
Reservation policy	Yes
Credit cards	Accepted
Price Range	Affordable
Style	Smart casual
Cuisine	Classic French
Recommended for	Worth the travel

Kevin Dundon is a familiar face on Irish television, and now diners can walk in and chat to him as he cooks in the new open kitchen of his country house restaurant. The luxurious dining room, which looks out over the gardens of the 121-hectare (300-acre) estate, is pleasantly relaxing and Dundon's precise cooking makes the most of produce plucked from the garden, locally reared meat and fish from the day boats at nearby Duncannon harbour. With classic French leanings, there's a formality to the plating of the food, but it avoids being too 'cheffy' and always delivers on flavour.

'Brilliant food, great technique and exceptional utilization of regional products.'

RICHARD EKKEBUS P248

NETHERLANDS

'INDONESIAN RESTAURANTS HAVE BECOME A DUTCH PHENOMENON AND THIS PLACE REMINDS US WHY.'

AGUS HERMAWAN P253

'GREAT COCKTAILS AND TAPAS. THEY COOK IN SUCH A SPECIAL WAY!'

MICHAEL WOLF P248

'Pure creativity, daring combinations and flavours.'

JEAN BEDDINGTON

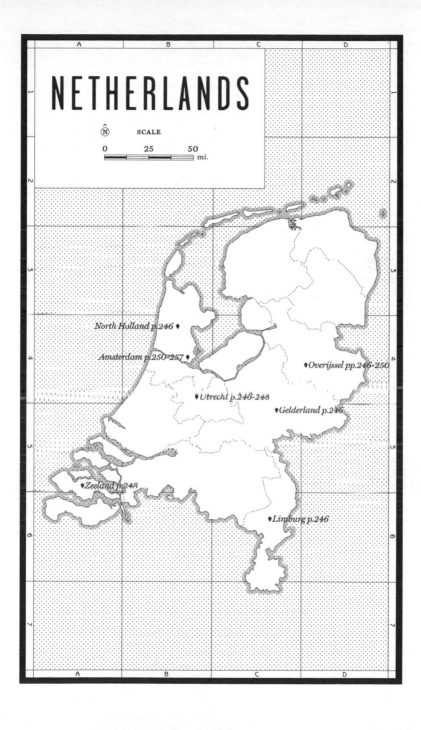

NETHERLANDS

N SCALE

0   25   50 mi.

North Holland p.246 ♦

Amsterdam p.250-257 ♦

♦ Overijssel pp.246-250

♦ Utrecht p.246-248

♦ Gelderland p.246

♦ Zeeland p.248

♦ Limburg p.246

'T NONNETJE

Vischmarkt 38
Harderwijk
Gelderland 3841 BG
+31 341415848
www.hetnonnetje.nl

Opening hours.............3 days for lunch and 6 days for dinner
Reservation policy...Yes
Reservation email.................................info@hetnonnetje.nl
Credit cards..Accepted
Price range...Affordable
Style...Smart casual
Cuisine..French
Recommended for..Worth the travel

This small restaurant is on a charming little square, formerly the fish market, in the north of Harderwijk. Completely renovated in 2009, 't Nonnetje is now a sleek, air-conditioned space with a slate tile floor, grey walls, polished mirrors and comfortable purple banquettes. They do a reasonable *Verleiding* (Temptation) menu on weekdays, and the food is French international. This includes old standbys such as hare à la royale, as well as more modern combinations such as lobster dim sum broth with roast Peking Duck. The cheese wagon, which displays a choice of twenty different varieties, is a highlight.

BELUGA

Centre Céramique 12
Plein 1992
Maastricht
Limburg 6221 JP
+31 433213364
www.rest-beluga.com

Opening hours.............4 days for lunch and 5 days for dinner
Reservation policy...Yes
Credit cards..Accepted
Price range..Expensive
Style...Smart casual
Cuisine..International
Recommended for..Worth the travel

THE RED SUN

Huizerweg 3
Blaricum
North Holland 1261 AR
+31 355336996
www.theredsun.nl

Opening hours.............5 days for lunch and 6 days for dinner
Reservation policy...Yes
Credit cards..Accepted
Price range...Affordable
Style...Smart casual
Cuisine...Modern Asian
Recommended for............................Regular neighbourhood

Red Sun's regulars tend to be Dutch VIPs and celebrities, many of whom live nearby. As such, this expensive and fashionable restaurant gets very busy on Friday and Saturday nights. The walls are red and lined in black lacquer, with black chandeliers hanging above and mismatched gold Buddhas dotted about the room. The sushi and sashimi are excellent and served in trendy iced bowls, the wagyu is well sourced, and there's an excellent sake list. Since portions can be quite small, they recommend you have at least three courses. Commendably, for such a trendy place, staff are friendly and down to earth.

BAI YOK

Diezerpoortenplas 3
Zwolle
Overijssel 8011 VV
+31 384229882
www.baiyok.nl

Opening hours...6 days for dinner
Reservation policy...Yes
Credit cards...Accepted but not AMEX
Price range..Budget
Style..Casual
Cuisine..Thai
Recommended for............................Regular neighbourhood

Eight years old, Bai Yok is Zwolle's only Thai restaurant and one of the better ones in Holland. Its chef, originally from Chiang Mai, does an excellent pad thai with quail; equally well-regarded is his deep-fried catfish with dried coconut in red curry sauce. They even run a cookery course for locals who want to prepare better Thai food at home. There's a shaded, tree-lined terrace at the back looking out over the water — a lovely place in the summertime to slurp a glass noodle and fish ball soup.

DE LINDENHOF

Recommended by
Jonnie Boer

Beulakerweg 77
Giethoorn
Overijssel 8355 AC
+31 521361444
www.restaurantdelindenhof.nl

Opening hours	5 days for lunch and dinner
Reservation policy	Yes
Reservation email	info@restaurantDeLindenhof.nl
Credit cards	Accepted
Price range	Expensive
Style	Smart casual
Cuisine	Modern European
Recommended for	High end

Giethoorn is one of the prettiest villages in Holland. Cars used to be banned here, and most people still get around by bike or by boat on the canals. The best way to arrive at De Lindenhof is by canal boat, with the ducks flapping out of the way and a glass of champagne waiting for you at your destination. For high-end dining, things are fairly relaxed here – menus range between four and twelve courses. The restaurant is an old thatched farmhouse and has two elegant suites upstairs. The gardens are delightful and produce many of the kitchen's herbs.

RESTAURANT DE LIBRIJE

Recommended by
Dave De Belder, Gert de
Mangeleer, Martin Wishart

Broerenkerkplein 13-15
Zwolle
Overijssel 8011 TW
+31 384212083
www.librije.com

Opening hours	4 days for lunch and dinner
Reservation policy	Yes
Reservation email	info@librije.com
Credit cards	Accepted
Price range	Expensive
Style	Smart casual
Cuisine	French
Recommended for	High end

'T AMSTERDAMMERTJE

Recommended by
Onno Kokmeijer

Rijksstraatweg 119
Loenen Aan de Vecht
Utrecht 3632 AB
www.restaurantamsterdammertje.nl

Opening hours	4 days for lunch and 5 days for dinner
Reservation policy	Yes
Credit cards	Accepted
Price range	Expensive
Style	Smart casual
Cuisine	International
Recommended for	Worth the travel

Having occupied another site since the 1980s, chef André Gerrits reopened Het Amsterdammertje in a beautiful old Loenen farmhouse in 2008. It's named after the one-metre-high (three feet) steel bollards that are a traditional symbol of Amsterdam, and which date to the city's golden age in the seventeenth century. Gerrits's food is light, daring and modern, with dishes including lobster with breaded frogs' legs in lobster and orange sauce (€32.50; £26; $40). The new site has seventy-five covers and has been a tremendous success, the restaurant receiving its first Michelin star in 2010.

GRAND RESTAURANT KAREL V

Recommended by
Agus Hermawan

Geertebolwerk 1
Binnenstad
Utrecht 3511 XA
+31 302337575
www.grandrestaurantkarelv.nl

Opening hours	6 days for dinner
Reservation policy	Yes
Credit cards	Accepted
Price range	Expensive
Style	Smart casual
Cuisine	French
Recommended for	Worth the travel

'A great and inspiring chef and maitre d' run the show.'—Agus Hermawan

JASMIJN & IK

Kanaalstraat 219
Utrecht 3531 CH
+31 302938907
www.jasmijnenik.nl

Opening hours	5 days for dinner
Reservation policy	Yes
Reservation email	info@jasmijnenik.nl
Credit cards	Accepted
Price range	Affordable
Style	Smart casual
Cuisine	Asian
Recommended for	Regular neighbourhood

'It's mostly Chinese, Indonesian and Thai food. They cook with fair trade, organic products.'—Michael Wolf

DE KROMME WATERGANG

Slijkplaat 6
Hoofdplaat
Zeeland 4513 KK
+31 117348696
www.krommewatergang.nl

Opening hours	5 days for lunch and dinner
Reservation policy	Yes
Reservation email	info@krommewatergang.nl
Credit cards	Accepted
Price range	Affordable
Style	Smart casual
Cuisine	Modern European
Recommended for	Worth the travel

OUD SLUIS

Beestenmarkt 2
Sluis
Zeeland 4524 EA
+31 117461269
www.oudsluis.nl

Opening hours	4 days for lunch and 5 days for dinner
Reservation policy	Yes
Reservation email	contact@oudsluis.nl
Credit cards	Accepted
Price range	Expensive
Style	Formal
Cuisine	Seafood
Recommended for	High end

'Brilliant food, great technique and exceptional utilization of regional products.'—Richard Ekkebus

PIZZERIA RISTORANTE ROMAGNA

Kaai 7
Sluis
Zeeland 4524 CL
+31 117462438
www.pizzeriaromagna.com

Opening hours	5 days for lunch and dinner
Reservation policy	Yes
Credit cards	Accepted
Price range	Budget
Style	Casual
Cuisine	Pizza
Recommended for	Bargain

'My favourite dish is the carpaccio and rucola pizza.'—Filip Claeys

PURE C

Strand Hotel
Boulevard de Wielingen 49
Cadzand
Zeeland 4506 JK
+31 117396036
www.sergioherman.com

Opening hours	5 days for lunch and dinner
Reservation policy	Yes
Credit cards	Accepted
Price range	Affordable
Style	Smart casual
Cuisine	French
Recommended for	Wish I'd opened

'Great cocktails and tapas. They cook in such a special way!'—Michael Wolf

Sergio Herman achieved world-class form with his first restaurant Oud Sluis, and has done it again with Pure C, an airy beach bar and restaurant in Cadzand, on the island of Zeeland, with incredible views over the stormy North Sea. With the superlative ingredients of his native countryside and inspired by international flavours and techniques, Herman's menu and his head chef Syrco Bakker won Pure C a Michelin star in only a year and a half, since opening in 2010, with such dishes as Zeeland shellfish, oyster, dashi and chervil root, and roe deer, salsify, wholewheat ravioli and rocket (arugula).

'GOOD SIMPLE FOOD AND
A RELAXED MEETING PLACE
IN A BUSY CITY.'

MICHAEL WOLF P252

'Try the *broodje
croquette* or *broodje
warmvlees* – very
traditional Dutch
snacks.'

JEAN BEDDINGTON P252

AMSTERDAM

'The best
Italian in town
and easily the
best in the
Netherlands.'

AGUS HERMAWAN P253

'Wonderful
seasonal
menus and
perfect
service.'

JEAN BEDDINGTON P256

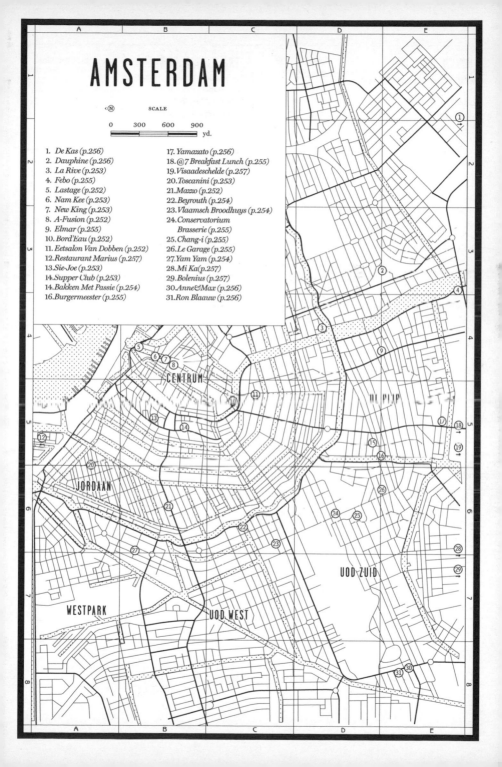

AMSTERDAM

N SCALE

0   300   600   900   yd.

1. *De Kas (p.256)*
2. *Dauphine (p.256)*
3. *La Rive (p.253)*
4. *Febo (p.255)*
5. *Lastage (p.252)*
6. *Nam Kee (p.253)*
7. *New King (p.253)*
8. *A-Fusion (p.252)*
9. *Elmar (p.255)*
10. *Bord'Eau (p.252)*
11. *Eetsalon Van Dobben (p.252)*
12. *Restaurant Marius (p.257)*
13. *Sie-Joe (p.253)*
14. *Supper Club (p.253)*
14. *Bakken Met Passie (p.254)*
16. *Burgermeester (p.255)*
17. *Yamazato (p.256)*
18. *@7 Breakfast Lunch (p.255)*
19. *Visaadeschelde (p.257)*
20. *Toscanini (p.253)*
21. *Mazzo (p.252)*
22. *Beyrouth (p.254)*
23. *Vlaamsch Broodhuys (p.254)*
24. *Conservatorium Brasserie (p.255)*
25. *Chang-i (p.255)*
26. *Le Garage (p.255)*
27. *Yam Yam (p.254)*
28. *Mi Ka (p.257)*
29. *Bolenius (p.257)*
30. *Anne&Max (p.256)*
31. *Ron Blaauw (p.256)*

CENTRUM

DE PIJP

JORDAAN

WESTPARK

OUD WEST

OUD ZUID

A-FUSION

Zeedijk 130
Binnenstad
Amsterdam 1012 BC
+31 203304068
www.a-fusion.nl

Opening hours	7 days for lunch and dinner
Reservation policy	Yes
Credit cards	Accepted
Price range	Budget
Style	Casual
Cuisine	Asian
Recommended for	Bargain

An unpretentious pan-Asian joint a short distance from Nieuwmarkt, A-Fusion is decorated with reddish woods, cream-coloured walls and little touches of blue. Orchids shoot from elegant vases. A projection TV displays Japanese and Hong Kong commercials, which works in this setting surprisingly well. They serve good sushi, hot and sour soup, dim sum, udon, chicken satay, marinated octopus, lamb in black pepper sauce – so don't come here expecting rigorous authenticity, but do come for good, reasonably priced cooking that ranges across the Far East. The bubble tea with tapioca balls is very popular for dessert.

BORD'EAU

Hotel de L'Europe
Nieuwe Doelenstraat 2-14
Binnenstad
Amsterdam 1012 CP
+31 205311705
www.leurope.nl/bord-eau

Opening hours	5 days for dinner
Reservation policy	Yes
Reservation email	bordeau@leurope.nl
Credit cards	Accepted
Price range	Expensive
Style	Smart casual
Cuisine	Contemporary French
Recommended for	High end

EETSALON VAN DOBBEN

Korte Reguliersdwardsstraat 5-7-9
Binnenstad
Amsterdam 1017 BH
www.eetsalonvandobben.nl

Opening hours	7 days for brunch and dinner
Reservation policy	No
Reservation email	info@eetsalonvandobben.nl
Credit cards	Not accepted
Price range	Budget
Style	Casual
Cuisine	Dutch
Recommended for	Local favourite

'Go for their broodje croquette or broodje warmvlees – a very traditional Dutch snack.'—Jean Beddington

LASTAGE

Geldersekade 29
Binnenstad
Amsterdam 1011 EJ
+31 207370811
www.restaurantlastage.nl

Opening hours	5 days for dinner
Reservation policy	Yes
Credit cards	Accepted
Price range	Affordable
Style	Smart casual
Cuisine	French
Recommended for	High end

MAZZO

Rozengracht 114
Binnenstad
Amsterdam 1016 NH
+31 203446402
www.mazzoamsterdam.nl/en

Opening hours	7 days from breakfast until late
Reservation policy	Yes
Credit cards	Accepted
Price range	Affordable
Style	Smart casual
Cuisine	Italian
Recommended for	Worth the travel

'Good simple food and a relaxed meeting place.'
—Michael Wolf

NAM KEE

Recommended by
Onno Kokmeijer

Zeedijk 111-113
Binnenstad
Amsterdam 1012 AV
+31 206243470
www.namkee.net

Opening hours	7 days for lunch and dinner
Reservation policy	Yes
Credit cards	Accepted
Price range	Budget
Style	Casual
Cuisine	Chinese
Recommended for	Bargain

Nam Kee is perhaps Holland's most famous Chinese restaurant, immortalized in a book and latterly a film called Oysters at Nam Kee's. That dish is indeed rather special – beautifully fresh oysters bathed in silky black bean sauce. The restaurant, which opened in 1981 and now has two other branches, is something of an icon, and was recently redecorated following a handsome stone and wood aesthetic. Main courses range from €8.50 to €18.50 (£7–£15; $11–$23) and include Peking duck, char siu, and salt and pepper squid – all relatively cheap for somewhere so famous. They do an excellent takeaway (takeout), too.

NEW KING

Recommended by
Julius Jaspers

Zeedijk 115-117
Binnenstad
Amsterdam 1012 AV
+31 206252180
www.newking.nl

Opening hours	7 days for lunch and dinner
Reservation policy	Yes
Credit cards	Accepted
Price range	Budget
Style	Casual
Cuisine	Chinese
Recommended for	Bargain

LA RIVE

Recommended by
Jean Beddington

Intercontinental Hotel
Professor Tulpplein 1
Binnenstad
Amsterdam 1018 GX
+31 205203264
www.restaurantlarive.nl

Opening hours	4 days for lunch and 5 days for dinner
Reservation policy	Yes
Reservation email	larive@ihg.com
Credit cards	Accepted
Price range	Expensive
Style	Smart casual
Cuisine	Fusion
Recommended for	Worth the travel

SIE-JOE

Recommended by
Agus Hermawan

Gravenstraat 24a
Binnenstad
Amsterdam 1012 NM
www.siejoe.com

Opening hours	6 days for lunch and dinner
Reservation policy	No
Credit cards	Not accepted
Price range	Budget
Style	Casual
Cuisine	Indonesian
Recommended for	Regular neighbourhood

'Indonesian restaurants have become a Dutch phenomenon and Sie-Joe reminds us why.'
—Agus Hermawan

TOSCANINI

Recommended by
Sergio Herman, Agus Hermawan,
Julius Jaspers, Sue Zemanick

Lindengracht 75
Binnenstad
Amsterdam 1015 KD
+31 206232813
www.restauranttoscanini.nl

Opening hours	6 days for dinner
Reservation policy	Yes
Credit cards	Accepted
Price range	Affordable
Style	Casual
Cuisine	Italian
Recommended for	Regular neighbourhood

'The best Italian in town, and that makes it the best in the Netherlands.'—Agus Hermawan

SUPPER CLUB

Recommended by
Michael Guerrieri

Jonge Roelensteeg 21
Burgwallen Nieuwe Zijde
Amsterdam 1012 PL
+31 203446400
www.supperclub.com

Opening hours	7 days for dinner
Reservation policy	Yes
Credit cards	Accepted
Price range	Expensive
Style	Smart casual
Cuisine	International
Recommended for	Wish I'd opened

'I love the concept and originality behind the design. Foot massage, palm reading, stress release … you name it … all the services you could want in between meals.'—Michael Guerrieri

YAM YAM

Recommended by
Robert J.K. Kranenborg

Frederik Hendrikstraat 88-90
Frederik Hendrikbuurt
Amsterdam 1052 HZ
+31 206815097
www.yamyam.nl

Opening hours	6 days for dinner
Reservation policy	Yes
Credit cards	Accepted
Price range	Affordable
Style	Casual
Cuisine	Italian
Recommended for	Bargain

BEYROUTH

Recommended by
Jean Beddington

Kinkerstraat 18
Oud-West
Amsterdam 1053 DV
+31 206160635
www.restaurant-beyrouth.nl

Opening hours	7 days for dinner
Reservation policy	Yes
Credit cards	Accepted
Price range	Affordable
Style	Casual
Cuisine	Lebanese
Recommended for	Regular neighbourhood

'Really good mezzes.'—Jean Beddington

VLAAMSCH BROODHUYS

Recommended by
Julius Jaspers,
Michael Wolf

Eerste Constantijn Huygensstraat 64
Oud-West
Amsterdam 1013 BR
www.vlaamschbroodhuys.nl

Opening hours	6 days for breakfast and lunch
Reservation policy	No
Credit cards	Not accepted
Price range	Budget
Style	Casual
Cuisine	Café
Recommended for	Breakfast

'I like sweet things in the morning and here they make their own jam.'—Michael Wolf

BAKKEN MET PASSIE

Recommended by
Robert J. K. Kranenborg

Albert Cuypstraat 51-53
Oud-Zuid
Amsterdam 1072 CM
+31 206701376
www.bakkenmetpassie.nl

Opening hours	5 days for breakfast and lunch
Reservation policy	No
Credit cards	Accepted
Price range	Budget
Style	Casual
Cuisine	Bakery
Recommended for	Breakfast

BURGERMEESTER

Recommended by
Alfredo Hoz

Albert Cuypstraat 48
Oud-Zuid
Amsterdam 1071 CV
+31 9002874377
www.burgermeester.eu

Opening hours	7 days for lunch and dinner
Reservation policy	Yes
Credit cards	Accepted
Price range	Budget
Style	Casual
Cuisine	Burgers
Recommended for	Bargain

CHANG-I

Recommended by
Agus Hermawan

Jan Willem Brouwersstraat 7
Oud-Zuid
Amsterdam 1071 LH
+31 204701700
www.chang-i.nl

Opening hours	7 days for dinner
Reservation policy	Yes
Credit cards	Accepted
Price range	Affordable
Style	Smart casual
Cuisine	Modern Chinese
Recommended for	Late night

'Best Chinese in Amsterdam!'—Agus Hermawan

CONSERVATORIUM BRASSERIE

Recommended by
Jean Beddington

Conservatorium Hotel
Van Baerlestraat 27
Oud-Zuid
Amsterdam 1071 AN
www.conservatoriumhotel.com

Opening hours	7 days for breakfast, lunch and dinner
Reservation policy	Yes
Credit cards	Accepted
Price range	Expensive
Style	Casual
Cuisine	French
Recommended for	Breakfast

'Wonderful location.'—Jean Beddington

ELMAR

Recommended by
Alfredo Hoz

Van Woustraat 110
Oud-Zuid
Amsterdam 1073 LS
+31 206646629
www.restaurantelmar.nl

Opening hours	5 days for lunch and dinner
Reservation policy	Yes
Reservation email	info@restaurantelmar.nl
Credit cards	Accepted
Price range	Affordable
Style	Casual
Cuisine	French
Recommended for	Regular neighbourhood

FEBO

Recommended by
Jonnie Boer

Amsteldijk 132-133
Oud-Zuid
Amsterdam 1078 RT
www.febodelekkerste.nl

Opening hours	7 days for lunch and dinner
Reservation policy	No
Credit cards	Not accepted
Price range	Budget
Style	Casual
Cuisine	Fast Food
Recommended for	Late night

Something of a legend among connoisseurs of late-night Amsterdam munchies, Febo is a large fast-food chain, with twenty-two branches in the capital alone. It's most famous for its coin-operated automat machines: you pop the money in the slot, unlocking a door from which you can remove a *kroket* – a deep-fried Dutch delicacy made from beef, veal, cheese or chicken. Prices are remarkably cheap and the places are open even when many of the bars have shut. The company slogan is 'the best', and at a certain time of night it would be hard to disagree.

LE GARAGE

Recommended by
Julius Jaspers,
Robert J. K. Kranenborg

Ruysdaelstraat 54-56
Oud-Zuid
Amsterdam 1071 XE
+31 206797176
www.restaurantlegarage.nl

Opening hours	5 days for lunch and 7 days for dinner
Reservation policy	Yes
Credit cards	Accepted
Price range	Affordable
Style	Casual
Cuisine	International
Recommended for	Late night

RON BLAAUW

Recommended by
Agus Hermawan,
Julius Jaspers

Sophialaan 55
Oud-Zuid
Amsterdam 1075 BP
+31 351234567
www.ronblaauw.nl

Opening hours..............4 days for lunch and 5 days for dinner
Reservation policy..Yes
Reservation email.......................................info@ronblaauw.nl
Credit cards..Accepted
Price range...Expensive
Style..Smart casual
Cuisine..Modern French
Recommended for..Wish I'd opened

'Great atmosphere, wonderful and beautifully
presented food!'—Agus Hermawan

YAMAZATO

Recommended by
Jean Beddington

Okura Hotel
Ferdinand Bolstraat 333
Oud-Zuid
Amsterdam 1072 LH
+31 206787450
www.yamazato.nl

Opening hours..................7 days for lunch and dinner
Reservation policy..Yes
Credit cards..Accepted
Price range...Expensive
Style..Smart casual
Cuisine..Japanese
Recommended for...High end

'Wonderful seasonal menus and perfect
service.'—Jean Beddington

ANNE&MAX

Recommended by
Agus Hermawan

Amstelveenseweg 196
Schinkel Buua
Amsterdam 1075 XS
www.annemax.nl

Opening hours..................7 days for breakfast, lunch and tea
Reservation policy...No
Credit cards..Not accepted
Price range...Affordable
Style...Casual
Cuisine..Café
Recommended for..Breakfast

'Just really good.'—Agus Hermawan

DAUPHINE

Recommended by
Julius Jaspers

Prins Bernhardplein 175
Watergraafsmeer
Amsterdam 1097 BL
+31 204621646
www.caferestaurantdauphine.nl

Opening hours..................7 days for brunch and dinner
Reservation policy..Yes
Credit cards..Accepted
Price range...Affordable
Style..Smart casual
Cuisine..International
Recommended for...Bargain

DE KAS

Recommended by
Jonnie Boer, Julius Jaspers,
Robert J. K. Kranenborg

Kamerlingh Onneslaan 3
Watergraafsmeer
Amsterdam 1097 DE
+31 204624562
www.restaurantdekas.nl

Opening hours..............5 days for lunch and 6 days for dinner
Reservation policy..Yes
Reservation email............................info@restaurantdekas.nl
Credit cards..Accepted
Price range...Affordable
Style...Formal
Cuisine...Mediterranean
Recommended for..Wish I'd opened

Saved from the wrecking ball and soulless
redevelopment by chef Gert Jan Hageman,
this municipal nursery on the southern edge of
Amsterdam opened as his restaurant in 2001. The
restored 1926 hothouse, its brick chimney preserved,
is now a spacious modern dining room showered
with natural light. Given the setting, Hagemen
decided the best way forward was to become a
grower, with vegetables and herbs for the seriously
seasonal, Mediterranean-inspired menu either grown
on site or on their own land 10 km (6 miles) away.
Book the chef's table for a tasting menu that makes
the most of all those fresh vegetables and herbs.

RESTAURANT MARIUS

Recommended by
Alfredo Hoz,
Robert J. K. Kranenborg

Barentszstraat 243
Westerpark
Amsterdam 1013 NH
+31 204227880

Opening hours...5 days for dinner
Reservation policy..Yes
Credit cards...Not accepted
Price range..Affordable
Style..Casual
Cuisine...International
Recommended for.................................Local favourite

@7 BREAKFAST LUNCH TEA

Recommended by
Onno Kokmeijer

Scheldestraat 92
Zuideramstel
Amsterdam 1078 GN
+31 0206709295
www.at7online.nl

Opening hours.........................7 days for breakfast and lunch
Reservation policy..Yes
Credit cards..Accepted
Price range...Budget
Style..Casual
Cuisine...Café
Recommended for.......................................Breakfast

@7 is so named because it serves food seven days
a week and opens at 7.00 a.m. Monday to Friday.
(The doors don't open until 8.00 a.m. and 9.00 a.m.
on Saturday and Sunday mornings respectively.) It's
a bright café serving fresh coffee, homemade apple
pie and muffins, wild smoked fish and excellent
brunch. But perhaps it's most famous for its Brazilian
health shakes at around €5 (£4; $6) apiece. @7 is
hugely dog and child-friendly: they'll provide water
and treats for pets and there's a special play area,
with toys, for youngsters. Around the corner is
Amstelpark, which has a kid's playground and a
city farm.

BOLENIUS

Recommended by
Robert J. K. Kranenborg

George Gershwinlaan 30
Zuideramstel
Amsterdam 1082 MT
+31 204044411
www.bolenius-restaurant.nl

Opening hours...............................6 days for lunch and dinner
Reservation policy..Yes
Credit cards..Accepted
Price range..Affordable
Style..Smart casual
Cuisine...Modern European
Recommended for................................Regular neighbourhood

MI KA

Recommended by
Jean Beddington

Buitenveldertselaan 158a
Zuideramstel
Amsterdam 1081 AB

Opening hours...6 days for dinner
Reservation policy..No
Credit cards...Not accepted
Price range...Budget
Style..Casual
Cuisine...Asian
Recommended for...Bargain

'A nice mixture of traditional home-style dishes from
Korea and Japan.'—Jean Beddington

VISAANDESCHELDE

Recommended by
Julius Jaspers

Scheldeplein 4
Zuideramstel
Amsterdam 1078 GR
+31 206751583
www.visaandeschelde.nl

Opening hours.............5 days for lunch and 7 days for dinner
Reservation policy..Yes
Credit cards..Accepted
Price range..Affordable
Style..Smart casual
Cuisine...Seafood
Recommended for................................Regular neighbourhood

'THIS IS THE BEST EXAMPLE OF BELGIAN "TERROIR" AND SEASONAL COOKING.'

PETER GOOSSENS P261

'A BARGAIN? FRENCH FRIES. THEY'RE ON ALMOST EVERY CORNER OF THE FLEMISH STREETS.'

ROGER VAN DAMME

BELGIUM

'Traditional Flemish and French cooking in a authentic setting. You always start off the meal with some pâté, rillette, pork fat, bread and pickles.'

KOBE DESRAMAULTS P268

'PROBABLY THE BEST 4 CHEESES MACARONI IN BELGIUM AND SERVED ALL NIGHT LONG...'

SANGHOON DEGEIMBRE P267

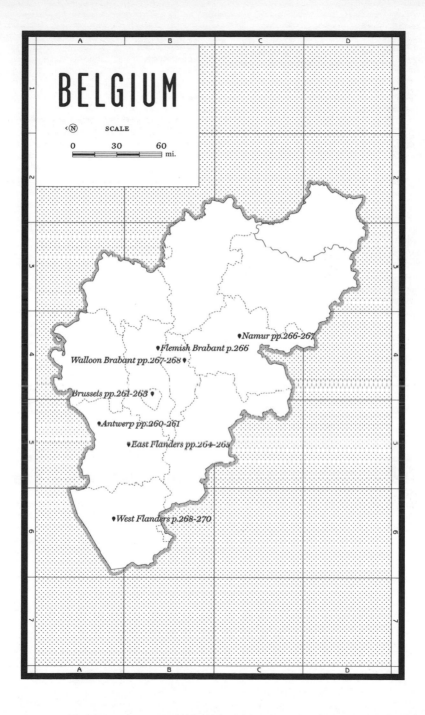

BELGIUM

N   SCALE

0   30   60 mi.

Namur pp.266-267

Flemish Brabant p.266

Walloon Brabant pp.267-268

Brussels pp.261-263

Antwerp pp.260-261

East Flanders pp.264-265

West Flanders p.268-270

DE PASTORALE

Laarstraat 22
Rumst
Antwerp 2840
+32 038446526
www.depastorale.be

Opening hours	5 days for brunch and 4 days dinner
Reservation policy	Yes
Reservation email	info@depastorale.be
Credit cards	Accepted
Price range	Expensive
Style	Smart casual
Cuisine	Contemporary French
Recommended for	Worth the travel

'De Pastorale in Reet: creativity, technique, art!'—Sang-Hoon Degeimbre

Pastorale is one of the more famous restaurants in Belgium, having held two Michelin stars since 2007. Chef Bart de Pooter opened it twenty years ago in a former monastery, outside Antwerp, dating to 1830. The decor is stylish and modern: wooden sculptures by Arne Quinze adorn the main dining room and flat-screen TVs display shifting images of modern art. The lunch menu costs €75 (£60; $93) but the twelve-course tasting menus are the highlight and can last four or five hours for patient, lingering customers. Expect barbecued Anjou pigeon with cherries or langoustine with cabbage; desserts are renowned for their balance.

FINJAN

Graaf van Hoornestraat 1
Antwerp 2000
+32 32487714
www.finjan.be

Opening hours	7 days for lunch and dinner
Reservation policy	Yes
Credit cards	Accepted
Price range	Budget
Style	Casual
Cuisine	Middle Eastern
Recommended for	Late night

THE GLORIOUS INN

De Burburestraat 4a
Antwerp 2000
+32 32370613
www.theglorious.be

Opening hours	5 days for breakfast, lunch and dinner
Reservation policy	Yes
Reservation email	info@theglorious.be
Credit cards	Accepted
Price range	Affordable
Style	Casual
Cuisine	Modern European
Recommended for	Local favourite

This split-level bistro is in Antwerp's fashionable, busy Zuid, a district that's full of antique shops, boutiques and art galleries. Inspired by its environment in terms of design and by New York-style deluxe bistros in terms of the food, veteran restaurateur Jurgen Lijcops has brought in chef Johan Van Raes to do bistro the Belgian way — with a bit of Italian thrown in. Dishes such as grilled sea bass with white asparagus and lamb's ears and beurre blanc sit alongside Lijcops's stunning wine list. There's a terrace on which, afterwards, you can enjoy a malt whisky and a fine cigar.

HET GEBAAR

Leopoldstraat 24
Antwerp 2000
+32 32323710
www.hetgebaar.be

Opening hours	5 days for lunch
Reservation policy	Yes
Reservation email	info@hetgebaar.be
Credit cards	Accepted
Price range	Affordable
Style	Formal
Cuisine	International
Recommended for	Worth the travel

'The best desserts in the world!'—Filip Claeys

JAM

Recommended by
Dave De Belder,
Ben Roche

Wolstraat 47
Antwerp 2000

Opening hours	5 days for breakfast and lunch
Reservation policy	Yes
Credit cards	Not accepted
Price range	Budget
Style	Casual
Cuisine	International
Recommended for	Breakfast

LAM EN YIN

Recommended by
Dave De Belder,
Roger van Damme

Reyndersstraat 17
Antwerp 2000
+32 32328838
www.lam-en-yin.be

Opening hours	5 days for dinner
Reservation policy	Yes
Credit cards	Accepted
Price range	Affordable
Style	Casual
Cuisine	Chinese
Recommended for	Regular neighbourhood

LUNG WAH

Recommended by
Roger van Damme

Van Wesenbekestraat 38
Antwerp 2060

Opening hours	6 days for lunch and dinner
Reservation policy	No
Credit cards	Not accepted
Price range	Budget
Style	Casual
Cuisine	Chinese
Recommended for	Local favourite

PAZZO

Recommended by
Dave De Belder

Oude Leeuwenrui 12
Antwerp 2000
+32 32328682
www.pazzo.be

Opening hours	5 days for lunch and dinner
Reservation policy	Yes
Credit cards	Accepted
Price range	Affordable
Style	Casual
Cuisine	Fusion
Recommended for	Bargain

'T FORNUIS

Recommended by
Peter Goossens,
Roger van Damme

Reynderstraat 24
Antwerp 2000
+32 32336270

Opening hours	5 days for lunch and dinner
Reservation policy	Yes
Credit cards	Accepted
Price range	Expensive
Style	Smart casual
Cuisine	French
Recommended for	Regular neighbourhood

'It takes me every time by surprise by its simplicity. Johan Segers' style of cuisine is very solid. This is the best example of Belgian "Terroir" and seasonal cooking.'—Peter Goossens

FRITURE RENÉ

Recommended by
Roger van Damme

Place de la Résistance 14
Anderlecht
Brussels 1070
+32 25232876
www.friturerene.be

Opening hours	5 days for lunch and dinner
Reservation policy	No
Credit cards	Accepted
Price range	Affordable
Style	Casual
Cuisine	Belgian
Recommended for	Regular neighbourhood

LA PAIX

Recommended by
Dave De Belder

Rue Ropsy-Chaudron 49
Anderlecht
Brussels 1070
+32 25230958
www.lapaix1892.com

Opening hours	5 days for lunch and 1 day for dinner
Reservation policy	Yes
Credit cards	Accepted
Price range	Affordable
Style	Smart casual
Cuisine	French Brasserie
Recommended for	Worth the travel

BON BON

Recommended by
Kobe Desramaults,
Tomoyasu Kamo

Avenue de Tervueren 453
Etterbeek
Brussels 1150
www.bon-bon.be

Opening hours.............4 days for lunch and 5 days for dinner
Reservation policy...Yes
Credit cards...Accepted
Price range...Expensive
Style...Smart casual
Cuisine...Modern Mediterranean
Recommended for..High end

'Here I had the most amazing sea bass ever, baked
in a crust of broken oyster shells and seaweed.
—Kobe Desramaults

Christophe Hardiquest is among the most celebrated
younger chefs in Belgium; at Bon Bon his wife
Stéphanie manages front of house. There's no menu:
diners choose from a blackboard whose dishes
change daily according to what looked best in the
market that morning. The wood-floored dining room,
with its chandeliers, red curtains and grey chairs,
evokes a kind of utilitarian luxury. Diners enjoy
dishes such as roasted langoustines with confit
of bacon and Sarazen sauce, or sesame-coated Anjou
pigeon in spiced consommé. The seven-course tasting menu isn't cheap, but there's a reasonably priced
lunch deal.

HET KRIEKSKE

Recommended by
Tomoyasu Kamo

Kapittel 10b
Halle
Brussels 1500
+32 23801421

Opening hours.................................5 days for lunch and dinner
Reservation policy...Yes
Credit cards...Accepted
Price range...Affordable
Style...Casual
Cuisine...Traditional Belgian
Recommended for..................................Regular neighbourhood

ORIENTALIA

Recommended by
Tomoyasu Kamo

Chaussée de Charleroi 277
Saint-Gilles
Brussels 1060
+32 25207575

Opening hours.............6 days for breakfast, lunch and dinner
Reservation policy...Yes
Credit cards...Accepted
Price range...Affordable
Style...Casual
Cuisine...Lebanese
Recommended for...............................Regular neighbourhood

LE CHALET DE LA FORÊT

Recommended by
Tomoyasu Kamo

Drève de Lorraine 43
Uccle
Brussels 1180
+32 23745416
www.lechaletdelaforet.be

Opening hours.................................5 days for lunch and dinner
Reservation policy...Yes
Credit cards...Accepted
Price range...Expensive
Style...Smart casual
Cuisine...Modern French
Recommended for.....................................Worth the travel

LA BRASSERIE DE BRUXELLES

Recommended by
Lionel Rigolet

Place de la Vieille Halle aux Blés 39
Ville de Bruxelles
Brussels 1000
+32 25139812

Opening hours.................................6 days for lunch and dinner
Reservation policy...Yes
Credit cards...Accepted
Price range...Affordable
Style...Casual
Cuisine...Belgian Brasserie
Recommended for...............................Regular neighbourhood

LE PAIN QUOTIDIEN

Recommended by
Gert de Mangeleer

Dansaertstraat 16a
Ville de Bruxelles
Brussels 1000
www.lepainquotidien.be

Opening hours	7 days for breakfast and lunch
Reservation policy	No
Credit cards	Accepted
Price range	Budget
Style	Casual
Cuisine	Café-Bakery
Recommended for	Breakfast

LE PERROQUET

Recommended by
Lionel Rigolet

Rue Watteau 31
Ville de Bruxelles
Brussels 1000

Opening hours	7 days for lunch and dinner
Reservation policy	No
Credit cards	Accepted
Price range	Budget
Style	Casual
Cuisine	Café
Recommended for	Bargain

PIERRE MARCOLINI

Recommended by
Arabelle Meirlaen

Rue des Minimes
Place du Grand Sablon
Ville de Bruxelles
Brussels 1000
www.marcolini.be

Opening hours	7 days
Reservation policy	No
Credit cards	Accepted
Price range	Affordable
Style	Casual
Cuisine	Chocolaterie
Recommended for	High end

RESTAURANT LE CHAT NOIR

Recommended by
Tomoyasu Kamo

Rue Jules Van Praetstraat 8
Ville de Bruxelles
Brussels 1000
+32 25121077
www.restolechatnoir.be

Opening hours	7 days for lunch and dinner
Reservation policy	Yes
Credit cards	Accepted
Price range	Affordable
Style	Casual
Cuisine	Belgian
Recommended for	Late night

LE SI BÉMOL

Recommended by
Lionel Rigolet

Rue Aux Fleurs 20
Ville de Bruxelles
Brussels 1000
+32 22196378
www.lesibemol.be

Opening hours	6 days for dinner
Reservation policy	Yes
Credit cards	Accepted
Price range	Affordable
Style	Casual
Cuisine	French
Recommended for	Late night

DE LIEVE

Recommended by
Kobe Desramaults

Sint-Margrietstraat 1
Gent
East Flanders 9000
+32 92232947
www.eetkaffee-delieve.be

Opening hours	5 days for lunch and dinner
Reservation policy	Yes
Credit cards	Accepted
Price range	Budget
Style	Casual
Cuisine	Belgian
Recommended for	Bargain

'An institution for years. Go in for a quick lunch – traditional food, lots of it and it's cheap too.' —Kobe Desramaults

Eetkaffee De Lieve, on the corner of Lievestraat and Sint-Margrietstraat, is an old favourite among Ghent natives. The large café has been going since the mid-1980s, serving good food at excellent prices. It's always been popular with students, artists and tourists. The genial owners command proceedings effectively, and the kitchen claims to take its inspiration from no less a figure than Escoffier. On the menu are a great prawn (shrimp) cocktail, some stews, meatballs, and haddock in mustard sauce, and a fabulous Dame Noire for dessert. Potatoes are a notable highlight, either as chips (fries), mashed or croquettes.

HOF VAN CLEVE

Recommended by
David Martin, Arabelle Meirlaen,
Lionel Rigolet, Roger van Damme

Riemegemstraat 1
Kruishoutem
East Flanders 9770
+32 93835848
www.hofvancleve.com

Opening hours	4 days for lunch and 5 days for dinner
Reservation policy	Yes
Credit cards	Accepted
Price range	Expensive
Style	Smart casual
Cuisine	Modern Belgian
Recommended for	High end

J.E.F.

Recommended by
Kobe Desramaults

Lange Streenstraat 10
Gent
East Flanders 9000
+32 93368058
www.j-e-f.be

Opening hours	4 days for lunch and 5 days for dinner
Reservation policy	Yes
Credit cards	Accepted
Price range	Budget
Style	Casual
Cuisine	Belgian
Recommended for	Regular neighbourhood

'Down to earth but creative cooking in a cool setting.'—Kobe Desramaults

J.E.F. is named after Jason Blanckaert and his girlfriend Femke Dequidt, who set up the restaurant in the middle of Ghent's old town. The off-white walls and aged, bare tables give the place a clean and sturdy look – it's not fancy, but the food is innovative, on-trend and very reasonably priced. Hare royale comes with cabbage, quince and shallots, smoked trout with yogurt, radish and cucumber, and they have a dessert of apple verjuice with nuts and almond. The set lunch has two choices for each course and there's a cracking selection of Belgian beers.

MARTINO

Recommended by
Kobe Desramaults

Vlaanderenstraat 125
Gent
East Flanders 9000
+32 92250104

Opening hours	5 days for dinner
Reservation policy	Yes
Credit cards	Accepted
Price range	Budget
Style	Casual
Cuisine	American
Recommended for	Late night

'In Gent there is a place called Martino that's been in the family for a few generations. It opens at 6 p.m. and closes at 1.30 a.m. Order cheese and eggs – amazing (definitely after some beers).'—Kobe Desramaults

Martino was recently refurbished, and the old neon signs were stripped away. It's now a brightly lit and functional late-night café, serving great pasta carbonara, spaghetti Bolognese, cheeseburgers (often with egg), sandwiches, steak tartare and so on, typically with copious quantities of chips (fries). The place is rather an institution among Ghent's students and clubbers – who, let's face it, often overlap – lingering over a final drink and a burger at the end of a night out. Perhaps the most famous dish is the steak martino, which sees the beef smothered in a rich, spicy sauce.

NIEUW STADION

Recommended by
Peter Goossens

Brusselsesteenweg 664
Gent
East Flanders 9050
+32 92308833
www.nieuwstadion.be

Opening hours	5 days for lunch and 6 days for dinner
Reservation policy	Yes
Credit cards	Accepted
Price range	Affordable
Style	Smart casual
Cuisine	French
Recommended for	Bargain

'Serve quality meats and traditional Belgian cuisine.'—Kobe Desramaults

SIMON SAYS

Recommended by
Kobe Desramaults

Sluizeken 8
Gent
East Flanders 9000
+32 92330343
www.simon-says.be

Opening hours	6 days for breakfast and lunch
Reservation policy	Yes
Reservation email	info@simon-says.be
Credit cards	Accepted
Price range	Budget
Style	Casual
Cuisine	Café
Recommended for	Breakfast

'This is great place for breakfast in Gent. Watch out, this place is always packed with cool crowds but has a warm environment.'—Kobe Desramaults

Simon Says is a new and stylish bed and breakfast in the middle of Ghent's Patershol district, where many of the city's best restaurants are clustered. The dining room is painted in turquoise, while handsome gold objects from Antwerp artist Panamarenko

hang from the walls. For breakfast: freshly baked croissants and other pastries from the local baker, cereals and good marmalade, and they do organic brunches with Fairtrade Belgian chocolate as well. The café is closed to non-residents on Monday, allowing bed and breakfast guests to enjoy breakfast whenever they like.

'T OVERHAMME

Recommended by
Kristof Coppens

Brusselse Steenweg 163
Aalst
East Flanders 9300
+32 53778599
www.toverhamme.be

Opening hours	4 days for lunch and dinner
Reservation policy	Yes
Reservation email	overhamme@skynet.be
Credit cards	Accepted
Price range	Affordable
Style	Smart casual
Cuisine	French
Recommended for	Regular neighbourhood

VOLTA

Recommended by
Kobe Desramaults

Nieuwe Wandeling 2b
Gent
East Flanders 9000
+32 93240500
www.volta-gent.be

Opening hours	5 days for lunch and dinner
Reservation policy	Yes
Credit cards	Accepted
Price range	Affordable
Style	Casual
Cuisine	Modern European
Recommended for	Regular neighbourhood

'Down to earth but creative cooking in a cool setting.'—Kobe Desramaults

One of the most exciting restaurants in Belgium, Volta is a huge former turbine hall a few minutes' walk from the centre of Ghent. Chef Olly Ceulenaere serves a seven-course tasting menu in the evenings, while a cleverly designed lunch menu sees an appetizer of four tapas plus a main course. Expect crunchy white cabbage with smoked eel and parsley root, or red potato with sand carrot and lettuce. When the weather is fine they open the sixty-cover terrace, and there's a wood-beamed private dining room upstairs. Surprisingly for such original cooking, Volta is very popular with families.

DE KUIPER

Vissersstraat 51
Vilvoorde
Flemish Brabant 1800
+32 22511387

Opening hours	5 days for lunch and dinner
Reservation policy	No
Credit cards	Accepted
Price range	Affordable
Style	Casual
Cuisine	Belgian
Recommended for	Bargain

DE ZOGERAA

Kasteelbrakelsesteenweg 492
Lembeek
Flemish Brabant 1502
+32 23060075
www.dezogeraa.be

Opening hours	5 days for lunch and dinner
Reservation policy	Yes
Credit cards	Accepted
Price range	Affordable
Style	Casual
Cuisine	Belgian
Recommended for	Regular neighbourhood

L'AIR DU TEMPS

Chaussée de Louvain 181
Noville-sur-Méhaigne
Namur 5310
+32 81813048
www.airdutemps.be

Opening hours	5 days for lunch and 5 days for dinner
Reservation policy	Yes
Reservation email	info@airdutemps.be
Credit cards	Accepted
Price range	Expensive
Style	Smart casual
Cuisine	Contemporary French
Recommended for	Worth the travel

'Abroad, the one I have enjoyed the most is
Sang-Hoon Degeimbre's restaurant L'Air duTemps.'
—Quinque Dacosta

True to its name, L'Air du Temps is an avant-garde
restaurant with a sensory mission. Having been a
butcher before becoming a sommelier, Korean-born

chef Sang-Hoon Degeibre moved to modernist
cookery methods. Fastidious research and a menu
that has been perfected over time earned the chef
first one Michelin star, then two. Unlike many
gastronomic innovators the chef's menu is
accessible, where the likes of kimchi is cleverly
paired with more conventional European ingredients.
The menu dégustation comes as a series of artfully
garnished and technicoloured creations. Provenance
is central to this developmental venture.

BRASSERIE FRANÇOIS

Place Saint-Aubain 3
Namur 5000
+32 81221123
www.brasseriefrancois.be

Opening hours	7 days for lunch and dinner
Reservation policy	Yes
Credit cards	Accepted
Price range	Affordable
Style	Casual
Cuisine	French
Recommended for	Regular neighbourhood

Brasserie François is a beautiful early nineteenth-
century building, designed in Napoleon III style,
next to Namur's celebrated baroque cathedral.
The restaurant has two floors: a brasserie
downstairs with a wood and brass bar and a seafood
counter, and a huge panelled room upstairs with
7-metre (23-feet) high walls. The food is classic
Parisian bistro: foie gras terrine with fig compote
(€15.50; £12; $19); snails in pastry with mushrooms
and garlic (€13.50; £11; $17); or veal brains with
sauce ravigote (€13.50; £11; $17) for the more
adventurous. If the weather is fine the covered
terrace outside is lovely – with a cold Belgian beer.

CHEZ CHEN

Chaussée de Dinant 873
Wepion
Namur 5100
+32 81747441
www.chezchen.be

Opening hours	6 days for lunch and dinner
Reservation policy	Yes
Credit cards	Accepted
Price range	Affordable
Style	Casual
Cuisine	Chinese
Recommended for	Bargain

Chez Chen is perhaps the best Chinese restaurant in Namur, if not southern Belgium. Open since 1985, it lies on the banks of the Meuse River, over whose cliffs and babbling water it offers splendid views. Set menus start at less than €30 (£24; $37) and include soup, salad and at least three other dishes – such as chicken with sweet and sour fruit or minced (ground) beef with vegetables – plus dessert. It also serves excellent Beijing-style duck and Chinese fondues, which must be ordered one day in advance. The aesthetic – white and cream walls, minimal extraneous decor and elegant black chairs – is clean and peaceful, thereby matching the setting.

LE FOU EST BELGE

Recommended by
Arabelle Meirlaen

24 route de Givet
Heure-en-Famenne
Namur 5377
+32 86322812
www.lefouestbelge.be

Opening hours	4 days for lunch and dinner
Reservation policy	Yes
Credit cards	Accepted
Price range	Affordable
Style	Casual
Cuisine	Belgian
Recommended for	Local favourite

LE SCALDIA 'CHEZ PIPPO'

Recommended by
Sang-Hoon Degeimbre

13 place Maurice Servais
Namur 5000

Opening hours	6 days for breakfast, lunch and dinner
Reservation policy	No
Credit cards	Not accepted
Price range	Budget
Style	Casual
Cuisine	Café
Recommended for	Late night

'Pippo's…probably the best four cheeses macaroni in Belgium, served all night long… With Orval beer…'—Sang-Hoon Degeimbre

Chez Pippo is unlikely to win any awards for its atmosphere – it is full of harsh lighting, McDonald's-like tiled floors, crane-grabbing toy machines, clumsy murals and uncomfortable furniture – but it serves some of the best *frites* in Charleroi and is famous among the city's inhabitants, known as Carolos.

These chips (fries) are well seasoned, never pre-frozen, and are served with a good dollop of Belgian mayonnaise. Children are very welcome. Since it's in the centre of town it's a perfect spot to grab a late lunch after sightseeing. It closes at 3.00 p.m. Monday to Thursday and at 6.30 p.m. on Saturday evenings.

FRUITS DE LA PASSION

Recommended by
Sang-Hoon Degeimbre

Chaussée de Charleroi 6
Thorembais-les-Beguines
Perwez
Walloon Braban 1360
+32 10880806
www.fruitsdelapassion.be

Opening hours	3 days for lunch and dinner
Reservation policy	Yes
Credit cards	Accepted
Price range	Affordable
Style	Casual
Cuisine	Bavarian
Recommended for	Local favourite

'A wine cellar owned by a passionate. In the kitchen dishes are based on bio product where the healthy way is the most important.'—Sang-Hoon Degeimbre

Feted by the Gault Millau guide on the boat now opening of 2012, Les Fruits de la Passion is proving very popular among local wine enthusiasts. Owner Vincent Damien has a vast knowledge of French wine and constructs the list around unusual bottles from 'little corners of France', as he puts it. It's a relaxed, country place – about 30 km (20 miles) outside Brussels – with wooden tables and paper napkins. Chef François Gérard makes exquisite cassoulet, pâtés and saucissons to complement the ecletic wine list.

WATARO

Recommended by
David Martin

Chaussée de Bruxelles 399
Waterloo
Walloon Brabant 1410
+32 23530134

Opening hours	5 days for lunch and 6 days for dinner
Reservation policy	Yes
Credit cards	Accepted
Price range	Affordable
Style	Casual
Cuisine	Japanese
Recommended for	Bargain

L'AUBERGE IN DE ZON

Recommended by
Kobe Desramaults

Dikkebusstraat 80
De Klijte
West Flanders 8950
+32 57212626
www.indezon.be

Opening hours	4 days for lunch and 5 days for dinner
Reservation policy	Yes
Credit cards	Accepted
Price range	Affordable
Style	Casual
Cuisine	Belgian
Recommended for	Local favourite

'Serves traditional Flemish and French food in an authentic setting. Start off the meal with some pâté, rilette, pork fat, bread and pickles. It has some very good draught (draft) beers!'—Kobe Desramaults

L'Auberge In De Zon is a handsome tavern a mile or so from the French border. Brown-bricked, with a red-tiled roof it overlooks a lush garden. A bright and soulful place with stained-glass windows and bare brick, there's often a band playing with an accordion and a double bass. The food is infinitely better than you might expect for a venue like this: appetizers of young snails with cauliflower and mains of osso bucco, crown of lamb with parsley and garlic butter, or veal kidney and eel in buttermilk. The set menu even includes half a bottle of wine per person.

BISTRO CHRISTOPHE

Recommended by
Filip Claeys,
Gert de Mangeleer

Garenmarkt 34
Bruges
West Flanders 8000
+32 50344892
www.christophe-brugge.be

Opening hours	5 days for dinner
Reservation policy	Yes
Credit cards	Accepted
Price range	Affordable
Style	Casual
Cuisine	French Bistro
Recommended for	Late night

'Christophe Bruges' place is only open in the evening and serves traditional Belgian food.'—Filip Claeys

BISTRO DE KRUIDEN MOLEN

Recommended by
Filip Claeys,
Gert de Mangeleer

Dorpsstraat 1
Klemskerke
West Flanders 8420
+32 59235178
www.kruidenmolen.be

Opening hours	5 days for lunch and dinner
Reservation policy	Yes
Credit cards	Not accepted
Price range	Affordable
Style	Casual
Cuisine	Belgian
Recommended for	Regular neighbourhood

'The best bistro of Belgium!'—Filip Claeys

DE JONKMAN

Recommended by
Kristof Coppens,
James 'Jockey' Petrie

Maalsesteenweg 438
Sint Kruis
Bruges
West Flanders 8310
+32 50360767
www.dejonkman.be

Opening hours	5 days for lunch and dinner
Reservation policy	Yes
Reservation email	info@dejonkman.be
Credit cards	Accepted
Price range	Expensive
Style	Smart casual
Cuisine	Modern Belgian
Recommended for	Worth the travel

DE SIPHON

Recommended by
Filip Claeys, Sergio Herman

Damse Vaart-Oost 1
Damme
West Flanders 8340
+32 50620202
www.siphon.be

Opening hours	5 days for lunch and dinner
Reservation policy	Yes
Reservation email	info@siphon.be
Credit cards	Not accepted
Price range	Affordable
Style	Casual
Cuisine	French
Recommended for	Local favourite

'A traditional Flemish kitchen and the third generation of owners.'—Filip Claeys

FRITUUR BOSRAND

Recommended by
Gert de Mangeleer

Koning Albert I Laan 108
Sint Michiels
Bruges
West Flanders 8200
www.frituurbosrand.be

Opening hours	7 days for lunch and dinner
Reservation policy	No
Credit cards	Not accepted
Price range	Budget
Style	Casual
Cuisine	Fast Food
Recommended for	Bargain

FRITUUR RAKONTIKI

Recommended by
Filip Claeys

Maalsesteenweg 391
Sint-Kruis
Bruges
West Flanders 8310
www.rakontiki.be

Opening hours	6 days for lunch and dinner
Reservation policy	No
Credit cards	Accepted
Price range	Budget
Style	Casual
Cuisine	Burgers
Recommended for	Bargain

HERTOG JAN

Recommended by
Julius Jaspers, Lisa Muncan

Torhoutsesteenweg 479
Bruges
West Flanders 8200
+32 50673446
www.hertog-jan.com

Opening hours	5 days for lunch and dinner
Reservation policy	Yes
Credit cards	Accepted
Price range	Expensive
Style	Formal
Cuisine	Modern European
Recommended for	Worth the travel

HOSTELLERIE ST NICOLAS

Recommended by
Kristof Coppens

Nicolas Hotel
Veurnseweg 532
Elverdinge
West Flanders 8906
+32 57200622
www.hostellerie-stnicolas.com

Opening hours.................................5 days for lunch and dinner
Reservation policy...Yes
Credit cards...Accepted
Price range...Affordable
Style..Smart casual
Cuisine..Belgian
Recommended for...High end

ROCK FORT

Recommended by
Gert de Mangeleer

Langestraat 15
Bruges
West Flanders 8000
+32 50334113
www.rock-fort.be

Opening hours.................................5 days for lunch and dinner
Reservation policy...Yes
Credit cards...Accepted
Price range...Affordable
Style...Casual
Cuisine..Belgian
Recommended for.............................Regular neighbourhood

IN DE WULF

Recommended by
Sven Chartier, Alexandre
Gauthier, Stephen Harris,
David Martin, Arabelle Meirlaen

Wulvestraat 1
Heuvelland
Dranouter
West Flanders 8950
+32 57445567
www.indewulf.be

Opening hours..............3 days for lunch and 5 days for dinner
Reservation policy...Yes
Credit cards...Accepted
Price range...Expensive
Style...Casual
Cuisine..Belgian
Recommended for...Worth the travel

Kobe Desramaults' hideaway isn't the most
accessible of places, tucked away 160 km (100
miles) north of the French–Belgian border, but you'll
be glad you tracked down this former farm turned
restaurant with rooms. Its wild location is a suitable
backdrop for what's offered: a procession of small
dishes often made with unpronounceable ingredients
(*kerremelkstampers* or *Keiemtaler*, anyone?) plucked
from the farm's environs. Hardened gastronomes
will know the score – whelks balancing on pebbles,
salads of foraged herbs and fennel pollen aplenty, all
impeccably presented on a baffling array of dinnerware. Could this be Belgium's answer to Noma?
In a word, (whisper it), yes.

'A MOUNTAIN BISTRO IN THE MIDDLE OF NOWHERE WITH A WARM AND RUSTIC ATMOSPHERE.'

EMMANUEL RENAUT P289

'SITUATED IN ONE OF THE PRETTIEST HOUSES IN CHAMPAGNE.'

ESTHER SHAM P279

'All the spirit of Southwest cuisine: simple, great products and superb atmosphere.'

PASCAL AUSSIGNAC P274

FRANCE & MONACO

'VERY GOOD CUISINE NICOISE.'

MAURO COLAGRECO P285

'DON'T FORGET TO LEAVE WITH SOME SEAWEED BREAD TO EAT WITH OYSTERS ON THE PORT.'

GUILLAUME MONJUR P277

'ALWAYS AT THE TOP OF THEIR GAME AND THEIR FOIE GRAS IS THE BEST IN THE WORLD!'

LORI GRANITO P274

FRANCE
& MONACO

N SCALE

0   75   150
mi.

L'AUBERGE DE L'ILL

Recommended by
Lori Granito, Jean Joho

2 Rue de Collonges au Mont d'Or
Illhaeusern
Alsace 68970
+33 389718900
www.auberge-de-l-ill.com

Opening hours	5 days for lunch and dinner
Reservation policy	Yes
Credit cards	Accepted
Price range	Expensive
Style	Smart casual
Cuisine	Alsatian
Recommended for	Worth the travel

'The Haeberlin family are always at the top of their game and their foie gras is the best in the world!'
—Lori Granito

LE COCHON VOLANT

Recommended by
Michel Portos

22 Place des Capucins
Bordeaux
Aquitaine 33800
+33 557591000
www.bordeaux-restaurant-cochon-volant.com

Opening hours	6 days for dinner
Reservation policy	Yes
Credit cards	Accepted
Price range	Affordable
Style	Casual
Cuisine	French bistro
Recommended for	Late night

While some of the major foodie capitals lack decent late-night dining spots, Bordeaux night owls and locals on the late shift never have that problem. Most of the after hours operations are located near the bustling Marché des Capucins. 'Pigs Might Fly' – this aptly named bistro in a former butcher's shop – is typical in its deferral of last orders until 3.00 a.m. The appealing red and white tiled room is classically French – right down to its self-confessed moody patron – and offers generous portions of classics such as duck rillettes and roasted Camembert alongside vintage wines from the famous Bordeaux appellation.

GRAVELIER

Recommended by
Michel Troisgros

114 Cours de Verdun
Bordeaux
Aquitaine 33000
+33 556481715
www.gravelier.fr

Opening hours	5 days for lunch and dinner
Reservation policy	Yes
Credit cards	Accepted
Price range	Affordable
Style	Casual
Cuisine	Modern French
Recommended for	Bargain

LA TUPINA

Recommended by
Pascal Aussignac

6-8 Rue Porte de la Monnaie
Aquitaine 33800
+33 556915637
www.latupina.com

Opening hours	7 days for lunch and dinner
Reservation policy	Yes
Credit cards	Accepted
Price range	Affordable
Style	Casual
Cuisine	Southwest French
Recommended for	Worth the travel

'All the spirit of Southwest cuisine is at La Tupina. Great produce and superb atmosphere.'
—Pascal Aussignac

LA CAPE

Recommended by
Michel Portos

9 Allée Morlette
Cenon
Aquitaine 33150
+33 0557802425
www.restaurant-lacape.com

Opening hours	5 days for lunch and dinner
Reservation policy	Yes
Credit cards	Accepted
Price range	Expensive
Style	Smart casual
Cuisine	Modern French
Recommended for	Regular neighbourhood

In his grandparents' day, his family ran the old Cenon institution Rancho, so one-star chef Nicholas Magie had no great dilemma about settling on a location when it was time to start his own venture.

The suburban bungalow with cream-painted shutters and picket fence – inside there's a long and contemporary leather-panelled room – adds a touch of chic to what remains very much a friends and family affair. On the menu, Aquitaine specialities make the most of local produce, while Nicholas's time in Paris's fine-dining establishments means he retains a love for truffles and other upmarket *produits nobles*.

LA GRANDE CUISINE ETOILÉE

Recommended by
Josean Alija,
Daniel Boulud

Les Prés d'Eugénie
334 Rue René Vielle
Eugenie les Bains
Aquitaine 40320
+33 558050607
www.michelguerard.com

Opening hours	2 days for lunch and 6 days for dinner
Reservation policy	Yes
Reservation email	reservation@michelguerard.com
Credit cards	Accepted
Price range	Expensive
Style	Formal
Cuisine	Modern French
Recommended for	Wish I'd opened

HEGIA

Recommended by
Tom Aikens

Chemin de Curutcheta
Quartier Celhai
Hasparren
Aquitaine 64240
+33 55929678
www.hegia.com

Opening hours	7 days for breakfast and dinner
Reservation policy	Yes
Reservation email	info@hegia.com
Credit cards	Accepted
Price range	Expensive
Style	Smart casual
Cuisine	Modern French
Recommended for	Worth the travel

LE RELAIS DE LA POSTE

Recommended by
Julien Duboué

24 Avenue de Maremne
Magescq
Aquitaine 40140
+33 558477025
www.relaisposte.com

Opening hours	5 days for lunch and dinner
Reservation policy	Yes
Reservation email	poste@relaischateaux.com
Credit cards	Accepted
Price range	Expensive
Style	Smart casual
Cuisine	Southwest French
Recommended for	High end

AU BON COIN LES PIEDS DE COCHON

Recommended by
Julien Duboué

223 Rue de Château
Peyrehorade
Aquitaine 40300
+33 558730045
www.auboncoin40.fr

Opening hours	7 days for lunch
Reservation policy	Yes
Credit cards	Not accepted
Price range	Affordable
Style	Casual
Cuisine	Pig trotters
Recommended for	Local favourite

'One of the things I treasure most is the experience of eating pork trotters (feet) at the restaurant Pieds de Cochon in my hometown. This experience is best on Wednesday mornings because of the street market that goes on. All the farmers from the near by towns come here to eat.'—Julien Duboué

L'AUBERGE DU PAS DE VENT

Recommended by
Julien Duboué

281 Avenue Pas de Vent
Pouillon
Aquitaine 40350
www.auberge-dupasdevent.com

Opening hours	6 days for lunch and 4 days for dinner
Credit cards	Accepted
Price range	Affordable
Style	Casual
Cuisine	Southwest French
Recommended for	Local favourite

'Fresh, traditional cuisine from Les Landes.'
—Julien Duboué

LA FERME D'ORTHE

Recommended by
Julien Duboué

9 Rue de la Fontaine
Orthevielle
Aquitaine 40300
+33 558730103
www.lafermedorthe.fr

Opening hours.............6 days for lunch and 3 days for dinner
Reservation policy...Yes
Credit cards...Accepted
Price range...Budget
Style...Casual
Cuisine...French Bistro
Recommended for...Bargain

'Here you'll get a very good, well made,
simple meal.'—Julien Duboué

MICHEL TRAMA

Recommended by
Ollie Couillaud

52 Rue Royale
Puymirol
Aquitaine 47270
+33 553953146
www.aubergade.com

Opening hours.............5 days for lunch and 7 days for dinner
Reservation policy...Yes
Reservation email.......................reservation@aubergade.com
Credit cards...Accepted
Price range..Expensive
Style...Smart casual
Cuisine...Modern French
Recommended for..Worth the travel

MAISON DÉCORET

Recommended by
Pascal Barbot, Jacques
Marcon

15 Rue du Parc
Vichy
Auvergne 03200
+33 470976506
www.jacquesdecoret.com

Opening hours..............................5 days for lunch and dinner
Reservation policy...Yes
Reservation email.......................decoret@relaischateaux.com
Credit cards...Accepted
Price range..Expensive
Style...Smart casual
Cuisine...Modern French
Recommended for................................Regular neighbourhood

It might seem a little out of the way in the slow-paced, chintzy town of Vichy, but there's nothing provincial about rising star Jacques Décoret's cooking. The former winner of the coveted Ouvrier de France award set up this one-star venture with the help of his wife Martine, who was behind the restaurant's chic white interiors. (The Napoleon III-era chalet also boasts five tasteful guest rooms.) The *menu confiance* allows Décoret carte blanche to explore his sophisticated flavour combinations, but he's not immune to fun: breaded and deep-fried eggs with bacon-infused foam, say, or a certain penchant for plastic TV trays.

CRÊPERIE DU PUITS

Recommended by
Gwendal Le Ruyet

11 Rue de la Vallée du Loch
Brandivy
Brittany 56390
+33 297560416

Opening hours...7 days for dinner
Reservation policy...Yes
Credit cards...Accepted
Price range...Budget
Style...Casual
Cuisine...Crêpes
Recommended for................................Regular neighbourhood

Located in the pretty village of Morbihan, far from the urban sprawl, this family-run crêperie is permanently over-subscribed, purely thanks to word of mouth. Many of those pulling up a perch in the humble tiled room are repeat customers on summer vacations. Arrive early during the height of the season, when it can grow rather rowdy. The menu covers the whole savoury and sweet scale: well-priced buckwheat galettes with ham and cheese; wheat flour crêpes filled with sugar, Chantilly and caramelized apple. Tradition continues with the homemade cider – Brittany's typical accompaniment to its regional dish – which arrives in an earthenware vessel.

GRAIN DE VANILLE

12 Place Victoire
Cancale
Brittany 35260
+33 468806455
www.maisons-de-bricourt.com

Opening hours	5 days for breakfast, lunch and tea
Reservation policy	No
Credit cards	Accepted
Price range	Budget
Style	Casual
Cuisine	Bakery-Café
Recommended for	Breakfast

'Don't forget to leave with some seaweed bread to eat oysters with on the port.'—Guillaume Monjuré

RESTAURANT PATRICK JEFFROY

L'Hôtel de Carantec
20 Rue du Kelenn
Carantec
Brittany 29660
+33 298670047
www.hoteldecarantec.com

Opening hours	5 days for lunch and dinner
Reservation policy	Yes
Credit cards	Accepted
Price range	Affordable
Style	Smart casual
Cuisine	Modern French
Recommended for	High end

CRÊPERIE DES PROMENADES

18 Rue des Promenades
Saint-Brieuc
Brittany 22000
www.creperie-des-promenades.com

Opening hours	5 days for brunch and 1 day for dinner
Reservation policy	Yes
Credit cards	Accepted
Price range	Budget
Style	Casual
Cuisine	Café
Recommended for	Regular neighbourhood

VICTOR'INN

12 Rue Saint Gilles
Saint-Brieuc
Brittany 22000
+33 296613635

Opening hours	5 days for lunch and 4 days for dinner
Reservation policy	Yes
Credit cards	Accepted
Price range	Budget
Style	Casual
Cuisine	Italian Deli-Café
Recommended for	Bargain

LE CONTRE QUAI

Rue Saint-Nicolas
Sauzon
Brittany 56360
+33 297316060

Opening hours	6 days for dinner
Reservation policy	Yes
Credit cards	Accepted
Price range	Affordable
Style	Casual
Cuisine	Seafood
Recommended for	Local favourite

'Great food and atmosphere.'—Pierre Gagnaire

LE COQUILLAGE

Château Richeux
D115 Route du Mont St Michel
St-Méloir des Ondes
Brittany 35350
+33 299896476
www.maisons-de-bricourt.com

Opening hours	7 days for lunch and dinner
Reservation policy	Yes
Credit cards	Accepted
Price range	Expensive
Style	Smart casual
Cuisine	Northwest French
Recommended for	Wish I'd opened

LE CRAPAUD ROUGE

Recommended by
Jean Marie Baudic

28 Rue Port Goret
Tréveneuc
Brittany 22410
+33 296703621
www.lecrapaudrouge.com

Opening hours	7 days for lunch and dinner
Reservation policy	Yes
Credit cards	Not accepted
Price range	Budget
Style	Casual
Cuisine	French Bistro
Recommended for	Local favourite

BISSOH

Recommended by
Tomoyasu Kamo

1a Rue du Faubourg St Jacques
Beaune
Burgundy 21200
+33 699219950
www.bissoh.com

Opening hours	5 days for lunch and dinner
Reservation policy	Yes
Credit cards	Accepted
Price range	Affordable
Style	Smart casual
Cuisine	Japanese-French
Recommended for	Wish I'd opened

CAVES MADELEINE

Recommended by
Josep Roca

8 Rue Faubourg Madeleine
Beaune
Burgundy 21200
+33 380229330

Opening hours	5 days for lunch and dinner
Reservation policy	Yes
Credit cards	Accepted
Price range	Affordable
Style	Smart casual
Cuisine	Burgundian
Recommended for	Wish I'd opened

Very much off the track beaten by those devoted to the Red Guide, this rural French bistro has been popularized via word of mouth and because of an ability to pair excellent wines with brilliantly cooked classic French dishes. The usual suspects are all done very well. From confit duck to andouille and boeuf bourguignon to snail cassolette, the regional authenticity always feels nourishing. Net curtains drape in the windows of a fairly unsuspecting facade, behind which diners sit cheek by jowl on communal wooden tables. Wines are available to take away; a mere €6 (£5; $7) corkage is charged for consumption in house.

MAISON LAMELOISE

Recommended by
Jeremy Charles, Bruce
Poole, Heinz Winkler

36 Place d'Armes
Chagny
Burgundy 71150
+33 385876565
www.lameloise.fr

Opening hours	5 days for lunch and dinner
Reservation policy	Yes
Reservation email	reception@lameloise.fr
Credit cards	Accepted
Price range	Expensive
Style	Smart casual
Cuisine	Modern French
Recommended for	Worth the travel

'A lovely three-Michelin-starred restaurant with beautifully judged and friendly service.'
—Bruce Poole

A fifteenth-century coaching inn of character with gleaming wood floors, thick stone walls, rugged beams and wrought-iron screens is the setting for this gracious three-Michelin-starred restaurant with – conveniently – sixteen bedrooms and a memorably decadent cellar. Chef Éric Pras, whose motto is 'simplicity is the key to flavour', curates and updates dishes from the venue's nine decades in the tenure of the welcoming Lameloise family. These could include substantial blue lobster with violet artichokes, fibrous morels and tarragon, and local roast pigeon with aromatic almonds. Ensure you leave room to plunder the two-tier cheese trolley.

LA CÔTE SAINT JACQUES

Recommended by
Morgan Meunier

14 Faubourg de Paris
Joigny
Burgundy 89300
+33 386620970
www.cotesaintjacques.com

Opening hours	5 days for lunch and 6 days for dinner
Reservation policy	Yes
Reservation email	lorain@relaischateaux.com
Credit cards	Accepted
Price range	Expensive
Style	Formal
Cuisine	Modern French
Recommended for	Worth the travel

'Jean Michel Lorain is an exceptional chef. Located by the river, the hotel is fantastic for a weekend break away from the stress of city life.'—Morgan Meunier

RELAIS BERNARD LOISEAU

Recommended by
Guy Savoy

2 Rue d'Argentine
Saulieu
Burgundy 21210
+33 380905353
www.bernard-loiseau.com

Opening hours	5 days for lunch and dinner
Reservation policy	Yes
Credit cards	Accepted
Price range	Expensive
Style	Smart casual
Cuisine	Modern French
Recommended for	Worth the travel

LE PARC

Recommended by
Esther Sham

Domaine Les Crayères
64 Boulevard Henry Vasnier
Reims
Champagne-Ardenne 51100
+33 326249000
www.lescrayeres.com

Opening hours	5 days for lunch and dinner
Reservation policy	Yes
Credit cards	Accepted
Price range	Expensive
Style	Formal
Cuisine	Modern French
Recommended for	Wish I'd opened

'Situated in what I think is one of the prettiest houses in Champagne.'—Esther Sham

L'ASSIETTE CHAMPENOISE

Recommended by
Jean Joho, Yvonnick Lalle

40 Avenue Paul-Vaillant-Couturie
Tinqueux
Champagne-Ardenne 51430
+33 326846464
www.assiettechampenoise.com

Opening hours	5 days for lunch and 6 days for dinner
Reservation policy	Yes
Reservation email	Assiette.champenoise@wanadoo.fr
Credit cards	Accepted
Price range	Expensive
Style	Smart casual
Cuisine	Modern French
Recommended for	Worth the travel

MARIE ROSÉ

Recommended by
Armand Arnal

13 Rue Pasteur
Aigues-Mortes
Languedoc-Roussillon 30220
+33 466537984

Opening hours	4 days for dinner
Reservation policy	Yes
Credit cards	Accepted
Price range	Affordable
Style	Casual
Cuisine	Southern French
Recommended for	Regular neighbourhood

LES TEMPLIERS

L'Hôtel les Templiers
23 Rue République
Aigues-Mortes
Languedoc-Rousillon 30220
+33 466536656

Opening hours	6 days for dinner
Reservation policy	Yes
Credit cards	Accepted
Price range	Affordable
Style	Casual
Cuisine	Southern French
Recommended for	Regular neighbourhood

Replete with *objets d'art* and an impressive wine cellar, this eighteenth-century merchant's house with dipping pool and airy terrace is inside the old fortifications of Aigues-Mortes. By night the courtyard restaurant attracts a jovial crowd of regulars. The cooking sticks to regional and traditional cuisine – this Camargue city is particularly famed for its sea salt and asparagus – and eschews a formal menu for a daily selection of dishes based on market produce.

CAN MARCEL

1 Rue Pasteur
Canet
Languedoc-Rousillon 66140

Opening hours	6 days for lunch and 5 days for dinner
Reservation policy	Yes
Credit cards	Accepted
Price range	Affordable
Style	Casual
Cuisine	Seafood
Recommended for	Worth the travel

'Fresh fish cooked by a lunatic chef/owner with a great heart. It's fresh fish with no extras, cooked to perfection.'—Jérôme Tauvron

GILLES GOUJON

Auberge du Vieux Puits
5 Avenue Saint Victor
Fontjoncouse
Languedoc-Rousillon 11360
+33 468440737
www.aubergeduvieuxpuits.fr

Opening hours	5 days for lunch and 4 days for dinner
Reservation policy	Yes
Reservation email	reception@aubergeduvieuxpuits.fr
Credit cards	Accepted
Price range	Expensive
Style	Smart casual
Cuisine	French Mediterranean
Recommended for	Regular neighbourhood

Gilles Goujon shed a few tears when the Auberge du Vieux Puits finally racked up its third Michelin star in 2010. Eighteen years earlier it had opened with a staff of just two: Goujon and his wife Marie-Christine. Tucked away in the tiny village of Fontjoncouse in the backwaters of the Aude, the renovated wine cellar (with pool and sunny terrace) needed something very special to escape obscurity. The answer was top-notch Mediterranean food with a firm accent on the terroir: specialities include roasted partridge, black pork and eggs served with truffle purée. Not bad for a village that houses only a hundred or so souls.

LA RÉSERVE RIMBAUD

820 Avenue St Maur
Montpellier
Languedoc-Rousillon 34000
+33 467725253
www.reserve-rimbaud.com

Opening hours	6 days for lunch and dinner
Reservation policy	Yes
Credit cards	Accepted
Price range	Affordable
Style	Smart casual
Cuisine	Southern French
Recommended for	Worth the travel

'A very pleasant waterfront restaurant with great cuisine by the chef Charles Fontes.'— Julien Duboué

WASABI SUSHI BAR

Recommended by
Lisa Muncan

53 Avenue Georges Pompidou
Nîmes
Languedoc-Rousillon 30900

Opening hours.................................5 days for lunch and dinner
Reservation policy...Yes
Credit cards...Accepted
Price range..Budget
Style...Casual
Cuisine..Japanese
Recommended for..Bargain

L'HUÎTRE ET LA VIGNE

Recommended by
Lisa Muncan

Route de Saint Hilaire
Saint-Hilaire-d'Ozilhan
Languedoc-Rousillon 30210
+33 608056357
www.lhuitreetlavigne.com

Opening hours.................................7 days for lunch and dinner
Reservation policy...Yes
Credit cards...Accepted
Price range..Affordable
Style...Casual
Cuisine..Seafood
Recommended for...........................Regular neighbourhood

'You sit in the middle of a vineyard – love it!'
—Lisa Muncan

The marriage of an oyster seller and a winemaker, this well-liked Mediterranean venture ten minutes from the Pont du Gard is tucked away on the owners' private vineyard. Although it was recently struck by lightning, neighbours and regulars banded together, and the romantic spot is back in business. The menu – best enjoyed with a sunset or with the sound of crickets in the background – takes in tapas, shellfish platters and oysters, expertly shucked by Anne-Sophie. (Lobster is also on the menu if you order in advance.) Meanwhile, affable Belgian Benoît offers tastings of his own wines, which – like the shellfish – are available to take away.

LE RENAISSANCE

Recommended by
Lisa Muncan

6 Place des Herbes
Uzès
Languedoc-Rousillon 30700
+33 466031182
www.restaurant-lerenaissance.fr

Opening hours.............7 days for breakfast, lunch and dinner
Reservation policy...Yes
Credit cards...Accepted
Price range..Budget
Style...Casual
Cuisine...Southern French
Recommended for..Breakfast

LOUIS ALLARD

Recommended by
Gwendal Le Ruyet

2 Rue Chaussée St Pierre
Angers
Loire 49100

Opening hours.........................7 days from breakfast until late
Reservation policy..No
Credit cards...Accepted
Price range..Affordable
Style...Casual
Cuisine..Pastries
Recommended for..High end

'For their paté aux prunes.'—Gwendal Le Ruyet

L'ARNSBOURG

Recommended by
Andreas Caminada, Harald
Wohlfahrt

Hôtel K
18 Untermuhlthal
Baerenthal
Lorraine 57230
+33 0387065085
www.arnsbourg.com

Opening hours.................................5 days for lunch and dinner
Reservation policy...Yes
Credit cards...Accepted
Price range..Expensive
Style...Formal
Cuisine...Modern French
Recommended for.....................................Worth the travel

SAQUANA

22 Place Hamelin
Honfleur
Lower Normandy 14600
+33 231894080
www.alexandre-bourdas.com

Recommended by
Pascal Barbot,
Marc-André Jetté

Opening hours	4 days for lunch and dinner
Reservation policy	Yes
Credit cards	Accepted
Price range	Expensive
Style	Casual
Cuisine	Modern French
Recommended for	Worth the travel

BRAS

Route de l'Aubrac
Laguiole
Midi-Pyrenees 12210
+33 565511820
www.bras.fr

Recommended by
Ferran Adrià, Andoni Luis Aduriz, Massimiliano Alajmo, Josean Alija, Stefano Baiocco, Pascal Barbot, Jean Marie Baudic, Anton Bjuhr, Andreas Caminada, Enrico Crippa, Sang-Hoon Degeimbre, Marcus Eaves, Pierre Gagnaire, Peter Gilmore, Claus Moller Henriksen, Thomas Herman, Daniel Humm, Katsumi Ishida, Timothy Johnson, Dylan Jones and Bo (Duangporn) Songvisava, Gwendal Le Ruyet, David Martin, Arabelle Meirlaen, Magnus Nilsson, Enrique Olvera, Peeter Pihel, Thomas Rode Anderson, Pekka Terävä

Opening hours	6 days for lunch and dinner
Reservation policy	Yes
Credit cards	Accepted
Price range	Expensive
Style	Formal
Cuisine	Modern French
Recommended for	Wish I'd opened

'The best meal we have ever had.'—Dylan Jones and
Bo (Duangporn) Songvisava

LA COUR DE RÉMI

1 Rue Baillet
Bermicourt
Nord Pas-de-Calais 62130
+33 321033333
www.lacourderemi.com

Recommended by
Alexandre Gauthier

Opening hours	6 days for lunch and dinner
Reservation policy	Yes
Reservation email	sebastien@lacourderemi.com
Credit cards	Accepted
Price range	Affordable
Style	Smart casual
Cuisine	Northern French
Recommended for	Regular neighbourhood

LE CHATILLON

6 Rue Charles Tellier
Boulogne-sur-Mer
Nord Pas-de-Calais 62200
+33 321314395
www.le-chatillon.com

Recommended by
Alexandre Gauthier

Opening hours	5 days for breakfast and lunch
Reservation policy	Yes
Credit cards	Accepted
Price range	Budget
Style	Casual
Cuisine	Seafood
Recommended for	Local favourite

LA GRENOUILLÈRE

Rue de la Grenouillère
La Madelaine-sous-Montreuil
Nord Pas-de-Calais 62170
www.lagrenouillere.fr

Recommended by
Armand Arnal,
Daniel Boulud,
Yves Camdeborde,
Kobe Desramaults,
Arabelle Meirlaen, Carlo
Mirarchi, Michel Troisgros

Opening hours	4 days for lunch and 6 days for dinner
Reservation policy	Yes
Reservation email	contact@lagrenouillere.fr
Credit cards	Accepted
Price range	Expensive
Style	Formal
Cuisine	Modern French
Recommended for	Local favourite

'I was dazzled by the meal I had here – daring cooking
but oh so great. The whole place is an experience.'
—Kobe Desramaults

The Auberge de la Grenouillère opened as early as 1920 in the pretty village of Montreuil-sur-Mer, a few miles from Le Touquet. It once specialized in dishes involving frogs but, at least since 2003 – when chef Alexandre Gauthier (then just twenty-three years old) took over the kitchen from his father – the cuisine has ranged far wider. Gauthier's cooking is bold and vigorous: Norway lobster comes with vanilla and galangal, Licques pigeon with crisp asparagus, a whole baby squid with fig purée and chives. One of the best restaurants in this part of France.

CAFÉ DES FÉDÉRATIONS

Recommended by
Henry Harris

8 Rue du Major-Martin
Le Touquet
Nord Pas-de-Calais 69001
+33 478282600
www.lesfedeslyon.com

Opening hours	6 days for lunch and dinner
Reservation policy	Yes
Credit cards	Accepted
Price range	Budget
Style	Casual
Cuisine	Lyonnaise
Recommended for	Bargain

LES CIMAISES

Recommended by
Alexandre Gauthier

Westminster Hotel and Spa
Avenue du Verger
Le Touquet
Nord Pas-de-Calais 62520
+33 321054848
www.westminster.fr

Opening hours	7 days for breakfast, lunch and dinner
Reservation policy	Yes
Credit cards	Accepted
Price range	Affordable
Style	Casual
Cuisine	Northern French
Recommended for	Breakfast

COUTANCEAU

Recommended by
Philippe Rochat

Plage de la Concurrence
La Rochelle
Poitou-Charentes 17000
+33 546414819
www.coutanceaularochelle.com

Opening hours	6 days for lunch and dinner
Reservation policy	Yes
Reservation email	coutanceau@relaischateaux.com
Credit cards	Accepted
Price range	Expensive
Style	Smart casual
Cuisine	Modern French
Recommended for	Worth the travel

L'ATELIER DE JEAN LUC RABANEL

Recommended by
Christophe Michalak

7 Rue des Carmes
Arles
Provence-Alps-Côte d'Azur 13200
+33 490910769
www.rabanel.com

Opening hours	5 days for lunch and dinner
Reservation policy	Yes
Reservation email	contact@rabanel.com
Credit cards	Accepted
Price range	Expensive
Style	Casual
Cuisine	Modern French
Recommended for	Worth the travel

'I tasted Jean-Luc Rabanel's cooking (all organic) and I was totally amazed.'—Christophe Michalak

With a fourth address just opened, it looks like Jean-Luc Rabanel is playing real-life Monopoly on Rue des Carmes, a cute, paved pedestrian street in the heart of old Arles. After his much acclaimed experimental gastro L'Atelier (two Michelin stars), in 2009, came A Coté, cooking probably the best Camargue bull steak in the region – and it is everywhere. At Iode, a neo-fishmongers squished between the two, you can eat in à la plancha, take away the gorgeous seafood platters or have them sent over if you're staying in town. And now l'hyperchef gives us Le Bar à Nel's, a champagne and dessert bar open to members of Le Cercle Rouge, designed to start or prolong an evening spent in one of the next doors.

LE GIBOLIN

Recommended by
Armand Arnal

13 Rue des Porcelets
Arles
Provence-Alps-Côte d'Azur 13200
+33 488654314

Opening hours	5 days for lunch and dinner
Reservation policy	Yes
Credit cards	Not accepted
Price range	Affordable
Style	Casual
Cuisine	French Bistro
Recommended for	Regular neighbourhood

LE GRAND RESTAURANT

Recommended by
Jerome Lorvellec

Auberge La Fenière
Route de Lourmarin
Cadenet
Provence-Alpes-Côte d'Azur 84160
+33 490681179
www.reinesammut.com

Opening hours	5 days for lunch and dinner
Reservation policy	Yes
Reservation email	contact@aubergelafeniere.com
Credit cards	Accepted
Price range	Expensive
Style	Smart casual
Cuisine	Mediterranean
Recommended for	Local favourite

RESTAURANT XAVIER MATHIEU

Recommended by
Chakall

Le Phébus & Spa
Route de Murs
Joucas
Provence-Alpes-Côte d'Azur 84220
+33 490057883
www.lephebus.com

Opening hours	4 days for lunch and 7 days for dinner
Reservation policy	Yes
Credit cards	Accepted
Price range	Expensive
Style	Smart casual
Cuisine	Mediterranean
Recommended for	High end

OUSTAU DE BAUMANIÈRE

Recommended by
Armand Arnal

Les Baux-de-Provence
Provence-Alpes-Côte d'Azur 13520
+33 490543307
www.oustaudebaumaniere.com

Opening hours	7 days for lunch and dinner
Reservation policy	Yes
Credit cards	Accepted
Price range	Expensive
Style	Smart casual
Cuisine	Modern French
Recommended for	High end

CHEZ SAUVEUR

Recommended by
Michel Portos

10 Rue d'Aubagne
Marseille
Provence-Alpes-Côte d'Azur 13001
+33 491543396
www.chezsauveur.fr

Opening hours	5 days for lunch and dinner
Reservation policy	No
Credit cards	Accepted
Price range	Budget
Style	Casual
Cuisine	Pizza
Recommended for	Regular neighbourhood

One of Marseille's oldest pizzerias, nothing much has changed at Chez Sauveur since it opened back in 1943. The wood-fired pizzas still come out of the original oven, and are prepared to exactly the same recipe – the only difference being that these days the ads lining the walls have become fashionably 'vintage'. Although the young owner has attracted a hipper clientele of late, this remains a family-friendly neighbourhood favourite, with diners of all ages enjoying Sicilian specialities like chaussons and calzoni. If too packed to find a place, you can also get your Marguerite or Meridionale to go.

LE PETIT NICE PASSÉDAT

Recommended by
Michel Portos

Anse de Maldormé
Corniche J.F. Kennedy
Marseille
Provence-Alps-Côte d'Azur 13007
www.petitnice-passedat.com

Opening hours	6 days for lunch and dinner
Reservation policy	Yes
Credit cards	Accepted
Price range	Expensive
Style	Smart casual
Cuisine	Seafood
Recommended for	Wish I'd opened

Gérald Passédat was born in this neo-Greek villa, purchased by his grandfather, and continues to draw inspiration from its spectacular views of the Mediterranean. Apt to go into a paean about the personality of the little-known fish (the 'solitary' comber, the 'flirtatious' wrasse) that form the basis of his three-star cooking, Passédat reserves his greatest passion for his cult take on southern favourite bouillabaisse. The corner table has impressive panoramic views – as does the terrace where you can swim and sip pastis, should you opt for a night in one of the hotel's restful suites.

LE MIRAZUR

Recommended by
Sasu Laukkonen

30 Avenue Aristide Briand
Menton
Provence-Alps-Côte d'Azur 06500
www.mirazur.fr

Opening hours	5 days for lunch and dinner
Reservation policy	Yes
Credit cards	Accepted
Price range	Expensive
Style	Formal
Cuisine	Modern Provençal
Recommended for	Worth the travel

Le Mirazur overlooks the gleaming Côte d'Azur, metres (yards) from Italy's border. 'Food's aromas awaken the oldest memories' believes Argentinian head chef Mauro Colagreco, who left home for France to learn the 'building blocks of cuisine' with Alain Ducasse, Alain Passard and the late Bernard Loiseau. He breathed life back into a shell that had been closed for years, sowing an edible garden in the process. Colagreco's South American heritage is evident in ingredients such as quinoa, mate (for macaroons) and dulce de leche, although dishes such as the deconstructed Vietnamese spring roll show Colagreco's increasing interest in Asia.

LA BASTIDE DE MOUSTIERS

Recommended by
Michael Kempf

Chemin de Quinson
Moustiers-Sainte-Marie
Provence-Alps-Côte d'Azur 04360
+33 492704747
www.bastide-moustiers.com

Opening hours	7 days for lunch and dinner
Reservation policy	Yes
Credit cards	Accepted
Price range	Expensive
Style	Smart casual
Cuisine	Provençal
Recommended for	Worth the travel

LA MERENDA

Recommended by
Mauro Colagreco

4 Rue Raoul Bosio
Nice
Provence-Alpes-Côte d'Azur 06000

Opening hours	5 days for lunch and dinner
Reservation policy	Yes
Credit cards	Not accepted
Price range	Affordable
Style	Casual
Cuisine	Niçoise
Recommended for	Local favourite

'Very good Cuisine Niçoise.'—Mauro Colagreco

Cash only, no phone, closed every weekend, tiny and quirky, La Merenda in Nice's Old Town is one of a kind. Dominique Le Stanc, who previously ran the star-studded Le Chantecler, took it over in the mid-1990s as a going concern that had been serving simple Niçoise cuisine for some twenty years. He changed very little. All the cooking is done solo from the simple, open kitchen at the back. The menu, scrawled on a blackboard, is a short selection of local classics that, depending on the time of year, might include *pâtes au pistou*, *tripes à la Niçoise* and *tarte aux blettes*.

VOYAGEUR NISSART

Recommended by
Alexis Gauthier

19 Rue Alsace Lorraine
Nice
Provence-Alpes-Côte d'Azur 06000
+33 493821960
www.voyageurnissart.com

Opening hours..............5 days for lunch and 6 days for dinner
Reservation policy..Yes
Credit cards...Accepted
Price range..Budget
Style...Casual
Cuisine...Niçoise
Recommended for..Bargain

LE BISTROT DU PARADOU

Recommended by
Henry Harris

57 Avenue Vallée des Baux
Paradou
Provence-Alps-Côte d'Azur 13520
+33 490543270

Opening hours......................5 days for lunch and dinner
Reservation policy..Yes
Credit cards...Accepted
Price range..Affordable
Style...Casual
Cuisine..Provençal
Recommended for.....................................Worth the travel

LA REMISE

Recommended by
Jacques Marcon

Le Pont de l'Huile
Antraigues-sur-Volane
Rhone-Alps 07530
+33 475387074

Opening hours......................7 days for lunch and dinner
Reservation policy..Yes
Credit cards...Accepted
Price range..Affordable
Style...Casual
Cuisine..Eastern French
Recommended for...Wish I'd opened

Run by former rally racer Yves Jouanny, this temple
to Ardèche cuisine is the pit stop of choice for Monte
Carlo sports stars and their glittering entourage – if
you arrive in mid-January expect the hum of motors
out front. Jean Ferrat, the singer and poet, was a
friend of the establishment, and the rustic grange
– replete with majestic Formica counter – bears the

portraits of La Remise's many famous patrons. When
he's not charming the clientele, the mythic Jouanny
tends to a menu – such as pork terrine, asparagus
soufflé and fruit tart – based on the availability of
seasonal, local ingredients, washed down with
robust regional wines.

L'AUBERGE DU PONT DE COLLONGES

Recommended by
Pierre Koffmann,
Jean-François Piège,
Mathieu Rostaing-Tayard

40 Quai de la Plage
Collonges-au-Mont-d'Or
Rhone-Alpes 69660
+33 472429090
www.bocuse.fr

Opening hours..................................7 days for lunch and dinner
Reservation policy..Yes
Credit cards...Accepted
Price range..Expensive
Style..Smart casual
Cuisine..French
Recommended for..................................Wish I'd opened

'Wow, a genius.'—Pierre Koffmann

LE BOIS FLEURI

Recommended by
Guillaume Monjuré

L'Hôtel du Golf
Les Ritons
Corrençon-en-Vercors
Rhone-Alps 38250
+33 476958484
www.hotel-du-golf-vercors.fr

Opening hours..............2 days for lunch and 7 days for dinner
Reservation policy..Yes
Credit cards...Accepted
Price range..Expensive
Style..Smart casual
Cuisine..Modern French
Recommended for..................................Regular neighbourhood

'Family atmosphere and a superb wine list.'
—Guillaume Monjuré

HOSTELLERIE DU PORT DE GROSLÉE

Recommended by
Guy Savoy

Le Port
Groslée
Rhone-Alps 01680
+33 474397101
www.hostellerieduportdegroslee.fr

Opening hours	7 days for lunch and 6 days for dinner
Reservation policy	Yes
Credit cards	Accepted
Price range	Affordable
Style	Casual
Cuisine	Eastern French
Recommended for	Bargain

LA BRASSERIE GEORGES

Recommended by
Mathieu Rostaing-Tayard

30 Cours de Verdun Perrache
Lyon
Rhone-Alps 69002
+33 472565454
www.brasseriegeorges.com

Opening hours	7 days for lunch and dinner
Reservation policy	Yes
Credit cards	Accepted
Price range	Affordable
Style	Casual
Cuisine	Lyonnaise
Recommended for	Late night

This shrine to Lyonnaise gastronomy, the oldest brasserie in the city, does everything on a large scale – be it the 650-odd covers, or the fact that it once served the biggest sauerkraut in the world. Beneath the lustrous frescoes of this Art Deco brasserie, Ernest Hemingway, Paul Verlaine and Jacques Brel spent many a night nursing the Brasserie's home brew – a tradition since its inception, when Lyon water was considered of impeccable quality. These days the luminaries may be gone, but Brasserie Georges remains a buzzing place to while away an evening over regional specialities like tripe with *pommes Lyonnais* and Lyon sausage with pistachio.

GEORGES FIVE

Recommended by
Guillaume Monjuré

32 Rue du Boeuf
Lyon
Rhone-Alps 69005
+33 472402330
www.georgesfive.com

Opening hours	5 days for dinner
Reservation policy	Yes
Credit cards	Accepted
Price range	Affordable
Style	Casual
Cuisine	Mediterranean
Recommended for	Local favourite

'Excellent meats and cheeses, superb selection of wine by the glass.'—Guillaume Monjuré

L'OURSON QUI BOIT

Recommended by
Guillaume Monjuré,
Roberta Sudbrack

23 Rue Royale
Lyon
Rhone-Alps 69001
+33 478272337

Opening hours	5 days for lunch and dinner
Reservation policy	Yes
Credit cards	Accepted
Price range	Budget
Style	Casual
Cuisine	Japanese-French
Recommended for	Worth the travel

'A spectacular chef, remarkable, honest and brave cooking.'—Roberta Sudbrack

LE PALÉGRIÉ

Recommended by
Mathieu Rostaing-Tayard

8 Rue Palais Grillet
Lyon
Rhone-Alps 69002
+33 478929484
www.palegrie.fr

Opening hours	5 days for lunch and 6 days for dinner
Reservation policy	Yes
Credit cards	Accepted
Price range	Affordable
Style	Casual
Cuisine	French bistro
Recommended for	Bargain

Owners Guillaume Monjuré and Chrystel Barnier have an impressive pedigree: he was head chef of Parisian bistro Le Goupil, and she was the first ever female sommelière in Morocco, during the time the pair spent at Marrakesh's Mamounia. Their first venture is a welcome addition to Lyon's thriving bistronomy scene, with a very reasonable set menu and, as you'd expect from Barnier's presence, a decent selection of regional wines. Dishes – salmon carpaccio, saddle of rabbit bone – are strictly dictated by the seasons, and such is the mustachioed Monjuré's delight in experimentation, they tend to evolve daily, inviting repeat visits.

LE POTAGER DES HALLES

Recommended by
Mathieu Rostaing-Tayard

3 Rue de la Martinière
Lyon
Rhone-Alps 69001
www.lepotagerdeshalles.com

Opening hours	5 days for lunch and dinner
Reservation policy	Yes
Credit cards	Accepted
Price range	Affordable
Style	Casual
Cuisine	Mediterranean
Recommended for	Regular neighbourhood

Having extended the Paris bistronomy trend south-wards, Bocuse disciple Frank Delhoum and his chef Floriant Rémont have conquered the palates of Lyon locals, even adding a brasserie next door in 2010. Wrench your eyes from the view – the vast Fresque des Lyonnais, a trompe-l'oeil mural of an entire building, lies opposite – and there's plenty to admire

on the daily blackboard set menu too. Flavours tend towards the Mediterranean with an accent on fresh market produce, and Delhoum prides himself on grandmother-style hospitality, so portions are generous. For more finicky eaters, there's an à la carte menu available in the evenings.

RESTAURANT DANIEL ET DENISE

Recommended by
Mathieu
Rostaing-Tayard

156 Rue de Créqui
Lyon
Rhone-Alps 69003
+33 478606653
www.daniel-et-denise.fr

Opening hours	5 days for lunch and dinner
Reservation policy	Yes
Credit cards	Accepted
Price range	Affordable
Style	Casual
Cuisine	Lyonnaise
Recommended for	Regular neighbourhood

For those in search of real Lyonnaise cuisine, this venue in the city's historic *bouchon* tradition is a pretty good place to start. Set up in medieval times to cater for workers' appetites, *bouchons* are as offal (variety meat)-heavy as the nose to tail brigade, so lovers of veal brain, sweetbreads, tripe and the like will have their pick of the menu. The desserts – crème brûlée and île flottante – are as reassuring as the red and white chequered tablecloths, making the place so popular with locals you'll need to reserve in advance. It's a shame for weekenders that it's closed on Saturdays and Sundays.

RUE LE BEC

Recommended by
Mathieu Rostaing-Tayard

43 Quai Rambaud
Lyon
Rhone-Alps 69002
+33 478928787
www.nicolaslebec.com

Opening hours	6 days for lunch and 5 days for dinner
Reservation policy	Yes
Credit cards	Accepted
Price range	Affordable
Style	Casual
Cuisine	Modern French
Recommended for	Breakfast

Europe's largest urban redevelopment project – La Confluence, situated at the junction of the Rhône and Saône rivers – needed a suitably slick eatery, and in Nicholas Le Bec's two-star concept establishment, that's just what it got. Stylishly modelled on a local shopping street, it features a deli, *boulangerie*, florist and pottery store, with a mezzanine encircling the downstairs restaurant area. If you just want a glass of Beaujolais and wagyu beef, it's sufficiently casual, but gourmets particularly rate the Sunday brunch. The fixed-price menu isn't cheap, but you can take your pick from a vast buffet, including top-quality champagne, tuna tartare and prime French cheese.

FLOCONS DE SEL

Recommended by
Eric Frechon, Jacques
Marcon, Guillaume Monjuré,
Mathieu Rostaing-Tayard

1775 Route de Leutaz
Megève
Rhone-Alps 74120
+33 450214999
www.floconsdesel.com

Opening hours	5 days for lunch and dinner
Reservation policy	Yes
Credit cards	Accepted
Price range	Expensive
Style	Smart casual
Cuisine	Modern French
Recommended for	Worth the travel

'Perfect for a getaway. Have the vegetable millefeuille, fera fish from Lake Geneva, and finish with the chocolate dome flambéed with Pear William.'
—Guillaume Monjuré

Having manned the kitchens at Paris's uber-luxury Hotel Crillon and London's Claridge's, Emmanuel Renaut sought a more tranquil canvas for his talents. His choice – an alpine chalet with a handful of high-end design rooms and a spa offering treatments based on the chef's favourite plants – paid off, and in 2012 he scooped a third Michelin star. Today, skiers and gourmets from Geneva can get a workout with the two-and-a-quarter hour, nine-course 'hike' menu, typically immersed in the locale, with Lake Geneva fish, Savoie biscuit (cracker) and mountain cheese. Up here the air is rarefied, but, then again, so is Renaut's cuisine.

LE REFUGE

Recommended by
Emmanuel Renaut

2615 Route Leutaz
Megève
Rhone-Alps 74120
+33 450212304
www.refuge-megeve.com

Opening hours	7 days for lunch and dinner
Reservation policy	Yes
Credit cards	Accepted
Price range	Budget
Style	Casual
Cuisine	French bistro
Recommended for	Bargain

'A mountain bistro in the middle of nowhere with a warm and rustic atmosphere. The chef offers traditional, simple and tasty cuisine at an inexpensive price. It is a very good set up.'—Emmanuel Renaut

LA SAUVAGEONNE

Recommended by
Emmanuel Renaut

Hameau du Leutaz
Megève
Rhone-Alps 74120
+33 450919081
www.sauvageonne-megeve.com

Opening hours	7 days for lunch and dinner
Reservation policy	Yes
Credit cards	Accepted
Price range	Affordable
Style	Smart casual
Cuisine	French-Asian
Recommended for	Late night

'The hot spot for nights in Megève.'—Emmanuel Renaut

AUX ANGES

Recommended by
Michel Troisgros

6 Place Georges Clemenceau
Roanne
Rhone-Alps 42300
+33 477781985
www.aux-anges.com

Opening hours	6 days for lunch and 5 days for dinner
Reservation policy	Yes
Credit cards	Accepted
Price range	Affordable
Style	Smart casual
Cuisine	Modern French
Recommended for	Regular neighbourhood

MAISON TROISGROS

Place Jean Troisgros
Roanne
Rhone-Alps 42300
+33 477716697
www.troisgros.fr

Recommended by
Armand Arnal, Yves
Camdeborde, Claus Meyer,
Christophe Michalak, Lisa
Muncan, Patrick O'Connell,
Michel Portos, Theo Randall,
Josep Roca, Takuji Takahashi

Opening hours	5 days for lunch and dinner
Reservation policy	Yes
Reservation email	info@troisgros.com
Credit cards	Accepted
Price range	Expensive
Style	Formal
Cuisine	French
Recommended for	Worth the travel

'Some of the most incredible food I have eaten.
Absolute perfection but still very interesting. '
—Theo Randall

Maison Troisgros represents the epitome of the
finest and most traditional haute cuisine. The Trois
gros family is one of France's best-known culinary
dynasties, with a cooking heritage spanning more
than eighty years, of which their flagship restaurant
has held three Michelin stars for an impressive
forty-five. With Michel behind the stove the cooking
has become less fussy but no less produce focused.
Many restaurants today make great boasts of
creating menus 'according to what is available in
the market' but MT was doing it when they were
still in their infancy and is still the master of ad
hoc hospitality.

LA TABLE DU TERROIR

L'Auberge Jean-François Chanéac
Sagnes-et-Goudoulet
Rhone-Alps 07450
www.auberge-chaneac.fr

Recommended by
Jacques Marcon

Opening hours	5 days for lunch and dinner
Reservation policy	Yes
Credit cards	Accepted
Price range	Affordable
Style	Casual
Cuisine	Eastern French
Recommended for	Bargain

It's not hard to imagine what Jean-François
Chanéac's grandfather saw in the location of this
auberge, set amid the unspoiled nature of the
Ardèche. Two generations on, the former tavern
with rooms has a fine line in local cuisine, too, with

the picturesque backdrop doubling as a local larder
(pantry). Chef-owner Jean-François's generous
menu, inspired by the ingredients discovered on his
countryside walks, sticks to traditional classics such
as marbled foie gras and Ardèche trout. In winter,
with the open fire roaring, fans come in numbers for
his Maôche: a dish of pig stomach stuffed with
cabbage, it's almost as old as the mountains.

LE NEUVIÈME ART

Place du 19 Mars 1962
Saint-Just-Saint-Rambert
Rhone-Alps 42170
+33 477558715
www.leneuviemeart.com

Recommended by
Jacques Marcon

Opening hours	5 days for lunch and dinner
Reservation policy	Yes
Reservation email	reservation@leneuviemeart.com
Credit cards	Accepted
Price range	Expensive
Style	Smart casual
Cuisine	Modern French
Recommended for	Worth the travel

It's a fair bet that many who make the trip to
Christophe Roure's two-star establishment, located
in a former train station with tracks out front, would
be prepared to quibble with the 'ninth art' designating
comic strips. The restaurant was founded in 2003, but
the minimal space, decorated with abstract art, has
been gaining increasing attention for its brand of
contemporary French cuisine. A disciple of Paul
Bocuse and Pierre Gagnaire, the talented Roure uses
the best suppliers in the business – like top cheese
house Fromagerie Mons – to craft visually creative
dishes such as crab cannelloni with basmati rice
mousse, nori algae and Kristal caviar.

UMIA

Domaine Gambert de Loche
2 Rue de la Petite Pierrelle
Tain l'Hermitage
Rhone-Alps 26600
+33 475091985
www.umia.fr

Recommended by
Riki Mizukami

Opening hours	4 days for lunch and 5 days for dinner
Reservation policy	Yes
Credit cards	Accepted
Price range	Affordable
Style	Casual
Cuisine	French-Japanese
Recommended for	Wish I'd opened

MAISON PIC

285 Avenue Victor Hugo
Valence
Rhone-Alps 26000
+33 475441532
www.pic-valence.fr

Opening hours	5 days for lunch and dinner
Reservation policy	Yes
Credit cards	Accepted
Price range	Expensive
Style	Formal
Cuisine	Modern French
Recommended for	High end

Located on the Route Nationale 7 (the road provides the name of the trendy on-site bistro), the century-old Maison Pic has always been on gastro-tourists' radar. Home to one of France's oldest kitchen dynasties, these days it's run by Ann-Sophie Pic – the only woman in France with three Michelin stars (although her ancestors had already won and lost that many twice). Such pedigree is worked into the boutique hotel's design, which features the Pic family's photo archive. In the restaurant, the 'Pic Collection' menu exemplifies Ann-Sophie's perfectionist streak, with dishes like moules marinières with liquorice striving to outdo the over-achieving Pics of the past.

NOUVELLE MAISON DE MARC VEYRAT

13 Vieille Route des Pensieres
Veyrier-Du-Lac
Rhone-Alps 74290
www.yoann-conte.com

Opening hours	5 days for lunch and 4 days for dinner
Reservation policy	Yes
Credit cards	Accepted
Price range	Expensive
Style	Formal
Cuisine	Modern French
Recommended for	High end

GEORGES BLANC

Place du Marché
Vonnas
Rhone-Alps 01540
+33 474509090
www.georgesblanc.com

Opening hours	3 days for lunch and 5 days for dinner
Reservation policy	Yes
Reservation email	reservation@georgesblanc.com
Credit cards	Accepted
Price range	Expensive
Style	Smart casual
Cuisine	French
Recommended for	Worth the travel

LE LOUIS XV

Place du Casino
Monte-Carlo
Monaco 9800
+377 98068864
www.alain-ducasse.com

Opening hours	5 days for lunch and dinner
Reservation policy	Yes
Credit cards	Accepted
Price range	Expensive
Style	Formal
Cuisine	Mediterranean
Recommended for	High end

'My expectations before I ate here were very high but the whole experience exceeded them.'
—Nathan Outlaw

The ultimate expression of Monégasque glamour, Le Louis XV, an opulent Versailles grand siècle-inspired palace of pleasure, opened in 1987, is perhaps the greatest achievement and defining project of Alain Ducasse's star-studded career. Leaving aside the swan-like service, a dining room in which Marie-Antoinette would have felt at home, the gilded handbag stools, the custom-made dinnerware and silverware, the 400,000-bottle cellar and a mineral water list longer then the average bistro's *carte du vin* – it's the quality of Riviera-led cooking, which takes the very best from sea, garden and farm, that remains at its luxurious heart.

PARIS

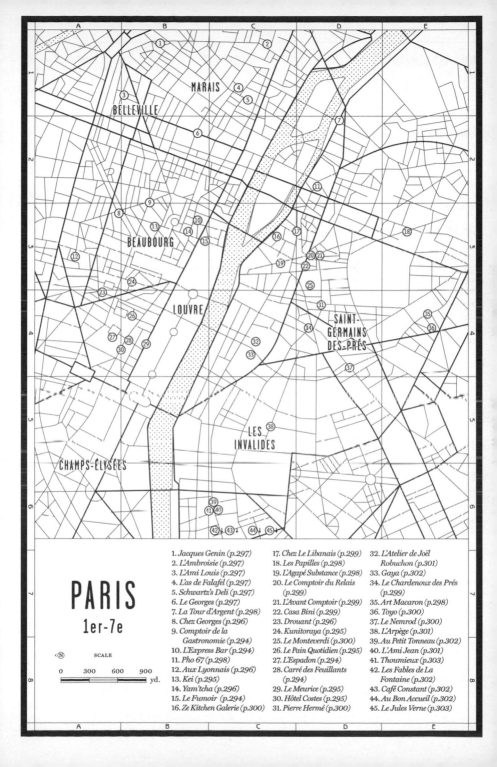

PARIS

1er–7e

‹N› SCALE

0   300   600   900
yd.

CARRÉ DES FEUILLANTS

Recommended by
Chakall

14 Rue de Castiglione
Paris 75001
+33 142868282
www.carredesfeuillants.fr

Opening hours.............5 days for lunch and 6 days for dinner
Reservation policy...Yes
Credit cards...Accepted
Price range...Expensive
Style...Smart casual
Cuisine...French
Recommended for.............................Worth the travel

'Amazing.'—Chakall

Never one to court the guidebooks or the French celebrity chef scene, preferring the corrida and rugby stadiums to Parisian kowtowing, Alain Dutournier stands resolutely firm with his two-Michelin-starred Carré des Feuillants. In its Alberto Bali decor, Dutournier's frank, jovial musketeer cooking, full of truffles, roast chicken, foie gras and epic cheeses, reassures the faithful clientele. Meanwhile, a second Pinxo – Dutournier's gastro-tapas concept – has opened nine years after the first, in Saint Germain des Prés, where a younger crowd squeeze together in a finger-licking, shared-plate scrum of Arcachon oysters, duck hearts grilled on the plancha and Landaise pie with prune ice cream.

COMPTOIR DE LA GASTRONOMIE

Recommended by
Paul Qui

34 Rue Montmartre
Paris 75001
+33 142333132
www.comptoirdelagastronomie.com

Opening hours.......................6 days for lunch and dinner
Reservation policy...Yes
Credit cards...Accepted
Price range...Affordable
Style..Casual
Cuisine..French bistro
Recommended for.............................Worth the travel

L'ESPADON

Recommended by
Jerome Lorvellec, Jean-
François Piège, Emmanuel
Renaut

Ritz Hotel
15 Place Vendôme
Paris 75001
+33 143163030
www.ritzparis.com

Opening hours.................................7 days for lunch and dinner
Reservation policy...Yes
Credit cards...Accepted
Price range...Expensive
Style...Formal
Cuisine...French
Recommended for..High end

'The French luxury which emanates from this place makes every moment exceptional and unforgettable.'—Jean-François Piège

L'EXPRESS BAR

Recommended by
Yves Camdeborde

23 Rue Roule
Paris 75001

Opening hours.......................6 days for lunch and dinner
Reservation policy..No
Credit cards...Not accepted
Price range..Budget
Style..Casual
Cuisine..French bistro
Recommended for...Late night

LE FUMOIR

Recommended by
Lisa Muncan

6 Rue de l'Amiral Coligny
Paris 75001
www.lefumoir.com

Opening hours.......................7 days for lunch and dinner
Reservation policy...Yes
Credit cards...Accepted
Price range...Affordable
Style..Casual
Cuisine..International
Recommended for.............................Worth the travel

One of the first of Paris's lounge generation, Le Fumoir has held its own so well it's becoming an institution. The tall windows of the restaurant and British club feel in the library bar pour some cool on the lofty surroundings. It's great for lazy newspaper reading over brunch, or for a sexier half-lit dinner which should leave you enough euros for a few cocktails at the bar afterwards. The risotto, pork belly with oysters and frozen cheesecake are very correct as they say in Paris. The efficient, verging on robotic, service goes with the territory.

HÔTEL COSTES

Recommended by
Paul Pairet

239 Rue Saint-Honoré
Paris 75001
+33 142445000
www.hotelcostes.com

Opening hours	7 days for breakfast, lunch and dinner
Reservation policy	Yes
Credit cards	Accepted
Price range	Expensive
Style	Smart casual
Cuisine	French
Recommended for	Worth the travel

KEI

Recommended by
Lisa Muncan

5 Rue Coq Héron
Paris 75001
+33 142331474
www.restaurant-kei.fr

Opening hours	5 days for lunch and dinner
Reservation policy	Yes
Credit cards	Accepted but not AMEX and Diners
Price range	Affordable
Style	Smart casual
Cuisine	French-Japanese
Recommended for	Wish I'd opened

KUNITORAYA

Recommended by
Mauro Colagreco

39 Rue Sainte-Anne
Paris 75001
www.kunitoraya.com

Opening hours	7 days for lunch and dinner
Reservation policy	No
Credit cards	Not accepted
Price range	Affordable
Style	Casual
Cuisine	Japanese
Recommended for	Bargain

'Good, simple, fast and cheap.'—Mauro Colagreco

Twenty years ago Japanese chef Masafumi Nomoto introduced Parisians to the delights of slurping cheap, fat udon noodles in his packed out, no-reservations canteen, Kunitoraya. Now it's been re-christened Kunitoraya 1, as Nomoto has taken over Chez Pauline, the famous ex-*haut lieu* of Burgundy cuisine across the street. The noodle, hot or cold, remains the star, but in this unlikely decor of imposing 1900s brasserie mirrors, wall clocks and dark wood panelling you can now book a table for excellent tempura or *onigiri*. In the evenings the chef sends out his small-plate feast of sashimis, whelks and leeks in miso sauce or grated radish with broad (fava) beans.

LE MEURICE

Recommended by
Walter Manzke,
Esther Sham

Meurice Hotel
228 Rue de Rivoli
Paris 75001
+33 144581055
www.lemeurice.com

Opening hours	5 days for breakfast, lunch and dinner
Reservation policy	Yes
Credit cards	Accepted
Price range	Expensive
Style	Formal
Cuisine	Modern French
Recommended for	Worth the travel

'I love chef Yannick Alléno's style of cuisine, so full of flavour and yet delicately light.'—Esther Sham

LE PAIN QUOTIDIEN

Recommended by
Christian Ebbe

18 Place du Marché Saint Honoré
Paris 75001
www.lepainquotidien.co.uk

Opening hours	7 days from breakfast until late
Reservation policy	No
Credit cards	Accepted
Price range	Budget
Style	Casual
Cuisine	Bakery-Café
Recommended for	Breakfast

YAM'TCHA

Recommended by
Eduardo Moreno

4 Rue Sauval
Paris 75001
+33 140260807
www.yamtcha.com

Opening hours	5 days for lunch and dinner
Reservation policy	Yes
Credit cards	Accepted
Price range	Affordable
Style	Smart casual
Cuisine	French-Chinese
Recommended for	Wish I'd opened

Adeline Grattard spent three years with Pascal Barbot at L'Astrance, and three in restaurants in China. In 2009 she pitched her twenty-cover, verging-on-austere restaurant perfectly as Paris moved on from traditional French high-end formality and woke up to post-sushi Asian diversity and raffinement. With her husband Chi Wan, cooking from a minuscule open kitchen – 'we want to stay in touch with our clients as if we were all at home' – she offers just one service an evening. Like a sommelier, Chi Wan matches his teas (there's a wine list too) to Grattard's breathtakingly sensual cooking – Challans duck, aubergines (eggplants) *à la schezuanaise*, cockles sautéed with black soya.

AUX LYONNAIS

Recommended by
Kamal Mouzawak

32 Rue Saint Marc
Paris 75002
+33 142966504
www.auxlyonnais.com

Opening hours	4 days for lunch and 5 days for dinner
Reservation policy	Yes
Reservation email	auxlyonnais@free.fr
Credit cards	Accepted
Price range	Affordable
Style	Smart casual
Cuisine	French bistro
Recommended for	Worth the travel

CHEZ GEORGES

Recommended by
Fergus Henderson,
Jeremy Lee

1 Rue du Mail
Paris 75002
+33 0142600711

Opening hours	5 days for lunch and dinner
Reservation policy	Yes
Credit cards	Accepted
Price range	Affordable
Style	Casual
Cuisine	French bistro
Recommended for	Worth the travel

Paris is coming down with establishments that go by the name of Chez Georges. While the Latin Quarter's Chez Georges old school caves bar is certainly worth stopping by for *un verre* or *deux*, the chances are that if anyone recommends a Chez Georges they're most likely talking about this Bourse bistro. Opened by Georges Brouillet back in 1964, you get the impression that very little has changed since – from the menu crammed with comforting bourgeois classics to its well-heeled regulars. Although, admittedly, the latter now have to grudgingly share the invariably packed, long narrow room with camera-happy tourists.

DROUANT

Recommended by
Raphael Dworak

16-18 Place Gaillon
Paris 75002
+33 142651516
www.drouant.com

Opening hours	7 days for lunch and dinner
Reservation policy	Yes
Credit cards	Accepted
Price range	Expensive
Style	Formal
Cuisine	French
Recommended for	Regular neighbourhood

'I like its cuisine-simple and gourmande.'
—Raphael Dworak

L'AMI LOUIS

32 Rue du Vertbois
Paris 75003
+33 148877748

Recommended by
Yves Camdeborde, Eric
Frechon, Francis Mallmann,
Ruth Rogers, Guy Savoy,
Mitchell Tonks

Opening hours..................................5 days for lunch and dinner
Reservation policy...Yes
Credit cards...Accepted
Price range...Expensive
Style...Smart casual
Cuisine...French bistro
Recommended for...High end

JACQUES GENIN

133 Rue de Turenne
Paris 75003
www.jacquesgenin.fr

Recommended by
Eduardo Moreno

Opening hours..................................6 days for lunch and dinner
Reservation policy..No
Credit cards...Accepted
Price range..Affordable
Style..Casual
Cuisine...Pastries
Recommended for.......................................Worth the travel

'If you're after something sweet, you have to try the
mango-passion fruit caramels at Jacques Genin.'
—Eduardo Moreno

L'AMBROISIE

9 Place des Vosges
Paris 75004
+33 142785145
www.ambroisie-placedesvosges.com

Recommended by
Eric Frechon, Daniel Humm,
Patrick O'Connell

Opening hours..................................5 days for lunch and dinner
Reservation policy...Yes
Credit cards...Accepted
Price range...Expensive
Style...Formal
Cuisine...French
Recommended for.......................................Worth the travel

'Dining at L'Ambroisie is like going back in time.
Although the food is very French and very classic,
it still has a sense of modernity to it. The setting
hasn't changed all that much which is part of the
appeal. Whenever I go there, I feel like it grounds
me in some sense, like it's taking me back to my roots.
I truly love going there—no other restaurant celebrates
luxury ingredients as well as L'Ambroisie does.'
—Daniel Humm

L'AS DE FALAFEL

34 Rue des Rosiers
Paris 75004
+33 148876360

Recommended by
Petter Nilsson

Opening hours..................................6 days for lunch and dinner
Reservation policy..No
Credit cards...Accepted
Price range...Budget
Style..Casual
Cuisine..North African
Recommended for..Bargain

LE GEORGES

Center Georges Pompidou
19 Rue Beaubourg
Paris 75004
+33 144784799
www.maisonthierrycostes.com

Recommended by
Jacques and Laurent Pourcel

Opening hours..................................6 days for lunch and dinner
Reservation policy...Yes
Credit cards...Accepted
Price range..Affordable
Style...Smart casual
Cuisine..International
Recommended for..Late night

SCHWARTZ'S DELI

16 Rue des Ecouffes
Paris 75004
www.schwartzsdeli.fr

Recommended by
Thierry Marx

Opening hours..................................7 days for lunch and dinner
Reservation policy..No
Credit cards...Accepted
Price range..Affordable
Style..Casual
Cuisine...American
Recommended for..Bargain

Now that Paris has not only discovered but begun
producing its very own gourmet burgers, Schwartz's
has faded somewhat into a comfortable semi-has-
been-ness. But the burgers are still among the best
value in Paris, and chefs nostalgic for New York diner
food can get big food, fast. At all three addresses the
menu includes all the usual American standards —
bagels, cheesecake, pastrami, Dr. Pepper — served
on red-checked tablecloths or at a high zinc bar.
A comforting cliché, with big portioned, unchalleng-
ing food that won't start a riot, perfect for hungry
chefs who sometimes need to switch off their brains
and palates, and simply get fed.

LES PAPILLES

Recommended by
Yves Camdeborde

30 Rue Gay-Lussac
Paris 75005
+33 143252079
www.lespapillesparis.fr

Opening hours	5 days for lunch and dinner
Reservation policy	Yes
Credit cards	Accepted
Price range	Affordable
Style	Casual
Cuisine	French bistro
Recommended for	Bargain

PHO 67

Recommended by
Eduardo Moreno

59 Rue Galande
Paris 75005

Opening hours	7 days for lunch and dinner
Reservation policy	No
Credit cards	Not accepted
Price range	Budget
Style	Casual
Cuisine	Vietnamese
Recommended for	Worth the travel

LA TOUR D'ARGENT

Recommended by
Pierre Gagnaire,
Alexis Gauthier

15 Quai de la Tournelle
Paris 75005
+33 143542331
www.latourdargent.com

Opening hours	5 days for lunch and dinner
Reservation policy	Yes
Credit cards	Accepted
Price range	Expensive
Style	Formal
Cuisine	French
Recommended for	Wish I'd opened

'For the constant show of pressing ducks in the dining room.'—Alexis Gauthier

L'AGAPÉ SUBSTANCE

Recommended by
Enrico & Roberto Cerea,
Eduardo Moreno

66 Rue Mazarine
Paris 75006
+33 143293383
www.agapesubstance.com

Opening hours	5 days for lunch and dinner
Reservation policy	Yes
Credit cards	Accepted
Price range	Affordable
Style	Smart casual
Cuisine	Modern French
Recommended for	Worth the travel

'Weird and vanguardist. There's only one table, which is large and high, it's uncomfortable, dark and expensive ... but it's worth the experience.'
— Eduardo Moreno

The concept of the open kitchen takes a leap forward at L'Agapé Substance, where, in a narrow Saint-Germain dining room, you effectively sit in the kitchen, perched either side of a long twenty-four-seat bench. David Toutain, whose credentials include spells at L'Arpège and, perhaps more tellingly, Mugaritz, is the envelope-pushing young chef at the helm. While its name – what's the best translation? Love Stuff? Material Love? – sounds like it's trying way too hard (it doesn't trip off the tongue any easier in French), the creative, market-driven menus that trawl the globe for inspiration don't come across as forced – rather, inspired.

ART MACARON

Recommended by
Julien Duboué

129 Boulevard du Montparnasse
Paris 75006
+33 143213249

Opening hours	6 days from breakfast until late
Reservation policy	Yes
Credit cards	Accepted
Price range	Budget
Style	Casual
Cuisine	Café
Recommended for	Breakfast

'A special place that is still part of the undiscovered paris. The excellent French toast and hot chocolate are a highlight. The macarons, the house speciality, are delicious.'—Julien Duboué

L'AVANT COMPTOIR

Recommended by
Julien Duboué, Alexandre
Gauthier

Relais Saint-Germain Hotel
9 Carrefour de l'Odéon
Paris 75006
www.hotel-paris-relais-saint-germain.com

Opening hours	7 days for lunch and dinner
Reservation policy	No
Credit cards	Accepted but not AMEX and Diners
Price range	Budget
Style	Smart casual
Cuisine	Small plates
Recommended for	Regular neighbourhood

'A place I go regularly with friends for it's tapas by the
star chef Ives Camdeborde. They have great natural
wines on their menu.'—Julien Duboué

CASA BINI

Recommended by
Pierre Gagnaire

36 Rue Grégoire de Tours
Paris 75006
+33 146340560
www.casabini.fr

Opening hours	5 days for lunch and dinner
Reservation policy	Yes
Credit cards	Accepted
Price range	Affordable
Style	Casual
Cuisine	Italian
Recommended for	Bargain

LE CHARDENOUX DES PRÉS

Recommended by
Jean-François Piège

27 Rue du Dragon
Paris 75006
+33 145482968
www.restaurantlechardenouxdespres.com

Opening hours	7 days for lunch and dinner
Reservation policy	Yes
Credit cards	Accepted
Price range	Affordable
Style	Smart casual
Cuisine	French
Recommended for	Local favourite

'Without a doubt this place represents Paris.'
—Jean-François Piège

A decade ago, Cyril Lignac became France's Jamie
Oliver by reproducing Jamie's TV formats in French.
The industry sneered, but for the past few years
Lignac has been gutsily earning back his chef's
colours by opening real, solid restaurants. His
sensitive takeover of Le Chardenoux des Prés has
been a success among the hard to please and
famously tight-fisted Germanopratins. Prices for
bistro favourites made chichi – croque monsieur de
luxe, raspberry and brioche pain perdu – soar if you
take the à la carte, but lunchtime's two-dish *prix fixe*
will take you for a good value stroll around the day's
market.

CHEZ LE LIBANAIS

Recommended by
Eduardo Moreno

35 Rue St-André-des-Arts
Paris 75006
+33 140460739
www.chezlelibanais.com

Opening hours	7 days from breakfast until late
Reservation policy	Yes
Credit cards	Accepted
Price range	Budget
Style	Casual
Cuisine	Lebanese
Recommended for	Late night

LE COMPTOIR DU RELAIS

Recommended by
Josef Centeno, Andreas
Dahlberg, Thierry Marx,
Carlo Mirarchi, Jean-
François Piège,
Emmanuel Renaut

Relais Saint Germain Hotel
9 Carrefour de l'Odéon
Paris 75006
+33 0144270797
www.hotel-paris-relais-saint-germain.com

Opening hours	7 days for lunch and dinner
Reservation policy	Yes
Credit cards	Accepted
Price range	Expensive
Style	Smart casual
Cuisine	French bistro
Recommended for	Worth the travel

'You can get lucky at lunch without a reservation and
I always recommend the pig's trotter (foot).'—Josef
Centeno

Yves Camdeborde is one of the founding fathers of
la bistronomie, the movement that dismissed starry
codes in favour of simple bistro cuisine made
gastronomic. Camdeborde's Comptoir has been a
Basque trailblazer of all things pig and has not
emptied since the day it opened. Such is Camdeborde's fame and reputation, you'll be hard pushed
to get a table. But he has thoughtfully opened a hotel
on one side – where you can stay and wait a day or
two to pounce – and the great Avant Comptoir, a
small plate and tapas stand-up counter, on the other,
when shoulder to shoulder's what you're after.

LE MONTEVERDI

5-7 Rue Guisarde
Paris 75006
+33 142345590
www.lemonteverdi.com

Opening hours	6 days for lunch and dinner
Reservation policy	Yes
Credit cards	Accepted
Price range	Affordable
Style	Smart casual
Cuisine	Italian
Recommended for	Regular neighbourhood

LE NEMROD

51 Rue du Cherche-Midi
Paris 75006
+33 145481705
www.lenemrod.com

Opening hours	7 days from breakfast until late
Reservation policy	Yes
Credit cards	Accepted but not AMEX and Diners
Price range	Affordable
Style	Casual
Cuisine	French bistro
Recommended for	Local favourite

PIERRE HERMÉ

72 Rue Bonaparte
Paris 75006
www.pierreherme.com

Opening hours	7 days from breakfast until late
Reservation policy	No
Credit cards	Accepted
Price range	Expensive
Style	Smart casual
Cuisine	Sweets-Pastries
Recommended for	High end

'Expensive but perfect! Certainly the best macaroons in the world.'—Christophe Michalak

TOYO

17 Rue Jules Chaplain
Paris 75006
+33 143542803

Opening hours	5 days for lunch and dinner
Reservation policy	Yes
Credit cards	Accepted but not AMEX and Diners
Price range	Affordable
Style	Smart casual
Cuisine	French-Japanese
Recommended for	Worth the travel

'Precise and delicate cooking.'—Roberta Sudbrack

ZE KITCHEN GALERIE

4 Rue des Grands-Augustins
Paris 75006
+33 144320032
www.zekitchengalerie.fr

Opening hours	5 days for lunch and 6 days for dinner
Reservation policy	Yes
Credit cards	Accepted
Price range	Expensive
Style	Smart casual
Cuisine	French-Asian
Recommended for	Worth the travel

William Ledeuil was one of the first French chefs to cook some sense into the existing chilli, cumin and lemongrass Asian fusion cacophony. When he opened Ze Kitchen Galerie in 2001 he had never been to the countries whose food was the foundation of his menu, learning everything from cookbooks and whatever he could glean from suppliers in Paris's 13th arrondissement. After years of researching, refining and spending time in the Far East, he won his Michelin star in 2008 and Gault et Millau Chef of the Year in 2010 for his cuisine, largely built around light, fragrant broths and emulsions. His restaurant filled with contemporary art brings flashes of ballsy colour to the hallowed greyness of Saint Germain des Prés.

L'AMI JEAN

27 Rue Malar
Paris 75007
+33 147058689
www.lamijean.fr

Opening hours	7 days for lunch and dinner
Reservation policy	Yes
Credit cards	Accepted
Price range	Affordable
Style	Casual
Cuisine	French bistro
Recommended for	Wish I'd opened

'It's an inspirational restaurant for me, not only because of Stephane Jego's food but the elbow-to-elbow energy of the place, and everyone enjoying every minute of it.'—Josef Centeno

Stéphane Jégo's pedigree (Christian Constant at the Crillon and Camdeborde at La Régalade) and talent make it tough to get a place at L'Ami Jean's famous farm table. Renowned for his roasts and braises, some of his meat dishes — like the Kobe Côté de boeuf or half-raw quail with head and beak intact — border on downright filthy. The decor is a bistro-punk layering of weird brown junk, in a room lit like a dentist's surgery (office). But clients' eyes are on their plates and, although prices are soaring, you get the feeling they'd gladly pay twice as much for another shot at Jégo's mythical rice pudding.

L'ARPÈGE

84 Rue de Varenne
Paris 75007
+33 0147050906
www.alain-passard.com

Opening hours	5 days for lunch and dinner
Reservation policy	Yes
Credit cards	Accepted
Price range	Expensive
Style	Formal
Cuisine	Modern French
Recommended for	High end

'Chef Passard is cooking on a completely different level right now and L'Arpège continues to be my 'must stop' whenever I'm in Paris.'—David Kinch

In 2001, Alain Passard raised an eyebrow or two among his countrymen when he took red meat off the menu at L'Arpège, pledging instead to explore the virtues of veg. Michelin didn't seem to mind. Chef Passard kept his trio of stars, bought a kitchen garden 230 km (140 miles) outside Paris and now ferries his organic harvest to the city early each morning to grace plates in the hushed dining room the same afternoon. There's flesh too — the duck is particularly fine — and the much-imitated 'hot-cold egg'. It all comes at a three-star price, so it's worth noting that the lunch *dégustation*, at less than half the price of the evening menu, is a more affordable way in.

L'ATELIER DE JOËL ROBUCHON

15 Rue de Montalembert
Paris 75007
+33 142225656
www.joel-robuchon.net

Opening hours	7 days for lunch and dinner
Reservation policy	Yes
Credit cards	Accepted but not Diners
Price range	Expensive
Style	Smart casual
Cuisine	French
Recommended for	High end

The concept may be dated now but the Asian feel, small-plate, chef-gawking counter that Robuchon created in 2003 conquered a sceptical Paris clientele. L'Atelier's door opens from the inside out, meaning staff control entry, and its booking system is a pain, but once inside its black lacquer cocoon with the sleek brigade busy making gorgeous five-bite morsels, all's well. No wonder the Ateliers took off — the menu allows clients a bit of luxurious every-thing. About twenty tasting plates on one side; on the other, larger mains and desserts. Stick to the small ones! After foie gras with verjuiced peppers, sweet-breads with bay and rosemary, and a couple of other taste poppers, the yuzu soufflé is a no-brainer.

AU BON ACCUEIL

14 Rue de Monttessuy
Paris 75007
+33 147054611
www.aubonaccueilparis.com

Opening hours	5 days for lunch and dinner
Reservation policy	Yes
Credit cards	Accepted
Price range	Affordable
Style	Casual
Cuisine	French bistro
Recommended for	Worth the travel

AU PETIT TONNEAU

20 Rue Surcouf
Paris 75007
+33 147050901

Opening hours	6 days for lunch and dinner
Reservation policy	Yes
Credit cards	Accepted
Price range	Affordable
Style	Casual
Cuisine	French bistro
Recommended for	Bargain

'A true Parisian bistro where you can eat good, traditional French food that's good value for money.'—Eric Frechon

CAFE CONSTANT

139 Rue Saint-Dominique
Paris 75007
+33 147537334
www.cafeconstant.com

Opening hours	6 days for breakfast, lunch and dinner
Reservation policy	No
Credit cards	Accepted
Price range	Affordable
Style	Casual
Cuisine	French bistro
Recommended for	Bargain

LES FABLES DE LA FONTAINE

131 Rue Saint Dominique
Paris 75007
+33 144183755
www.lesfablesdelafontaine.net

Opening hours	7 days for lunch and dinner
Reservation policy	Yes
Credit cards	Accepted
Price range	Affordable
Style	Smart casual
Cuisine	Seafood
Recommended for	Regular neighbourhood

'A small cosy Michelin starred restaurant where I go to eat when I'm looking for great seafood. The chef Sebastien Gravè is a good friend and a great cook.'—Julien Duboué

GAYA

44 Rue du Bac
Paris 75007
+33 145447373
www.pierre-gagnaire.com

Opening hours	6 days for lunch and dinner
Reservation policy	Yes
Reservation email	gaya8@wanadoo.fr
Credit cards	Accepted
Price range	Affordable
Style	Smart casual
Cuisine	Seafood
Recommended for	Wish I'd opened

'The young team at Gaya, led by Nicolas Fontaine, is full of passion and energy and is delivering great food!'—Tim Lai

LE JULES VERNE

Recommended by
Emmanuel Renaut

Eiffel Tower
Avenue Gustave Eiffel
Paris 75007
+33 145556144
www.lejulesverne-paris.com

Opening hours	7 days for lunch and dinner
Reservation policy	Yes
Credit cards	Accepted
Price range	Expensive
Style	Formal
Cuisine	Modern French
Recommended for	Wish I'd opened

'This restaurant always fascinates me. To open a restaurant in such a symbolic location is more than a chef can dream of.'—Emmanuel Renaut

THOUMIEUX

Recommended by
Yves Camdeborde, Julius
Jaspers, Pierre Koffmann,
Onno Kokmeijer, Christophe
Michalak

79 Rue Saint-Dominique
Paris 75007
+33 0147054975
www.thoumieux.fr

Opening hours	5 days for dinner
Reservation policy	Yes
Credit cards	Accepted
Price range	Expensive
Style	Smart casual
Cuisine	French bistro
Recommended for	Local favourite

'A top creative and modern kitchen.'
—Christophe Michalak

When wunderkind Thierry Costes (Café Etienne Marcel, Café Marly, Georges) teamed up with brazen ex-Crillon chef Jean-François Piège to transform this classic brasserie in the 7th arrondissement, the locals grumbled and the critics sneered but everybody else flocked. When they subsequently opened the excellent chef's table above the restaurant – instantly gaining two Michelin stars – revamped the rooms and Piège became a judge on French TV's Top Chef, things got serious. Now that the place is deliciously dark, noisy and louche, no one really cares whether they can see their (comfort) food. *Calamars à la carbonara*, eggiest crème caramel with dainty *langues de chat*, a type of biscuit (cookie), and stellar tartes are picked at by *le beau monde*.

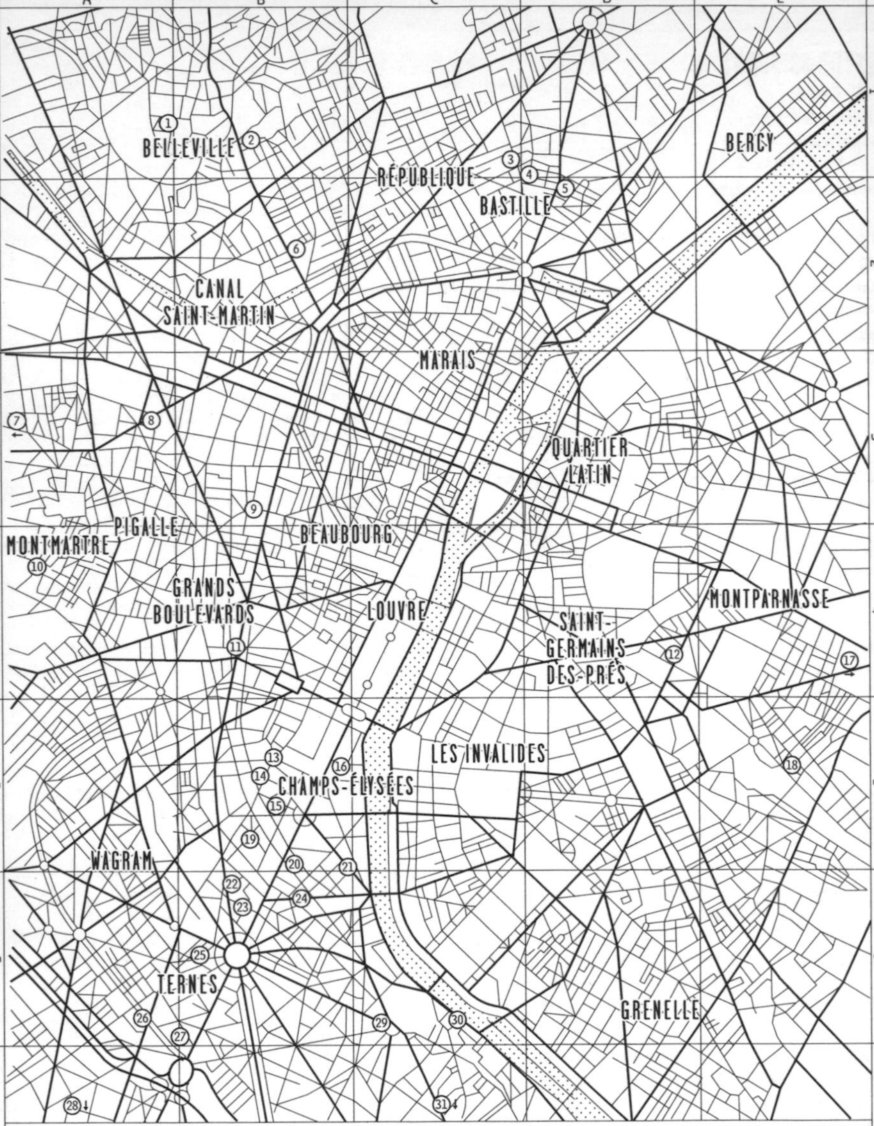

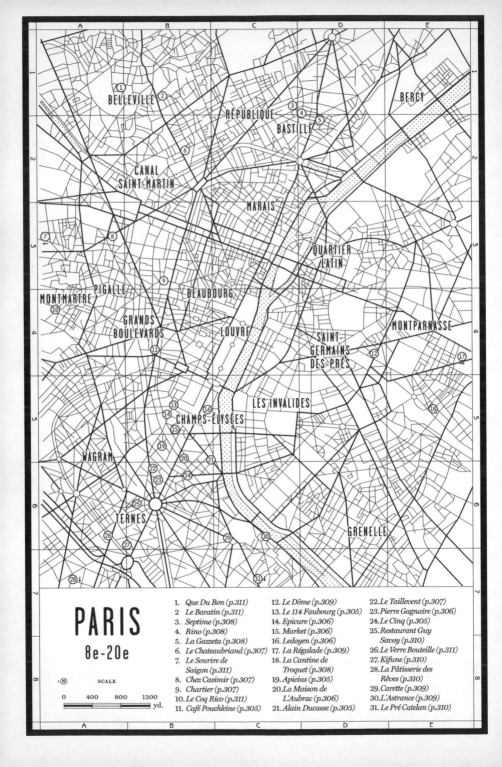

PARIS

8e-20e

SCALE

0 400 800 1200 yd.

1. *Que Du Bon (p.311)*
2 *Le Baratin (p.311)*
3. *Septime (p.308)*
4. *Rino (p.308)*
5. *La Gazzeta (p.308)*
6. *Le Chateaubriand (p.307)*
7. *Le Sourire de Saigon (p.311)*
8. *Chez Casimir (p.307)*
9. *Chartier (p.307)*
10. *Le Coq Rico (p.311)*
11. *Café Pouchkine (p.305)*
12. *Le Dôme (p.309)*
13. *Le 114 Faubourg (p.305)*
14. *Epicure (p.306)*
15. *Market (p.306)*
16. *Ledoyen (p.306)*
17. *La Régalade (p.309)*
18. *La Cantine de Troquet (p.308)*
19. *Apicius (p.305)*
20. *La Maison de L'Aubrac (p.306)*
21. *Alain Ducasse (p.305)*
22. *Le Taillevent (p.307)*
23. *Pierre Gagnaire (p.306)*
24. *Le Cinq (p.305)*
25. *Restaurant Guy Savoy (p.310)*
26. *Le Verre Bouteille (p.311)*
27. *Kifune (p.310)*
28. *La Pâtisserie des Rêves (p.310)*
29. *Carette (p.309)*
30. *L'Astrance (p.309)*
31. *Le Pré Catelan (p.310)*

LE 114 FAUBOURG

Bristol Hotel
114 Rue du Faubourg Saint-Honoré
Paris 75008
+33 153434444
www.lebristolparis.com

Opening hours.............7 days for breakfast, lunch and dinner
Reservation policy...Yes
Reservation email................114faubourg@lebristolparis.com
Credit cards..Accepted
Price range...Expensive
Style...Smart casual
Cuisine...Modern French
Recommended for.....................................Worth the travel

ALAIN DUCASSE

Plaza Athenee Hotel
25 Avenue Montaigne
Paris 75008
+33 153676500
www.plaza-athenee-paris.com

Opening hours.............2 days for lunch and 5 days for dinner
Reservation policy...Yes
Credit cards..Accepted
Price range...Expensive
Style...Formal
Cuisine..French
Recommended for..High end

'Classic French style.'—Mauro Colagreco

APICIUS

20 Rue d'Artois
Paris 75008
+33 143801966
www.restaurant-apicius.com

Opening hours...................................5 days for lunch and dinner
Reservation policy...Yes
Credit cards..Accepted
Price range...Expensive
Style...Formal
Cuisine..French
Recommended for..High end

'Try the Millefeuille of beef, spinach and caviar and the
hot chocolate soufflé.'—Guillaume Monjuré

CAFÉ POUCHKINE

Printemps Department Store
64 Boulevard Haussmann
Paris 75008

Opening hours...........................6 days for breakfast until late
Reservation policy..No
Credit cards..Accepted
Price range..Affordable
Style...Smart casual
Cuisine...Pastries
Recommended for.....................................Worth the travel

'Truly artistic, the essence of real French cooking,
baking and presentation philosophy.'—Gençay Üçok

LE CINQ

Four Seasons Hotel
31 Avenue George V
Paris 75008
+33 149527154
www.fourseasons.com

Opening hours.............7 days for breakfast, lunch and dinner
Reservation policy...Yes
Credit cards..Accepted
Price range...Expensive
Style...Formal
Cuisine..French
Recommended for...Breakfast

EPICURE

Recommended by
Yves Camdeborde, Alyn
Williams

Le Bristol Hotel
112 Rue du Faubourg Saint-Honoré
Paris 75008
+33 53434340
www.lebristolparis.com

Opening hours	7 days for lunch until late
Reservation policy	Yes
Reservation email	epicure@lebristolparis.com
Credit cards	Accepted
Price range	Expensive
Style	Formal
Cuisine	French
Recommended for	High end

'Éric Frechon at the Bristol in Paris is a master of
French haute cuisine.'—Alyn Williams

The grand restaurant at L'Hôtel Le Bristol, relaunched as Epicure in 2011 in the dramatically but
classically refurbished garden room of the five-star
luxury hotel, is the quintessential Parisian multi-
Michelin-starred haute cuisine experience. Headed
up by Chevalier de la Légion d'Honneur Eric Frechon,
a friend of former French President Nicolas Sarkozy,
it's the place to go for the seriously luxurious
ingredients synonymous with smart French nosh:
think foie gras, caviar, lobster, frogs' legs and grand
cru chocolate. For sheer impact, however, try the
Bresse chicken *en vessie* (stuffed with truffles and
cooked inside a pig's bladder).

LA MAISON DE L'AUBRAC

Recommended by
Eric Frechon, Guillaume
Monjuré, Michel Troisgros

37 Rue Marbeuf
Paris 75008
+33 143590514
www.maison-aubrac.com

Opening hours	7 days for 24 hours
Reservation policy	Yes
Credit cards	Accepted but not AMEX and Diners
Price range	Affordable
Style	Casual
Cuisine	Steakhouse
Recommended for	Late night

'Beautiful meat at all hours with a good glass
of wine.'—Guillaume Monjuré

MARKET

Recommended by
Christophe Michalak

15 Avenue Matignon
Paris 75008
+33 156434090
www.jean-georges.com

Opening hours	7 days for brunch and dinner
Reservation policy	Yes
Credit cards	Accepted but not AMEX and Diners
Price range	Affordable
Style	Smart casual
Cuisine	International
Recommended for	Regular neighbourhood

'The cuisine of Jean Georges is masterful'
—Christophe Michalak

LEDOYEN

Recommended by
Alexis Gauthier

1 Avenue Dutuit
Paris 75008
+33 153051000
www.ledoyen.com

Opening hours	4 days for lunch and 5 days for dinner
Reservation policy	Yes
Credit cards	Accepted
Price range	Expensive
Style	Formal
Cuisine	French
Recommended for	High end

'Mind-blowingly expensive, but well worth it.'
—Alexis Gauthier

PIERRE GAGNAIRE

Recommended by
Jordi Butrón Melero, André
Chiang, Andrew Fairlie,
Alexandre Gauthier, Esben
Holmboe Bang, Katsumi
Ishida, Alberto Landgraf,
Lisa Muncan, Michel Portos,
Joan Roca, Kevin Thornton

6 Rue Balzac
Paris 75008
+33 158361250
www.pierre-gagnaire.com

Opening hours	5 days for lunch and dinner
Reservation policy	Yes
Credit cards	Accepted
Price range	Expensive
Style	Formal
Cuisine	Modern French
Recommended for	High end

LE TAILLEVENT

Recommended by
Homaro Cantu

15 Rue Lamennais
Paris 75008
+33 144951501
www.taillevent.com

Opening hours	5 days for lunch and dinner
Reservation policy	Yes
Reservation email	reservation@taillevent.com
Credit cards	Accepted
Price range	Expensive
Style	Formal
Cuisine	French
Recommended for	Worth the travel

'Perfect classic French gastronomy.'—Homaro Cantu

CHARTIER

Recommended by
Michel Portos

7 Rue du Faubourg
Paris 75009
www.bouillon-chartier.com

Opening hours	7 days for lunch and dinner
Reservation policy	No
Credit cards	Accepted
Price range	Budget
Style	Casual
Cuisine	French bistro
Recommended for	Bargain

Parisian time-machine Chartier opened in 1896 and hasn't changed a scrap since. Its purpose was and is to feed the workers – quickly and cheaply – so do not expect gourmet anything and count yourself lucky if your waiter cracks a smile. It's simple, classic French food, steak frites, oeuf mayo, snails, leeks vinaigrette, frisée aux lardons, homemade Chantilly cream… Most of the entrées cost less than €3 (£2; $3) and mains less than €10 (£8; $12). There's no booking so *manger comme des poules* (before 7.00 p.m.) is the only way to avoid queuing (lining up) in the evening. The decor is spectacular – enjoy the show and delight in no-nonsense, real food.

CHEZ CASIMIR

Recommended by
Yves Camdeborde

6 Rue de Belzunce
Paris 75010
+33 148782880

Opening hours	7 days for lunch and dinner
Reservation policy	Yes
Credit cards	Accepted
Price range	Affordable
Style	Casual
Cuisine	French bistro
Recommended for	Bargain

LE CHATEAUBRIAND

Recommended by
Alex Atala, Ettore Botrini,
Massimo Bottura, Christian
Ebbe, Katsumi Ishida,
Tom Kerridge, Tony Maws,
Andrew McConnell, Magnus
Nilsson, Petter Nilsson, Íñigo
Peña, René Redzepi

129 Avenue Parmentier
Paris 75011
+33 0143574595

Opening hours	5 days for dinner
Reservation policy	Yes
Credit cards	Accepted
Price range	Affordable
Style	Casual
Cuisine	French bistro
Recommended for	Worth the travel

'The tasting menu at Chateaubriand blows my mind. Hats off to Inaki, Laurant and the whole crew.'
—Massimo Bottura

Sat on a sycamore-shaded Avenue in Belleville, Le Chateaubriand occupies a handsome old bistro, its 1930s facade and interior largely unchanged. With its lack of airs and graces, championing of pungent natural wines and a take-it-or-leave-it five-course fixed price menu at dinner – there are those who don't get why it's created such a stir since opening in 2006. But that's their loss, because the cooking, which keeps things as raw and unadulterated as possible while mixing French staples with less familiar foreign flavours, makes it clear why chef-owner Inaki Aizpitarte has become the poster boy for the 'bistronomique' movement.

RINO

Recommended by
Isaac McHale,
Jean-François Piège

46 Rue Trousseau
Paris 75011
+33 148069585
www.rino-restaurant.com

Opening hours	2 days for lunch and 5 days for dinner
Reservation policy	Yes
Credit cards	Accepted
Price range	Affordable
Style	Smart casual
Cuisine	Italian
Recommended for	Bargain

'Giovanni Passerini serves outstanding cuisine for reasonable prices.'—Jean-François Piège

If you're in Paris looking for first-class modern European cuisine in unpretentious surroundings, head over to the arty Sainte-Marguerite quartier in the 11th arrondissement, where Rome's Giovanni 'Rino' Passerini is cooking up a storm. In a small, well-managed dining room with light-coloured walls, some bare brick and simple wooden furniture, you can choose from a daily changing menu that combines influences and ingredients from all over Europe in a highly imaginative and often surprising way. Rino has a genuine talent for marrying textures and flavours in dishes befitting fine dining, without the fine dining price.

SEPTIME

Recommended by
Sven Chartier, Isaac McHale

80 Rue de Charonne
Paris 75011
+33 143673829
www.septime-charonne.fr

Opening hours	4 days for lunch and 5 days for dinner
Reservation policy	Yes
Credit cards	Accepted but not AMEX and Diners
Price range	Affordable
Style	Casual
Cuisine	Modern French
Recommended for	Wish I'd opened

Rarely has a restaurant in Paris condensed and combined so many world trends. The room is industrial/loft, the waiters kindly attentive, carefully unshaven and if they don't have tattoos yet they're just about to. Bernard Grébaut is eminently celebable, good-looking, speaks his mind, loves poetry, was trained by Passard and pocketed a Michelin star at only twenty-seven years old. His gentle, sensitive

cuisine enfolds the new Nordic codes in solid French technique – petit-suisse tarte with vanilla and lemon, white asparagus, sauce gribiche, oysters, plus flowers everywhere. Although despairingly hip and hard to book, it's exhilarating to witness the emergence of a blazing new talent.

LA GAZZETTA

Recommended by
Andreas Dahlberg, Robert
J. K. Kranenborg, Jacques
and Laurent Pourcel

29 Rue de Cotte
Paris 75012
+33 143474705
www.lagazzetta.fr

Opening hours	5 days for lunch and dinner
Reservation policy	Yes
Credit cards	Accepted
Price range	Affordable
Style	Smart casual
Cuisine	Modern French
Recommended for	Bargain

This elegant 1930s bistro was given a new lease of life in 2006 with the arrival of chef Petter Nilsson and the team from Le Fumoir. Close to the marché d'Aligre, Paris's hippest market, the lunch is magically priced: three small plates from a choice of four to team with salad or charcuterie and le dessert du jour, all for less than €20 (£16; $25). In the evening a more sparkly but still tight, and fantastically good value, evening menu – asparagus and bonito with verbina butter; duck foie gras with new potatoes, saffron and mustard; hay and chicory ice cream – has made Nilsson a rising star among the new legion of fiercely independent young French chefs.

LA CANTINE DU TROQUET

Recommended by
Yves Camdeborde

101 Rue de L'Ouest
Paris 75014
+33 145400498

Opening hours	5 days for dinner
Reservation policy	No
Credit cards	Accepted
Price range	Affordable
Style	Casual
Cuisine	Basque
Recommended for	Regular neighbourhood

LE DÔME

108 Boulevard Montparnasse
Paris 75014
+33 14263481

Recommended by
Pierre Gagnaire

Opening hours.................7 days for lunch and dinner
Reservation policy.......................................Yes
Credit cards................................Not accepted
Price range.....................................Expensive
Style...Smart casual
Cuisine..Seafood
Recommended for...........................Late night

LA RÉGALADE

14 Avenue Jean-Moulin
Paris 75014
+33 145456858

Recommended by
Julien Duboué, Guillaume
Monjuré, Eduardo Moreno,
Bradley Turley

Opening hours............4 days for lunch and 5 days for dinner
Reservation policy...Yes
Credit cards..Accepted
Price range..Affordable
Style..Smart casual
Cuisine...French bistro
Recommended for....................................Bargain

'Everything you order is guaranteed to be delicious and
if you order it all with truffles, it's even better.'
—Eduardo Moreno

Ferocious talent Yves Camdeborde sent shock waves
through Paris kitchens when he left behind the starry
Hôtel de Crillon in 1992 to open a tiny bistro in the
14th arrondissement. Credited as the forerunner of
the *la bistronomique* movement, his quaint tiled
bistro touted haute skills and ingredients at bistro
prices. Camdeborde has sinced moved on (to Le
Comptoir) but new owner Bruno Doucet keeps the
generous spirit alive, inviting guests to dig in to
homemade terrine ahead of an unashamedly Gallic
feast of coquilles Saint-Jacques with herb butter,
pork belly and lentils and Grand Marnier soufflé. A
second Régalade opened on the Rue Saint-Honoré
in 2010.

L'ASTRANCE

4 Rue Beethoven
Paris 75016
+33 14050844

Recommended by
André Chiang, Mauro
Colagreco, Sang-Hoon
Degeimbre, Anatoly Komm,
Virgilio Martinez, Philippe
Rochat, Michel Troisgros

Opening hours.................4 days for lunch and dinner
Reservation policy.......................................Yes
Credit cards................................Accepted
Price range.....................................Expensive
Style...Formal
Cuisine....................................Modern French
Recommended for...................Worth the travel

'The taste mixes and the creations surprise me.
The service is also very impressive. All is
perfect.'—Mauro Colagreco

This small (but tall!), out of the way, airy, three-
Michelin-starred restaurant is soaked in relaxed
confidence, as is Pascal Barbot's concise cooking.
Root vegetables, flowers and herbs are very much
the stars, sitting together raw, fermented and
poached, or spiked with notes of smoke, citrus and
pickle. Barbot rightly prides himself on the very
careful pairing of wine with the tasting menu (for
instance, Challans duck and raspberries, with a
Gevrey Chambertin 'Vieilles Vignes' 2005) and, unlike
many lazier *grandes tables*, here it would be a shame
not to let yourself be guided from start to finish.
You're in good hands.

CARETTE

4 Place du Trocadéro
Paris 75016
+33 147279885
www.carette-paris.com

Recommended by
Pierre Gagnaire, Thierry
Marx, Christophe Michalak

Opening hours.................7 days from breakfast until late
Reservation policy.......................................Yes
Credit cards................................Accepted
Price range..Affordable
Style...Casual
Cuisine..Pastries
Recommended for.................................Breakfast

'The best tarts and pastries.'—Christophe Michalak

LA PÂTISSERIE DES RÊVES

111 Rue de Longchamp
Paris 75016
www.lapatisseriedesreves.com

Opening hours	6 days from breakfast until late
Reservation policy	No
Credit cards	Accepted
Price range	Budget
Style	Casual
Cuisine	Pastries
Recommended for	Local favourite

LE PRÉ CATELAN

Route de Suresnes
Bois de Boulogne
Paris 75016
+33 144144114
www.restaurant-precatelan.com

Opening hours	5 days for lunch and dinner
Reservation policy	Yes
Credit cards	Accepted
Price range	Expensive
Style	Formal
Cuisine	French
Recommended for	High end

Frédéric Anton reigns supreme over one of Paris's most prestigious gastro-temples, built in 1905 in a section of the Bois de Boulogne dedicated to Théophile Catelan, Louis XVI's *capitaine des chasses*. Anton, with his Kojak looks and smoky regard, former second to Joel Robuchon, to whom he 'owes everything', was awarded three Michelin stars in 2007. When he became MasterChef judge in 2010, Anton was already so much part of the firmament that the media deluge merely strengthened his aura. His refined, lofty take on the most noble of French produce – sole, artichoke purée, caviar, souffléd green apple filled with caramel ice cream and cider – has the menu reading like a poem.

KIFUNE

44 Rue St-Ferdinand
Champs-Élysées
Paris 75017
+33 145721119

Opening hours	5 days for lunch and dinner
Reservation policy	Yes
Credit cards	Accepted
Price range	Affordable
Style	Casual
Cuisine	Japanese
Recommended for	Regular neighbourhood

RESTAURANT GUY SAVOY

18 Rue Troyon
Paris 75017
+33 143804061
www.guysavoy.com

Opening hours	4 days for lunch and 5 days for dinner
Reservation policy	Yes
Reservation email	reserv@guysavoy.com
Credit cards	Accepted
Price range	Expensive
Style	Formal
Cuisine	French
Recommended for	Worth the travel

'The soulful approach to three-Michelin-starred cuisine and the skill at which they transform classic French cooking is amazing.'—Mark Sullivan

Guy Savoy is spending his last days at the famous Rue Troyon address before moving his belle maison to a new, Rive Gauche location. Just like Pierre Gagnaire and Joel Robuchon, Savoy has grown a global empire, opening in Las Vegas and Singapore, from this intimate three-Michelin-starred restaurant where the service is ultra-personalized from the minute the client opens the door. Elsewhere in Paris, three modern bistro/brasseries – Le Chiberta, Les Bouquinistes and L'Atelier Maître Albert – serve simpler versions of Savoy's classicism but his artichoke soup with black truffles, Parmesan and mushroom brioche with black truffle butter remains one of France's most celebrated dishes. Chefs return again and again to soak up the Savoy magic and inspiration.

LE VERRE BOUTEILLE

85 Avenue des Ternes
Paris 75017
+33 145740102
www.leverrebouteille.com

Opening hours	5 days for lunch and dinner
Reservation policy	Yes
Credit cards	Accepted
Price range	Affordable
Style	Casual
Cuisine	French bistro
Recommended for	Late night

'The cheese ravioli is deadly!'—Christophe Michalak

LE COQ RICO

98 Rue Lepic
Paris 75018
+33 142598289
www.lecoqrico.com

Opening hours	7 days for lunch and dinner
Reservation policy	Yes
Credit cards	Accepted
Price range	Affordable
Style	Casual
Cuisine	Chicken
Recommended for	Wish I'd opened

'It's all about the chicken – in many different styles. A must see when in Paris.'—Raphael Dworak

LE SOURIRE DE SAIGON

54 Rue du Mont Cenis
Paris 75018
+33 42233116
www.souriredesaigon.com

Opening hours	7 days for dinner
Reservation policy	Yes
Credit cards	Accepted
Price range	Affordable
Style	Smart casual
Cuisine	Vietnamese
Recommended for	Regular neighbourhood

Parisians and film stars happily cross half a dozen arrondissements for Monsieur Dang's Vietnamese fair, yet the room retains a real neighbourhood family feel. The dim sum and nem sharing plates fill your table with clutter and clatter, adding to the place's noisy informality. The Saigon ribs, pho and chicken in tamarind are not to be missed. But it is when you watch, mesmerized, as one of the silk-encased waitresses peels back the edges of a bamboo pipe to reveal Le Sourire's famous sticky rice that you understand the restaurant's true artistry.

QUE DU BON

22 Rue du Plateau
Paris 75019
+33 1428381865

Opening hours	6 days for lunch and 5 days for dinner
Reservation policy	Yes
Credit cards	Accepted
Price range	Affordable
Style	Casual
Cuisine	French bistro
Recommended for	Bargain

LE BARATIN

3 Rue Jouye-Rouve
Paris 75020
+33 143493970

Opening hours	4 days for lunch and 5 days for dinner
Reservation policy	Yes
Credit cards	Accepted but not AMEX and Diners
Price range	Affordable
Style	Casual
Cuisine	French bistro
Recommended for	Regular neighbourhood

Raquel Carena and Philipppe 'Pinuche' Pinoteau have admirably ridden the wave of global fame and *New York Times* profiles to keep Le Baratin the way it has always been – a crammed, no-nonsense, local bistro with a splash of charm, plus slavish, personal devotion to the highest quality wine and ingredients. Chefs love revitalizing their tired palates with Raquel's motherly, delicate handling of fish and vegetables from Breton superstar Annie Bertin. She holds their awe and respect as much as the Passards and Ducasses for the dozens of remarkably inventive dishes that spring from her heart and tiny kitchen every day.

SPAIN

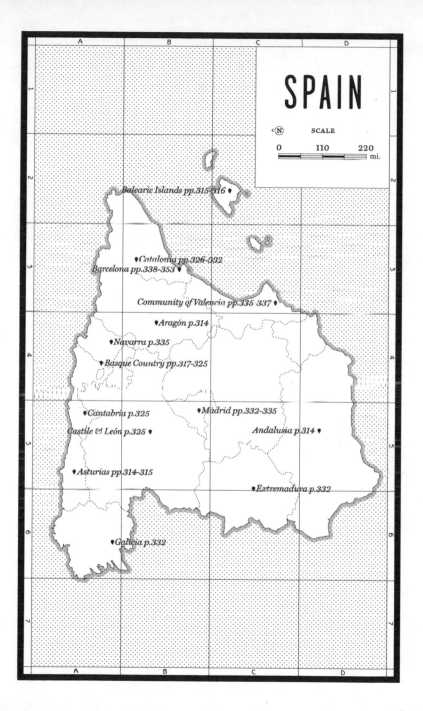

SPAIN

N SCALE

0   110   220 mi.

Balearic Islands pp.315–316 ♥

♥ Catalonia pp.326–002
Barcelona pp.338–353 ♥

Community of Valencia pp.335–337 ♥

♥ Aragón p.314

♥ Navarra p.335

♥ Basque Country pp.317–325

♥ Cantabria p.325   ♥ Madrid pp.332–335
Castile & León p.325 ♥   Andalusia p.314 ♥

♥ Asturias pp.314–315

                                 ♥ Extremadura p.332

♥ Galicia p.332

APONIENTE

Recommended by
Quique Dacosta,
Paco Morales

Calle Puerto Escondido 6
El Puerto de Santa María
Cádiz
Andalusia 11500
+34 956851870
www.aponiente.com

Opening hours................................5 days for lunch and dinner
Reservation policy...Yes
Reservation email...............................info@aponiente.com
Credit cards...Accepted
Price range..Expensive
Style...Smart casual
Cuisine...Modern Spanish
Recommended for......................................Worth the travel

EL CAMPERO

Recommended by
Samantha & Samuel Clark

Avenida Constitución Local 5c
Barbate
Cádiz
Andalusia 11160
+34 956432300
www.restauranteelcampero.es

Opening hours................................7 days for lunch and dinner
Reservation policy...Yes
Credit cards...Accepted
Price range...Affordable
Style...Casual
Cuisine..Seafood
Recommended for......................................Worth the travel

'El Campero is in the heart of the traditional tuna
fishing region of Jerez and during tuna fishing season
serves a mouth-watering tuna tasting menu.'
—Samantha and Samuel Clark

EL ASADOR DE NATI

Recommended by
Paco Morales

Avenida de Miguel de Unamuno 14
Fuensanta
Córdoba
Andalusia 14010
+34 957435918

Opening hours................................6 days for lunch and dinner
Reservation policy...Yes
Credit cards...Accepted
Price range...Budget
Style...Casual
Cuisine...Andalusian
Recommended for...Bargain

CALIMA

Recommended by
Paco Morales

Calle Jose Melia
Marbella
Málaga
Andalusia 29602
www.restaurantecalima.es

Opening hours.............4 days for lunch and 5 days for dinner
Reservation policy...Yes
Credit cards...Accepted
Price range...Affordable
Style...Smart casual
Cuisine...Modern Spanish
Recommended for......................................Worth the travel

LA LOBERA DE MARTÍN

Recommended by
Hugh Acheson

Calle de Don Mariano Supervía 58
Zaragoza
Aragón 50006
+34 976359659
www.laloberademartin.org

Opening hours................................7 days for lunch and dinner
Reservation policy...Yes
Credit cards...Accepted
Price range...Budget
Style...Casual
Cuisine...Tapas
Recommended for......................................Worth the travel

CASA GERARDO

Recommended by
Quique Dacosta

Antigua Carretera AS-19
Prendes
Carreño
Asturias 33438
www.casa-gerardo.com
+34 985887797

Opening hours.............6 days for lunch and 2 days for dinner
Reservation policy...Yes
Credit cards...Accepted
Price range...Affordable
Style...Smart casual
Cuisine...Asturian
Recommended for......................................Worth the travel

EL HÓRREO

Recommended by
Alberto Chicote

Antigua Carretera AS-239
Antromero
Gozón
Asturias 33449
+34 985871470

Opening hours	7 days for lunch and dinner
Reservation policy	Yes
Credit cards	Accepted
Price range	Affordable
Style	Casual
Cuisine	Seafood
Recommended for	Wish I'd opened

'They serve the best seafood I have ever tasted.'
—Alberto Chicote

JUAN Y ANDREA

Recommended by
Sergio Herman

Playa de Illetas
San Francisco Javier
Formentera
Balearic Islands 07860
+34 971187130
www.juanyandrea.com

Opening hours	7 days for lunch and dinner
Reservation policy	Yes
Credit cards	Accepted
Price range	Expensive
Style	Casual
Cuisine	Seafood
Recommended for	Wish I'd opened

CROISSANT SHOW

Recommended by
Sergio Herman

Plaça de la Constitució 2
Ibiza
Balearic Islands 07800
www.croissant-show.com

Opening hours	7 days from breakfast until late
Reservation policy	No
Credit cards	Accepted
Price range	Budget
Style	Casual
Cuisine	Bakery
Recommended for	Breakfast

ES XARCU

Recommended by
Joan Roca

Cala Es Xarcu
Porroig
Ibiza
Balearic Islands 07830
www.esxarcu.com

Opening hours	7 days for lunch
Reservation policy	Yes
Reservation email	restaurante@esxarcu.com
Credit cards	Accepted
Price range	Affordable
Style	Casual
Cuisine	Ibicencan
Recommended for	Local favourite

Few restaurants can boast a terrace with a view as picturesque as Es Xarcu's, which is located directly on the sandy shores of a Sant Josep cove. Locals don't come for the view alone, however, but for the traditional food that is cooked simply over a flame for maximum flavour. The menu is comfortingly basic, with appetizers such as hand-carved *jamón* (ham), *boquerones* and fresh prawns (shrimp) *a la plancha* making way for simple mains of freshly caught fish that are merely thrown on the grill. There are no delusions of grandeur here, with the cheap plastic chairs and the daily lunchtime scramble only adding to the experience.

RESTAURANT ES TORRENT

Recommended by
Filip Claeys, Sergio Herman

Platja d'es Torrent
Sant Josep de sa Talaia
Ibiza
Balearic Islands 07839
+34 971802160
www.estorrent.net

Opening hours	7 days for lunch and dinner
Reservation policy	Yes
Credit cards	Accepted
Price range	Expensive
Style	Casual
Cuisine	Seafood
Recommended for	Wish I'd opened

'A magical place right on the beach with excellent food.'—Filip Claeys

ZARANDA

Hilton Sa Torre Mallorca Hotel
Cami de Sa Torre 8
Llucmajor
Mallorca
Balearic Islands 07609
+34 971010450
www.zaranda.es

Opening hours...5 days for dinner
Reservation policy...Yes
Reservation email................................zaranda@zaranda.es
Credit cards..Accepted
Price range...Expensive
Style...Smart casual
Cuisine...Majorcan
Recommended for..High end

EL BUNGALOW

Carrer d'Esculls
Palma de Mallorca
Balearic Islands 07007
+34 971262738

Opening hours...............6 days for lunch and 5 day for dinner
Reservation policy..Yes
Credit cards..Accepted
Price range..Affordable
Style...Casual
Cuisine...Seafood
Recommended for...................................Regular neighbourhood

'The food is incredibly simple, but the cuttlefish rice
and the salt-baked sea bass are great. It's the perfect
place to arrive early in the evening, sit on the terrace
and watch the sunset over the Mediterranean.'
—Marc Fosh

FIBONACCI

Vicario Joaquin Fuster 95
Palma de Mallorca
Balearic Islands 07006
www.fibonaccibakery.com

Opening hours.........................7 days from breakfast until late
Reservation policy...No
Credit cards..Accepted
Price range..Budget
Style...Casual
Cuisine...Bakery-Café
Recommended for...Breakfast

'Great coffee and homemade pastries and breads that
are to die for. Being right next to the Mediterranean
sea completes the experience.'—Marc Fosh

MESÓN CA'N PEDRO

Calle Rector Vives 4
Gènova
Palma de Mallorca
Balearic Islands 07015
+34 971402479
www.mesoncanpedro.com

Opening hours................................7 days for lunch and dinner
Reservation policy...Yes
Credit cards..Accepted
Price range..Budget
Style...Casual
Cuisine...Majorcan
Recommended for..Wish I'd opened

'The food is really basic and the waiters never smile
but somehow this place manages to pack in over
500 covers every service. '—Marc Fosh

CA NA TONETA

Horitzó 21
Caimari
Selva
Mallorca
Balearic Islands 07314
+34 971515226
www.canatoneta.com

Opening hours...7 days for dinner
Reservation policy...Yes
Credit cards..Accepted
Price range..Affordable
Style...Casual
Cuisine...Majorcan
Recommended for...Local favourite

'Two sisters cook up traditional Majorcan recipes
with home-grown produce from their farm. It's simple,
country food at its best!'—Marc Fosh

ARBOLAGAÑA

Recommended by
Alexandra Raij

Museum of Fine Arts
Plaza del Museo 2
Bilbao
Basque Country 48011
+34 944424657

Opening hours.............6 days for lunch and 3 days for dinner
Reservation policy...Yes
Credit cards..Accepted
Price range..Expensive
Style...Smart casual
Cuisine...Modern Spanish
Recommended for..................................Worth the travel

'Time and time again I am impressed with Aitor Bassabe's dishes at Arbolagaña in the Museo de Bellas Artes in Bilbao. His food is so tasty and soulful and without pretension. He really offers a full experience. Also the wine list is great - it represents great value.'—Alexandra Raij

ASADOR INDUSI

Recommended by
Josean Alija

Calle Maestro García Rivero 7
Bilbao
Basque Country 48011

Opening hours....................7 days for lunch and dinner
Reservation policy..Yes
Credit cards..Accepted
Price range...Affordable
Style...Smart casual
Cuisine..Basque
Recommended for.............................Regular neighbourhood

'A brasserie specializing in amazing grilled meats.'—Josean Alija

BAITA GAMINIZ

Recommended by
Josean Alija

Calle Alameda de Mazarredo 20
Bilbao
Basque Country 48001
+34 944242267
www.baitagaminiz.com

Opening hours.............6 days for lunch and 4 days for dinner
Reservation policy...Yes
Reservation email.....................baitagaminiz@gmail.com
Credit cards..Accepted
Price range..Affordable
Style..Casual
Cuisine..Basque
Recommended for.........................Regular neighbourhood

'A restaurant with a cuisine sourced from its surroundings and specializing in fish.'—Josean Alija

It might lie within sight of the Guggenheim, but this Bilbao favourite has won fans far closer to home than hungry tourists looking for a lunch spot. Legions of loyal locals testify to the keen pricing – €50 (£40; $63) for the tasting menu – as well as the comfortable, calm ambience and the excellence of the cooking. Chef Aitor Elizegi uses traditional Basque cuisine as a springboard to original creations. *Bacalao* (salt cod) is the reason to come. If you've enjoyed it in the restaurant, you can buy twenty varieties of it in the Baita Gaminiz shop next door. Book in advance, particularly if you're aiming to score a table on the pretty riverside terrace.

MUGI ARDO TXOKO

Recommended by
Josean Alija

Licenciado Poza 55
Bilbao
Basque Country 48013

Opening hours........................6 days from breakfast until late
Reservation policy..No
Credit cards..Not accepted
Price range..Budget
Style..Casual
Cuisine..Tapas
Recommended for...Breakfast

'Mugi is a special place to meet. I usually have a coffee but it also sells fabulous ham.'—Josean Alija

NERUA

Recommended by
Víctor Arguinzóniz,
Quique Dacosta

Guggenheim Bilbao Museum
Avenida Abandoibarra 2
Bilbao
Basque Country 48001
+34 944000430
www.nerua.com

Opening hours............6 days for lunch and 4 days for dinner
Reservation policy...Yes
Reservation email.................................reservas@nerua.com
Credit cards...Accepted
Price range..Expensive
Style..Casual
Cuisine..Modern Basque
Recommended for...Worth the travel

ELKANO

Recommended by
Andoni Luis Aduriz,
Martín Berasategui

Calle de Herrerieta 2
Getaria
Gipuzcoa
Basque Country 20808
+34 943140024
www.restauranteelkano.com

Opening hours............6 days for lunch and 4 days for dinner
Reservation policy...Yes
Credit cards...Accepted
Price range..Expensive
Style..Casual
Cuisine...Seafood
Recommended for................................Regular neighbourhood

'I love going to the local fish grills. This is an example of one of the best. It's most representative in this area in terms of the traditions that characterize us.'
—Martín Berasategui

The philosophy at Elkano, which sits on the seafront at Getaria, an hour west of San Sebastián, is quite simple: fresh fish, chargrilled. Except some strange alchemy seems to occur when the piscine produce of the Guipuzcoan coast meets Pedro Arregui's coals in the open air. Superlative turbot and hake are delivered unadorned to clothed tables in the unselfconsciously old-fashioned dining room – terracotta tiles, dark wooden beams. Lobster, clams, baby squid and coral-pink prawns (shrimp) all receive the same treatment, partnered by a compact selection of Spanish wines, including the region's own dry sparkling Chacolí. Round off with another local speciality – indulgent custard-filled *Panchineta*.

KAIA KAIPE

Recommended by
Martín Berasategui, Íñigo
Peña, Pedro Subijana

General Arnao 4
Getaria
Gipuzkoa
Basque Country 20808
+34 943140500
www.kaia-kaipe.com

Opening hours.................................7 days for lunch and dinner
Reservation policy...Yes
Credit cards...Accepted
Price range..Expensive
Style..Smart casual
Cuisine...Seafood
Recommended for...High end

Situated about 25 km (15 miles) along the coast from San Sebastián, Getaria catches the eye for the rocky outcrop that juts out into the sea, attached by a spit of land. On this spit, overlooking the little harbour, stands Kaia Kaipe. You can imagine how fresh the fish is. If you get a table outside, you can watch it coming in. Turbot, hake, langoustines, lobster... cooked as well as any fish you will ever have the pleasure of eating. This speciality brings in the local regulars, as well as fish fanciers from far and wide, which all makes for a very rewarding experience.

MARTÍN BERASATEGUI

Recommended by
Fausto Luigi Airoldi, Luis
Baena, Ettore Botrini,
Arabelle Meirlaen, Íñigo
Peña, Lionel Rigolet,
Ljubomir Stanisic,
Pedro Subijana

Loidi Kalea 4
Lasarte-Oria
Gipuzkoa
Basque Country 20160
+34 943366471
www.martinberasategui.com

Opening hours............5 days for lunch and 4 days for dinner
Reservation policy...Yes
Credit cards...Accepted
Price range..Expensive
Style..Casual
Cuisine...Modern Spanish
Recommended for...Worth the travel

'I think it's the best restaurant in Spain.'—Íñigo Peña

As if you need another reason for going to San Sebastián, a visit to Martin Berasategui is the cherry on the icing on the cake. And a warm toasted almond cake at that. Located a short drive outside the Basque capital, the restaurant is a haven of calm simplicity, while in the kitchen an orchestra of sous-chefs plays tirelessly to Berasategui's score. Not one for gilding the lily, he has become a master at extracting the maximum from his pure ingredients. Expect not a lavish feast, but delicate portions of intense flavour that melt in the mouth and leave a long-lasting impression.

MUGARITZ

Otazulueta Baserria
Aludura Aldea 20
Errenteria
Gipuzkoa
Basque Country 20100
+34 943522455
www.mugaritz.com

Recommended by
Josean Alija, Víctor Arguinzóniz, Juan Mari & Elena Arzak, Anton Bjuhr, Massimo Bottura, Wylie Dufresne, Alexandre Gauthier, Peter Gilmore, Mehmet Gürs, Rodolfo Guzman, Christoffer Hruskova, Dan Hunter, Anatoly Komm, Paolo Lopriore, Nuno Mendes, Paco Morales, Eduardo Moreno, Uwe Opocensky, Neil Perry, Albert Raurich, Perfecto Roger, Thomas Rode Anderson, Pedro Subijana

Opening hours...............5 days for lunch and dinner
Reservation policy...Yes
Reservation email........................info@mugaritz.com
Credit cards...Accepted
Price range...Expensive
Style..Casual
Cuisine...Modern Spanish
Recommended for.............................Wish I'd opened

'Andoni's food really brings out my emotions and each meal that I have had there is a very intense experience.'—Nuno Mendes

The smell of barbecue greets visitors to this cutting-edge restaurant tucked away in the hills outside San Sebastián, where head chef Andoni Luis Aduriz believes it's a universal childhood aroma. It's academic, really, as everything you're served once seated in the bright and spacious dining room is unrecognizable – designed to startle, amaze and even challenge your ideas about food. The techno-emotional cooking approach means a succession of wildly creative dishes such as "edible stones". There are no Basque favourites such as hake and salsa verde on the menu. In fact, there isn't even a menu – you simply put yourself at the kitchen's mercy.

YALDE

Oialume Bidea 34
Astigarraga
Gipuzcoa
Basque Country 20115
+34 943330530
www.chuletillasyalde.com

Recommended by
Andoni Luis Aduriz

Opening hours.............5 days for lunch and 3 days for dinner
Reservation policy...Yes
Credit cards...Accepted
Price range..Affordable
Style...Casual
Cuisine...Basque
Recommended for...Bargain

A fifteen-minute circuitous drive to the outskirts of San Sebastián takes you to Yalde – an honest, rustic restaurant serving authentic Basque cuisine. There is a menu but it's better to do as the locals – gastronomes with finely calibrated taste buds – and accept what the chef decides to prepare. A cold plate of chorizo and sheep's milk cheese to start, followed by fish and a Basque-style scrambled eggs. The apogee is a heap of expertly grilled lamb cutlets brought atop steaming vines. Sip on Bierzo – its liquorice and spicy notes are a suitable match for the cooking's savoury piquancy. This is a relatively unknown gem in the midst of a culinary Mecca.

ZUBEROA

Recommended by
Víctor Arguinzóniz, Juan
Mari & Elena Arzak, Martín
Berasategui, Íñigo Peña,
Pedro Subijana

Araneder Bidea
Barrio Iturriotz
Oiartzun
Gipuzkoa
Basque Country 20180
www.zuberoa.com

Opening hours	5 days for lunch and dinner
Reservation policy	Yes
Credit cards	Accepted
Price range	Expensive
Style	Smart casual
Cuisine	Basque
Recommended for	Wish I'd opened

The setting – a convivial old stone building in a 600-year-old village outside San Sebastián – may be quaint, but there is nothing quaint about the cooking. This is traditional Basque food brought bang up to date by chef Hilario Arbelaitz, who stakes his reputation on the quality of his ingredients and his ability to arrange them enticingly on the plate. Seafood plays the lead role, as you would expect in this part of the world, and the flavours are rich and warming, but Arbelaitz is not afraid to throw in the odd exotic ingredient, such as coconut or pineapple, or even both.

A FUEGO NEGRO

Recommended by
Ollie Couillaud,
Julien Duboué

Calle del Treinta y Uno de Agosto 31
San Sebastián
Basque Country 20003
+34 650135373
www.afuegonegro.com

Opening hours	6 days for lunch and dinner
Reservation policy	Yes
Reservation email	jan@afuegonegro.com
Credit cards	Accepted
Price range	Budget
Style	Casual
Cuisine	Tapas
Recommended for	Worth the travel

AKELADE

Recommended by
Víctor Arguinzóniz, Juan
Mari & Elena Arzak, Marc
Fosh, Ben Tish

Paseo Padre Orcoloaga 56
San Sebastián
Basque Country 20008
+34 943311209
www.akelarre.net

Opening hours	6 days for lunch and 5 days for dinner
Reservation policy	Yes
Reservation email	restaurante@akelarre.net
Credit cards	Accepted
Price range	Expensive
Style	Casual
Cuisine	Modern Basque
Recommended for	Wish I'd opened

'The best fish course of my life.'—Marc Fosh

Should you tire of San Sebastián's abundant *pintxos* (Basque tapas) bars, venture a little out of town for an altogether more ethereal and quirky demonstration of Basque hospitality. Admired by professional chefs the world over, Pedro Subijana of the three-Michelin-starred Akelade is one of the founding fathers of New Basque cuisine. Injecting much needed humour into high-concept cooking, his restaurant – perched above the Bay of Biscay – has pursued culinary innovation and technical perfection with tongue firmly in cheek for over thirty years. Two tasting menus, one based on *Aranori* (fish) and one on *Bekarki* (meat), are beautifully conceived and pleasingly playful.

ARZAK

Recommended by
Akmal Anuar, Josean Alija,
Víctor Arguinzóniz, Derry
Clarke, José Cordeiro, Ollie
Couillaud, Paco Guzmán,
Alfredo Hoz, Matias Palomo
Reyes, Pedro Subijana

Avenida Alcalde José Elósegui 273
San Sebastián
Basque Country 20015
+34 943285593
www.arzak.es

Opening hours	5 days for lunch and dinner
Reservation policy	Yes
Credit cards	Accepted
Price range	Expensive
Style	Casual
Cuisine	Modern Basque
Recommended for	Worth the travel

'I really admire Arzak. It's the perfect mix of tradition and modernity, and after years it's still one of the best restaurants in the world.'—Matias Palomo Reyes

Despite its three Michelin stars, there are no Arzak franchises – Juan Mari and his daughter Elena stay behind the stove, where the Arzak family has been for over 100 years. The cooking has come some distance since the building's former incarnation as a wine tavern, built by Juan Mari's grandparents. The monochrome dining room provides an urbane backdrop for the 'New Basque' cuisine, which works classic local ingredients into avant-garde compilations: deep blue duck with ginger and liquorice; sea bass with vegetable confetti; a 'moon stone' dessert. Fish – particularly hake – is exquisite. Book the chef's table to observe the father-daughter team at work.

ASADOR PORTUETXE

Recommended by
Wylie Dufresne

Portuetxe Kalea 43
San Sebastián
Basque Country 20018
+34 943219604
www.asadorportuetxe.com

Opening hours	7 days for lunch and dinner
Reservation policy	Yes
Credit cards	Accepted
Price range	Affordable
Style	Casual
Cuisine	Basque
Recommended for	Worth the travel

'They serve simple Spanish fare. I wouldn't miss the cuttlefish and caramelized onions.'—Wylie Dufresne

In the heart of the spirited Basque region of northern Spain, this traditional restaurant, replete with huge decorative wine barrels and ancient wooden beams, specializes in fresh fish and large hunks of meat cooked over charcoal grills. Portuetxe is in the style of a Basque farmhouse (the building is four hundred years old) and is diligent in the preparation of seasonal vegetables and offers an impressive wine list with over 350 bins. This is classic but casual – resistant to the modernism that has characterized some of San Sebastián's more famed restaurants. To accompany the meat and fish try the artichokes for which it is well known.

BARKAIZTEGI

Recommended by
Pedro Subijana

Paseo de Barkaiztegi 42
Martutene
San Sebastián
Basque Country 20014
+34 943455501
www.barkaiztegi.com

Opening hours	6 days for lunch and dinner
Reservation policy	Yes
Credit cards	Accepted
Price range	Affordable
Style	Casual
Cuisine	Basque
Recommended for	Local favourite

BERNARDINA VINOTECA

Recommended by
Juan Mari & Elena Arzak

Calle de Vitoria-Gasteiz 6
San Sebastián
Basque Country 20018
+34 943314899
www.vinotecabernadina.com

Opening hours	6 days for brunch and 5 days for dinner
Reservation policy	Yes
Credit cards	Accepted
Price range	Budget
Style	Casual
Cuisine	Basque
Recommended for	Wish I'd opened

BERNARDO ETXEA

Recommended by
Pedro Subijana

Calle del Puerto 7
San Sebastián
Basque Country 20003
+34 943422055
www.bernardoetxea.com

Opening hours	6 days for lunch and 5 days for dinner
Reservation policy	Yes
Credit cards	Accepted
Price range	Affordable
Style	Smart casual
Cuisine	Basque
Recommended for	High end

LA BODEGA DONOSTIARRA

Calle Peña y Goñi 13
San Sebastián
Basque Country 20002
+34 943011380
www.bodegadonostiarra.com

Opening hours	6 days for breakfast and lunch
Reservation policy	Yes
Credit cards	Accepted
Price range	Budget
Style	Casual
Cuisine	Tapas
Recommended for	Local favourite

Enjoy a traditional San Sebastián bar experience, while avoiding the heaving streets of the old town, at old-timer Bodega Donostiarra, established in 1928 in the district of Gros. Behind the undistinguished blue frontage and frosted glass windows is a real locals' local, though it receives a huge influx of non-Donostiarras during the International Film Festival at the nearby Kursaal. A mouth-watering menu of *pintxos* (Basque tapas) and meaty grills, including the 800 g (28 oz) chuleta steak, goes down well with a *txikito* of wine or two. Don't miss the tuna, anchovy and *guindilla* (pepper) *pintxo*, a celebration of the region's traditional canned seafood.

BODEGON ALEJANDRO

Calle de Fermín Calbetón 4
San Sebastián
Basque Country 20003
+34 943427158
www.bodegonalejandro.com

Opening hours	6 days for lunch and 4 days for dinner
Reservation policy	Yes
Reservation email	info@bodegonalejandro.com
Credit cards	Accepted
Price range	Affordable
Style	Casual
Cuisine	Basque
Recommended for	Bargain

CALONGE SAGARDOTEGIA

Paseo Orkolaga 8
Igledo
San Sebastián
Basque Country 20008
+34 943213251
www.sidreriacalonge.com

Opening hours	6 days for lunch and dinner
Reservation policy	Yes
Reservation email	sidreriacalonge@gmail.com
Credit cards	Accepted
Price range	Affordable
Style	Casual
Cuisine	Basque
Recommended for	Local favourite

LA ESPIGA

Calle San Marcial 48
San Sebastián
Basque Country 20006
www.barlaespiga.com

Opening hours	7 days for lunch and dinner
Reservation policy	No
Credit cards	Accepted
Price range	Affordable
Style	Smart casual
Cuisine	Tapas
Recommended for	Late night

GANBARA JATETXEA

Calle de San Jeronimo 21
San Sebastián
Basque Country 20003
+34 943422575
www.ganbarajatetxea.com

Opening hours	6 days for lunch and 5 days for dinner
Reservation policy	Yes
Credit cards	Accepted
Price range	Budget
Style	Casual
Cuisine	Tapas
Recommended for	Regular neighbourhood

GANDARIAS

Recommended by
Pedro Subijana

Calle del Treinta y Uno de Agosto 23
San Sebastián
Basque Country 20003
+34 943426362
www.restaurantegandarias.com

Opening hours	7 days from breakfast until late
Reservation policy	Yes
Reservation email	gandarias@casagandarias.com
Credit cards	Accepted but not AMEX
Price range	Affordable
Style	Casual
Cuisine	Basque
Recommended for	Late night

San Sebastián's old town is awash with atmospheric bars, their counters loaded with *pintxos* (Basque tapas) and hams hanging from their ceilings. Gandarias is one such establishment and is as essential a stop on a serious gourmet tour of the city as it is on a late-night bar crawl. Its restaurant is known for its bloody, marbled steaks and excellent wine cellar (strong on Riojas), while the always lively bar is recommended for its classic *pintxos* and blackboard specials. Specialities include the *brocheta de chipirón* (squid), *ensaladilla rusa* (Russian salad) and, of course, the celebrated acorn-fed Joselito ham.

HAIZEA BAR

Recommended by
Brendan McGill

Calle de Aldamar 8
San Sebastián
Basque Country 20003

Opening hours	7 days for lunch and 6 days for dinner
Reservation policy	No
Credit cards	Not accepted
Price range	Budget
Style	Casual
Cuisine	Tapas
Recommended for	Worth the travel

IBAI

Recommended by
Víctor Arguinzóniz,
Íñigo Peña

Calle de Getaria 15
San Sebastián
Basque Country 20005
+34 943428764

Opening hours	5 days for lunch
Reservation policy	Yes
Credit cards	Not accepted
Price range	Expensive
Style	Casual
Cuisine	Basque
Recommended for	Local favourite

'They work with the best seasonal products and whenever Ferran Adrià pays a visit to our city, he goes to have a meal here.'—Íñigo Peña

If Ibai had silver service, it would be regarded as one of the finest restaurants in the world. Instead, tucked away beneath a Donostia tapas bar, it's a secret, unpretentious gem, a rustic dining room with five cloth-clad and heavily subscribed tables. In fact, you need to persevere if you want to get a table because the locals snap them up fast. This is due to the food and the high quality of the ingredients. Ibai serves the freshest of fresh fish (either fried or slow-cooked in the oven), shellfish and vegetables, embellished with local truffles, local wine and good old local hospitality.

MARUGAME CAFÉ BAR

Recommended by
Íñigo Peña

Plaza Marugame
Bajo
San Sebastián
Basque Country 20018
www.barmarugame.com

Opening hours	7 days from breakfast until late
Reservation policy	Yes
Credit cards	Accepted
Price range	Budget
Style	Casual
Cuisine	Basque
Recommended for	Breakfast

The Japanese name comes from the square in which this chic little café bar resides, which in turn comes from a town in Japan, twinned with San Sebastián. The food, though, is quintessentially Spanish, or rather Basque: excellent *pintxos* (Basque tapas), *bocatas* (sandwiches) and mixed platters are available any time and it's a popular place for the locals to kick off their day. This is social eating in the finest Iberian tradition. From the location to the music to the art, for which the restaurant doubles as an exhibition space, Marugame is cool, relaxed and a joyous place to hang out.

TAMBORIL

Recommended by
Juan Mari & Elena Arzak

Calle Pescaderia 2
San Sebastián
Basque Country 20003
www.bartamboril.com

Opening hours	5 day for lunch and 7 days for dinner
Reservation policy	No
Credit cards	Accepted
Price range	Budget
Style	Casual
Cuisine	Tapas
Recommended for	Bargain

VA BENE DISCO BURGER

Recommended by
Andoni Luis Aduriz, Martín
Berasategui, Íñigo Peña

Blas de Lezo 4
Amara Viejo
San Sebastián
Basque Country 20007

Opening hours	7 days from lunch until late
Reservation policy	No
Credit cards	Accepted
Price range	Budget
Style	Casual
Cuisine	Burgers
Recommended for	Late night

'Great hamburgers using meat from the Basque country.'—Andoni Luis Aduriz

ASADOR ETXEBARRI

Recommended by
Andoni Luis Aduriz, Josean Alija,
Pascal Barbot, Juan Mari & Elena
Arzak, Alberto Chicote, Quique
Dacosta, Mathias Dahlgren,
Matthew Dillon, Henry Harris,
Jacob Holmstrom, Katsumi
Ishida, David Martin, Neil Perry,
Didem Şenol, Joachim Wissler

Plaza San Juan 1
Atxondo
Viscaya
Basque Country 48291
+34 946583042
www.asadoretxebarri.com

Opening hours	6 days for lunch and 1 day for dinner
Reservation policy	Yes
Reservation email	reservas@asadoretxebarri.com
Credit cards	Accepted
Price range	Expensive
Style	Formal
Cuisine	Basque Grill
Recommended for	Worth the travel

'Victor Arguinzóniz is a poet with wood and coals and takes grilling to the highest form. Quite extraordinary.'—Neil Perry

There's no food without fire at Victor Arguinzoniz's homage to the Iberian-born tradition of the *asador* (grill restaurant). It sits in the bucolic Basque Country village of Axpe, nestled at the foot of Mount Alluitz, halfway between San Sebastián and Bilbao. Every dish that makes it onto Arguinzoniz's strictly seasonal tasting menu is flavoured with a smoky kiss from his charcoal-fired grill: seafood, marbled beef, vegetables, eggs, cheese, butter – even the desserts – smoked milk often making an appearance. Ingredients are predominantly sourced from the surrounding unfairly fertile Atxondo Valley – even the charcoal for the grill, made from local oak.

AZURMENDI

Azurmendi Barrio Leguina s/n
Larrabetzu
Viscaya
Basque Country 48195
+34 944558866
www.azurmendi.biz

Opening hours.............6 days for lunch and 2 days for dinner
Reservation policy...Yes
Credit cards...Accepted
Price range..Expensive
Style..Casual
Cuisine..Modern Basque
Recommended for...Worth the travel

Eneko Atxa is Azurmendi's young, passionate and impressively earringed chef. The restaurant opened in 2005 in a warehouse-style building ten minutes outside Bilbao. The dining room is brightly lit, with tall windows, and the decor is stylish and modern – sensible lighting and an open, airy space. Atxa's food is bold and experimental, his dishes bearing names such as 'the garden' (edible soil with young vegetables) or 'heart of the countryside', but there are nods to a more rustic Basque heritage in a dish of Ibérian pork cheek with mushroom duxelles and roasted peppers. They serve an excellent txakoli wine produced by their own winery

BODEGA DEL RIOJANO

Calle del Río de la Pila 5
Santander
Cantabria 39003
+34 942216750
www.bodegadelriojano.com

Opening hours.............7 days for lunch and 6 days for dinner
Reservation policy...Yes
Credit cards...Accepted
Price range..Affordable
Style..Casual
Cuisine...Northern Spanish
Recommended for...Local favourite

EL SERBAL

Calle de Andrés del Río 7
Santander
Cantabria 39004
+34 942222515
www.elserbal.com

Opening hours.............6 days for lunch and 5 days for dinner
Reservation policy...Yes
Reservation email...............................elserbal@elserbal.com
Credit cards...Accepted
Price range..Affordable
Style..Smart casual
Cuisine...Modern Spanish
Recommended for...High end

LERA

Posada Senda de los Frailes
Castroverde de Campos
Zamora
Castile and León 49110
+34 980664653
www.restaurantelera.com

Opening hours...............................7 days for lunch and dinner
Reservation policy...Yes
Credit cards...Accepted
Price range..Affordable
Style..Smart casual
Cuisine...Modern Spanish
Recommended for...Worth the travel

'A great restaurant in such an unexpected place.'
—Martin Berasategui

BAR DEL PUERTO

Zona Portuaria s/n
Arenys de Mar
Barcelona
Catalonia 08350
+34 937921483
www.bardelpuerto.com

Opening hours..............6 days for lunch and 5 days for dinner
Reservation policy...Yes
Reservation email................bardelpuerto@bardelpuerto.com
Credit cards..Accepted
Price range...Affordable
Style..Casual
Cuisine..Catalan
Recommended for..Bargain

What Bar del Puerto lacks in interior design flair it
more than makes up for in its charming port location,
complete with boats bobbing on the turquoise
Mediterranean Sea. More than this, its stone's-
throw-from-the-ocean coordinates mean that fresh
fish is predominant on the menu. In the Barcelona
municipality of Arenys de Mar, the restaurant offers
simple and unadulterated Catalonian cuisine. A welcome break from fussy, etiquette-ridden dining, Bar
del Puerto serves immaculately cooked fish and
decent quaffing wine. With its reasonable prices and
fortifying offering, this is a break from the hustle and
pretence of the inner city.

HISPANIA

Cami Ral 54
Arenys de Mar
Barcelona
Catalonia 08350
+34 937910306
www.restauranthispania.com

Opening hours..............7 days for lunch and 5 days for dinner
Reservation policy..Yes
Reservation email.............hispania@restauranthispania.com
Credit cards..Accepted
Price range..Expensive
Style..Casual
Cuisine..Catalan
Recommended for...Local favourite

COLLSACREU

Carretera Sant Celoni 7
Arenys de Munt
Barcelona
Catalonia 08358
+34 937938499
www.restaurante-collsacreu.com

Opening hours..............6 days for breakfast, lunch and dinner
Reservation policy...Yes
Credit cards..Accepted
Price range...Affordable
Style..Casual
Cuisine..Catalan
Recommended for..Bargain

LA QUADRA

Carrer Raval 8
Calella
Barcelona
Catalonia 08370
+34 937661951
www.laquadra.net

Opening hours...3 days for dinner
Reservation policy...Yes
Credit cards..Accepted
Price range...Budget
Style..Casual
Cuisine...Tapas
Recommended for..Late night

'An interesting place with music, ham, cheese, bread
with tomato, wine, Cava and Champagne.'
—Carme Ruscalleda

CAN JUBANY

Carreterra de Sant Hilari
Calldetenes
Barcelona
Catalonia 08506
+34 938891023
www.canjubany.com

Recommended by
Carles Abellan, Albert Adrià

Opening hours	5 days for lunch and 4 days for dinner
Reservation policy	Yes
Credit cards	Accepted
Price range	Expensive
Style	Casual
Cuisine	Modern Catalan
Recommended for	Worth the travel

A disciple of the modernist Catalonian school of gastronomy, Nandu Jubany has created a picturesque retreat that masterfully showcases the produce of his own farm and gardens. Like many of his contemporaries, his dishes often start at a traditional base before being reinterpreted by modern molecular innovations. This includes the likes of grilled peas with *botifarra* (a type of sausage) and pork belly or roasted monkfish with pumpkin gnocchi. Precise craft and immaculate service wow and please equally throughout. Outside is rural Catalonia; inside is serenity, with minimalist design resting tastefully within the building's historical character. Jubany has mastered the marriage of old and new in all aspects of his restaurant.

ELS CASALS

Els Casals Hotel
Camí de la Guàrdia
Sagás (Berguedà)
Barcelona
Catalonia 08517
www.hotelelscasals.com

Recommended by
Albert Adrià, Josep Roca

Opening hours	7 days for lunch
Reservation policy	Yes
Credit cards	Accepted
Price range	Expensive
Style	Smart casual
Cuisine	Modern Spanish
Recommended for	High end

Head about 90 km (55 miles) north of Barcelona and you'll find the small town of Sagàs in the Pre-Pyrenees and this rural ten-bedroom hotel surrounded by its own farmland, which has its restaurant in a converted stable building. Dozens of varieties of vegetables and herbs, including Sant Pau beans, Blanca de Bufet potatoes and Montserrat tomatoes, grow in the garden, and the fields are home to free-range cattle and other livestock. All of which is used well — along with other local, seasonable produce — by chef Oriol Rovira, who serves dishes such as roast beef with peppers and baked potatoes.

CAN FABES

Carrer Sant Joan 6
Sant Celoni
Barcelona
Catalonia 08470
+34 938672851
www.canfabes.com

Recommended by
Albert Adrià, Christian
Domschitz, Carrie
Nahabedian, Michael Wolf

Opening hours	5 days for Lunch and 4 days for Dinner
Reservation policy	Yes
Reservation email	canfabes@canfabes.com
Credit cards	Accepted
Price range	Expensive
Style	Smart casual
Cuisine	Modern Catalan
Recommended for	Wish I'd opened

'Every time I go I have the best food ever. It's got a modern interior but has wood on the ceiling. It's like you're a king when you sit there.'—Michael Wolf

SANT PAU

Carrer Nou 10
Sant Pol de Mar
Barcelona
Catalonia 08395
+34 937600662
www.ruscalleda.com

Recommended by
Riki Mizukami

Opening hours	4 days for lunch and 5 days for dinner
Reservation policy	Yes
Credit cards	Accepted
Price range	Expensive
Style	Smart casual
Cuisine	Modern Spanish
Recommended for	Worth the travel

CAL CAMPANER

Recommended by
Albert Adrià

Calle Mossèn Carles Feliu 23
Roses
Girona
Catalonia 17480
+34 972256954

Opening hours	5 days for lunch and 7 days for dinner
Reservation policy	Yes
Credit cards	Not accepted
Price range	Expensive
Style	Casual
Cuisine	Seafood
Recommended for	Wish I'd opened

CAL TET

Recommended by
Joan Roca

Carrer Santa Anna 38
Girona
Catalonia 17258
+34 972751179
www.caltet.com

Opening hours	7 days for lunch and dinner
Reservation policy	Yes
Credit cards	Accepted
Price range	Affordable
Style	Casual
Cuisine	Catalan
Recommended for	Regular neighbourhood

Eating out on Spain's Costa Brava is not a simple toss up between eye-popping molecular gastronomy à la Ferran Adrià and greasy calamares in a beachfront bar. The *marisqueria* (seafood restaurant) Cal Tet, in the fishing village-turned-resort of L'Estartit, is where local families go to enjoy their region's traditional dishes. Since 1971 the Giménez family have staked their reputation on dazzling shellfish from local and Galician waters, serving Catalan classics such as *mariscada* (seafood stew of sea snails, winkles and mussels) and *fideuada* (pasta 'paella'), for parties of two or more, accompanied by the local Empordà wine.

CAN MARQUÈS

Recommended by
Joan Roca, Josep Roca

Plaça Calvet i Rubalcaba 3
Girona
Catalonia 17001
+34 972201001
www.canmarques.com

Opening hours	6 days for lunch and 5 days for dinner
Reservation policy	Yes
Credit cards	Accepted
Price range	Affordable
Style	Casual
Cuisine	Catalan
Recommended for	Breakfast

It describes itself as 'one of the most traditional restaurants in Girona'. Currently overseen by the fourth generation of the founding family, Can Marques's interior subtly pays tribute to the innovations of restaurant design. It strikes a careful balance between old and new, modern furniture sitting comfortably among traditional wooden dressers and cabinets stacked with wine bottles and glassware. Exceptional value can be found in the *menú del día* – three courses with a drink for €13.50 (£11; $17). It is in part defined by its proximity to the city market, which lies opposite and which elicits a wealth of exciting produce. For breakfast try the scrambled eggs with prawns (shrimp) and garlic.

CAN ROCA

Recommended by
Jordi Cruz, Joan Roca,
Jordi Roca, Josep Roca

Carretera de Taialà 42
Girona
Catalonia 17007

Opening hours	5 days for lunch and dinner
Reservation policy	Yes
Credit cards	Accepted
Price range	Budget
Style	Casual
Cuisine	Catalan
Recommended for	Local favourite

EL CELLER DE CAN ROCA

Can Sunyer 48
Girona
Catalonia 17007
+34 972222157
www.cellercanroca.com

Opening hours...............................7 days for lunch and dinner
Reservation policy..Yes
Reservation email.................restaurant@cellercanroca.com
Credit cards..Accepted
Price range..Expensive
Style..Casual
Cuisine..Modern Catalan
Recommended for..............................Worth the travel

'A mind-blowing lunch that saw a perfect harmony
of flavour, colour, texture, execution, wine-pairing
and service. Each course is etched into my memory.'
—Brad Holmes

While molecular gastronomy fans flocked to elBulli
and The Fat Duck, the pioneering trio of brothers at
El Celler de Can Roca in Girona remained Spain's
little secret. Eating in the clean-cut Scandi-style
dining room is an experience that plays with mood
and memory. Traditional Catalonian ingredients are
given innovative treatment to create playful dishes
such as caramelized olives hanging from a bonsai
tree or the famous Journey to Havana – a tobacco-
flavoured 'cigar' sitting on an 'ashtray' – or desserts
that replicate Calvin Klein or Lancôme scents. Having
achieved a third star in 2009, the €130 (£104; $168)
seven-course menu looks like very good value.

LES COLS

Mas les Cols
Carretera de la Canya
Olot
Girona
Catalonia 17800
+34 972269209
www.lescols.com

Opening hours..............7 days for lunch and 5 days for dinner
Reservation policy..Yes
Reservation email.....................................lescols@lescols.com
Credit cards..Accepted
Price range..Expensive
Style..Casual
Cuisine...Modern Spanish
Recommended for..............................Local favourite

'An exceptional place.'—Carme Ruscalleda

EL MOTEL

Avenida Salvador Dalí i Domènech 170
Figueres
Girona
Catalonia 17600
+34 972500562
www.elmotel.cat

Opening hours...............................7 days for lunch and dinner
Reservation policy..Yes
Credit cards..Accepted
Price range..Affordable
Style...Smart casual
Cuisine..Modern Catalan
Recommended for..............................Local favourite

OCCI

Recommended by
Jordi Roca

Carrer dels Mercaders 3
Girona
Catalonia 17004
www.restaurantocci.com

Opening hours	6 days for lunch and dinner
Reservation policy	Yes
Credit cards	Accepted
Price range	Affordable
Style	Casual
Cuisine	Modern Catalan
Recommended for	Late night

Occi is a modernist Catalan restaurant with a typically youthful personality. Walls double as blackboards, which artfully list the daily-changing fare. Its application of the methods of Spain's *nueva cocina* and assortment of exquisite carpaccios is juxtaposed against the traditional architecture of Girona's old quarter. Presentation is magnificent and gratefully doesn't act as a barrier to portion generosity. A conscientious effort is made here to optimize the availability of good local produce. The subterranean interior is a moody blend of black and red such as befits an after-dinner cocktail or two.

RAFA'S

Recommended by
Albert Adrià

Calle Sant Sebastià 56
Roses
Girona
Catalonia 17480
+34 972254003

Opening hours	5 days for lunch and dinner
Reservation policy	Yes
Credit cards	Accepted
Price range	Affordable
Style	Casual
Cuisine	Seafood
Recommended for	Wish I'd opened

The second most-famous restaurant to open in the vicinity of Roses on the Costa Brava has long been celebrated as a favourite of the brothers Adrià of elBulli fame. When Ferran Adrià let slip that it was his favourite place to eat when he wasn't in his kitchen, a meal at Rafa's quickly became part of the pilgrimage for those en route to elBulli. There's no menu, the fantastically fresh *plancha*-kissed seafood offered being whatever has come in that morning. Call ahead because it opens and closes according to the quality of the catch available each day.

LA SIRENA

Recommended by
Paco Morales

Call, s/n
Cadaqués
Girona
Catalonia 17488
+34 972258974

Opening hours	6 days for lunch and dinner
Reservation policy	Yes
Credit cards	Accepted
Price range	Affordable
Style	Casual
Cuisine	Seafood
Recommended for	Regular neighbourhood

RESTAURANT CAN XIFRA

Recommended by
Jordi Roca

Mas Artigas
Cartellà, Sant Gregori
Girona
Catalonia 17199
www.canxifra.com

Opening hours	7 days for lunch and dinner
Reservation policy	Yes
Credit cards	Accepted
Price range	Budget
Style	Casual
Cuisine	Catalan
Recommended for	Local favourite

Styled in the inviting farmhouse aesthetic of rural Catalonia, Can Xifra has rustic terracotta-tiled flooring, open brick walls and wooden-beamed ceilings. It is a simple affair situated within view of the outstanding Rocacorba Mountain, about 7 km (4 miles) outside Girona. Bold food, such as roasted shoulder of lamb, braised wild boar and stewed rabbit, is served in positively unpretentious surroundings. An obvious aim to provide robust sustenance with unfussy house wines is a welcome reminder that, despite innovations from Ferran Adrià loyalists all over Spain, there remains a place for the hearty traditionalists.

RESTAURANTE TAJ

Recommended by
Jordi Roca

Carrer de Cort Reial 6
Girona
Catalonia 17004

Opening hours..................................6 days for lunch and dinner
Reservation policy..Yes
Credit cards..Accepted
Price range..Budget
Style..Casual
Cuisine..Indian
Recommended for..Bargain

RESTAURANT VILLA MAS

Recommended by
Josep Roca

Passeig San Pol 95
San Feliu de Guíxols
Girona
Catalonia 17220

Opening hours..................................7 days for lunch and dinner
Reservation policy..Yes
Credit cards..Accepted
Price range..Expensive
Style..Smart casual
Cuisine..Modern Spanish
Recommended for..Worth the travel

In the summer, you dine in the courtyard of this early
twentieth-century modernist villa set in the bay of
Sant Feliu de Guíxols, an hour north of Barcelona.
Former DJ and now chef Carlos Orta serves the
freshest seafood, such as red prawns (shrimp) from
Palamos, scorpion fish, grilled grouper and marinated sardines on potato confit. There are regional
specialities, including *salmorejo* (a type of gazpacho),
and inventive pairings such as pig's trotter (feet)
with sea cucumber. For wine lovers there's an internationally noted selection of Burgundy vintages
pegged at close-to-retail prices, although you'll still
need deep pockets to enjoy them.

MIRAMAR

Recommended by
Jordi Cruz

Passeig Marítim 7
Llançà
Catalonia 17490
+34 972380132
www.restaurantmiramar.com

Opening hours.............6 days for lunch and 5 days for dinner
Reservation policy..Yes
Reservation email.............reservas@restaurantmiramar.com
Credit cards..Accepted
Price range..Expensive
Style..Smart casual
Cuisine..Modern Spanish
Recommended for..Worth the travel

LA TAVERNA DEL MAR

Recommended by
Joan Roca

Platja de S'Agaró 140
Catalonia 17220
www.latavernadelmar.com

Opening hours..................................7 days for lunch and dinner
Reservation policy..Yes
Reservation email.................reservas@latavernadelmar.com
Credit cards..Accepted
Price range..Affordable
Style..Smart casual
Cuisine..Seafood
Recommended for..Late night

JOAN GATELL

Recommended by
Michael Mina

Passeig de Miramar 26
Cambrils
Tarragona
Catalonia 43850
+34 977360057
www.joangatell.com

Opening hours	7 days for lunch and 5 days for dinner
Reservation policy	Yes
Credit cards	Accepted
Price range	Expensive
Style	Casual
Cuisine	Catalan
Recommended for	Worth the travel

The port of Cambrils is well known throughout Catalonia for the quality of its fish restaurants and Joan Gatell is among the best. Owner Joan Gatell and his wife Fanni have run the restaurant since 1970 but the site has been serving food since 1914, originally under the Café Casa Gatell name, and head chef Joan Pedrell is now in charge of the piscine preparation. Most of the fish, which comes in the traditional Catalan style, is likely to have been landed by local fishermen and bought on the quayside, and is best eaten on the upstairs terrace with views overlooking the port.

ATRIO

Recommended by
Quique Dacosta,
José Pizarro

Atrio Hotel
Plaza de San Mateo 1
Cáceres
Extremadura 10003
+34 927242928
www.restauranteatrio.com

Opening hours	7 days for lunch and dinner
Reservation policy	Yes
Credit cards	Accepted
Price range	Expensive
Style	Formal
Cuisine	Spanish
Recommended for	Worth the travel

The new incarnation of chef Toño Pérez and José Polo's Atrio in Cáceres, Extremadura, designed by renowned architects Luis M. Mansilla and Emilio Tuñón Alvarez, opened in 2011. Situated on a small square beside the convent of San Pablo and the church of San Mateo in the beautiful, historic part of the city, black granite floors and white oak walls adorned with contemporary art are the setting for Pérez's famous creations — such as roast scallops with creamy boletus and truffle, and Ibérican ham with lobster, pimentón and garlic — and Polo's celebrated wine selection, kept in an incredible, purpose-built cellar.

EL FIGÓN DE EUSTAQUIO

Recommended by
José Pizarro

Plaza de San Juan 14
Cáceres
Extremadura 10003
+34 927244362
www.elfigondeeustaquio.com

Opening hours	5 days for lunch and dinner
Reservation policy	Yes
Reservation email	reservas@elfigondeeustaquio.com
Credit cards	Accepted
Price range	Affordable
Style	Smart casual
Cuisine	Modern Spanish
Recommended for	Bargain

CASA MARCELO

Recommended by
Jean Marie Baudic,
Eduardo Moreno

Rua Hortas 1
Santiago de Compostela
Galicia 15705
+34 981558580
www.casamarcelo.net

Opening hours	4 days for lunch and dinner
Reservation policy	Yes
Credit cards	Accepted
Price range	Expensive
Style	Smart casual
Cuisine	Galician
Recommended for	Worth the travel

CORRAL DE LA MORERIA

Recommended by
Dario Bassa

Calle de la Morería 17
Madrid 28005
+34 913658446
www.corraldelamoreria.com

Opening hours	6 days for dinner
Reservation policy	Yes
Credit cards	Accepted
Price range	Affordable
Style	Casual
Cuisine	Spanish
Recommended for	Local favourite

'Restaurant with best flamenco show in the world.'—Dario Bassa

DIVERXO

Recommended by
Carme Ruscalleda

Calle Pensamiento 28
Madrid 28020
+34 915700766
www.diverxo.com

Opening hours...............................5 days for lunch and dinner
Reservation policy..Yes
Credit cards...Accepted
Price range..Expensive
Style..Smart casual
Cuisine..Spanish-Asian
Recommended for..Worth the travel

EL FOGÓN DE TRIFÓN

Recommended by
Dario Bassa

Calle de Ayala 144
Madrid 28006
+34 914023794
www.elfogondetrifon.com

Opening hours.............6 days for lunch and 5 days for dinner
Reservation policy..Yes
Credit cards...Accepted
Price range..Affordable
Style...Casual
Cuisine...Madrileno
Recommended for...Bargain

JUANA LA LOCA

Recommended by
Roberta Sudbrack

Plaza de Puerta de Moros 4
Madrid 28005
+34 913640525

Opening hours.............6 days for lunch and 7 days for dinner
Reservation policy..Yes
Credit cards...Accepted
Price range..Affordable
Style...Casual
Cuisine...Tapas
Recommended for..Worth the travel

'Best tapas I've had in a long time.'—Roberta Sudbrack

MOULIN CHOCOLAT

Recommended by
Dario Bassa

Calle de Alcalá 77
Madrid 28009
www.moulinchocolat.com

Opening hours........................6 days from breakfast until late
Reservation policy...No
Credit cards...Accepted
Price range...Budget
Style...Casual
Cuisine...Café
Recommended for..Breakfast

O'CLOCK PUB & GARDEN

Recommended by
Dario Bassa

Calle de Juan Bravo 25
Madrid 28006
www.oclockpub.com

Opening hours...............................6 days from dinner until late
Reservation policy...No
Credit cards...Accepted
Price range..Affordable
Style...Casual
Cuisine...Tapas
Recommended for...Late night

'Where you can drink spectacular cocktails while
having some tapas.' —Dario Bassa

RAMÓN FREIXA MADRID

Recommended by
Dario Bassa, Carme
Ruscalleda, Henrique
Sá Pessoa

Calle Claudio Coello 67
Madrid 28001
+34 917818262
www.ramonfreixamadrid.com

Opening hours	5 days for lunch and dinner
Reservation policy	Yes
Reservation email	info@ramonfreixamadrid.com
Credit cards	Accepted
Price range	Expensive
Style	Casual
Cuisine	Modern Spanish
Recommended for	Worth the travel

Nothing says 'special occasion' quite like dinner at Ramon Freixa's ravishing Madrid restaurant. Jaws hit the floor at the first sight of the chandeliers, mosaic floor and magnificent mirrored ceiling. Classically trained Catalan chef Freixa backs up style with substance: his highly evolved cuisine was awarded two Michelin stars within two years of the restaurant opening in 2009. Both 'traditional' and 'modern' dishes are served – it's not often one finds hare à la royale and duck burger with mustard ice cream on the same menu. Cooking is in Freixa's blood – his father was a top chef and it's his excellent bread that's served here.

RESTAURANTE COMBARRO

Recommended by
Pedro Subijana

Calle Reina Mercedes 12
Madrid 28020
+34 915547784
www.combarro.com

Opening hours	7 days for lunch and dinner
Reservation policy	Yes
Reservation email	combarro@combarro.com
Credit cards	Accepted
Price range	Affordable
Style	Smart casual
Cuisine	Galician
Recommended for	High end

This elegant and refined dining room close to Madrid's city centre specializes in the cuisine of Galicia and especially its seafood. If you've never tried the scary looking but oh-so-delicious *percebes* (gooseneck barnacles) that are death defyingly harvested by hand from Galician cliff sides, this is place to eat them. There are other *outré* species such as the eel-like lamprey, but the more familiar dishes such as octopus and a range of grilled or baked fish

are equally attractive propositions. You don't have to indulge in full-on fine-dining though – there's tapas in the handsome wood-panelled bar with its impressive display of hanging hams.

SACHA

Recommended by
Alberto Chicote

Calle de Juan Hurtado de Mendoza 11
Madrid 28036
+34 913455952

Opening hours	6 days for lunch and dinner
Reservation policy	Yes
Credit cards	Accepted
Price range	Affordable
Style	Casual
Cuisine	Madrileno
Recommended for	Regular neighbourhood

SANTCELONI

Recommended by
Ollie Couillaud

Hesperia Hotel
Paseo de la Castellana 57
Madrid 28010
+34 912108840
www.restaurantesantceloni.com

Opening hours	5 days for lunch and 6 days for dinner
Reservation policy	Yes
Credit cards	Accepted
Price range	Expensive
Style	Smart casual
Cuisine	Madrileno
Recommended for	Worth the travel

SERGI AROLA GASTRO

Recommended by
Vicky Ratnani

Calle de Zurbano 31
Madrid 28010
+34 913102169
www.sergiarola.es

Opening hours	5 days for lunch and dinner
Reservation policy	Yes
Credit cards	Accepted
Price range	Expensive
Style	Formal
Cuisine	Modern Spanish
Recommended for	Worth the travel

TABERNA DE LA DANIELA

Recommended by
Omar Allibhoy

General Pardiñas 21
Madrid 28001
+34 915762091
www.tabernaladaniela.com

Opening hours................................7 days for lunch and dinner
Reservation policy...Yes
Credit cards..Accepted
Price range...Budget
Style...Casual
Cuisine..Madrileno
Recommended for...Local favourite

'This restaurant serves the best *Cocido Madrileño*.
It's a rich soup with thin angel hair pasta, chickpeas,
stewed beef in tomato sauce and seasonal greens. It's
a must try if you're in Madrid.'—Omar Allibhoy

LA TERRAZA

Recommended by
Alberto Chicote,
Eduardo Moreno

Casino de Madrid
Calle de Alcalá 15
Madrid 28014
+34 915321275
www.casinodemadrid.es

Opening hours............5 days for lunch and 6 days for dinner
Reservation policy...Yes
Reservation email....................terraza.casino@nh-hotels.com
Credit cards..Accepted
Price range..Expensive
Style...Formal
Cuisine...Modern Spanish
Recommend for...High end

LA MAÑUETA

Recommended by
Andoni Luis Aduriz

Calle Mañueta 10
Pamplona
Navarra 31001

Opening hours........7 days during San Fermín Festival in July
Reservation policy..No
Credit cards..Not accepted
Price range...Budget
Style...Casual
Cuisine..Churros
Recommended for...Breakfast

CASA FEDERICO

Recommended by
Quique Dacosta

Carrer de Ausiàs March 22
Dénia
Alicante
Community of Valencia 03700
+34 965783041

Opening hours................................7 days for lunch and dinner
Reservation policy...Yes
Credit cards..Accepted
Price range...Budget
Style...Casual
Cuisine..Seafood
Recommended for...Bargain

JOËL RESTAURANT BISTRONOMIC

Recommended by
Quique Dacosta

Avenida Alicante 19
Dénia
Alicante
Community of Valencia 03700
www.joelrestaurant.es

Opening hours................................6 days for lunch and dinner
Reservation policy...Yes
Credit cards..Accepted
Price range...Affordable
Style...Casual
Cuisine...Modern Spanish
Recommended for...Local favourite

PACO GANDÍA

Recommended by
Paco Morales

Carrer San Francisco 2
Pinoso
Alicante
Community of Valencia 3650
+34 965478023

Opening hours...7 days for lunch
Reservation policy...Yes
Credit cards..Accepted
Price range...Affordable
Style...Casual
Cuisine...Valencian
Recommended for...Local favourite

'Paco Gandia has to be the only place in the world
that serves rice with snails and rabbit roasted in
vine leaves.'—Paco Morales

PASTELERÍA TOTEL ELDA

Avenida de José Martínez González 101
Elda
Alicante
Community of Valencia 03600
www.torreblanca.net

Opening hours..........................7 days from breakfast until late
Reservation policy..No
Credit cards...Accepted
Price range..Affordable
Style..Casual
Cuisine..Modern pastries
Recommended for...Breakfast

'The world stops every time I am here.'
—Quique Dacosta

PEIX AND BRASES

Plaza Benidorm
Dénia
Alicante
Community of Valencia 03700
www.peixibrases.com

Opening hours.................................7 days for lunch and dinner
Reservation policy..Yes
Credit cards...Accepted
Price range..Affordable
Style..Smart casual
Cuisine..Modern Mediterranean
Recommended for....................................Local favourite

QUIQUE DACOSTA RESTAURANTE

Carreterra de les Marines
Dénia
Alicante
Community of Valencia 03700
+34 965784179
www.quiquedacosta.es

Opening hours.................................5 days for lunch and dinner
Reservation policy..Yes
Reservation email..............quiquedacosta@quiquedacosta.es
Credit cards...Accepted
Price range..Expensive
Style..Formal
Cuisine..Modern Spanish
Recommended for.......................................Worth the travel

'Amazing.'—Felipe Bronze

Chef Quique Dacosta takes his place among the
Spanish avant-garde giants such as Ferran Adrià due
to his desire to create truly original dishes. Following
elBulli's closure, his Costa Blanca restaurant has
become the new place of pilgrimage for globetrotting
gastronomes. Inside the glass and concrete building,
which resembles both a modern art gallery and a
rustic Spanish retreat, Dacosta experiments with
underutilized plants such as cacti, as well as more
traditional Spanish ingredients, in an attempt to
create an 'edible landscape'. As you might imagine,
dishes are colourful, often surprising and occasionally slightly whacky – but always memorable.

RESTAURANTE LA CUINA

Carreterra de les Marines
Dénia
Alicante
Community of Valencia 03700
+34 965787080

Opening hours.................................6 days for lunch and dinner
Reservation policy..Yes
Credit cards...Accepted
Price range..Budget
Style..Casual
Cuisine..Tapas
Recommended for....................................Local favourite

CAFETERÍA LA GELA

Recommended by
Paco Morales

Carrer de Santa Agueda
Bocairent
Community of Valencia 46880

Opening hours	6 days from breakfast until late
Reservation policy	No
Credit cards	Not accepted
Price range	Budget
Style	Casual
Cuisine	Café
Recommended for	Breakfast

RESTAURANT PACO MORALES

Recommended by
Matias Palomo Reyes

Ferrero Hotel
Carretera de Villena-Ontinyent 16
Bocairent
Community of Valencia 46880
+34 962355175
www.hotelferrero.com

Opening hours	7 days for lunch and dinner
Reservation policy	Yes
Credit cards	Accepted
Price range	Expensive
Style	Smart casual
Cuisine	Modern Spanish
Recommended for	Worth the travel

VUELVE CAROLINA

Recommended by
Dario Bassa

Carrer de Correos 8
Valencia
Community of Valencia 46002
+34 963218686
www.vuelvecarolina.com

Opening hours	6 days for lunch and dinner
Reservation policy	Yes
Credit cards	Accepted but not AMEX
Price range	Affordable
Style	Casual
Cuisine	Tapas
Recommended for	Worth the travel

PORTAL FOSC

Recommended by
Paco Morales

Carrer de Portal de Valencia 22
Xativa
Community of Valencia 46800

Opening hours	6 days for lunch and 4 days for dinner
Reservation policy	Yes
Credit cards	Accepted
Price range	Affordable
Style	Casual
Cuisine	Modern Spanish
Recommended for	Late night

The peregrinations of young talent Jordi Garrido have taken him from his hometown of Xàtiva near Valencia to top kitchens all over Spain and back again. Magpie-like, he's picked up a bit of everything along the way but, established at his townhouse restaurant Portal Fosc since 2008, his cooking is entirely his own. The fully open kitchen practises *cocina de proximidad* (market cooking) using organic vegetables from the kitchen garden and small local producers. Availability of dishes is season-dependent but monkfish liver with *cacau del collaret* (a local peanut championed by Slow Food) and Garrido's version of Arnadí, a Valencian pumpkin pie, have been hits.

'**Serves the best Ibérian ham sandwich.**'
ALBERT ADRIÀ P340

'LOCATED IN THE BOQUERIA MARKET THEY SERVE A GREAT FORK AND SPOON BREAKFAST.'
WILLY TRULLAS MORENO P342

'Traditional food from Galicia.'
PACO GUZMAN P340

BARCELONA

'GOOD BUTTER PLUS GOOD BAKER'S HANDS AND A LOT OF LOVE EQUALS A FANTASTIC BAKERY.'
ALBERT RAURICH P350

'**Grilled meats, snails, escalivada and bustle.**'
JACOB KENEDY P352

'IT'S IN FRONT OF THE MEDITERRANEAN SEA. SUN, A NEWSPAPER, COLD BEER AND ONE OF THE BEST PAELLAS IN CATALUNYA.'
ALBERT RAURICH P347

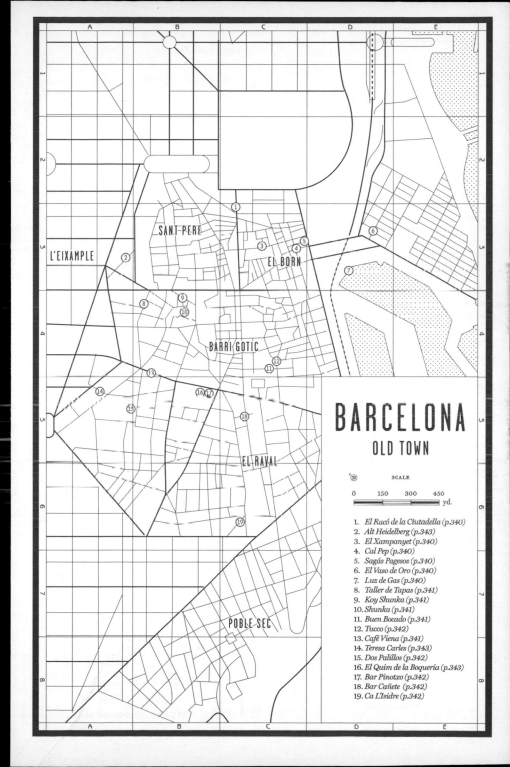

BARCELONA
OLD TOWN

LUZ DE GAS

Recommended by
Carles Abellán

Marina Port Vell
Muelle del depósito s/n
Barceloneta
Barcelona 08039
www.luzdegas.com

Opening hours	7 days for lunch and dinner
Reservation policy	No
Credit cards	Accepted
Price range	Budget
Style	Casual
Cuisine	Tapas
Recommended for	Late night

Luz de Gas is not so much a tapas joint as a floating barge-cum-nightclub, even though small plates remain a key part of its offer. Its prestigious location, so close to the yachts that you can almost board them, means that it regularly attracts a tourist crowd and on some nights can more resemble a frat party than your typical Barcelona night spot. But don't be put off – it's a fun place to let your hair down.

EL VASO DE ORO

Recommended by
Jordi Cruz

Carrer de Balboa 6
Barceloneta
Barcelona 08003
www.vasodeoro.com

Opening hours	7 days for breakfast, lunch and dinner
Reservation policy	No
Credit cards	Accepted
Price range	Affordable
Style	Casual
Cuisine	Tapas
Recommended for	Late night

CAL PEP

Recommended by
Jason Fox, Henry Harris,
Jacob Kenedy, Cal Peternell

Plaça de les Olles 8
El Born
Barcelona 08003
+34 933107961
www.calpep.com

Opening hours	5 days for lunch and 6 days for dinner
Reservation policy	Yes
Reservation email	calpep@calpep.com
Credit cards	Accepted
Price range	Affordable
Style	Casual
Cuisine	Tapas
Recommended for	Late night

'Infamous.'—Jacob Kenedy

EL RACÓ DE LA CIUTADELLA

Recommended by
Paco Guzmán

Carrer de la Princesa 50
El Born
Barcelona 08003

Opening hours	6 days for breakfast, lunch and dinner
Reservation policy	Yes
Credit cards	Accepted but not AMEX
Price range	Budget
Style	Casual
Cuisine	Tapas
Recommended for	Regular neighbourhood

El Racó de la Ciutadella looks like many other of the hundreds of tapas joints that crowd Spain's second city – too brightly lit, messy floors – but what sets it apart is the sheer breadth of food offered as well as the super-competitive prices. Money hasn't been spent on fancy decor – an old fruit machine and cheap metal furniture are proof – but on ensuring that the quality of ingredients surpasses that of its nearby rivals. This means that Galician-style squid and *pote* (a type of stew) are top-notch and the *jamón* (ham) and tortillas more than hold their own.

EL XAMPANYET

Recommended by
Albert Adrià

Carrer de Montcada 22
El Born
Barcelona 08004

Opening hours	6 days for lunch and 5 days for dinner
Reservation policy	No
Credit cards	Not accepted
Price range	Affordable
Style	Casual
Cuisine	Tapas
Recommended for	Local favourite

SAGÀS PAGESOS

Recommended by
Jordi Cruz

Plà del Palau 13
El Born
Barcelona 08003
+34 933300303

Opening hours	7 days for lunch and dinner
Reservation policy	Yes
Credit cards	Accepted
Price range	Affordable
Style	Casual
Cuisine	Spanish
Recommended for	Bargain

BUEN BOCADO

Carrer de Escudellers 31
El Gòtic
Barcelona 08002

Opening hours	6 days for lunch and dinner
Reservation policy	No
Credit cards	Not accepted
Price range	Budget
Style	Casual
Cuisine	North African
Recommended for	Late night

CAFÉ VIENA

La Rambla del Estudis 115
El Gòtic
Barcelona 08002
www.viena.es

Opening hours	7 days from breakfast until late
Reservation policy	No
Credit cards	Accepted
Price range	Budget
Style	Casual
Cuisine	Café
Recommended for	Bargain

'Serves the best Ibérian ham sandwich.'—Albert Adrià

KOY SHUNKA

Carrer de Copons 7
El Gòtic
Barcelona 08002
+34 934127939
www.koyshunka.com

Opening hours	6 days for lunch and 5 days for dinner
Reservation policy	Yes
Credit cards	Accepted
Price range	Affordable
Style	Smart casual
Cuisine	Japanese
Recommended for	Late night

Barcelona has acquired a healthy appetite for Japanese food in recent years. Following the success of their original restaurant Shunka, owners Hideki Matsuhisa and Xu Zhangchao opened Koy Shunka in 2008. Behind an anonymous door in an anonymous back alley in the gothic quarter lies a beautiful grey slate room dominated by a polished wood counter, where a maximum of twenty-four diners watch as

a series of stunning Japanese dishes are meticulously prepared before their eyes. It's not cheap, and a tasting menu can stretch well on into the night, but you won't hear any complaints from anyone lucky enough to score a reservation.

SHUNKA

Carrer dels Sagristans 5
El Gòtic
Barcelona 08002
+34 934124991

Opening hours	6 days for lunch and dinner
Reservation policy	Yes
Credit cards	Accepted
Price range	Affordable
Style	Smart casual
Cuisine	Japanese
Recommended for	Regular neighbourhood

TALLER DE TAPAS

Carrer Comtal 28
El Gòtic
Barcelona 08002
+34 934816233
www.tallerdetapas.com

Opening hours	7 days for lunch and dinner
Reservation policy	Yes
Credit cards	Accepted
Price range	Affordable
Style	Casual
Cuisine	Tapas
Recommended for	Wish I'd opened

'The food is so good and they have a huge menu. It's a major inspiration for me.'—Ken Oringer

TUCCO

Recommended by
Paco Guzmán

Carrer dels Còdols 27
El Gòtic
Barcelona 08002
www.tuccopastasfrescas.com

Opening hours....................................6 days for lunch and dinner
Reservation policy...No
Credit cards...Accepted
Price range...Budget
Style...Casual
Cuisine...Argentine-Italian
Recommended for.................................Regular neighbourhood

If you've worked up an appetite exploring Barcelona's gothic quarter, this cubbyhole of a restaurant is the perfect place for a pit stop. With just three tables and a blackboard menu listing a variety of freshly made pastas, this is about as simple and as cheap as dining in the Catalan capital gets. The numerous ravioli stuffings might include aubergine (eggplant) with balsamic vinegar, mushroom, chicken with bacon or goat's cheese with basil. There's a selection of savoury tarts and sandwiches and, if you've still got room after all those carbs, rich desserts such as Tiramisù and banana and chocolate pudding.

BAR CAÑETE

Recommended by
Albert Adrià

Carrer de la Unió 17
El Raval
Barcelona 08001
+34 932703458
www.antiguobarorgia.com

Opening hours....................................6 days for lunch and dinner
Reservation policy...Yes
Credit cards...Accepted
Price range...Affordable
Style...Casual
Cuisine...Tapas
Recommended for.......................................Local favourite

BAR PINOTXO

Recommended by
Albert Adrià, Ferran Adrià,
Pier Bussetti,
Sergio Herman,
Willy Trullas Moreno

Mercat de la Boqueria 466-467
Rambles 89
El Raval
Barcelona 08002
+34 933171731
www.boqueria.info

Opening hours..........................6 days for breakfast and lunch
Reservation policy...No
Credit cards..Not accepted
Price range...Affordable
Style...Casual
Cuisine...Tapas
Recommended for..Breakfast

'Located in the Boqueria market they serve a great fork and spoon breakfast.'—Willy Trullas Moreno

CA L'ISIDRE

Recommended by
Albert Adrià

Carrer de les Flors 12
El Raval
Barcelona 08001
+34 9344111
www.calisidre.com

Opening hours....................................6 days for lunch and dinner
Reservation policy...Yes
Reservation email..............................reservas@calisidre.com
Credit cards...Accepted
Price range..Expensive
Style...Smart casual
Cuisine..Modern Spanish
Recommended for.......................................Local favourite

DOS PALILLOS

Recommended by
Ferran Adrià,
Claus Moller Henriksen

Carrer d'Elisabets 9
El Raval
Barcelona 08001
+34 933040513
www.dospalillos.com

Opening hours.............2 days for lunch and 3 days for dinner
Reservation policy...Yes
Reservation email.......................dospalillos@dospalillos.com
Credit cards...Accepted
Price range...Affordable
Style...Casual
Cuisine...Asian small plates
Recommended for.................................Regular neighbourhood

You've been executive chef at the most renowned restaurant on the planet for the best part of a decade — what do you do next? The answer for Albert

Raurich, who ran the kitchen at elBulli from 1999 until 2007, is to open an Asian-inspired tapas bar. Located beside the Casa Camper hotel (with a second branch at their Berlin hotel), Dos Palillos serves small plates in its no-nonsense front bar, where you perch perilously on plastic crates. Behind the bead curtain at the back lies a more formal, low-lit dining room with counter seating that offers a multi-coursed menu of Asian-Ibérian dishes.

EL QUIM DE LA BOQUERIA

Mercat de la Boqueria
Rambles 91
El Raval
Barcelona 08002
www.elquimdelaboqueria.cat

Recommended by
Carles Abellan, Albert Adrià,
Jason Fox

Opening hours	5 days for breakfast and lunch
Reservation policy	No
Credit cards	Accepted
Price range	Affordable
Style	Casual
Cuisine	Tapas
Recommended for	Breakfast

Cava hangover be damned, the time to get to Barcelona's legendary food market, La Boqueria, is at 7.00 a.m., when its top bar, El Quim De La Boqueria (established 1987), fries its first egg. This is when the Catalan capital's top chefs gather for a breakfast beer and Quim Márquez Durán's famous eggs, practically deep-fried in olive oil and served with *chipirones* (baby squid) or foie gras and wild mushrooms. Quim's exceptional ingredients are the pick of the market. The eighteen stools at its modest counter are among the city's most sought after — it's strictly first come, first served.

TERESA CARLES

Carrer de Jovellanos 2
El Raval
Barcelona 08001
+34 933171829
www.teresacarles.com

Recommended by
Paco Guzmán

Opening hours	7 days from breakfast until late
Reservation policy	Yes
Credit cards	Accepted
Price range	Budget
Style	Casual
Cuisine	Catalan
Recommended for	Regular neighbourhood

'Desde 1979' reads the sign on the door at Teresa Carles in El Raval, though this chic glass-fronted and thoroughly modern café-restaurant only opened in 2011. In fact, 1979 is the year that self-taught chef Carles opened pioneering Catalan vegetarian restaurant, Paradís, in Lleida, thirty-two years before her business-savvy son and daughter persuaded her to come to Barcelona. She's now a fixture in the Catalan capital, where her tofu and sprout-laden salads, vibrant tapas, juices and seitan burgers put a youthful glow on the complexions of the city's beautiful people. Not just for lentil-loving veggies, it's very popular for brunch.

ALT HEIDELBERG

Ronda de la Universitat 5
Sant Pere
Barcelona 08007

Recommended by
Paco Guzmán

Opening hours	5 days from breakfast until late
Reservation policy	Yes
Credit cards	Accepted
Price range	Budget
Style	Casual
Cuisine	German
Recommended for	Bargain

'Alt Heidelberg…' begins the German folksong, '… none can with thee compare'. The song refers of course to the German city but it could apply to the bar of the same name in Barcelona, a local institution that's been grilling bratwurst since 1934. More than just a Bierkeller serving foaming Steins to students from the nearby university, the blue-tiled interior doubles up as a tapas bar selling Ibérian ham and tortilla alongside hefty classics of the German culinary canon including Eisbein (pickled pork knuckle) and sauerkraut. 'Echt' it ain't, but it's an atmospheric all-hours spot for good beer and good sausages.

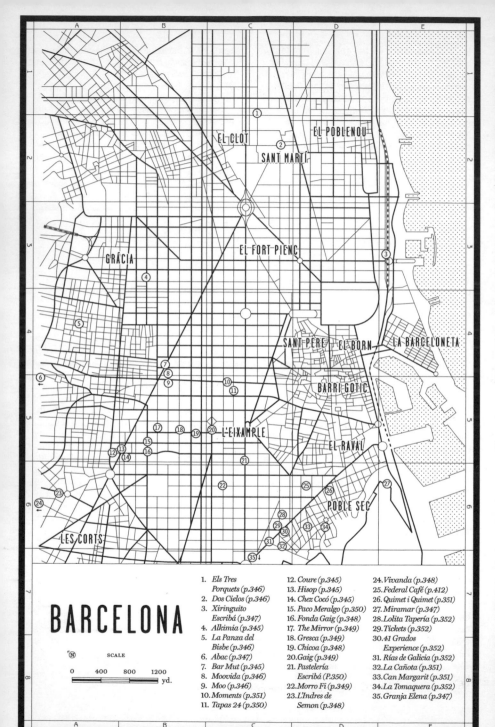

BARCELONA

SCALE

0   400   800   1200
yd.

ALKIMIA

Carrer Indústria 79
L'Eixample
Barcelona 08025
www.alkimia.cat

Opening hours	5 days for lunch and 1 day for dinner
Reservation policy	Yes
Credit cards	Accepted but not AMEX
Price range	Affordable
Style	Smart casual
Cuisine	Modern Catalan
Recommended for	High end

BAR MUT

Carrer Pau Claris 192
L'Eixample
Barcelona 08037
+34 932174338

Opening hours	7 days for brunch
Reservation policy	Yes
Credit cards	Accepted
Price range	Affordable
Style	Casual
Cuisine	Tapas
Recommended for	Late night

'If you're in Barcelona you must have tapas.
Bar Mut serves some of the best.'—Jordi Cruz

CHEZ COCÓ

Avinguda Diagonal 465
L'Eixample
Barcelona 08036
+34 934449822
www.chezcoco.es

Opening hours	6 days for lunch and dinner
Reservation policy	Yes
Credit cards	Accepted
Price range	Affordable
Style	Casual
Cuisine	Rotisserie
Recommended for	Worth the travel

The traditional Spanish roadside rotisserie is, despite
its obvious charms, rather inconsistent – order at
the right time and you'll be rewarded with a
succulent chicken heavily seasoned with salty herbs;
get the wrong end of service and you'll be stuck with
a dry old bird. Opened in 2012, Chez Cocó is
rotisserie gone gourmet – pigeon, duck, guinea fowl
and quail slowly spin next to more conventional
poultry in the impressive open-plan kitchen, and
there are people like head chef Enrique Valenti on
hand to make sure nothing – apart from the extravagant decor is overdone.

COURE

Passatge de Marimon 20
L'Eixample
Barcelona 08021

Opening hours	5 days for lunch and dinner
Reservation policy	No
Credit cards	Accepted
Price range	Affordable
Style	Casual
Cuisine	Modern Catalan
Recommended for	Regular neighbourhood

Barcelona's bistronomics movement is about ambitious chefs serving exciting food while keeping costs
to a minimum. The modern Catalan dishes chef Albert
Ventura produces in his basement restaurant are
aimed at the heights of Michelin-starred gastronomy,
but at just €35 (£28; $45) for a seasonal menu, this
classy cooking doesn't have to be a rare treat. On
the lower floor are squeezed ten stools at a small
tapas bar, where you can enjoy a taste of the
theatrics from below – without the white tablecloths
and for an even more reasonable chunk of cash.

HISOP

Passatge de Marimón 9
L'Eixample
Barcelona 08021

Opening hours	5 days for lunch and 6 days for dinner
Reservation policy	Yes
Credit cards	Accepted
Price range	Affordable
Style	Smart casual
Cuisine	Modern Spanish
Recommended for	Worth the travel

'Casual but sophisticated, and not at outrageous
prices.'—Jason Fox

MOO

Recommended by
Mustafa Cihan Kipçak

Omm Hotel
Carrer de Rosselló 265
L'Eixample
Barcelona 08008
+34 34934454000
www.hotelomm.es

Opening hours...............................6 days for lunch and dinner
Reservation policy..Yes
Credit cards...Accepted
Price range...Expensive
Style...Smart casual
Cuisine..Modern Catalan
Recommended for...Worth the travel

MOOVIDA

Recommended by
Josep Roca

Omm Hotel
Carrer de Rosselló 265
L'Eixample
Barcelona 08008
+34 934454000
www.hotelomm.es

Opening hours...............................7 days for lunch and dinner
Reservation policy..Yes
Reservation email..........................reservas@hotelomm.es
Credit cards...Accepted
Price range...Affordable
Style...Smart casual
Cuisine..International
Recommended for...Late night

Hip Barcelona residents, not known for early nights, join in-the-know visitors for a late supper at trendy Hotel Omm. The Eixample hotel, opened by the forward-thinking Grupo Tragaluz in 2003, has two restaurants: Michelin-starred Moo (overseen by the Roca brothers) and the less formal Moovida, just an olive's throw from the lobby bar. Food's served all day (handy for a bite before or after visiting Gaudí's La Pedrera) but it's around midnight that the joint really starts jumping. Regulars rate the apple tart and ginger ice cream, foie gras toast and 'Joan Roca's steak tartar' with mustard ice cream.

LA PANXA DEL BISBE

Recommended by
Paco Guzmán

Carrer de Rabassa 37
Gràcia
Barcelona 08024

Opening hours.............................5 days for lunch and dinner
Reservation policy..Yes
Credit cards...Accepted
Price range..Budget
Style...Casual
Cuisine..Tapas
Recommended for.............................Regular neighbourhood

DOS CIELOS

Recommended by
Albert Adrià,
Eduardo Moreno

Me Hotel
Carrer Pere IV 272-286
Poblenou
Barcelona 08005
+34 933672070
www.doscielos.com

Opening hours.............................5 days for lunch and dinner
Reservation policy..Yes
Credit cards...Accepted
Price range...Expensive
Style..Formal
Cuisine...Modern Spanish
Recommended for..High end

ELS TRES PORQUETS

Recommended by
Carles Abellan, Albert Adrià

Rambla del Poblenou 165
Poblenou
Barcelona 08018
www.elstresporquets.es

Opening hours.............6 days for breakfast, lunch and dinner
Reservation policy..Yes
Credit cards...Accepted
Price range...Affordable
Style...Smart casual
Cuisine..Tapas
Recommended for..High end

XIRINGUITO ESCRIBÀ

Ronda Litoral 42
Poblenou
Barcelona 08005
+34 932210729
www.escriba.es

Recommended by
Paco Guzmán, Albert Raurich

Opening hours	7 days for lunch and 3 days for dinner
Reservation policy	Yes
Reservation email	resereves@escriba.es
Credit cards	Accepted
Price range	Affordable
Style	Casual
Cuisine	Seafood
Recommended for	Regular neighbourhood

'It's in front of the Mediterranean sea. Sun, a newspaper, cold beer and one of the best paellas in Catalunya.'—Albert Raurich

If the tourist throng on Las Ramblas gets too much, just remember you're only ten minutes away from paella on a sandy white beach at this casual seaside joint in Barcelona's smart Olympic port neighbourhood. There's cuttlefish, octopus and Galician mussels in the classic seafood version, mushrooms and asparagus paella for vegetarians, and the Valencian take on the dish called *Fideuà* that's made with noodles instead of rice. But this isn't just any beach restaurant – with talented chef Joan Escribà in charge of the menu there's an imaginative range of dishes, including octopus with caramelized onion, potato and truffle.

GRANJA ELENA

Passeig Zona Franca 228
Poble Sec
Barcelona 08038
+34 933320241

Recommended by
Carles Abellan

Opening hours	5 days for lunch
Reservation policy	Yes
Credit cards	Accepted
Price range	Affordable
Style	Casual
Cuisine	Spanish
Recommended for	Bargain

Granja Elena has evolved from a small, unpretentious breakfast and snacks bar into a small, unpretentious à la carte restaurant, where you can feast on fantastically tender suckling pig or outrageously rich creamy rice with fresh morels and foie gras, and only pay around €50 (£40; $63) for the privilege. Not many tourists make it this far off La Rambla – we're talking the far side of Montjuïc here – but those who do are handsomely rewarded, not only by the quality of the food, which really is first class, but also by the welcome from Abel Sierra and his friendly, knowledgeable, English-speaking staff.

MIRAMAR

Carretera Miramar 40
Montjuic Poble Sec
Barcelona 08038
www.club-miramar.es

Recommended by
Albert Adrià

Opening hours	6 days for lunch
Reservation policy	Yes
Reservation email	info@club-miramar.es
Credit cards	Accepted
Price range	Affordable
Style	Formal
Cuisine	Mediterranean
Recommended for	High end

ABAC

ABaC Hotel
Avinguda del Tibidabo 1
Sarriá-Sant Gervasi
Barcelona 08022
+34 933196600
www.abacbarcelona.com

Recommended by
Albert Adrià,
Thrainn Freyr Vigfusson

Opening hours	6 days for lunch and dinner
Reservation policy	Yes
Reservation email	info@abacbarcelona.com
Credit cards	Accepted
Price range	Expensive
Style	Formal
Cuisine	Modern Catalan
Recommended for	High end

There is something of the Great Gatsby in the serene interior and Michelin-starred Catalonian cuisine of ABaC. It could be that chef Jordi Cruz is a youthful devotee to style and quality. Proof is in the fact that he received his first star at the age of twenty-five. Or it might be that the food is a successful meeting of tradition and innovation. The restaurant's elBulli-style cooking has given birth to an annual seasonal portfolio of tartares that should be on your to-order list. If you have a minute, between indulging in the pioneering molecular gastronomy, try to wander by the formidably modern, stainless steel kitchen to watch the action.

L'INDRET DE SEMON

Recommended by
Carme Ruscalleda

Carrer de Ganduxer 31
Sarriá-Sant Gervasi
Barcelona 08021
+34 932016931
www.semon.es

Opening hours	5 days for lunch and 4 days for dinner
Reservation policy	Yes
Credit cards	Accepted
Price range	Affordable
Style	Smart casual
Cuisine	Deli
Recommended for	Wish I'd opened

When we say that L'Indret de Semon is a deli restaurant, bear in mind that the deli (of the same name) happens to be Barcelona's most exclusive. Expect the compact Catalan menu to be brimming with luxury ingredients – caviar, foie gras, sparkling seafood. The Benfumat salmon is worth the trip alone – order any dish that features it – but the light, luxe line-up also includes delights such as Alaska crab with lettuce hearts, spinach leaves, rocket (arugula) and artichokes. Open for lunch during the week and now dinner Thursday to Sunday, the grey-panelled dining room has all the breezy elegance of a million-aire's summer house. Advance booking is essential.

VIVANDA

Recommended by
Albert Adrià

Carrer Major de Sarrià 134
Sarriá-Sant Gervasi
Barcelona 08017
+34 932031918

Opening hours	6 days for lunch and 5 days for dinner
Reservation policy	Yes
Credit cards	Accepted
Price range	Affordable
Style	Casual
Cuisine	Catalan
Recommended for	Local favourite

CHICOA

Recommended by
Carles Abellan

Carrer d'Aribau 73
L'Eixample
Barcelona 08036
+34 934531123
www.chicoa.es

Opening hours	5 days for lunch and dinner
Reservation policy	Yes
Credit cards	Accepted
Price range	Affordable
Style	Casual
Cuisine	Catalan
Recommended for	Local favourite

Chicoa has been a favourite among Barcelona's locals for its no-nonsense Catalan cooking since 1969. An extensive menu features a good selection of meat dishes but the real star of the show is fish – in particular, cod – which is given main billing. The interior doesn't look like it has changed much in the forty or so years it's been open – wooden tables, exposed brickwork (though not Manhattan loft style) and rafters give an olde worlde feel to the place that can make it feel a bit like a contrived tourist trap. But set these preconceptions to one side and you'll experience a true taste of Catalonia.

FONDA GAIG

Recommended by
Jordi Cruz

Carrer de Còrsega 200
L'Eixample
Barcelona 08036
+34 934532020
www.fondagaig.com

Opening hours	7 days for lunch and 6 days for dinner
Reservation policy	Yes
Credit cards	Accepted
Price range	Affordable
Style	Casual
Cuisine	Modern Spanish
Recommended for	Regular neighbourhood

GAIG

Carrer d'Aragó 214
L'Eixample
Barcelona 08011
+34 934291017
www.restaurantgaig.com

Recommended by
Albert Adrià, Jordi Cruz

Opening hours	5 days for lunch and dinner
Reservation policy	Yes
Credit cards	Accepted
Price range	Expensive
Style	Smart casual
Cuisine	Modern Catalan
Recommended for	Local favourite

THE MIRROR

Carrer de Còrsega 255
L'Eixample
Barcelona 08036
+34 932028685
www.themirrorbarcelona.com

Recommended by
Jordi Cruz

Opening hours	7 days for breakfast, lunch and dinner
Reservation policy	Yes
Credit cards	Accepted
Price range	Affordable
Style	Smart casual
Cuisine	Seafood
Recommended for	Regular neighbourhood

GRESCA

Carrer de Provença 230
L'Eixample
Barcelona 8036
+34 934516193
www.gresca.net

Recommended by
Jordi Butrón

Opening hours	5 days for lunch and 6 days for dinner
Reservation policy	Yes
Credit cards	Accepted
Price range	Affordable
Style	Casual
Cuisine	Modern Spanish
Recommended for	Bargain

MORRO FI

Carrer del Consell de Cent 171
L'Eixample
Barcelona 08007

Recommended by
Paco Guzmán

Opening hours	2 days for lunch and 6 days for dinner
Reservation policy	No
Credit cards	Not accepted
Price range	Budget
Style	Casual
Cuisine	Tapas
Recommended for	Regular neighbourhood

With just twenty-six covers, the narrow, minimalist dining room with its white linen and white walls focuses the diner's full attention on the plate. Which is no bad thing as the dinnerware here is the canvas for talented and creative chef Rafael Peña. A graduate of the school of Spanish modernism sustained by both Ferran Adrià and Martín Berasategui, Peña's style of 'bistronomia' fuses traditional bistro food with the haute-cuisine ideals of gastronomy to produce dishes – a flower-shaped egg-white soufflé with soft yolk centre, for instance – that are as affordable as they are delicious.

PACO MERALGO

Carrer de Muntaner 171
L'Eixample
Barcelona 08036
+34 934309027
www.pacomeralgo.com

Recommended by
Albert Adrià

Opening hours	7 days for lunch and dinner
Reservation policy	Yes
Credit cards	Accepted
Price range	Affordable
Style	Casual
Cuisine	Tapas
Recommended for	Local favourite

The Eixample district is often described as having a monotonous block layout, but the same cannot be said of the food. Nestled between the Old Town and suburbs, Alta Taberna Paco Meralgo offers elegant tapas in an unassuming environment. Exposed brickwork, chunky high wooden tables, a blackboard and mirrors make up the contemporary decor of this neighbourhood favourite, which boasts Catalan small plates at good prices. *Montaditos* (mini sandwiches) are a speciality – adorned with the likes of steak tartare, *jamón ibérico* (naturally), fried artichokes, courgette (zucchini) blossoms stuffed with mozzarella, razor clams, prawns (shrimp), cockles and giant oysters. This local flair makes it well worth leaving the busy centro.

PASTELERIA ESCRIBÀ

Gran Via de les Corts Catalanes 546
L'Eixample
Barcelona 08011
www.escriba.es

Recommended by
Albert Raurich

Opening hours	6 days for lunch and dinner
Reservation policy	No
Credit cards	Accepted
Price range	Affordable
Style	Casual
Cuisine	Bakery
Recommended for	Breakfast

'Good butter plus good baker's hands and a lot of love equals a fantastic bakery.'—Albert Raurich

The name Escribà is known in sweet-toothed Barcelona circles both as a traditional family-run bakery dating back to 1906 and as the producer of avant-garde chocolate sculptures almost worthy of a Turner Prize. The Gran Vía flagship is a showcase for fourth generation pastry chef Christian Escriba's fashion-fabulous creations (including very wearable sugar rings and not-quite-so-practical chocolate shoes) as well as a great spot for coffee and a pastry. The flavoured croissants are famous: try *sobra-sada* (cured sausage) and honey, vanilla and rose or chocolate and banana. The gorgeous La Rambla shop, an Art Nouveau gem, is another must-see.

TAPAS 24

Carrer de la Diputació 269
L'Eixample
Barcelona 08007
+34 934880977
www.projectes24.com

Recommended by
Albert Adrià, Michael
Ferraro, Joan Roca

Opening hours	7 days for breakfast, lunch and dinner
Reservation policy	Yes
Credit cards	Accepted
Price range	Affordable
Style	Casual
Cuisine	Tapas
Recommended for	Bargain

'The super-fresh and perfectly executed seafood is very impressive.'—Michael Ferraro

The Eixample tapas bar from chef Carles Abellan, who did sixteen years under you-know-who of elBulli fame, and also runs the long-running and more experimental Commerc24, and Bravo24 in the W Hotel. In a small brightly lit basement, the short menu of crowd-pleasing snacks is designed as a cutlery wrapper and scrawled across mirrors and blackboards. These include classic salt cod croquettes, Catalan favourites such as tripe stew, and the trendy fast-food hits that are the Bikini – a ham and cheese toastie (griddled sandwich) flecked with black truffle – and the McFoie Burger – a beef and foie gras pâté in a crispy bun.

CAN MARGARIT

Carrer de la Concordia 21
Poble Sec
Barcelona 08004

Opening hours	6 days for dinner
Reservation policy	Yes
Credit cards	Accepted
Price range	Affordable
Style	Casual
Cuisine	Tapas
Recommended for	Late night

'A delightful beer den.'—Jacob Kenedy

LA CAÑOTA

Recommended by
Albert Adrià

Carrer de Lleida 7
Poble Sec
Barcelona 08004
+34 933259171
www.riasdegallcla.com

Opening hours	7 days for lunch and dinner
Reservation policy	Yes
Credit cards	Accepted
Price range	Affordable
Style	Casual
Cuisine	Tapas
Recommended for	Local favourite

MOMENTS

Recommended by
Carme Ruscalleda

Mandarin Oriental Hotel
Passeig de Gràcia 38-40
Poble Sec
Barcelona 08007
+34 931518781
www.mandarinoriental.com

Opening hours	5 days for lunch and dinner
Reservation policy	Yes
Reservation email	mobcn-moments@mohg.com
Credit cards	Accepted
Price range	Expensive
Style	Smart casual
Cuisine	Modern Spanish
Recommended for	Regular neighbourhood

QUIMET I QUIMET

Recommended by
Albert Adrià, Jacob Kenedy,
Willy Trullas Moreno

Poeta Cabanyes 25
Poble Sec
Barcelona 08004

Opening hours	6 days for lunch and 5 days for dinner
Reservation policy	No
Credit cards	Accepted
Price range	Affordable
Style	Casual
Cuisine	Tapas
Recommended for	Late night

'Tremendous tapas – all from tins.'—Jacob Kenedy

A prince among Barcelona tapas joints, Quimet i Quimet has been in the Quim family for four generations, since it was built at the start of the twentieth century. There are no chairs and just a couple of tables, and the walls are hung with bottles of wine and spirits from all over the world, and some of the best tinned foods in Spain. The specialities here are the *montaditos*, little open sandwiches of that Señor Quim improvises perhaps dozens every night – they might feature salmon with truffled honey or tuna with caviar and balsamic syrup. There's a vast selection of wines and house beer on tap.

RÍAS DE GALICIA

Carrer de Lleida 7
Poble Sec
Barcelona 08004
+34 933300303
www.riasdegalicia.com

Opening hours	7 days for lunch and dinner
Reservation policy	Yes
Credit cards	Accepted
Price range	Expensive
Style	Smart casual
Cuisine	Galician-Seafood
Recommended for	High end

'A formidable seafood restaurant.'—Ferran Adrià

The late 1980s/early 1990s time warp of a dining room aside, it's hard to fault anything else bar the steepness of the bill at this Galician seafood specialist, although these days that's the price of fish this rare. Aside from the vintage Joselito ham with which you can start you meal and the large range of cheeses with which you can finish, the only land food offered is simply prepared suckling pig, kid and veal. Indulge in the lengthiest list of wacky and wonderful shellfish delicacies you're ever likely to see this side of a high-end Tokyo sushi bar.

LA TOMAQUERA

Carrer de Margarit 58
Poble Sec
Barcelona 08004

Opening hours	5 days for lunch and dinner
Reservation policy	No
Credit cards	Not accepted
Price range	Affordable
Style	Casual
Cuisine	Catalan
Recommended for	Late night

'Grilled meats, snails, escalivada and bustle.'
—Jacob Kenedy

41 GRADOS EXPERIENCE

Avinguda Paral-lel 164
Sant Antoni
Barcelona 08015
www.41grados.es

Opening hours	5 days for dinner
Reservation policy	Yes
Reservation email	experience@41grados.es
Credit cards	Accepted but not Diners
Price range	Expensive
Style	Formal
Cuisine	Tapas
Recommended for	Worth the travel

'Fantastic place for high gastronomy.'—Albert Raurich

FEDERAL CAFÉ

Carrer del Parlament 39
Sant Antoni
Barcelona 08015
www.federalcafe.es

Opening hours	6 days from breakfast until late
Reservation policy	No
Credit cards	Accepted
Price range	Affordable
Style	Casual
Cuisine	Café
Recommended for	Breakfast

LOLITA TAPERIA

Recommended by
Albert Raurich

Tamarit 104
Local 2-4
Sant Antoni
Barcelona 08015
+34 934245231
www.lolitataperia.com

Opening hours	2 days for lunch and 5 days for dinner
Reservation policy	No
Reservation email	info@lolitataperia.com
Credit cards	Accepted
Price range	Budget
Style	Casual
Cuisine	Tapas
Recommended for	Bargain

'Good raw products, good philosophy and a nice place to eat informal tapas.'—Albert Raurich

The wildly popular Inopia, opened by Albert Adrià and Joan Martínez, quickly graduated from neighbourhood tapas bar to become one of Barcelona's most sought-after hang-outs when it opened in 2006. Now that Adrià has moved on and the restaurant has been renamed Lolita Taperia, the neighbourhood feel has returned — that's not to say that Martínez is letting standards slip. The familiar faces behind the counter are still as welcoming as ever, the laid-back decor as effortlessly cool and the food as appealing as it is unshowy. Long-term fans might recognize the potato-and-beef-filled Bomba d'Eixample. Other highlights include a tennis ball of *burrata* and the Gos d'Atura hot dog, all at down-to-earth prices.

TICKETS

Recommended by
Carles Abellan, Omar
Allibhoy, Felipe Bronze,
Pier Bussetti, Jordi Butrón
Melero, Jacob Kenedy,
Albert Raurich, Jordi Roca,
Perfecto Roger

Avinguda Paral-lel 164
Sant Antoni
Barcelona 08015
www.ticketsbar.es

Opening hours	1 day for lunch and 5 days for dinner
Reservation policy	Yes
Credit cards	Accepted
Price range	Affordable
Style	Casual
Cuisine	Tapas
Recommended for	Worth the travel

This is what the elBulli brothers did next. Their next trick, after running the most famously oversubscribed restaurant the world has every seen, was to open a tapas bar. Or, to be more precise, a tapas bar and a casual restaurant that does tapas, the way elBulli was a formal restaurant that did tapas. Sitting next to Tickets, 41 Grados Experience, closer to a traditional tapas bar in terms of the space, serves creative cocktails and snacks. Tickets itself is arranged with counters, colourful furniture and a series of stations that prepare everything from local seafood delicacies to wacky desserts.

'**Great ambience and brilliant fish.**'
MIGUEL CASTRO E SILVA P356

'**Simple and fresh food. You'll want to return and return and return.**'
LUIS BAENA P356

'**ORDER THE SARDINES.**'
OLIVIER DA COSTA P357

PORTUGAL

'*This is one of the restaurants that most represents my region in northern Portugal. You can eat wonderful local products, cooked to perfection.*'
JOSÉ CORDEIRO P356

'**The view is amazing.**'
MICHAEL WOLF P356

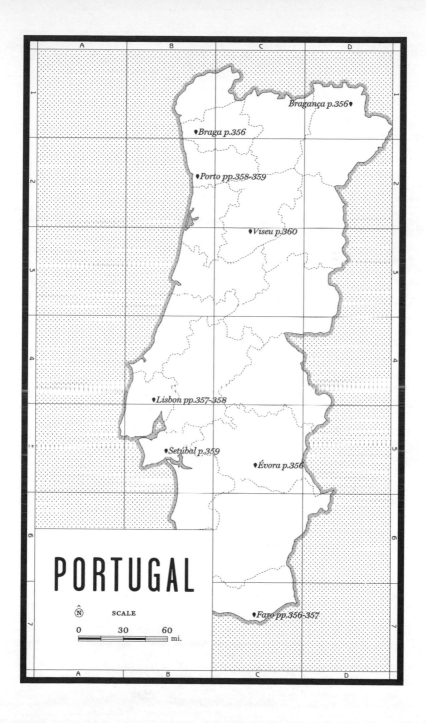

Bragança p.356

Braga p.356

Porto pp.358-359

Viseu p.360

Lisbon pp.357-358

Setúbal p.359

Évora p.356

Faro pp.356-357

PORTUGAL

N

SCALE

0   30   60
                mi.

CONFEITARIA COLONIAL

Largo Porta Nova 43
Barcelos
Braga 4750-329
+351 253811365

Opening hours............................7 days for breakfast and lunch
Reservation policy..No
Credit cards..Not accepted
Price range..Budget
Style..Casual
Cuisine...Bakery-Café
Recommended for...Breakfast

RESTAURANTE GEADAS

Rua do Loreto 32
Bragança 5300-189
+351 273324413
www.geadas.net

Opening hours.................................7 days for lunch and dinner
Reservation policy...Yes
Credit cards...Accepted
Price range..Affordable
Style..Casual
Cuisine...Portuguese
Recommended for..Local favourite

'Local wonderful products, cooked to perfection.'
—José Cordeiro

SÃO ROSAS

Largo Dom Dinis 11
Estremoz
Évora 7100-509
+351 268333345

Opening hours..............................6 days for lunch and dinner
Reservation policy...Yes
Reservation email...sao.rosas@hotmail.com
Credit cards...Accepted
Price range..Budget
Style..Casual
Cuisine...Portuguese
Recommended for..................................Regular neighbourhood

CANIÇO

Aldeamento da Prainha
Praia dos Três Irmãos
Alvor
Faro 8500-072
+351 282458503
www.canicorestaurante.com

Opening hours........................7 days from breakfast until late
Reservation policy...Yes
Credit cards........................Accepted but not AMEX and Diners
Price range..Affordable
Style..Casual
Cuisine..Mediterranean
Recommended for...Worth the travel

'The view is amazing.'—Michael Wolf

GIGI'S

Praia de Quinta do Lago
Almancil
Faro 8135-024
+351 964045178

Opening hours..7 days for lunch
Reservation policy...Yes
Reservation email......................................gigipraia@hotmail.com
Credit cards..Not accepted
Price range..Affordable
Style..Casual
Cuisine...Portuguese
Recommended for...Worth the travel

'Great ambience and brilliant fish.'
—Miguel Castro e Silva

NOÉLIA E JERÓNIMO

Avenida Ria Formosa
Edifício Cabanas-Mar
Cabanas de Tavira
Faro
8800-591
+351 281370649

Opening hours.................................7 days for lunch and dinner
Reservation policy...Yes
Credit cards...Accepted
Price range..Affordable
Style..Casual
Cuisine...Portuguese
Recommended for..................................Regular neighbourhood

'Simple and fresh food. You'll want to return
and return and return.'—Luis Baena

OCEAN

Vila Vita Parc Hotel
Rua Anneliese Pohl
Alporchinhos
Porches
Faro 8400-450
+351 282310100
www.vilavitaparc.com

Opening hours................................5 days for dinner
Reservation policy...Yes
Reservation email....................reservas@vilavitaparc.com
Credit cards.................Accepted but not AMEX and Diners
Price range...Expensive
Style..Formal
Cuisine......................................Modern Portuguese
Recommended for.............................Worth the travel

VILA JOYA

Vila Joya Hotel
Estrada da Praia da Galé
Albufeira
Faro 8201-917
+351 289591795
www.vilajoya.com

Opening hours.............7 days for breakfast, lunch and dinner
Reservation policy ....Yes
Reservation email...............................info@vilajoya.com
Credit cards..Accepted
Price range..Expensive
Style..Smart casual
Cuisine..Modern European
Recommended for...High end

'The energy and spirit of Vila Joya inspires me.'
—Normand Laprise

FORTALEZA DO GUINCHO

Fortaleza do Guincho Hotel
Estrada do Guincho
Cascais
Lisbon 2750-642
+351 214870491
www.guinchotel.pt

Opening hours.................7 days for lunch and dinner
Reservation policy..Yes
Reservation email...................restaurante@guinchotel.pt
Credit cards...Accepted
Price range...Expensive
Style...Formal
Cuisine..French-Portuguese
Recommended for...High end

'By the sea and with amazing food.'—José Cordeiro

A seventeenth-century fortress keeping watch over
the vast Atlantic from Cascais, due west of Lisbon,
Fortaleza do Guincho is now a five-star hotel and
Michelin-starred restaurant, under the creative hand
of celebrated Alsatian chef Antoine Westermann.
The style is essentially French but the ingredients
are largely Portuguese, and fourteen years at this
post has added a battery of local culinary knowledge
to Westermann's armoury. Whether you choose the
seasonal, à la carte or tasting menu – the latter
comprising six courses including *amuse-bouches*
and *mignardises* – expect a barrage of flavour and
exquisite texture, complemented by a suitably
excellent selection of wine.

MIDORI

Penha Longa Hotel Spa & Golf Resort
Estrada da Lagoa Azul
Sintra
Lisbon 2714-511
+351 219249000
www.penhalonga.com

Opening hours.................5 days for lunch and dinner
Reservation policy..Yes
Credit cards...Accepted
Price range..Affordable
Style..Smart casual
Cuisine...Japanese
Recommended for.....................................Wish I'd opened

MONTE MAR

Hotel Quinta da Marinha Resort
Avenida Nossa Senhora do Cabo 2845
Guincho
Cascais
Lisbon 2750-374
+351 214869270
www.montemar.pt

Opening hours.................................6 days for lunch and dinner
Reservation policy..Yes
Credit cards..Accepted
Price range..Expensive
Style..Smart casual
Cuisine..Portuguese
Recommended for.................................Regular neighbourhood

Restaurante Monte Mar on the Estoril Coast is part
of the swish Quinta da Marinha resort frequented
by well-heeled golf club-toting tourists, but at
5 km (3 miles) from the fairway, it has an alluring
and comparatively remote feel about it. Sunday
lunchtimes are best for people watching, as local
bigwigs arrive with their families for a feast of
exceptional fresh local shellfish, including Setúbal
oysters, prawns (shrimp), clams and dressed crab.
Sea bass in a salt crust for two is another show-
stopper. Choose a table on the terrace to watch
the sun set or the Atlantic waves crashing down
at your feet.

PORTO DE SANTA MARIA

Estrada do Guincho
Cascais
Lisbon 2750-640
+351 214879450
www.portosantamaria.com

Opening hours.................................6 days for lunch and dinner
Reservation policy..Yes
Reservation email................reservas@portosantamaria.com
Credit cards..Accepted
Price range..Affordable
Style..Smart casual
Cuisine..Portuguese-Seafood
Recommended for...High end

RISO-RISOTTORIA DEL MUNDO

Rua Santa Maria 274
Funchal
Madeira 9060-291
+351 291280360
www.riso.pai.pt

Opening hours.................................6 days for lunch and dinner
Reservation policy..Yes
Reservation email...................................reservas@riso-fx.com
Credit cards....................Accepted but not AMEX and Diners
Price range..Affordable
Style..Smart casual
Cuisine..Modern Mediterranean
Recommended for...Worth the travel

First you've got to get to Funchal on the Portuguese
island of Madeira, then you've got to haul yourself up
the quaint but vertiginous Rua Santa Maria, but once
you take your seat on the Riso terrace overlooking
the sea, you'll be glad you bothered. In a setting
this good, you can easily overlook the food, but in
this case it measures up to its surroundings and
lively atmosphere, which is further enhanced by the
cheerful service. As the name suggests, risotto is the
speciality and there's a fine array to choose from,
but there are other options. Whatever you choose,
save some room for dessert.

RESTAURANTE DOP

Palácio das Artes
Largo de São Domingos 18
Porto 4050-545
+351 222014313
www.ruipaula.com

Opening hours.............6 days for lunch and 5 days for dinner
Reservation policy..Yes
Reservation email...dop@ruipaula.com
Credit cards..Accepted
Price range..Affordable
Style..Smart casual
Cuisine..Modern Portuguese
Recommended for...Worth the travel

RESTAURANTE INÊS DO ALEIXO

Rua de Miraflor 20
Porto 4300-332
+351 225106988

Opening hours	7 days for lunch and 6 days for dinner
Reservation policy	Yes
Credit cards	Accepted but not AMEX and Diners
Price range	Budget
Style	Casual
Cuisine	Portuguese
Recommended for	Regular neighbourhood

'A lovely traditional restaurant.'—José Cordeiro

SHIS

Esplanada do Castelo
Foz do Douro
Porto 4150-623
+351 226189593
www.shisrestaurante.com

Opening hours	7 days for lunch and dinner
Reservation policy	Yes
Credit cards	Accepted
Price range	Affordable
Style	Smart casual
Cuisine	International
Recommended for	Wish I'd opened

THE YEATMAN

The Yeatman Hotel
Rua do Choupelo
Vila Nova de Gaia
Porto 4400-088
www.the-yeatman-hotel.com

Opening hours	7 days for lunch and dinner
Reservation policy	Yes
Reservation email	reception@theyeatman.com
Credit cards	Accepted
Price range	Expensive
Style	Smart casual
Cuisine	Modern Portuguese
Recommended for	High end

RESTAURANTE PRAIA DA RIVIERA

Costa de Caparica
Almada
Setúbal 2825-308
+351 212902423

Opening hours	7 days from breakfast until late
Reservation policy	No
Reservation email	praiadariviera@gmail.com
Credit cards	Not accepted
Price range	Budget
Style	Casual
Cuisine	Café
Recommended for	Local favourite

RESTAURANTE PRAIA DO CASTELO

Costa de Caparica
Almada
Setúbal 2825-308

Opening hours	7 days from breakfast until late
Reservation policy	No
Credit cards	Not accepted
Price range	Budget
Style	Casual
Cuisine	Portuguese
Recommended for	Local favourite

'Order the sardines.'—Olivier da Costa

VALE DO GAIO

Barragem Trigo de Morais
Torrão
Alcácer do Sal
Setúbal 7595-034
+351 265669610
www.valedogaio.com

Opening hours	7 days for breakfast, lunch and dinner
Reservation policy	Yes
Reservation email	reservas@valedogaio.com
Credit cards	Accepted
Price range	Affordable
Style	Smart casual
Cuisine	Portuguese
Recommended for	Local favourite

'By the sea and with amazing food.'
—Miguel Castro e Silva

O CORTIÇO

Recommended by
Luis Baena

Rua Augusto Hilário 43-47
Viseu 3500-089
+351 232423853
www.restaurantecortico.com

Opening hours..................................7 days for lunch and dinner
Reservation policy..Yes
Credit cards...Accepted
Price range..Budget
Style..Casual
Cuisine..Portuguese
Recommended for..Bargain

'Huge, obscene portions for really cheap.'—Luis Baena

RESTAURANTE DOC

Recommended by
José Cordeiro

Estrada Nacional 222
Folgosa
Armamar
Viseu 5110-204
+351 254858123
www.ruipaula.com

Opening hours..................................7 days for lunch and dinner
Reservation policy..Yes
Credit cards...Accepted
Price range...Expensive
Style...Smart casual
Cuisine..Modern Portuguese
Recommended for..Wish I'd opened

'Go for the location and the great culinary quality.'
—José Cordeiro

'The Portuguese don't really eat out for breakfast but they'll make an exception for coffee and pastries here.'

MIGUEL CASTRO E SILVA P367

LISBON

'A TRADITIONAL MEAL IN THE CENTRE OF THE CITY.'

JOSÉ CORDEIRO P367

'IT'S OBLIGATORY TO TRY THE GRILLED COD'

LUIS BAENA P366

'The owner is a master at working with fish.'

MICHAEL GUERRIERI P369

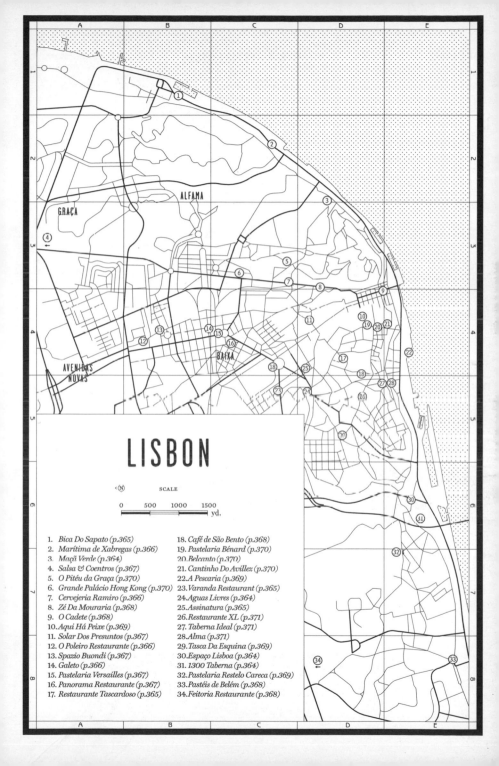

LISBON

‹N› SCALE

0   500   1000   1500
                        yd.

ALFAMA

GRAÇA

AVENIDAS
NOVAS

BAIXA

MAÇÃ VERDE

Recommended by
José Cordeiro

Rua dos Caminhos de Ferro 84
Maça Verde
Lisbon 1100-108
+351 218868780

Opening hours	6 days for lunch and dinner
Reservation policy	No
Credit cards	Not Accepted
Price range	Budget
Style	Casual
Cuisine	Portuguese
Recommended for	Bargain

'Fantastic meal for an honest price.'—José Cordeiro

1300 TABERNA

Recommended by
Henrique Sá Pessoa

Rua Rodrigues Faria 103
Lx Factory
Alicântara
Lisbon 1300-501
+351 213649170
www.1300taberna.com

Opening hours	5 days for lunch and dinner
Reservation policy	No
Reservation email	1300taberna@gmail.com
Credit cards	Accepted but not AMEX and Diners
Price range	Affordable
Style	Casual
Cuisine	Modern Portuguese
Recommended for	Wish I'd opened

Located in the hip LX factory development in Alcântara, which was previously home to a thriving textile business, 1300 Taberna is an achingly cool wine bar and restaurant that is as eclectic as they come. Spoons hang from light fittings, chairs come in all shapes and colours, and numerous clocks adorn the walls of this huge hipster hang-out. Chef Nuno Barros is on hand to cook classic dishes in his open kitchen, using as much local produce as possible from small producers – an ethos that is mirrored by the bar's wine selection, which features numerous small releases from largely unknown producers.

ESPAÇO LISBOA

Recommended by
José Cordeiro

Rua da Cozinha Económica 16
Alicântara
Lisbon 1300-149
+351 213610212
www.espacolisboa.pt

Opening hours	7 days for dinner
Reservation policy	Yes
Reservation email	reservas@espacolisboa.pt
Credit cards	Accepted
Price range	Affordable
Style	Casual
Cuisine	Portuguese
Recommended for	Late night

AGUAS LIVRES

Recommended by
Alexandre Silva

Calçada Bento da Rocha Cabral 18
Amoreiras
Lisbon 1250-047
+351 213878365

Opening hours	6 days for lunch and dinner
Reservation policy	No
Credit cards	Accepted
Price range	Budget
Style	Casual
Cuisine	Portuguese
Recommended for	Regular neighbourhood

This quintessentially Portuguese tasca serves classic cuisine to gatherings of families and friends at extremely reasonable prices. Charming and familiar service and lack of pretence ensure an experience of enjoyable authenticity. The decor is basic but comfortable, with red, blue and yellow gingham tablecloths adding to the rustic feel. The proprietors here aim to extend the conviviality of their own home and serve, from a concise menu, lovingly made *pataniscas de bacalhau* (fried salt cod cakes) and meats that are grilled over a wood fire. Curiously, special care is also taken over the seasoning of their excellent house salad.

ASSINATURA

Rua do Vale Pereiro 19
Amoreiras
Lisbon 1250-270
+351 213867696
www.assinatura.com.pt

Opening hours.............4 days for lunch and 6 days for dinner
Reservation policy..Yes
Reservation email.................restaurante@assinatura.com.pt
Credit cards...Accepted
Price range..Affordable
Style..Smart casual
Cuisine...Modern Portuguese
Recommended for..Worth the travel

RESTAURANTE TASCARDOSO

Rua do Século 242-4
Amoreiras
Lisbon 1200-439
+351 213475698

Opening hours.................6 days for lunch and dinner
Reservation policy..Yes
Credit cards..Not Accepted
Price range..Budget
Style...Casual
Cuisine...Portuguese
Recommended for...Bargain

VARANDA RESTAURANT

Four Seasons Ritz Hotel
Rua Rodrigo da Fonseca 88
Amoreiras
Lisbon 1099-039
+351 213811400
www.fourseasons.com

Opening hours.............7 days for breakfast, lunch and dinner
Reservation policy..Yes
Credit cards...Accepted
Price range..Expensive
Style..Smart casual
Cuisine...Portuguese
Recommended for...Breakfast

BICA DO SAPATO

Avenida Infante Dom Henrique
Armazem B
Cais da Pedra
Avenidas Novas
Lisbon 1900-436
+351 218810320
www.bicadosapato.com

Opening hours.............6 days for lunch and 7 days for dinner
Reservation policy..Yes
Reservation email.................info@bicadosapato.com
Credit cards...Accepted
Price range..Affordable
Style..Smart casual
Cuisine...Modern Portuguese
Recommended for...Wish I'd opened

On an old cobbled street in Lisbon's old town – alongside a tramway leading to the sea – is Bica Do Sapato, a warehouse-space restaurant, sushi bar and adjacent club co-owned by actor John Malkovich. The lofty, minimalist space and euro-vogue decor is mirrored in the restaurant's libertarian take on Portuguese classics. The coast location means that the sushi is fresh and fish, rightly, dominates the Bica Do Sapato menu. Conveniently located across the street, for post-dinner shape-throwing, is Club Lux where skilfully prepared cocktails and generously iced beverages are served to a young and undeniably hip crowd.

CERVEJARIA RAMIRO

Avenida Almirante Reis 1h
Avenidas Novas
Lisbon 1150-007
+351 218851024
www.cervejariaramiro.pt

Recommended by
José Avillez, Luis Baena,
Olivier da Costa,
Henrique Sá Pessoa

Opening hours.................................6 days for lunch and dinner
Reservation policy...No
Reservation email............................geral@cervejariaramiro.pt
Credit cards....................... Accepted but not AMEX and Diners
Price range...Affordable
Style...Casual
Cuisine..Seafood
Recommended for.....................................Local favourite

Cervejaria (meaning 'beerhouse') downplays the charms of this downtown seafood specialist. Sure, the scruffy neighbourhood and the 1970s decor are not pulls, but beer certainly isn't the main reason that, for over fifty years, Lisboetas have been waiting in line here. That accolade goes to the superb sea-food. Start with the house Pata Negra, before getting stuck into some super-size Portuguese *carabineiros* (shrimp), santola (crab) and sea-salty *percebes* (gooseneck barnacles). Leave room for the famous *prego* steak sandwich. Wash it all down with local beer or a bottle of ice-cold Vinho Verde. Seasoned staff are quick – the line moves fast – but always cheery.

GALETO

Avenida da República 14A
Nossa Senhora de Fátima
Avenidas Novas
Lisbon 1050-191
+351 213544444

Recommended by
Fausto Luigi Airoldi

Opening hours.........................7 days from breakfast until late
Reservation policy...No
Credit cards...Accepted
Price range...Affordable
Style...Casual
Cuisine..Portuguese
Recommended for...Late night

Night owls haunt Galeto, a frozen-in-aspic relic of 1960s Lisbon, open daily until 3.00 a.m., when the last bleary-eyed clubber or vintage design lover shuffles off home. This quintessential hang-out (founded in 1967) on the Avenida da República is like a Portuguese David Lynch's take on an American diner – if you can imagine that – manned by bow-tied waiters who serve literally hundreds of people a night at the bar that wraps around the immaculately preserved, windowless room. Though it serves all day, Galeto caters best for night-time cravings – burgers, fries, sandwiches and Portuguese steak dishes. Prices are hiked after 10.00 p.m.

MARÍTIMA DE XABREGAS

Rua Manutenção 40-42
Beato
Avenidas Novas
Lisbon 1900-320
www.restaurantemaritimadexabregas.com.pt

Recommended by
Luis Baena

Opening hours.................................6 days for lunch and dinner
Reservation policy...No
Credit cards...Accepted
Price range..Budget
Style...Casual
Cuisine..Seafood
Recommended for.....................................Local favourite

'It's obligatory to try the grilled cod fish.'—Luis Baena

O POLEIRO RESTAURANTE

Rua de Entrecampos 30a
Avenidas Novas
Lisbon 1700-158
+351 217976265
www.opoleiro.com

Recommended by
Chakall

Opening hours.................................6 days for lunch and dinner
Reservation policy..Yes
Credit cards...Accepted
Price range...Affordable
Style...Casual
Cuisine..Portuguese
Recommended for................................Regular neighbourhood

PANORAMA

Sheraton Lisbon Hotel & Spa
Rua Latino Coelho 1
Avenidas Novas
Lisbon 1069-025
+351 213120000
www.panorama-restaurante.com

Opening hours.............5 days for lunch and 7 days for dinner
Reservation policy...Yes
Reservation email.................sheraton.lisboa@sheraton.com
Credit cards...Accepted
Price range...Expensive
Style...Smart casual
Cuisine..Modern Portuguese
Recommended for..High end

PASTELARIA VERSAILLES

Avenue da República 15a
Nossa Senhora de Fátima
Avenidas Novas
Lisbon 1050-185
+357 213546340

Opening hours...........................7 days for breakfast until late
Reservation policy..No
Credit cards...Accepted
Price range..Budget
Style...Casual
Cuisine..Bakery-Café
Recommended for......................................Breakfast

'The Portuguese don't really eat out for breakfast,
maybe just for coffee and a pastry but Pastelaria
Versailles is a good option.'—Miguel Castro e Silva

Breakfast is all too often relegated to gastronomy's
second division – a rushed attempt to jolt the system
awake with caffeine and to stave off hunger pangs
until lunch. Here you can savour the first meal of the
day in premiership style. Established in 1922, the
imposing stone frontage of this grand café with its
Corinthian columns and sculptured bronze signage
gives way to a glorious ornate interior with crystal
chandeliers and marble floors. Go native with a
psteis de nata (custard tart) and espresso, standing
at the bar, or take a seat and appreciate a cup of
black tea from Mozambique, the house speciality.

SALSA & COENTROS

Rua Coronel Marques Leitão 12
Avenidas Novas
Lisbon 1700-125
+351 218410990
www.salsaecoentros.com

Opening hours................................6 days for lunch and dinner
Reservation policy..Yes
Credit cards.....................Accepted but not AMEX and Diners
Price range...Budget
Style..Casual
Cuisine..Portuguese
Recommended for....................................Local favourite

SOLAR DOS PRESUNTOS

Rua das Portas de Santo Antão 150
Avenidas Novas
Lisbon 1150-269
+351 213424253
www.solardospresuntos.com

Opening hours................................6 days for lunch and dinner
Reservation policy..Yes
Credit cards...Accepted
Price range..Affordable
Style..Casual
Cuisine..Modern Portuguese
Recommended for....................................Local favourite

SPAZIO BUONDI

Avenida Sacadura Cabral 53b
Alvalade
Avenidas Novas
Lisbon 1000-273
+351 217970760

Opening hours.............6 days for lunch and 7 days for dinner
Reservation policy..Yes
Reservation email.....................spazio_buondi@hotmail.com
Credit cards...Accepted
Price range..Affordable
Style..Casual
Cuisine..Portuguese
Recommended for....................................Local favourite

'A traditional meal in the centre of the city.'
—José Cordeiro

ZÉ DA MOURARIA

Recommended by
Alexandre Silva

Rua João Outeiro 24
Avenidas Novas
Lisbon 1100-292
+351 218865436

Opening hours	6 days for lunch
Reservation policy	Yes
Credit cards	Not accepted
Price range	Budget
Style	Casual
Cuisine	Portuguese
Recommended for	Local favourite

O CADETE

Recommended by
Ljubomir Stanisic

Rua dos Correeiros 36-38
Baixa
Lisbon 1100-166
+351 213465367
www.restauranteocadete.com

Opening hours	6 days for lunch and dinner
Reservation policy	Yes
Credit cards	Accepted but not AMEX and Diners
Price range	Budget
Style	Casual
Cuisine	Portuguese
Recommended for	Bargain

CAFÉ DE SÃO BENTO

Recommended by
Miguel Castro e Silva, José
Cordeiro, Olivier da Costa,
Ljubomir Stanisic

Rua de São Bento 212
Bairro Alto
Lisbon 1200-821
+351 213952911
www.cafesaobento.com

Opening hours	5 days for lunch and 7 days for dinner
Reservation policy	Yes
Reservation email	reservas@cafesaobento.com
Credit cards	Accepted
Price range	Affordable
Style	Smart casual
Cuisine	Steakhouse
Recommended for	Late night

With its typically Portuguese blue and white ceramic tiles, you might walk straight past this very modest-looking joint. But that would be a mistake, because they've been serving some of the best steak in the city here for over thirty years. A re-creation of a traditional Lisbon café, the low ceiling, wood-panelled bar and red leather bucket seats create a clubby feel, ideal for a late night feast. They've improved on the nineteenth-century classic *Bife á Marrare* (steak in pepper sauce) by replacing rump with fillet (tenderloin) and tweaking and refining the sauce to piquant, creamy perfection.

FEITORIA

Recommended by
Luis Baena

Altis Belém Hotel & Spa
Doca do Bom Sucesso
Belém
Lisbon 1400-038
+351 210400200
www.restaurantefeitoria.com

Opening hours	6 days for lunch and dinner
Reservation policy	Yes
Reservation email	reservations@altisbelemhotel.com
Credit cards	Accepted
Price range	Affordable
Style	Smart casual
Cuisine	Modern Portuguese
Recommended for	Regular neighbourhood

'Don't miss the fish dishes.'—Luis Baena

PASTÉIS DE BELÉM

Recommended by
Vítor Sobral

Rua de Belém 84-92
Belém
Lisbon 1300-085
+351 213637423
www.pasteisdebelem.pt

Opening hours	7 days from breakfast until late
Reservation policy	Yes
Credit cards	Accepted
Price range	Budget
Style	Casual
Cuisine	Bakery-Café
Recommended for	Breakfast

PASTELARIA RESTELO CARECA

Recommended by
Henrique Sá Pessoa

Rua Duarte Pacheco Pereira 11d
Santa Maria de Belém
Belém
Lisbon 1400-139
www.pastelaria-restelo.pai.pt

Opening hours..........................6 days from breakfast until late
Reservation policy...No
Credit cards..Accepted
Price range..Affordable
Style...Casual
Cuisine..Bakery-Café
Recommended for...Breakfast

TASCA DA ESQUINA

Recommended by
Luis Baena, Henrique Sá
Pessoa, Ljubomir Stanisic

Rua Domingos Sequeira 41c
Campo de Ourique
Lisbon 1350-119
+351 919837255
www.tascadaesquina.com

Opening hours..............5 days for lunch and 6 days for dinner
Reservation policy..Yes
Reservation email...........................info@tascadaesquina.com
Credit cards..Accepted
Price range..Affordable
Style..Smart casual
Cuisine..Portuguese
Recommended for...............................Regular neighbourhood

Chef Vitor Sobral masterminded Tasca da Esquina,
a minimalistic corner restaurant that has raised the
bar of tapas joints in the capital since its inception
in 2007. Sobral is largely recognized as one of the
pioneers of national *petiscos* – the Portuguese
sibling of Spanish tapas – of which there are plenty
to nibble on as you watch the world go by through
the restaurant's vast glass frontage. Opt either for
the *Hoje Há* (on the menu today) of daily changing
dishes or, if you want something more traditional,
pick from the *Há Lá Carta*, a fixed menu of classics
that seldom changes.

A PESCARIA

Recommended by
Michael Guerrieri

Cais da Ribeira Nova 18-19
Armazém B
São Paulo
Chiado
Lisbon 1200-109
+351 213463588

Opening hours..........6 days for brunch and 5 days for dinner
Reservation policy..Yes
Credit cards..Accepted
Price range..Budget
Style...Casual
Cuisine..Seafood
Recommended for...............................Worth the travel

'The owner is a master at working with fish.'
—Michael Guerrieri

AQUI HÁ PEIXE

Recommended by
Miguel Castro e Silva

Rua da Trindade 18a
Chiado
Lisbon 1200-468
+351 213432154
www.aquihapeixe.pt

Opening hours..............4 days for lunch and 6 days for dinner
Reservation policy..Yes
Credit cards..Accepted
Price range..Affordable
Style...Casual
Cuisine..Seafood
Recommended for...............................Regular neighbourhood

BELCANTO

Largo de São Carlos 10
Mártires
Chiado
Lisbon 1200-410
+351 213420607
www.belcanto.pt

Recommended by
Fausto Luigi Airoldi,
Miguel Castro e Silva

Opening hours.........................5 days for lunch and dinner
Reservation policy...Yes
Credit cards..Accepted
Price range..Affordable
Style...Smart casual
Cuisine..Modern Portuguese
Recommended for...Wish I'd opened

'Impressive experimental cooking.'
—Miguel Castro e Silva

Chef José Avillez has taken over the space that formerly played host, in the form of a gentleman's club, to opera patrons and artists from the nearby Teatro Nacional de São Carlos. It has been designed to act as an arena in which this promising chef – who has worked under both Ferran Adrià and Alain Ducasse – can flourish. A formal and sophisticated makeover has retained some signs of the past, such as bookshelves, wood panelling and grand lighting. Modern Portuguese cuisine, however, has replaced the pole dancers of old. The likes of partridge escabeche, *açorda de bacalhau* and trotters (feet) in coriander (cilantro) come from a menu that aims – ambitiously – to tell stories and stir emotions.

CANTINHO DO AVILLEZ

Rua dos Duques de Bragança 7
Mártires
Chiado
Lisbon 1200-162
+351 211992369
www.cantinhodoavillez.pt

Recommended by
José Avillez

Opening hours.................................6 days for lunch and dinner
Reservation policy...Yes
Credit cards..Accepted
Price range..Affordable
Style...Smart casual
Cuisine..Modern Portuguese
Recommended for..Late night

PASTELARIA BÉNARD

Rua Garrett 104
Chiado
Lisbon 1200-205

Recommended by
Fausto Luigi Airoldi,
José Avillez

Opening hours.........................6 days from breakfast until late
Reservation policy...No
Credit cards..Accepted
Price range..Budget
Style...Casual
Cuisine..Bakery-Café
Recommended for..Breakfast

GRANDE PALÁCIO HONG KONG

Rua Pascoal de Melo 8a
São Jorge de Arroios
Graça
Lisbon 1170-294
www.restaurante-chines.com

Recommended by
José Avillez

Opening hours.................................7 days for lunch and dinner
Reservation policy...Yes
Credit cards..Accepted
Price range..Budget
Style...Casual
Cuisine..Chinese
Recommended for..Bargain

O PITÉU DA GRAÇA

Recommended by
Ljubomir Stanisic

Largo da Graça 95-96
Graça
Lisbon 1170-165
+351 218871067

Opening hours	6 days for lunch and 5 days for dinner
Reservation policy	Yes
Credit cards	Accepted
Price range	Budget
Style	Casual
Cuisine	Portuguese
Recommended for	Local favourite

Buzzy restaurant O Pitéu is as old-school Portuguese as they come, complete with noisy families excitedly discussing the day's proceedings, gilt-edged mono-grammed plates, plates hanging on the wall and the obligatory TV in the corner (with the sound muted), which is probably why it continues to be such a hit among the locals. As you'd expect, the food is fresh and without pomp, with a good selection of meat and fish dishes, including specialities such as baked kid and *cozido* (meat and veg stew), served in hearty portions and with only a scant regard to presentation – making it all the more enjoyable.

RESTAURANTE XL

Recommended by
Luís Baena

Calçada da Estrela 57-63
Lapa
Lisbon 1200-661
+351 213956118

Opening hours	6 days for dinner
Reservation policy	Yes
Credit cards	Accepted
Price range	Affordable
Style	Casual
Cuisine	Portuguese
Recommended for	Late night

ALMA

Recommended by
José Cordeiro

Calçada Marquês de Abrantes 92
Santos
Lisbon 1200-720
+351 213963527
www.alma.co.pt

Opening hours	5 days for dinner
Reservation policy	Yes
Reservation email	reservas@alma.co.pt
Credit cards	Accepted but not AMEX and Diners
Price range	Affordable
Style	Smart casual
Cuisine	Modern Portuguese
Recommended for	Worth the travel

TABERNA IDEAL

Recommended by
Miguel Castro e Silva

Rua da Esperança 112-114
Santos
Lisbon 1200-658
+351 213962744

Opening hours	1 day for lunch and 5 days for dinner
Reservation policy	Yes
Credit cards	Not accepted
Price range	Budget
Style	Casual
Cuisine	Portuguese
Recommended for	Bargain

'I DON'T HAVE THE POSSIBILITY TO EAT HERE REGULARLY BUT I LOVE THIS PLACE.'

HEINZ BECK P374

GERMANY

'IT'S A TRADITIONAL GERMAN RESTAURANT WHERE YOU CAN FIND GREAT DISHES LIKE BLOOD SAUSAGE, MASHED POTATOES AND GLAZED APPLES WITH ONION. THEY ALSO OFFER OVER 2,000 DIFFERENT LABELS ON THE WINE LIST.'

TIM RAUE P382

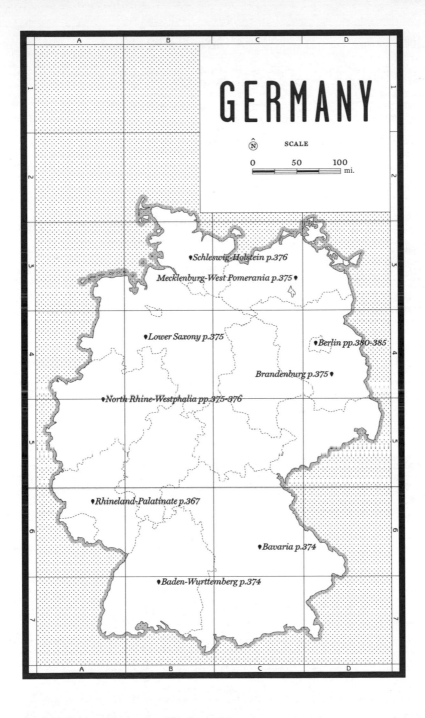

GERMANY

$\hat{N}$ SCALE

0   50   100 mi.

♦Schleswig-Holstein p.376

Mecklenburg-West Pomerania p.375 ♦

♦Lower Saxony p.375

♦Berlin pp.380-385

Brandenburg p.375 ♦

♦North Rhine-Westphalia pp.375-376

♦Rhineland-Palatinate p.367

♦Bavaria p.374

♦Baden-Wurttemberg p.374

ANITASTUBE

Sackmann Hotel
Murgtalstrasse 602
Baiersbronn
Baden-Wurttemberg 72270
+49 74472890
www.hotel-sackmann.de

Opening hours..................................7 days for lunch and dinner
Reservation policy...Yes
Credit cards...Accepted
Price range..Affordable
Style...Smart casual
Cuisine...Baden
Recommended for..Bargain

SILBERBERG

Traube Tonbach Hotel
Tonbachstrasse 237
Baiersbronn
Baden-Wurttemberg 72270
+49 7442492665
www.traube-tonbach.de

Opening hours.............7 days for breakfast, lunch and dinner
Reservation policy...Yes
Reservation email......tischreservierung@traube-tonbach.de
Credit cards...Accepted
Price range..Affordable
Style...Casual
Cuisine...International
Recommended for..Breakfast

GASTHOF MESSERSCHMIED

Grassauertrasse 1
Rottau
Bavaria 83224
+49 86412562
www.gasthof-messerschmied.de

Opening hours.............5 days for breakfast, lunch and dinner
Reservation policy...Yes
Credit cards...Not accepted
Price range..Budget
Style...Casual
Cuisine...Bavarian
Recommended for..Bargain

RESIDENZ HEINZ WINKLER

Kirchplatz 1
Aschau im Chiemgau
Bavaria 83229
+49 805217990
www.residenz-heinz-winkler.de

Opening hours..................................7 days for lunch and dinner
Reservation policy...Yes
Credit cards...Accepted
Price range..Expensive
Style...Formal
Cuisine...Modern German
Recommended for...Local favourite

'Unfortunately I don't have the possibility to go here
regularly, but I love this place.'—Heinz Beck

TANTRIS

Johann-Fichte Strasse 7
Munich
Bavaria 80805
+49 893619590
www.tantris.de

Opening hours..................................5 days for lunch and dinner
Reservation policy...Yes
Reservation email...info@tantris.de
Credit cards...Accepted
Price range..Expensive
Style...Smart casual
Cuisine...Modern European
Recommended for...Local favourite

Property magnate Fritz Eichbauer could have bought
a castle for what he invested in Tantris, his impos-
sibly extravagant temple of fine dining and Pop art
— 'but then where would I have gone to eat?' Back in
1971, Eichbauer's accountant doubtless balked at the
expenditure lavished on stone carvings, orange
carpet for the floor and walls, and avant-garde
exposed concrete and steel for the exterior, but
Tantris has become a fiercely protected icon of 1970s
design. Chef Hans Haas's elegant modern European
cuisine, honoured with two Michelin stars, is positively understated by comparison. Go for broke with
the eight-course gourmet menu.

TRATTORIA TOSCANA

Recommended by
Hendrik Otto

Dorfaue 12
Grossbeeren
Brandenburg 14979
+49 3370190955
www.trattoria-toscana.com

Opening hours	7 days for lunch and dinner
Reservation policy	Yes
Credit cards	Accepted
Price range	Budget
Style	Casual
Cuisine	Italian
Recommended for	Regular neighbourhood

AQUA

Recommended by
Marco Müller

Ritz-Carlton Hotel
Parkstrasse 1
Wolfsburg
Lower Saxony 38440
+49 5361606056
www.restaurant-aqua.com

Opening hours	5 days for dinner
Reservation policy	Yes
Credit cards	Accepted
Price range	Expensive
Style	Formal
Cuisine	Modern European
Recommended for	Worth the travel

STRANDHALLE BINZ

Recommended by
Hendrik Otto

Strandpromenade 5
Ostseebad Binz
Mecklenburg-West Pomerania 18609
+49 3839331564
www.strandhalle-binz.de

Opening hours	7 days for lunch and dinner
Reservation policy	Yes
Credit cards	Accepted
Price range	Affordable
Style	Casual
Cuisine	German
Recommended for	Worth the travel

LERBACH

Recommended by
Michael Kempf

Schloss Lerbach Hotel
Lerbacher Weg
Bergisch Gladbach
North Rhine-Westphalia 51465
+49 2202204962
www.schlosshotel-lerbach.com

Opening hours	5 days for lunch and dinner
Reservation policy	Yes
Credit cards	Accepted
Price range	Expensive
Style	Smart casual
Cuisine	Modern German
Recommended for	Worth the travel

VENDÔME

Recommended by
Michael Kempf, Uwe
Opocensky, Hendrik Otto

Schloss Bensberg Hotel
Kadettenstrasse
Bergisch Gladbach
North Rhine-Westphalia 51429
+49 2204421941
www.schlossbensberg.com

Opening hours	5 days for lunch and dinner
Reservation policy	Yes
Credit cards	Accepted
Price range	Expensive
Style	Formal
Cuisine	Modern German
Recommended for	Wish I'd opened

Although the name might have originated from Paris's Place Vendôme, any French connection ends there. In fact, chef Joachim Wissler is, unlike many of his countrymen, more concerned with the 'treasures of our own neglected cuisine', so diners might well come across workaday German ingredients such as sauerkraut and Knäckebrot (crispbread) in his 'New German' cooking. However, this being the three-star restaurant of a luxury hotel set in a baroque castle, regional culinary traditions are elevated by molecular cooking techniques and vibrant presentation, delivered, perhaps, in a twenty-five-course menu. Set in the hills above Cologne, the dining room, refurbished in 2007, is light-filled and more approachable than you'd imagine.

LE MOISSONNIER

Recommended by
Joachim Wissler

Krefelderstrass 25
Cologne
North Rhine-Westphalia 50670
+49 221729479
www.lemoissonnier.de

Opening hours	5 days for lunch and dinner
Reservation policy	Yes
Credit cards	Accepted
Price range	Expensive
Style	Smart casual
Cuisine	French
Recommended for	Regular neighbourhood

VICTOR'S

Recommended by
Filip Claeys

Victor's Residenz Hotel Schloss Berg
Schlossstrasse 27-29
Perl-Nenning
Mosel
Rhineland-Palatinate 66706
+49 686679118
www.victors-gourmet.de

Opening hours	2 days for lunch and 5 days for dinner
Reservation policy	Yes
Reservation email	reservierung@victors-gourmet.de
Credit cards	Accepted
Price range	Expensive
Style	Formal
Cuisine	Modern European
Recommended for	Worth the travel

LA BELLE EPOQUE

Recommended by
Tim Raue

Columbia Hotel
Kaiserallee 2
Travemünde
Lübeck
Schleswig-Holstein 23570
+49 45023080
www.columbia-hotels.com

Opening hours	5 days for dinner
Reservation policy	Yes
Credit cards	Accepted
Price range	Expensive
Style	Formal
Cuisine	Modern European
Recommended for	Worth the travel

The restaurant inside Lubeck-Travemunde's Columbia Hotel is avant-garde by nature, if not by name. Chef Kevin Fehling has been hailed for creating wholly original dishes, bent on mastering intricate techniques with the use of carefully selected ingredients — though not at the expense of a strong concept. Crustacean macaron with basil pesto and aioli, goose liver ice cream with Jerusalem artichoke, sherry vinegar and figs, and carpaccio of scallops with Périgord truffles and Granny Smith are just a handful of this young chef's innovations. The new marriage of so many tastes can be enjoyed looking over the beach and sea beyond.

'YOU'LL ONLY FIND SOMETHING SIMILAR IN CHINA.'
CHAKALL P383

'I was blown away by the food here.'
HYWEL JONES P385

BERLIN

'IN BERLIN YOU HAVE TO GO FOR A SAUSAGE WITH CURRY KETCHUP AND FRENCH FRIES WITH MAYONNAISE.'
TIM RAUE P381

BERLIN

N   SCALE

0   650   1300   1950
                          yd.

GOOD FRIENDS

Kantstrasse 30
Charlottenburg
Berlin 10623
+49 303132659
www.goodfriends-berlin.de

Opening hours	7 days for lunch and dinner
Reservation policy	Yes
Credit cards	Accepted
Price range	Affordable
Style	Casual
Cuisine	Chinese
Recommended for	Regular neighbourhood

KUCHI

Kantstrasse 30
Charlottenburg
Berlin 10623
+49 3031507815
www.kuchi.de

Opening hours	7 days for lunch and dinner
Reservation policy	Yes
Credit cards	Accepted
Price range	Affordable
Style	Casual
Cuisine	Japanese
Recommended for	Regular neighbourhood

MOON THAI

Kantstrasse 32
Charlottenburg
Berlin 10625
+49 3031809743
www.moonthai-restaurant.de

Opening hours	7 days for lunch and dinner
Reservation policy	Yes
Credit cards	Accepted
Price range	Affordable
Style	Casual
Cuisine	Thai
Recommended for	Bargain

LE COQ D'OR

Boxhagener Strasse 27
Friedrichshain
Berlin 12045
+49 3021237959
www.lecoqdor-berlin.de

Opening hours	7 days for lunch and dinner
Reservation policy	Yes
Credit cards	Accepted
Price range	Budget
Style	Casual
Cuisine	Asian
Recommended for	Bargain

In spite of the French name, Berlin's Coq d'Or is a useful pan-Asian all-rounder in up and coming Friedrichshain. It's the quality-price ratio that has, more than anything, won it the plaudits. Colourful salads and attractive noodle and rice dishes from Vietnam, Thailand and Japan cost around €5 (£4; $6), decent selections of sushi only double that, plus they don't stiff you on the extras (summer rolls, satay). No wonder some regulars eat here more often than they do at home. Bench seating, sexy lighting and a bonsai tree by way of decoration strike the right notes with young urbanites on a budget.

IL RITROVO

Wühlischrasse 29
Friedrichshain
Berlin 10245
+49 3029364130

Opening hours	5 days for lunch and 7 days for dinner
Reservation policy	Yes
Credit cards	Not accepted
Price range	Budget
Style	Casual
Cuisine	Italian
Recommended for	Worth the travel

SAPORITO

Recommended by
Chakall

Strassmannstrasse 21
Friedrichshain
Berlin 10249
+49 3060930450
www.saporito-berlin.de

Opening hours	2 days for lunch and 7 days for dinner
Reservation policy	Yes
Credit cards	Accepted
Price range	Affordable
Style	Casual
Cuisine	Italian
Recommended for	Late night

'Simple but really good quality food.'—Chakall

First with their pizzeria Pomodorino and now with their postage-stamp-sized trattoria Saporito, located next door, Gerardo Amendola and Marcello Calenda have brought their unique brand of Italian Gemütlichkeit to Berlin's hip Friedrichshain. Saporito, opened in spring 2011, does what all good restaurants should do: namely, a few things well. Go for the fresh homemade pasta from the brief, weekly changing menu – perhaps fusilli with wild boar ragù or rocket (arugula) tagliolini with squid and bottarga – accompanied by a bottle of Italian wine chosen from the shelves that line the walls. Finish with a grappa and a sigh of satisfaction.

RESTAURANTSCHIFF PATIO

Recommended by
Marco Müller

Helgoländer Ufer
Kirchstrasse 13a
Hansaviertel
Berlin 10557
+49 3040301700
www.patio-berlin.de

Opening hours	7 days for brunch and dinner
Reservation policy	Yes
Credit cards	Accepted
Price range	Affordable
Style	Smart casual
Cuisine	European
Recommended for	Breakfast

BURGERMEISTER

Recommended by
Michael Kempf

Oberbaumstrasse 8
Kreuzberg
Berlin 10997
+49 3022436493
www.burger-meister.de

Opening hours	7 days for lunch and dinner
Reservation policy	No
Credit cards	Accepted
Price range	Budget
Style	Casual
Cuisine	Burgers
Recommended for	Late night

CURRY 36

Recommended by
Hendrik Otto
Tim Raue

Mehringdamm 36
Kreuzberg
Berlin 10961
+49 302517368
www.curry36.de

Opening hours	7 days for breakfast, lunch and dinner
Reservation policy	No
Credit cards	Not accepted
Price range	Budget
Style	Casual
Cuisine	Fast Food
Recommended for	Late night

'In Berlin you have to go for a "sausage with curry ketchup and chips (fries) with mayonnaise". My favourite is Curry 36.'—Tim Raue

In a city with countless stalls and even a museum dedicated to the Berlin-born cult of the currywurst – sliced pork sausage coated with spicy ketchup – this Imbiss, opened back in 1980, has somehow managed to gain favour over much of the competition. Perhaps it's the convenient location near Mehringdamm U-Bahn station or the long hours they keep – the late-night queues (lines) include a diverse mix of tourists, taxi drivers and loyal locals. You'll always be asked *mit oder ohne*, with or without, referring to your sausage and its skin. Undecided? Order a mixed double to get one of each.

HASIR

Recommended by
Marco Müller

Adalbertstrasse 10
Kreuzberg
Berlin 10999
+49 306142373
www.hasir.de

Opening hours	7 days for lunch and dinner
Reservation policy	Yes
Credit cards	Not accepted
Price range	Affordable
Style	Casual
Cuisine	Turkish
Recommended for	Late night

HENNE

Recommended by
Hendrik Otto

Leuschnerdamm 25
Kreuzberg
Berlin 10999
+49 306147730
www.henne-berlin.de

Opening hours	6 days for dinner
Reservation policy	Yes
Credit cards	Accepted
Price range	Affordable
Style	Casual
Cuisine	German
Recommended for	Worth the travel

BANDOL SUR MER

Recommended by
Marco Müller

Torstrasse 167
Mitte
Berlin 10115
+49 3076302051

Opening hours	7 days for dinner
Reservation policy	Yes
Credit cards	Not accepted
Price range	Affordable
Style	Casual
Cuisine	French Bistro
Recommended for	Local favourite

BOCCA DI BACCO

Recommended by
Hendrik Otto

Friedrichstrasse 167-168
Mitte
Berlin 10117
+49 3020672828
www.boccadibacco.de

Opening hours	6 days for lunch and 7 days for dinner
Reservation policy	Yes
Credit cards	Accepted
Price range	Affordable
Style	Casual
Cuisine	Italian
Recommended for	High end

DOS PALILLOS

Recommended by
Claus Moller Henriksen

Weinmeisterstrasse 1
Mitte
Berlin 10178
+49 3020003413
www.dospalillos.com

Opening hours	3 days for lunch and 5 days for dinner
Reservation policy	Yes
Reservation email	dospalillosservice@casacamper.com
Credit cards	Accepted
Price range	Affordable
Style	Casual
Cuisine	Asian small plates
Recommended for	Worth the travel

CHIPPS

Recommended by
Michael Kempf

Jägerstrasse 35
Mitte
Berlin 10117
+49 3036444588
www.chipps.eu

Opening hours	7 days for breakfast, lunch and dinner
Reservation policy	Yes
Reservation email	happy@chipps.de
Credit cards	Accepted
Price range	Affordable
Style	Casual
Cuisine	International
Recommended for	Breakfast

LUTTER & WEGNER

Recommended by
Tim Raue

Charlottenstrasse 56
Mitte
Berlin 10117
+49 302029540
www.l-w-berlin.de

Opening hours	7 days for lunch and dinner
Reservation policy	Yes
Credit cards	Accepted
Price range	Affordable
Style	Casual
Cuisine	German
Recommended for	Local favourite

'It's a traditional German restaurant where you can find great dishes like black pudding (blood sausage), mashed potatoes and glazed apples with onion. They also offer over 2,000 different labels on the wine list.'—Tim Raue

Berliners don't come to this two-hundred-year-old Mitte institution for the views over the cathedral-flanked Gendarmenmarkt square, the neatly pressed waiters or even the excellent house Riesling. They come for one thing only: the best Wiener schnitzel in Berlin. The size and thickness of a dinner plate, the veal is dusted in fine crumbs, fried to crispy perfection and served with a simple potato and cucumber salad. It is best enjoyed in the wood-panelled dining room – former meeting place of the city's Bohemians – on one of Berlin's famously bleak winter days. Vegetarian diners are welcome only if they like potatoes (a lot).

MARGAUX BERLIN

Recommended by
Michael Kempf
Tim Raue

Unter den Linden 78
Mitte
Berlin 10117
+49 3022652611
www.margaux-berlin.de

Opening hours	5 days for dinner
Reservation policy	Yes
Credit cards	Accepted
Price range	Expensive
Style	Casual
Cuisine	Modern European
Recommended for	High end

MING DYNASTIE

Recommended by
Chakall

Brückenstrasse 6
Mitte
Berlin 10179
+49 3030875680
www.ming-dynastie.de

Opening hours	7 days for lunch and dinner
Reservation policy	Yes
Credit cards	Accepted
Price range	Affordable
Style	Casual
Cuisine	Chinese
Recommended for	Local favourite

'You'll only find something similar in China.'—Chakall

The original Ming Dynastie in Berlin, aka Ming I, opposite the Chinese Embassy, is a benchmark for Chinese food in the German capital. The ten-year-old restaurant's many Chinese regulars eschew the buffet – as should you – in favour of classic dim sum and authentic Szechuan and Huaiyang cuisine. Choose from more challenging dishes such as pig's ear with chilli oil, Szechuan-style tripe, and chicken gizzard and kidney with hot sauce or go for one of the 'greatest hits' menus featuring the likes of hot and sour soup, spring rolls and crispy duck. Ming II, opened in 2009, is at the Europa shopping centre.

PAULY SAAL

Recommended by
Marco Müller

Auguststrasse 11-13
Mitte
Berlin 10117
+49 3033006070
www.paulysaal.com

Opening hours	7 days for lunch and dinner
Reservation policy	Yes
Reservation email	office@paulysaal.com
Credit cards	Accepted
Price range	Expensive
Style	Smart casual
Cuisine	German
Recommended for	Wish I'd opened

VAU

Recommended by
Chakall

Jägerstrasse 54-55
Mitte
Berlin 10117
+49 302029730
www.vau-berlin.de

Opening hours................................6 days for lunch and dinner
Reservation policy..Yes
Credit cards...Accepted
Price range..Expensive
Style...Formal
Cuisine...Modern French
Recommended for.............................Regular neighbourhood

When Kolja Kleeberg opened Vau in Mitte in 1997 it
was a case of right chef, right place, right time.
Kleeberg's light touch with German regional ingredients wedded to French culinary traditions was bang
on too, winning a Michelin star, which it has held
since the year of opening. The American walnut and
stucco lustro dining room, designed by architect
Meinhard von Gerkan (of Berlin Hauptbahnhof fame),
welcomes local movers and shakers and serious
foodies. Savour such delights as sweetbreads,
morels and white asparagus or Hainanese-style
poulet noir with superb Old World wines – but brace
yourself for the bill.

LAVANDERIA VECCHIA

Recommended by
Michael Kempf

Flughafenstrasse 46
Neukölln
Berlin 12053
+49 3062722152
www.lavanderiavecchia.de

Opening hours..............4 days for lunch and 5 days for dinner
Reservation policy..Yes
Reservation email..........reservierung@lavanderiavecchia.de
Credit cards...Accepted
Price range..Affordable
Style...Casual
Cuisine...Italian
Recommended for...Bargain

ANNA BLUME

Recommended by
Hendrik Otto

Kollwitzstrasse 83
Prenzlauer Berg
Berlin 10405
+49 3044048749
www.cafe-anna-blume.de

Opening hours.........................7 days for breakfast and lunch
Reservation policy..Yes
Credit cards...Accepted
Price range..Affordable
Style...Casual
Cuisine...Café
Recommended for..Breakfast

THE BIRD

Recommended by
Marco Müller

Am Falkplatz 5
Prenzlauer Berg
Berlin 10435
+49 3051053283
www.thebirdinberlin.com

Opening hours.....................................7 days for dinner
Reservation policy..Yes
Reservation email................thebirdreservations@gmail.com
Credit cards..Not accepted
Price range..Affordable
Style...Casual
Cuisine...Steakhouse
Recommended for...Bargain

FILETSTÜCK

Recommended by
Gwendal Le Ruyet

Schönhauser Allee 45
Prenzlauer Berg
Berlin 10435
+49 3048820304
www.filetstueck-berlin.de

Opening hours.............6 days for lunch and 7 days for dinner
Reservation policy..Yes
Reservation email..........schoenhauser@filetstueck-berlin.de
Credit cards..Not accepted
Price range..Affordable
Style...Casual
Cuisine...Steakhouse
Recommended for...Worth the travel

A glance through the window of Prenzlauer Berg's
Filetstück reveals twinkling chandeliers, polished
glass vitrines, ornamental green tiles and, on display
at the back, bloody great slabs of beef. Filetstück,
opened in 2009, enjoys a double life as classy deli-
resto-butchers by day and chichi bistro by night. It
specializes in dry-aged beef of impeccable quality

from Germany, Ireland and as far afield as Iowa, as well as lamb specialities such as Eiderland salt-marsh lamb, sold over the counter or on a judiciously brief, if expensive, menu of cuts, sauces, gourmet sides and wines. A second branch opened in Wilmersdorf in 2011.

TAURO

Recommended by
Chakall

Schönhauser Allee 176
Prenzlauer Berg
Berlin 10119
+49 3040056048
www.tauro-berlin.de

Opening hours	7 days for brunch and dinner
Reservation policy	Yes
Credit cards	Accepted
Price range	Affordable
Style	Casual
Cuisine	Spanish
Recommended for	Breakfast

'A nice place for brunch.'—Chakall

Tauro is a cavernous three-level eating and drinking complex in the former Pfeffer brewery in rapidly gentrifying Prenzlauer Berg. The brewery itself has a fascinating history – producing beer, then chocolate, bread and later munitions – but is now a cultural centre promising galleries, studios and, since December 2009, great tapas. Tauro has a beer garden, bar, deli and two restaurants: one American steakhouse and one traditionally tiled Spanish restaurant, now established as Berlin's favourite destination for paella and *jamón* (ham). The majestic Sunday brunch buffet is a feast for the eyes of ham, cured meats, cheese, tapas, paella and even a chocolate fountain.

SISSI

Recommended by
Michael Kempf

Motzstrasse 34
Schöneberg
Berlin 10777
+49 3021018101
www.sissi-berlin.de

Opening hours	7 days for lunch and dinner
Reservation policy	Yes
Credit cards	Accepted
Price range	Affordable
Style	Casual
Cuisine	Austrian
Recommended for	Regular neighbourhood

FACIL

Recommended by
Hywel Jones, Marco Müller

Mandala Hotel
Potsdamer Strasse 3
Tiergarten
Berlin 10785
+49 30590051234
www.facil.de

Opening hours	5 days for lunch and dinner
Reservation policy	Yes
Reservation email	welcome@facil.de
Credit cards	Accepted
Price range	Expensive
Style	Smart casual
Cuisine	Modern European
Recommended for	Worth the travel

'I was blown away by the food here.'—Hywel Jones

PAMFILYA

Recommended by
Cristiano Rienzner

Luxemburger Strasse 1
Wedding
Berlin 13353
www.pamfilya-restaurant.de

Opening hours	7 days for lunch and dinner
Reservation policy	No
Credit cards	Accepted
Price range	Budget
Style	Casual
Cuisine	Turkish
Recommended for	Regular neighbourhood

BIEBERBAU

Recommended by
Marco Müller

Durlacher Strasse 15
Wilmersdorf
Berlin 10715
+49 308532390
www.bieberbau-berlin.de

Opening hours	5 days for dinner
Reservation policy	Yes
Reservation email	restaurant@bieberbau-berlin.de
Credit cards	Not accepted
Price range	Affordable
Style	Smart casual
Cuisine	Modern European
Recommended for	High end

SWITZERLAND

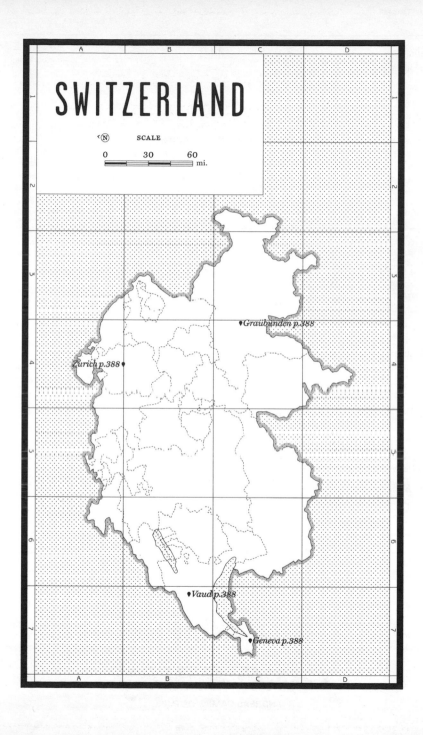

SWITZERLAND

N SCALE

0 30 60 mi.

Graubunden p.388

Zürich p.388

Vaud p.388

Geneva p.388

LE LEXIQUE
Recommended by
Philippe Rochat

Rue de la Faucille 14
Grottes
Geneva 1201
+41 227333131
www.lelexique.ch

Opening hours.............4 days for lunch and 5 days for dinner
Reservation policy..Yes
Credit cards...Accepted
Price range..Affordable
Style...Casual
Cuisine..French
Recommended for...............................Regular neighbourhood

WALDHEIM
Recommended by
Andreas Caminada

Via Runs 6
Laax
Graubünden 7031
+41 081921415
www.restaurant-waldheim.ch

Opening hours..................................5 days for dinner
Reservation policy..No
Reservation email.........................waldheimlaax@bluewin.ch
Credit cards...Accepted
Price range..Affordable
Style...Casual
Cuisine...Swiss
Recommended for.................................Local favourite

'It serves an authentic cuisine from Graubunden.'
—Andreas Caminada

AU CHAT NOIR
Recommended by
Philippe Rochat

Rue Beau-Séjour 27
Lausanne
Vaud 1003
+41 213129585

Opening hours.................................5 days for lunch and dinner
Reservation policy..Yes
Credit cards...Accepted
Price range..Expensive
Style...Casual
Cuisine..French
Recommended for...............................Regular neighbourhood

HILTL
Recommended by
Andreas Caminada

Sihlstrasse 28
Zurich 8001
+41 0442277000
www.hiltl.ch

Opening hours........................7 days from breakfast until late
Reservation policy..Yes
Reservation email..................................info@hiltl.ch
Credit cards...Accepted
Price range..Affordable
Style...Casual
Cuisine...Vegetarian
Recommended for...............................Regular neighbourhood

TIBITS
Recommended by
Andreas Caminada

Seefeldstrasse 7
Zurich 8008
www.tibits.ch

Opening hours........................7 days from breakfast until late
Reservation policy..No
Credit cards...Accepted
Price range..Affordable
Style...Casual
Cuisine...Vegetarian
Recommended for...............................Regular neighbourhood

'A vegetarian restaurant with a great buffet
for take away.'
—Andreas Caminada

'The *tutto crudo* menu was fabulous and the restaurant is practically in the sea!'
JEAN BEDDINGTON P406

'PERFECT PILLOWS OF GNOCCHI.'
ŞEMSA DENIZSEL P398

ITALY

'One of the oldest bakeries in Rome.'
HEINZ BECK P398

'EXCELLENT EXPRESSO.'
EMANUELE SCARELLO P396

'I go here for *tigelle*, a cheap, quick, on-the-go kind of meal. It is very typical Modenese.'
MASSIMO BOTTURA P394

'THE BEST RISOTTO EVER - BY FAR!'
MARC FOSH P415

'It combines local gastronomy, art, culture and traditions in the most beautiful wine region, Nobile.'
NIKOS POULIASIS P411

ITALY

Trentino-Alto p.410

Friuli-Venezia Giulia pp.396-397

Lombardy pp.401-404

Veneto pp.412-415

Piedmont pp.406-407

Emilia Romagna p.393-395

Liguria pp.400-401

Tuscany pp.410-412

Marche p.404-406

Latium pp.397-400

Puglia p.408

Campania pp.392-393

Sardinia p.408

Calabria p.392

Sicily pp.408-409

N

SCALE

0   80   160
mi.

RISTORANTE L'APPRODO

Cala del Porto Hotel
Via Roma 22
Vibo Marina
Vibo Valentia
Calabria 89811
+39 0963577763
www.lapprodo.com

Opening hours................................7 days for lunch and dinner
Reservation policy..Yes
Reservation email...info@lapprodo.com
Credit cards..Accepted
Price range..Affordable
Style..Smart casual
Cuisine..Calabrian
Recommended for..Worth the travel

LA CONCA DEL SOGNO

Via San Marciano 9
Nerano
Massa Lubrense
Naples
Campania 80061
+39 0818081036
www.concadelsogno.it

Opening hours................................7 days for lunch and dinner
Reservation policy..Yes
Reservation policy.............................info@concadelsogno.it
Credit cards..Accepted
Price range..Affordable
Style..Casual
Cuisine...Seafood
Recommended for..............................Regular neighbourhood

DA DORA

Via Fernando Palasciano 30
Chiaia
Naples
Campania 80122

Opening hours..............5 days for lunch and 6 days for dinner
Reservation policy..Yes
Credit cards..Accepted
Price range..Affordable
Style..Casual
Cuisine...Seafood
Recommended for..Wish I'd opened

'I reckon it's the best seafood restaurant in
the world.'—Jacob Kenedy

DON ALFONSO

Relais Don Alfonso Hotel
Corso Sant'Agata 11-13
Sant'Agata Sui Due Golfi
Naples
Campania 80064
+39 0818780026
www.donalfonso.com

Opening hours...5 days for dinner
Reservation policy..Yes
Credit cards..Accepted
Price range..Expensive
Style..Formal
Cuisine..Modern Mediterranean
Recommended for...Wish I'd opened

'An unforgettable experience. The perfect mix of talent,
passion and empathy.'—Emanuele Scarello

LO SCOGLIO DA TOMMASO

Lo Scoglio Hotel
Piazze delle Sirene 115
Massa Lubrense
Naples
Campania 80061
+39 0818081026
www.hotelloscoglio.com

Opening hours..............7 days for breakfast, lunch and dinner
Reservation policy..Yes
Reservation email.........................info@hotelloscoglio.com
Credit cards..Accepted
Price range..Affordable
Style..Casual
Cuisine...Campanian
Recommended for..Local favourite

PIZZERIA GINO SORBILLO

Via dei Tribunali 32
Naples
Campania 80138
+39 081446643
www.accademiadellapizza.it

Opening hours........................6 days from breakfast until late
Reservation policy..No
Credit cards..Accepted
Price range..Budget
Style..Casual
Cuisine..Pizza
Recommended for..Bargain

RISTORANTE QUATTRO PASSI

Via Amerigo Vespucci 13
Località Nerano
Massa Lubrense
Naples
Campania 80061
+39 0818082800
www.ristorantequattropassi.com

Opening hours	6 days for lunch and dinner
Reservation policy	Yes
Credit cards	Accepted
Price range	Expensive
Style	Smart casual
Cuisine	Modern Italian
Recommended for	Worth the travel

TAVERNA DEL CAPITANO

Piazza delle Sirene 10-11
Località Marina del Cantone
Massalubrense
Naples
Campania 80061
+39 0818081028
www.tavernadelcapitano.it

Opening hours	6 days for lunch and dinner
Reservation policy	Yes
Credit cards	Accepted
Price range	Affordable
Style	Casual
Cuisine	Mediterranean
Recommended for	Worth the travel

TORRE DEL SARACINO

via Torretta 9
Località Marina d'Aequa
Vico Equense
Naples
Campania 80069
+39 0818028555
www.torredelsaracino.it

Opening hours	6 days for lunch and 5 days for dinner
Reservation policy	Yes
Reservation email	prenotazioni@torredelsaracino.it
Credit cards	Accepted
Price range	Expensive
Style	Smart casual
Cuisine	Modern Italian
Recommended for	High end

'The chef always gives me happiness at the table. '
—Filippo La Mantia

ROSSELLINIS

Palazzo Sasso Hotel
Via San Giovanni del Toro 28
Ravello Salerno
Campania 84010
+39 089818181
www.palazzosasso.com

Opening hours	7 days for dinner
Reservation policy	Yes
Reservation email	food.beverage@palazzosasso.com
Credit cards	Accepted
Price range	Expensive
Style	Formal
Cuisine	Modern Italian
Recommended for	Worth the travel

SANTA ROSA RISTORANTE

Monastero Santa Rosa Hotel & Spa
Via Roma 2
Conca dei Marini
Salerno
Campania 84010
+39 0898321199
www.monasterosantarosa.com

Opening hours	7 days for breakfast, lunch and dinner
Reservation policy	Yes
Credit cards	Accepted
Price range	Expensive
Style	Smart casual
Cuisine	Campanian
Recommended for	Worth the travel

GELATAURO

Via San Vitale 98
Bologna
Emilia-Romagna 40125
+39 051230049
www.gelatauro.com

Opening hours	6 days from lunch until late
Reservation policy	No
Credit cards	Not accepted
Price range	Budget
Style	Casual
Cuisine	Ice cream
Recommended for	Worth the travel

'Easily the best *gelato* in the world.'—Jacob Kenedy

RISTORANTE MARCONI

Via Porrettana 291
Sasso Marconi
Bologna
Emilia-Romagna 40037
+39 051846216
www.ristorantemarconi.it

Opening hours	6 days for lunch and 5 days for dinner
Reservation policy	Yes
Credit cards	Accepted
Price range	Affordable
Style	Smart casual
Cuisine	Bolognese
Recommended for	Worth the travel

'The food is very creative but still keeps the traditional Bologna spirit in the back ground. Great wine cellar.'—Hiro Sone

BAR FRAGOLA CORTA

Via Giardini 144
Modena
Emilia-Romagna 41100

Opening hours	6 days for breakfast and lunch
Reservation policy	No
Credit cards	Not accepted
Price range	Budget
Style	Casual
Cuisine	Café
Recommended for	Breakfast

'At around 10.30 a.m. I always go to Fragola Corta for Federica's amazing moccacciono or a fresh-squeezed orange juice and Morena's special toasted sandwich with prosciutto and artichokes. I go there not only for the food but to talk about the football team – Inter – with Vasco, who has owned the bar for fifty years. Food, after all, is not only about nurturing the body, but the soul.'—Massimo Bottura

BRASSERIE FRANCECHETTA 58

Via Vignolese 58
Modena
Emilia-Romagna 41124
+39 0593091008
www.franceschetta58.it

Opening hours	6 days for dinner
Reservation policy	Yes
Credit cards	Accepted but not AMEX and Diners
Price range	Affordable
Style	Smart casual
Cuisine	Bar-Bistro
Recommended for	Late night

'It's usually buzzing untill quite late. I always stop by to say hello to the staff and remaining guests. A couple of slices of culatello or a cheese plate is just perfect at that hour.'—Massimo Bottura

LA CHERSENTA

Via Luigi Albinelli 36-38
Modena
Emilia-Romagna 41100
www.lachersenta.it

Opening hours	5 days for lunch until late
Reservation policy	No
Credit cards	Not accepted
Price range	Budget
Style	Casual
Cuisine	Bakery-Café
Recommended for	Bargain

'I go here for *tigelle*, a cheap, quick, on-the-go kind of meal. It is very typical Modenese. *Tigelle* are round flat breads that are cooked between two hot stones. When it is still warm it is sliced in half and you can put almost anything you want in it as filling. The traditional garnish is a lard, rosemary and garlic mixture with freshly grated Parmigiano Reggiano. The filling melts just enough to bring out the flavours.' —Massimo Bottura

HOSTERIA GIUSTI

Recommended by
Steve Samson

Via Luigi Carlo Farini 75
Modena
Emilia-Romagna 41100
+39 059222533
www.hosteriagiusti.it

Opening hours	5 days for lunch
Reservation policy	Yes
Reservation email	info@hosteriagiusti.it
Credit cards	Accepted
Price range	Affordable
Style	Casual
Cuisine	Modenese
Recommended for	Worth the travel

L'OSTERIA FRANCESCANA

Recommended by
Corrado Assenza, Enrico
Crippa, Anatoly Komm,
Ross Lewis, Davide Oldani,
Michel Portos, Mathieu
Rostaing-Tayard,
Emanuele Scarello

Via Stella 22
Modena
Emilia-Romagna 41121
+39 059210118
www.osteriafrancescana.it

Opening hours	5 days for lunch and 6 days for dinner
Reservation policy	Yes
Credit cards	Accepted
Price range	Expensive
Style	Smart casual
Cuisine	Modern Italian
Recommended for	Worth the travel

Deconstruction, reinterpretation and concentration are recurring themes at Massimo Bottura's Modena restaurant, where even the most traditional of dishes from the Emilia-Romagna region is given the modern treatment. The jazz-loving chef, like his beloved music, mixes things up in unconventional ways – his take on mortadella sees its key ingredients stripped out and served separately – yet he also adheres strictly to tradition when it counts, particularly in his peerless pasta dishes. Bottura's effervescent personality pervades Osteria Francescana: seldom is he seen without his trademark trainers (sneakers), which enable him to bound around the kitchen with an energy that would put an athlete to shame.

NUOVO GAMBERO ROSSO

Recommended by
Massimo Bottura

Via Vignolese 292
Modena
Emilia-Romagna 41125

Opening hours	7 days for lunch and dinner
Reservation policy	No
Credit cards	Accepted
Price range	Budget
Style	Casual
Cuisine	Pizza
Recommended for	Regular neighbourhood

'They make a special pizza that is neither square nor round, but oval-shaped. The dough has only natural raising (leavening) agents so it is easy to digest, crunchy but soft, and very satisfying.'
—Massimo Bottura

TRATTORIA AI DUE PLATANI

Recommended by
Gualtiero Marchesi

Via Budellungo 104
Parma
Emilia-Romagna 43123

Opening hours	6 days for lunch and 5 days for dinner
Reservation policy	Yes
Credit cards	Accepted
Price range	Affordable
Style	Casual
Cuisine	Parmese
Recommended for	Regular neighbourhood

'In September and October they make the best pumpkin ravioli I know. A good reason to visit is also the ice cream, served every evening at 10.00 p.m.'
—Gualtiero Marchesi

TRATTORIA AI CIODI

Località Anfora di Grado
Grado Gorizia
Friuli-Venezia Giulia
+39 03357522209
www.portobusoaiciodi.it

Opening hours...................................7 days for lunch and dinner
Reservation policy..Yes
Credit cards...Not accepted
Price range...Affordable
Style...Casual
Cuisine..Seafood
Recommended for..Local favourite

'You can only reach it by boat, open from April to October, serves freshly caught fish in a traditional way.'—Emanuele Scarello

LA PRIMULA

Via San Rocco 47
San Quirino
Pordenone
Friuli-Venezia Giulia 33080
+39 43491005
www.ristorantelaprimula.it

Opening hours................1 day for lunch and 5 days for dinner
Reservation policy..Yes
Reservation policy.........................info@ristorantelaprimula.it
Credit cards...Accepted
Price range...Affordable
Style...Smart casual
Cuisine..Modern Italian
Recommended for..................................Regular neighbourhood

AGLI AMICI

Via Liguria 250
Udine
Friuli-Venezia Giulia 33100
+39 432565411
www.agliamici.it

Opening hours..............6 days for lunch and 5 days for dinner
Reservation policy..Yes
Credit cards...Accepted
Price range...Affordable
Style...Smart casual
Cuisine..Modern Italian
Recommended for..................................Regular neighbourhood

AI BINTARS

Viale Trento e Trieste 63
San Daniele del Friuli
Udine
Friuli-Venezia Giulia 33038
+39 0432957322
www.aibintars.com

Opening hours...............................6 days for lunch and dinner
Reservation policy..Yes
Credit cards...Accepted
Price range...Budget
Style...Casual
Cuisine..Friulani
Recommended for...Bargain

CAFFÈ OTTELIO

Piazza Giacomo Matteotti 11a
Udine
Friuli-Venezia Giulia 33100

Opening hours...........................7 days for breakfast until late
Reservation policy...No
Credit cards...Accepted
Price range...Budget
Style...Casual
Cuisine...Café-Bar
Recommended for...Late night

'For great ham, cheese and wine.'—Emanuele Scarello

GROSMI CAFFÈ

Piazza Giacomo Matteotti 6
Udine
Friuli-Venezia Giulia 33100
www.grosmicaffe.it

Opening hours...........................6 days for breakfast and lunch
Reservation policy...No
Credit cards...Accepted
Price range...Budget
Style...Casual
Cuisine...Café
Recommended for..Breakfast

'Excellent expresso.'—Emanuele Scarello

NIÙ

Via Nazionale 40
Tavagnacco
Udine
Friuli-Venezia Giulia 33010
+39 0432484739
www.niudine.it

Opening hours.................................6 days for lunch and dinner
Reservation policy...Yes
Credit cards..Accepted
Price range..Budget
Style..Casual
Cuisine..Friulani
Recommended for..Late night

OSTERIA ALTRAN

Località Cortona, 19
Ruda, Udine
Friuli-Venezia Giulia 33050
+39 0431969402

Opening hours..5 days for dinner
Reservation policy...Yes
Reservation email..............................osteria.altran@libero.it
Credit cards..Accepted
Price range...Affordable
Style..Smart casual
Cuisine..Friulani
Recommended for...Local favourite

Sandwiched between the Adriatic and the Alps, and just a stone's throw from the Slovenian border, Udine's Osteria Altran serves up big, distinctive Friulian flavours to its local following. Theirs is a kitchen celebrating local raw materials — oysters in pastry on a bed of creamy salt cod, fried rabbit and escarole soup, to name but a few. There's Friulian wine in abundance, too, where the Austro-Hungarian influence comes into play — try a Verduzzo, a local Chardonnay or a Tocai with dessert, which range from lemon mousse to caramel cream. White tablecloths and terracotta tiles rightly put the spotlight on the meal itself, available à la carte or as a tasting menu.

PASTICCERIA SIMENONI

Via Francesco Mantica 15
Udine
Friuli-Venezia Giulia 33100
+39 0432502505
www.simeonipasticceria.com

Opening hours........................7 days from breakfast until late
Reservation policy..No
Credit cards..Not accepted
Price range..Budget
Style..Casual
Cuisine...Bakery-Café
Recommended for..Breakfast

'Superb croissants and cakes.'—Emanuele Scarello

00100 PIZZA

Via Giovanni Branca 88
Rome
Latium 00100
www.00100pizza.com

Opening hours.................................7 days for lunch and dinner
Reservation policy..No
Credit cards..Not accepted
Price range..Budget
Style..Casual
Cuisine...Pizza
Recommended for...Worth the travel

From the same crew behind Sforno, which many pizza pundits swear is Rome's best, comes this much more basic slice-punting outpost near Piazza di Santa Maria Liberatrice, Testaccio. It's cutely named after the Roman postcode combined with the grade of semolina flour used in their various pizzas, focacce pugliesi and trademark tramezzini. The latter triangular pockets of bread play to the local love of offal (variety meats) in combinations such as tripe, tomato and mint; braised oxtail, celery and carrots; and tongue with parsley and garlic. There are a handful of places to perch in the shop but it's primarily a takeaway (takeout).

ANTICO FORNO ROSCIOLI
Recommended by
Heinz Beck

Via dei Chiavari 34
Rome
Latium 00186
www.salumeriaroscioli.com

Opening hours.........................6 days from breakfast until late
Reservation policy...No
Credit cards..Accepted
Price range...Budget
Style...Casual
Cuisine..Bakery
Recommended for.................................Breakfast

'One of the oldest bakeries in Rome.'—Heinz Beck

L'ARCANGELO
Recommended by
Şemsa Denizsel

Via Giuseppe Gioacchino Belli 59
Rome
Latium 00193
+39 063210992

Opening hours.............5 days for lunch and 6 days for dinner
Reservation policy...Yes
Credit cards..Accepted
Price range...Affordable
Style...Smart casual
Cuisine..Roman
Recommended for.................................Worth the travel

'For its perfect pillows of gnocchi.'—Şemsa Denizsel

BRÒ PORTA PORTESE
Recommended by
Heinz Beck

Largo Alessandro Toja 2-3
Trastevere
Rome
Latium 00153
+39 065813500
www.broportaportese.it

Opening hours................................6 days for lunch and dinner
Reservation policy...Yes
Reservation email.........................info@broportaportese.it
Credit cards..Accepted
Price range...Affordable
Style...Smart casual
Cuisine..Roman
Recommended for.................................Bargain

IMÀGO
Recommended by
Rahul Akerkar

Hassler Hotel
Piazza Trinità dei Monti 6
Rome
Latium 00187
+39 0669934726
www.imagorestaurant.com

Opening hours.................................7 days for dinner
Reservation policy...Yes
Reservation email...............................imago@hotelhassler.it
Credit cards..Accepted
Price range...Expensive
Style...Formal
Cuisine..Modern Italian
Recommended for.................................Worth the travel

Located on the top floor of the Hotel Hassler, at the summit of the Spanish Steps, Imàgo offers stunning views of spectacular Rome. In fact, it takes something very special to divert one's attention from what's outside the window to what's being served within, but Neapolitan chef Francesco Apreda comes up with the goods. His cooking reflects a versatility and fine eye for detail garnered in London and Tokyo and an affinity with his native cuisine that keeps the locals coming back for more. Save room for dessert — Apreda's first love.

LA PERGOLA
Recommended by
Tomaž Kavčič, Heinz Winkler

Rome Cavalieri Hotel
Via Roberto Cadlolo 101
Rome
Latium 00136
+39 0635091
www.romecavalieri.com/lapergola.php

Opening hours.................................5 days for dinner
Reservation policy...Yes
Credit cards..Accepted
Price range...Expensive
Style...Formal
Cuisine..Mediterranean
Recommended for.................................Wish I'd opened

RISTORANTE CESARE

Recommended by
Francis Mallmann

Via Crescenzio 13
Rome
Latium 00193
+39 0668130351
www.ristorantecesare.com

Opening hours	7 days for lunch and 6 days for dinner
Reservation policy	Yes
Credit cards	Accepted
Price range	Affordable
Style	Smart casual
Cuisine	Roman
Recommended for	Regular neighbourhood

ROSCIOLI

Recommended by
Massimo Bottura,
Şemsa Denizsel

Via dei Giubbonari 21
Rome
Latium 00186
+39 066875287
www.salumeriaroscioli.com

Opening hours	6 days for lunch and dinner
Reservation policy	Yes
Credit cards	Accepted
Price range	Affordable
Style	Smart casual
Cuisine	Bar-Bistro-Deli
Recommended for	Worth the travel

'Roscioli is my favourite Roman getaway. It's a gourmet pizza place with amazing quality products, wine and the occasional plate of pasta as well. '
—Massimo Bottura

Run by the Roscioli family for over forty years, this renowned deli in the heart of Rome is the kind of place you dream of discovering. Allesandro and Pierluigi transformed their father Marco's deli into a wine bar and restaurant in 2002. Behind the formidable shopfront bursting with artisan cheeses and cold cuts sits a small dining room, where chefs conjure up unfussy Roman food of a freshness and quality that makes the eyes water: the decadent burrata and spaghetti carbonara are legendary. The Rosciolis also run Antico Forno Roscioli, a historic bakery, around the corner – Bianca, their classic Roman pizza, is rightfully a cult favourite.

SAPORE DI MARE

Recommended by
Michael Schwartz

Via del Piè di Marmo 36
Rome
Latium 00186
+39 066780968
www.saporedimarearoma.it

Opening hours	2 days for lunch and 7 days for dinner
Reservation policy	Yes
Credit cards	Accepted
Price range	Affordable
Style	Smart casual
Cuisine	Seafood
Recommended for	Worth the travel

'Flavors of the sea, literally.'—Michael Schwartz

SOMO

Recommended by
Filippo La Mantia

Via Goffredo Mameli 5
Trastevere
Rome
Latium 00153
+39 065882060
www.somo.asia

Opening hours	6 days for dinner
Reservation policy	Yes
Reservation email	reservations@somo.asia
Credit cards	Accepted
Price range	Affordable
Style	Smart casual
Cuisine	Japanese-Mediterranean
Recommended for	Regular neighbourhood

SORA LELLA

Recommended by
Heinz Beck

Via Ponte Quattro Capi 16
Rome
Latium 00186
+39 066861601
www.soralella.com

Opening hours	7 days for lunch and dinner
Reservation policy	Yes
Reservation email	trattoriasoralella@libero.it
Credit cards	Accepted
Price range	Affordable
Style	Casual
Cuisine	Roman
Recommended for	Regular neighbourhood

'In Rome, when I have the chance, I like to eat at Sora Lella, one of the historical Restaurants in Rome.'—Heinz Beck

TRATTORIA DA MARCELLO

Recommended by
Jacob Kenedy

Via dei Campani 12
San Lorenzo
Rome
Latium 00185
+39 064463311

Opening hours	7 days for lunch and dinner
Reservation policy	Yes
Credit cards	Accepted
Price range	Affordable
Style	Casual
Cuisine	Roman
Recommended for	Wish I'd opened

'Amazing, typical food and an atypically amazing wine list.'—Jacob Kenedy

TRATTORIA DA TEO

Recommended by
Rowley Leigh

Piazza dei Ponziani 7
Trastevere
Rome
Latium 00153
+39 065818355

Opening hours	7 days for lunch and dinner
Reservation policy	Yes
Credit cards	Accepted
Price range	Affordable
Style	Casual
Cuisine	Roman
Recommended for	Worth the travel

O MAGAZIN

Recommended by
Robert Marchetti

Calata Marconi 34
Portofino
Genoa
Liguria 16034
+39 0185269178

Opening hours	6 days for lunch and dinner
Reservation policy	Yes
Credit cards	Accepted
Price range	Affordable
Style	Casual
Cuisine	Seafood
Recommended for	Worth the travel

'Try the tiny anchovies, the very best *spaghetti vongole*, and the incredible salt-baked whole sea bass with new potatoes and Ligurian olives.'—Robert Marchetti

TRATTORIA DA LAURA

Recommended by
Ruth Rogers

Near San Fruttuoso Abbey
San Fruttuoso
Camogli
Genoa
Liguria
+39 0185772589

Opening hours	7 days for lunch
Reservation policy	Yes
Credit cards	Not accepted
Price range	Budget
Style	Casual
Cuisine	Ligurian
Recommended for	Wish I'd opened

'A shack on the beach in Liguria serving only fish and *lasagnette al pesto*.'—Ruth Rogers

LA SPIAGGETTA

Recommended by
Mauro Colagreco

Via Romana Antica s/n
Grimaldi di Ventimiglia
Imperia
Liguria 18039
+39 184227020
www.balzirossi.it

Opening hours	5 days for brunch and 6 days for dinner
Reservation policy	Yes
Credit cards	Not accepted
Price range	Affordable
Style	Smart casual
Cuisine	Ligurian
Recommended for	Breakfast

'Beautiful place to relax.'—Mauro Colagreco

LA VECCHIA OSTAIA

Recommended by
Mauro Colagreco

via Provinciale, 34
San Biagio della Cima
Imperia
Liguria 18036
+39 0184289249

Opening hours	6 days for lunch and dinner
Reservation policy	Yes
Credit cards	Not accepted
Price range	Affordable
Style	Casual
Cuisine	Ligurian
Recommended for	Regular neighbourhood

'It's a family restaurant and the pasta is fresh, very good and made by Mama Angela.'—Mauro Colagreco

You will soon forget the tortuous, winding roads once you arrive at Mamma Angela's Vecchia Ostaia, beside a clear stream at the fringe of San Biagio della Cima, a colourful Ligurian hamlet. Working under urgently spinning fans, the soulful singing cook is beloved by locals and intrepid internationals alike for her *Menu Degustivo*. Served on floral dinnerware, this may include slow-cooked rabbit in local wine, a dish that at least one visitor rated as rivalling (in flavour, if not aesthetics) that of Alain Ducasse in nearby Monaco. From the dessert trolley, ripe fruit tarts – including Angela's fig tart – glisten under sweet candied crusts.

GIANNI FRANZI

Recommended by
Ruth Rogers

Piazza San Giovanni Battista
Vernazza
La Spezia
Liguria 19020
+39 0187821003
www.giannifranzi.it

Opening hours	6 days for lunch and dinner
Reservation policy	Yes
Credit cards	Accepted
Price range	Affordable
Style	Casual
Cuisine	Ligurian
Recommended for	Worth the travel

DA VITTORIO

Recommended by
Albert Raurich,
Emanuele Scarello

Via Cantalupa 17
Brusaporto Bergamo
Lombardy 24060
+39 035681024
www.davittorio.com

Opening hours	6 days for lunch and 7 days for dinner
Reservation policy	Yes
Credit cards	Accepted
Price range	Expensive
Style	Casual
Cuisine	Lombardian
Recommended for	High end

'Is a pleasure for the senses in an amazing place.'
—Albert Raurich

MC MAIER'S

Recommended by
Enrico & Roberto Cerea

Via Italia, 87
Seriate
Bergamo
Lombardy 24068
+39 035294459
www.mcmaiers.com

Opening hours	6 days for dinner
Reservation policy	Yes
Credit cards	Accepted
Price range	Affordable
Style	Casual
Cuisine	Lombardian
Recommended for	Late night

DISPENSA PANI E VINI

Recommended by
Gualtiero Marchesi

Via Principe Umberto, 23
Torbiato di Adro
Brescia
Lombardy 25030
+39 0307450757
www.dispensafranciacorta.com

Opening hours	6 days for lunch and dinner
Reservation policy	Yes
Credit cards	Accepted
Price range	Budget
Style	Casual
Cuisine	Bar-Bistro
Recommended for	Bargain

'Perfect for when you feel like cheeses and meats.'
—Gualtiero Marchesi

OSTERIA DELLA VILLETTA

Recommended by
Gualtiero Marchesi

Via Guglielmo Marconi 104
Palazzolo sull'Oglio
Brescia
Lombardy 25036
+39 0307401899
www.osteriadellavilletta.it

Opening hours	5 days for lunch and 3 days for dinner
Reservation policy	Yes
Credit cards	Accepted
Price range	Affordable
Style	Casual
Cuisine	Lombardian
Recommended for	Late night

'A real restaurant where the chef makes simple, clean and almost naive dishes, in a reassuring way.'
—Gualtiero Marchesi

PASTICCERIA CAVOUR

Via Gombito 7a
Bergamo
Lombardy 24129
+39 035243418

Opening hours............................6 days from breakfast until late
Reservation policy...Yes
Credit cards..Accepted
Price range...Affordable
Style..Casual
Cuisine..Bakery-Café
Recommended for...Breakfast

DAL PESCATORE

Località Runate
Riserva del Parco Oglio Sud
Canneto sull'Oglio
Mantua
Lombardy 46013
+39 0376723001
www.dalpescatore.com

Opening hours.............4 days for lunch and 5 days for dinner
Reservation policy...Yes
Reservation email..........................santini@dalpescatore.com
Credit cards..Accepted
Price range...Expensive
Style...Smart casual
Cuisine..Mantuan
Recommended for....................................Local favourite

'Where else can you eat the most exquisite fried frogs
legs, snail soup and Nadia's singular pumpkin-filled
tortelli? Nowhere in the world!'—Massimo Bottura

Sit back and stay awhile – you'll be reluctant to
leave! The Santini family are renowned for treating
customers like old friends at their world-class
restaurant, set in isolated splendour an hour's drive
from Milan. Dal Pescatore, originally a humble
osteria, has been in the same hands for three
generations. Serving refined Mantuan cuisine, the
three-Michelin-starred kitchen is run by Nadia
Santini, considered one of Italy's finest chefs, along
with her son Giovanni and mother-in-law Bruna.
Produce takes pride of place, and rigorously indigenous dishes such as tortelli di zucca, snails with
porcini and agnolini in brodo often feature on the two
tasting menus: the *Primavera* and *Campagna*.

ALICE RISTORANTE

Via Adige 9
Milan
Lombardy 20135
+39 025462930
www.aliceristorante.it

Opening hours................................7 days for lunch and dinner
Reservation policy...Yes
Reservation policy.................alice@aliceristorante.it
Credit cards..Accepted
Price range...Affordable
Style...Smart casual
Cuisine...Mediterranean
Recommended for..Worth the travel

ANTICA OSTERIA MAGENES

Via Cavour 7
Barate di Gaggiano
Milan
Lombardy 20083
+39 029085125
www.osteriamagenes.it

Opening hours...............1 day for lunch and 6 days for dinner
Reservation policy...Yes
Credit cards..Accepted
Price range...Affordable
Style..Casual
Cuisine..Lombardian
Recommended for...Bargain

BIFFI

Corso Magenta 87
Milan
Lombardy 20123
+39 025462930
www.biffipasticceria.it

Opening hours............................7 days from breakfast until late
Reservation policy...Yes
Credit cards..Accepted
Price range...Affordable
Style..Casual
Cuisine..Bakery-Café
Recommended for...Breakfast

Opened by Paolo Biffi, the inventor of panettone, in
1847, this Milan institution has sold 'that famous
cake' ever since. A *pasticceria* and *offelleria*, it has
long been a site of pilgrimage for coffee addicts and
those in need of a little morning refreshment, and
has changed little since its Art Deco heyday. Patrons

seeking sanctuary in its opulent interior from the fashion-hungry crowds of the Corso Vercelli are just as likely to be sophisticated Milanese regulars as camera-toting tourists. A frothy cappuccino and *spremuta*, freshly squeezed juice, with brioche or cream cake at the bar makes for an indulgent breakfast, arguably worth the exorbitant cost.

CALIFORNIA BAKERY

Recommended by
Davide Oldani

Piazza Sant'Eustorgio 4
Milan
Lombardy 20122
+39 0239811538
www.californiabakery.it

Opening hours	7 days for breakfast until late
Reservation policy	No
Credit cards	Accepted
Price range	Affordable
Style	Casual
Cuisine	Bakery-Café
Recommended for	Breakfast

CRACCO

Recommended by
Massimo Bottura, Davide Oldani, Emanuele Scarello

Via Victor Hugo 4
Milan
Lombardy 20123
+39 028767/4
www.ristorantecracco.it

Opening hours	4 days for lunch and 6 days for dinner
Reservation policy	Yes
Reservation email	rosa@ristorantecracco.it
Credit cards	Accepted
Price range	Affordable
Style	Smart casual
Cuisine	Modern Italian
Recommended for	Worth the travel

'Genius.'—Emanuele Scarello

Carlo Cracco's elegant vault of a dining room opened in 2001 as Cracco-Peck, a partnership with the famous Milanese food store that plies its reassuring expensive wares just around the corner. In a city where tradition tends to triumph over creativity in terms of restaurants, Cracco, who parted with Peck in 2007, has carved out a niche and courted controversy, as an innovator and risk taker, by embracing avant-garde techniques and – appropriately, in that this is Milan – fashion. Leave aside the à la carte and the 'traditional' tasting menu and, instead, go 'creative' to experience his latest collection of dishes.

TRATTORIA AL CARRETTO

Recommended by
Gualtiero Marchesi

Via Milano 28
Bonirola
Gaggiano
Milan
Lombardy 20083
+39 029085254

Opening hours	6 days for lunch and dinner
Reservation policy	Yes
Credit cards	Not accepted
Price range	Affordable
Style	Casual
Cuisine	Pugliese
Recommended for	Local favourite

'They source everything including the wine from farmers. I would recommend it, an emotional experience.'—Gualtiero Marchesi

D'O

Recommended by
Andrea Berton,
Filippo La Mantia

Via Magenta 18
San Pietro all'Olmo
Milan
Lombardy 20010
+39 029362209
www.cucinapop.do

Opening hours	5 days for lunch and dinner
Reservation policy	Yes
Reservation email	info@cucinapop.do
Credit cards	Not accepted
Price range	Affordable
Style	Smart casual
Cuisine	Italian
Recommended for	Wish I'd opened

IL LUOGO DI AIMO E NADIA

Recommended by
Corrado Assenza,
Massimo Bottura,
Rodrigo Oliveira,
Emanuele Scarello

Via Privata Raimondo Montecuccoli 6
Milan
Lombardy 20147
+39 02416886
www.aimoenadia.com

Opening hours	5 days for lunch and 6 days for dinner
Reservation policy	Yes
Credit cards	Accepted
Price range	Expensive
Style	Smart casual
Cuisine	Modern Italian
Recommended for	Worth the travel

'The meal of my life.'—Rodrigo Oliveira

RISTORANTE TEATRO ALLA SCALA

Piazza della Scala
Angolo dei Filodrammatici
Milan
Lombardy 20121
+39 0272094338
www.ilmarchesino.it

Opening hours	6 days for dinner
Reservation policy	Yes
Credit cards	Accepted
Price range	Expensive
Style	Smart casual
Cuisine	Modern Italian
Recommended for	Late night

TRATTORIA DEL NUOVO MACELLO

Via Cesare Lombroso 20
Milan
Lombardy 20137
+39 025457714
www.trattoriadelnuovomacello.it

Opening hours	6 days for lunch and 5 days for dinner
Reservation policy	Yes
Reservation email	info@trattoriadelnuovomacello.it
Credit cards	Not accepted
Price range	Affordable
Style	Casual
Cuisine	Lombardian
Recommended for	Regular neighbourhood

TRUSSARDI ALLA SCALA

Piazza della Scala 5
Milan
Lombardy 20121
+39 0280688201
www.trussardiallascala.com

Opening hours	5 days for lunch and 6 days for dinner
Reservation policy	Yes
Reservation email	ristorante@trussardiallascala.com
Credit cards	Accepted
Price range	Expensive
Style	Smart casual
Cuisine	Modern Italian
Recommended for	Regular neighbourhood

ZERO

Corso Magenta 87
Milan
Lombardy 20123
+39 245474733
www.zeromagenta.it

Opening hours	6 days for dinner
Reservation policy	Yes
Credit cards	Accepted
Price range	Expensive
Style	Smart casual
Cuisine	Modern Japanese
Recommended for	Late night

BISTRÒ 2

Lungomare Leonardo Da Vinci 8
Senigallia
Ancona
Marche 60019
+39 0717926281

Opening hours	7 days from breakfast until late
Reservation policy	No
Credit cards	Not accepted
Price range	Budget
Style	Casual
Cuisine	Bar-Bistro
Recommended for	Late night

LA MADONNINA DEL PESCATORE

Via Lungomare Italia 11
Senigallia
Ancona
Marche 60019
+39 071698267
www.morenocedroni.it

Opening hours	6 days for lunch and dinner
Reservation policy	Yes
Credit cards	Accepted
Price range	Expensive
Style	Smart casual
Cuisine	Seafood
Recommended for	Worth the travel

OSTERIA DEL TEATRO
Via Fratelli Bandiera 70
Senigallia
Ancona
Marche 60019
+39 07160517

Opening hours	5 days for lunch and 6 days for dinner
Reservation policy	Yes
Credit cards	Accepted
Price range	Affordable
Style	Casual
Cuisine	Marchese
Recommended for	Regular neighbourhood

OSTERIA SARA
Corso Italia 9
Sirolo
Ancona
Marche 60020
+39 0719330716

Opening hours	6 days for lunch and dinner
Reservation policy	Yes
Credit cards	Accepted but not AMEX and Diners
Price range	Budget
Style	Casual
Cuisine	Marchese
Recommended for	Local favourite

'Go for the traditional fish recipes.'—Moreno Cedroni

OSTERIA TEATRO STRABACCO
Via Guglielmo Oberdan 2-2a
Ancona
Marche 60100
+39 07156748
www.osteriastrabacco.it

Opening hours	6 days for lunch and dinner
Reservation policy	Yes
Credit cards	Accepted
Price range	Affordable
Style	Casual
Cuisine	Marchese
Recommended for	Late night

'When I have the opportunity to stay in my hometown, Ancona, I always go to the Osteria Strabacco, where they serve typical regional dishes.'—Stefano Baiocco

RISTORANTE DA GIACCHETTI
Via Portonovo 171
Ancona
Marche 60020
+39 071801384
www.ristorantedagiacchetti.it

Opening hours	7 days for lunch and dinner
Reservation policy	Yes
Credit cards	Accepted
Price range	Affordable
Style	Casual
Cuisine	Seafood
Recommended for	Regular neighbourhood

RISTORANTE EMILIA
Baia di Portonovo
Ancona
Marche 60129
+39 071801328
www.ristoranteemilia.it

Opening hours	6 days for lunch and dinner
Reservation policy	Yes
Reservation email	info@ristoranteemilia.it
Credit cards	Accepted
Price range	Affordable
Style	Casual
Cuisine	Seafood
Recommended for	Local favourite

SAFFI CAFFÈ
Piazza Saffi 18
Senigallia
Ancona
Marche 60019
+39 07160053
www.safficaffe.it

Opening hours	6 days from breakfast until late
Reservation policy	No
Credit cards	Accepted
Price range	Budget
Style	Casual
Cuisine	Café
Recommended for	Breakfast

ULIASSI

Recommended by
Matthew Accarrino
Jean Beddington

Banchina di Levante 6
Senigallia
Ancona
Marche 60019
+39 07165463
www.uliassi.it

Opening hours	6 days for lunch and dinner
Reservation policy	No
Credit cards	Accepted
Price range	Expensive
Style	Smart casual
Cuisine	Modern Italian
Recommended for	Worth the travel

'Chef Mauro Uliassi successfully blends the seafood of the region in a unique way that both satisfies and surprises. '—Matthew Accarrino

CÀ DEL RE

Recommended by
Russell Moore

Castello di Verduno
Via Umberto I 14
Verduno
Cuneo
Piedmont 12060
+39 0172470281
www.castellodiverduno.com

Opening hours	2 days for lunch and 6 days for dinner
Reservation policy	Yes
Credit cards	Accepted
Price range	Affordable
Style	Casual
Cuisine	Piedmontese
Recommended for	Wish I'd opened

OPEN BALADIN

Recommended by
Pier Bussetti

Via Statale 68
Santa Vittoria d'Alba
Cuneo
Piedmont 12069
+39 0172479287
www.openbaladin.com

Opening hours	7 days for dinner
Reservation policy	Yes
Reservation email	openbaladin@gmail.com
Credit cards	Accepted
Price range	Budget
Style	Casual
Cuisine	Fast food
Recommended for	Late night

'They make burgers with Piedmontese *Fassone* veal and great bread made by an artisanal baker.'
—Pier Bussetti

OSTERIA DEL BOCCONDIVINO

Recommended by
Jonathan Jones

Via Mendicità 14
Bra
Cuneo
Piedmont 12042
+39 0172425674
www.osteriadellarco.it

Opening hours	5 days for lunch and dinner
Reservation policy	Yes
Credit cards	Accepted
Price range	Affordable
Style	Casual
Cuisine	Piedmontese
Recommended for	Worth the travel

LA PIOLA

Recommended by
Enrico Crippa

Piazza Risorgimento 4
Alba
Cuneo
Piedmont 12051
+39 0173442800
www.lapiola-alba.it

Opening hours	6 days for lunch and 5 days for dinner
Reservation policy	Yes
Reservation email	info@lapiola-alba.it
Credit cards	Accepted
Price range	Budget
Style	Casual
Cuisine	Piedmontese
Recommended for	Bargain

The brainchild of Piedmontese wine entrepreneurs the Ceretto family and Milan chef Enrico Crippa, La Piola is the more modest sister restaurant of Alba's two-Michelin-starred El Duomo. Dedicated to promoting the fruits of Piedmont both traditionally and affordably, La Piola serves up northern Italian classics like truffle-laden fried egg, raw veal and egg pastas — all best experienced during the annual White Truffle Festival in October. Guests choose their truffle by weight at a reasonable €5 (£4; $6) per gram and bottles of world-famous local wines — Barolo, Barbera, Barbaresco — start at €14 (£11; $17) each. Stark (yet sleek) marble tables and dark wooden chairs let the food and wine do the talking.

RISTORANTE ALL'ENOTECA

Recommended by
Scott Conant

Via Roma 57
Canale
Cuneo
Piedmont 12043
+39 017395857
www.davidepalluda.it

Opening hours	5 days for lunch and 6 days for dinner
Reservation policy	Yes
Credit cards	Accepted
Price range	Expensive
Style	Smart casual
Cuisine	Modern Italian
Recommended for	Worth the travel

'Simple and refined food.'—Scott Conant

RISTORANTE PIAZZA DUOMO

Recommended by
Massimo Bottura

Piazza Risorgimento 4
Alba
Cuneo
Piedmont 12051
+39 0173366167
www.piazzaduomoalba.it

Opening hours	6 days for lunch and 5 days for dinner
Reservation policy	Yes
Credit cards	Accepted
Price range	Expensive
Style	Formal
Cuisine	Modern Italian
Recommended for	Worth the travel

'I was very impressed by Enrico Crippa's talent and restraint.'—Massimo Bottura

AL PASSATORE

Recommended by
Alfredo Russo

Via Giuseppe Barbaroux 10
Turin
Piedmont 10122

Opening hours	6 days for lunch early dinner
Reservation policy	No
Credit cards	Not accepted
Price range	Budget
Style	Casual
Cuisine	Bar-Café
Recommended for	Bargain

'They make a fantastic *piadina*.'—Alfredo Russo

With Turin's baroque boulevards and arcades full to bursting with cafés, bars and takeaways (takeouts), recommendations are gold dust. A badly kept secret among locals, this cheap bijou pit stop hidden on a narrow cobbled street in central Turin has been plying a brisk trade for over twenty years. For less than €5 (£4; $6), grab yourself one of their famous grilled *piadina romagnola*, Piedmontese flatbread, filled with sliced meat and soft squacquarone cheese, or smothered with chocolate spread, but be prepared to wait when it's deluged at lunchtime. Shell out a fraction more to occupy a bar seat with a carafe of local wine.

COMBAL.ZERO

Recommended by
Emanuele Scarello

Piazzale Mafalda di Savoia
Rivoli
Turin
Piedmont 10098
+39 0119565225
www.combal.org

Opening hours	5 days for dinner
Reservation policy	Yes
Credit cards	Accepted
Price range	Expensive
Style	Smart casual
Cuisine	Modern Italian
Recommended for	Worth the travel

LIBERY

Recommended by
Pier Bussetti

Via Legnano 14
Turin
Piedmont 10128
+39 0114546040

Opening hours	4 days for lunch and 6 days for dinner
Reservation policy	Yes
Credit cards	Accepted
Price range	Budget
Style	Casual
Cuisine	Pizza
Recommended for	Regular neighbourhood

Cavernous, whitewashed, full of wrought-iron furniture and always bustling (evening bookings are essential), this gourmet pizzeria really flies the flag for northern Italian pizza. We're talking thin sourdough base with blackened chunky crusts, gilded with, for instance, burrata, sausage and artichoke. Given the ingredients are cherry-picked from local suppliers – such as eggs from Parisi and flour from Gragano – this is good value for a standout meal. That and the much-loved Baladin, the local beer that arrives in carafes from the taps.

AQUA E SALE

Recommended by
Theo Randall

Via Peppino Orlando 2
Ostuni
Brindisi
Puglia 72017
+39 0831330302
www.ristoranteacquasale.it

Opening hours	7 days for lunch and dinner
Reservation policy	Yes
Credit cards	Accepted
Price range	Affordable
Style	Casual
Cuisine	Mediterranean
Recommended for	Worth the travel

'The best meal I had last year.'—Theo Randall

PANTAGRUELE

Recommended by
Saul G. Bolton

Via Salita di Ripalta 1
Brindisi
Puglia 72100
+39 0831560605

Opening hours	5 days for lunch and 6 days for dinner
Reservation policy	Yes
Credit cards	Accepted
Price range	Budget
Style	Casual
Cuisine	Pugliese
Recommended for	Worth the travel

SU FURRIADROXU

Recommended by
Anna Hansen

Via XXIV Maggio
S'arruga de su Soddu 11
Pula
Cagliari
Sardinia 09010
+39 0709246148
www.sufurriadroxu.it

Opening hours	6 days for lunch and dinner
Reservation policy	Yes
Reservation email	info@sufurriadroxu.it
Credit cards	Accepted
Price range	Budget
Style	Casual
Cuisine	Sardinian
Recommended for	Worth the travel

'Rows of slowly roasting sucking pigs, cured mutton, wild boar, fresh cheeses and plenty of chilled fruity red ... and all consumed under the stars. Perfect!'
—Anna Hansen

LA MADIA

Recommended by
Massimiliano Alajmo,
Stefano Baiocco

Corso Filippo Re Capriata 22
Licata
Agrigento
Sicily 92027
+39 0922771443
www.ristorantelamadia.it

Opening hours	6 days for lunch and dinner
Reservation policy	Yes
Reservation email	info@ristorantelamadia.it
Credit cards	Accepted but not Diners
Price range	Expensive
Style	Smart casual
Cuisine	Modern Sicilian
Recommended for	Worth the travel

Licata, a nondescript town in southern Sicily barely mentioned in travel guides, is an odd place to find a high-end (nay, trailblazing) kitchen. It is, however, the birthplace of Michelin-starred chef Pino Cuttaia, who opened La Madia in 2000 and quickly gained a reputation as one of the best chefs on the island. Be warned – few navigation systems can find the place and there's no obvious signage, so seek help from a local when you reach the town. A simple, modern take on traditional Sicilian cuisine is the hallmark of Cuttaia: his tasting menus offer clever and dazzlingly presented riffs on classics such as arancini and cannoli, plus an adventurous pine-cone-smoked fish.

CHARLESTON

Recommended by
Heinz Beck

Via Generale Vincenzo Magliocco 15
Palermo
Sicily 90141
+39 091450171
www.ristorantecharleston.com

Opening hours	6 days for lunch and dinner
Reservation policy	Yes
Reservation email	info@ristorantecharleston.com
Credit cards	Accepted
Price range	Affordable
Style	Smart casual
Cuisine	Modern Italian
Recommended for	Wish I'd opened

'I love this restaurant for its architectural beauty and its location, in the sea ... beautiful.'—Heinz Beck

TRATTORIA BIONDO
Recommended by
Filippo La Mantia
Via Giosuè Carducci 15
Libertà
Palermo
Sicily 90141
+39 091583662
www.ristoratoribiondo.com

Opening hours	6 days for dinner
Reservation policy	Yes
Credit cards	Accepted but not AMEX and Diners
Price range	Affordable
Style	Casual
Cuisine	Sicilian
Recommended for	Local favourite

'Captures the very soul of my region.'
—Filippo La Mantia

LA GAZZA LADRA
Recommended by
Corrado Assenza
Via Blandini, 5
Modica
Ragusa
Sicily 97015
+39 0932755655
www.ristorantelagazzaladra.it

Opening hours	5 days for dinner
Reservation policy	Yes
Credit cards	Accepted
Price range	Affordable
Style	Smart casual
Cuisine	Sicilian
Recommended for	High end

RISTORANTE MARIA FIDONE
Recommended by
Corrado Assenza
Via Gianforma 6
Frigintini, Modica
Ragusa
Sicily 97015
+39 0932901135
www.mariafidone.com

Opening hours	6 days for dinner
Reservation policy	Yes
Credit cards	Not accepted
Price range	Affordable
Style	Casual
Cuisine	Sicilian
Recommended for	Bargain

CAFFÈ SICILIA
Recommended by
Massimiliano Alajmo
Corso Vittorio Emanuele III 125
Noto
Syracuse
Sicily 96017
+39 0931835013
www.infioratadinoto.it

Opening hours	7 days for breakfast, lunch and dinner
Reservation policy	No
Credit cards	Accepted
Price range	Affordable
Style	Casual
Cuisine	Café
Recommended for	Breakfast

'Go for a brioche filled with coffee granita.'
—Massimilano Alajmo

In the baroque Sicilian town of Noto, Caffè Sicilia promises to set you up for the day with a vast selection of baked goods and local favourites, all proudly displayed in colourful rows on their counter. Owners and brothers Carlo and Corrado Assenza create local classics with an edge. Try brioche with a refreshing almond *granita*, a semi-frozen dessert. Alternatively, take coffee with a *cannolo*, a tube-like Sicilian pastry enveloping flavoured custard fillings, which range from basil to lemon and saffron. Also on offer are famous desserts: *cassata*, ricotta dessert with marzipan, or double *panna cotta* with figs. Breakfast on the honey-hued terrace makes a very sweet start to the day.

ZUBEBI
Recommended by
Roberta Sudbrack
Zubebi Resort
Contrada Zubebi
Isola de Pantelleria
Trapani
Sicily 91017
+39 0923913653
www.zubebi.com

Opening hours	7 days from breakfast until late
Reservation policy	Yes
Credit cards	Accepted
Price range	Affordable
Style	Smart casual
Cuisine	International
Recommended for	Wish I'd opened

'A different menu is prepared every day with what is available at the market. Super simple and no doubt the most memorable food of my life.'—Roberta Sudbrack

LOCANDA MARGON

Recommended by
Andrea Berton

Via Margone di Ravina 15
Trento
Trentino-Alto 38123
+39 0461349401
www.locandamargon.it

Opening hours	6 days for lunch and 5 days for dinner
Reservation policy	Yes
Credit cards	Accepted
Price range	Affordable
Style	Smart casual
Cuisine	Modern Italian
Recommended for	Worth the travel

For an oenologist with a love of food, this fine-dining hilltop salotto overlooking Trento has to be a utopian prospect. Many Italian wine producers convert farmhouses into informal restaurants but the Lunelli family, owners of the Ferrari winery, has been rather more ambitious. Since Alfio Ghezzi took over the kitchen and won them a Michelin star, Locanda Margon has thronged with gastro tourists and wine lovers. Imaginative wine pairings are suggested throughout and seasonally changing menus might include ziti with razor clams or roe deer loin with coffee polenta. For a truly immersive experience fit in a cellar tour and wine tasting beforehand.

MASO CANTANGHEL

Recommended by
Zach Pollack

Via Madonnina 33
Civezzano
Trento
Trentino-Alto 38045
+39 0461858714
www.masocantanghel.eu

Opening hours	5 days for lunch and dinner
Reservation policy	Yes
Credit cards	Accepted
Price range	Affordable
Style	Smart casual
Cuisine	Trentino
Recommended for	Worth the travel

ENOTECA PINCHIORRI

Recommended by
Alfonso & Ernesto Iaccarino

Via Ghibellina, 87
Santa Croce
Florence
Tuscany 50122
+39 055242757
www.enotecapinchiorri.com

Opening hours	5 days for dinner
Reservation policy	Yes
Reservation email	ristorante@enotecapinchiorri.com
Credit cards	Accepted
Price range	Expensive
Style	Formal
Cuisine	Modern Italian
Recommended for	Worth the travel

IL PALAGIO

Recommended by
Italo Bassi

Four Seasons Hotel
Borgo Pinti 99
Florence
Tuscany 50121
+39 05526261
www.fourseasons.com/florence

Opening hours	7 days for breakfast and dinner
Reservation policy	Yes
Credit cards	Accepted
Price range	Expensive
Style	Smart casual
Cuisine	Tuscan
Recommended for	High end

OSTERIA DEL VICARIO

Recommended by
Alfred Prasad

via Rivellino 3
Certaldo
Florence
Tuscany 50052
+39 0571668228
www.osteriadelvicario.it

Opening hours	7 days for lunch and dinner
Reservation policy	Yes
Credit cards	Accepted
Price range	Expensive
Style	Smart casual
Cuisine	Tuscan
Recommended for	Wish I'd opened

'So quaint, beautiful and with fantastic valley views, it is very special.'—Alfred Prasad

This converted Tuscan monastery in the medieval town of Certaldo wins hearts with its antiquated setting and varied menu. It is widely praised for a wide choice of traditional Tuscan dishes such as crespelle fiorentine and gnocchi. That said, it's a more gourmet experience than the rustic connotations of *Osteria* and a regional cuisine might suggest. Their sommelier will match your choice of food to the perfect wine – one local to Tuscany perhaps, or from further afield in Piedmont, where Barolos abound. The former cloister's terrace and the colonnade-clad balcony offer panoramic views of the Chianti hills, making this a unique spot for special meal.

TRATTORIA CAMMILLO

Recommended by
Ollie Dabbous

Borgo San Jacopo 57r
Florence
Tuscany 50125
+39 055212427

Opening hours	5 days for lunch and dinner
Reservation policy	Yes
Credit cards	Accepted
Price range	Affordable
Style	Smart casual
Cuisine	Tuscan
Recommended for	Worth the travel

TRATTORIA FRATELLI BRIGANTI

Recommended by
Italo Bassi

Piazza Giovanbattista Giorgini, 12
Florence
Tuscany 50134
+39 055475255

Opening hours	5 days for lunch and 6 days for dinner
Reservation policy	Yes
Credit cards	Not accepted
Price range	Budget
Style	Casual
Cuisine	Italian Bistro
Recommended for	Local favourite

DA CAINO

Recommended by
Paolo Lopriore

Via della Chiesa 4
Montemerano
Manciano
Grosseto
Tuscany 58050
+39 0564602817
www.dacaino.it

Opening hours	6 days for lunch and dinner
Reservation policy	Yes
Credit cards	Accepted
Price range	Expensive
Style	Smart casual
Cuisine	Tuscan
Recommended for	Local favourite

ARNOLFO

Recommended by
Kristof Coppens

Via XX Settembre 50-52
Colle di Val d'Elsa
Siena
Tuscany 53034
+39 0577920549
www.arnolfo.com

Opening hours	5 days for lunch and dinner
Reservation policy	Yes
Credit cards	Accepted
Price range	Expensive
Style	Smart casual
Cuisine	Modern Italian
Recommended for	Worth the travel

CAFFÈ POLIZIANO

Recommended by
Nikos Pouliasis

Via Voltaia del Corso 27-29
Montepulciano
Siena
Tuscany 53045
+39 0578758615
www.caffepoliziano.it

Opening hours	7 days for breakfast, lunch and dinner
Reservation policy	Yes
Credit cards	Accepted
Price range	Budget
Style	Smart casual
Cuisine	Tuscan
Recommended for	Wish I'd opened

'It combines local gastronomy, art, culture and traditions in the most beautiful wine region, Nobile.'—Nikos Pouliasis

ENOTECA I TERZI

Recommended by
Paolo Lopriore

Via dei Termini 7
Siena
Tuscany 53100
+39 057744329
www.enotecaiterzi.it

Opening hours	6 days for lunch and dinner
Reservation policy	Yes
Credit cards	Accepted
Price range	Budget
Style	Casual
Cuisine	Bar-Bistro
Recommended for	Late night

Named for its location at the junction of three roads, Enoteca I Terzi is a Sienese wine bar with timeless appeal, which keeps its doors open until 1.00 a.m. Well-informed service and a chintz-free old town location maintain the constant sea of locals, accompanied by occasional tides of visitors. A rustic menu – think *Bistecca alla Fiorentina* (from local Chianina cattle), carpaccio and Gorgonzola, and spaghetti with clams – supports a robust Tuscan wine list of around 1,800 *vini*. These are stored in a cavernous thirteenth-century cellar beneath the high-ceilinged drinking space, where guests can order by the glass or bottle.

OSTERIA DA TROMBICCHE

Recommended by
Paolo Lopriore

Via delle Terme 66
Siena
Tuscany 53100
+39 0577288089
www.trombicche.it

Opening hours	6 days for breakfast, lunch and dinner
Reservation policy	Yes
Credit cards	Not accepted
Price range	Budget
Style	Casual
Cuisine	Tuscan
Recommended for	Bargain

OSTERIA DEL ROSSI

Recommended by
Paolo Lopriore

Via Del Rossi 79-81
Siena
Tuscany 53100
+39 0577287592

Opening hours	6 days for lunch and dinner
Reservation policy	Yes
Credit cards	Accepted
Price range	Affordable
Style	Casual
Cuisine	Tuscan
Recommended for	Regular neighbourhood

LE CALANDRE

Recommended by
Umberto Bombana

Via Liguria 1
Sarmeola di Rubano
Padua
Veneto 35030
+39 049630303
www.calandre.com

Opening hours	5 days for lunch and dinner
Reservation policy	Yes
Reservation email	info@alajmo.it
Credit cards	Accepted
Price range	Expensive
Style	Smart casual
Cuisine	Modern Italian
Recommended for	Worth the travel

Helmed by Massimiliano Alajmo, the youngest ever chef to receive three Michelin stars, Le Calandre has 'foodie pilgrimage' written all over it. Ignore the unlovely location in the Paduan suburbs and you'll find regional classics given a molecular spin, such as Veneto staple risotto with a sprinkling of powdered liquorice. For more experimental fare, there's the *In.gredienti* menu: this is also the name of the restaurant's gourmet grocery, which stocks pure essences produced in collaboration with a master perfumer. Alajmo's mother Rita taught him everything he knows: head next door to casual sibling venue Il Calandrino for her famous zuccotto.

TRATTORIA AL SASSO

Recommended by
Massimiliano Alajmo

Via Ronco 11
Castelnuovo di Teolo
Padua
Veneto 35037
+39 499925073
www.trattorialsasso.it

Opening hours	6 days for lunch and dinner
Reservation policy	Yes
Reservation email	alsasso@gmail.com
Credit cards	Accepted but not AMEX and Diners
Price range	Affordable
Style	Casual
Cuisine	Veneto
Recommended for	Regular neighbourhood

AL GATTO NERO DA RUGGERO

Recommended by
Mitchell Tonks

Via Giudecca 88
Burano
Venice
Veneto 30142
+39 041730120
www.gattonero.com

Opening hours	6 days for lunch and dinner
Reservation policy	Yes
Credit cards	Accepted
Price range	Affordable
Style	Casual
Cuisine	Venetian
Recommended for	Worth the travel

ALLE TESTIERE

Recommended by
Tom Oldroyd

Calle del Mondo Novo
Castello 5801
Venice
Veneto 30122
+39 0415227220
www.osterialletestiere.it

Opening hours	5 days for lunch and dinner
Reservation policy	Yes
Reservation email	info@osterialletestiere.it
Credit cards	Accepted
Price range	Affordable
Style	Casual
Cuisine	Venetian
Recommended for	Worth the travel

'The perfect finish to an arduous *giro di ombre*, bacaro crawl, is ending the evening with dinner here.'
—Tom Oldroyd

There are only twenty-four seats spread over nine tables at this tiny *osteria* and most of them are usually filled with Venetians. One of the notable exceptions to the generally accepted wisdom that Venice is one of the hardest places in Italy to find a decent meal, Alle Testiere, specializes in serving local seafood. Typically taxing to track down, despite its proximity to St Mark's and the Rialto, it's housed in a beautiful old bacaro, its tables covered with brown paper instead of white cloth. Despite this informality there's sophistication from the kitchen and a serious wine list that focuses on quirky local producers.

LA CANTINA

Recommended by
Tom Oldroyd

Cannaregio 3689
Campo San Felice
Venice
Veneto 30121

Opening hours	6 days from breakfast until late
Reservation policy	Yes
Credit cards	Accepted
Price range	Affordable
Style	Smart casual
Cuisine	Venetian
Recommended for	High end

CORTE SCONTA

Recommended by
Tom Oldroyd

Calle del Pestrin 3886
Venice
Veneto 30122
www.veneziaristoranti.it

Opening hours	5 days for lunch and dinner
Reservation policy	Yes
Reservation email	corte.sconta@yahoo.it
Credit cards	Accepted
Price range	Affordable
Style	Smart casual
Cuisine	Venetian
Recommended for	High end

HARRY'S BAR

Recommended by
Cristiano Rienzner,
Mitchell Tonks

San Marco 1323
Calle Vallaresso
Venice
Veneto 30124
+39 0415285777
ww.cipriani.com

Opening hours	7 days for lunch and dinner
Reservation policy	Yes
Reservation email	harrysbar@cipriani.com
Credit cards	Accepted
Price range	Expensive
Style	Smart casual
Cuisine	Bar-Bistro
Recommended for	Wish I'd opened

LA MASCARETA

Recommended by
Massimiliano Alajmo

Calle Lunga Santa Maria Formosa
Castello 5183
Venice
Veneto 30122
+39 0415230744
www.ostemaurolorenzon.it

Opening hours	6 days for dinner
Reservation policy	Yes
Credit cards	Accepted
Price range	Budget
Style	Casual
Cuisine	Italian
Recommended for	Late night

The offspring of established Venetian osteria Al
Mascaron, this intimate enoteca (wine bar) has over
time proved more popular than its forebear. Owner
Mauro Lorenzon, famously charismatic and always
wearing a bow tie, will match your choice of cicchetti
(Venetian tapas) with the perfect wine. Many rave
about the prosciutto here, not to mention the cheese-
board, crostini, traditional bean soups, cuttlefish
pasta and baccalà served in antipasti-sized portions.
Whether it's a late-night bite and ombra (literally
'shadow', a white wine to follow food) or anything
else from a hefty wine list, menu and ambience
conspire for fun well into the early hours.

PIZZERIA DU DE COPE

Recommended by
Albert Adrià

Galleria Pellicciai 10
Verona
Veneto 37121
+39 045595562
www.pizzeriadudecope.it

Opening hours	7 days for lunch and dinner
Reservation policy	Yes
Credit cards	Accepted
Price range	Affordable
Style	Casual
Cuisine	Pizza
Recommended for	Worth the travel

Just because chef Giancarlo Perbellini holds two
Michelin stars (for his eponymous restaurant in Isola
Rizza) doesn't mean that pizza is beneath him. At his
busy, rather groovily tiled, Pizzeria Du De Cope
(established 2004) in central Verona, he happily
eschews cheffy 'twists' in favour of good, honest
artisan produce that genuinely has a place on a
wood-fired sourdough base. Campanian buffalo
mozzarella and Cantabrian anchovies grace the
Romana, one of just fifteen pizzas available. Italian
craft beer is the accompaniment of choice. Perbellini
hails from a family of pastry-makers so stick around
for dessert and a cream-filled millefoglie pastry.

IL RIDOTTO

Recommended by
Armand Arnal

Castello 4509
Campo S.S. Filippo e Giacomo
Venice
Veneto 30122
+39 0415208280
www.ilridotto.com

Opening hours	5 days for lunch and dinner
Reservation policy	Yes
Reservation email	info@ilridotto.com
Credit cards	Accepted
Price range	Affordable
Style	Smart casual
Cuisine	Modern Italian
Recommended for	Worth the travel

RISTORANTE OSTELLO

Recommended by
Bradley Turley

Venissa Hotel
Fondamenta Santa Caterina 3
Isola di Mazzorbo
Venice
Veneto 30170
+39 0415272281
www.venissa.it

Opening hours	6 days for lunch and dinner
Reservation policy	Yes
Credit cards	Accepted
Price range	Expensive
Style	Smart casual
Cuisine	Modern Italian
Recommended for	Worth the travel

TRATTORIA DA ROMANO

Recommended by
Marc Fosh

Via San Martino 221
Burano
Venice
Veneto 30012
+39 041730030
www.daromano.it

Opening hours	7 days for lunch and 6 days for dinner
Reservation policy	Yes
Credit cards	Accepted
Price range	Affordable
Style	Casual
Cuisine	Venetian
Recommended for	Worth the travel

'Their risotto "Go" is the best risotto ever – by far!'
—Marc Fosh

LOCANDA 4 CUOCHI

Recommended by
Italo Bassi

Via Alberto Mario 12
Verona
Veneto 37121
+39 0458030311
www.locanda4cuochi.it

Opening hours	6 days for lunch and dinner
Reservation policy	Yes
Credit cards	Accepted
Price range	Affordable
Style	Smart casual
Cuisine	Modern Italian
Recommended for	Local favourite

TRATTORIA IL POMPIERE

Recommended by
Tim Siadatan

Vicolo Regina d'Ungheria 5
Verona
Veneto 37121
+39 0458030537
www.alpompiere.tv

Opening hours	6 days for lunch and dinner
Reservation policy	Yes
Credit cards	Accepted
Price range	Affordable
Style	Casual
Cuisine	Veronese
Recommended for	Worth the travel

AUSTRIA, CZECH REPUBLIC, HUNGARY & SLOVENIA

AUSTRIA, CZECH REPUBLIC, HUNGARY & SLOVENIA

‹Ⓝ› SCALE

0   60   120
mi.

HUNGARY

♦Budapest p.420

Vienna pp.418-419♥
Lower Austria p.418♥

Prekmurje p.420♥

CZECH REPUBLIC

Prague pp.419-420♥

AUSTRIA

SLOVENIA

Primorska p.421♥

WEINBAU ÖSTERREICHER

Recommended by
Raphael Dworak

Bahngasse 19
Pfaffstätten
Lower Austria 2511
Austria
www.heuriger-oesterreicher.at

Opening hours...................................7 days for lunch and dinner
Reservation policy..Yes
Credit cards..Accepted
Price range...Affordable
Style...Casual
Cuisine...Austrian
Recommended for.................................Local favourite

'A nice, comfortable and cosy *Heurige* (wine bar) that serves good, traditional Austrian food, accompanied by a wide choice of regional wine.'—Raphael Dworak

MRAZ & SOHN

Recommended by
Christian Domschitz

Wallensteinstrasse 59
Brigittenau
Vienna 1200
Austria
www.mrazundsohn.at

Opening hours...................................5 days for lunch and dinner
Reservation policy..Yes
Credit cards..Accepted
Price range...Affordable
Style...Smart casual
Cuisine...Austrian
Recommended for.................................Worth the travel

MEIXNER

Recommended by
Christian Domschitz

Buchengasse 64
Favoriten
Vienna 1100
Austria
+43 16042710
www.meixners-gastwirtschaft.at

Opening hours...................................7 days for lunch and dinner
Reservation policy..Yes
Credit cards..Accepted
Price range...Affordable
Style...Casual
Cuisine...Austrian
Recommended for.................................Regular neighbourhood

AMARANTIS

Recommended by
Christian Domschitz

Babenbergerstrasse 5
Innere Stadt
Vienna 1010
Austria
+43 15852439
www.amarantis.at

Opening hours...................................6 days for lunch and dinner
Reservation policy..Yes
Credit cards..Accepted
Price range...Affordable
Style...Casual
Cuisine...Mediterranean
Recommended for...Late night

HOLY MOLY

Recommended by
Christian Domschitz

Donaukanallände
Schwedenplatz and Urania
Innere Stadt
Vienna 1010
Austria
www.badeschiff.at

Opening hours..6 days for dinner
Reservation policy..Yes
Reservation email........................reservierung@badeschiff.at
Credit cards..Accepted
Price range...Affordable
Style...Casual
Cuisine...Austrian
Recommended for.................................Local favourite

SILVIO NICKOL

Recommended by
Raphael Dworak, Harald
Wohlfahrt, Michael Wolf

Palais Coburg Residenz
Coburgbastei 4
Innere Stadt
Vienna 1010
Austria
+43 51818800
www.coburg.at

Opening hours..5 days for dinner
Reservation policy..Yes
Credit cards..Accepted
Price range...Expensive
Style...Formal
Cuisine...Modern European
Recommended for.................................Worth the travel

'It's in the Coburg Palace and looks amazing. It's really special that there's a restaurant there.'—Michael Wolf

STEIRERECK

Recommended by
Christian Domschitz, Michael
Tusk, Heinz Winkler

Am Heumarkt 2a
Stadtpark
Landstraße
Vienna 1030
Austria
www.steirereck.at

Opening hours	5 days for lunch and dinner
Reservation policy	Yes
Credit cards	Accepted
Price range	Expensive
Style	Smart casual
Cuisine	Modern Austrian
Recommended for	Worth the travel

DÉCOR

Recommended by
Raphael Dworak

Obere Augartenstraße 1
Leopoldstadt
Vienna 1020
Austria
+43 12123888
www.decor-augarten.at

Opening hours	7 days for brunch and 6 days for dinner
Reservation policy	Yes
Credit cards	Accepted
Price range	Affordable
Style	Smart casual
Cuisine	Modern European
Recommended for	Breakfast

'Situated at the Augarten, a nice park. Ideal for sunny weather.' Raphael Dworak

SCHNITZELWIRT

Recommended by
Raphael Dworak

Neubaugasse 52
Neubau
Vienna 1070
Austria
+43 15233771
www.schnitzelwirt.co.at

Opening hours	6 days for lunch and dinner
Reservation policy	Yes
Credit cards	Not accepted
Price range	Budget
Style	Casual
Cuisine	Austrian
Recommended for	Bargain

'A very good place to go if you are very hungry as they serve big portions.'—Raphael Dworak

CAFÉ DE PARIS

Recommended by
Gwendal Le Ruyet

Maltézské Náměstí 4
Malá Strana
Prague 118 00
Czech Republic
+420 603160718
www.cafedeparis.cz

Opening hours	7 days for lunch and dinner
Reservation policy	Yes
Credit cards	Accepted
Price range	Budget
Style	Casual
Cuisine	French
Recommended for	Late night

CUKR KÁVA LIMONÁDA

Recommended by
Gwendal Le Ruyet

Lázeňská 7
Malá Strana
Prague 118 00
Czech Republic
+420 257225396
www.cukrkavalimonada.com

Opening hours	7 days for breakfast and lunch
Reservation policy	Yes
Reservation email	info@cukrkavalimonada.com
Credit cards	Accepted
Price range	Budget
Style	Casual
Cuisine	Café
Recommended for	Breakfast

In the heart of the beautifully baroque Lesser Quarter, not far from the tourist traps around Maltese Square, sits this refreshing café in a quiet courtyard. Reasonably priced for the area, it's a cosy contemporary space in a sensitively refurbished old building, all clean lines, pretty painted floral ceiling and simple modern furniture. Named after the nursery rhyme (sugar, coffee, lemonade) used in the Czech version of the playground game of statues, the service is warm and friendly, and the breakfast, from quality patisserie via savoury pancakes to eggs and ham, a cut above the average Prague café experience.

ICHNUSA BOTEGA & BISTRO

Recommended by
Gwendal Le Ruyet

Plaska 5
Malá Strana
Prague 150 00
Czech Republic
+420 605525748

Opening hours	7 days for dinner
Reservation policy	Yes
Credit cards	Accepted
Price range	Budget
Style	Casual
Cuisine	Sardinian
Recommended for	Regular neighbourhood

This bijou backstreet Italian is christened after the hoppy Sardinian lager of the same name. There's no menu and the service is charmingly hands-on with the Czech chef-proprietor Ivo Koudelka, who trained in Sardinia, making his way to your table to discuss your likes and dislikes, and telling you what he has to offer that day before you then negotiate exactly what it is you're going to eat. Your meal invariably starts with a plate of ham and cheese served with *pane carasau* (crispy Sardinian bread) and ends with either a glass of Limoncello or of Mirto, the distinctive Sardinian myrtle liqueur.

PAUL

Recommended by
Gwendal Le Ruyet

Jugoslávská 6
Vinohrady
Prague 120 00
Czech Republic
www.paul-international.com

Opening hours	7 days from breakfast until late
Reservation policy	No
Credit cards	Accepted
Price range	Budget
Style	Casual
Cuisine	Café
Recommended for	Bargain

'For their ham and cheese sandwich'
—Gwendal Le Ruyet

ONYX RESTAURANT

Recommended by
Brett Barnes

Vörösmarty tér 7-8
Budapest 1051
Hungary
+36 305080622
www.onyxrestaurant.hu

Opening hours	4 days for lunch and 5 days for dinner
Reservation policy	Yes
Credit cards	Accepted
Price range	Affordable
Style	Formal
Cuisine	Modern European
Recommended for	Worth the travel

GOSTILNA RAJH

Recommended by
Tomaž Kavčič

Bakovci
Soboška Ulica 32
Murska Sobota 9000
Prekmurje
Slovenia
+386 25439098
www.rajh.si

Opening hours	6 days for lunch and 5 days for dinner
Reservation policy	Yes
Reservation email	info@rajh.si
Credit cards	Accepted
Price range	Affordable
Style	Smart casual
Cuisine	Slovenian
Recommended for	Worth the travel

In the eastern-most corner of Slovenia, lies Prekmurje, a culturally defined region of the country with its own culinary traditions. Gostilna Rajh is a Prekmurje countryside inn, in the village of Bakovci near the city of Murska Sobota. Run by the Rajh family since 1886, great-grandmother Marija Rajh still keeps an eye on what comes out of the kitchen. The menu changes with the seasons but a five-strong selection of soups, dandelion salad, Bograč goulash made with pork, beef, venison and cured bacon, and the distinctive layered cake that is Prekmurska *gi-banica*, are some of the traditional specialities offered.

GOSTILNA ŽEJA

Ozeljan 321
Šempas
Nova Gorica 5261
Primorska
Slovenia
+386 53088459

Opening hours............6 days for lunch and 5 days for dinner
Reservation policy..Yes
Credit cards..Accepted
Price range..Affordable
Style..Smart casual
Cuisine..Slovenian
Recommended for..Worth the travel

VIPAVSKI HRAM

Vinarska Cesta 5
Vipava 5271
Primorska
Slovenia
+386 53671245
www.vipavskihram.si

Opening hours................................5 days for lunch and dinner
Reservation policy..Yes
Credit cards..Accepted
Price range..Budget
Style..Casual
Cuisine..Slovenian
Recommended for..Bargain

'Has a really cool scene and some amazing Asian flavours.'

BEN POLLINGER P426

'A MEDIEVAL RESTAURANT IN THE OLD CITY.'

MARTINS RITINS P425

ESTONIA, LATVIA & RUSSIA

'THIS CLASSIC CAFÉ IN THE MIDDLE OF HISTORIC MOSCOW CAPTURES THE FEELING OF PRE-COMMUNIST RUSSIA, LIKE IN THE TIME OF THE TSARS. IT OFFERS TRUE ELEGANT RUSSIAN CUISINE AND ATTITUDE.'

JARROD VERBIAK P426

'Filled with authentic antiques and has its own kitchen garden.'

MARTINS RITINS P425

'Not only is the cooking marvellous, but this restaurant also has the total package, with luxury hotel, spa and its own organic garden.'

FILIP LANGHOFF P424

ESTONIA,
LATVIA &
RUSSIA

SCALE

0   140   280
                  mi.

Harjumaa p.424
Saaremaa p.424
ESTONIA
Kurzeme p.425
Riga p.425
LATVIA

RUSSIA

Moscow p.426

ALEXANDER

Recommended by
Filip Langhoff

Padaste Manor
Muhu Island
Saaremaa 94716
Estonia
+372 4548800
www.padaste.ee

Opening hours.................................7 days for lunch and dinner
Reservation policy..Yes
Reservation email..................................info@padaste.ee
Credit cards..Accepted
Price range...Expensive
Style..Smart casual
Cuisine..Modern Nordic
Recommended for.................................Worth the travel

'Not only is Peeter Pihel's cooking marvellous, but this restaurant also has the total package, with luxury hotel, spa and it's own organic garden.'—Filip Langhoff

LA BOTTEGA

Recommended by
Vladislav Djatsuk

Vene 4
Tallinn
Harjumaa 10123
Estonia
+372 6277733
www.labottega.ee

Opening hours.................................7 days for lunch and dinner
Reservation policy..Yes
Credit cards..Accepted
Price range...Affordable
Style..Smart casual
Cuisine..Italian
Recommended for.................................Late night

CHEDI

Recommended by
Vladislav Djatsuk

Sulevimägi 1
Tallinn
Harjumaa 10123
Estonia
+372 6461676
www.chedi.ee

Opening hours.................................7 days for lunch and dinner
Reservation policy..Yes
Reservation email..................................info@chedi.ee
Credit cards..Accepted
Price range...Expensive
Style..Smart casual
Cuisine..Modern Asian
Recommended for.................................Regular neighbourhood

KOHVIK MOON

Recommended by
Vladislav Djatsuk

Võrgu 3
Tallinn
Harjumaa 10415
Estonia
+372 6314575
www.kohvikmoon.ee

Opening hours.................................6 days for lunch and dinner
Reservation policy..Yes
Reservation email..................................kohvik@kohvikmoon.ee
Credit cards..Accepted
Price range...Budget
Style..Casual
Cuisine..Russian
Recommended for.................................Bargain

LEIB RESTO JA AED

Recommended by
Vladislav Djatsuk

Uus tn 31
Tallinn
Harjumaa 10111
Estonia
+372 6119026
www.leibresto.ee

Opening hours.................................7 days for lunch and dinner
Reservation policy..Yes
Credit cards..Accepted
Price range...Budget
Style..Casual
Cuisine..European
Recommended for.................................Worth the travel

NOP

Recommended by
Peeter Pihel

Köleri 1
Tallinn
Harjumaa 10150
Estonia
+372 6032270
www.nop.ee

Opening hours.................................7 days for breakfast and lunch
Reservation policy..Yes
Credit cards..Accepted
Price range...Budget
Style..Casual
Cuisine..Deli
Recommended for.................................Breakfast

KUKŠI MANOR HOUSE
Kuksas
Jaunsatu, Tukuma
Kurzeme 3128
Latvia
+371 63181545
www.kuksumuiza.lv

Opening hours.............7 days for breakfast, lunch and dinner
Reservation policy..No
Credit cards..Accepted
Price range..Expensive
Style...Casual
Cuisine...Latvian
Recommended for...Wish I'd opened

'Filled with authentic antiques and has it's own kitchen garden.'—Martins Ritins

RESTAURANT EIROPA
Eiropa Guest House
Baltezers, Adaži
Riga 2164
Latvia
+371 26135917
www.vneiropa.lv

Opening hours...............................7 days for lunch and dinner
Reservation policy..Yes
Credit cards..Accepted
Price range..Affordable
Style...Casual
Cuisine...Latvian
Recommended for..................................Regular neighbourhood

'The chef cooks fish to perfection.'—Martins Ritins

FOODBOX
Antonijas ielā 6a-20
Krišjāña Barona ielā 31
Riga 1010
Latvia
+371 28205998

Opening hours................................6 days for lunch and dinner
Reservation policy..Yes
Credit cards..Not accepted
Price range..Budget
Style...Casual
Cuisine...Turkish
Recommended for...Bargain

'The owner bakes his own pittas and makes his own giros.'—Martins Ritins

ROSENGRALS
Rozena 1
Riga 1050
Latvia
+371 67224748
www.rozengrals.lv

Opening hours................................7 days for lunch and dinner
Reservation policy..Yes
Reservation email..................................info@rozengrals.lv
Credit cards..Accepted
Price range..Affordable
Style...Casual
Cuisine...Historic
Recommended for.....................................Local favourite

'A medieval restaurant in the old city.'—Martins Ritins

RUMENE MANOR HOUSE
Kandava
Rumene
Riga 3120
Latvia
+371 67770900
www.rumene.lv

Opening hours.............7 days for breakfast, lunch and dinner
Reservation policy..Yes
Reservation email..................................rumene@hotelbergs.lv
Credit cards..Accepted
Price range..Expensive
Style..Smart casual
Cuisine...Latvian
Recommended for.....................................Worth the travel

VINA STUDIJA
Elizabetes iela 10
Riga 1010
Latvia
+371 67283205
www.vinastudija.lv

Opening hours................................7 days for lunch and dinner
Reservation policy..Yes
Credit cards..Accepted
Price range..Affordable
Style...Casual
Cuisine..Bar-Small plates
Recommended for...Late night

CAFE PUSHKIN

Recommended by
Jarrod Verbiak

Tverskoi Bulvar 26a
Tverskaya
Moscow 125009
Russia
+7 4957390033
www.cafe-pushkin.ru

Opening hours..............7 days for breakfast, lunch and dinner
Reservation policy...Yes
Credit cards..Accepted
Price range...Expensive
Style...Formal
Cuisine...Russian
Recommended for..Worth the travel

'This classic café in the middle of historic Moscow captures the feeling of pre-Communist Russia, like in the time of the Tsars, and it offers true elegant Russian cuisine and attitude.'—Jarrod Verbiak

KHACHAPURI

Recommended by
Petter Nilsson

Bolshoi Gnezdnikovsky Pereulok 10
Tverskaya
Moscow 125009
Russia
+7 9857643118
www.hacha.ru

Opening hours...........................7 days for breakfast until late
Reservation policy...Yes
Credit cards..Accepted
Price range..Budget
Style..Casual
Cuisine...Georgian
Recommended for..Worth the travel

NEDALNY VOSTOK

Recommended by
Ben Pollinger

Tverskoy Bulvar 15
Building 2
Tverskaya
Moscow 103009
Russia
+7 4956940641
www.novikovgroup.ru

Opening hours.................................7 days for lunch and dinner
Reservation policy..No
Credit cards..Accepted
Price range..Affordable
Style...Smart casual
Cuisine...Asian
Recommended for..Worth the travel

'Has a really cool scene and some amazing Asian flavours. '—Ben Pollinger

'Real Greek food, in an amazing location looking over the Aegean Sea.'

DOMINIC CHAPMAN P430

'A NICE FISH TAVERN AT PERIVOLOS BEACH WHERE THEY SERVE FRESH LOCAL FISH AND SEAFOOD ALL YEAR AROUND. THEY ALSO HAVE LOCAL SANTORINIAN SPECIALITIES.'

NIKOS POULIASIS P430

GREECE TURKEY & CYPRUS

'FOR THE MOST WONDERFUL SEAFOOD MEZES AND FORAGED GREENS.'

ŞEMSA DENIZSEL P432

'THE BEST PLACE TO DRINK OUZO AND FEEL YOU ARE IN GREECE.'

NIKOS POULIASIS P430

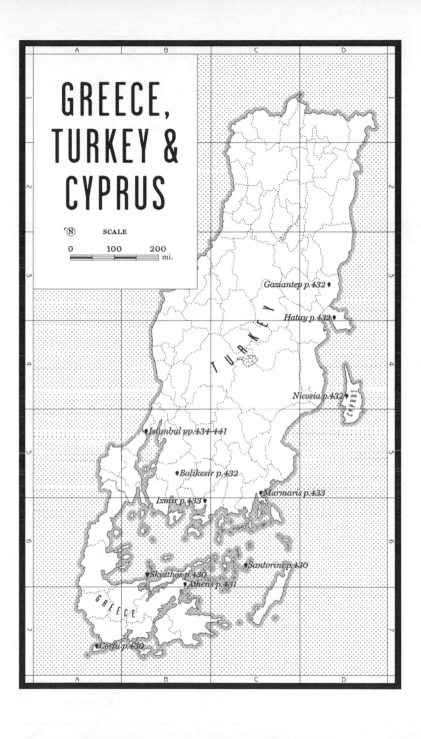

GREECE, TURKEY & CYPRUS

 SCALE

0   100   200 mi.

Gaziantep p.432 ♥

Hatay p.432 ♥

TURKEY

Nicosia p.432 ♥   CYPRUS

Istanbul pp.434–441 ♥

Balıkesir p.432 ♥

Marmaris p.433 ♥

Izmir p.433 ♥

Santorini p.430 ♥

Skiathos p.430 ♥
Athens p.431 ♥

GREECE

Corfu p.430 ♥

KLIMATARIA

Recommended by
Ettore Botrini

Benitses
Achilleio
Corfu 49084
Greece
+30 2661071201
www.klimataria-restaurant.gr

Opening hours	7 days for lunch and dinner
Reservation policy	Yes
Credit cards	Accepted
Price range	Affordable
Style	Casual
Cuisine	Corfiot
Recommended for	Local favourite

SUNSET

Recommended by
Nikos Pouliasis

Ammoudi
Oia
Santorini 84702
Greece
+30 2286071614
www.sunset-ammoudi.gr

Opening hours	7 days for lunch and dinner
Reservation policy	Yes
Reservation email	info@sunset-ammoudi.gr
Credit cards	Accepted
Price range	Affordable
Style	Casual
Cuisine	Santorinian
Recommended for	Local favourite

'A unique location under the cliff, where they serve fish and seafood right by the water. The best place to drink ouzo and feel you are in Greece.'—Nikos Pouliasis

TA DICHTIA

Recommended by
Nikos Pouliasis

Agios Georgios
Perivolos
Santorini 84703
Greece
+30 2286082818
www.tadichtia.com

Opening hours	7 days for lunch and dinner
Reservation policy	Yes
Reservation email	info@tadichtia.com
Credit cards	Accepted
Price range	Affordable
Style	Casual
Cuisine	Santorinian Seafood
Recommended for	Regular neighbourhood

'Here they serve fresh local fish and seafood all year round. They also have local specialities such as baked and smoked Santorinian white aubergine (eggplant) salad, broad (fava) beans, squid with bulgur cooked in its ink.'—Nikos Pouliasis

AGNADIO

Recommended by
Dominic Chapman

By the Monastery of Evangelistria
Skiathos 37002
Greece
+30 2427022016

Opening hours	7 days for dinner
Reservation policy	Yes
Credit cards	Accepted
Price range	Affordable
Style	Casual
Cuisine	Greek
Recommended for	Worth the travel

'Real Greek food, in an amazing location overlooking the Aegean Sea. Excellent service and a good wine list.'—Dominic Chapman

BOTRINI'S

Recommended by
Nikos Pouliasis

Vasileos Georgiou 24
Halandri
Athens 15233
Greece
+30 2106857323
www.botrinis.com

Opening hours	1 day for lunch and 5 days for dinner
Reservation policy	Yes
Reservation email	reservations@botrinis.com
Credit cards	Accepted
Price range	Affordable
Style	Casual
Cuisine	Modern Greek
Recommended for	Worth the travel

'Hector Botrini's creativity is really impressive.'
—Nikos Pouliasis

KRITIKOS

Recommended by
Nikos Pouliasis

Aiolou 49
Kantza
Athens 15351
Greece
+30 2106659061

Opening hours	7 days for lunch and dinner
Reservation policy	Yes
Credit cards	Accepted
Price range	Budget
Style	Casual
Cuisine	Greek
Recommended for	Bargain

'Go and enjoy Greek meat together with excellent
house red wine.'—Nikos Pouliasis

SPONDI RESTAURANT

Recommended by
Nikos Pouliasis

Pyrronos 5
Pangrati
Athens 11636
Greece
+30 2107564021
www.spondi.gr

Opening hours	7 days for dinner
Reservation policy	Yes
Reservation email	info@spondi.gr
Credit cards	Accepted
Price range	Expensive
Style	Smart casual
Cuisine	Mediterranean
Recommended for	High end

NEW TASTE

Recommended by
Jerome Lorvellec

New Hotel
Filellinon 16
Syntagma Square
Athens 10557
Greece
+30 2103273000
www.yeshotels.gr

Opening hours	7 days for breakfast, lunch and dinner
Reservation policy	Yes
Credit cards	Accepted
Price range	Affordable
Style	Casual
Cuisine	Mediterranean
Recommended for	Breakfast

ZANETTOS

Recommended by
Ettore Botrini

Trikoupi 65
Nicosia 1015
Cyprus
+357 22765501
www.zanettos.com

Opening hours	6 days for dinner
Reservation policy	Yes
Credit cards	Accepted
Price range	Budget
Style	Casual
Cuisine	Cypriot
Recommended for	Worth the travel

BAY NIHAT - LALE

Recommended by
Şemsa Denizsel

Sahil Yolu 21
Ayvalik
Balikesir 10405
Turkey
+90 2663271063
www.baynihat.com.tr

Opening hours	7 days for lunch and dinner
Reservation policy	Yes
Reservation email	restoran@baynihat.com.tr
Credit cards	Accepted
Price range	Affordable
Style	Smart casual
Cuisine	Meze
Recommended for	Worth the travel

'For the most wonderful seafood mezes
and foraged greens.'—Şemsa Denizsel

METANET LOKANTASI

Recommended by
Şemsa Denizsel

Kozluca Caddessi 11
Sahinbey
Gaziantep
Turkey

Opening hours	7 days for lunch
Reservation policy	No
Credit cards	Not accepted
Price range	Budget
Style	Casual
Cuisine	Turkish
Recommended for	Worth the travel

'They make the most wonderful *beyran*, a local
breakfast staple, which is actually a spicy rice and lamb
soup with tons of garlic.'—Şemsa Denizsel

KARDEŞLER ET LOKANTASI

Recommended by
Mehmet Gürs

Asi Caddessi 29
Güzelburç
Antakya
Hatay
Turkey

Opening hours	6 days for lunch and dinner
Reservation policy	No
Credit cards	Not accepted
Price range	Budget
Style	Casual
Cuisine	Turkish
Recommended for	Worth the travel

'A very simple place but the flavours are
still with me.'—Mehmet Gürs

SELÇUK KÖFTECISI

Recommended by
Gençay Üçok

Şahabettin Dede Caddesi
Selçuk
Izmir 35920
Turkey
+90 2328926696

Opening hours.................................7 days for lunch and dinner
Reservation policy...No
Credit cards......................Accepted but not AMEX and Diners
Price range...Budget
Style..Casual
Cuisine...Turkish
Recommended for................................Worth the travel

'Honest family food, smiling faces everywhere. Very
fresh high quality produce. Simple but awesome dishes
like chilli meatballs and wild greens sauteed with olive
oil and garlic.'—Gençay Üçok

KAPLAN DAG

Recommended by
Didem Şenol

Kaplan Dağ
Tire
Izmir 35900
Turkey
+90 2325126652
www.kaplandag.com

Opening hours.................................6 days for lunch and dinner
Reservation policy...Yes
Credit cards...Not accepted
Price range...Budget
Style..Casual
Cuisine...Turkish
Recommended for................................Worth the travel

ÇINAR

Recommended by
Mustafa Cihan Kipçak

Çinar Hotel
Camli Köyü
Marmaris 48700
Turkey
+90 2524958080
www.cinarmuglaevleri.com

Opening hours.............7 days for breakfast, lunch and dinner
Reservation policy...Yes
Credit cards...Not accepted
Price range...Budget
Style..Casual
Cuisine...Turkish
Recommended for..Breakfast

ORFOZ

Recommended by
Didem Şenol

Adatepe
Bozburun
Marmaris 48700
Turkey
+90 2524562209
www.orfoz.com

Opening hours...7 days for dinner
Reservation policy...Yes
Credit cards...Not accepted
Price range...Affordable
Style..Casual
Cuisine...Seafood
Recommended for................................Worth the travel

'Especially good on a sunny weekend morning for a long lazy, ceremonial Turkish breakfast while enjoying the views of the Bosphorus.'
GENÇAY ÜÇOK P441

'THIS PLACE IS A FOOD PALACE. MAGNIFICENT KEBABS. ONE OF THE CULT RESTAURANTS OF ISTANBUL WHICH HAS BEEN OPERATING SINCE THE 1940S.'
GENÇAY ÜÇOK P436

ISTANBUL

'Try any of the great meatball trucks scattered around Istanbul.'
MEHMET GÜRS P440

'THE FOOD IS IMPRESSIVE, THE SERVICE FLAWLESS, THE VIEW STUNNING. I THINK IT IS THE ONLY WORLD-CLASS FINE-DINING RESTAURANT IN ISTANBUL.'
ŞEMSA DENIZSEL P438

'IT LOOKS VERY ANTIPODEAN IN DESIGN BUT IT'S DEFINITELY TURKISH IN MENU INFLUENCE. TRY THE SCRAMBLED EGGS ON TOAST WITH PRESERVED QUINCE, OR A SLICE OF BROWNIE WITH TURKISH COFFEE.'
PETER GORDON P440

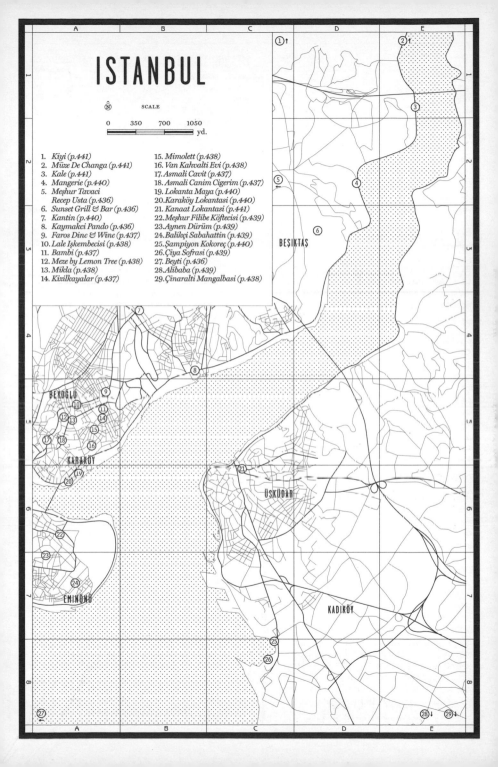

ISTANBUL

N̂   SCALE

0   350   700   1050
yd.

1. *Kiyi (p.441)*
2. *Müze De Changa (p.441)*
3. *Kale (p.441)*
4. *Mangerie (p.440)*
5. *Meşhur Tavaci Recep Usta (p.436)*
6. *Sunset Grill & Bar (p.436)*
7. *Kantin (p.440)*
8. *Kaymakci Pando (p.436)*
9. *Faros Dine & Wine (p.437)*
10. *Lale Işkembecisi (p.438)*
11. *Bambi (p.437)*
12. *Meze by Lemon Tree (p.438)*
13. *Mikla (p.438)*
14. *Kizilkayalar (p.437)*
15. *Mimolett (p.438)*
16. *Van Kahvalti Evi (p.438)*
17. *Asmali Cavit (p.437)*
18. *Asmali Canim Cigerim (p.437)*
19. *Lokanta Maya (p.440)*
20. *Karaköy Lokantasi (p.440)*
21. *Kanaat Lokantasi (p.441)*
22. *Meşhur Filibe Köftecisi (p.439)*
23. *Aynen Dürüm (p.439)*
24. *Balileçi Sabahattin (p.439)*
25. *Sampiyon Kokoreç (p.440)*
26. *Çiya Sofrasi (p.439)*
27. *Beyti (p.436)*
28. *Alibaba (p.439)*
29. *Çinaralti Mangalbasi (p.438)*

BEŞIKTAŞ

BEYOĞLU

KARAKÖY

ÜSKÜDAR

EMINÖNÜ

KADIKÖY

BEYTI

Recommended by
Mustafa Cihan Kipçak,
Didem Şenol, Gençay Üçok

Orman Sokak 8
Florya
Bakirkoy
Istanbul 34153
+90 2126632990
www.beyti.com

Opening hours	6 days for lunch and dinner
Reservation policy	Yes
Reservation email	rezervasyon@beyti.com
Credit cards	Accepted
Price range	Affordable
Style	Smart casual
Cuisine	Turkish
Recommended for	Wish I'd opened

'This place is a food palace. Magnificent kebabs. These people really know how to work with meat. Sort of VIP fine dining feel. One of the cult restaurants of Istanbul which has been operating since 1940s.'—Gençay Üçok

KAYMAKCI PANDO

Recommended by
Şemsa Denizsel

Beşiktaş Carsisi
Beşiktaş
Istanbul 34357

Opening hours	7 days for breakfast
Reservation policy	No
Credit cards	Not accepted
Price range	Budget
Style	Casual
Cuisine	Café
Recommended for	Breakfast

'The owner Pando is probably 100 years old and still there. It's the tiniest eatery with only buffalo-milk *kaymak*, eggs, fresh bread and milk. Even the tea comes from outside. It's a very basic place but so good you barely notice the grime.'—Şemsa Denizsel

How much this *kaymak* specialist in Beşiktaş market has changed since it opened back in 1895, it's hard to say. A thick clotted cream made from skimming simmered buffalo milk, *kaymak* is a Turkish breakfast delight, and Kaymakci Pando does the very best in Istanbul. Run by eighty-seven-year-old Pando, it's an unapologetically scruffy place but its four inside tables and – assuming it's not raining – those on the pavement (sidewalk) outside, are never empty. Freshly baked white bread, dipped in *kaymak* with honey, and a side of fried eggs drowning in butter, with hot milk or a cup of black tea – way to go.

MEŞHUR TAVACI RECEP USTA

Recommended by
Gençay Üçok

Lavinya Sokak 2
Levent
Beşiktaş
Istanbul 34340
+90 2122800425
www.tavacirecepusta.com

Opening hours	4 days for lunch and 7 days for dinner
Reservation policy	Yes
Reservation email	bilgi@tavacirecepusta.com
Credit cards	Not accepted
Price range	Budget
Style	Casual
Cuisine	Turkish
Recommended for	Regular neighbourhood

'Beautiful garden and superb service. You can often come across many Turkish celebrities here but among tourists it is not known at all. They do only lamb dishes. *Sac tava*, *kuzu dolma* and dried aubergines (eggplants) stuffed with seasonal pilaf and minced (ground) lamb are true wonders.'—Gençay Üçok

SUNSET GRILL & BAR

Recommended by
Gençay Üçok

Adnan Saygun Caddesi
Yol Sokak 2 Ulus Parki
Beşiktaş
Istanbul 34340
+90 2122870358
www.sunsetgrillbar.com

Opening hours	6 days for lunch and 7 days for dinner
Reservation policy	Yes
Credit cards	Accepted
Price range	Expensive
Style	Smart casual
Cuisine	International
Recommended for	High end

'A rich wine cellar, good food, great for occasions and celebrations.'—Gençay Üçok

ASMALI CANIM CIGERIM

Istiklal Caddessi 162
Beyoğlu
Istanbul 34420
www.asmalicanimcigerim.com

Opening hours	7 days for lunch and dinner
Reservation policy	No
Credit cards	Accepted
Price range	Budget
Style	Casual
Cuisine	Turkish
Recommended for	Bargain

'Grilled skewered liver to perfection.'—Mehmet Gürs

ASMALI CAVIT

Asmalımescit Sokak 16d
Beyoğlu
Istanbul 34830
+90 2122924950

Opening hours	6 days for dinner
Reservation policy	Yes
Credit cards	Accepted
Price range	Budget
Style	Casual
Cuisine	Meze
Recommended for	Regular neighbourhood

BAMBI

Siraselviler Caddesi 9
Beyoğlu
Istanbul 34437
+90 2122932121
www.bambicafe.com.tr

Opening hours	7 days from breakfast until late
Reservation policy	No
Credit cards	Not accepted
Price range	Budget
Style	Casual
Cuisine	Fast food
Recommended for	Late night

'Order the grilled tongue and cheese sandwiches with *ayran* (sour salted yogurt or buttermilk) or *şalgam suyu* (pickled turnip and beetroot [beet] juice) to wash it down.'—Peter Gordon

FAROS DINE & WINE

Cumhuriyet Caddesi 31a
Elmadag
Taksim
Beyoğlu
Istanbul 34373
+90 2122976077
www.farosrestaurants.com

Opening hours	7 days for lunch and dinner
Reservation policy	Yes
Reservation email	info@farostaksim.com
Credit cards	Accepted
Price range	Affordable
Style	Smart casual
Cuisine	Italian
Recommended for	Regular neighbourhood

KIZILKAYALAR

Siraselviler Caddessi 6
Taksim
Beyoğlu
Istanbul 34373
www.kizilkayalar.com.tr

Opening hours	7 days for 24 hours
Reservation policy	No
Credit cards	Not accepted
Price range	Budget
Style	Casual
Cuisine	Fast food
Recommended for	Late night

'Wet burgers that are very garlicky.'—Şemsa Denizsel

Kizilkayalar first managed to distinguish itself from Istanbul's vast sea of fast-food stands in the late 1970s, when some bright spark, noting that the doner market was somewhat flooded, came up with the concept of the Islak Burger (wet burger). Their sweetly pungent smell first hits you as you wait outside. The burgers are doused in an oily, tomato sauce, containing relationship-ending quantities of garlic, then steamed for several hours inside their sticky bun to produce the world's slipperiest slider. Order two right from the start, as putting your hand back into your pocket after your first is a very messy business.

LALE IŞKEMBECISI

Tarlabaşı Bulvarı 13
Taksim
Beyoğlu
Istanbul 34437
www.laleiskembecisi.com.tr/ana_sayfa.html

Opening hours	7 days for 24 hours
Reservation policy	No
Credit cards	Accepted but not AMEX and Diners
Price range	Budget
Style	Casual
Cuisine	Tripe
Recommended for	Late night

'Serves very garlicky tripe soup.'—Şemsa Denizsel

MEZE BY LEMON TREE

Meşrutiyet Caddesi 83b
Asmalımescit
Beyoğlu
Istanbul
+90 2122528302
www.mezze.com.tr

Opening hours	7 days for dinner
Reservation policy	Yes
Credit cards	Accepted
Price range	Affordable
Style	Smart casual
Cuisine	Meze
Recommended for	Worth the travel

'Small, tasty plates. Based on mezze obviously but with a nod towards modernity. A small place, very laid back.'—Peter Gordon

MIKLA

Marmara Pera Hotel
Meşrutiyet Caddesi 15
Beyoğlu
Istanbul 34430
+90 2122935656
www.miklarestaurant.com

Opening hours	6 days for dinner
Reservation policy	Yes
Reservation email	reservations@miklarestaurant.com
Credit cards	Accepted
Price range	Expensive
Style	Smart casual
Cuisine	Modern Turkish
Recommended for	High end

'The food is impressive, the service flawless, the view stunning. I think it is the only world-class fine-dining restaurant in Istanbul.'—Şemsa Denizsel

MIMOLETT

Siraselviler Caddesi 55a
Cihangir
Beyoğlu
Istanbul 34433
+90 02122459858
www.mimolett.com.tr

Opening hours	6 days for dinner
Reservation policy	Yes
Credit cards	Accepted
Price range	Expensive
Style	Formal
Cuisine	French-Mediterranean
Recommended for	High end

VAN KAHVALTI EVI

Defterdar Yokuşu 52
Kılıç Ali Paşa
Cihangir
Beyoğlu
Istanbul 34425
www.vankahvalti-evi.com

Opening hours	7 days from breakfast until late
Reservation policy	No
Credit cards	Accepted but not AMEX and Diners
Price range	Affordable
Style	Casual
Cuisine	Turkish breakfast
Recommended for	Breakfast

ÇINARALTI MANGALBAŞI

Kasaplar Çarşısı g2
Altıntepe
Bostanci
Istanbul 34840
www.cinaraltimangalbasi.com

Opening hours	1 day for lunch and 7 days for dinner
Reservation policy	Yes
Credit cards	Accepted
Price range	Affordable
Style	Casual
Cuisine	Turkish
Recommended for	Worth the travel

'There's something about this place. It's filled with tables set around copper hoods and bbqs. If football (soccer) is on, you'll be watching it along with everyone else, and the room, near the ferries on the Asian side looking out towards the Princes Islands, is full of Turks all having a rowdy fun time.'—Peter Gordon

ALIBABA

Recommended by
Peter Gordon

Büyükada-Maden
Istanbul 34970
+90 2163823733
www.alibababuyukada.com

Opening hours	7 days for lunch and dinner
Reservation policy	Yes
Reservation email	rezervasyon@alibababuyukada.com
Credit cards	Accepted
Price range	Expensive
Style	Smart casual
Cuisine	Seafood
Recommended for	Worth the travel

'The most impressive selection of mezze and the freshest grilled or fried wild sea bass.'—Pete Gordon

AYNEN DÜRÜM

Recommended by
Gençay Üçok

Muhafazacilar 33
Grand Bazaar
Fatih
Istanbul 34710

Opening hours	7 days for lunch
Reservation policy	No
Credit cards	Not accepted
Price range	Budget
Style	Casual
Cuisine	Turkish
Recommended for	Bargain

'Sit on a tiny stool by the side of the market and enjoy *adana durum* (a spicy long meatball grilled on charcoal and wrapped in a smoking pitta bread), garnishes of pickles, grilled pepper, parsley and radish all served on a nylon sheet.'—Gençay Üçok

BALIKÇI SABAHATTIN

Recommended by
Peter Gordon

Seyit Hasan Kuyu Sokak
Cankurtaran
Eminönü
Fatih
Istanbul 34110
+90 2124581824
www.balikcisabahattin.com

Opening hours	7 days for lunch and dinner
Reservation policy	Yes
Credit cards	Accepted
Price range	Affordable
Style	Smart casual
Cuisine	Seafood
Recommended for	Worth the travel

'A fish restaurant in an old wooden building in the old town. It serves pretty much just that: fish. And bread. Plus a few specialized mezze plates.'—Peter Gordon

MEŞHUR FILIBE KÖFTECISI

Recommended by
Şemsa Denizsel

Ankara Caddesi 112
Sirkeci
Fatih
Istanbul 34112

Opening hours	6 days for lunch and dinner
Reservation policy	No
Credit cards	Not accepted
Price range	Budget
Style	Casual
Cuisine	Turkish
Recommended for	Bargain

'Delicious, cheap and satisfying. It serves simply grilled meatballs with a bean salad.'—Şemsa Denizsel

ÇIYA SOFRASI

Recommended by
Anita Lo, Jockey Petrie

Güneşlibahçe Sokak 43
Kadiköy
Istanbul 34710
+90 2163303190
www.ciya.com.tr

Opening hours	7 days for lunch and dinner
Reservation policy	Yes
Credit cards	Accepted but not AMEX
Price range	Budget
Style	Smart casual
Cuisine	Turkish
Recommended for	Worth the travel

KARAKÖY LOKANTASI

Recommended by
Didem Şenol

Kemankes Caddessi 37a
Kadiköy
Istanbul 34425
www.karakoylokantasi.com

Opening hours	6 days for lunch and dinner
Reservation policy	Yes
Credit cards	Accepted
Price range	Budget
Style	Casual
Cuisine	Turkish
Recommended for	Local favourite

LOKANTA MAYA

Recommended by
Şemsa Denizsel

Kemankeş Caddessi 35a
Kadiköy
Istanbul 34710
+90 2122526884
www.lokantamaya.com

Opening hours	6 days for lunch and 5 days for dinner
Reservation policy	Yes
Reservation email	info@lokantamaya.com
Credit cards	Accepted
Price range	Affordable
Style	Casual
Cuisine	Modern Turkish
Recommended for	Regular neighbourhood

'The young chef-owner, Didem Senol,
does seafood beautifully, just not traditionally.'
—Şemsa Denizsel

ŞAMPIYON KOKOREÇ

Recommended by
Didem Şenol

Rıhtım Caddessi 34
Rasimpaça
Kadıköy
Istanbul 34710
www.sampiyonkokorec.com.tr

Opening hours	7 days for lunch and dinner
Reservation policy	No
Credit cards	Not accepted
Price range	Budget
Style	Casual
Cuisine	Fast food
Recommended for	Late night

MANGERIE

Recommended by
Peter Gordon

Cevdet Paşa Caddesi 69
Küçük Bebek
Istanbul 34342
+90 2122635199
www.mangeriebebek.com

Opening hours	7 days from breakfast until late
Reservation policy	Yes
Credit cards	Accepted
Price range	Affordable
Style	Smart casual
Cuisine	Modern Turkish
Recommended for	Breakfast

'It looks very Antipodean in design but it's definitely
Turkish in menu influence. Try the scrambled eggs on
toast with preserved quince, or a slice of brownie with
Turkish coffee.'—Peter Gordon

KANTIN

Recommended by
Mehmet Gürs

Akkavak Sokağı 30
Nişantaşı
Istanbul 34365
+90 2122193114
www.kantin.biz

Opening hours	6 days for lunch and dinner
Reservation policy	No
Credit cards	Accepted
Price range	Affordable
Style	Smart casual
Cuisine	Modern Turkish
Recommended for	Local favourite

'Great for contemporary and super tasty food. The chef,
Şemsa Denizsel, is great with her seasonal, simple and
refined food. Great bread too.'—Mehmet Gürs

KALE

Recommended by
Gençay Üçok

Yahya Kemal Caddesi 16
Rumelihisar
Istanbul 34470
www.kalecafe.com

Opening hours	7 days for brunch and 4 days for dinner
Reservation policy	No
Credit cards	Accepted
Price range	Budget
Style	Casual
Cuisine	Turkish
Recommended for	Breakfast

'Especially good on a sunny weekend morning for a long lazy, ceremonial Turkish breakfast while enjoying the views of the Bosphorus. Scrambled eggs with pastrami, fresh thick clotted cream with honey and lots of feta cheese to be accompanied with fresh tomatoes are musts. Avoid weekend noon times due to extreme crowds and traffic.'—Gençay Üçok

KIYI

Recommended by
Mehmet Gürs, Didem Şenol

Kefeliköy Caddesi 126
Tarabya
Sariyer
Istanbul 34457
+90 2122620002
www.kiyi.com.tr

Opening hours	7 days for lunch and dinner
Reservation policy	Yes
Credit cards	Accepted
Price range	Budget
Style	Casual
Cuisine	Meze-Seafood
Recommended for	Regular neighbourhood

'A lazy lunch here when the weather is great is fabulous. Ask for a window table on the second floor.'—Mehmet Gürs

A mezze and seafood restaurant on the European side of the Bosporus, ramshackle Kiyi eclipses its better-groomed competitors by 'maximizing the full potential of seasonal fish'. This is fresh, traditional Turkish cuisine, with mezze of squid, prawns (shrimp) and mussels, and vine leaves, sea beans and cheesy cigarette pastries. Choose from a long fish menu that changes seasonally, including grilled gurnard (sea robin), scorpion fish or lightly floured red mullet. Open since 1964, Kiyi's history of local custom, a sea view and decor of wood panels and creeping vines gives eating seafood here a dash of shabby chic.

MÜZE DE CHANGA

Recommended by
Didem Şenol

Sakip Sabanci Caddesi 42
Emirgan
Sariyer
Istanbul 34467
+90 2123230901
www.changa-istanbul.com

Opening hours	6 days for lunch and dinner
Reservation policy	Yes
Credit cards	Accepted
Price range	Affordable
Style	Smart casual
Cuisine	Modern Turkish
Recommended for	Breakfast

KANAAT LOKANTASI

Recommended by
Gençay Üçok

Selmani Pak Cadessi 25
Tembel Hacı Mehmet
Üsküdar
Istanbul 34672
+90 2165533791
www.kanaatlokantasi.com.tr

Opening hours	7 days for lunch and dinner
Reservation policy	No
Credit cards	Not accepted
Price range	Budget
Style	Casual
Cuisine	Turkish
Recommended for	Local favourite

'Homemade one-pot food, cold dishes of vegetables cooked with olive oil, great traditional desserts. There is something for everyone in Kanaat. Very vegetarian friendly too.'—Gençay Üçok

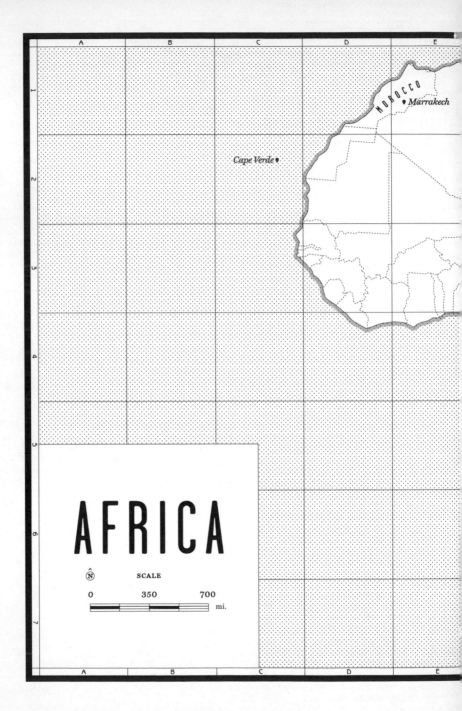

MOROCCO

• Marrakech

Cape Verde •

AFRICA

N

SCALE

0   350   700
▭▭▭▭▭▭▭▭ mi.

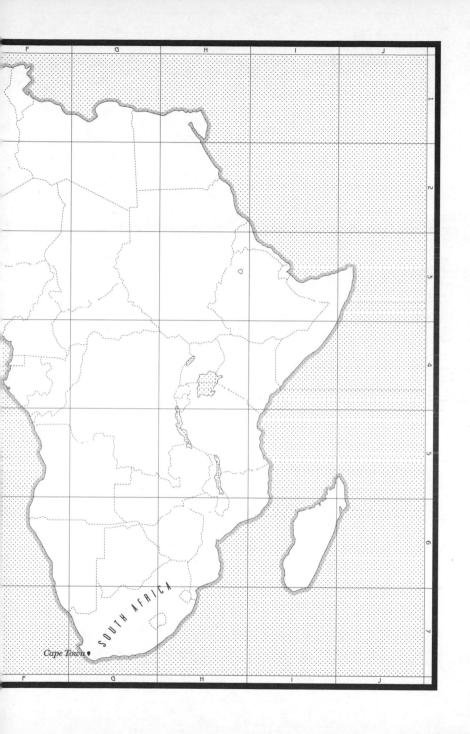

'FINE WINE, DELICIOUS MEATS AND TEMPTING DESSERTS.'

PETER TEMPELHOFF

'An oasis in the middle of the desert.'

GUILLAUME MONJURÉ P466

'SOME OF THE BEST BREADS I'VE EVER TASTED.'

SCOT KIRTON P449

CAPE VERDE, MOROCCO & SOUTH AFRICA

'IT'S A TRADITIONAL SOUTH AFRICAN PLACE.'

SCOT KIRTON P477

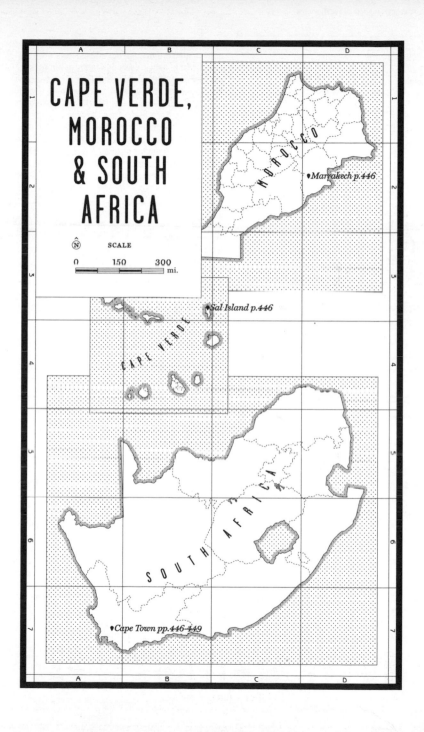

CAPE VERDE, MOROCCO & SOUTH AFRICA

SCALE

0   150   300 mi.

MOROCCO

●Marrakech p.446

●Sal Island p.446

CAPE VERDE

SOUTH AFRICA

●Cape Town pp.446-449

CAFÉ CREOLE

Recommended by
Adam Byatt

Porto Antigo
Santa Maria
Sal Island
Cape Verde
+238 9953690

Opening hours	7 days from breakfast until late
Reservation policy	Yes
Credit cards	Not accepted
Price range	Budget
Style	Casual
Cuisine	Creole
Recommended for	Worth the travel

LA PAUSE

Recommended by
Guillaume Monjuré

Douar Lmih Laroussiène
Commune Agafay
Marrakech
Morocco
+212 661306494
www.lapause-marrakech.com

Opening hours	7 days for breakfast, lunch and dinner
Reservation policy	Yes
Credit cards	Not accepted
Price range	Affordable
Style	Casual
Cuisine	Moroccan
Recommended for	Worth the travel

'An oasis in the middle of the desert.'
—Guillaume Monjuré

THE AZURE

Recommended by
José Pizarro

Twelve Apostles Hotel and Spa
Victoria Road
Camps Bay
Cape Town 8040
South Africa
+27 0214379029
www.12apostleshotel.com

Opening hours	7 days for breakfast, lunch and dinner
Reservation policy	Yes
Reservation email	azure@12apostles.co.za
Credit cards	Accepted
Price range	Affordable
Style	Smart casual
Cuisine	International
Recommended for	Worth the travel

The Azure at the 12 Apostle's Hotel in Camps Bay is aptly named – there are incredible views over the Atlantic from its windows and terrace. The recipes of hotelier, chef and writer Bea Tollman, amassed during her travels, form half the international menu, and those of executive chef Henrico Grobbelaar the other. Using fresh herbs from the hotel's garden, vegetables and meat from the local market and sustainable seafood, The Azure draws crowds from nearby Cape Town for dishes such as Springbok Tenderloin, preserved carrots, candied turnips, quinoa, date paste and ginger infused jus, plus a list of South Africa's best wines.

CARNE

Recommended by
Luke Dale-Roberts

70 Keerom Street
Cape Town 8000
South Africa
+27 214243460
www.carne-sa.com

Opening hours	6 days for dinner
Reservation policy	Yes
Credit cards	Accepted
Price range	Affordable
Style	Smart casual
Cuisine	Italian-Steakhouse
Recommended for	Wish I'd opened

THE GREENHOUSE

Recommended by
Luke Dale-Roberts,
Scot Kirton

Cellars-Hohenort Hotel
93 Brommersvlei Road
Constantia
Cape Town 7800
South Africa
+27 217942137
www.cellars-hohenort.com/greenhouse

Opening hours	5 days for dinner
Reservation policy	Yes
Reservation email	reception@cellars-hohenort.co.za
Credit cards	Accepted
Price range	Expensive
Style	Smart casual
Cuisine	Modern South African
Recommended for	High end

MELISSA'S

Recommended by
Luke Dale-Roberts

Shop 1 & 2 Constantia Courtyard
Main Road
Constantia
Cape Town 7806
South Africa
www.melissas.co.za

Opening hours.........................7 days from breakfast until late
Reservation policy..No
Credit cards...Accepted
Price range..Budget
Style...Casual
Cuisine...Deli-Café
Recommended for...Breakfast

Mark and Melissa van Hoogstraten opened their first Melissa's in 1996 and now have seven of their upscale continental deli-cafés around Cape Town. The third branch in lush leafy 'Constantia Village' does a roaring brunch trade. Tuck into the breakfast buffet of fruit salads, omelettes, pastries and so on, or go à la carte for the wildly popular Eggs Benedict with toasted Turkish bread or enamel 'breakfast mug' of baked eggs, bacon, tomato and mascarpone. Have a peak at the gourmet goodies on the shelves while you eat: Melissa's own-made preserves, quiches and cakes are practically de rigueur at Capetonian parties.

COL'CACCHIO PIZZERIA

Recommended by
Luke Dale-Roberts

2 Redefine North Wharf
42 Hans Strijdom Avenue
Foreshore
Cape Town 8001
South Africa
+27 214194848
www.colcacchio.co.za

Opening hours.............5 days for lunch and 7 days for dinner
Reservation policy..Yes
Credit cards...Accepted
Price range..Budget
Style...Casual
Cuisine...Pizza
Recommended for..................................Regular neighbourhood

MZOLI'S

Recommended by
Scot Kirton

NY155, Shop 3
Gugulethu
Cape Town 7751
South Africa

Opening hours.................................7 days for lunch and dinner
Reservation policy..No
Credit cards...Not accepted
Price range..Budget
Style...Casual
Cuisine..Barbecue
Recommended for..Local favourite

'It's a traditional South African place.'—Scot Kirton

MASSIMO'S

Recommended by
Scot Kirton

Oakhurst Farm Park
Main Rd
Hout Bay
Cape Town 7806
South Africa
+27 217905648
www.pizzaclub.co.za

Opening hours.............2 days for lunch and 5 days for dinner
Reservation policy..Yes
Reservation email   info@massimos.co.za
Credit cards...Accepted
Price range..Affordable
Style...Casual
Cuisine...Italian
Recommended for...........................Regular neighbourhood

OLYMPIA CAFÉ

Recommended by
Scot Kirton

134 Main Road
Kalk Bay
Cape Town 7975
South Africa
+27 217886396

Opening hours.............7 days for breakfast, lunch and dinner
Reservation policy..No
Credit cards...Accepted
Price range..Budget
Style...Casual
Cuisine..Café
Recommended for...Breakfast

'Olympia Café is a favourite.'—Scot Kirton

BORRUSO'S

Recommended by
Scot Kirton,
Peter Tempelhoff

Corner Main Road and Mains Avenue
Kenilworth
Cape Town 7708
South Africa
www.borrusos.net

Opening hours	7 days for dinner
Reservation policy	No
Credit cards	Accepted
Price range	Budget
Style	Casual
Cuisine	Pizza
Recommended for	Bargain

BIHARI

Recommended by
Luke Dale-Roberts

Southern Sun Hotel
7 Main Road
Newlands
Cape Town 7700
South Africa
+27 216747186
www.bihari.co.za

Opening hours	7 days for lunch and dinner
Reservation policy	Yes
Credit cards	Accepted
Price range	Budget
Style	Casual
Cuisine	Indian
Recommended for	Bargain

Bihari Newlands was a labour of love for London-born founder Donna Ross, who wanted to introduce the fiery north Indian tandoori cuisine she knew from the UK to Cape Town. Fortunately she borrowed little from UK 'curry house' design, and has given Bihari, which opened at the Southern Sun Hotel in 2009, an upscale look with heavy carved wooden doors and wrought-iron lanterns. Bihari's well priced menu makes the most of the tandoor oven, where fresh ingredients – including paneer, courgettes (zucchini) and lamb chops – all get the hot coals treatment in the hands of the India-trained chefs. The local wines can more than stand up to the spice.

PIRATES STEAKHOUSE

Recommended by
Scot Kirton

160 Main Road
Plumstead
Cape Town 7801
South Africa
+27 217975659
www.piratessteakhouse.co.za

Opening hours	7 days for lunch and dinner
Reservation policy	Yes
Credit cards	Accepted
Price range	Budget
Style	Casual
Cuisine	Steakhouse
Recommended for	Late night

'After a good night out, I occasionally stop for a late night burger at Pirates steakhouse.'—Scot Kirton

BELEZA

Recommended by
Scot Kirton

Kloof Nek Road
Tamboerskloof
Cape Town 8001
South Africa
+27 214260795
www.belezarestaurant.co.za

Opening hours	6 days from breakfast until late
Reservation policy	Yes
Reservation email	info@belezarestaurant.co.za
Credit cards	Accepted
Price range	Budget
Style	Casual
Cuisine	Italian-Portuguese
Recommended for	Bargain

NOBU

Recommended by
Peter Tempelhoff

One & Only Resort
Dock Road
Victoria & Alfred Waterfront
Cape Town 8001
South Africa
+27 214314511
www.oneandonlyresorts.com

Opening hours	7 days for dinner
Reservation policy	Yes
Credit cards	Accepted
Price range	Expensive
Style	Smart casual
Cuisine	Modern Japanese
Recommended for	High end

THE POT LUCK CLUB

Recommended by
Peter Tempelhoff

104a The Old Biscuit Mill
375 Albert Road
Woodstock
Cape Town 7915
South Africa
+27 214470804
www.thepotluckclub.co.za

Opening hours................1 day for lunch and 5 days for dinner
Reservation policy...Yes
Reservation email............reservations@thepotluckclub.co.za
Credit cards..Accepted
Price range...Budget
Style...Casual
Cuisine...International small plates
Recommended for...Wish I'd opened

Luke Dale-Roberts has been busy since he stepped
down from running the kitchen at La Colombe,
Cape Town's most acclaimed restaurant, to open
his own. In late 2010 he launched The Test Kitchen
to widespread acclaim. This more casual follow-
up, opened next door in early 2012, is in the same
development — what was an old biscuit (cookie)
factory. The menu does small plates designed for
sharing that trawl across Asia and Europe and
beyond for inspiration — from fish tacos to Chinese-
style ribs. The space doubles as a contemporary
art gallery.

THE TEST KITCHEN

Recommended by
Scot Kirton, Peter Tempelhoff

104a The Old Biscuit Mill
375 Albert Road
Woodstock
Cape Town 7915
South Africa
+27 2144/2337
www.thetestkitchen.co.za

Opening hours...................................5 days for lunch and dinner
Reservation policy...Yes
Reservation email............reservations@thetestkitchen.co.za
Credit cards..Accepted
Price range..Affordable
Style...Smart casual
Cuisine..Modern South African
Recommended for...Wish I'd opened

SUNRISE CHIP AND RANCH

Recommended by
Peter Tempelhoff

89 Sparks Road
Asherville
Durban 4067
South Africa

Opening hours.............7 days for breakfast, lunch and dinner
Reservation policy...No
Credit cards..Not accepted
Price range...Budget
Style...Casual
Cuisine..Fast food
Recommended for...Late night

OVERTURE

Recommended by
Peter Tempelhoff

Hidden Valley Estate
Annandale Road
Stellenbosch 7600
South Africa
| 27 218802721
www.dineatoverture.co.za

Opening hours.............6 days for lunch and 2 days for dinner
Reservation policy...Yes
Credit cards..Accepted
Price range..Affordable
Style..Smart casual
Cuisine..Modern South African
Recommended for................................Regular neighbourhood

ILE DE PAIN

Recommended by
Scot Kirton

Thesen's Island Street
Knysna
Western Cape 6571
South Africa
+27 443025707
www.iledepain.co.za

Opening hours............................6 days for breakfast and lunch
Reservation policy...No
Credit cards..Accepted
Price range...Budget
Style...Casual
Cuisine...Bakery-Café
Recommended for...Worth the travel

'Some of the best breads I've ever tasted.'—Scot Kirton

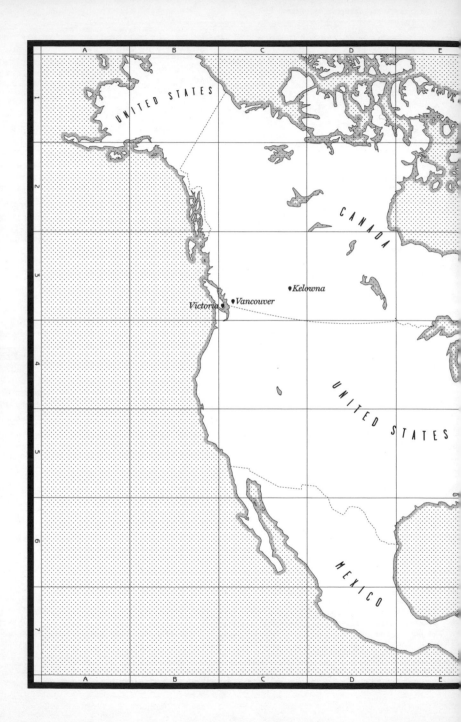

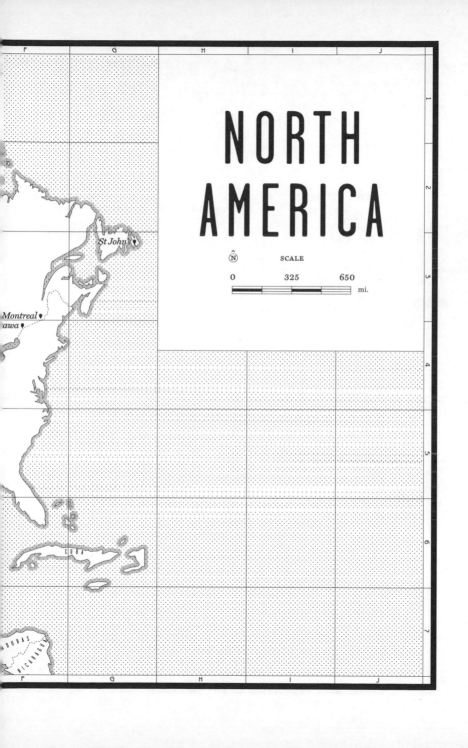

NORTH AMERICA

$\hat{N}$

SCALE

0   325   650

mi.

St John's

Montreal
awa

CUBA

DURAS
NICARAGUA

'In the summer months the produce of the Okanagan Valley shines in the chef's hands.'
LEE COOPER P454

'Eat a delicious dinner with local wine watching the sun set over the ocean from the original dining room.'
BRAD HOLMES P454

'Has a wood burning oven. Sit on the deck overlooking the ocean.'
JEREMY CHARLES P455

'AMAZING. THIS GUY BUILT HIS OWN OVEN, MILLS HIS OWN FLOUR AND MAKES GREAT PASTRIES AND CONFECTIONS TO BOOT.'
TED ANDERSON P455

CANADA

'Well-executed French brasserie food with a touch of West Coast. A definite go-to.'
BRAD HOLMES P454

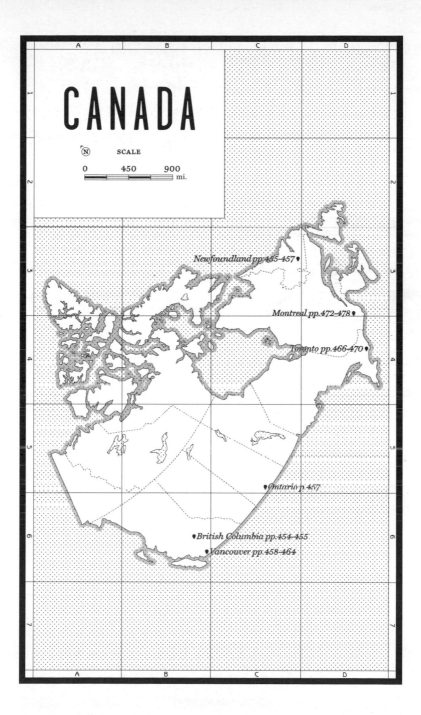

CANADA

N   SCALE

0   450   900 mi.

WATERFRONT RESTAURANT

Recommended by
Lee Cooper

104-1180 Sunset Drive
Kelowna
British Columbia V1Y 9W6
+1 2509791222
www.waterfrontrestaurant.ca

Opening hours	6 days for dinner
Reservation policy	Yes
Credit cards	Accepted
Price range	Affordable
Style	Smart casual
Cuisine	International
Recommended for	Worth the travel

'In the summer months the produce of the Okanagan Valley shines in chef Mark Filat's hands. He has an amazing garden at his house where he grows some of the produce served at the restaurant. Fried squid with tamarind dipping sauce is a favourite.'
—Lee Cooper

POINT-NO-POINT RESORT

Recommended by
Brad Holmes

10829 West Coast Road
Shirley
British Columbia V9Z 1G9
+1 2506462020
www.pointnopointresort.com

Opening hours	7 days for lunch and 5 days for dinner
Reservation policy	Yes
Credit cards	Accepted
Price range	Affordable
Style	Casual
Cuisine	International
Recommended for	High end

'Rent one of their rustic cabins with a fireplace and an outdoor hot tub. Eat a delicious dinner with local wine, watching the sun set over the ocean from the original dining room (sixty years in operation).'—Brad Holmes

SOOKE HARBOUR HOUSE

Recommended by
Brad Holmes

1528 Whiffin Spit Road
Sooke
British Columbia V9Z 0T4
+1 2506423421
www.sookeharbourhouse.com

Opening hours	1 day for lunch and 5 days for dinner
Reservation policy	Yes
Reservation email	reservations@sookeharbourhouse.com
Credit cards	Accepted
Price range	Affordable
Style	Casual
Cuisine	Seafood
Recommended for	Local favourite

'Hyper-local long before the term "100-mile diet" was coined. Foraging for mushrooms, seaweed and other indigenous edibles is the cornerstone of their cuisine.'—Brad Holmes

BRASSERIE L'ECOLE

Recommended by
Brad Holmes

1715 Government Street
Victoria
British Columbia V8W 1Z4
+1 2054756260
www.lecole.ca

Opening hours	5 days for dinner
Reservation policy	No
Credit cards	Accepted
Price range	Affordable
Style	Casual
Cuisine	French
Recommended for	Late night

'Well-executed French brasserie food with a touch of West Coast and open later than most places in Victoria. A definite go-to.'—Brad Holmes

FOL EPI

Recommended by
Ted Anderson, Brad Holmes

398 Harbour Road
Victoria
British Columbia V9A 0B7
+1 205 477 8882
www.folepi.ca

Opening hours	5 days for breakfast and lunch
Reservation policy	No
Credit cards	Accepted
Price range	Budget
Style	Casual
Cuisine	Bakery-Café
Recommended for	Worth the travel

'The bakery Fol Epi is amazing. This guy built his own oven, mills his own flour and makes great pastries and confections to boot.'—Ted Anderson

PIZZERIA PRIMA STRADA

Recommended by
Ted Anderson, Brad Holmes

2960 Bridge Street
Victoria
British Columbia V8T 4T3
+1 2505904380
www.pizzeriaprimastrada.com

Opening hours	5 days for lunch and dinner
Reservation policy	Yes
Credit cards	Accepted
Price range	Budget
Style	Casual
Cuisine	Pizza
Recommended for	Worth the travel

'Excellent Neapolitan wood-fired pizza.'—Brad Holmes

RELISH

Recommended by
Brad Holmes

920 Pandora Avenue
Victoria
British Columbia V8V 3P3
+1 2505908464
www.relishfoodcoffee.com

Opening hours	5 days for breakfast and lunch
Reservation policy	No
Credit cards	Accepted
Price range	Budget
Style	Casual
Cuisine	Café
Recommended for	Bargain

'Delicious breakfast and lunch from a daily changing menu. Everything is made in-house and with care.'
—Brad Holmes

BONAVISTA SOCIAL CLUB

Recommended by
Jeremy Charles

Upper Amherst Cove
Bonavista
Newfoundland A0C 2A0
+1 7094455556
www.bonavistasocialclub.com

Opening hours	6 days for lunch and dinner
Reservation policy	Yes
Credit cards	Accepted
Price range	Budget
Style	Casual
Cuisine	Bakery-Café
Recommended for	Local favourite

'Has a wood-burning oven. Sit on the deck overlooking the ocean.'—Jeremy Charles

Upper Amherst Cove is a unique area that practises a holistic version of farming, using traditional methods wherever possible. The Bonavista Social Club fits there perfectly, its kitchen using local organic honey and local produce wherever possible, and recycling and composting much of its waste. The restaurant has the only commercial wood-fired oven in Newfoundland, baking rye bread, sourdough, baguettes, multigrain loaves and bagels daily, as well as excellent pizzas. The moose burger – which includes partridgeberry ketchup, sautéed wild mushrooms, bacon and spinach – has been recognized as one of the five best in Canada.

BASHO

Recommended by
Jeremy Charles

283 Duckworth Street
St. John's
Newfoundland A1C 1G9
+1 7095764600

Opening hours	5 days for lunch and 6 days for dinner
Reservation policy	Yes
Credit cards	Accepted
Price range	Expensive
Style	Smart casual
Cuisine	Japanese-International
Recommended for	Regular neighbourhood

**'I highly recommend the Toby Platter.'
—Jeremy Charles**

You wouldn't necessarily expect to find a restaurant like Basho in St. John's – it's a large and trendy Japanese fusion place that opened in 2006, with hanging baskets and Corinthian columns flanking the door. The venue is on two floors, with the dining room downstairs. Chef Tak Ishiwata is a first-generation Canadian who serves filet mignon with sweet potato chips (fries) for those unused to sushi, and fantastically fresh salmon tartare, or lobster with black beans and sake sauce for people who are keen on Asian food. There's also a great cocktail list with an emphasis on martinis.

BLUE ON WATER

Recommended by
Jeremy Charles

319 Water Street
St. John's
Newfoundland A1C 1B9
+1 8774312583
www.blueonwater.com

Opening hours	7 days for breakfast, lunch and dinner
Reservation policy	Yes
Reservation email	info@blueonwater.com
Credit cards	Accepted
Price range	Affordable
Style	Smart casual
Cuisine	Canadian
Recommended for	Breakfast

'I highly recommend the fish cakes with mustard pickles.'—Jeremy Charles

Blue on Water is perhaps Newfoundland's leading boutique hotel, located in downtown St. John's on the oldest street in North America. The decor is functional, urban and a little bit smart: stiff white linen, a blue-painted ceiling, bare bulbs and exposed brickwork. Brunch here is equally popular among guests and non-guests. They do a great bacon-infused burger with smoked Gouda and caramelized onion, a gorgeous crab bisque, lobster Eggs Benedict with potato rösti (hash browns), or citrus, cinnamon and maple French toast. The well-stocked bar mixes a great Caesar.

DUKE OF DUCKWORTH

Recommended by
Jeremy Charles

325 Duckworth Street
St. John's
Newfoundland A1C 1H5
+1 7097396344
www.dukeofduckworth.com

Opening hours	7 days for lunch and dinner
Reservation policy	No
Credit cards	Accepted
Price range	Budget
Style	Casual
Cuisine	Bar-Bistro
Recommended for	Bargain

'Choose the fish and chips.'—Jeremy Charles

VENICE PIZZERIA

Recommended by
Jeremy Charles

81 Military Road
St. John's
Newfoundland A1C 2C8
+1 7097387373

Opening hours	7 days for lunch and dinner
Reservation policy	No
Credit cards	Accepted
Price range	Budget
Style	Casual
Cuisine	Pizza
Recommended for	Late night

'Order thin crust.'—Jeremy Charles

ATLANTICA RESTAURANT

The Beach House
38 Beachy Cove Road
Portugal Cove
St. Philip's
Newfoundland A1M 1N3
+1 7098951251
www.atthebeachhouse.ca

Opening hours	6 days for dinner
Reservation policy	Yes
Reservation email	reservations@atthebeachhouse.ca
Credit cards	Accepted
Price range	Expensive
Style	Smart casual
Cuisine	Modern European
Recommended for	High end

RESTAURANT 18

18 York Street
Ottawa
Ontario K1N 5T5
+1 6132441188
www.restaurant18.com

Opening hours	7 days for dinner
Reservation policy	Yes
Credit cards	Accepted
Price range	Expensive
Style	Smart casual
Cuisine	Steakhouse-Seafood
Recommended for	Worth the travel

THE WHALESBONE

430 Bank Street
Ottawa
Ontario K2P 1Y8
+1 6132318569
www.thewhalesbone.com

Opening hours	6 days for lunch and 7 days for dinner
Reservation policy	Yes
Credit cards	Accepted
Price range	Affordable
Style	Casual
Cuisine	Seafood
Recommended for	Worth the travel

'The atmosphere is not for everyone,' insists The Whalesbone's own blurb, intriguingly. Ottawa's Whalesbone Oyster House, opened in 2005, is not your ritzy champagne and crustacea bar; this rowdy shoebox-sized *boîte* isn't so very many notches above 'spit and sawdust'. What you'll find is exposed brick walls, a fish skeleton suspended above the bar, affable bartenders and a pumping soundtrack. But if you want luxury, order some food. How's about half a dozen Colville Bay oysters on the half shell? Or make it spaghetti with clams or walleye with polenta and lemon caper butter. Although not the hectoring type, The Whalesbone takes sustainable fishing very seriously indeed.

HAISAI

794079 County Road 124
Singhampton
Ontario N0C 1M0
+1 7054452748
www.haisairestaurantbakery.com

Opening hours	2 days for brunch and 4 days for dinner
Reservation policy	Yes
Credit cards	Not accepted
Price range	Expensive
Style	Casual
Cuisine	Bakery-Café
Recommended for	Wish I'd opened

Owner-chef Michael Stadtländer is an environmentalist, farmer and something of a visionary. He owns the nearby Elgensinn farm, which supplies Haisai with much of its produce, and he built the venue's furniture by hand. The enterprise is both restaurant and bakery, a wooden barn adjoining a brick building covered in solar panels. The place is constructed entirely from local materials – stone, clay and wood – and the food is rigorously local: even the wine list is one hundred per cent Ontario. There's a daily-changing, fixed-price, ten-course menu, while the wood-fired oven serves great pizza and superb prune pastries.

'Large portions and the Yukon style bacon is amazing. Also serves the best hamburgers in town.'

LEE COOPER P464

'Local ingredients executed with finesse and great technique. They have hit the nail on the head for what Vancouver wants.'

TED ANDERSON 462

VANCOUVER

'Very Vancouver. It is elegant while still staying informal. The cooking is European in technique while using West Coast products and allows Asian influences to shine through in some dishes.'

LEE COOPER P464

'DURING CRAB SEASON, CHOOSE THE BIGGEST CRAB THEY HAVE AND GET AS MANY PREPARATIONS AS POSSIBLE. AWESOME.'

TED ANDERSON P463

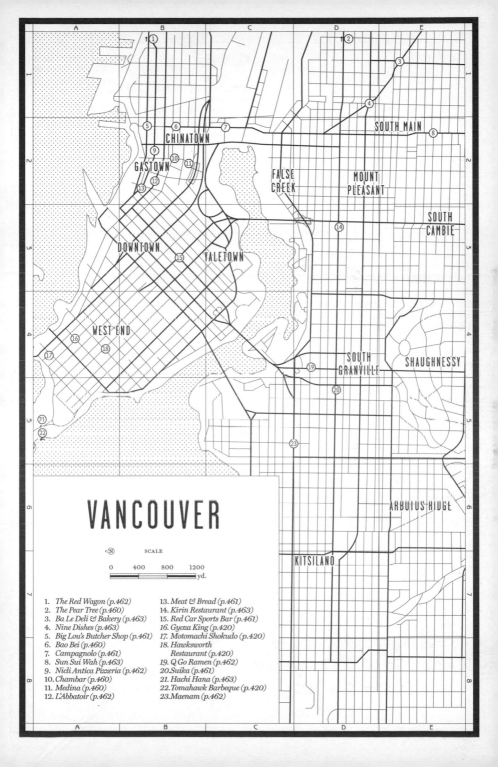

VANCOUVER

SCALE

0   400   800   1200
yd.

CHINATOWN
GASTOWN
SOUTH MAIN
FALSE CREEK
MOUNT PLEASANT
SOUTH CAMBIE
DOWNTOWN
YALETOWN
WEST END
SOUTH GRANVILLE
SHAUGHNESSY
ARBUTUS RIDGE
KITSILANO

THE PEAR TREE

Recommended by
Lee Cooper, Vikram Vij

4120 East Hastings Street
Burnaby
Vancouver
British Columbia V5C 2J4
+1 6042992772
www.peartreerestaurant.net

Opening hours	5 days for dinner
Reservation policy	Yes
Credit cards	Accepted
Price range	Expensive
Style	Smart casual
Cuisine	Modern European
Recommended for	Worth the travel

'The Pear Tree is an amazing restaurant tucked away in a neighbourhood where one might not be looking to find a world class meal. Chef Scott Jaeger is one of Canada's premiere talents in the kitchen. The dining room is tasteful and the service warm and professional. The food is executed as close to perfection as you can get. Sensible flavour combinations, modern yet rooted in classic technique. Roast scallops with bacon risotto is a classic Pear Tree dish but you can't go wrong with any menu items.'—Lee Cooper

BAO BEI

Recommended by
Vikram Vij

163 Keefer Street
Chinatown
Vancouver
British Columbia V6A 1X3
+1 6046880876
www.bao-bei.ca

Opening hours	6 days for dinner
Reservation policy	No
Credit cards	Accepted
Price range	Budget
Style	Casual
Cuisine	Chinese
Recommended for	Late night

CHAMBAR

Recommended by
Lee Cooper

562 Beatty Street
Crosstown
Vancouver
British Columbia V6B 2N7
+1 6048797119
www.chambar.com

Opening hours	7 days for dinner
Reservation policy	Yes
Credit cards	Accepted
Price range	Affordable
Style	Casual
Cuisine	Modern European
Recommended for	Wish I'd opened

'Chambar is a model of success. They seem to be able to keep the restaurant full consistently night after night. Schuermans cooks simple dishes with bold flavours. The lounge is bustling yet comfortable and easily the best place for a drink and bite to eat – mussels and chips (fries) are the best – pre- and post-event as it is located right near the stadium/arena. After over five years of being open Chambar seems to only get busier. To own a restaurant that consistently has their guests leave happy and return year after year is something that most restauranteurs can only dream of.'—Lee Cooper

MEDINA

Recommended by
Vikram Vij

556 Beatty Street
Crosstown
Vancouver
British Columbia V6B 2L3
+1 6048793114
www.medinacafe.com

Opening hours	7 days for breakfast and lunch
Reservation policy	Yes
Credit cards	Accepted
Price range	Budget
Style	Casual
Cuisine	Café
Recommended for	Breakfast

MEAT & BREAD

Recommended by
Brad Holmes

370 Cambie Street
Downtown
Vancouver
British Columbia V6B 2N3
www.meatandbread.ca

Opening hours	6 days for lunch
Reservation policy	No
Credit cards	Accepted
Price range	Budget
Style	Casual
Cuisine	Sandwiches
Recommended for	Wish I'd opened

'Delicious. Genius.'—Brad Holmes

RED CARD SPORTS BAR

Recommended by
David Hawksworth

900 Seymour Street
Downtown
Vancouver
British Columbia V6B 3L9
+1 6046894460
www.redcardsportsbar.ca

Opening hours	7 days for lunch and dinner
Reservation policy	Yes
Reservation email	info@redcardsportsbar.ca
Credit cards	Accepted
Price range	Affordable
Style	Casual
Cuisine	Italian
Recommended for	Late night

BIG LOU'S BUTCHER SHOP

Recommended by
Ted Anderson

269 Powell Street
Downtown Eastside
Vancouver
British Columbia V6A 0B6
+1 6045669229
www.biglousbutchershop.com

Opening hours	7 days for breakfast and lunch
Reservation policy	No
Credit cards	Accepted
Price range	Budget
Style	Casual
Cuisine	Sandwiches
Recommended for	Bargain

'Try the porchetta sandwich.'—Ted Anderson

Why open a restaurant in an old butcher's shop, as many have done, when you can open a butcher with a restaurant within it? That seems to have been the logic behind Big Lou's Butcher Shop, a quality meat shop with a sandwich counter that's also bookable as a fourteen-seat 'Bouchery' private dining room boasting a menu that keeps out vegetarians. Opened in early 2011, Lou's supplies meat to many on the Vancouver restaurant scene, and their sandwiches, including the already legendary porchetta and the crispy pork belly with chimichurri, pack a considerably meaty punch for not a lot of greenbacks.

CAMPAGNOLO

Recommended by
Marc-André Jetté,
Vikram Vij

1020 Main Street
Downtown Eastside
Vancouver
British Columbia V6A 2W1
+1 5064846018
www.campagnolorestaurant.ca

Opening hours	7 days for lunch and dinner
Reservation policy	Yes
Credit cards	Accepted
Price range	Affordable
Style	Casual
Cuisine	Italian
Recommended for	Regular neighbourhood

SUIKA

Recommended by
Ted Anderson

1626 West Broadway
Fairview
Vancouver
British Columbia V6J 1X6
+1 6047301678
www.suika-snackbar.com

Opening hours	6 days for lunch and 7 days for dinner
Reservation policy	Yes
Credit cards	Accepted
Price range	Budget
Style	Casual
Cuisine	Japanese
Recommended for	Late night

'Great Izakaya food – the ma-po rice cakes are wicked – and a fun atmosphere.'—Ted Anderson

L'ABBATOIR

Recommended by
Ted Anderson

217 Carrall Street
Gastown
Vancouver
British Columbia V6B 2J2
+1 6045681701
www.labattoir.ca

Opening hours	7 days for dinner
Reservation policy	Yes
Credit cards	Accepted
Price range	Affordable
Style	Casual
Cuisine	Modern French-Canadian
Recommended for	Local favourite

'L'Abbatoir in Gastown is pretty unique. Chef Lee Cooper has come up with an amazing, succinct menu of local ingredients, executed with finesse and great technique. The restaurant is casual in setting, but high class in all that they do. They have hit the nail on the head for what Vancouver wants.'—Ted Anderson

NICLI ANTICA PIZZERIA

Recommended by
Lee Cooper

62 East Cordova Street
Gastown
Vancouver
British Columbia V6A 1K2
+1 6046696985
www.nicli-antica-pizzeria.ca

Opening hours	7 days for lunch and dinner
Reservation policy	No
Credit cards	Accepted
Price range	Budget
Style	Casual
Cuisine	Pizza
Recommended for	Regular neighbourhood

'Authentic pizza made in a wood-fired oven that was imported from Italy. Simple classic toppings with a chewy and slightly blistered crust. All the pizzas are outstanding and they are open until 12.00 a.m. This is a regular post-work stop.'—Lee Cooper

THE RED WAGON

Recommended by
Ted Anderson

2296 East Hastings Street
Hastings-Sunrise
Vancouver
British Columbia V5L 1V4
+1 6045684565
www.redwagoncafe.com

Opening hours	7 days for brunch and 5 days for dinner
Reservation policy	No
Credit cards	Accepted
Price range	Budget
Style	Casual
Cuisine	Diner-Café
Recommended for	Breakfast

MAENAM

Recommended by
Ted Anderson

1938 West 4th Avenue
Kitsilano
Vancouver
British Columbia V6J 1M5
+1 6047305579
www.maenam.ca

Opening hours	5 days for lunch and 7 days for dinner
Reservation policy	Yes
Credit cards	Accepted
Price range	Budget
Style	Casual
Cuisine	Thai
Recommended for	Regular neighbourhood

Q GO RAMEN

Recommended by
Ted Anderson

1443 West Broadway
Kitsilano
Vancouver
British Columbia V6H 1H6
+1 6045689916

Opening hours	7 days for lunch and dinner
Reservation policy	No
Credit cards	Not accepted
Price range	Budget
Style	Casual
Cuisine	Japanese
Recommended for	Bargain

BA LE DELI & BAKERY

Shop 21, 701 Kingsway
Mt Pleasant
Vancouver
British Columbia V5T 2R7
+1 6048750088

Opening hours	7 days for breakfast and lunch
Reservation policy	No
Credit cards	Not accepted
Price range	Budget
Style	Casual
Cuisine	Vietnamese
Recommended for	Bargain

'Great *bánh mì* sandwiches.'—Ted Anderson

KIRIN RESTAURANT

201 City Square
Mt Pleasant
555 West 12th Avenue
Vancouver
British Columbia V5Z 3X7
+1 6048798038
www.kirinrestaurants.com

Opening hours	7 days for lunch and dinner
Reservation policy	Yes
Credit cards	Accepted
Price range	Affordable
Style	Casual
Cuisine	Chinese
Recommended for	Regular neighbourhood

'Excellent dim sum.'—David Hawksworth

NINE DISHES

960 Kingsway
Mt Pleasant
Vancouver
British Columbia V5V 3C4
+1 7782828699

Opening hours	7 days for dinner
Reservation policy	Yes
Credit cards	Not accepted
Price range	Budget
Style	Casual
Cuisine	Chinese
Recommended for	Late night

'Cheap beer, awesome tripe with spicy chillies and
peanuts, and you help yourself to rice.'—Ted Anderson

SUN SUI WAH

3888 Main Street
Mt Pleasant
Vancouver
British Columbia V5V 3N9
+1 6048728822
www.sunsuiwah.com

Opening hours	7 days for lunch and dinner
Reservation policy	Yes
Credit cards	Accepted
Price range	Affordable
Style	Casual
Cuisine	Chinese
Recommended for	High end

'During crab season, choose the biggest crab they
have and get as many preparations as possible.
Awesome.'—Ted Anderson

HACHI HANA

1426 Lonsdale Avenue
North Vancouver
Vancouver
British Columbia V7M 2J1
+1 6049900081

Opening hours	6 days for lunch and dinner
Reservation policy	Yes
Credit cards	Accepted
Price range	Affordable
Style	Casual
Cuisine	Japanese
Recommended for	Bargain

'Neighbourhood sushi joint. Reliable, fresh, good-
quality fish. Standard menu. Always cheap and they do
takeaways (takeouts).'—Lee Cooper

TOMAHAWK BARBEQUE

Recommended by
Lee Cooper

1550 Philip Avenue
North Vancouver
Vancouver
British Columbia V7P 2V8
+1 6049882612
www.tomahawkrestaurant.com

Opening hours	7 days for breakfast, lunch and dinner
Reservation policy	No
Credit cards	Accepted
Price range	Budget
Style	Casual
Cuisine	Diner-Café
Recommended for	Breakfast

'This restaurant has been around for over eighty years. It is packed on weekends so the best time to visit is mid-week. Large portions and the Yukon-style bacon is amazing. Also serves the best burgers in town during the afternoon.'—Lee Cooper

GYOZA KING

Recommended by
Lee Cooper,
David Hawksworth

1508 Robson Street
West End
Vancouver
British Columbia V6G 1C2
+1 6046698278
www.gyokingroup.com

Opening hours	3 days for lunch and 7 days for dinner
Reservation policy	Yes
Credit cards	Accepted
Price range	Budget
Style	Casual
Cuisine	Japanese
Recommended for	Late night

'An Izakaya-style restaurant serving Japanese pub fare. It's open until 2.00 a.m. and is a local hang-out for cooks just finishing their long day in the kitchen. The beer here is always the best while eating large amounts of their homemade gyoza.'—Lee Cooper

HAWKSWORTH RESTAURANT

Recommended by
Lee Cooper, Brad Holmes,
Vikram Vij

801 West Georgia Street
West End
Vancouver
British Columbia V6P 1C7
+1 6046737000
www.hawksworthrestaurant.com

Opening hours	7 days for breakfast, lunch and dinner
Reservation policy	Yes
Credit cards	Accepted
Price range	Affordable
Style	Smart casual
Cuisine	Modern Canadian
Recommended for	Worth the travel

'Hawksworth Restaurant is very "Vancouver". It is elegant while still staying informal. You can go there wearing a suit or jeans and feel comfortable either way. The cooking is European in technique while using West Coast products and allows Asian influences to shine through in some dishes. The combination of these things make Hawksworth a restaurant that embodies Vancouver on several levels. The sweetbread dish is a killer.'—Lee Cooper

MOTOMACHI SHOKUDO

Recommended by
David Hawksworth

740 Denman Street
West End
Vancouver
British Columbia V6G 2L5
+1 6046090310

Opening hours	6 days for lunch and dinner
Reservation policy	No
Credit cards	Not accepted
Price range	Budget
Style	Casual
Cuisine	Japanese
Recommended for	Bargain

'The best ramen noodle shop.'—David Hawksworth

'AMAZING FRESH OYSTERS AND MUSSELS.'

PAUL NEWMAN P469

'I get mad cravings for their Pad Thai'

CLAUDIO APRILE P469

TORONTO

'FREE-RANGE, ONTARIO, GRASS-FED BONE-IN RIBEYE. THE BEST STEAK I HAVE EVER EATEN.'

MARC FOSH P470

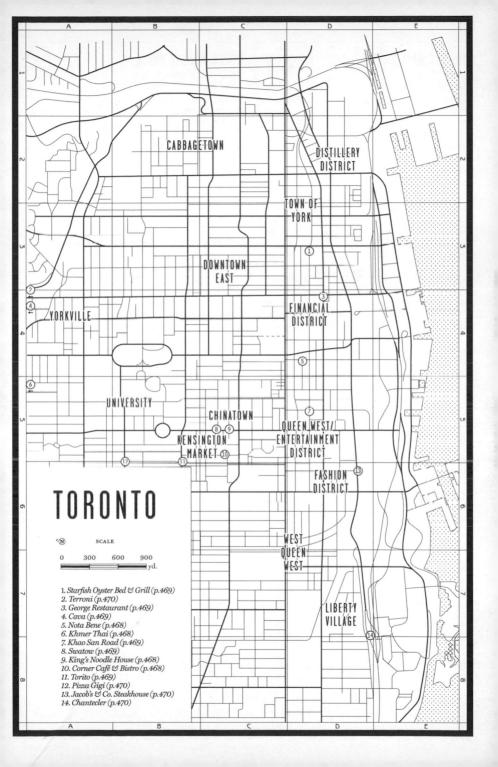

TORONTO

N SCALE

0   300   600   900
yd.

CABBAGETOWN

DISTILLERY
DISTRICT

TOWN OF
YORK

DOWNTOWN
EAST

FINANCIAL
DISTRICT

YORKVILLE

UNIVERSITY

CHINATOWN

KENSINGTON
MARKET

QUEEN WEST/
ENTERTAINMENT
DISTRICT

FASHION
DISTRICT

WEST
QUEEN
WEST

LIBERTY
VILLAGE

CORNER CAFÉ & BISTRO

The Drake Hotel
1150 Queen Street West
Beaconsfield Village
Toronto
Ontario M6J 1J3
+1 4165315042
www.thedrakehotel.ca

Opening hours...........7 days for brunch and 2 days for dinner
Reservation policy..Yes
Reservation email................specialevents@thedrakehotel.ca
Credit cards...Accepted
Price range..Affordable
Style..Casual
Cuisine..Café
Recommended for...Breakfast

Built in 1890, the Drake hotel started to go downhill in the 1960s. From the 1970s until the end of the millennium it saw action as a flophouse, a punk bar and a rave den. Reborn in 2004 as a boutique hotel, an arty hub with a club in its basement and a bar on its rooftop, it's been a catalyst for the ongoing gentrification of the surrounding neighbourhood. Its Corner Café, which morphs into a bistro in the evenings, is a popular breakfast destination for its freshly baked scones, croissants, muffins and doughnuts, eggs, filled bagels, biscuits (cookies) and burritos.

KHMER THAI

1018 Saint Clair Avenue West
Cedarvale
Toronto
Ontario M6E 1A4
+1 4166540609
www.khmerthai.com

Opening hours..............4 days for lunch and 7 days for dinner
Reservation policy...No
Credit cards...Accepted
Price range..Budget
Style..Casual
Cuisine...Thai-Cambodian
Recommended for...Bargain

KING'S NOODLE HOUSE

296 Spadina Avenue
Chinatown
Toronto
Ontario M5T 2E7
+1 4165981817

Opening hours.................................6 days for lunch and dinner
Reservation policy...No
Credit cards...Not accepted
Price range..Budget
Style..Casual
Cuisine...Chinese
Recommended for................................Regular neighbourhood

Longstanding, reliable and affordable Cantonese in the heart of Chinatown that stays open all day, every day (bar Wednesdays), from congee at breakfast to small hours' noodles. So brightly lit since its refurbishment several years ago that the photosensitive should bring their shades. It can get chaotically busy at peak times, with long queues (lines) not uncommon during the lunch rush and late at night. The various barbequed meats in the window are not just there for display, the duck and pork coming highly recommended. Be prepared to share and do play nice if you're put on one of the communal tables.

NOTA BENE

180 Queen Street West
Chinatown
Toronto
Ontario M5V 3X3
+1 4169776400
www.notabenerestaurant.com

Opening hours.............5 days for lunch and 6 days for dinner
Reservation policy..Yes
Credit cards...Accepted
Price range..Expensive
Style...Smart casual
Cuisine...International
Recommended for...Wish I'd opened

SWATOW

Recommended by
Claudio Aprile

309 Spadina Avenue
Chinatown
Toronto
Ontario M5T 2E6
+1 41669770601

Opening hours................................7 days for lunch and dinner
Reservation policy...No
Credit cards...Not accepted
Price range..Budget
Style...Casual
Cuisine..Chinese
Recommended for..Late night

'For my late-night guilty pleasure I go to Swatow for
the General Tso chicken and cold tea.'—Claudio Aprile

CAVA

Recommended by
Michael Steh

1560 Yonge Street
Deer Park
Toronto
Ontario M4T 2S9
+1 4169799918
www.cavarestaurant.ca

Opening hours...7 days for dinner
Reservation policy...Yes
Credit cards...Accepted
Price range..Affordable
Style...Casual
Cuisine..Spanish
Recommended for...High end

KHAO SAN ROAD

Recommended by
Claudio Aprile

326 Adelaide Street West
Entertainment District
Toronto
Ontario M5V 1P7
+1 6473525773
www.khaosanroad.ca

Opening hours................................6 days for lunch and dinner
Reservation policy...No
Reservation email...................reservations@khaosanroad.ca
Credit cards...Accepted
Price range..Budget
Style...Casual
Cuisine...Thai
Recommended for...Bargain

'I get mad cravings for the Pad Thai.'—Claudio Aprile

GEORGE RESTAURANT

Recommended by
Paul Newman

111c Queen Street East
Garden District
Toronto
Ontario M5C 1S2
+1 4168636006
www.georgeonqueen.com

Opening hours................................5 days for lunch and dinner
Reservation policy...Yes
Credit cards...Accepted
Price range..Affordable
Style..Smart casual
Cuisine..International
Recommended for..Worth the travel

'Interesting menu compilations.'—Paul Newman

STARFISH OYSTER BED & GRILL

Recommended by
Paul Newman

100 Adelaide Street East
Garden District
Toronto
Ontario M5C 1K9
+1 4163667827
www.starfishoysterbed.com

Opening hours.............5 days for lunch and 7 days for dinner
Reservation policy...Yes
Credit cards...Accepted
Price range..Affordable
Style..Smart casual
Cuisine..Seafood
Recommended for..Worth the travel

'Amazing fresh oysters and mussels.'—Paul Newman

TORITO

Recommended by
Claudio Aprile

276 Augusta Avenue
Kensington Market
Toronto
Ontario M5T 2L9
+1 4169617373
www.toritorestaurant.com

Opening hours...7 days for dinner
Reservation policy...Yes
Credit cards...Accepted
Price range..Affordable
Style...Casual
Cuisine..Tapas
Recommended for..Local favourite

'When I need a Spanish fix I head here.'
—Claudio Aprile

PIZZA GIGI

Recommended by
Michael Steh

189 Harbord Street
Little Italy
Toronto
Ontario M5S 1H5
+1 4165354444
www.pizzagigi.ca

Opening hours	7 days for dinner
Reservation policy	No
Credit cards	Not accepted
Price range	Budget
Style	Casual
Cuisine	Pizza
Recommended for	Late night

Before it became the punch line to endless jokes involving college students and late night munchies, Gigi was Toronto's go-to joint for an old school pizza slice in the small hours. Back in 2011, despite the police finding C$1m-worth of marijuana (and various other drugs) on the premises, it re-opened less than a month later. A fixture on Harbord Street in the Annex neighbourhood since 1973, you can have your crust thin or thick, but the generously sloppy toppings remain unapologetically retro – they even do a Hawaiian. Just don't make any jokes about fresh herbs – they've heard them all before.

CHANTECLER

Recommended by
Claudio Aprile

1320 Queen Street West
Parkdale
Toronto
Ontario M6K 1L4
+1 4166283586
www.restaurantchantecler.ca

Opening hours	5 days for dinner
Reservation policy	No
Credit cards	Not accepted
Price range	Affordable
Style	Casual
Cuisine	European-Asian
Recommended for	High end

'The stand-out dish was the hen with oyster sauce. An incredible combination of flavours.'—Claudio Aprile

TERRONI

Recommended by
Claudio Aprile

1095 Yonge Street
Summerhill
Toronto
Ontario M4W 2L8
+1 4169254020
www.terroni.com

Opening hours	7 days for lunch and dinner
Reservation policy	Yes
Credit cards	Accepted
Price range	Budget
Style	Casual
Cuisine	Italian
Recommended for	Regular neighbourhood

'For the last ten years I've been ordering the same thing: insalata nizzarda and pizza marinara.' —Claudio Aprile

JACOB'S & CO. STEAKHOUSE

Recommended by
Marc Fosh

12 Brant Street
Trinity-Niagara
Toronto
Ontario M5V 2M1
+1 4163660200
www.jacobssteakhouse.com

Opening hours	7 days for lunch and dinner
Reservation policy	Yes
Reservation email	reservations@jacobssteakhouse.com
Credit cards	Accepted
Price range	Expensive
Style	Casual
Cuisine	Steakhouse
Recommended for	Worth the travel

'Free-range, Ontario, grass-fed bone-in ribeye. The best steak I have ever eaten.'—Marc Fosh

'THE CHEF COOKS WITH CONFIDENCE AND A GREAT KNOWLEDGE AND RESPECT FOR CANADIAN PRODUCE.'
LEE COOPER P476

'IT MAKES A SIMPLE, INEXPENSIVE BUT FANTASTIC SUNDAY BRUNCH.'
ELOI DION P475

MONTREAL

'Contemporary, slightly on the rustic side, with the addition of rare local ingredients, makes this place unique.'
ELOI DION P474

'THE BURGER WITH FOIE GRAS IS EVIL...'
CHRISTOPHE MICHALAK P475

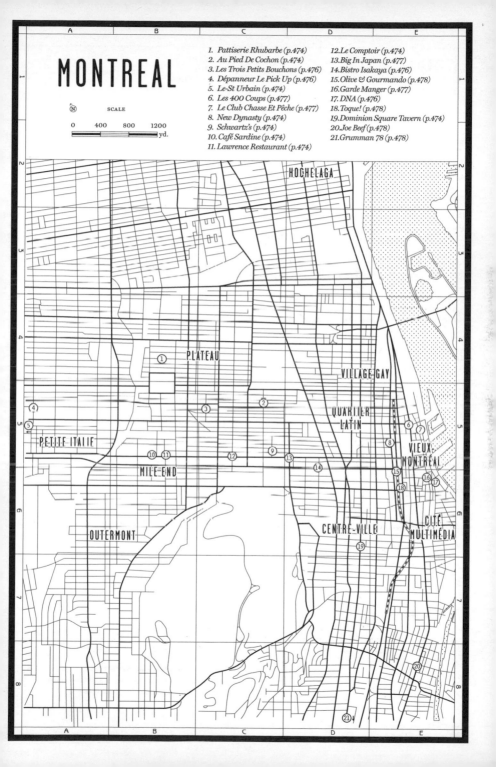

MONTREAL

SCALE

0   400   800   1200
|____|____|____|____| yd.

HOCHELAGA

PLATEAU

VILLAGE GAY

QUARTIER
LATIN

PETITE ITALIE

VIEUX
MONTRÉAL

MILE-END

OUTERMONT

CENTRE-VILLE

CITÉ
MULTIMÉDIA

LE ST-URBAIN

Recommended by
Eloi Dion

96 Rue Fleury Ouest
Ahuntsic-Cartierville
Montreal
Quebec H3L 1T2
+1 5145047700
www.lesturbain.com

Opening hours	4 days for lunch and 5 days for dinner
Reservation policy	Yes
Credit cards	Accepted
Price range	Affordable
Style	Casual
Cuisine	Modern Canadian
Recommended for	Local favourite

'Marc-André Royal's curiosity, taste and great knowledge of technique goes into every dish that is served in his restaurant. Contemporary, slightly on the rustic side, with the addition of rare local indigenous ingredients, makes this place unique. It's rare also to find more than fifty different wines by the glass.'—Eloi Dion

DOMINION SQUARE TAVERN

Recommended by
Marc-André Jetté

1243 Rue Metcalfe
Downtown
Montreal
Quebec H3B 2V5
+1 5145645056
www.dominiontavern.com

Opening hours	5 days for lunch and 7 days for dinner
Reservation policy	Yes
Credit cards	Accepted
Price range	Affordable
Style	Casual
Cuisine	French-Canadian Bistro
Recommended for	Regular neighbourhood

CAFÉ SARDINE

Recommended by
Eloi Dion, Marc-André Jetté

9 Avenue Fairmount Est
Mile End
Montreal
Quebec H2T 1C7
+1 5148028899
www.cafesardine.com

Opening hours	7 days for breakfast, lunch and dinner
Reservation policy	No
Credit cards	Accepted
Price range	Budget
Style	Casual
Cuisine	Café-Bar-Bistro
Recommended for	Late night

Packing them in like the fish from which it takes its name, newcomer Café Sardine in stylish Mile End is café by day, restaurant by night. As a café, it's no ordinary one, serving single origin coffee (from Calgary roasters Phil & Sebastian) and the likes of chocolate and fleur de sel doughnuts and a devilish good duck egg muffin. Things get even more exciting come evening time when the gin and tonics (with a hint of sage and chartreuse) flow until 1.00 a.m. and diners split orders of beetroot (beet), marjoram and buttermilk or smoked quail, red cabbage and juniper from Aaron Langille's creative small plates menu.

LE COMPTOIR

Recommended by
Eloi Dion,
Marc-André Jetté

4807 Boulevard Saint-Laurent
Mile End
Montreal
Quebec H2T 1R6
+1 5148448467
www.comptoircharcuteriesetvins.ca

Opening hours	5 days for brunch and 7 days for dinner
Reservation policy	Yes
Reservation email	info@comptoircharcuteriesetvins.ca
Credit cards	Accepted
Price range	Affordable
Style	Casual
Cuisine	European small plates
Recommended for	Regular neighbourhood

'I love their small-plates formula. There's a long counter in front of the open kitchen and it feels almost like you're sitting at a sushi bar, except in a contemporary, rustic decor. Recently I caved for roasted cauliflowers dipped in butter and set on warm anchovy paste – a reinvented bagna cauda.'—Eloi Dion

LAWRENCE RESTAURANT

Recommended by
Marc-André Jetté,
Ségué Lepage

5201 Boulevard Saint-Laurent
Mile End
Montreal
Quebec H2T 1S4
+1 5145031070
www.lawrencerestaurant.com

Opening hours	5 days for brunch and 4 days for dinner
Reservation policy	Yes
Reservation email	lawrence@lawrencerestaurant.com
Credit cards	Accepted
Price range	Affordable
Style	Casual
Cuisine	Modern French
Recommended for	Breakfast

NEW DYNASTY

Recommended by
Ségué Lepage

1110 Rue Clark
Mile End
Montreal
Quebec H2Z 1K3
+1 5148718778

Opening hours	7 days for lunch and dinner
Reservation policy	Yes
Credit cards	Accepted
Price range	Budget
Style	Casual
Cuisine	Chinese
Recommended for	Breakfast

AU PIED DE COCHON

Recommended by
Matthew Harris, Linton Hopkins,
Normand Laprise, Christophe
Michalak, Michael Steh

536 Avenue Duluth Est
Le Plateau-Mont-Royal
Montreal
Quebec H2L 1A9
+1 5142811114
www.restaurantaupieddecochon.ca

Opening hours	6 days for dinner
Reservation policy	Yes
Reservation email	aupieddecochon@qc.aira.com
Credit cards	Accepted
Price range	Affordable
Style	Smart casual
Cuisine	Modern French
Recommended for	Local favourite

'The burger with foie gras is evil...'
—Christophe Michalak

Martin Picard's cult Québécois outpost has carved out a decadent reputation for itself since opening in 2001. Picard made his name here with his pork and foie gras fixated menu, which incorporates these ingredients into everything – including the local delicacy that is poutine (chips [fries] topped with cheese curd and gravy), burgers, more typically French applications such as terrines and boudin noir tarts – and stuffing it generously inside the restaurant's namesake. Meanwhile, Picard's famous Duck-in-a-can is magret and more foie gras, cooked and brought to the table in said can and dumped on toast topped with celeriac purée.

PATISSERIE RHUBARBE

Recommended by
Eloi Dion

5091 Rue de Lanaudière
Le Plateau-Mont-Royal
Montréal
Quebec H2J 3P9
+1 5149033395
www.patisserierhubarbe.com

Opening hours	2 days for breakfast and 5 days for lunch
Reservation policy	No
Credit cards	Accepted but not AMEX
Price range	Budget
Style	Casual
Cuisine	Bakery-Café
Recommended for	Breakfast

'A lovely artisan patisserie in a popular Montreal neighbourhood, Rhubarbe makes a simple, inexpensive but fantastic Sunday brunch. It has a short menu including scones, good coffee and fresh orange juice.'—Eloi Dion

SCHWARTZ'S

Recommended by
Armand Arnal

3895 Boulevard Saint-Laurent
Le Plateau-Mont-Royal
Montreal
Quebec H2W 1X9
+1 5148424813
www.schwartzsdeli.com

Opening hours	7 days for breakfast, lunch and dinner
Reservation policy	No
Credit cards	Not accepted
Price range	Budget
Style	Casual
Cuisine	Deli-Café
Recommended for	Bargain

LES TROIS PETITS BOUCHONS

Recommended by
Ségué Lepage

4669 Rue Saint-Denis
Le Plateau-Mont-Royal
Montreal
Quebec H2J 2L5
+1 5142854444
www.lestroispetitsbouchons.com

Opening hours	6 days for dinner
Reservation policy	Yes
Credit cards	Accepted
Price range	Affordable
Style	Casual
Cuisine	French
Recommended for	Regular neighbourhood

BISTRO ISAKAYA

Recommended by
Normand Laprise

3469 Avenue du Parc
Quartier Milton-Parc
Montreal
Quebec H2X 2H6
+1 5148458226
www.bistroisakaya.com

Opening hours	4 days for lunch and 6 days for dinner
Reservation policy	Yes
Credit cards	Accepted
Price range	Budget
Style	Casual
Cuisine	Japanese
Recommended for	Bargain

DÉPANNEUR LE PICK UP

Recommended by
Eloi Dion, Ségué Lepage

7032 Rue Waverly
Rosemont-La Petite-Patrie
Montreal
Quebec H2S 3J2
+1 514 2718011
www.depanneurlepickup.com

Opening hours	7 days from breakfast until late
Reservation policy	No
Reservation email	lepickupevents@gmail.com
Credit cards	Not accepted
Price range	Budget
Style	Casual
Cuisine	Deli-Café
Recommended for	Bargain

Montréal's coolest 'dep' – Québécois slang for convenience store – is a uniquely Montrealais beast. Where else can one pop in for a six-pack of beer or some home-baked gluten-free biscuits (cookies), hang at the lunch counter over a chipotle club sandwich, attend a butchery workshop or backyard pop-up supper? Very 'now' it may be, but Le Pick Up oozes old-school charm. Opened in 2008, it inherited its vintage diner counter from the previous owners (along with a killer steak hero recipe) and now brings in a mix of old regulars, artists and slackers, united by their love of pulled pork sandwiches laced with chipotle mayo.

DNA

Recommended by
Lee Cooper, Vikram Vij

355 Rue Marguerite D'Youville
Vieux-Montréal
Montreal
Quebec H2Y 2C4
+1 5142873362
www.dnarestaurant.com

Opening hours	5 days for dinner
Reservation policy	Yes
Reservation email	info@dnarestaurant.com
Credit cards	Accepted
Price range	Affordable
Style	Casual
Cuisine	Canadian-European
Recommended for	Worth the travel

'When in Montreal I always make a point of dining at DNA restaurant. Derek Dammann is a tremendous chef who cooks with confidence and a great knowledge and respect for Canadian produce, especially fish and meat. It has an Italian-influenced menu – his pasta dishes and charcuterie programme are excellent. Last I heard he was using almost exclusively Canadian products in his kitchen.'—Lee Cooper

LES 400 COUPS

Recommended by
Eloi Dion, Ségué Lepage

400 Rue Notre-Dame Est
Ville-Marie
Montreal
Quebec H2Y 1C8
+1 5149850400
www.les400coups.ca

Opening hours	1 day for lunch and 5 days for dinner
Reservation policy	Yes
Reservation email	info@les400coups.ca
Credit cards	Accepted
Price range	Affordable
Style	Casual
Cuisine	Modern French
Recommended for	Wish I'd opened

'Perfect size, location, decor and ambiance. And of
course I admire the demonstration of talent by these
two chefs. It all makes this place wonderful.'
—Eloi Dion

BIG IN JAPAN

Recommended by
Normand Laprise

3723 Boulevard Saint-Laurent
Ville-Marie
Montreal
Quebec H2X 2V7
| 1 5148472222
www.biginjapan.ca

Opening hours	5 days for lunch and 7 days for dinner
Reservation policy	Yes
Credit cards	Accepted
Price range	Budget
Style	Casual
Cuisine	Japanese
Recommended for	Bargain

LE CLUB CHASSE ET PÊCHE

Recommended by
Jeremy Charles

423 Rue Saint-Claude
Ville-Marie
Montreal
Quebec H2Y 3B6
+1 5148611112
www.leclubchasseetpeche.com

Opening hours	5 days for dinner
Reservation policy	Yes
Credit cards	Accepted
Price range	Affordable
Style	Smart casual
Cuisine	Modern Canadian
Recommended for	Worth the travel

Since it opened in late 2004, Le Club Chasse et Pêche
has become known as one of the best restaurants
in Montreal. Set back from a cobbled street in the
city's old quarter, with a crest of antlers and fish
hanging by the door, it serves fresh and modern
Canadian cuisine with a special emphasis – as the
name suggests – on game and fish. The surf and
turf includes Kobe beef and lobster tail, and they
do a great scallop and braised piglet risotto. It's
a loud and boisterous place popular with
young Montrealers.

GARDE MANGER

Recommended by
Carles Abellan

408 Rue Saint-François-Xavier
Ville-Marie
Montreal
Quebec H2Y 2S9
+1 5146785044
www.crownsalts.com/gardemanger

Opening hours	6 days for dinner
Reservation policy	Yes
Credit cards	Accepted
Price range	Expensive
Style	Smart casual
Cuisine	International
Recommended for	Worth the travel

Tattooed and talented, young turk Chuck Hughes
opened Garde Manger in Vieux-Montréal in 2006,
on a mission to serve great food in edgy, clubby
surroundings. Although, as an Iron Chef American
winner, he's now what you'd call a bona fide celebrity
chef, Hughes still runs a happening, credible joint.
Blackboard menus change daily to allow for seasonal
changes, though there's an outcry whenever the
lobster poutine, tomato and fried Cheddar salad or
deep-fried Mars Bar are off. Reservations go fast,
so be sure to book a month ahead. When/if you get
in, don't miss the Bloody Caesar cocktail with snow
crab garnish.

OLIVE & GOURMANDO

Recommended by
Mindy Segal

351 Saint-Paul West
Ville-Marie
Montreal
Quebec H2Y 2A7I

Opening hours	5 days for breakfast and lunch
Reservation policy	No
Credit cards	Accepted
Price range	Budget
Style	Casual
Cuisine	Bakery-Café
Recommended for	Worth the travel

TOQUÉ!

Recommended by
Eloi Dion

900 Place Jean Paul Riopelle
Ville-Marie
Montreal
Quebec H2Z 2B2
+1 5144992084
www.restaurant-toque.com

Opening hours	4 days for lunch and 5 days for dinner
Reservation policy	Yes
Credit cards	Accepted
Price range	Expensive
Style	Smart casual
Cuisine	Modern French-Canadian
Recommended for	High end

'A real gastronomic restaurant. Normand Laprise
and his brigade are working with very high-end
products; most of them are from the region.'
—Eloi Dion

GRUMMAN 78

Recommended by
Marc-André Jetté

630 Rue de Courcelle
Westmount
Montreal
Quebec H4C 3C7
+1 5142905125
www.grumman78.com

Opening hours	5 days for lunch and dinner
Reservation policy	Yes
Credit cards	Accepted
Price range	Budget
Style	Casual
Cuisine	Mexican
Recommended for	Bargain

JOE BEEF

Recommended by
Normand Laprise,
Gabriel Rucker

2491 Rue Notre-Dame Ouest
Westmount
Montreal
Quebec H3J 1N6
+1 5149356504
www.joebeef.ca

Opening hours	5 days for dinner
Reservation policy	Yes
Credit cards	Accepted
Price range	Affordable
Style	Casual
Cuisine	Steakhouse-Seafood
Recommended for	Local favourite

'A beautiful, modern Napa Valley restaurant.'

MITCHELL ROSENTHAL P484

'The people watching is great late at night.'

MITCHELL ROSENTHAL P482

USA WEST

'This place in Phoenix gave me the courage to open a restaurant that maintains a strong point of view.'

RUSSELL MOORE P482

'IT'S SET RIGHT ON THE BAY WITH BEAUTIFUL SUNSETS. THE INGREDIENTS IN HAWAII ARE SOME OF THE BEST AND THE FOOD IS OUT OF THIS WORLD. THE OPEN KITCHEN IS A CHEF'S DREAM!'

BRADLEY TURLEY P485

'Just about everything there is farmed, fished or foraged locally and tastes delicious.'

JASON FOX P485

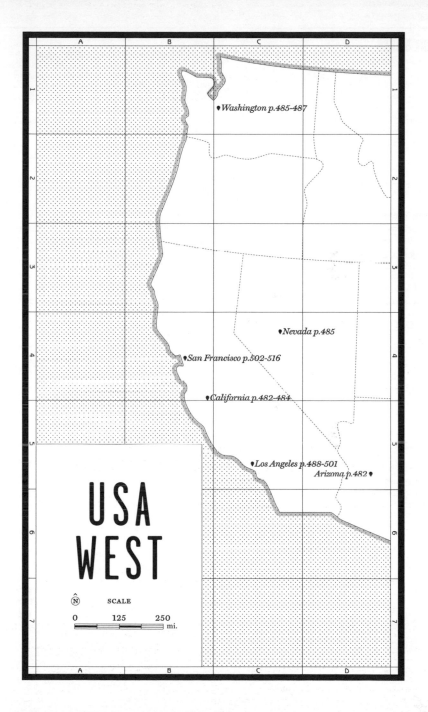

USA
WEST

N   SCALE

0   125   250
mi.

PIZZERIA BIANCO

Recommended by
Russell Moore

623 East Adams Street
Phoenix
Arizona 85004
www.pizzeriabianco.com

Opening hours	6 days for lunch and dinner
Reservation policy	No
Credit cards	Accepted
Price range	Budget
Style	Casual
Cuisine	Pizza
Recommended for	Wish I'd opened

'I am really inspired by restaurants that take a stand and feel personal. Restaurants like Pizzeria Bianco in Phoenix gave me the courage to open a restaurant that maintains a strong point of view.'—Russell Moore

IN-N-OUT

Recommended by
Walter Manzke, Mitchell
Rosenthal, Keith Silverton

13850 Francisquito Avenue
Baldwin Park
California 91706
+1 8007861000
www.in-n-out.com

Opening hours	7 days for breakfast, lunch and dinner
Reservation policy	No
Credit cards	Accepted
Price range	Budget
Style	Casual
Cuisine	Burgers
Recommended for	Late night

'Nothing tastes better then a Double-Double Cheeseburger and side of chips (fries). The people watching is great late at night.'—Mitchell Rosenthal

MANRESA

Recommended by
Mauro Colagreco, Peter
Doyle, Dan Hunter,
Steve Samson

320 Village Lane
Los Gatos
California 95030
+1 4083544330
www.manresarestaurant.com

Opening hours	5 days for dinner
Reservation policy	Yes
Credit cards	Accepted
Price range	Expensive
Style	Smart casual
Cuisine	Modern American
Recommended for	Wish I'd opened

'I admire David's philosophy. His cuisine is refined and absolutely delicious. Bravo!'—Mauro Colagreco

Nestled in a well-heeled San Jose suburb, Manresa might be easily missed by the unobservant but it is no culinary wallflower. Enigmatic and humble, chef-proprietor David Kinch has been thrilling diners with his unfussy yet inventive presentations of California's bounty for over ten years. A 'chef's chef', his two-Michelin-star food defies categorization, though a tip o' the hat to Alice Waters at Chez Panisse might give you an idea of what to expect. The ingredient-led tasting menu, which champions produce supplied by local biodynamic growers at Love Apple Farm, and shuns sous vide, siphons and molecular experimentation, has won Manresa widespread acclaim.

TINTO

Recommended by
Ben Roche

Saguaro Hotel
1800 East Palm Canyon Drive
Palm Springs
California 92264
+1 7603221900
www.jdvhotels.com

Opening hours	7 days for breakfast, lunch and dinner
Reservation policy	Yes
Credit cards	Accepted
Price range	Affordable
Style	Smart casual
Cuisine	Basque
Recommended for	Worth the travel

HANA

Recommended by
Michael Mina

101 Golf Course Drive
Rohnert Park
California 94928
+1 7075860270
www.hanajapanese.com

Opening hours	6 days for lunch and 7 days for dinner
Reservation policy	Yes
Credit cards	Accepted
Price range	Affordable
Style	Casual
Cuisine	Japanese
Recommended for	Regular neighbourhood

MARINUS

Recommended by
Michael Ferraro

415 West Carmel Valley Road
Carmel Valley
San Diego
California 93924
+1 8316583595
www.bernardus.com

Opening hours	5 days for dinner
Reservation policy	Yes
Credit cards	Accepted
Price range	Affordable
Style	Smart casual
Cuisine	Modern American
Recommended for	Worth the travel

THE RESTAURANT

Recommended by
Tim Cushman,
Jason Fox

Meadowood Hotel
900 Meadowood Lane
St. Helena
California 94574
+1 7079671205
www.meadowood.com

Opening hours	6 days for dinner
Reservation policy	Yes
Reservation email	reservations@meadowood.com
Credit cards	Accepted
Price range	Expensive
Style	Smart casual
Cuisine	Modern American
Recommended for	High end

TWO BIRD CAFÉ

Recommended by
Michael Mina

625 San Geronimo Valley Drive
San Geronimo
California 94963
+1 4154880105
www.twobirdcafe.com

Opening hours	7 days for brunch and 5 days for dinner
Reservation policy	Yes
Credit cards	Accepted
Price range	Affordable
Style	Casual
Cuisine	American
Recommended for	Breakfast

Just outside the Roy's Redwoods Open Space Preserve, and in the Marin coast's pretty hamlet of San Geronimo, the Two Bird Café serves some of the best breakfasts north of San Francisco. They've won an award for their brunches, which include fluffy omelettes, blueberry pancakes, pan-fried trout with eggs, grilled lamb chops with potatoes and terrific eggs benedict – diners frequently don't need to eat again that day. The dining room has an open fire in winter and the beautiful gardens are perfect for a stroll in summer. A rustic and welcome place with comfortable beds.

RESTAURANTE LOS PINOS

Recommended by
David Kinch

2019 North Pacific Avenue
Santa Cruz
California 95060
www.lospinosrestaurante.com

Opening hours	7 days for breakfast, lunch and dinner
Reservation policy	No
Credit cards	Accepted
Price range	Budget
Style	Casual
Cuisine	Mexican
Recommended for	Regular neighbourhood

'A cool little Mexican place where the quality is up a notch. They make a beautiful guacamole to order, and it is worth the wait.'—David Kinch

SOIF WINE BAR

Recommended by
Brett Barnes, David Kinch

105 Walnut Avenue
Santa Cruz
California 95060
+1 8314232020
www.soifwine.com

Opening hours	7 days for dinner
Reservation policy	Yes
Credit cards	Accepted
Price range	Affordable
Style	Casual
Cuisine	Bar-Bistro
Recommended for	Regular neighbourhood

'A little wine bar not far from my house that I frequent for a glass of wine and a simple plate of food.'
—David Kinch

BOTTEGA RISTORANTE

Recommended by
Carrie Nahabedian

6525 Washington Street
Yountville
California 94599
+1 7079451050
www.botteganapavalley.com

Opening hours	6 days for lunch and 7 days for dinner
Reservation policy	Yes
Credit cards	Accepted
Price range	Affordable
Style	Casual
Cuisine	Italian
Recommended for	Worth the travel

BOUCHON

Recommended by
Timothy Johnson,
Jarrod Verbiak

6534 Washington Street
Yountville
California 94599
+1 7079448037
www.bouchonbistro.com

Opening hours	7 days for lunch and dinner
Reservation policy	Yes
Credit cards	Accepted
Price range	Affordable
Style	Smart casual
Cuisine	French
Recommended for	Wish I'd opened

'A classic and simplistic approach to French bistro cooking.'—Jarrod Verbiak

THE FRENCH LAUNDRY

Recommended by
Matthew Accarrino, Andoni Luis
Aduriz, Jason Atherton, Daniel
Boulud, Mathias Dahlgren,
Christian Domschitz, Raphael
Dworak, Paul Foster, André
Garrett, Gerald Hirigoyen, Onno
Kokmeijer, Corey Lee, Carrie
Nahabedian, Uwe Opocensky,
Jockey Petrie, Gabriel Rucker,
Michael Tusk

6640 Washington Street
Yountville
California 94599
+1 7079442380
www.frenchlaundry.com

Opening hours	3 days for lunch and 7 days for dinner
Reservation policy	Yes
Credit cards	Accepted
Price range	Expensive
Style	Formal
Cuisine	Modern American
Recommended for	Wish I'd opened

'Having worked for Chef Keller, I experienced first hand the impact he has had on chefs and dining in America. It is a legacy any chef would be honoured to have created.'—Matthew Accarrino

REDD

Recommended by
Mitchell Rosenthal

6480 Washington Street
Yountville
California 94599
+1 7079442222
www.reddnapavalley.com

Opening hours	7 days for lunch and dinner
Reservation policy	Yes
Credit cards	Accepted
Price range	Affordable
Style	Smart casual
Cuisine	Modern American
Recommended for	Wish I'd opened

'A beautiful, modern Napa Valley restaurant run by an old friend, Richard Reddington.'—Mitchell Rosenthal

ROY'S

Recommended by
Bradley Turley

6600 Kalanianaole Highway
Honolulu
Hawaii 96825
+1 8083967697
www.roysrestaurant.com

Opening hours	7 days for dinner
Reservation policy	Yes
Credit cards	Accepted
Price range	Affordable
Style	Smart casual
Cuisine	Hawaiian Asian
Recommended for	Wish I'd opened

'It's set right on the bay with beautiful sunsets. The ingredients in Hawaii are some of the best and Roy's food is out of this world. The open kitchen is a chef's dream!'—Bradley Turley

L'ATELIER DE JOEL ROBUCHON

Recommended by
Bruce Bromberg,
Adam Horton

MGM Grand Hotel Casino
3799 Las Vegas Boulevard South
The Strip
Las Vegas
Nevada 89109
+1 7028917358
www.mgmgrand.com/restaurants

Opening hours	7 days for dinner
Reservation policy	Yes
Credit cards	Accepted
Price range	Expensive
Style	Smart casual
Cuisine	French
Recommended for	High end

'Incredible.'—Adam Horton

SAGE

Recommended by
Bruce Bromberg,
Bradley Turley

Aria Hotel Casino
3730 Las Vegas Boulevard
The Strip
Las Vegas
Nevada 89158
+1 8772302742
www.arialasvegas.com/dining/sage.aspx

Opening hours	6 days for dinner
Reservation policy	Yes
Credit cards	Accepted
Price range	Expensive
Style	Smart casual
Cuisine	Modern American
Recommended for	Worth the travel

THE WILLOWS INN

Recommended by
Andrew Carmellini,
Jason Fox

2579 West Shore Drive
Lummi Island
Washington 98262
+1 3607582620
www.willows-inn.com

Opening hours	5 days for dinner
Reservation policy	Yes
Credit cards	Accepted
Price range	Expensive
Style	Smart casual
Cuisine	Modern American
Recommended for	Worth the travel

'Just about everything there is farmed, fished or foraged locally and tastes delicious.'—Jason Fox

BELLTOWN PIZZA

Recommended by
Blaine Wetzel

2422 1st Avenue
Belltown
Seattle
Washington 98121
www.belltownpizza.net

Opening hours...........2 days for brunch and 7 days for dinner
Reservation policy..No
Credit cards..Accepted
Price range...Budget
Style..Casual
Cuisine..Pizza
Recommended for...Late night

LA BÊTE

Recommended by
Brendan McGill

1802 Bellevue Avenue
Capitol Hill
Seattle
Washington 98122
+1 2063294047
www.labeteseattle.com

Opening hours................................6 days for dinner
Reservation policy...Yes
Credit cards..Accepted
Price range..Affordable
Style..Casual
Cuisine...Northwest American
Recommended for.................................Wish I'd opened

'Chef-owned restaurant serving imaginative refined
food in a beautiful room. An industry hang-out.'
—Brendan McGill

CAFÉ PRESSE

Recommended by
Brendan McGill

1117 12th Avenue
Central Business District
Seattle
Washington 98122
+1 2067097674
www.cafepresseseattle.com

Opening hours..............7 days for breakfast, lunch and dinner
Reservation policy...Yes
Credit cards..Accepted
Price range...Budget
Style..Casual
Cuisine..French
Recommended for...Breakfast

CANLIS

Recommended by
Blaine Wetzel

2576 Aurora Avenue North
East Queen Anne
Seattle
Washington 98109
+1 2062833313
www.canlis.com

Opening hours................................6 days for dinner
Reservation policy...Yes
Credit cards..Accepted
Price range...Expensive
Style..Formal
Cuisine...Modern American
Recommended for..................................Worth the travel

MAEKAWA BAR

Recommended by
Brendan McGill

601 South King Street
International District
Seattle
Washington 98104
+1 2066220634

Opening hours................................6 days for dinner
Reservation policy...Yes
Credit cards..Accepted
Price range...Budget
Style..Casual
Cuisine..Japanese
Recommended for...Late night

MANEKI

Recommended by
Matthew Dillon

304 6th Avenue South
International District
Seattle
Washington 98104
+1 2066222631
www.manekirestaurant.com

Opening hours................................6 days for dinner
Reservation policy...Yes
Credit cards..Accepted
Price range...Budget
Style..Casual
Cuisine..Japanese
Recommended for................................Regular neighbourhood

GOODIES MARKET

13721 Lake City Way North East
Lake City
Seattle
Washington 98125
+1 2063622694

Opening hours.........................7 days from breakfast until late
Reservation policy...No
Credit cards...Accepted
Price range...Budget
Style...Casual
Cuisine...Mediterranean
Recommended for...Bargain

'A Lebanese-owned food market with amazing *moutabal* (charcoal-grilled aubergine [eggplant] with tahini and garlic), flatbread, *makdous* (pickled young aubergine [eggplant] stuffed with walnuts and peppers) and great *sujuk* (Arabic beef salami).'
—Matthew Dillon

EZELL'S FAMOUS CHICKEN

501 23rd Avenue
Minor
Seattle
Washington 98122
www.ezellschicken.com

Opening hours..........................7 days for lunch and dinner
Reservation policy...No
Credit cards...Accepted
Price range...Budget
Style..Style
Cuisine..Southern American
Recommended for...Bargain

THE WALRUS AND THE CARPENTER

4743 Ballard Avenue Northwest
Old Ballard
Seattle
Washington 98107
www.thewalrusbar.com

Opening hours.................................7 days for dinner
Reservation policy...No
Credit cards...Accepted
Price range...Affordable
Style...Casual
Cuisine...Seafood
Recommended for.....................................Worth the travel

An oyster bar on Rain City's Ballard Avenue, The Walrus and the Carpenter oozes utilitarian elegance with its stripped floorboards, whitewashed walls and baskets of fruit, oysters and liquor decorating the steel bar. The daily-changing menu promises a choice of around eight varieties of fresh oyster and even more of them on the fish menu (fried and gratinéed), which also includes zingy dishes such as white anchovy tartine with avocado. Salads and desserts are equally bright and original – imagine Tom Thumb greens with grapefruit citronette, and roasted Medjool dates with olive oil and sea salt. The wine list is a mixture of French, Italian and West Coast American options designed to complement seafood.

QUINN'S PUB

1001 East Pike Street
Pike/Pine
Seattle
Washington 98122
www.quinnspubseattle.com

Opening hours...7 days for dinner
Reservation policy...No
Credit cards...Accepted
Price range...Affordable
Style...Casual
Cuisine..Bar-Bistro
Recommended for...Late night

GREEN LEAF

418 8th Avenue South
Yesler Terrace
Seattle
Washington 98104
www.greenleaftaste.com

Opening hours.................................7 days for lunch and dinner
Reservation policy...No
Credit cards...Accepted
Price range...Budget
Style...Casual
Cuisine..Vietnamese
Recommended for................................Regular neighbourhood

'THE ULTIMATE DINING EXPERIENCE IN LOS ANGELES.'
STEVE SAMSON P490

'TRUE, HONEST CALIFORNIA CUISINE.'
GOVIND ARMSTRONG P490

'NOT ONLY IS THE FOOD GOOD, THE SERVICE MAKES YOU FEEL JUST LIKE THE STARS THAT ARE SITTING NEXT TO YOU.'
CHRISTIAN PAGE P493

LOS ANGELES

'Snails, pig tails, veal brains, beef tongue, confit rabbit, oh my! Some seriously inspired dishes.'
BRAD FARMERIE P499

'What makes dining in LA so special is the sheer number of ethnicities that define the local food scene.'
ZACH POLLACK

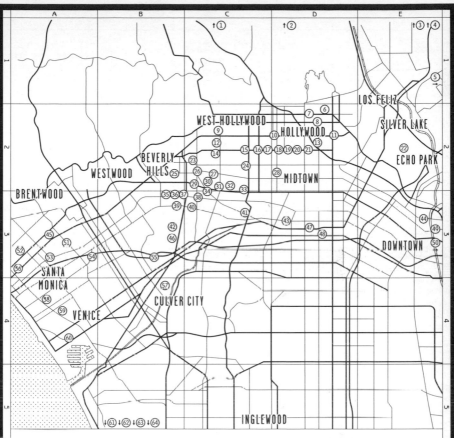

LOS ANGELES

SCALE

0   1500   3000   4500
                              yd.

BOUCHON
235 North Canon Drive
Beverly Hills
Los Angeles
California 90210
+1 3102719910
www.bouchonbistro.com

Recommended by
Govind Armstrong

Opening hours	7 days for lunch and dinner
Reservation policy	Yes
Credit cards	Accepted
Price range	Affordable
Style	Smart casual
Cuisine	French
Recommended for	High end

RED MEDICINE
8400 Wilshire Boulevard
Beverly Hills
Los Angeles
California 90211
+1 3236515500
www.redmedicinela.com

Recommended by
Claus Meyer, Steve Samson

Opening hours	7 days for dinner
Reservation policy	Yes
Credit cards	Accepted
Price range	Affordable
Style	Casual
Cuisine	Vietnamese
Recommended for	Bargain

'Medicine is mind-blowing.'—Claus Meyer

SCARPETTA
225 North Canon Drive
Beverly Hills
Los Angeles
California 90210
+1 3108607970
www.montagebeverlyhills.com

Recommended by
Adam Horton

Opening hours	1 day for brunch and 7 days for dinner
Reservation policy	Yes
Credit cards	Accepted
Price range	Expensive
Style	Smart casual
Cuisine	Italian
Recommended for	Breakfast

URASAWA
218 North Rodeo Drive
Beverly Hills
Los Angeles
California 90210
+1 3102478939

Recommended by
Tim Cushman, Neal Fraser,
Corey Lee, Steve Samson,
Ricardo Zarate

Opening hours	5 days for dinner
Reservation policy	Yes
Credit cards	Accepted
Price range	Expensive
Style	Smart casual
Cuisine	Japanese
Recommended for	High end

'Chef Urasawa is totally dedicated to his craft. He serves only ten guests a night so he is able to focus on giving the ultimate dining experience in Los Angeles.'—Steve Samson

CAMPANILE
624 South La Brea Avenue
Los Angeles
La Brea
California 90036
+1 3239381447
www.campanilerestaurant.com

Recommended by
Govind Armstrong

Opening hours	7 days for lunch and dinner
Reservation policy	Yes
Credit cards	Accepted
Price range	Affordable
Style	Smart casual
Cuisine	Italian
Recommended for	Local favourite

'True, honest California cuisine.'—Govind Armstrong

VINCENTI
11930 San Vicente Boulevard
Brentwood
Los Angeles
California 90049
+1 3102070127
www.vincentiristorante.com

Recommended by
Matt Molina

Opening hours	1 day for lunch and 6 days for dinner
Reservation policy	Yes
Credit cards	Accepted
Price range	Expensive
Style	Smart casual
Cuisine	Italian
Recommended for	Regular neighbourhood

CRAFT

Recommended by
James 'Jockey' Petrie

10100 Constellation Boulevard
Century City
Los Angeles
California 90067
+1 3102794180
www.craftrestaurantsinc.com

Opening hours	5 days for lunch and 6 days for dinner
Reservation policy	Yes
Credit cards	Accepted
Price range	Expensive
Style	Smart casual
Cuisine	Modern American
Recommended for	Worth the travel

AKASHA

Recommended by
Ricardo Zarate

9543 Culver Boulevard
Culver City
Los Angeles
California 90232
+1 3108451700
www.akasharestaurant.com

Opening hours	6 days for brunch and 7 days for dinner
Reservation policy	Yes
Credit cards	Accepted
Price range	Affordable
Style	Casual
Cuisine	Café
Recommended for	Breakfast

BÄCO MERCAT

Recommended by
Matt Molina

408 South Main Street
Downtown
Los Angeles
California 90013
+1 2136878808
www.bacomercat.com

Opening hours	7 days for brunch and dinner
Reservation policy	Yes
Credit cards	Accepted
Price range	Budget
Style	Casual
Cuisine	Spanish
Recommended for	Worth the travel

SHIN-SEN-GUMI

Recommended by
Steve Samson

18517 South Western Avenue
Gardena
Los Angeles
California 90248
+1 3107151588
www.shinsengumigroup.com

Opening hours	5 days for lunch and 7 days for dinner
Reservation policy	No
Credit cards	Accepted
Price range	Budget
Style	Casual
Cuisine	Japanese
Recommended for	Regular neighbourhood

CANELÉ

Recommended by
Christian Page

3219 Glendale Boulevard
Glendale
Los Angeles
California 90039
www.canele-la.com

Opening hours	2 days for brunch and 6 days for dinner
Reservation policy	No
Credit cards	Accepted
Price range	Affordable
Style	Casual
Cuisine	International
Recommended for	Worth the travel

'OMG what a brunch.'—Christian Page

CACTUS TACOS

Recommended by
Josef Centeno

950 Vine Street
Hollywood
Los Angeles
California 90038
+1 3234645865
www.cactustacos.com

Opening hours	7 days for lunch and dinner
Reservation policy	No
Credit cards	Not accepted
Price range	Budget
Style	Casual
Cuisine	Mexican
Recommended for	Late night

'They're always open and the tacos are always
reliably good.'—Josef Centeno

JITLADA

Recommended by
Zach Pollack

5233 West Sunset Boulevard
Hollywood
Los Angeles
California 90027
+1 3236633104
www.Jitladala.com

Opening hours	6 days for lunch and dinner
Reservation policy	Yes
Credit cards	Accepted
Price range	Budget
Style	Casual
Cuisine	Thai
Recommended for	Regular neighbourhood

LOTERIA GRILL

Recommended by
Neal Fraser

6627 Hollywood Boulevard
Hollywood
Los Angeles
California 90028
+1 3234652500
www.loteriagrill.com

Opening hours	7 days for breakfast, lunch and dinner
Reservation policy	Yes
Credit cards	Accepted
Price range	Budget
Style	Casual
Cuisine	Mexican
Recommended for	Regular neighbourhood

THE RESTAURANT

Recommended by
Josef Centeno, Jean-
François Piège

Chateau Marmont
8221 Sunset Boulevard
Hollywood
Los Angeles
California 90046
+1 3238485908
www.chateaumarmont.com

Opening hours	7 days for breakfast, lunch and dinner
Reservation policy	Yes
Credit cards	Accepted
Price range	Expensive
Style	Smart casual
Cuisine	American
Recommended for	Breakfast

'The quietness of Château Marmont is unequalled. The breakfast there is very special.'—Jean-François Piège

There's not an official dress code at Chateau Marmont, but best bring your sunglasses, otherwise you might feel left out. Built on Sunset Boulevard in 1927, modelled loosely on a Loire Valley château, breakfast in its restaurant provides an accessible hit of Hollywood hotel glamour for those who can't afford to cough up for a room – and somewhere to start the day for those who can. The menu takes in the usual American classics: buttermilk pancakes, two types of French toast (one plain brioche, the other almond crunchy) and a soft-boiled egg that they describe as coming with 'accoutrements' rather than toast.

SANAMLUANG CAFÉ

Recommended by
Adam Horton

5170 Hollywood Boulevard
Hollywood
Los Angeles
California 90027
+1 3236608006

Opening hours	7 days for lunch and dinner
Reservation policy	No
Credit cards	Not accepted
Price range	Budget
Style	Casual
Cuisine	Thai
Recommended for	Regular neighbourhood

'Great grilled pork.'—Adam Horton

SQUARE ONE DINING

Recommended by
Steve Samson

4854 Fountain Avenue
Hollywood
Los Angeles
California 90029
+1 3236611109
www.squareonedining.com

Opening hours	7 days for breakfast and lunch
Reservation policy	No
Credit cards	Accepted
Price range	Budget
Style	Casual
Cuisine	American
Recommended for	Breakfast

STREET

Recommended by
Scott Conant,
Jean-François Piège

742 North Highland Avenue
Hollywood
Los Angeles
California 90038
+1 3232030500
www.eatatstreet.com

Opening hours	3 days for lunch and 7 days for dinner
Reservation policy	Yes
Credit cards	Accepted
Price range	Budget
Style	Casual
Cuisine	International Small plates
Recommended for	Worth the travel

YAI

Recommended by
Neal Fraser

5757 Hollywood Boulevard
Hollywood
Los Angeles
California 90028
www.yai.menutoeat.com

Opening hours	7 days for lunch and dinner
Reservation policy	No
Credit cards	Not accepted
Price range	Budget
Style	Casual
Cuisine	Thai
Recommended for	Late night

DAIKOKUYA

Recommended by
Christian Page

327 East 1st Street
Little Tokyo
Los Angeles
California 90012
+1 2136261680
www.dkramen.com

Opening hours	7 days for lunch and dinner
Reservation policy	No
Credit cards	Not accepted
Price range	Budget
Style	Casual
Cuisine	Japanese
Recommended for	Bargain

SUSHI GEN

Recommended by
Ricardo Zarate

422 East 2nd Street
Little Tokyo
Los Angeles
California 90012
+1 2136170552
www.sushigenla.com

Opening hours	5 days for lunch and 6 days for dinner
Reservation policy	Yes
Credit cards	Accepted
Price range	Affordable
Style	Casual
Cuisine	Japanese
Recommended for	Regular neighbourhood

MANHATTAN BEACH POST

Recommended by
Steve Samson

1142 Manhattan Avenue
Manhattan Beach
Los Angeles
California 90266
+1 3105455405
www.eatmbpost.com

Opening hours	2 days for brunch and 7 days for dinner
Reservation policy	Yes
Credit cards	Accepted
Price range	Affordable
Style	Casual
Cuisine	American
Recommended for	Local favourite

'Good, unique food and a laid-back and friendly
atmosphere, by the beach.'—Steve Samson

OSTERIA MOZZA

Recommended by
Govind Armstrong,
Christian Page

6602 Melrose Avenue
Melrose
Los Angeles
California 90038
+1 3232970100
www.osteriamozza.com

Opening hours	7 days for dinner
Reservation policy	Yes
Credit cards	Accepted
Price range	Expensive
Style	Smart casual
Cuisine	Italian
Recommended for	High end

'Not only is the food good, the service makes you feel
just like the stars that are sitting next to you.'
—Christian Page

ANGELINI OSTERIA

Recommended by
Walter Manzke

7313 Beverly Boulevard
Mid-City West
Los Angeles
California 90036
+1 3232970070
www.angeliniosteria.com

Opening hours	4 days for lunch and 6 days for dinner
Reservation policy	Yes
Reservation email	info@angeliniosteria.com
Credit cards	Accepted
Price range	Affordable
Style	Casual
Cuisine	Italian
Recommended for	Regular neighbourhood

FŌNUTS

Recommended by
Christina Tosi

8104 West 3rd Street
Mid-City West
Los Angeles
California 90048
www.fonuts.com

Opening hours	6 days for breakfast and lunch
Reservation policy	No
Credit cards	Accepted
Price range	Budget
Style	Casual
Cuisine	Bakery-Café
Recommended for	Wish I'd opened

'Waylynn is a genius and I wish it were my idea
every time I bite into one of her confections!
SO genius.'—Christina Tosi

ROBATA JINYA

Recommended by
Neal Fraser

8050 West 3rd Street
Mid-City West
Los Angeles
California 90048
+1 3236538877
www.jinya-la.com

Opening hours	7 days for lunch and dinner
Reservation policy	Yes
Credit cards	Accepted
Price range	Affordable
Style	Casual
Cuisine	Japanese
Recommended for	Bargain

SHORT CAKE

Recommended by
Christian Page

6333 West 3rd Street
Mid-City West
Los Angeles
California 90036
+1 3237617976
www.shortcakela.com

Opening hours	7 days for brunch and 6 days for dinner
Reservation policy	No
Credit cards	Accepted
Price range	Budget
Style	Casual
Cuisine	Bakery-Café
Recommended for	Breakfast

SON OF A GUN

Recommended by
Marcus Samuelsson, Keith
Silverton, Christina Tosi

8370 West 3rd Street
Mid-City West
Los Angeles
California 90048
+1 3237829033
www.sonofagunrestaurant.com

Opening hours	5 days for lunch and 7 days for dinner
Reservation policy	Yes
Credit cards	Accepted
Price range	Affordable
Style	Casual
Cuisine	Seafood
Recommended for	Worth the travel

'It's this perfect balance of great hospitality and service
– small enough so it's cool and intimate but vast
enough that the food is diverse in range, flavor, texture
and thoughtfulness.'—Christina Tosi

ASTRO BURGER

Recommended by
Matt Molina

5601 Melrose Avenue
Mid-Wilshire
Los Angeles
California 90038
+1 3234691924
www.astroburger.com

Opening hours	7 days for breakfast, lunch and dinner
Credit cards	Not accepted
Price range	Budget
Style	Casual
Cuisine	Burgers
Recommended for	Regular neighbourhood

KOBAWOO HOUSE
Recommended by
Russell Moore
698 South Vermont Avenue
Koreatown
Mid-Wilshire
Los Angeles
California 90005
+1 2133897300

Opening hours	7 days for lunch and dinner
Reservation policy	No
Credit cards	Accepted
Price range	Affordable
Style	Casual
Cuisine	Korean
Recommended for	Worth the travel

'Best for *bo ssam*.'—Russell Moore

MARIO'S
Recommended by
Perfecto Roger
5786 Melrose Avenue
Mid-Wilshire
Los Angeles
California 90038
+1 3234664181

Opening hours	7 days for lunch and dinner
Reservation policy	No
Credit cards	Accepted
Price range	Budget
Style	Casual
Cuisine	Peruvian
Recommended for	Regular neighbourhood

PARK'S BBQ
Recommended by
Ricardo Zarate
995 South Vermont Avenue
Koreatown
Mid-Wilshire
Los Angeles
California 90006
+1 2133801717
www.parksbbq.com

Opening hours	7 days for lunch and dinner
Reservation policy	Yes
Credit cards	Accepted
Price range	Affordable
Style	Casual
Cuisine	Korean
Recommended for	Late night

PEET'S COFFEE & TEA
Recommended by
Matt Molina
124 North Larchmont Boulevard
Mid-Wilshire
Los Angeles
California 90004
+1 3239781003
www.peets.com

Opening hours	7 days from breakfast until late
Reservation policy	No
Credit cards	Accepted
Price range	Budget
Style	Casual
Cuisine	Café
Recommended for	Breakfast

POLLO A LA BRASA
Recommended by
Matt Molina
764 South Western Avenue
Mid-Wilshire
Los Angeles
California 90005
+1 2133871531

Opening hours	6 days for lunch and dinner
Reservation policy	No
Credit cards	Accepted
Price range	Budget
Style	Casual
Cuisine	Peruvian
Recommended for	Bargain

PROVIDENCE
Recommended by
Adam Horton, Perfecto
Roger, Steve Samson,
Ricardo Zarate
5955 Melrose Avenue
Mid-Wilshire
Los Angeles
California 90038
+1 3234604170
www.providencela.com

Opening hours	1 day for lunch and 7 days for dinner
Reservation policy	Yes
Credit cards	Accepted
Price range	Expensive
Style	Smart casual
Cuisine	Seafood
Recommended for	High end

'The tasting menus are incredible.'—Adam Horton

EL CHATO TACO TRUCK

Recommended by
Zach Pollack

5300 West Olympic Boulevard
Miracle Mile
Los Angeles
California 90036
www.elchatotacotruck.com

Opening hours	6 days for dinner
Reservation policy	No
Credit cards	Not accepted
Price range	Budget
Style	Style
Cuisine	Mexican
Recommended for	Late night

KRUA THAI

Recommended by
Adam Horton

13130 Sherman Way
North Hollywood
Los Angeles
California 91605
+1 8187597998

Opening hours	7 days for lunch and dinner
Reservation policy	No
Credit cards	Accepted
Price range	Budget
Style	Casual
Cuisine	Thai
Recommended for	Late night

N/NAKA

Recommended by
Hiro Sone

3455 South Overland Avenue
Palms
Los Angeles
California 90034
+1 3108366252
www.n-naka.com

Opening hours	5 days for dinner
Reservation policy	Yes
Credit cards	Accepted
Price range	Expensive
Style	Smart casual
Cuisine	Modern Japanese
Recommended for	Worth the travel

'Serves a *Kaiseki*-style prix fixe menu, pairing it
with sake, beer and wines. Great service in a
relaxed atmosphere.'—Hiro Sone

BLUE PLATE

Recommended by
Govind Armstrong

1415 Montana Avenue
Santa Monica
Los Angeles
California 90403
+1 3102608877
www.blueplatesantamonica.com

Opening hours	7 days for breakfast, lunch and dinner
Reservation policy	No
Credit cards	Accepted
Price range	Budget
Style	Casual
Cuisine	American
Recommended for	Wish I'd opened

LA CABAÑA

Recommended by
Perfecto Roger

738 Rose Avenue
Santa Monica
Los Angeles
California 90291
+1 3103927973
www.lacabanavenice.com

Opening hours	7 days for lunch and dinner
Reservation policy	Yes
Credit cards	Accepted
Price range	Budget
Style	Casual
Cuisine	Mexican
Recommended for	Late night

MARISCOS GUILLEN LA PLAYITA

Recommended by
Perfecto Roger

3306 Lincoln Boulevard
Santa Monica
Los Angeles
California 90405

Opening hours	7 days for lunch and dinner
Reservation policy	No
Credit cards	Not accepted
Price range	Budget
Style	Casual
Cuisine	Mexican
Recommended for	Bargain

MÉLISSE

Recommended by
Matt Molina, Perfecto Roger

1104 Wilshire Boulevard
Santa Monica
Los Angeles
California 90401
+1 3103950881
www.melisse.com

Opening hours..5 days for dinner
Reservation policy...Yes
Credit cards...Accepted
Price range...Expensive
Style...Smart casual
Cuisine...French
Recommended for..High end

MILO AND OLIVE

Recommended by
Christian Page

2723 Wilshire Boulevard
Santa Monica
Los Angeles
California 90403
www.miloandolive.com

Opening hours..............7 days for breakfast, lunch and dinner
Reservation policy..No
Credit cards...Accepted
Price range..Affordable
Style...Casual
Cuisine..Bakery-Pizza
Recommended for.........................Regular neighbourhood

'I go where ever Walter Manzke is cooking –
he has been moving around a lot. Milo and Olive
as of recent.'—Christian Page

THE PENTHOUSE

Recommended by
Keith Silverton

Huntley Hotel
1111 2nd Street
Santa Monica
Los Angeles
California 90403
+1 3103938080
www.thehuntleyhotel.com

Opening hours..............7 days for breakfast, lunch and dinner
Reservation policy...Yes
Credit cards...Accepted
Price range..Affordable
Style...Smart casual
Cuisine..Modern American
Recommended for...Local favourite

'It's right next to the farmers' market so it's extremely
fresh, Californian cuisine.'—Keith Silverton

PHO CAFÉ

Recommended by
Matt Molina

2841 West Sunset Boulevard
Silver Lake
Los Angeles
California 90026

Opening hours................................7 days for lunch and dinner
Reservation policy...No
Credit cards...Not accepted
Price range...Budget
Style...Casual
Cuisine..Vietnamese
Recommended for...Local favourite

ASANEBO

Recommended by
Josef Centeno

11941 Ventura Boulevard
Studio City
Los Angeles
California 91604
+1 8187603348
www.asanebo-restaurant.com

Opening hours............4 days for lunch and 6 days for dinner
Reservation policy...Yes
Credit cards...Accepted
Price range..Affordable
Style...Casual
Cuisine..Japanese
Recommended for..High end

FATBURGER

Recommended by
Adam Horton

10600 1/2 Ventura Boulevard
Studio City
Los Angeles
California 91604
www.fatburger.com

Opening hours................................7 days for lunch and dinner
Reservation policy...No
Credit cards...Accepted
Price range...Budget
Style...Casual
Cuisine...Burgers
Recommended for...Late night

RAMEN YAMADAYA

Recommended by
Ricardo Zarate

3118 West 182nd Street
Torrance
Los Angeles
California 90504
+1 3103805555
www.ramen-yamadaya.com

Opening hours	7 days for lunch and dinner
Reservation policy	No
Credit cards	Not accepted
Price range	Budget
Style	Casual
Cuisine	Japanese
Recommended for	Bargain

TORIHEI

Recommended by
Zach Pollack

1757 West Carson Street
Torrance
Los Angeles
California 90501
+1 3107819407
www.torihei-usa.com

Opening hours	7 days for dinner
Reservation policy	Yes
Credit cards	Accepted
Price range	Affordable
Style	Casual
Cuisine	Japanese
Recommended for	Bargain

PHO 999

Recommended by
Adam Horton

6411 Sepulveda Boulevard
Van Nuys
Los Angeles
California 91411

Opening hours	7 days for breakfast, lunch and dinner
Reservation policy	No
Credit cards	Accepted
Price range	Budget
Style	Casual
Cuisine	Vietnamese
Recommended for	Bargain

GJELINA

Recommended by
Josef Centeno,
David Hawksworth

1429 Abbot Kinney Boulevard
Venice
Los Angeles
California 90291
+1 3104501429
www.gjelina.com

Opening hours	7 days for brunch and dinner
Reservation policy	Yes
Credit cards	Accepted
Price range	Affordable
Style	Casual
Cuisine	American
Recommended for	Regular neighbourhood

'The seasonality of everything is amazing and the selection of farmers' market produce reflects Southern California's food scene.'—Josef Centeno

Gjelina's the hip Venice hang-out that caused a stir by turning down a pregnant Victoria Beckham's special request. Gjelina's Cali-Med salads, sexy brunches and wood-oven pizzas are just right as they are, thank you very much. When it opened in 2008 it was the dream neighbourhood joint. Now that word's got out of its guanciale and green olive pizza, braised artichokes with burrata, and butterscotch pot de crème, there are almost more out-of-towners than there are local artists and surfers. Tables in the backyard have the edge – just – over the industrial chic interior. Reservations are like gold dust but there's always GTA (Gjelina Take Away) next door.

ANIMAL

435 North Fairfax Avenue
West Hollywood
Los Angeles
California 90036
+1 3237829225
www.animalrestaurant.com

Opening hours	7 days for dinner
Reservation policy	Yes
Credit cards	Accepted
Price range	Affordable
Style	Casual
Cuisine	Steakhouse
Recommended for	Worth the travel

'I went to Animal on my last trip to LA and figured that it couldn't live up to the hype, and yet it did. We gorged ourselves on a whole laundry list of unique deliciousness - snails, pig tails, veal brains, beef tongue, confit rabbit, oh my! Some seriously inspired dishes.'
—Brad Farmerie

Jon Shook and Vinny Dotolo's 2008 launch, Animal, has been an unlikely La La Land hit. Stick-thin Angelenos hunt for a light salad here in vain; there's barely a dish that doesn't contain meat – usually pig – in some form (to wit, the much talked about bacon chocolate crunch bar). The Floridian duo's modestly priced 'dude food' is best exemplified by upscale riffs on comfort food such as a foie gras-topped biscuit with maple sausage gravy and pig head with hush puppies (deep-fried cornbread balls) and pickled ramps (wild leeks). Loud music and late hours also win the dude vote. A spin-off, Son Of A Gun, opened in 2011.

BLD

7450 Beverly Boulevard
West Hollywood
Los Angeles
California 90036
+1 3239309744
www.bldrestaurant.com

Opening hours	7 days for breakfast, lunch and dinner
Reservation policy	Yes
Credit cards	Accepted
Price range	Affordable
Style	Casual
Cuisine	American
Recommended for	Breakfast

CECCONI'S

8764 Melrose Avenue
West Hollywood
Los Angeles
California 90069
+1 3104322000
www.cecconiswesthollywood.com

Opening hours	7 days for breakfast, lunch and dinner
Reservation policy	Yes
Credit cards	Accepted
Price range	Affordable
Style	Smart casual
Cuisine	Italian
Recommended for	Breakfast

EVELEIGH

8752 West Sunset Boulevard
West Hollywood
Los Angeles
California 90069
+1 4242391630
www.theeveleigh.com

Opening hours	3 days for brunch and 7 days for dinner
Reservation policy	Yes
Reservation email	reservations@theeveleigh.com
Credit cards	Accepted
Price range	Affordable
Style	Casual
Cuisine	American
Recommended for	Worth the travel

INK.

8360 Melrose Avenue
West Hollywood
Los Angeles
California 90069
+1 3236515866
www.mvink.com

Opening hours	7 days for dinner
Reservation policy	Yes
Credit cards	Accepted
Price range	Expensive
Style	Casual
Cuisine	International
Recommended for	Wish I'd opened

LUCQUES

Recommended by
Russell Moore

8474 Melrose Avenue
West Hollywood
Los Angeles
California 90048
+1 3236556277
www.lucques.com

Opening hours............5 days for lunch and 7 days for dinner
Reservation policy...Yes
Credit cards...Accepted
Price range..Affordable
Style..Smart casual
Cuisine..International
Recommended for...Late night

NISHIMURA

Recommended by
Josef Centeno

8684 Melrose Avenue
West Hollywood
Los Angeles
California 90069
+1 3106594770

Opening hours............5 days for lunch and 6 days for dinner
Reservation policy...Yes
Credit cards...Accepted
Price range...Expensive
Style..Casual
Cuisine..Japanese
Recommended for..High end

PINK'S HOT DOGS

Recommended by
Walter Manzke

709 North La Brea Avenue
West Hollywood
Los Angeles
California 90038
+1 3239314223
www.pinkshollywood.com

Opening hours............7 days for breakfast, lunch and dinner
Reservation policy..No
Credit cards...Not accepted
Price range..Budget
Style..Casual
Cuisine..Hot Dogs
Recommended for..Local favourite

PIZZERIA MOZZA

Recommended by
Josef Centeno

641 North Highland Avenue
West Hollywood
Los Angeles
California 90036
+1 3232970101
www.pizzeriamozza.com

Opening hours.................................7 days for lunch and dinner
Reservation policy...Yes
Credit cards...Accepted
Price range..Affordable
Style..Casual
Cuisine...Pizza
Recommended for............................Regular neighbourhood

'Go between lunch and dinner when you're most likely to be able to find an open seat at the bar. Order the chicken livers with guanciale, bone marrow *al forno* and a pizza with anchovy and tomatoes.'
—Josef Centeno

TOMATO PIE PIZZA JOINT

Recommended by
Govind Armstrong

7751 1/2 Melrose Avenue
West Hollywood
Los Angeles
California 90046
+1 3236539993
www.tomatopiepizzajoint.com

Opening hours.................................7 days for lunch and dinner
Reservation policy..No
Credit cards...Accepted
Price range..Budget
Style..Casual
Cuisine...Pizza
Recommended for...Bargain

PICCA

9575 West Pico Boulevard
West Los Angeles
Los Angeles
California 90035
+1 3102770133
www.piccaperu.com

Opening hours	7 days for dinner
Reservation policy	Yes
Credit cards	Accepted
Price range	Affordable
Style	Casual
Cuisine	Peruvian
Recommended for	Local favourite

'The food is cutting edge, different but without being crazy. It's heavily influenced by Latin and Japanese food.'—Neal Fraser

SOTTO

9575 West Pico Boulevard
West Los Angeles
Los Angeles
California 90035
+1 3102770210
www.sottorestaurant.com

Opening hours	3 days for lunch and 6 days for dinner
Reservation policy	Yes
Credit cards	Accepted
Price range	Affordable
Style	Casual
Cuisine	Italian
Recommended for	Worth the travel

TSUJITA

2057 Sawtelle Boulevard
West Los Angeles
Los Angeles
California 90025
+1 3102317373
www.tsujita-la.com

Opening hours	7 days for lunch and dinner
Reservation policy	Yes
Credit cards	Not accepted
Price range	Budget
Style	Casual
Cuisine	Japanese
Recommended for	Bargain

'Wow, the dough, the dough, the dough. It's God's pizza.'
MATTHEW DILLON P516

'JUST PUT YOURSELF IN THEIR HANDS AND YOU CAN'T GO WRONG.'
JASON FOX P505

'It's the best Chinese food in San Francisco.'
MITCHELL ROSENTHAL P504

'The best burger in town.'
DANIEL PATTERSON P505

'WHEN I EAT HERE I HAVE A VERY SERIOUS CASE OF RESTAURANT ENVY!'
GABRIELLE HAMILTON P507

SAN FRANCISCO

'I LOVE THEIR CHICKEN LIVER, AND THEIR PASTAS ARE UNRIVALED IN THE CITY.'
CHRISTOPHER THOMPSON P509

'The hot and cold foie gras is ridiculous.'
CHRISTOPHER THOMPSON P509

'Head here if you're in the Mission, for something sweet.'
MATTHEW ACCARRINO P510

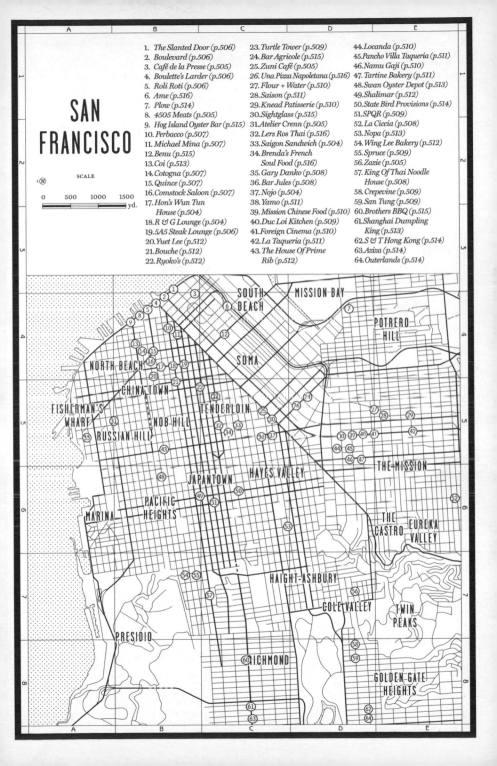

SAN FRANCISCO

SCALE

0   500   1000   1500
yd.

HON'S WUN TUN HOUSE

Recommended by
Gerald Hirigoyen

648 Kearny Street
Chinatown
San Francisco
California 94108
+1 4154333966

Opening hours	6 days for lunch and dinner
Reservation policy	No
Credit cards	Not accepted
Price range	Budget
Style	Casual
Cuisine	Chinese
Recommended for	Bargain

R&G LOUNGE

Recommended by
Corey Lee, Michael Mina,
Mitchell Rosenthal

631 Kearny Street
Chinatown
San Francisco
California 94108
+1 4159827877
www.rnglounge.com

Opening hours	7 days for lunch and dinner
Reservation policy	Yes
Credit cards	Accepted
Price range	Affordable
Style	Casual
Cuisine	Chinese
Recommended for	Regular neighbourhood

'It's the best Chinese food in San Francisco and my kids love it as much as I do. I recommend the salt and pepper fried crab.'—Mitchell Rosenthal

NOJO

Recommended by
Jason Fox, Hiro Sone

231 Franklin Street
Civic Center
San Francisco
California 94102
+1 4158964587
www.nojosf.com

Opening hours	4 days for brunch and 6 days for dinner
Reservation policy	Yes
Credit cards	Accepted
Price range	Budget
Style	Casual
Cuisine	Japanese
Recommended for	Worth the travel

'Daily visits to the farmers' market shine through in this Japanese-influenced, farm-to-table concept restaurant. Everything is very fresh and seasonal, light but very tasty - you will be feeling good after the meal.'—Hiro Sone

SAIGON SANDWICH

Recommended by
Matthew Accarrino

560 Larkin Street
Civic Center
San Francisco
California 94102
+1 4154745698

Opening hours	7 days from breakfast until late
Reservation policy	No
Credit cards	Not accepted
Price range	Budget
Style	Casual
Cuisine	Vietnamese
Recommended for	Bargain

After a refurbishment in 2011, Saigon Sandwich is once again serving some of the best *bánh mì* in North America. The tiny place – just two seats – has stood on a rough stretch of Larkin Street, at the western edge of the Tenderloin district, for over thirty years. They do about ten varieties of *bánh mì* of which the best is the gloriously fatty roast pork, stuffed into a freshly baked and crusty baguette, generously smeared in chicken liver pâté, with lightly pickled vegetables and a load of fresh coriander (cilantro). Chicken and tofu are also available. A perfect cheap lunch if you're on the march.

ZUNI CAFÉ

Recommended by
Craig Stoll, Michel Troisgros

1658 Market Street
Civic Center
San Francisco
California 94102
+1 4155522522
www.zunicafe.com

Opening hours	6 days for lunch and dinner
Reservation policy	Yes
Credit cards	Accepted
Price range	Affordable
Style	Casual
Cuisine	International
Recommended for	Local favourite

CAFÉ DE LA PRESSE

Recommended by
Gerald Hirigoyen

352 Grant Avenue
Downtown
San Francisco
California 94108
+1 4153982680
www.cafedelapresse.com

Opening hours	7 days for brunch and dinner
Reservation policy	Yes
Credit cards	Accepted
Price range	Budget
Style	Casual
Cuisine	French
Recommended for	Breakfast

ZAZIE

Recommended by
David Taylor

941 Cole Street
Cole Valley
San Francisco
California 94117
+1 4155645332
www.zaziesf.com

Opening hours	7 days for brunch and dinner
Reservation policy	Yes
Credit cards	Accepted
Price range	Affordable
Style	Casual
Cuisine	French
Recommended for	Breakfast

4505 MEATS

Recommended by
Daniel Patterson,
Michael Tusk

Farmers Market
Embarcadero
1 Ferry Building
San Francisco
California 94105
www.4505meats.com

Opening hours	2 days for lunch
Reservation policy	No
Credit cards	Not accepted
Price range	Budget
Style	Casual
Cuisine	American
Recommended for	Bargain

ATELIER CRENN

Recommended by
Jason Fox, Guy Savoy

3127 Fillmore Street
Cow Hollow
San Francisco
California 94123
+1 4154400460
www.ateliercrenn.com

Opening hours	5 days for dinner
Reservation policy	Yes
Credit cards	Accepted
Price range	Expensive
Style	Formal
Cuisine	French
Recommended for	High end

'Just put yourself in their hands and you can't go wrong.'—Jason Fox

'The best burger in town.'—Daniel Patterson

Chef turned artisan butcher Ryan Farr – pusher of prime cuts of beef, superior sausages and classy *chicharrones* – gets behind the grill twice a week to serve up meaty staples at his Ferry Plaza Farmer's Market stall. There's no shortage of takers every Thursday and Saturday for his rotating lunch menu, which always includes the near legendary (and award-winning) 4505 cheeseburger – a dry-aged, grass-fed beef, quarter-pound patty sat on a buttery Parmesan, spring onion (scallion) and sesame seed bun, topped with melted Gruyère, red onion, crispy iceberg and – as seems to be the case with all great burgers – its own secret sauce.

BOULETTE'S LARDER

Recommended by
Mitchell Rosenthal,
Mark Sullivan

1 Ferry Building Marketplace
Embarcadero
San Francisco
California 94111
+1 4153991155
www.bouletteslarder.com

Opening hours	6 days for breakfast and lunch
Reservation policy	Yes
Credit cards	Accepted
Price range	Affordable
Style	Casual
Cuisine	Deli-Café
Recommended for	Breakfast

'Perfectly cooked eggs every time.'
—Mitchell Rosenthal

BOULEVARD

Recommended by
Jason Fox

1 Mission Street
Embarcadero
San Francisco
California 94105
+1 4155436084
www.boulevardrestaurant.com

Opening hours	5 days for lunch and 7 days for dinner
Reservation policy	Yes
Reservation email	reservations@boulevardrestaurant.com
Credit cards	Accepted
Price range	Expensive
Style	Smart casual
Cuisine	International
Recommended for	Local favourite

HOG ISLAND OYSTER BAR

Recommended by
Corey Lee

One Ferry Building
Embarcadero
San Francisco California 94111
+1 4153917117
www.hogislandoysters.com

Opening hours	7 days for lunch and 5 days for dinner
Reservation policy	No
Credit cards	Accepted
Price range	Affordable
Style	Casual
Cuisine	Seafood
Recommended for	Local favourite

'It's a great example of how people in the Bay Area are interested in food. The view of the Bay is pretty iconic as well.'—Corey Lee

ROLI ROTI

Recommended by
Michael Mina

Farmers Market
1 Ferry Building
Embarcadero
San Francisco
California 94105
+1 5107800300
www.roliroti.com

Opening hours	2 from breakfast until late
Reservation policy	No
Credit cards	Not accepted
Price range	Budget
Style	Casual
Cuisine	Rotisserie
Recommended for	Bargain

THE SLANTED DOOR

Recommended by
Miles Kirby

1 Ferry Building
Embarcadero
San Francisco
California 94111
+1 4158618032
www.slanteddoor.com

Opening hours	7 days for lunch and dinner
Reservation policy	Yes
Credit cards	Accepted
Price range	Affordable
Style	Casual
Cuisine	Vietnamese
Recommended for	Worth the travel

5A5 STEAK LOUNGE

Recommended by
Paul Newman

244 Jackson Street
Financial Disctrict
San Francisco
California 94111
+1 4159892539
www.5a5stk.com

Opening hours	7 days for dinner
Reservation policy	Yes
Reservation email	rsvp@5a5stk.com
Credit cards	Accepted
Price range	Expensive
Style	Smart casual
Cuisine	Steakhouse
Recommended for	Worth the travel

'Very contemporary and fun. Fantastic steaks!'
—Paul Newman

COMSTOCK SALOON

Recommended by
Jason Fox

155 Columbus Avenue
Financial Disctrict
San Francisco
California 94133
+1 4156170071
www.comstocksaloon.com

Opening hours	7 days for dinner
Reservation policy	Yes
Credit cards	Accepted
Price range	Budget
Style	Casual
Cuisine	American
Recommended for	Late night

'Order the pot pie or rabbit, if it's on the menu.'
—Jason Fox

COTOGNA

Recommended by
Josef Centeno, Gabrielle
Hamilton, Gerald Hirigoyen

490 Pacific Avenue
Financial Disctrict
San Francisco
California 94133
+1 4157758508
www.cotognasf.com

Opening hours	6 days for lunch and 7 days for dinner
Reservation policy	Yes
Credit cards	Accepted
Price range	Affordable
Style	Smart casual
Cuisine	Italian
Recommended for	Worth the travel

'When I eat here I have a very serious case of
restaurant envy!'—Gabrielle Hamilton

MICHAEL MINA

Recommended by
Bradley Turley

252 California Street
Financial District
San Francisco
California 94111
+1 4153979222
www.michaelmina.net

Opening hours	5 days for lunch and 7 days for dinner
Reservation policy	Yes
Credit cards	Accepted
Price range	Expensive
Style	Smart casual
Cuisine	Japanese-French
Recommended for	High end

PERBACCO

Recommended by
David Taylor

230 California Street
Financial District
San Francisco
California 94111
+1 4159550663
www.perbaccosf.com

Opening hours	5 days for lunch and 6 days for dinner
Reservation policy	Yes
Credit cards	Accepted
Price range	Affordable
Style	Smart casual
Cuisine	Italian
Recommended for	Wish I'd opened

QUINCE

Recommended by
Jason Fox, Carrie
Nahabedian, David Taylor

470 Pacific Avenue
Financial District
San Francisco
California 94133
+1 4157758500
www.quincerestaurant.com

Opening hours	6 days for dinner
Reservation policy	Yes
Credit cards	Accepted
Price range	Expensive
Style	Formal
Cuisine	Mediterranean
Recommended for	High end

'Just put yourself in their hands and you can't go
wrong.'—Jason Fox

GARY DANKO

800 North Point
Hyde Street
Fisherman's Wharf
San Francisco
California 94109
+1 4157492060
www.garydanko.com

Opening hours	7 days for dinner
Reservation policy	Yes
Credit cards	Accepted
Price range	Expensive
Style	Formal
Cuisine	American
Recommended for	High end

'For the best blini and caviar in town.'
—**Matthew Accarrino**

Gary Danko's eponymous San Francisco restaurant has become a go-to for traditional cooking that makes the most of America's high-quality produce without any fuss. First impressions reveal little to make it stand out from other middle-class destinations of its type: crisp white linen, hushed tones and a laden cheese trolley which is ceremoniously pushed around the room. But that's the point. The reassuringly familiar package leaves you under no illusion of what you're going to get, which is a polished haute-cuisine meal, the kind of which you'd happily eat every day if only your arteries could stand it.

LA CICCIA

291 30th Street
Glen Park
San Francisco
California 94131
+1 4155508114
www.laciccia.com

Opening hours	6 days for dinner
Reservation policy	Yes
Credit cards	Accepted
Price range	Affordable
Style	Casual
Cuisine	Italian
Recommended for	Wish I'd opened

BAR JULES

609 Hayes Street
Hayes Valley
San Francisco
California 94102
+1 4156215482
www.barjules.com

Opening hours	6 days for brunch and 5 days for dinner
Reservation policy	Yes
Credit cards	Accepted
Price range	Affordable
Style	Casual
Cuisine	Café
Recommended for	Worth the travel

KING OF THAI NOODLE HOUSE

639 Clement Street
Inner Richmond
San Francisco
California 94118
+1 4157525198

Opening hours	7 days for lunch and dinner
Reservation policy	No
Credit cards	Not accepted
Price range	Budget
Style	Casual
Cuisine	Thai
Recommended for	Late night

'Gets a lot of my late night business.'
—**Christopher Thompson**

WING LEE BAKERY

503 Clement Street
Inner Richmond
San Francisco
California 94118
+1 4156689481

Opening hours	7 days for breakfast and lunch
Reservation policy	No
Credit cards	Not accepted
Price range	Budget
Style	Casual
Cuisine	Chinese
Recommended for	Bargain

CREPEVINE

Recommended by
David Taylor

624 Irving Street
Inner Sunset
San Francisco
California 94121
+1 4156815858
www.crepevine.com

Opening hours	7 days for breakfast, lunch and dinner
Reservation policy	No
Credit cards	Accepted
Price range	Budget
Style	Casual
Cuisine	Crepes
Recommended for	Bargain

TURTLE TOWER

Recommended by
Cal Peternell

631 Larkin Street
Little Saigon
San Francisco
California 94109
+1 4154093333
www.turtletowersf.com

Opening hours	7 days for breakfast and lunch
Reservation policy	No
Credit cards	Not accepted
Price range	Budget
Style	Casual
Cuisine	Vietnamese
Recommended for	Bargain

SAN TUNG

Recommended by
Corey Lee

1031 Irving Street
Inner Sunset
San Francisco
California 94122
+1 4152420828
www.santungrestaurant.com

Opening hours	6 days for lunch and dinner
Reservation policy	Yes
Credit cards	Accepted
Price range	Budget
Style	Casual
Cuisine	Chinese
Recommended for	Bargain

'Order the black bean noodles and fried chicken.'
—Corey Lee

SPQR

Recommended by
Jason Fox,
Christopher Thompson

1911 Fillmore Street
Lower Pacific Heights
San Francisco
California 94115
+1 4157717779
www.spqrsf.com

Opening hours	2 days for lunch and 7 days for dinner
Reservation policy	Yes
Credit cards	Accepted
Price range	Affordable
Style	Casual
Cuisine	Modern Italian
Recommended for	Local favourite

'I love their chicken liver, and their pastas are
unrivalled in the city.'—Christopher Thompson

SPRUCE

Recommended by
Christopher Thompson

3640 Sacramento Street
Laurel Heights
San Francisco
California 94118
+1 4159315100
www.sprucesf.com

Opening hours	5 days for lunch and 7 days for dinner
Reservation policy	Yes
Credit cards	Accepted
Price range	Expensive
Style	Smart casual
Cuisine	Modern American
Recommended for	High end

'The hot and cold foie gras is ridiculous.'
—Christopher Thompson

DUC LOI KITCHEN

Recommended by
Jason Fox

2200 Mission Street
Mission
San Francisco
California 94110
+1 4155511772

Opening hours	7 days from breakfast until late
Reservation policy	No
Credit cards	Accepted
Price range	Budget
Style	Casual
Cuisine	Vietnamese Sandwiches
Recommended for	Bargain

FLOUR + WATER

Recommended by
Jason Fox

2401 Harrison Street
Mission
San Francisco
California 94110
+1 4158267000
www.flourandwater.com

Opening hours	7 days for dinner
Reservation policy	Yes
Credit cards	Accepted
Price range	Affordable
Style	Casual
Cuisine	Italian
Recommended for	Local favourite

LOCANDA

Recommended by
Mark Sullivan

557 Valencia Street
Mission
San Francisco
California 94110
+1 4158636800
www.locandasf.com

Opening hours	7 days for dinner
Reservation policy	Yes
Credit cards	Accepted
Price range	Affordable
Style	Smart casual
Cuisine	Italian
Recommended for	Regular neighbourhood

FOREIGN CINEMA

Recommended by
Craig Stoll

2534 Mission Street
Mission
San Francisco
California 94110
+1 4156487600
www.foreigncinema.com

Opening hours	2 days for brunch and 7 days for dinner
Reservation policy	Yes
Credit cards	Accepted
Price range	Affordable
Style	Casual
Cuisine	International
Recommended for	Regular neighbourhood

MISSION CHINESE FOOD

Recommended by
Russell Moore

2234 Mission Street
Mission
San Francisco
California 94110
+1 4154316268
www.missionchinesefood.com

Opening hours	5 days for lunch and dinner
Reservation policy	No
Credit cards	Accepted
Price range	Budget
Style	Casual
Cuisine	Modern Chinese
Recommended for	Bargain

KNEAD PATISSERIE

Recommended by
Matthew Accarrino

3111 24th Street
Mission
San Francisco
California 94110
+1 4156553024
www.kneadpatisserie.com

Opening hours	6 days for breakfast and lunch
Reservation policy	No
Credit cards	Accepted
Price range	Budget
Style	Casual
Cuisine	Bakery
Recommended for	Bargain

'Head here if you're in the Mission, for something sweet. '—Matthew Accarrino

NAMU GAJI

Recommended by
Russell Moore

499 Dolores Street
Mission
San Francisco
California 94110
www.namusf.com

Opening hours	7 days for lunch and 6 days for dinner
Reservation policy	No
Credit cards	Accepted
Price range	Affordable
Style	Casual
Cuisine	Korean
Recommended for	Late night

'I like their *dolsot bibimbap* and grilled fish parts.'—Russell Moore

PANCHO VILLA TAQUERIA

Recommended by
Christopher Thompson

3071 16th Street
Mission
San Francisco
California 94103
+1 4158648840
www.sfpanchovilla.com

Opening hours	7 days for lunch and dinner
Reservation policy	No
Credit cards	Accepted
Price range	Budget
Style	Casual
Cuisine	Mexican
Recommended for	Late night

'If I find myself in the Mission I go to Pancho Villa's for carnitas.'—Christopher Thompson

SAISON

Recommended by
Walter Manzke,
Mitchell Rosenthal

2124 Folsom Street
Mission
San Francisco
California 94110
+1 4158287990
www.salsonsf.com

Opening hours	5 days for dinner
Reservation policy	Yes
Credit cards	Accepted
Price range	Expensive
Style	Casual
Cuisine	French-American
Recommended for	High end

'Best interpretation of modern fine dining.'
—Mitchell Rosenthal

LA TAQUERIA

Recommended by
Tim Cushman

2889 Mission Street
Mission
San Francisco
California 94110
+1 4152857117

Opening hours	7 days for lunch and dinner
Reservation policy	No
Credit cards	Not accepted
Price range	Budget
Style	Casual
Cuisine	Mexican
Recommended for	Bargain

TARTINE BAKERY

Recommended by
Matthew Accarrino, Mitchell
Rosenthal, Craig Stoll

600 Guerrero Street
Mission
San Francisco
California 94110
+1 4154872600
www.tartinebakery.com

Opening hours	7 days for breakfast, lunch and dinner
Reservation policy	No
Credit cards	Accepted
Price range	Affordable
Style	Casual
Cuisine	Bakery-Café
Recommended for	Breakfast

'Chad Robertson bakes the best bread in the world.'—Mitchell Rosenthal

YAMO

Recommended by
Jason Fox

3406 18th Street
Mission
San Francisco
California 94110
+1 4155538911

Opening hours	7 days for lunch and dinner
Reservation policy	No
Credit cards	Not accepted
Price range	Budget
Style	Casual
Cuisine	Burmese
Recommended for	Bargain

YUET LEE

Recommended by
Gerald Hirigoyen, Craig Stoll

1300 Stockton Street
North Beach
San Francisco
California 94133
+1 4159826020

Opening hours	6 days for lunch and dinner
Reservation policy	No
Credit cards	Accepted
Price range	Affordable
Style	Casual
Cuisine	Chinese
Recommended for	Late night

Yuet Lee, in the North Beach area of San Francisco, is often described as one of the city's 'best kept secrets' but it's actually a no-frills food joint that has been blogged about so frequently that it's actually better known than most other places. Yet it's easy to believe that this Chinatown favourite remains undiscovered, such is the modest interior and cash-only policy that doesn't go down well with tourists. But not so for the late-night revellers who can regularly be seen winding down in the small hours to a steaming bowl of frog rice pudding, braised duck feet or the legendary salt and pepper squid.

BOUCHE

Recommended by
Jason Fox

603 Bush Street
Nob Hill
San Francisco
California 94108
+1 4159560396
www.bouchesf.com

Opening hours	6 days for dinner
Reservation policy	Yes
Credit cards	Accepted
Price range	Affordable
Style	Casual
Cuisine	French
Recommended for	Late night

THE HOUSE OF PRIME RIB

Recommended by
Gerald Hirigoyen

1906 Van Ness Avenue
Nob Hill
San Francisco
California 94109
+1 4158854605
www.houseofprimerib.net

Opening hours	7 days for dinner
Reservation policy	Yes
Credit cards	Accepted
Price range	Affordable
Style	Smart casual
Cuisine	Steakhouse
Recommended for	Local favourite

RYOKO'S

Recommended by
David Taylor, Christopher
Thompson

619 Taylor Street
Nob Hill
San Francisco
California 94102
+1 4157751028
www.ryokos.com

Opening hours	7 days for dinner
Reservation policy	Yes
Credit cards	Accepted
Price range	Affordable
Style	Casual
Cuisine	Japanese
Recommended for	Late night

'Awesome servers and a DJ-dominated dining room. Good rolls.'—Christopher Thompson

SHALIMAR

Recommended by
Mitchell Rosenthal

1409 Polk Street
Nob Hill
San Francisco
California 94109
+1 4157764642
www.shalimarsf.com

Opening hours	7 days for lunch and dinner
Reservation policy	No
Credit cards	Not accepted
Price range	Budget
Style	Casual
Cuisine	Indian
Recommended for	Bargain

'Smoke from the tandoori oven, music blasting and all types of people.'—Mitchell Rosenthal

SWAN OYSTER DEPOT

1517 Polk Street
Nob Hill
San Francisco
California 94109
+1 4156731101

Opening hours	6 days for breakfast and lunch
Reservation policy	No
Credit cards	Not accepted
Price range	Affordable
Style	Casual
Cuisine	Seafood
Recommended for	Local favourite

'Has great fresh seafood classics like crab Louis and oysters on the half shell.'—Matthew Accarrino

Not many restaurants get to celebrate a century in business. The Depot didn't take credit cards or reservations when they opened in 1912 – and they don't now. Open from breakfast through to late afternoon, the lunchtime line for the twenty stools at the marble counter moves quickly. Many regulars just pop in for a plate of oysters, a cup of chowder or the Swan Special – a prawn (shrimp) cocktail and a beer – and are gone. Beyond that it's simply prepared seafood, from dressed crab to various salads and cocktails. There's no wine list but they have Anchor Steam Beer, a fine foil for anything on the menu.

COI

373 Broadway
North Beach
San Francisco
California 94133
+1 4153939000
www.coirestaurant.com

Opening hours	5 days for dinner
Reservation policy	Yes
Credit cards	Accepted
Price range	Expensive
Style	Smart casual
Cuisine	Modern American
Recommended for	Wish I'd opened

'Watching the chefs at Coi always gives me envy: everything is always perfect and rarely rushed. The food and dining room really match each other; that's extremely hard to do.'—Sean Brock

NOPA

560 Divisadero Street
North Panhandle
San Francisco
California 94117
+1 4158648643
www.nopasf.com

Opening hours	2 days for lunch and 7 days for dinner
Reservation policy	Yes
Credit cards	Accepted
Price range	Affordable
Style	Casual
Cuisine	European
Recommended for	Late night

'Serves until 1.00 a.m. so it's the perfect after-work industry hang-out.'—Daniel Patterson

This bustling neighbourhood joint north of the Panhandle – hence the name – is popular with restaurant workers after a little post-shift sustenance. Located in an old bank, well served by a series of 3.6-m (12-foot) tall windows, it's an evening-only operation, except on weekends when it opens for brunch. The menu, which focuses on delivering comfort from seasonal farm-sourced organic produce and a wood-fired grill, is what chef Laurence Jossel bills as 'urban rustic'. The balcony level is best for watching the scene unfold in the dining room below; the large communal table or the bar for being a part of it.

SHANGHAI DUMPLING KING

3319 Balboa Street
Outer Richmond
San Francisco
California 94121
+1 4153872088

Opening hours	6 days for lunch and dinner
Reservation policy	Yes
Credit cards	Accepted
Price range	Budget
Style	Casual
Cuisine	Chinese
Recommended for	Bargain

OUTERLANDS

Recommended by
Matthew Accarrino

4001 Judah Street
Outer Sunset
San Francisco
California 94122
+1 4156616140
www.outerlandssf.com

Opening hours	6 days for lunch and 4 days for dinner
Reservation policy	No
Credit cards	Accepted
Price range	Affordable
Style	Casual
Cuisine	Bakery-Café
Recommended for	Breakfast

'They bake great bread and work it into the menu.'
—Matthew Accarrino

S & T HONG KONG

Recommended by
Jason Fox

2578 Noriega Street
Outer Sunset
San Francisco
California 94122
+1 4156658338

Opening hours	7 days for lunch and dinner
Reservation policy	Yes
Credit cards	Accepted
Price range	Affordable
Style	Casual
Cuisine	Chinese
Recommended for	Bargain

STATE BIRD PROVISIONS

Recommended by
Jason Fox, Mark Sullivan

1529 Fillmore Street
Pacific Heights
San Francisco
California 94115
+1 4157951272
statebirdsf.com

Opening hours	6 days for dinner
Reservation policy	Yes
Credit cards	Accepted
Price range	Affordable
Style	Casual
Cuisine	American Small plates
Recommended for	Bargain

'This fun restaurant offers inventive, chef-inspired American cooking served dim sum-style. Customers don't have to over commit themselves to a large menu, and items are priced anywhere from $2-$7 (£1.50-£4.50)!'—Mark Sullivan

Its name cheekily conjures up California's state bird, the quail, a crunchy deep-fried version of which, served with wafer-thin slices of onion stewed in lemon and rosemary, is a trademark dish. Opened in 2012 by husband and wife, Stuart Brioza and Nicole Krasinski – formerly chefs at the now defunct Rubicon – the open kitchen of this bijou, darkly lit and basically decorated forty-five seater (exposed concrete, pinboard (tackboard) covered walls, simple wooden chairs and tables) overlooks Fillmore from a large plate-glass window. The shtick? A reasonably priced, short selection of creative dishes punted around the room by waiters pushing dim sum-style trolleys.

PLOW

Recommended by
Walter Manzke

1299 18th Street
Potrero Hill
San Francisco
California 94107
+1 4158217569
www.eatatplow.com

Opening hours	6 days for brunch
Reservation policy	No
Reservation email	info@eatatplow.com
Credit cards	Accepted
Price range	Budget
Style	Casual
Cuisine	Café
Recommended for	Breakfast

AZIZA

Recommended by
Matthew Accarrino,
Jason Fox

5800 Geary Boulevard
Richmond
San Francisco
California 94121
+1 4157522222
www.aziza-sf.com

Opening hours	6 days for dinner
Reservation policy	Yes
Credit cards	Accepted
Price range	Affordable
Style	Casual
Cuisine	Moroccan
Recommended for	Regular neighbourhood

'For a creative drink and distinctive modern Moroccan food in an intimate, sedate setting.'
—Matthew Accarrino

BROTHERS BBQ

Recommended by
Christopher Thompson

4128 Geary Boulevard
Richmond
San Francisco
California 94118
+1 4153877991

Opening hours	3 days for lunch and 7 days for dinner
Reservation policy	Yes
Credit cards	Accepted
Price range	Budget
Style	Casual
Cuisine	Korean
Recommended for	Regular neighbourhood

'The *doenjang*, fermented soy bean paste, is the best I've ever had. It has an odd blue cheese-like characteristic. Coined by fellow industry folks as "bean-cheese".'—Christopher Thompson

BAR AGRICOLE

Recommended by
Jason Fox, Gerald Hirigoyen, Russell Moore, Michael Tusk

355 11th Street
SoMa
San Francisco
California 94103
+1 4153559400
www.baragricole.com

Opening hours	7 days for dinner
Reservation policy	Yes
Credit cards	Accepted
Price range	Affordable
Style	Casual
Cuisine	Bar-Bistro
Recommended for	Local favourite

'Bar Agricole is a good representation of the Bay Area. The food has a sense of place; mostly because of the ingredients they use but also because they extend those purchasing practices to the bar programme as well, taking what the area is known for one step further.'—Russell Moore

BENU

Recommended by
Matthew Accarrino, David Chang, Jason Fox, David Kinch, Carlo Mirarchi, Daniel Patterson, Paul Qui

22 Hawthorne Street
SoMa
San Francisco
California 94105
+1 4156854860
www.benusf.com

Opening hours	5 days for dinner
Reservation policy	Yes
Reservation email	party@benusf.com
Credit cards	Accepted
Price range	Expensive
Style	Casual
Cuisine	Asian-American
Recommended for	High end

'Wonderful, highly personal, and an expensive treat.'—Daniel Patterson

A bold monument to modernism, Benu is high-achiever Corey Lee's first restaurant since leaving The French Laundry fold. Complex and thought-provoking, Lee's dishes make light work of classic techniques, injecting Asian flavours into immaculate dishes. (Lee even designs the plates and bowls himself.) Gels and foams feature widely on the ambitious tasting menu, which changes daily but always begins with a thousand-year-old quail egg. Benu treads a fine line between high-concept cooking and customer satisfaction, yet Lee's contemporaries are resoundingly gushing in their praise. Needless to say, innovation and exceptional craftsmanship comes at a price — you've been warned.

SIGHTGLASS

Recommended by
Corey Lee

270 7th Street
SoMa
San Francisco
California 94103
+1 4158611313
www.sightglasscoffee.com

Opening hours	7 days for breakfast and lunch
Reservation policy	No
Credit cards	Accepted
Price range	Budget
Style	Casual
Cuisine	Café
Recommended for	Breakfast

UNA PIZZA NAPOLETANA

Recommended by
Matthew Dillon

210 11th Street
SoMa
San Francisco
California 94103
+1 4158613444
www.unapizza.com

Opening hours	4 days for dinner
Reservation policy	No
Credit cards	Accepted
Price range	Affordable
Style	Casual
Cuisine	Pizza
Recommended for	Worth the travel

'Wow, the dough, the dough, the dough.
It's God's pizza.'—Matthew Dillon

AME

Recommended by
Mara Salles

689 Mission Street
South Beach
San Francisco
California 94103
+1 4152844040
www.amerestaurant.com

Opening hours	7 days for dinner
Reservation policy	Yes
Credit cards	Accepted
Price range	Expensive
Style	Formal
Cuisine	Japanese-American
Recommended for	Worth the travel

BRENDA'S FRENCH SOUL FOOD

Recommended by
Matthew Accarrino,
Christopher Thompson

652 Polk Street
Tenderloin
San Francisco
California 94102
+1 4153458100
www.frenchsoulfood.com

Opening hours	7 days from Breakfast until late
Reservation policy	No
Credit cards	Accepted
Price range	Affordable
Style	Casual
Cuisine	French-Creole
Recommended for	Breakfast

'Their prawn (shrimp) *beignets* are out of control: cheese, prawns and spring onions (scallions) on the inside and covered in paprika and garlic powder on the outside. The *croque monsieur* is also legit.'
—Christopher Thompson

LERS ROS THAI

Recommended by
Matthew Accarrino

730 Larkin Street
Tenderloin
San Francisco
California 94109
+1 4159316917
www.lersros.com

Opening hours	7 days for lunch and dinner
Reservation policy	No
Credit cards	Accepted
Price range	Affordable
Style	Casual
Cuisine	Thai
Recommended for	Regular neighbourhood

Originally intended as a late-night haunt for local Thai residents working in the industry, Lers Ros (pronounced 'lerhh rohh') transcends its location in Tenderloin, San Francisco's most rough and ready neighbourhood. Set up in 2008 by chef-owner Tom Silargorn — who is usually seen dexterously manning the wok — it's all about the balance of flavours, with dishes like pad Thai and roast duck larb mercifully avoiding concessions to the saccharine Western palate. Silargorn's success has meant recent expansion into the hip Hayes Valley — just five minutes away, but with an entirely different demographic.

IPPUKU

Recommended by
Russell Moore

2130 Center Street
Berkeley
California 94704
+1 5106651969
www.ippukuberkeley.com

Opening hours	5 days for lunch and 7 days for dinner
Reservation policy	Yes
Credit cards	Accepted
Price range	Affordable
Style	Casual
Cuisine	Japanese
Recommended for	Regular neighbourhood

'They make perfect soba noodles for lunch and then are an izakaya at night. I particularly like the yaki onigiri, rice porridge and chicken shoulder blade skewers. And they have lots of different shochu, which is kind of fun.'—Russell Moore

LITTLE SAIGON

Recommended by
Cal Peternell

1717 University Avenue
Berkeley
California 94703
+1 5105499594

Opening hours	7 days for lunch and dinner
Reservation policy	No
Credit cards	Accepted
Price range	Budget
Style	Casual
Cuisine	Vietnamese
Recommended for	Bargain

VIK'S CHAAT & MARKET

Recommended by
Russell Moore, Cal Peternell

2390 4th Street
Berkeley
California 94710
+1 5106444412
www.vikschaatcorner.com

Opening hours	7 days for lunch and 3 days for dinner
Reservation policy	No
Credit cards	Accepted
Price range	Budget
Style	Casual
Cuisine	Indian Street food
Recommended for	Bargain

KOI PALACE

Recommended by
Michael Tusk

365 Gellert Boulevard
Daly City
California 94015
+1 6509929000
www.koipalace.com

Opening hours	7 days for breakfast, lunch and dinner
Reservation policy	Yes
Credit cards	Accepted
Price range	Budget
Style	Casual
Cuisine	Chinese
Recommended for	Bargain

BOOT AND SHOE SERVICE

Recommended by
Daniel Patterson

3308 Grand Avenue
Grand Lake
Oakland
California 94610
www.bootandshoeservice.com

Opening hours	6 days for brunch and dinner
Reservation policy	No
Credit cards	Accepted
Price range	Affordable
Style	Casual
Cuisine	Pizza
Recommended for	Regular neighbourhood

'They have pizza. I have kids.'—Daniel Patterson

The sequel to Pizzaiolo does the same thing with quality wood-fired Neapolitan-style pizzas for the Oakland neighbourhood of Grand Lake that its older sibling does up in Temescal. Unlike Pizzaiolo, they don't take reservations here, but their bar is a rather pleasant holding pen when waiting for a table. The name has been recycled from the business that previously occupied the premises, the old shoe repair shop's sign and much of the building's original character – exposed bricks, beamed ceiling and scuffed floor – retained. A breakfast and brunch café in adjoining premises was added to the mix in 2011.

CAMINO

Recommended by
Cal Peternell,
Fernando Trocca

3917 Grand Avenue
Grand Lake
Oakland
California 94610
+1 5105475035
www.caminorestaurant.com

Opening hours	2 days for brunch and 6 days for dinner
Reservation policy	Yes
Credit cards	Accepted
Price range	Affordable
Style	Casual
Cuisine	Modern American
Recommended for	Local favourite

COMMIS

3859 Piedmont Avenue
Piedmont
Oakland
California 94611
+1 5106533902
www.commisrestaurant.com

Recommended by
Jason Fox, Dan Hunter, David
Kinch, Corey Lee, Russell
Moore, Daniel Patterson

Opening hours..5 days for dinner
Reservation policy...Yes
Credit cards..Accepted
Price range...Expensive
Style...Smart casual
Cuisine..Modern American
Recommended for...High end

'Wonderful and very personal.'—Daniel Patterson

Understated and gastronomically ambitious, James
Syhabout's Commis immediately demanded attention
when it opened in 2009. Not least for Syhabout's
credentials, which includes stretches at The Fat Duck
and elBulli before he returned to California to help
open Daniel Patterson's Coi in San Francisco and
work under David Kinch at Manresa in Los Gatos.
Raised in Oakland, the son of a Thai mother and a
Chinese father, his menus take a cerebral approach
to Northern California's ample larder (pantry),
combining modern European flair with the occasional
Asian technique. Try and claim a sought-after berth
at the six-seat counter overlooking the open kitchen.

EL PAISA

4610 International Boulevard
East Oakland
Oakland
California 94620

Recommended by
Russell Moore

Opening hours...................7 days for lunch and dinner
Reservation policy..No
Credit cards..Accepted
Price range..Budget
Style...Casual
Cuisine...Mexican
Recommended for...Bargain

PIZZAIOLO

5008 Telegraph Avenue
North Oakland
Oakland
California 94609
+1 5106524888
www.pizzaiolooakland.com

Recommended by
Daniel Patterson, Mark
Sullivan

Opening hours..6 days for dinner
Reservation policy...Yes
Credit cards..Accepted
Price range...Affordable
Style...Casual
Cuisine...Pizza
Recommended for...Late night

'Great atmosphere, late-night music and food.'
—Mark Sullivan

Charlie Hallowell, 'child of Chez Panisse' inspired by
his eight years in the kitchen at Alice Water's seminal
Berkeley restaurant, opened Pizzaiolo in Oakland in
2005. Located on Telegraph Avenue, in the maple-
lined heart of the Temescal district of the city, it has
developed a cult following for its simple menu built
around a line-up of antipasti, a handful of pasta
dishes, the occasional large plate and – the main
event – a selection of wood-fired Neapolitan-style
pizzas, made with organic flour and almost
exclusively topped with seasonal sustainably farmed
produce directly sourced from local farmers. Alice
must be very proud.

PYEONG CHANG TOFU HOUSE

4701 Telegraph Avenue
North Oakland
Oakland
California 94609
+1 5106589040

Recommended by
Russell Moore

Opening hours...................7 days for lunch and dinner
Reservation policy..No
Credit cards..Accepted
Price range..Budget
Style...Casual
Cuisine...Korean
Recommended for...Bargain

'Amazing iced coffee that keeps you wired for hours.'
JARROD VERBIAK P525

The quintessential Miami restaurant!
DOUGLAS RODRIGUEZ P528

'INCREDIBLE VIBE, FUN ATMOSPHERE AND AWESOME FOOD.'
ADAN SOBEL P524

USA EAST

'Shrimps and grits! This dish is such a Charleston staple and I can't get enough of it.'
SEAN BROCK P539

'They serve all the parts that make most people squirm, like testicles and brains, but they prepare it in a Southern context.'
SEAN BROCK P529

'THEY PRACTICE A TOUGH LOVE SERVICE STYLE BUT IT JUST KEEPS ME COMING BACK FOR MORE.'
MICHAEL SCHWARTZ P525

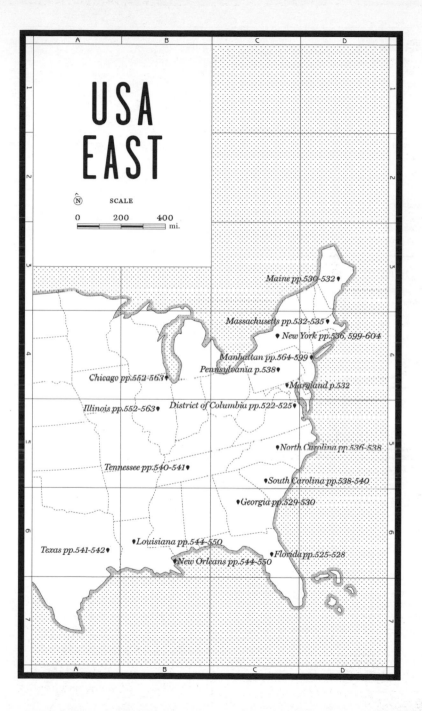

USA
EAST

N SCALE

0   200   400
mi.

Maine pp.530-532 ♦

Massachusetts pp.532-535 ♦

♦ New York pp.536, 599-604

Manhattan pp.564-599 ♦

Pennsylvania p.538 ♦

Chicago pp.552-563 ♦

♦ Maryland p.532

Illinois pp.552-563 ♦   District of Columbia pp.522-525 ♦

♦ North Carolina pp.536-538

Tennessee pp.540-541 ♦

♦ South Carolina pp.538-540

♦ Georgia pp.529-530

Texas pp.541-542 ♦   ♦ Louisiana pp.544-550

♦ Florida pp.525-528

New Orleans pp.544-550

TOKI UNDERGROUND

1234 H Street Northeast
Atlas District
Washington, D.C. 20002
+1 2023883086
www.tokiunderground.com

Opening hours...7 days for dinner
Reservation policy...No
Credit cards...Accepted
Price range...Affordable
Style...Style
Cuisine...Taiwanese
Recommended for.................................Wish I'd opened

'I love cooking Asian street food and this is something I would do in a heartbeat.'—Adam Sobel

RUSTIK TAVERN

84 T Street Northwest
Bloomingdale
Washington, D.C. 20001
+1 2022902936
www.rustikdc.com

Opening hours.............................7 days for brunch and dinner
Reservation policy...No
Credit cards...Accepted
Price range...Budget
Style...Casual
Cuisine...Italian
Recommended for...Breakfast

'Chorizo rösti (hash) and sunnyside eggs.'
—Matthew Kuhn

JOHNNY'S HALF SHELL

400 North Capitol Street Northwest
Capitol Hill
Washington, D.C. 20001
+1 2027370400
www.johnnyshalfshell.net

Opening hours.............5 days for lunch and 6 days for dinner
Reservation policy...Yes
Credit cards...Accepted
Price range...Affordable
Style...Casual
Cuisine...Seafood
Recommended for.................................Local favourite

PHO DC

608 H Street Northwest
Chinatown
Washington, D.C. 20001
+1 2025062888
www.phodc.com

Opening hours.........................7 days for lunch and dinner
Reservation policy...Yes
Credit cards...Accepted
Price range...Budget
Style...Casual
Cuisine...Vietnamese
Recommended for...Bargain

2AMYS

3715 Macomb Street Northwest
Cleveland Park
Washington, D.C. 20016
www.2amyspizza.com

Opening hours.............6 days for lunch and 7 days for dinner
Reservation policy...No
Credit cards...Accepted
Price range...Budget
Style...Casual
Cuisine...Pizza
Recommended for.................................Worth the travel

'Great pizza, and the back bar has excellent seasonal small plates and charcuterie.'—Matthew Kuhn

BIBIANA

1100 New York Avenue Northwest
Downtown
Washington, D.C. 20005
+1 2022169550
www.bibianadc.com

Opening hours.............5 days for lunch and 6 days for dinner
Reservation policy...Yes
Credit cards...Accepted
Price range...Expensive
Style...Formal
Cuisine...Modern Italian
Recommended for...High end

'Nick Stefanelli mixes refinement with Italian simplicities. The result is fantastic.'—Adam Sobel

OLD EBBITT GRILL

Recommended by
Matthew Kuhn

675 15th Street Northwest
Downtown
Washington, D.C. 20005
+1 2023474800
www.ebbitt.com

Opening hours	7 days from breakfast until late
Reservation policy	Yes
Credit cards	Accepted
Price range	Affordable
Style	Casual
Cuisine	American
Recommended for	Late night

'Go for the Pumpernickle pastrami, Muenster cheese and coleslaw.'—Matthew Kuhn

THE SOURCE

Recommended by
Adam Sobel

575 Pennsylvania Avenue Northwest
Downtown
Washington, D.C. 20001
+1 2026376100
www.wolfgangpuck.com

Opening hours	6 days for lunch and dinner
Reservation policy	Yes
Credit cards	Accepted
Price range	Expensive
Style	Formal
Cuisine	Asian-American
Recommended for	Regular neighbourhood

'Scott Drewno makes really delicious food, and the service is always outstanding. I love this restaurant.'
—Adam Sobel

OBELISK

Recommended by
Matthew Kuhn

2029 P Street Northwest
Dupont Circle
Washington, D.C. 20036
+1 2028721180

Opening hours	5 days for dinner
Reservation policy	Yes
Credit cards	Accepted
Price range	Expensive
Style	Smart casual
Cuisine	Italian
Recommended for	High end

'Simple, rustic Italian food. Very underrated.'
—Matthew Kuhn

PIZZERIA PARADISO

Recommended by
Matthew Kuhn

2003 P Street Northwest
Dupont Circle
Washington, D.C. 20036
www.eatyourpizza.com

Opening hours	7 days for lunch and dinner
Reservation policy	No
Credit cards	Accepted
Price range	Budget
Style	Casual
Cuisine	Pizza
Recommended for	Regular neighbourhood

'Ramp pesto pizza and a craft beer.'—Matthew Kuhn

BANDOLERO

Recommended by
Adam Sobel

3241 M Street Northwest
Georgetown
Washington, D.C. 20007
+1 2026254488
www.bandolerodc.com

Opening hours	7 days for dinner
Reservation policy	Yes
Credit cards	Accepted
Price range	Affordable
Style	Casual
Cuisine	Mexican
Recommended for	Late night

SEASONS

Recommended by
Adam Sobel

Four Seasons Hotel
2800 Pennsylvania Avenue Northwest
Georgetown
Washington, D.C. 20007
+1 2029442000
www.fourseasons.com

Opening hours	7 days for breakfast and 2 days for lunch
Reservation policy	Yes
Credit cards	Accepted
Price range	Expensive
Style	Smart casual
Cuisine	International
Recommended for	Breakfast

'This is a restaurant that knows how to do breakfast and is a typical meeting place for the most powerful people in D.C.'—Adam Sobel

GRAFFIATO

Recommended by
Adam Sobel

707 6th Street Northwest
Penn Quarter
Washington, D.C. 20001
+1 2022893600
www.graffiatodc.com

Opening hours	7 days for lunch and dinner
Reservation policy	Yes
Credit cards	Accepted
Price range	Expensive
Style	Smart casual
Cuisine	Italian
Recommended for	Late night

'Mike Isabella has two great restaurants that do late night and have an incredible vibe, fun atmosphere and awesome food, of course.'—Adam Sobel

RASIKA ✓

Recommended by
Adam Sobel

633 D Street Northwest
Penn Quarter
Washington, D.C. 20004
+1 2026371222
www.rasikarestaurant.com

Opening hours	5 days for lunch and 6 days for dinner
Reservation policy	Yes
Credit cards	Accepted
Price range	Affordable
Style	Smart casual
Cuisine	Modern Indian
Recommended for	Local favourite

'Rasika could possibly be the best Indian restaurant in the U.S. This is a Washington, D.C. staple.'
—Adam Sobel

THE AMERICAN ICE CO.

Recommended by
Matthew Kuhn

917 V Street Northwest
Shaw
Washington, D.C. 20001
+1 2027583562
www.amicodc.com

Opening hours	2 days for lunch and 7 days for dinner
Reservation policy	No
Credit cards	Accepted
Price range	Budget
Style	Casual
Cuisine	American
Recommended for	Wish I'd opened

'They serve craft beer and great BBQ. Late night they have $5 (£3) hot pork and cheese sandwiches. Awesome!'—Matthew Kuhn

ROGUE 24

Recommended by
Jesse Schenker

922 N Street Northwest
Shaw ✓
Washington, D.C. 20001
+1 2024089724
www.rogue24.com

Opening hours	5 days for dinner
Reservation policy	Yes
Credit cards	Accepted
Price range	Expensive
Style	Smart casual
Cuisine	Modern American
Recommended for	Worth the travel

'Super-interesting because the kitchen and dining room are in one room.'—Jesse Schenker

Chef and James Beard Award winner R. J. Cooper is America's answer to Heston Blumenthal – if anything, a little more theatrical. He's taken a former car body shop located down an alleyway and turned it into an arena of 'no parameters' fine dining. Shed your preconceptions, abandon control and gird your loins for sixteen or twenty-four courses of culinary curiosity (onion ice cream anybody?), each like a miniature stage set, prepared with quiet meticulousness amid puffs of steam on four work stations in the middle of the dining room. The whole experience is a sensory adventure to somewhere far from the norm.

STANDARD

Recommended by
Adam Sobel

1801 14th Street Northwest
Shaw
Washington, D.C. 20009
www.standarddc.com

Opening hours	2 days for lunch and 6 days for dinner
Reservation policy	No
Credit cards	Accepted
Price range	Affordable
Style	Casual
Cuisine	Barbecue
Recommended for	Bargain

'Amazing BBQ Brisket Sandwiches.'—Adam Sobel

RIS

Recommended by
Patrick O'Connell

2275 L Street Northwest
West End
Washington, D.C. 20037
+1 2027302500
www.risdc.com

Opening hours	6 days for lunch and dinner
Reservation policy	Yes
Credit cards	Accepted
Price range	Expensive
Style	Smart casual
Cuisine	Modern American
Recommended for	Regular neighbourhood

SUSHI ROCK CAFÉ

Recommended by
Patrick O'Connell

1515 East Las Olas Boulevard
Fort Lauderdale
Florida 33301
+1 9544625541

Opening hours	7 days for lunch and dinner
Reservation policy	No
Credit cards	Accepted
Price range	Affordable
Style	Casual
Cuisine	Japanese
Recommended for	Bargain

ENRIQUETA'S SANDWICH SHOP

Recommended by
Michael Schwartz

2830 Northeast 2nd Avenue
Miami
Florida 33137

Opening hours	6 days for breakfast and lunch
Reservation policy	No
Credit cards	Accepted
Price range	Budget
Style	Casual
Cuisine	Cuban
Recommended for	Breakfast

'I come here for breakfast, a Cuban sandwich and of course the obligatory *cortadito*. They practise a tough love service style but it just keeps me coming back for more.'—Michael Schwartz

ETERNITY COFFEE ROASTERS

Recommended by
Jarrod Verbiak

117 Southeast 2nd Avenue
Miami
Florida 33131
+1 3053507761
www.eternitycoffeeroasters.com

Opening hours	6 days for breakfast and lunch
Reservation policy	No
Credit cards	Accepted
Price range	Budget
Style	Casual
Cuisine	Cafe
Recommended for	Breakfast

'I am not a big breakfast person but I love coffee. Eternity Coffee Roasters make an amazing iced coffee that keeps you wired for hours. They roast their own beans, so the coffee always tastes just right. You can also indulge in a great pastry or homemade cake when you are there.'—Jarrod Verbiak

GIGI

Recommended by
Michael Schwartz

3470 North Miami Avenue
Miami
Florida 33127
+1 3055731520
www.giginow.com

Opening hours	7 days for lunch and dinner
Reservation policy	No
Credit cards	Accepted
Price range	Affordable
Style	Casual
Cuisine	Asian
Recommended for	Late night

'Duck confit, house-made pickles, any bun they've got, I'm eating. Late night!'—Michael Schwartz

MANDOLIN

Recommended by
Michael Schwartz

4312 Northeast 2nd Avenue
Miami
Florida 33137
+1 3055766066
www.mandolinmiami.com

Opening hours	7 days for lunch and dinner
Reservation policy	Yes
Credit cards	Accepted
Price range	Affordable
Style	Casual
Cuisine	Greek-Turkish
Recommended for	Regular neighbourhood

'It is so simple; everything beautiful about the Mediterranean on a plate.'—Michael Schwartz

LA MOON

Recommended by
Jarrod Verbiak

97 Southwest 8th Street
Miami
Florida 33130
+1 3053795617
www.lamoonrestaurantmiami.com

Opening hours	7 days for lunch and dinner
Reservation policy	No
Credit cards	Accepted
Price range	Budget
Style	Casual
Cuisine	Columbian
Recommended for	Late night

'They are famous for their *Perros Colombianos* – Colombian hot dogs. These things are just what you need at 3.00 a.m. when you are on your way home from a fun night in Miami. They come with over twelve toppings including crisps (chips) and lots of special sauces.'—Jarrod Verbiak

PUBBELLY

Recommended by
Jarrod Verbiak

1418 20th Street
Miami
Florida 33139
+1 3055327555
www.pubbelly.com

Opening hours	6 days for dinner
Reservation policy	No
Credit cards	Accepted
Price range	Affordable
Style	Casual
Cuisine	Bar-Bistro
Recommended for	Local favourite

'Great decor, simple concept and well-executed menu and service.'—Jarrod Verbiak

PUBBELLY SUSHI

Recommended by
Jarrod Verbiak

1424 20th Street
Miami
Florida 33139
+1 3055319282
www.pubbellysushi.com

Opening hours	5 days for lunch and 6 days for dinner
Reservation policy	No
Credit cards	Accepted
Price range	Affordable
Style	Casual
Cuisine	Japanese
Recommended for	Local favourite

SAKAYA KITCHEN

Recommended by
Jarrod Verbiak

125 Southeast 3rd Avenue
Miami
Florida 33131
+1 3053712511
www.sakayakitchen.com

Opening hours	7 days from breakfast until late
Reservation policy	No
Credit cards	Accepted
Price range	Affordable
Style	Casual
Cuisine	Korean food truck
Recommended for	Regular neighbourhood

SUGARCANE RAW BAR GRILL

Recommended by
Khalid Mohammed

3250 Northeast 1st Avenue
Miami
Florida 33127
+1 7863690353
www.sugarcanerawbargrill.com

Opening hours................................7 days for lunch and dinner
Reservation policy..Yes
Credit cards..Accepted
Price range...Affordable
Style..Casual
Cuisine...Asian-Latin American
Recommended for.................................Worth the travel

BARCELONETA

Recommended by
Jarrod Verbiak

1400 20th Street
Miami Beach
Florida 33139
+1 3055389299
www.barcelonetarestaurant.com

Opening hours............1 day for brunch and 7 days for dinner
Reservation policy..No
Credit cards..Accepted
Price range...Affordable
Style..Casual
Cuisine..Spanish
Recommended for.................................Worth the travel

'I feel like I am on holiday (vacation) when I eat here.'
—Jarrod Verbiak

CASA TUA

Recommended by
Bryn Williams

1700 James Avenue
Miami Beach
Florida 33139
+1 3056731010
www.casatualifestyle.com

Opening hours..6 days for dinner
Reservation policy...Yes
Reservation email...........................info@casatualifestyle.com
Credit cards..Accepted
Price range..Expensive
Style...Smart casual
Cuisine...Italian
Recommended for.................................Worth the travel

'This is an exquisite Italian restaurant. To this day, I
have never tasted gnocchi so good.'—Bryn Williams

CECCONI'S

Recommended by
Michael Schwartz

Soho Beach House
4385 Collins Avenue
Miami Beach
Florida 33140
+1 7865077902
www.cecconismiamibeach.com

Opening hours.............7 days for breakfast, lunch and dinner
Reservation policy...Yes
Reservation email.................miami@cecconisrestaurant.com
Credit cards..Accepted
Price range...Affordable
Style...Smart casual
Cuisine...Italian
Recommended for..Breakfast

'Immaculately designed with every detail crafted to
perfection. Hit the second floor bar of Soho Beach
House for a classic cocktail before you jump in the
pool.'—Michael Schwartz

HAKKASAN

Recommended by
Michael Schwartz

4441 Collins Avenue
Miami Beach
Florida 33140
+1 7862761388
www.hakkasan.com/miami

Opening hours...5 days for dinner
Reservation policy...Yes
Credit cards..Accepted
Price range..Expensive
Style...Smart casual
Cuisine..Modern Chinese
Recommended for..High end

'Best prawn (shrimp) dumplings and plenty
more.'—Michael Schwartz

JOE'S STONE CRAB

11 Washington Avenue
Miami Beach
Florida 33139
+1 3056730365
www.joesstonecrab.com

Opening hours	5 days for lunch and 7 days for dinner
Reservation policy	No
Credit cards	Accepted
Price range	Affordable
Style	Smart casual
Cuisine	Seafood
Recommended for	Local favourite

'The quintessential Miami restaurant!'
—Douglas Rodriguez

EL PALACIOS DE LOS JUGOS

5721 West Flagler Street
Miami Beach
Florida 33144

Opening hours	7 days from breakfast until late
Reservation policy	No
Credit cards	Accepted
Price range	Budget
Style	Casual
Cuisine	Cuban
Recommended for	Bargain

'It does not get more Miami than this.'
—Michael Schwartz

SCARPETTA

Fountainebleu Hotel
4441 Collins Avenue
Miami Beach
Florida 33140
+1 3055382000
www.fontainebleau.com

Opening hours	7 days for dinner
Reservation policy	Yes
Credit cards	Accepted
Price range	Expensive
Style	Smart casual
Cuisine	Italian
Recommended for	High end

'I especially like the Scialatielli with Key West pink
prawns (shrimp), calamari and English peas – it's a
tasty blend of flavors and textures.'—Jarrod Verbiak

SHAKE SHACK

1111 Lincoln Road
Miami Beach
Florida 33139
+1 3054347787
www.shakeshack.com

Opening hours	7 days for lunch and dinner
Reservation policy	No
Credit cards	Accepted
Price range	Budget
Style	Casual
Cuisine	Burgers
Recommended for	Wish I'd opened

'Thank goodness I don't have to head to Manhattan
anymore when I want my favourite burger, with a side
of Danny Meyer service.'—Michael Schwartz

YARDBIRD

1600 Lenox Avenue
Miami Beach
Florida 33139
+1 3055385220
www.runchickenrun.com

Opening hours	7 days for brunch and dinner
Reservation policy	Yes
Credit cards	Accepted
Price range	Affordable
Style	Casual
Cuisine	Southern American
Recommended for	Worth the travel

BUCCAN

350 South County Road
Palm Beach
Florida 33480
+1 5618333450
www.buccanpalmbeach.com

Opening hours	7 days for dinner
Reservation policy	Yes
Credit cards	Accepted
Price range	Affordable
Style	Smart casual
Cuisine	Modern American
Recommended for	Worth the travel

'Very innovative small plates. I like the wood-fired
Brussels sprouts.'—Paul Newman

PEACHES FINE FOODS

Recommended by
Hugh Acheson

840 West Broad Street
Athens
Georgia 30601
+1 7066135334
www.peachesfinefoods.com

Opening hours	5 days for lunch
Reservation policy	No
Credit cards	Accepted
Price range	Budget
Style	Casual
Cuisine	Southern American
Recommended for	Local favourite

BACCHANALIA

Recommended by
Linton Hopkins

1198 Howell Mill Road
Atlanta
Georgia 30318
+1 4043650410
www.starprovisions.com

Opening hours	6 days for dinner
Reservation policy	Yes
Credit cards	Accepted
Price range	Expensive
Style	Formal
Cuisine	Modern American
Recommended for	High end

CARVER'S COUNTRY KITCHEN

Recommended by
Linton Hopkins

1118 West Marietta Street Northwest
Atlanta
Georgia 30318
+1 4047944410
www.carverscountrykitchen.com

Opening hours	5 days for lunch
Reservation policy	No
Credit cards	Not accepted
Price range	Budget
Style	Casual
Cuisine	Southern American
Recommended for	Local favourite

'Meat and three, Southern style.'—Linton Hopkins

HOLEMAN & FINCH PUBLIC HOUSE

Recommended by
Hugh Acheson,
Sean Brock,
Andrea Reusing

2277 Peachtree Road
Atlanta
Georgia 30309
+1 40494811751
www.holeman-finch.com

Opening hours	1 day for lunch and 6 days for dinner
Reservation policy	No
Credit cards	Accepted
Price range	Affordable
Style	Casual
Cuisine	Southern American
Recommended for	Worth the travel

'Really casual and the food is daring but still very Southern. They serve all the parts that make most people squirm, like testicles and brains, but they prepare it in a Southern context. Oh, and did I mention that they make the best cocktails ever?!'—Sean Brock

MILLER UNION

Recommended by
Harold Dieterle

999 Brady Avenue
Atlanta
Georgia 30318
+1 6787338550
www.millerunion.com

Opening hours	5 days for lunch and 6 days for dinner
Reservation policy	Yes
Credit cards	Accepted
Price range	Affordable
Style	Casual
Cuisine	American
Recommended for	Worth the travel

The Georgia chapter of the South's fledgling farm-to-table movement has been well represented by Miller Union since 2009. Located in the heart of what's now known as the Railroad Historic District, it takes its name from the stockyards that served the railway from 1881 until the 1970s. The large purpose-built space is divided into a series of intimate dining areas and a bar, thereby avoiding the din that can be the curse of warehouse dining. The harvest-driven menu changes weekly, the emphasis on simple, rustic-styled dishes – particularly on the third Tuesday of every month, when they serve a family-style 'Harvest dinner'.

THE VARSITY

Recommended by
Linton Hopkins

61 North Avenue Northwest
Atlanta
Georgia 30308
www.thevarsity.com

Opening hours	7 days from breakfast until late
Reservation policy	No
Credit cards	Accepted
Price range	Budget
Style	Casual
Cuisine	Fast food
Recommended for	Bargain

WHITE HOUSE

Recommended by
Linton Hopkins

3172 Peachtree Road
Atlanta
Georgia 30305
+1 404237760
www.whitehouserestaurant.net

Opening hours	7 days for brunch and 5 days for dinner
Reservation policy	No
Credit cards	Accepted
Price range	Budget
Style	Casual
Cuisine	Diner-Café
Recommended for	Breakfast

'A Greek-owned diner in Buckhead. They really know how to poach eggs and they make strong coffee.'—Linton Hopkins

UMAIDO

Recommended by
Hugh Acheson

2790 Lawrenceville Suwanee Road
Suwanee
Georgia 30024
+1 6783188568
www.umaidos.com

Opening hours	7 days for lunch and dinner
Reservation policy	No
Credit cards	Accepted
Price range	Budget
Style	Casual
Cuisine	Japanese
Recommended for	Regular neighbourhood

THE LOST KITCHEN

Recommended by
Sam Hayward

108 Main Street
Belfast
Maine 04915
+1 2079302055

Opening hours	5 days for dinner
Reservation policy	Yes
Credit cards	Accepted
Price range	Affordable
Style	Casual
Cuisine	International
Recommended for	Worth the travel

'Hard-to-find, upstairs restaurant in a resurgent waterfront town. Excellent cooking based on fresh produce from Maine's farms and fisheries.'
—Sam Hayward

EL CAMINO

Recommended by
Sam Hayward

15 Cushing Street
Brunswick
Maine 04011
+1 2077258228
www.elcaminomaine.com

Opening hours	5 days for dinner
Reservation policy	No
Credit cards	Accepted
Price range	Affordable
Style	Casual
Cuisine	Mexican
Recommended for	Bargain

'Very good Mexican-based cooking and border-town kitsch elevated to art.'—Sam Hayward

BOYNTON-MCKAY

Recommended by
Sam Hayward

30 Main Street
Camden
Maine 04843
+1 2072362465
www.boynton-mckay.com

Opening hours	7 days for breakfast and lunch
Reservation policy	No
Credit cards	Accepted
Price range	Budget
Style	Casual
Cuisine	Café
Recommended for	Breakfast

'The finest doughnuts in Maine, totally unencumbered by surface gloop or inner sludge. Plain and perfect.'
—Sam Hayward

BODA

671 Congress Street
Portland
Maine 04101
+1 2073477557
www.bodamaine.com

Recommended by
Rob Evans, Sam Hayward

Opening hours	6 days for dinner
Reservation policy	No
Credit cards	Accepted
Price range	Budget
Style	Casual
Cuisine	Thai small plates
Recommended for	Late night

'Excellent bites and small plates until 1.00 a.m.'
—Sam Hayward

BRESCA

111 Middle Street
Portland
Maine 04101
+1 2077721004
www.restaurantbresca.com

Recommended by
Rob Evans

Opening hours	4 days for dinner
Reservation policy	Yes
Credit cards	Accepted
Price range	Affordable
Style	Smart casual
Cuisine	Modern Italian
Recommended for	High end

FORE STREET

288 Fore Street
Portland
Maine 04101
+1 2077752717
www.forestreet.biz

Recommended by
Rob Evans, Peter Hoffman

Opening hours	7 days for dinner
Reservation policy	Yes
Credit cards	Accepted
Price range	Affordable
Style	Casual
Cuisine	Modern American
Recommended for	Local favourite

GORGEOUS GELATO

434 Fore Street
Portland
Maine 04101
+1 2076994309
www.GorgeousGelato.com

Recommended by
Rob Evans

Opening hours	7 days
Reservation policy	No
Credit cards	Accepted
Price range	Budget
Style	Casual
Cuisine	Ice cream
Recommended for	Wish I'd opened

HOT SUPPA!

703 Congress Street
Portland
Maine 04102
+1 2078715005
www.hotsuppa.com

Recommended by
Rob Evans, Sam Hayward

Opening hours	7 days for brunch and 5 days for dinner
Reservation policy	No
Credit cards	Accepted
Price range	Budget
Style	Casual
Cuisine	American
Recommended for	Breakfast

'Small neighbourhood joint with excellent, robust home cooking.'—Sam Hayward

OTTO PIZZA

576 Congress Street
Portland
Maine 04101
+1 2077737099
www.ottoportland.com

Recommended by
Rob Evans

Opening hours	7 days for lunch and dinner
Reservation policy	No
Credit cards	Accepted
Price range	Budget
Style	Casual
Cuisine	Pizza
Recommended for	Bargain

PAI MEN MIYAKE

Recommended by
Rob Evans

188 Street
Portland
Maine 04101
+1 2075419204
www.miyakerestaurants.com

Opening hours	7 days for lunch and dinner
Reservation policy	Yes
Credit cards	Accepted
Price range	Budget
Style	Casual
Cuisine	Japanese
Recommended for	Regular neighbourhood

PETITE JACQUELINE

Recommended by
Sam Hayward

190 Street
Portland
Maine 04101
+1 2075537044
www.bistropj.com

Opening hours	7 days for brunch and dinner
Reservation policy	Yes
Credit cards	Accepted
Price range	Affordable
Style	Casual
Cuisine	French
Recommended for	Regular neighbourhood

'Well executed classic bistro cooking.'—Sam Hayward

PRIMO

Recommended by
Alex Young

2 South Main Street
Rockland
Maine 04841
+1 2075960770
www.primorestaurant.com

Opening hours	5 days for dinner
Reservation policy	Yes
Credit cards	Accepted
Price range	Affordable
Style	Casual
Cuisine	Mediterranean
Recommended for	Wish I'd opened

THE SLIPWAY

Recommended by
Sam Hayward

24 Public Landing
Thomaston
Maine 04861
+1 2073544155
www.maine-slipway.com

Opening hours	6 days for breakfast, lunch and dinner
Reservation policy	Yes
Credit cards	Accepted
Price range	Affordable
Style	Casual
Cuisine	Seafood
Recommended for	Local favourite

'Classic Maine coast "summer food" (lobsters, steamers, chowders) with some creative embellishments.'—Sam Hayward

LEVEL

Recommended by
Ben Roche

69 West Street
Annapolis
Maryland 21401
+1 4102680003
www.levelsmallplateslounge.com

Opening hours	7 days for dinner
Reservation policy	Yes
Credit cards	Accepted
Price range	Affordable
Style	Casual
Cuisine	American Small plates
Recommended for	Worth the travel

GOURMET DUMPLING HOUSE

Recommended by
Ken Oringer

52 Beach Street
Boston
Massachusetts 02111
+1 6173386223
www.gourmetdumpling.com

Opening hours	7 days for lunch and dinner
Reservation policy	No
Credit cards	Accepted
Price range	Affordable
Style	Casual
Cuisine	Chinese
Recommended for	Regular neighbourhood

'One of my favourite spots in Boston. They have this spicy Szechuan fish soup with peppercorns and fiery chillies that I get every time I go – it's amazing. Other dishes to get there are the spring onion (scallion) pancakes, tofu skin, and pork soup dumplings. Some of the best Chinese food I've had in the USA.'
—Ken Oringer

GRILL 23

Recommended by
Tony Maws

161 Berkeley Street
Boston
Massachusetts 02117
+1 6175422255
www.grill23.com

Opening hours	7 days for dinner
Reservation policy	Yes
Credit cards	Accepted
Price range	Expensive
Style	Smart casual
Cuisine	Modern American
Recommended for	High end

HAMERSLEY'S BISTRO

Recommended by
Sam Hayward

553 Tremont Street
Boston
Massachusetts 02116
+1 6174232700
www.hamersleysbistro.com

Opening hours	1 day for brunch and 7 days for dinner
Reservation policy	Yes
Credit cards	Accepted
Price range	Expensive
Style	Smart casual
Cuisine	French
Recommended for	Wish I'd opened

'Chef Gordon Hamersley is a true gentleman who has maintained exceptional standards over more than two decades.'—Sam Hayward

KUPEL'S BAKERY

Recommended by
Tony Maws

421 Harvard Street
Brookline
Boston
Massachusetts 02446
+1 6175669528
www.kupelsbakery.com

Opening hours	6 days from breakfast until late
Reservation policy	No
Credit cards	Accepted
Price range	Budget
Style	Casual
Cuisine	Bakery-Café
Recommended for	Breakfast

JUMBO SEAFOOD

Recommended by
Tony Maws

5 Hudson Street
Boston
Massachusetts 02111
+1 6175422823
www.NewJumboSeafoodRestaurant.com

Opening hours	7 days for breakfast, lunch and dinner
Reservation policy	Yes
Credit cards	Accepted
Price range	Budget
Style	Casual
Cuisine	Chinese
Recommended for	Regular neighbourhood

NEPTUNE OYSTER

Recommended by
Tony Maws

63 Salem Street
Boston
Massachusetts 02110
+1 6177423474
www.neptuneoyster.com

Opening hours	7 days for lunch and dinner
Reservation policy	No
Credit cards	Accepted
Price range	Affordable
Style	Casual
Cuisine	Seafood
Recommended for	Wish I'd opened

OISHII BOSTON

Recommended by
Ken Oringer

1166 Washington Street
Boston
Massachusetts 02118
+1 6174828868
www.oishiiboston.com

Opening hours	6 days for lunch and dinner
Reservation policy	Yes
Credit cards	Accepted
Price range	Expensive
Style	Casual
Cuisine	Japanese
Recommended for	Worth the travel

'They do a lot of great things with seasonal and exotic Japanese fish.'—Ken Oringer

PARISH CAFE

Recommended by
Tim Cushman

361 Boylston Street
Boston
Massachusetts 02116
+1 6172474777
www.parishcafe.com

Opening hours	7 days from lunch until late
Reservation policy	No
Credit cards	Accepted
Price range	Budget
Style	Casual
Cuisine	Bar-Café
Recommended for	Late night

PHO VIET

Recommended by
Tony Maws

1095 Commonwealth Avenue
Boston
Massachusetts 02228
+1 6175628828

Opening hours	7 days for lunch and dinner
Reservation policy	No
Credit cards	Accepted
Price range	Budget
Style	Casual
Cuisine	Vietnamese
Recommended for	Bargain

'Go for their *pho sate* and their *banh mi*.'—Tony Maws

SUPER DOG

Recommended by
Tony Maws

46 Newmarket Square
Roxbury
Boston
Massachusetts 02118
www.bostonspeeddog.com

Opening hours	7 days for lunch
Reservation policy	No
Credit cards	Not accepted
Price range	Budget
Style	Casual
Cuisine	Hot Dogs
Recommended for	Wish I'd opened

CRAIGIE ON MAIN

Recommended by
Ben Pollinger

853 Main Street
Cambridge
Massachusetts 02139
+1 6174975511
www.craigieonmain.com

Opening hours	1 day for brunch and 6 days for dinner
Reservation policy	Yes
Credit cards	Accepted
Price range	Affordable
Style	Casual
Cuisine	Modern American
Recommended for	Worth the travel

'Really great flavours!'—Ben Pollinger

EAST COAST GRILL

Recommended by
Ken Oringer

1271 Cambridge Street
Cambridge
Massachusetts 02139
+1 6174916568
www.eastcoastgrill.net

Opening hours	2 days for brunch and 7 days for dinner
Reservation policy	Yes
Credit cards	Accepted
Price range	Affordable
Style	Casual
Cuisine	Steakhouse-Seafood
Recommended for	Local favourite

'Great local seafood, like oysters and clams on the half shell.'—Ken Oringer

OLEANA

Recommended by
Tim Cushman,
Mitchell Rosenthal

134 Hampshire Street
Cambridge
Massachusetts 02139
+1 6176610505
www.oleanarestaurant.com

Opening hours	7 days for dinner
Reservation policy	Yes
Credit cards	Accepted
Price range	Budget
Style	Casual
Cuisine	Middle Eastern-Mediterranean
Recommended for	Worth the travel

'Delicious interpretation of Turkish food.'
—Mitchell Rosenthal

SAPPORO RAMEN

Recommended by
Ken Oringer

1815 Massachusetts Avenue
Cambridge
Massachusetts 02140
+1 6178764805

Opening hours	7 days for lunch and dinner
Reservation policy	No
Price range	Budget
Style	Casual
Cuisine	Japanese
Recommended for	Bargain

'A little street kiosk with just two items on the menu:
ramen and gyoza. I love it.'—Ken Oringer

THE BITE

Recommended by
Tony Maws

29 Basin Road
Menemsha
Massachusetts 02552
+1 5086459339
www.thebitemenemsha.com

Opening hours	6 days for breakfast and lunch
Reservation policy	No
Credit cards	Not accepted
Price range	Budget
Style	Casual
Cuisine	Seafood
Recommended for	Local favourite

'It's the place to go for fried clams out of a shack on
Martha's Vineyard.'—Tony Maws

HIGHLAND KITCHEN

Recommended by
Tony Maws

150 Highland Avenue
Somerville
Massachusetts 02143
+1 6176251131
www.highlandkitchen.com

Opening hours	1 day for brunch and 7 days for dinner
Reservation policy	Yes
Credit cards	Accepted
Price range	Affordable
Style	Casual
Cuisine	Modern American
Recommended for	Regular neighbourhood

RED WING DINER

Recommended by
Tim Cushman

2235 Providence Highway
Walpole
Massachusetts 02081
+1 5086680453
www.redwingdiner.net

Opening hours	7 days for lunch and dinner
Reservation policy	No
Credit cards	Accepted
Price range	Budget
Style	Casual
Cuisine	Diner-Café
Recommended for	Local favourite

⁄ BLUE HILL AT STONE BARNS

Recommended by
Sean Brock, Scott
Conant, Mikael Einarsson,
Brad Farmerie, Peter Gilmore,
Jacob Holmström, Claus
Meyer, Khalid Mohammed,
Masato Shimizu, Michael Tusk

630 Bedford Road
Pocantico Hills
New York 10591
+1 9143669600
www.bluehillfarm.com

Opening hours..............1 day for lunch and 5 days for dinner
Reservation policy...Yes
Credit cards..Accepted but not Diners
Price range...Expensive
Style..Formal
Cuisine...Modern American
Recommended for..Worth the travel

'The meal I had here may just have been the best meal I had ever eaten. Dan is a pure genius. We ate for hours and hours, course after course. Each one better than the next. The menu was very vegetable driven. In fact, we had very little protein. I just love that. I am a vegetable fiend. This meal was over the top, and I'll never forget it.'—Sean Brock

A pioneer of localism and 'eco-cuisine', Dan Barber is a perennial chefs' favourite. His commitment to serving produce only from the verdant Hudson Valley – the setting for his 32-hectare (80-acre) biodynamic farm – and his culinary wizardry has him hailed as 'pure genius'. Clarity of flavour is Barber's hallmark, and gastro-tourists travel from far and wide to savour ingredients that taste manifestly of themselves – elegant and fiercely seasonal offerings that yield so willingly to the fork that they hardly require mastication. Throwing the traditional menu to the wind, his field-to-fork multi-course Farmer's Feast is based on the day's harvest.

NICK TAHOU HOTS

Recommended by
Daniel Taylor

320 West Main Street
Rochester
New York 14608
www.garbageplate.com

Opening hours............6 days for breakfast, lunch and dinner
Reservation policy...No
Credit cards...Accepted
Price range...Budget
Style..Casual
Cuisine..American
Recommended for...Late night

'Best for ambiance and sustaining, stabilizing food.'—Daniel Tayler

ESTIA'S LITTLE KITCHEN

Recommended by
Scott Conant

1615 Sag Harbor
Bridgehampton Turnpike
Sag Harbor
New York 11963
+1 6317251045
www.estiaslittlekitchen.com

Opening hours...........7 days for brunch and 3 days for dinner
Reservation policy..Yes
Reservation email......................info@estiaslittlekitchen.com
Credit cards...Accepted
Price range...Budget
Style..Casual
Cuisine..American
Recommended for..Breakfast

'It's a little café with simple, straightforward food. Get the red flannel hash with chorizo, peppers, sweet potatoes and local eggs. '—Scott Conant

NEAL'S DELI

Recommended by
Andrea Reusing

100 East Main Street
Carrboro
North Carolina 27510
+1 9199672185
www.nealsdeli.com

Opening hours..........................6 days for breakfast and lunch
Reservation policy...No
Credit cards...Accepted
Price range...Budget
Style..Casual
Cuisine..Deli-Café
Recommended for..Breakfast

CROOK'S CORNER

Recommended by
Andrea Reusing

610 West Franklin Street
Chapel Hill
North Carolina 27516
+1 9199297643
www.crookscorner.com

Opening hours............1 day for brunch and 6 days for dinner
Reservation policy..Yes
Credit cards...Accepted
Price range...Affordable
Style..Casual
Cuisine...Southern American
Recommended for...............................Regular neighbourhood

SCRATCH

Recommended by
Andrea Reusing

111 Orange Street
Durham
North Carolina 27701
+1 9199565200
www.piefantasy.com

Opening hours	6 days for breakfast and lunch
Reservation policy	No
Credit cards	Accepted
Price range	Budget
Style	Casual
Cuisine	Bakery
Recommended for	Local favourite

TOAST

Recommended by
Andrea Reusing

345 West Main Street
Durham
North Carolina 27701
+1 9196832183
www.toast-fivepoints.com

Opening hours	6 days from lunch until late
Reservation policy	No
Credit cards	Accepted
Price range	Budget
Style	Casual
Cuisine	Italian Sandwiches
Recommended for	Bargain

VIN ROUGE

Recommended by
Daniel Taylor

2010 Hillsborough Road
Durham
North Carolina 27705
+1 9194160466
www.vinrougerestaurant.com

Opening hours	1 day for brunch and 6 days for dinner
Reservation policy	Yes
Credit cards	Accepted
Price range	Budget
Style	Casual
Cuisine	French
Recommended for	Worth the travel

'Matt Kelly cooks traditional French cuisine with American soul.'—Daniel Taylor

PANCIUTO

Recommended by
Andrea Reusing

110 South Churton Street
Hillsborough
North Carolina 27278
+1 9197326261
www.panciuto.com

Opening hours	4 days for dinner
Reservation policy	Yes
Credit cards	Accepted
Price range	Affordable
Style	Casual
Cuisine	Modern Italian
Recommended for	High end

DOS TAQUITOS

Recommended by
Daniel Taylor

5629 Creedmoor Road
Raleigh
North Carolina 27612
+1 9197873373
www.dostaquitosnc.com

Opening hours	5 days for lunch and 6 days for dinner
Reservation policy	Yes
Reservation email	info@dostaquitosnc.com
Credit cards	Accepted
Price range	Budget
Style	Casual
Cuisine	Mexican
Recommended for	Regular neighbourhood

'The best and most authentic Mexican food I know.'—Daniel Taylor

POOLE'S DINER

Recommended by
Alexandra Raij, Andrea Reusing

426 South McDowell Street
Raleigh
North Carolina 27601
+1 9198324477
www.poolesdowntowndiner.com

Opening hours	1 day for brunch and 5 days for dinner
Reservation policy	No
Credit cards	Accepted
Price range	Affordable
Style	Casual
Cuisine	Diner-Cafe
Recommended for	Worth the travel

'A great expression of place.'—Alexandra Raij

PORTER'S

Recommended by
Daniel Taylor

2412 Hillsborough Street
Raleigh
North Carolina 27607
+1 9198212133
www.porterstavern.com

Opening hours	7 days for lunch and dinner
Reservation policy	Yes
Credit cards	Accepted
Price range	Budget
Style	Casual
Cuisine	Bar-Bistro
Recommended for	Breakfast

'Consistently impressive.'—Daniel Taylor

OYSTER HOUSE

Recommended by
Douglas Rodriguez

1516 Sansom Street
Philadelphia
Pennsylvania 19102
+1 2155677683
www.oysterhousephilly.com

Opening hours	6 days for lunch and dinner
Reservation policy	Yes
Credit cards	Accepted
Price range	Affordable
Style	Casual
Cuisine	Seafood
Recommended for	Regular neighbourhood

PARC

Recommended by
Douglas Rodriguez

227 South 18th Street
Philadelphia
Pennsylvania 19103
+1 2155452262
www.parc-restaurant.com

Opening hours	7 days for breakfast, lunch and dinner
Reservation policy	Yes
Credit cards	Accepted
Price range	Affordable
Style	Casual
Cuisine	French
Recommended for	Breakfast

'Excellent croissants and bread.'—Douglas Rodriguez

PRIMANTI BROS

Recommended by
Brad Farmerie

46 18th Street
Pittsburgh
Pennsylvania 15222
www.primantibros.com

Opening hours	7 days from breakfast until late
Reservation policy	No
Credit cards	Not accepted
Price range	Budget
Style	Casual
Cuisine	Sandwiches
Recommended for	Bargain

BUTCHER & BEE

Recommended by
Sean Brock

654 King Street
Charleston
South Carolina 29403
+1 8436190202
www.butcherandbee.com

Opening hours	7 days for lunch and 3 days for dinner
Reservation policy	Yes
Reservation email	info@butcherandbee.com
Credit cards	Accepted
Price range	Budget
Style	Casual
Cuisine	Sandwiches
Recommended for	Late night

'It's designed to cater to people in the restaurant industry. So it's cooks cooking for cooks. That always rocks!'—Sean Brock

FIG

Recommended by
Anita Lo

232 Meeting Street
Charleston
South Carolina 29401
+1 8438055900
www.eatatfig.com

Opening hours	6 days for dinner
Reservation policy	Yes
Credit cards	Accepted
Price range	Affordable
Style	Casual
Cuisine	French-Italian
Recommended for	Worth the travel

THE GLASS ONION

Recommended by
Sean Brock

1219 Savannah Highway
Charleston
South Carolina 29407
+1 8432251717
www.ilovetheglassonion.com

Opening hours	6 days for breakfast, lunch and dinner
Reservation policy	No
Credit cards	Accepted
Price range	Affordable
Style	Casual
Cuisine	Southern American
Recommended for	Regular neighbourhood

'Clean, simple, honest and Southern. The menu changes often, most of it daily. Their focus is using super fresh ingredients at their peak and preparing them simply with a high level of skill.'—Sean Brock

HOMINY GRILL

Recommended by
Sean Brock

207 Rutledge Avenue
Charleston
South Carolina 29403
+1 8439370930
www.hominygrill.com

Opening hours	7 days for brunch and 6 days for dinner
Reservation policy	Yes
Credit cards	Accepted
Price range	Affordable
Style	Casual
Cuisine	Southern American
Recommended for	Breakfast

'I adore Hominy Grill's prawns (shrimps) and grits (a polenta-like porridge)! This dish is such a Charleston staple and I can't get enough of it.'—Sean Brock

HUSK

Recommended by
Hugh Acheson, Michael Tusk

76 Queen Street
Charleston
South Carolina 29401
+1 8435772500
www.huskrestaurant.com

Opening hours	7 days for lunch and dinner
Reservation policy	Yes
Credit cards	Accepted
Price range	Affordable
Style	Casual
Cuisine	Southern American
Recommended for	Worth the travel

Sean Brock's follow-up to McCrady's pursues the same farm-to-fork philosophy. The market-driven menu moves beyond South Carolina's larder (pantry) to make use of North Carolina smoked trout, Georgia beef and Tennessee truffles. But if it isn't a product of Southern pride, it doesn't make it near the wood-fired oven. The restored 1893 Queen Anne home with its columned porches has taken well to its new purpose: an open kitchen on street level and an upper-floor dining room that's as fetching as any in Dixie. The adjacent brick building houses a bar that touts craft bourbons and hand-carved Tennessee country hams.

MARTHA LOU'S KITCHEN

Recommended by
Sean Brock

1068 Morrison Drive
Charleston
South Carolina 29403
+1 8435779583

Opening hours	6 days for breakfast and lunch
Reservation policy	No
Credit cards	Not accepted
Price range	Budget
Style	Casual
Cuisine	Southern American
Recommended for	Bargain

'Martha Lou has been cooking here for twenty-five years on an old home stove. She has a magical way with elevating humble ingredients into life-changing moments of pure Southern bliss.'—Sean Brock

MCCRADY'S

Recommended by
Michael Anthony, Daniel Patterson

2 Unity Alley
Charleston
South Carolina 29401
+1 8435770025
www.mccradysrestaurant.com

Opening hours	7 days for dinner
Reservation policy	Yes
Credit cards	Accepted
Price range	Affordable
Style	Casual
Cuisine	Modern Southern American
Recommended for	Worth the travel

'When I travel, I want to taste something distinctive from that place. Sean Brock and his team bring the most innovative ideas to create dishes that are deeply rooted in the Southern dining experience.'
—Michael Anthony

Housed in a handsomely restored eighteenth-century tavern, McCrady's has been home to Sean Brock's antebellum-inspired new Southern culinary vision since 2006. Brock has established links with local farmers to revive heirloom crops and champion high welfare breeds. His menus combine these raw materials plus research from his vast collection of nineteenth-century Southern cookbooks with the latest high-tech techniques and more down-home methods such as pickling. Make sure to stop in the bar, which specializes in mixing pre-Prohibition cocktails, before making your way to a dining room that's a similarly smart concoction of exposed brick and crisp linen.

THOROUGHBRED CLUB

Recommended by
Hugh Acheson

Charleston Place Hotel
205 Meeting Street
Charleston
South Carolina 29401
+1 8437224900
www.charlestonplace.com

Opening hours	7 days for lunch and dinner
Reservation policy	Yes
Credit cards	Accepted
Price range	Affordable
Style	Casual
Cuisine	American small plates
Recommended for	High end

TRATTORIA LUCCA

Recommended by
Linton Hopkins

41 Bogard Street
Charleston
South Carolina 29403
+1 8439733323
www.luccacharleston.com

Opening hours	6 days for dinner
Reservation policy	Yes
Credit cards	Accepted
Price range	Affordable
Style	Smart casual
Cuisine	Italian
Recommended for	Worth the travel

'Amazing pasta.'—Linton Hopkins

TWO BOROUGHS LARDER

Recommended by
Gabrielle Hamilton

186 Coming Street
Charleston
South Carolina 29403
+1 8436373722
www.twoboroughslarder.com

Opening hours	5 days from breakfast until late
Reservation policy	No
Credit cards	Accepted
Price range	Budget
Style	Casual
Cuisine	American
Recommended for	Worth the travel

'Delicious food, expertly prepared.'
—Gabrielle Hamilton

GUS'S FRIED CHICKEN

Recommended by
Carlo Mirarchi

310 South Front Street
Memphis
Tennessee 38103
+1 90115274877

Opening hours	7 days for lunch and dinner
Reservation policy	No
Credit cards	Accepted
Price range	Budget
Style	Casual
Cuisine	Southern American
Recommended for	Worth the travel

THE BARN

Recommended by
Daniel Boulud

Blackberry Farm
1471 West Millers Cove Road
Walland
Tennessee 37886
+1 8006482348
www.blackberryfarm.com

Opening hours..7 days for dinner
Reservation policy...Yes
Credit cards...Accepted
Price range...Expensive
Style..Smart casual
Cuisine..Modern American
Recommended for...Worth the travel

BARTLETT'S

Recommended by
Tyson Cole

2408 West Anderson Lane
Austin
Texas 78757
+1 5124517333
www.bartlettsaustin.com

Opening hours...............................7 days for lunch and dinner
Reservation policy...Yes
Credit cards...Accepted
Price range..Affordable
Style...Casual
Cuisine..American
Recommended for.................................Regular neighbourhood

CONTIGO

Recommended by
Tyson Cole

2027 Anchor Lane
Austin
Texas 78723
+1 5126142260
www.contigotexas.com

Opening hours.............1 day for brunch and 7 days for dinner
Reservation policy...Yes
Credit cards...Accepted
Price range...Budget
Style...Casual
Cuisine..American
Recommended for.......................................Local favourite

FRANKLIN BARBECUE

Recommended by
Paul Qui, Andy Ricker

900 East 11th Street
Austin
Texas 78702
+1 5126531187
www.franklinbarbecue.com

Opening hours................................6 days for lunch and dinner
Reservation policy..No
Credit cards...Accepted
Price range...Budget
Style...Casual
Cuisine..Barbecue
Recommended for.......................................Local favourite

HOPDODDY BURGER BAR

Recommended by
Tyson Cole

1400 South Congress Avenue
Austin
Texas 78704
+1 5122437505
www.hopdoddy.com

Opening hours...............................7 days for lunch and dinner
Reservation policy..No
Credit cards...Accepted
Price range...Budget
Style...Casual
Cuisine..Burgers
Recommended for.................................Wish I'd opened

LILY'S SANDWICH

Recommended by
Paul Qui

10901 North Lamar Boulevard
Austin
Texas 78753
+1 5129739479

Opening hours.........................7 days from breakfast until late
Reservation policy..No
Credit cards...Not accepted
Price range...Budget
Style...Casual
Cuisine...Vietnamese
Recommended for...............................Regular neighbourhood

'My favorite *banh mi* in Austin. It's all about the bread
– make sure you eat it there while it is still hot.'
—Paul Qui

MUSASHINO

3407 Greystone Drive
Austin
Texas 78731
www.musashinosushi.com

Opening hours	4 days for lunch and 7 days for dinner
Reservation policy	Yes
Credit cards	Accepted
Price range	Affordable
Style	Casual
Cuisine	Japanese
Recommended for	High end

'I love nigiri and chef Kazu Fukumoto makes some of the best in town.'—Paul Qui

TAM DELI & CAFE

8222 North Lamar Boulevard
Austin
Texas 78753
+1 5128346458

Opening hours	6 days from breakfast until late
Reservation policy	No
Credit cards	Accepted
Price range	Budget
Style	Casual
Cuisine	Vietnamese
Recommended for	Breakfast

'I love eating their *banh cuon* for breakfast. It's light and tasty and gives me a great start to my day.' —Paul Qui

THAI KITCHEN

3009 Guadalupe Street
Austin
Texas 78705
+1 5124742575
www.thaikitchenofaustin.com

Opening hours	7 days for lunch and dinner
Reservation policy	No
Credit cards	Accepted
Price range	Budget
Style	Casual
Cuisine	Thai
Recommended for	Late night

BAGUETTE ET CHOCOLAT

Building 6
12101 Bee Cave Road
Bee Cave
Texas 78738
+1 5122638388
www.baguetteetchocolat.com

Opening hours	6 days for breakfast and lunch
Reservation policy	No
Credit cards	Accepted
Price range	Budget
Style	Casual
Cuisine	Bakery-Cafe
Recommended for	Breakfast

FEARING'S

Ritz Carlton Hotel
2121 McKinney Avenue
Dallas
Texas 75201
+1 2149224848
www.fearingsrestaurant.com

Opening hours	7 days for breakfast, lunch and dinner
Reservation policy	Yes
Credit cards	Accepted
Price range	Expensive
Style	Smart casual
Cuisine	American
Recommended for	Worth the travel

UNDERBELLY

1100 Westheimer Road
Houston
Texas 77006
+1 7135289800
www.underbellyhouston.com

Opening hours	5 days for lunch and 6 days for dinner
Reservation policy	Yes
Credit cards	Accepted
Price range	Affordable
Style	Smart casual
Cuisine	Modern American
Recommended for	Worth the travel

'A totally warming experience with a very passionate chef.'—Paul Qui

'BEST PIZZA IN NEW ORLEANS.
DON'T FORGET THE $2 (£1)
PITCHER OF BEER NIGHTS.'

TORY MCPHAIL P550

NEW ORLEANS

'I WASN'T SURE
WHETHER IT WOULD
LIVE UP TO THE
HYPE BUT IT WAS
AN INCREDIBLE
EXPERIENCE.'

LORI GRANITO P546

'Clean, elegant finger
food in a hip, vibrant
neighbourhood.'

TORY MCPHAIL P550

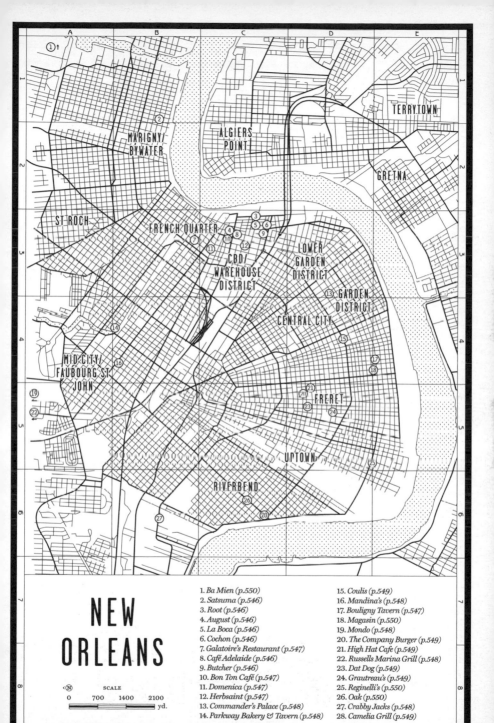

NEW ORLEANS

SCALE

0   700   1400   2100   yd.

SATSUMA
3218 Dauphine Street
Bywater
New Orleans
Louisiana 70117
+1 5043045962
satsumacafe.com

Opening hours............................7 days for breakfast and lunch
Reservation policy...No
Credit cards...Accepted
Price range..Budget
Style..Casual
Cuisine...Café
Recommended for...Breakfast

AUGUST
301 Tchoupitoulas Street
Central Business District
New Orleans
Louisiana 70130
+1 5042999777
www.restaurantaugust.com

Opening hours.............5 days for lunch and 7 days for dinner
Reservation policy...Yes
Credit cards...Accepted
Price range...Affordable
Style...Smart casual
Cuisine...French
Recommended for...Worth the travel

'I wasn't sure whether it would live up to the hype, but it was incredible experience.'—Lori Granito

LA BOCA
857 Fulton Street
Central Business District
New Orleans
Louisiana 70130
+1 5045258205
www.labocasteaks.com

Opening hours...6 days for dinner
Reservation policy..Yes
Credit cards...Accepted
Price range...Affordable
Style...Smart casual
Cuisine..Steakhouse
Recommended for..Late night

BUTCHER
930 Tchoupitoulas Street
Central Business District
New Orleans
Louisiana 70130
+1 5045887675
www.cochonbutcher.com

Opening hours.........................7 days from breakfast until late
Reservation policy...No
Credit cards...Accepted
Price range..Budget
Style..Casual
Cuisine..Sandwiches
Recommended for...Wish I'd opened

CAFÉ ADELAIDE
300 Poydras Street
Central Business District
New Orleans
Louisiana 70130
+1 5045953305
www.cafeadelaide.com

Opening hours.............7 days for breakfast, lunch and dinner
Reservation policy..Yes
Credit cards...Accepted
Price range...Affordable
Style..Casual
Cuisine..Creole
Recommended for..Local favourite

'Sit at the bar and get the best hand-crafted cocktails and the full menu from the restaurant.'—Tory McPhail

COCHON
930 Tchoupitoulas Street
Central Business District
New Orleans
Louisiana 70195
+1 5045882123
www.cochonrestaurant.com

Opening hours..............................6 days for lunch and dinner
Reservation policy..Yes
Credit cards...Accepted
Price range...Affordable
Style..Casual
Cuisine..Cajun
Recommended for...Worth the travel

DOMENICA

Recommended by
Susan Spicer

Roosevelt Hotel
123 Baronne Street
Central Business District
New Orleans
Louisiana 70112
+1 5046486020
www.domenicarestaurant.com

Opening hours	7 days for lunch and dinner
Reservation policy	Yes
Credit cards	Accepted
Price range	Affordable
Style	Casual
Cuisine	Italian
Recommended for	Late night

HERBSAINT

Recommended by
Susan Spicer

701 Saint Charles Avenue
Central Business District
New Orleans
Louisiana 70130
+1 5045244114
www.herbsaint.com

Opening hours	5 days for lunch and 6 days for dinner
Reservation policy	Yes
Credit cards	Accepted
Price range	Affordable
Style	Smart casual
Cuisine	French-Italian
Recommended for	Regular neighbourhood

ROOT

Recommended by
Stephen Stryjewski, Sue
Zemanick

200 Julia Street
Central Business District
New Orleans
Louisiana 70130
+1 5042529480
www.rootnola.com

Opening hours	5 days for lunch and 7 days for dinner
Reservation policy	Yes
Credit cards	Accepted
Price range	Affordable
Style	Casual
Cuisine	Modern American
Recommended for	Late night

BON TON CAFÉ

Recommended by
John Besh

401 Magazine Street
Downtown
New Orleans
Louisiana 70130
+1 5045243386
www.thebontoncafe.com

Opening hours	5 days for lunch and dinner
Reservation policy	Yes
Credit cards	Accepted
Price range	Affordable
Style	Smart casual
Cuisine	Cajun
Recommended for	Local favourite

BOULIGNY TAVERN

Recommended by
Tory McPhail

3641 Magazine Street
East Riverside
New Orleans
Louisiana 70115
+1 5048911810
www.boulignytavern.com

Opening hours	6 days for dinner
Reservation policy	No
Credit cards	Accepted
Price range	Affordable
Style	Smart casual
Cuisine	Bar-Small plates
Recommended for	Late night

GALATOIRE'S RESTAURANT

Recommended by
John Besh

209 Bourbon Street
French Quarter
New Orleans
Louisiana 70130
+1 5045252021
www.galatoires.com

Opening hours	6 days for lunch and dinner
Reservation policy	Yes
Credit cards	Accepted
Price range	Affordable
Style	Formal
Cuisine	Creole
Recommended for	High end

COMMANDER'S PALACE

1403 Washington Avenue
Garden District
New Orleans
Louisiana 70130
+1 5048998221
www.commanderspalace.com

Opening hours	7 days for brunch and dinner
Reservation policy	Yes
Credit cards	Accepted
Price range	Expensive
Style	Formal
Cuisine	Southern American-Creole
Recommended for	Breakfast

RUSSELLS MARINA GRILL

8555 Pontchartrain Boulevard
Lake View
New Orleans
Louisiana 70124
+1 5042829980
www.russellsmarinagrill.com

Opening hours	7 days for breakfast and lunch
Reservation policy	No
Credit cards	Accepted
Price range	Budget
Style	Casual
Cuisine	Diner-Cafe
Recommended for	Breakfast

CRABBY JACK'S

428 Jefferson Highway
Jefferson
New Orleans
Louisiana 70121
+1 5048332722
www.crabbyjacksnola.com

Opening hours	6 days from breakfast until late
Reservation policy	No
Credit cards	Accepted
Price range	Budget
Style	Casual
Cuisine	Southern American
Recommended for	Local favourite

MANDINA'S

3800 Canal Street
Mid-City
New Orleans
Louisiana 70119
+1 5044829179
www.mandinasrestaurant.com

Opening hours	7 days for lunch and dinner
Reservation policy	No
Credit cards	Accepted
Price range	Budget
Style	Casual
Cuisine	Creole-Italian
Recommended for	Local favourite

MONDO

900 Harrison Avenue
Lake View
New Orleans
Louisiana 70124
+1 5042242633
www.mondoneworleans.com

Opening hours	6 days for lunch and dinner
Reservation policy	Yes
Credit cards	Accepted
Price range	Affordable
Style	Casual
Cuisine	Modern American
Recommended for	Regular neighbourhood

PARKWAY BAKERY & TAVERN

538 Hagan Avenue
Mid-City
New Orleans
Louisiana 70119
+1 5044823047
www.parkwaypoorboys.com

Opening hours	6 days for lunch and dinner
Reservation policy	No
Credit cards	Accepted
Price range	Budget
Style	Casual
Cuisine	Sandwiches
Recommended for	Bargain

CAMELLIA GRILL

Recommended by
John Besh, Bruce Bromberg

626 South Carrollton Avenue
Uptown
New Orleans
Louisiana 70118
+1 5043092679

Opening hours.............7 days for breakfast, lunch and dinner
Reservation policy...No
Credit cards..Accepted
Price range..Budget
Style..Casual
Cuisine...Diner-Café
Recommended for...Late night

THE COMPANY BURGER

Recommended by
Stephen Stryjewski

4600 Freret Street
Uptown
New Orleans
Louisiana 70115
+1 5042670320
www.thecompanyburger.com

Opening hours...............................6 days for lunch and dinner
Reservation policy...No
Credit cards..Accepted
Price range..Budget
Style..Casual
Cuisine...Burgers
Recommended for.......................Regular neighbourhood

COULIS

Recommended by
Tory McPhail

3625 Prytania Street
Uptown
New Orleans
Louisiana 70115
+1 5043044265

Opening hours..........................7 days for breakfast and lunch
Reservation policy...No
Credit cards..Accepted
Price range..Budget
Style..Casual
Cuisine...Diner-Café
Recommended for...Breakfast

DAT DOG

Recommended by
Sue Zemanick

5030 Freret Street
Uptown
New Orleans
Louisiana 70115
+1 5048996883
www.datdognola.com

Opening hours...............................7 days from lunch until late
Reservation policy...No
Credit cards...Not accepted
Price range..Budget
Style..Casual
Cuisine...Hot dogs
Recommended for...................................Wish I'd opened

GAUTREAU'S

Recommended by
Tory McPhail

1728 Soniat Street
Uptown
New Orleans
Louisiana 70115
+1 5048997397
www.gautreausrestaurant.com

Opening hours...6 days for dinner
Reservation policy..Yes
Credit cards..Accepted
Price range..Expensive
Style...Smart casual
Cuisine...French
Recommended for...High end

HIGH HAT CAFE

Recommended by
Susan Spicer

4500 Freret Street
Uptown
New Orleans
Louisiana 70115
www.highhatcafe.com

Opening hours.............7 days for breakfast, lunch and dinner
Reservation policy...No
Credit cards..Accepted
Price range..Budget
Style..Casual
Cuisine...Southern American
Recommended for...............................Regular neighbourhood

MAGASIN

Recommended by
Sue Zemanick

4201 Magazine Street
Uptown
New Orleans
Louisiana 70115
+1 5048967611
www.magasincafe.com

Opening hours	6 days for lunch and dinner
Reservation policy	No
Credit cards	Accepted
Price range	Budget
Style	Casual
Cuisine	Vietnamese
Recommended for	Bargain

OAK

Recommended by
Tory McPhail

8118 Oak Street
Uptown
New Orleans
Louisiana 70118
+1 5043021485
www.oaknola.com

Opening hours	5 days for dinner
Reservation policy	No
Credit cards	Accepted
Price range	Affordable
Style	Smart casual
Cuisine	Bar-Small plates
Recommended for	Wish I'd opened

'Clean, elegant finger food in a hip, vibrant neighbourhood.'—Tory McPhail

This large, loud, dressy venue, with clean lines and live jazz piano, lounges at the edge of atmospheric Oak Street, by the broad Carrollton Avenue, known for its antique streetcar. Small plates by executive chef Aaron Burgau may include market-inspired Mississippi lamb meat pies with harissa yogurt, and Gulf prawn (shrimp) tacos with tortillas and lime crema. Of the house cocktails, prepared behind the glamorous marble counter, the Louisiana Lagniappe (white rum, agave syrup, citrus and cherries in brandy) delivers a decadent hit, while the wine list is curious, arranged not by variety, but feel, as is indicated by the heading 'Stones and Acid'.

REGINELLI'S

Recommended by
Tory McPhail

741 State Street
Uptown
New Orleans
Louisiana 70118
www.reginellis.com

Opening hours	7 days for lunch and dinner
Reservation policy	No
Credit cards	Accepted
Price range	Affordable
Style	Casual
Cuisine	Pizza
Recommended for	Bargain

'Best pizza in New Orleans Don't forget the $2 (£1) pitcher of beer nights.'—Tory McPhail

BA MIEN

Recommended by
John Besh

13235 Chef Menteur Highway
Willow Brook
New Orleans
Louisiana 70129
+1 5042550500
www.bamien.com

Opening hours	6 days from breakfast until late
Reservation policy	Yes
Credit cards	Accepted
Price range	Budget
Style	Casual
Cuisine	Vietnamese
Recommended for	Regular neighbourhood

'REPRESENTS A SENSE OF CREATIVITY AND PASSION THAT I HAVE NEVER SEEN AT ANY OTHER RESTAURANT.'
DANIEL HUMM P556

'THE BEST BBQ IN THE COUNTRY.'
HOMARO CANTU P556

'I took a trip to Chicago last fall after not having visited in ten years, and was pleasantly surprised by the vibrant food scene there. Options on every level.'
MATTHEW ACCARRINO

CHICAGO

'Ridiculous stuff here: pancakes, fried chicken and the best sticky buns ever.'
MICHAEL SCHWARTZ P563

'SUCH A SMALL SPACE AND THEY DO SUCH BIG THINGS. EVERYTHING I ATE WAS SOULFUL AND DELICIOUS.'
ADAM SOBEL P560

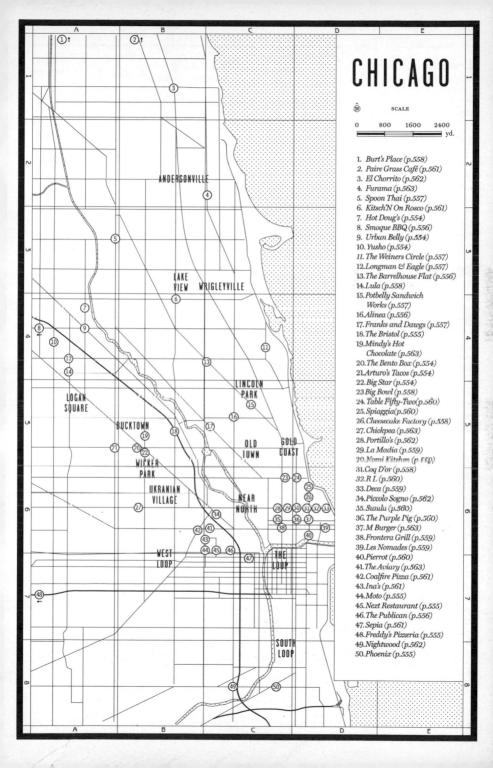

CHICAGO

$\hat{N}$ SCALE

0   800   1600   2400
yd.

HOT DOUG'S

3324 North California Avenue
Avondale
Chicago
Illinois 60618
+1 7732799550
www.hotdougs.com

Opening hours	6 days for breakfast and lunch
Reservation policy	No
Credit cards	Not accepted
Price range	Budget
Style	Casual
Cuisine	Hot Dogs
Recommended for	Local favourite

URBAN BELLY

3053 North California Avenue
Avondale
Chicago
Illinois 60618
www.urbanbellychicago.com

Opening hours	6 days for lunch and dinner
Reservation policy	No
Credit cards	Accepted
Price range	Affordable
Style	Casual
Cuisine	Asian
Recommended for	Regular neighbourhood

YUSHO

2853 North Kedzie Avenue
Avondale
Chicago
Illinois 60618
+1 7739048558
www.yusho-chicago.com

Opening hours	7 days for dinner
Reservation policy	Yes
Credit cards	Accepted
Price range	Budget
Style	Casual
Cuisine	Japanese
Recommended for	Regular neighbourhood

ARTURO'S TACOS

2001 North Western Avenue
Bucktown
Chicago
Illinois 60647
+1 7737724944
www.arturos-tacos.com/

Opening hours	7 days from breakfast until late
Reservation policy	No
Credit cards	Accepted
Price range	Budget
Style	Casual
Cuisine	Mexican
Recommended for	Late night

THE BENTO BOX

2246 West Armitage Avenue
Bucktown
Chicago
Illinois 60647
+1 7732783932
www.artisancateringchicago.com/box.html

Opening hours	6 days for lunch and dinner
Reservation policy	Yes
Credit cards	Accepted
Price range	Budget
Style	Casual
Cuisine	Asian
Recommended for	Regular neighbourhood

BIG STAR

1531 North Damen Avenue
Bucktown
Chicago
Illinois 60622
www.bigstarchicago.com

Opening hours	7 days for lunch and dinner
Reservation policy	No
Credit cards	Not accepted
Price range	Budget
Style	Casual
Cuisine	Mexican
Recommended for	Late night

THE BRISTOL

Recommended by
Ben Roche

2152 North Damen Avenue
Bucktown
Chicago
Illinois 60647
+1 7738625555
www.thebristolchicago.com

Opening hours	1 day for brunch and 7 days for dinner
Reservation policy	Yes
Credit cards	Accepted
Price range	Budget
Style	Casual
Cuisine	Mediterranean
Recommended for	Regular neighbourhood

PHOENIX

Recommended by
Jean Joho

2131 South Archer Avenue
Chinatown
Chicago
Illinois 60616
+1 3123280848
www.chinatownphoenix.com

Opening hours	7 days for breakfast, lunch and dinner
Reservation policy	Yes
Credit cards	Accepted
Price range	Budget
Style	Casual
Cuisine	Chinese
Recommended for	Local favourite

FREDDY'S PIZZERIA

Recommended by
Homaro Cantu

1600 South 61st Avenue
Cicero
Chicago
Illinois 60804
+1 7088639289
www.freddyspizza.com

Opening hours	6 days for lunch
Reservation policy	No
Credit cards	Not accepted
Price range	Budget
Style	Casual
Cuisine	Italian
Recommended for	Local favourite

'Best Italian-deli, home-style food I have ever had.'—Homaro Cantu

MOTO

Recommended by
Matthew Accarrino

945 West Fulton Market
Fulton Market
Chicago
Illinois 60607
+1 3124910058
www.motorestaurant.com

Opening hours	5 days for dinner
Reservation policy	Yes
Reservation email	motorestaurant@me.com
Credit cards	Accepted
Price range	Expensive
Style	Smart casual
Cuisine	Modern American
Recommended for	Worth the travel

If you're not a fan of molecular gastronomy, chef Homaro Cantu's temple to this style of cooking might not be for you; if you are, then you might just find culinary nirvana here. Described as part chef, part inventor, Cantu's *raison d'être* is to challenge culinary convention and take diners on a 'post-modern, interactive and fantastical gastronomical ride'. He turns home-spun American food on its head and inside out, so that savoury becomes dessert, the traditional enigmatic, and the overall dining experience an unknown quantity. Dishes have esoteric names such as 'smell the glove' and even the menu itself is edible.

NEXT RESTAURANT

Recommended by
Jeremy Charles,
Blaine Wetzel

953 West Fulton Market
Fulton Market
Chicago
Illinois 60607
www.nextrestaurant.com

Opening hours	5 days for dinner
Reservation policy	Yes
Reservation email	tickets@nextrestaurant.com
Credit cards	Accepted
Price range	Expensive
Style	Smart casual
Cuisine	International
Recommended for	Wish I'd opened

THE PUBLICAN

Recommended by
Ben Roche, Mindy Segal,
Jair Tellez

837 West Fulton Market
Fulton Market
Chicago
Illinois 60607
+1 3127339555
www.thepublicanrestaurant.com

Opening hours	2 days for brunch and 7 days for dinner
Reservation policy	Yes
Credit cards	Accepted
Price range	Affordable
Style	Casual
Cuisine	Bar-Bistro
Recommended for	Wish I'd opened

'It is such a self confident operation, they are extremely thorough in everything they do and still appear to be doing it in a cool and relaxed way.'
—Jair Tellez

Known in particular for its amazingly good brunches, this stripped-back, beer-led restaurant is all about immaculate produce served at its simplest and best. It comes courtesy of the team behind Chicago's much-loved, James Beard nominated Blackbird restaurant, but with a stark, hall-like interior – all straight wooden lines and flagstone – farmhouse fare and a vast beer list. The menus are split into pork-heavy 'meat', 'fish', which includes six types of oyster, and 'vegetable', with each section revealing impeccably sourced ingredients, be it the steamer clams from feminist novelist-turned-fishmonger Ingrid Bengis in Maine, or the 'ham chop in hay' from Becker Lane Organic Farm in Iowa.

SMOQUE BBQ

Recommended by
Homaro Cantu

3800 North Pulaski Road
Irving Park
Chicago
Illinois 60641
+1 7735457427
www.smoquebbq.com

Opening hours	6 days for lunch and dinner
Reservation policy	No
Credit cards	Accepted
Price range	Budget
Style	Casual
Cuisine	Barbecue
Recommended for	Wish I'd opened

'The best BBQ in the country.'—Homaro Cantu

ALINEA

Recommended by
Alberto Chicote, Jordi Cruz,
Daniel Humm, Timothy
Johnson, Carrie Nahabedian,
Martins Ritins, Alexandre
Silva, Thrainn Freyr
Vigfusson, Marcus Wareing

1723 North Halsted Street
Lincoln Park
Chicago
Illinois 60614
+1 3128670110
www.alinea-restaurant.com

Opening hours	5 days for dinner
Reservation policy	Yes
Credit cards	Accepted
Price range	Expensive
Style	Formal
Cuisine	Modern American
Recommended for	Worth the travel

'Alinea represents a sense of creativity and passion that I have never seen at any other restaurant. Whenever I dine there, I come back to New York inspired to push harder. It's a restaurant that has grown as its chef has grown, and, as a chef, that's what I aspire to do: to grow with my restaurants, to constantly evolve, to push my creativity.'—Daniel Humm

Alinea has been described as innovative, cutting edge and futuristic, but such words don't begin to describe the experience of having a chef 'paint' one's dessert directly onto the table, of eating an edible balloon filled with helium and tasting of apple, of a lamb dish with some eighty-six different components. The undisputed genius behind the sophisticated Lincoln Park restaurant, awarded three Michelin stars in 2010, is French Laundry-trained Grant Achatz, poster boy for progressive American cooking. Securing a reservation can take months. Achatz and partner Nick Kokonas have built on Alinea's success with a unique 'ticketed' restaurant, Next, and cocktail bar, Aviary.

THE BARRELHOUSE FLAT

Recommended by
Ben Roche

2624 North Lincoln Avenue
Lincoln Park
Chicago
Illinois 60614
+1 7738570421
www.barrelhouseflat.com

Opening hours	6 days for dinner
Reservation policy	No
Credit cards	Accepted
Price range	Budget
Style	Casual
Cuisine	Bar-Small plates
Recommended for	Late night

This cultish late-night drinking den is famed for its painstakingly crafted, seventy-strong cocktail list, and has become a favourite munch spot for chefs post-service thanks to Charlie Trotter alumnus Nick Hertel's concise but mouth-teasing menu of bar snacks and savouries. Wash down your perfectly crafted Sleepaway Camp (a delicious concoction of Beefeater gin, Campari, Amaro Ramazzotti, Crème de Violette, Orange Bitters and Absinthe) while enjoying a spot of pig-head poutine – a gourmet take on the French-Canadian dish of chips (French fries), gravy and cheese curd. Kitchen doors stay open until 4.00 a.m. on Saturdays; 3.00 a.m. on Thursdays and Fridays.

FRANKS 'N' DAWGS

Recommended by
Carrie Nahabedian

1863 North Clybourn Avenue
Lincoln Park
Chicago
Illinois 60614
+1 3122815187
www.franksndawgs.com

Opening hours	6 days for lunch and 5 days for dinner
Reservation policy	No
Credit cards	Accepted
Price range	Budget
Style	Casual
Cuisine	Hot Dogs
Recommended for	Bargain

POTBELLY SANDWICH WORKS

Recommended by
Mindy Segal

2264 North Lincoln Avenue
Lincoln Park
Chicago
Illinois 60614
+1 7735281405
www.potbelly.com

Opening hours	7 days from lunch until late
Reservation policy	No
Credit cards	Accepted
Price range	Budget
Style	Casual
Cuisine	Sandwiches
Recommended for	Bargain

THE WIENERS CIRCLE

Recommended by
Ben Roche, Bruce Sherman

2622 North Clark Street
Lincoln Park
Chicago
Illinois 60614
+1 7734777444
www.wienercircle.net

Opening hours	7 days for lunch and dinner
Reservation policy	No
Credit cards	Not accepted
Price range	Budget
Style	Casual
Cuisine	Hot dogs
Recommended for	Late night

SPOON THAI

Recommended by
Bruce Sherman

4608 North Western Avenue
Lincoln Square
Chicago
Illinois 60625
+1 7737691173
www.spoonthai.com

Opening hours	7 days for lunch and dinner
Reservation policy	Yes
Credit cards	Accepted
Price range	Budget
Style	Casual
Cuisine	Thai
Recommended for	Bargain

LONGMAN & EAGLE

Recommended by
Mindy Segal

2657 North Kedzie Avenue
Logan Square
Chicago
Illinois 60647
+1 7732767110
www.longmanandeagle.com

Opening hours	7 days from breakfast until late
Reservation policy	No
Credit cards	Accepted
Price range	Affordable
Style	Casual
Cuisine	Bar-Bistro
Recommended for	Breakfast

LULA

Recommended by
Ben Roche

2537 North Kedzie Boulevard
Logan Square
Chicago
Illinois 60647
+1 7734899554
www.lulacafe.com

Opening hours	7 days from breakfast until late
Reservation policy	Yes
Credit cards	Accepted
Price range	Budget
Style	Casual
Cuisine	Café
Recommended for	Breakfast

BURT'S PLACE

Recommended by
Homaro Cantu

8541 Ferris Avenue
Morton Grove
Chicago
Illinois 60053
+1 8479657997

Opening hours	3 days for lunch and 5 days for dinner
Reservation policy	Yes
Credit cards	Not accepted
Price range	Budget
Style	Casual
Cuisine	Pizza
Recommended for	Regular neighbourhood

BIG BOWL

Recommended by
Jean Joho

6 East Cedar
Near North
Chicago
Illinois 60611
+1 3126408888
www.bigbowl.com

Opening hours	7 days for lunch and dinner
Reservation policy	Yes
Credit cards	Accepted
Price range	Budget
Style	Casual
Cuisine	Asian
Recommended for	Regular neighbourhood

From banning bottled water and using naturally raised chicken, beef and sustainable seafood, to roasting all its own chillies, peanuts and spices in house, Big Bowl has built a reputation as an eco-aware restaurant group with a stringent back-to-basics ethos. Its fresh menu of soups, salads and noodle dishes includes pan-Asian staples like pad thai, kung pao chicken and clay pot prawns (shrimp) Panang, but its careful sourcing sets it apart from many neighbourhood Asians. Executive chef Marc Bernard has forged strong bonds with local farmers, resulting in the use of heirloom pork for barbecue ribs, wok-seared scallops from the East Coast, and Szechuan pork belly made with house-smoked bacon.

CHEESECAKE FACTORY

Recommended by
Carrie Nahabedian

875 North Michigan Avenue
Near North
Chicago
Illinois 60611
+1 3123371101
www.thecheesecakefactory.com

Opening hours	7 days from lunch until late
Reservation policy	Yes
Credit cards	Accepted
Price range	Budget
Style	Casual
Cuisine	Bakery-Cafe
Recommended for	Bargain

COQ D'OR

Recommended by
Carrie Nahabedian

Drake Hotel
140 East Walton Place
Near North
Chicago
Illinois 60611
+1 3129324622
www.thedrakehotel.com

Opening hours	7 days for lunch and dinner
Reservation policy	Yes
Credit cards	Accepted
Price range	Affordable
Style	Casual
Cuisine	Bar-Bistro
Recommended for	Regular neighbourhood

DECA

Recommended by
Carrie Nahabedian

Ritz Carlton Hotel
160 East Pearson Street
Near North
Chicago
Illinois 60611
+1 3125735160
www.decarestaurant.com

Opening hours	7 days for breakfast, lunch and dinner
Reservation policy	Yes
Credit cards	Accepted
Price range	Affordable
Style	Smart casual
Cuisine	Bar-Bistro
Recommended for	Breakfast

FRONTERA GRILL

Recommended by
Carrie Nahabedian

445 North Clark Street
Near North
Chicago
Illinois 60654
+1 3126611434
www.rickbayless.com/restaurants

Opening hours	5 days for lunch and dinner
Reservation policy	Yes
Credit cards	Accepted
Price range	Budget
Style	Casual
Cuisine	Mexican
Recommended for	Regular neighbourhood

LA MADIA

Recommended by
Carrie Nahabedian

59 West Grand Avenue
Near North
Chicago
Illinois 60654
+1 3123290400
www.dinelamadia.com

Opening hours	7 days for lunch and dinner
Reservation policy	Yes
Credit cards	Accepted
Price range	Budget
Style	Casual
Cuisine	Italian
Recommended for	Regular neighbourhood

LES NOMADES

Recommended by
Carrie Nahabedian,
Ben Roche

222 East Ontario Street
Near North
Chicago
Illinois 60611
+1 3126499010
www.lesnomades.net

Opening hours	5 days for dinner
Reservation policy	Yes
Credit cards	Accepted
Price range	Expensive
Style	Formal
Cuisine	Modern French
Recommended for	Wish I'd opened

NOMI KITCHEN

Recommended by
Jean Joho

Park Hyatt Hotel
800 North Michigan Avenue
Near North
Chicago
Illinois 60010
+1 3122394030
www.parkchicago.hyatt.com

Opening hours	7 days for brunch and 2 days for dinner
Reservation policy	Yes
Credit cards	Accepted
Price range	Expensive
Style	Smart casual
Cuisine	International
Recommended for	Breakfast

The mark of a good hotel is a breakfast feast, and the breakfast at NoMI Kitchen at Chicago's Park Hyatt hotel is superlative. Blending hearty American favourites with French classics, chef Ryan LaRoche serves morning food that is both fresh and indulgent, such as Eggs Blackstone with wilted rocket (arugula) and hollandaise, or brioche French toast with vanilla ricotta and blueberry compote. There's an interesting tension between LaRoche's insistence on produce from local artisans and the distinctly urban surroundings (black leather, long slanted windows, Chicago skyscape view), marking a departure from clinical hotel food. Marrying a metropolitan hotel setting with conscious eating, this is breakfast with a difference – best washed down with one of NoMI's bounteous Champagne cocktails.

PIERROT

Recommended by
Jean Joho

Peninsula Hotel
108 East Superior Street
Near North
Chicago
Illinois 60611
+1 3123372888
www.peninsula.com/chicago

Opening hours...........7 days for brunch and 6 days for dinner
Reservation policy...No
Credit cards...Accepted
Price range...Budget
Style...Casual
Cuisine..French
Recommended for...Breakfast

THE PURPLE PIG

Recommended by
Matthew Accarrino, Carrie
Nahabedian, Adam Sobel

500 North Michigan Ave
Near North
Chicago
Illinois 60611
+1 3124641744
www.thepurplepigchicago.com

Opening hours.................................7 days for lunch and dinner
Reservation policy..No
Credit cards...Accepted
Price range...Affordable
Style...Casual
Cuisine..Modern European
Recommended for.................................Worth the travel

'Such a small space and they do such big things.
Everything I ate was soulful and delicious.'
—Adam Sobel

R L

Recommended by
Carrie Nahabedian

115 East Chicago Avenue
Near North
Chicago
Illinois 60611
+1 3124751100
www.rlrestaurant.com

Opening hours...............................7 days for brunch and dinner
Reservation policy..Yes
Credit cards...Accepted
Price range...Affordable
Style...Smart casual
Cuisine...American
Recommended for..............................Wish I'd opened

SPIAGGIA

Recommended by
Carrie Nahabedian

980 North Michigan Avenue
Near North
Chicago
Illinois 60611
+1 3122802750
www.spiaggiarestaurant.com

Opening hours..7 days for dinner
Reservation policy..Yes
Credit cards...Accepted
Price range...Expensive
Style..Formal
Cuisine...Modern Italian
Recommended for.......................................High end

SUNDA

Recommended by
Carrie Nahabedian

110 West Illinois Street
Near North
Chicago
Illinois 60654
+1 3126440500
www.sundachicago.com

Opening hours.............5 days for lunch and 7 days for dinner
Reservation policy..Yes
Credit cards...Accepted
Price range...Affordable
Style...Casual
Cuisine...Modern Asian
Recommended for.......................................Late night

TABLE FIFTY-TWO

Recommended by
Chakall

52 West Elm Street
Near North
Chicago
Illinois 60610
+1 3125734000
www.tablefifty-two.com

Opening hours.............1 day for brunch and 7 days for dinner
Reservation policy..Yes
Reservation email................reservations@tablefifty-two.com
Credit cards...Accepted
Price range...Affordable
Style...Smart casual
Cuisine...American
Recommended for..............................Worth the travel

COALFIRE PIZZA

1321 West Grand Avenue
Near West
Chicago
Illinois 60642
+1 3122262625
www.coalfirechicago.com

Opening hours................................6 days for lunch and dinner
Reservation policy...No
Credit cards...Accepted
Price range...Budget
Style...Casual
Cuisine...Pizza
Recommended for..Bargain

INA'S

1235 West Randolph Street
Near West
Chicago
Illinois 60607
+1 3122268227
www.breakfastqueen.com

Opening hours..........................7 days for breakfast and lunch
Reservation policy..Yes
Credit cards...Accepted
Price range...Budget
Style...Casual
Cuisine..American
Recommended for...Breakfast

SEPIA

123 North Jefferson Street
Near West
Chicago
Illinois 60661
+1 3124411920
www.sepiachicago.com

Opening hours.............5 days for lunch and 7 days for dinner
Reservation policy..Yes
Credit cards...Accepted
Price range...Affordable
Style...Smart casual
Cuisine..Modern American
Recommended for...Worth the travel

'Delicious and creative food.'—Matthew Accarrino

Nostalgia isn't what it used to be at this converted nineteenth-century print shop in Chicago's fashionable downtown Fulton River District. Period memorabilia discreetly adorns the dining room, but the overall effect is as elegantly modern as chef Andrew Zimmerman's cooking. Chicken fried smoked sweetbreads are paired with an off-the-wall combination of rhubarb, celery and hoisin that works in a sweet and sour, salty and crispy way. The eye-catching list of 'libations', including a Death and Taxes cocktail made with whisky, brandy, oregano Earl Grey syrup, lemon, grapefruit and Creole Bitters, has won plaudits of its own.

PRAIRIE GRASS CAFÉ

601 Skokie Boulevard
Northbrook
Chicago
Illinois 60062
+1 8472054433
www.prairiegrasscafe.com

Opening hours.............................7 days for brunch and dinner
Reservation policy..Yes
Credit cards...Accepted
Price range...Budget
Style...Casual
Cuisine...Modern American
Recommended for...Local favourite

NIGHTWOOD

Recommended by
Ben Roche

2119 South Halsted Street
Pilsen
Chicago
Illinois 60608
+1 3125263385
www.nightwoodrestaurant.com

Opening hours.............1 day for brunch and 6 days for dinner
Reservation policy...Yes
Credit cards...Accepted
Price range..Affordable
Style..Casual
Cuisine.......................................Mediterranean-American
Recommended for..Breakfast

As well as his penchant for cooking whole hogs,
Nightwood's chef de cuisine Jason Vincent is
known for serving bold, produce-driven European
cuisine at this smart, cosy local in Chicago's Pilsen
neighbourhood. A sunny patio, crafty cocktail
selection and 'wow' breakfast menu mean this place
is the go-to weekend brunch spot, with crowds
drawn to the evil fresh doughnuts with bacon and
butterscotch, or rolled mushroom omelette with
eight-year matured Cheddar and straw (shoestring)
potatoes. Vincent works with speciality local
suppliers for meat, dairy and fresh veg, to give
Mediterranean-inspired ensembles such as the
deep-fried Michigan smelts with lemon and crème
fraiche a distinctively Midwestern accent.

PORTILLO'S

Recommended by
Carrie Nahabedian

100 West Ontario Street
River North
Chicago
Illinois 60654
www.portillos.com

Opening hours.............7 days for breakfast, lunch and dinner
Reservation policy...No
Credit cards...Accepted
Price range..Budget
Style..Casual
Cuisine...Diner-Cafe
Recommended for..Bargain

PICCOLO SOGNO

Recommended by
Homaro Cantu

464 North Halsted St
River West
Chicago
Illinois 60642
+1 3124210077
www.piccolosognorestaurant.com

Opening hours.............5 days for lunch and 7 days for dinner
Reservation policy...Yes
Credit cards...Accepted
Price range..Budget
Style..Casual
Cuisine..Italian
Recommended for...Worth the travel

EL CHORRITO

Recommended by
Bruce Sherman

6404 North Clark Street
Rogers Park
Chicago
Illinois 60626
+1 7733810902
www.elchorrito.com

Opening hours.........................7 days from breakfast until late
Reservation policy...No
Credit cards...Accepted
Price range..Budget
Style..Casual
Cuisine...Mexican
Recommended for..Late night

KITSCH'N ON ROSCOE

Recommended by
Homaro Cantu

2005 West Roscoe Street
Roscoe Village
Chicago
Illinois 60618
+1 7732487372
www.kitschn.com

Opening hours.........................7 days for breakfast and lunch
Reservation policy...No
Credit cards...Accepted
Price range..Budget
Style..Casual
Cuisine..American
Recommended for..Breakfast

M BURGER

Recommended by
Jean Joho

161 East Huron
Streeterville
Chicago
Illinois 60611
+1 3122548500
www.mburgerchicago.com

Opening hours	7 days for lunch and dinner
Reservation policy	Yes
Credit cards	Accepted
Price range	Budget
Style	Casual
Cuisine	Burgers
Recommended for	Bargain

What started as an enterprising lunchtime use of the chef's table at upscale French restaurant Tru has been expanded by Lettuce Entertain You Restaurants into Chicago's most cultish takeaway (takeout) burger joint – now with four locations across the city. The flagship E Huron site remains its cosiest, at just seven seats (with a capacity for forty on the outside patio) fought over by lunchers here for the signature M Burger, made with juicy, naturally raised meat, bacon, American cheese and pickles. All the sauces are made from scratch and in true In-N-Out Burger manner there's a secret menu, including the Doctor Betty – a meat patty version of its vegetarian Nurse Betty with beef (beefsteak) tomato, guacamole and pepper Jack cheese.

CHICKPEA

Recommended by
Ben Roche

2018 Chicago Avenue
Ukrainian Village
Chicago
Illinois 60622
+1 7733849930
www.chickpeaonthego.com

Opening hours	7 days for lunch and dinner
Reservation policy	No
Credit cards	Not accepted
Price range	Budget
Style	Casual
Cuisine	Middle Eastern
Recommended for	Bargain

FURAMA

Recommended by
Bruce Sherman

4936 North Broadway Street
Uptown
Chicago
Illinois 60640
+1 7732711161
www.furamachicago.com

Opening hours	7 days from breakfast until late
Reservation policy	Yes
Credit cards	Accepted
Price range	Budget
Style	Casual
Cuisine	Chinese
Recommended for	Breakfast

MINDY'S HOT CHOCOLATE

Recommended by
Michael Schwartz

1747 North Damen Avenue
Wicker Park
Chicago
Illinois 60647
+1 7734891747
www.hotchocolatechicago.com

Opening hours	5 days for brunch
Reservation policy	Yes
Credit cards	Accepted
Price range	Affordable
Style	Casual
Cuisine	American
Recommended for	Worth the travel

'Ridiculous stuff here: pancakes, fried chicken and the best sticky buns ever!'—Michael Schwartz

THE AVIARY

Recommended by
Adam Horton, Ben Roche

955 West Fulton Market
West Loop
Chicago
Illinois 60607
+1 3122260868
www.theaviary.com

Opening hours	5 days for dinner
Reservation policy	Yes
Reservation email	reservations@theaviary.com
Credit cards	Accepted
Price range	Expensive
Style	Smart casual
Cuisine	Bar-Small plates
Recommended for	Worth the travel

'The flavours were so intense I was shocked. It was an amazing experience.'—Adam Horton

'AN EXPENSIVE TREAT? NEW YORK! ANY OF MARIO BATALI'S RESTAURANTS.'
LUKE MANGAN P580

'SHOWS OFF THE DELICIOUS COOKING HAPPENING IN NEW YORK CITY BEFORE 10.00 A.M.'
MICHAEL ANTHONY P592

'The energy and feel is very New York.'
ERIC RIPERT P596

'JUST BECAUSE IT'S LATE DOESN'T MEAN STARVATION HAS TO KNOCK.'
CHRISTINA TOSI

NEW YORK

'A hot dog on any number of New York corners.'
WYLIE DUFRESNE

'WE ARE SPOILED IN NYC SO WE ARE EATING OUT ALL THE TIME AT DIFFERENT PLACES.'
ANDREW CARMELLINI

'I'M NOT REALLY SURE WHAT EXACTLY NEW YORK CUISINE IS BUT RICH TORRISI AND MARIO CARBONE HAVE CERTAINLY CAPTURED IT.'
DAVID CHANG P596

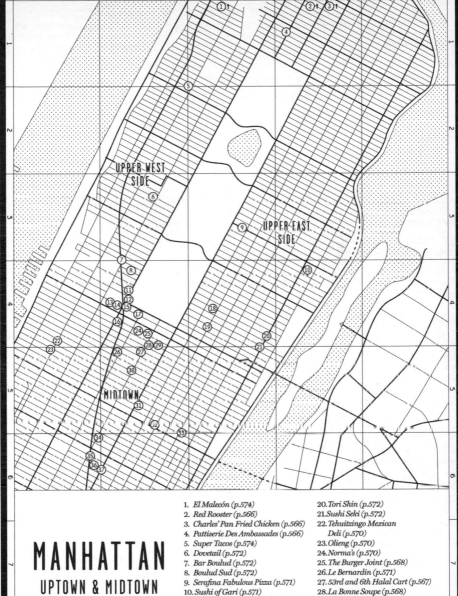

MANHATTAN

UPTOWN & MIDTOWN

UPPER WEST SIDE

UPPER EAST SIDE

MIDTOWN

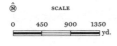

N̂

SCALE

0   450   900   1350
yd.

1. *El Malecón (p.574)*
2. *Red Rooster (p.566)*
3. *Charles' Pan Fried Chicken (p.566)*
4. *Pattiserie Des Ambassades (p.566)*
5. *Super Tacos (p.574)*
6. *Dovetail (p.572)*
7. *Bar Boulud (p.572)*
8. *Boulud Sud (p.572)*
9. *Serafina Fabulous Pizza (p.571)*
10. *Sushi of Gari (p.571)*
11. *Nougatine at Jean-Georges (p.570)*
12. *Jean Georges (p.573)*
13. *Per Se (p.574)*
14. *Masa (p.575)*
15. *Marea (p.569)*
16. *Yakitori Totto (p.570)*
17. *Petrossian (p.570)*
18. *Daniel (p.571)*
19. *540 Park (p.572)*
20. *Tori Shin (p.572)*
21. *Sushi Seki (p.572)*
22. *Tehuitzingo Mexican Deli (p.570)*
23. *Olieng (p.570)*
24. *Norma's (p.570)*
25. *The Burger Joint (p.568)*
26. *Le Bernardin (p.571)*
27. *53rd and 6th Halal Cart (p.567)*
28. *La Bonne Soupe (p.568)*
29. *Michael's Restaurant (p.569)*
30. *Sake Bar Hagi (p.566)*
31. *DB Bistro Moderne (p.568)*
32. *Grand Central Oyster Bar (p.567)*
33. *Sushi Yasuda (p.567)*
34. *Keens Steakhouse (p.569)*
35. *Gahm Mi Oak (p.568)*
36. *Mandoo Bar (p.567)*
37. *Kunjip (p.569)*

CHARLES' PAN FRIED CHICKEN

Recommended by
Ben Pollinger, Marcus
Samuelsson

2841 Frederick Douglass Boulevard
Harlem
Manhattan
New York 10039
+1 2122811800

Opening hours................................7 days for lunch and dinner
Reservation policy...No
Credit cards...Accepted
Price range..Budget
Style...Casual
Cuisine...Southern American
Recommended for..Bargain

'Some of my favourite fried chicken.'
—Marcus Samuelsson

PATISSERIE DES AMBASSADES

Recommended by
Marcus Samuelsson

2200 Frederick Douglass Boulevard
Harlem
Manhattan
New York 10026
www.patisseriedesambassades.com

Opening hours........................7 days from breakfast until late
Reservation policy...No
Credit cards..................................Accepted but not Diners
Price range..Budget
Style...Casual
Cuisine..Bakery-Café
Recommended for...Breakfast

'A West African patisserie serving the best croissants.
And the playlist is always fun: Bob Marley, Mariah Carey
and Phil Collins. It never changes. Sussudio blasting
in the morning is a great wake-up call.'
—Marcus Samuelsson

RED ROOSTER

Recommended by
Margot Henderson

310 Lenox Avenue
Harlem
Manhattan
New York 10027
+1 2127929001
www.redroosterharlem.com

Opening hours................................7 days for lunch and dinner
Reservation policy..Yes
Credit cards..................................Accepted but not Diners
Price range..Affordable
Style...Casual
Cuisine...Southern American
Recommended for..Worth the travel

It took an expat Ethiopian-Swede to open Harlem's
first very successful restaurant since gentrification
began in the mid-1990s. Combining a sense of the
area's proud African-American past with its future
and a touch of Scandinavian style, Martin Samuel-
son's Red Rooster has been a hit since it opened
in 2011. Sitting not far from the soul-food legend
that is Sylvia's, it serves a brand of elevated home
cooking that satisfies both Harlem's fashionable
newcomers and its long-standing residents. On the
menu, corn bread, prawns (shrimp) and dirty rice,
and spring (collard) greens sit alongside Swedish
meatballs and gravlax.

SAKE BAR HAGI

Recommended by
Daniel Humm, David
Pasternack, Jesse Schenker

152 West 49th Street
Midtown Center
Manhattan
New York 10019

Opening hours.....................................7 days for dinner
Reservation policy...No
Credit cards..................................Accepted but not Diners
Price range..Budget
Style...Casual
Cuisine..Japanese
Recommended for..Late night

GRAND CENTRAL OYSTER BAR

Recommended by
Daniel Boulud

Grand Central Station
89 East 42nd Street
Midtown East
Manhattan
New York 10017
+1 2124906650
www.oysterbarny.com

Opening hours	6 days for lunch and dinner
Reservation policy	Yes
Credit cards	Accepted
Price range	Affordable
Style	Casual
Cuisine	Seafood
Recommended for	Local favourite

SUSHI YASUDA

Recommended by
Marc Fosh, Didem Şenol

204 East 43rd Street
Midtown East
Manhattan
New York 10017
+1 2129721001
www.sushiyasuda.com

Opening hours	5 days for lunch and 6 days for dinner
Reservation policy	Yes
Credit cards	Accepted but not Diners
Price range	Expensive
Style	Smart casual
Cuisine	Modern Japanese
Recommended for	Worth the travel

53RD AND 6TH HALAL CART

Recommended by
Alex Young

53rd Street & 6th Avenue
Midtown West
Manhattan
New York 10019

Opening hours	7 days for dinner
Reservation policy	No
Credit cards	Not accepted
Price range	Budget
Style	Casual
Cuisine	Middle Eastern
Recommended for	Late night

MANDOO BAR

Recommended by
Daniel Humm

2 West 32nd Street
Midtown West
Manhattan
New York 10001
+1 2122793075
www.mandoobarnyc.com

Opening hours	7 days for lunch and dinner
Reservation policy	No
Credit cards	Accepted but not Diners
Price range	Budget
Style	Casual
Cuisine	Korean
Recommended for	Bargain

'I love their Korean dumplings, ramen and seafood pancakes. I've been going for years. It's great comfort food.'—Daniel Humm

It's all about the *mandoo* (dumplings) at Mandoo, handmade in the front window of this bijou Korea-town bar and prepared in a number of interesting ways, including vegetable and steamed kimchee or pan-fried with pork and minced cabbage. The industrial decor is functional, but brisk and friendly service means you can generally find a place to sit even during busy evening hours and the very reasonable prices ($11/£7 for ten *mandoo*) are bargains by Midtown standards. Don't forget to finish with their only dessert — a green-tea ice cream — to sooth the effects of all that Sriracha sauce.

LA BONNE SOUPE

Recommended by
Eric Ripert

48 West 55th Street
Midtown West
Manhattan
New York 10019
+1 2125867650
www.labonnesoupe.com

Opening hours	7 days for lunch and dinner
Reservation policy	Yes
Credit cards	Accepted
Price range	Budget
Style	Casual
Cuisine	French
Recommended for	Bargain

'Everyday food à la French.'—Eric Ripert

They certainly pack 'em in at La Bonne Soupe but Manhattanites put up with the rather, er, 'cosy' seating arrangements for the chance to eat very authentic Parisian bistro fare in equally authentic surroundings. A feature of Midtown for going on thirty years, its proximity to Broadway makes it ideal for wallet-friendly pre-theatre, and the well-heeled (and somewhat mature) crowd don't seem to mind sharing elbow space with their fellow diners. Appropriately, particularly recommended is the French onion soup, although if you really do prefer a bit of breathing space, try and get a table on the balcony upstairs.

THE BURGER JOINT

Recommended by
Andrew Fairlie

Le Parker Meridien Hotel
119 West 56th Street
Midtown West
Manhattan
New York 10019
+1 2127087414
www.parkermeridien.com

Opening hours	7 days for lunch and dinner, until late
Reservation policy	No
Credit cards	Not accepted
Price range	Budget
Style	Casual
Cuisine	Burgers
Recommended for	Wish I'd opened

'It has queues (lines) all day long, no advertising, blisteringly simple, you have to be in the know to find it. It sells burgers or cheeseburgers, chips (fries) and sodas. Menu states, "If you don't see it, we don't have it" I love the confidence.'—Andrew Fairlie

DB BISTRO MODERNE

Recommended by
Michael Ferraro,
Armin Leitgeb

55 West 44th Street
Midtown West
Manhattan
New York 10036
+1 2123912400
www.danielnyc.com/dbbistro.html

Opening hours	7 days for breakfast, lunch and dinner
Reservation policy	Yes
Credit cards	Accepted
Price range	Affordable
Style	Smart casual
Cuisine	French-American
Recommended for	High end

**'Have the original DB Bistro sirloin burger.'
—Michael Ferraro**

The name might be rather opaque ('DB' is chef and owner Daniel Boulud, who also heads a Michelin-star-studded worldwide restaurant empire, and a 'Bistro Moderne', which is – er, we'll get back to you on that) but there's nothing obscure about the appeal of this buzzing, beautifully designed, theatre district restaurant. The 'db Burger', filled with braised short ribs, foie gras and black truffle, has been much imitated but never equalled and sets the tone: familiar and approachable food that you want to eat again and again, but with enough thrilling luxury to ensure you won't get bored.

GAHM MI OAK

Recommended by
Andrew Carmellini,
Corey Lee

43 West 32nd Street
Midtown West
Manhattan
New York 10001
+1 2126954113
www.gahmmioak.com

Opening hours	7 days for 24 hours
Reservation policy	No
Credit cards	Accepted
Price range	Affordable
Style	Casual
Cuisine	Korean
Recommended for	Late night

KEENS STEAKHOUSE

72 West 36th Street
Midtown West
Manhattan
New York 10018
+1 2129473636
www.keens.com

Opening hours.............5 days for lunch and 7 days for dinner
Reservation policy...Yes
Credit cards..Accepted
Price range..Expensive
Style..Smart casual
Cuisine...Steakhouse
Recommended for...Wish I'd opened

KUNJIP

9 West 32nd Street
Midtown West
Manhattan
New York 10001
+1 2122169487
www.kunjip.net

Opening hours..7 days for 24 hours
Reservation policy...Yes
Credit cards..Accepted
Price range...Affordable
Style...Casual
Cuisine...Korean
Recommended for...Late night

'In the winter, they give you free tea and black pudding
(blood sausage) if there is a long wait for a table.'
—April Bloomfield

MAREA

240 Central Park South
Midtown West
Manhattan
New York 10019
+1 2125825100
www.marea-nyc.com

Opening hours.............6 days for lunch and 7 days for dinner
Reservation policy...Yes
Credit cards...Accepted but not Diners
Price range..Expensive
Style..Smart casual
Cuisine..Modern Italian
Recommended for...High end

'I most love the places that are still comfortable
and friendly even though they are utterly expert
and high-end—Marea does that for me.'
—Gabrielle Hamilton

MICHAEL'S RESTAURANT

24 West 55th Street
Midtown West
Manhattan
New York 10019
+1 2127670555
www.michaelsnewyork.com

Opening hours.............5 days for breakfast, lunch and dinner
Reservation policy...Yes
Credit cards..Accepted
Price range..Affordable
Style..Smart casual
Cuisine...Modern American
Recommended for...Breakfast

'It's great to start the day with this kind of elegance.'
—Ben Pollinger

NORMA'S

Recommended by
Keith Silverton

Le Parker Meridien Hotel
119 West 56th Street
Midtown West
Manhattan
New York 10019
+1 2127087460
www.parkermeridien.com

Opening hours	7 days for breakfast and lunch
Reservation policy	Yes
Credit cards	Accepted but not Diners
Price range	Affordable
Style	Casual
Cuisine	American
Recommended for	Breakfast

NOUGATINE AT JEAN GEORGES

Recommended by
Bradley Turley

1 Central Park West
Midtown West
Manhattan
New York 10023
+1 2122993900
www.jean-georges.com

Opening hours	7 days for breakfast, lunch and dinner
Reservation policy	Yes
Credit cards	Accepted but not Diners
Price range	Affordable
Style	Smart casual
Cuisine	French
Recommended for	Regular neighbourhood

OLIENG

Recommended by
Michael Guerrieri

644 10th Avenue
Midtown West
Manhattan
New York 10036
+1 2123079388
www.olieng.com

Opening hours	7 days for lunch and dinner
Reservation policy	No
Credit cards	Accepted
Price range	Budget
Style	Casual
Cuisine	Thai
Recommended for	Regular neighbourhood

PETROSSIAN

Recommended by
Michael Mina

182 West 58th Street
At 7th Avenue
Midtown West
Manhattan
New York 10019
+1 2122452214
www.petrossian.com

Opening hours	7 days for dinner
Reservation policy	Yes
Credit cards	Accepted but not Diners
Price range	Expensive
Style	Smart casual
Cuisine	French-Russian
Recommended for	High end

TEHUITZINGO MEXICAN DELI

Recommended by
Carlo Mirarchi

695 10th Avenue
Midtown West
Manhattan
New York 10036
+1 2123975956

Opening hours	7 days for lunch and dinner
Reservation policy	No
Credit cards	Not accepted
Price range	Budget
Style	Casual
Cuisine	Mexican
Recommended for	Bargain

YAKITORI TOTTO

Recommended by
Michael Anthony, Eric Ripert

251 West 55th Street
Midtown West
Manhattan
New York 10019
+1 2122454555
www.tottonyc.com

Opening hours	7 days for lunch and dinner
Reservation policy	Yes
Credit cards	Accepted
Price range	Budget
Style	Casual
Cuisine	Japanese
Recommended for	Late night

'Very authentic and delicious - you feel transported to Tokyo immediately.'—Eric Ripert

LE BERNARDIN

155 West 51st Street
Times Square
Manhattan
New York 10019
+1 2125541515
www.le-bernardin.com

Opening hours	5 days for lunch and 7 days for dinner
Reservation policy	Yes
Credit cards	Accepted
Price range	Expensive
Style	Formal
Cuisine	Seafood
Recommended for	Wish I'd opened

'For most of my professional cooking career, fine dining seafood has been my personal favourite, so a smaller version of Eric Ripert's Le Bernardin would be a dream restaurant of mine.'—Michael Ferraro

DANIEL

60 East 65th Street
Upper East Side
Manhattan
New York 10065
+1 2122880033
www.danielnyc.com

Opening hours	6 days for dinner
Reservation policy	Yes
Credit cards	Accepted
Price range	Expensive
Style	Formal
Cuisine	Modern French
Recommended for	High end

Daniel Boulud's increased international focus has seen him open less formal cafés, bistros and bars around the world, but at his eponymous spot in the heart of Manhattan's Upper East Side he flexes his high-end muscles with refined yet imaginative cooking. The opulent dining room, refurbished by the same design agency behind Thomas Keller's Per Se, is the scene for dishes that are rooted in the French chef's native Lyon but which have a distinctive American twang thanks to the use of local ingredients. The result is a supremely slick operation that remains one of Manhattan's culinary hot spots among the city's high rollers.

SERAFINA FABULOUS PIZZA

1022 Madison Avenue
Upper East Side
Manhattan
New York 10021
+1 2127342676
www.serafinarestaurant.com

Opening hours	7 days for lunch and dinner
Reservation policy	No
Credit cards	Accepted
Price range	Affordable
Style	Casual
Cuisine	Italian
Recommended for	Regular neighbourhood

When the great and good of Manhattan's Upper East Side want pizza they head to Serafina Fabulous, the Madison Avenue original of the ever-growing chain. Homemade soup and spaghetti pomodoro sit alongside luxury ingredients such as burrata and truffle ravioli on the extensive 'Northern Italian' menu. However, regulars stick to the pizza, which is thin and crisp of crust, slicked with plenty of tomato sauce and topped with dollops of the house mozzarella. There are glossier branches dotted across the city, but there's a cosy homespun feel to this two-floor dining room set back one block from Central Park – and service is warm too.

SUSHI OF GARI

402 East 78th Street
Upper East Side
Manhattan
New York 10075
+1 2125175340
www.sushiofgari.com

Opening hours	7 days for dinner
Reservation policy	Yes
Credit cards	Accepted but not Diners
Price range	Affordable
Style	Smart casual
Cuisine	Japanese
Recommended for	Worth the travel

SUSHI SEKI

Recommended by
Gwendal Le Ruyet,
Ben Pollinger

1143 1st Avenue
Upper East Side
Manhattan
New York 10021
+1 2123710238

Opening hours...................................6 days for dinner
Reservation policy...Yes
Credit cards........................Accepted but not Diners
Price range..Affordable
Style...Casual
Cuisine...Japanese
Recommended for............................Worth the travel

TORI SHIN

Recommended by
Takashi Inoue

1193 1st Avenue
Upper East Side
Manhattan
New York 10065
+1 2129888408
www.torishinny.com

Opening hours.................7 days for lunch and dinner
Reservation policy...Yes
Credit cards........................Accepted but not Diners
Price range..Affordable
Style...Smart casual
Cuisine...Japanese
Recommended for.......................Regular neighbourhood

540 PARK

Recommended by
Daniel Boulud

Loews Regency Hotel
540 Park Avenue
Upper West Side
Manhattan
New York 10065
+1 2123394050
www.loewshotels.com

Opening hours........7 days for breakfast and 5 days for lunch
Reservation policy...Yes
Credit cards..Accepted
Price range..Affordable
Style...Smart casual
Cuisine...Modern American
Recommended for....................................Breakfast

BAR BOULUD

Recommended by
Mark Sullivan

1900 Broadway
Upper West Side
Manhattan
New York 10023
+1 2125950303
www.barboulud.com

Opening hours.................7 days for lunch and dinner
Reservation policy...Yes
Credit cards..Accepted
Price range..Affordable
Style...Smart casual
Cuisine..French
Recommended for............................Worth the travel

'The skill with which they prepare charcuterie is the best in the country.'—Mark Sullivan

BOULUD SUD

Recommended by
Susan Spicer

20 West 64th Street
Upper West Side
Manhattan
New York 10023
+1 2125951313
www.danielnyc.com/boulud_sud.html

Opening hours.................7 days for lunch and dinner
Reservation policy...Yes
Credit cards..Accepted
Price range..Expensive
Style...Smart casual
Cuisine...Mediterranean
Recommended for......................................High end

DOVETAIL

Recommended by
Harold Dieterle,
Ben Pollinger

103 West 77th Street
Upper West Side
Manhattan
New York 10024
+1 2123623800
www.dovetailnyc.com

Opening hours............1 day for brunch and 7 days for dinner
Reservation policy...Yes
Credit cards..Accepted
Price range..Affordable
Style...Smart casual
Cuisine...Modern American
Recommended for............................Wish I'd opened

Dovetail's intimate dining room with its contrasting rugged bare brick columns, sleek dove-grey leather chairs and crisp white linen is one worth dressing up for. And the artfully presented food of multi-award-winning chef John Fraser (whose credentials include a stint at Thomas Keller's legendary The French Laundry) would suit a special occasion. But at heart this is a neighbourhood restaurant, albeit it one with a Michelin star, that serves a great value brunch menu and a 'Sunday Suppa' of halibut confit, broad (fava) beans and spring onions (scallions) as well as gourmet creations like rabbit and foie gras terrine with fennel mostarda.

JEAN GEORGES

1 Central Park West
Upper West Side
Manhattan
New York 10023
+1 2122993900
www.jean-georges.com

Recommended by
Daniel Boulud, Scott Conant,
Jean Joho, Ben Pollinger,
Vicky Ratnani, Eric Ripert,
Marcus Samuelsson,
Susan Spicer

Opening hours.................................7 days for lunch and dinner
Reservation policy...Yes
Credit cards...Accepted
Price range..Expensive
Style...Formal
Cuisine..French-Asian
Recommended for...Worth the travel

Born in Alsace but now a long-term U.S. citizen, there's nothing conventional about Jean Georges' rise up the culinary ladder, not least because his primarily Asian-influenced cuisine is a far cry from his Gallic roots. The JG empire has swelled to almost twenty establishments in recent years, serving all manner of styles of cuisine, but to taste him at his best go to his Central Park flagship, where classics such as peekytoe crab dumplings and yellow fin tuna ribbons make a regular appearance. Prices for the dinner menu can be quite hefty, but lunchtime offers a more affordable taste of what's offered.

MASA

Time Warner Center
10 Columbus Circle
Upper West Side
Manhattan
New York 10019
+1 2128239800
www.masanyc.com

Recommended by
Josean Alija, Quique
Dacosta, David Hawksworth,
Daniel Lindeberg, Eric Ripert,
Joan Roca

Opening hours.....................4 days for lunch 6 days for dinner
Reservation policy..Yes
Reservation email.........................reservation@masanyc.com
Credit cards...Accepted but not Diners
Price range..Expensive
Style...Smart casual
Cuisine..Modern Japanese
Recommended for...High end

'Exquisite.'—David Hawksworth

The best seats in the (Zen-like) house at Masayoshi Takayama's twenty-six-seat sushi restaurant are at the counter, under the watchful eye of Masa himself. Take a moment to caress the hinoki wood tabletop (sanded daily, apparently), before immersing yourself in the Masa omakase experience – one of the world's most expensive dining events. Forget you're in the Time Warner Center shopping mall, and concentrate on the luxury: tuna tartare with equal parts toro (flown in from Tokyo's Tsukiji Market) and osetra caviar, wagyu beef tataki with summer truffles, and truffle ice cream. Bar Masa next door (and in Vegas) offers luxury for less.

PER SE

Time Warner Center
10 Columbus Circle
Upper West Side
Manhattan
New York 10019
+1 2128239335
www.perseny.com

Opening hours..............3 days for lunch and 7 days for dinner
Reservation policy...Yes
Credit cards..Accepted
Price range...Expensive
Style..Formal
Cuisine...Modern American
Recommended for...............................Worth the travel

'Hands down one of the best meals I've had. The precision and quality, from the wine to the china to the ambiance, combined with the hand-craftsmanship of the food, was outstanding.'—Tory McPhail

Coming here is not about the money. It is excruciatingly expensive, but pleasure comes at a price, and chef-owner Thomas Keller is no artful dodger. Pleasure is Per Se's *raison d'être* – if the view of Central Park doesn't take your breath away, they'll sweat blood and tears to make sure the food does. A temple to sous vide, Keller's East Coast urban interpretation of the legendary French Laundry pulls out all the stops to make its food memorable. Chef de cuisine Eli Kaimeh has been running the kitchen since 2010 and his tasting menus change daily, although exquisite 'oysters and pearls' with caviar is a regular feature.

SUPER TACOS

97th Street
Upper West Side
Manhattan
New York 10025
+1 9178370866

Opening hours..............2 days for lunch and 7 days for dinner
Reservation policy...No
Credit cards...Not accepted
Price range...Budget
Style...Casual
Cuisine...Mexican
Recommended for.......................................Late night

EL MALECÓN

4141 Broadway
Washington Heights
Manhattan
New York 10033

Opening hours..............7 days for breakfast, lunch and dinner
Reservation policy...No
Credit cards..Accepted
Price range...Budget
Style...Casual
Cuisine...Cuban
Recommended for..Bargain

'A Cuban hole-in-the-wall near Times Square.'
—Daniel Boulud

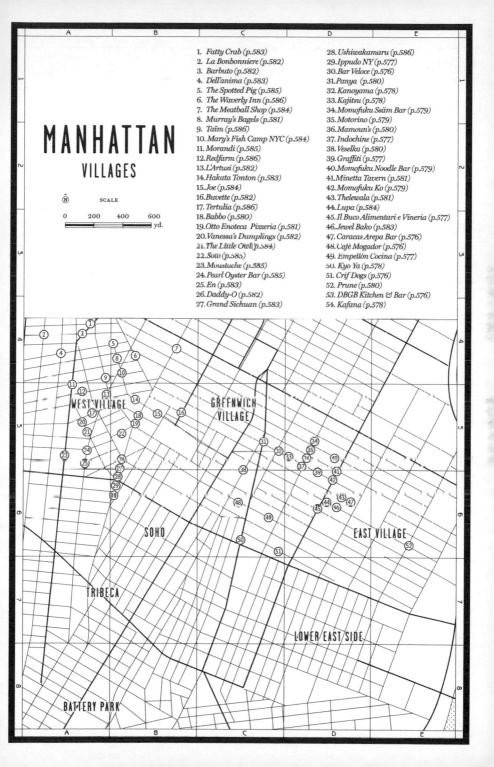

MANHATTAN
VILLAGES

SCALE

0   200   400   600 yd.

WEST VILLAGE

GREENWICH VILLAGE

SOHO

EAST VILLAGE

TRIBECA

LOWER EAST SIDE

BATTERY PARK

BAR VELOCE

Recommended by
Wylie Dufresne

175 2nd Avenue
East Village
Manhattan
New York 10003
www.barveloce.com

Opening hours..........................7 days from breakfast until late
Reservation policy..No
Credit cards..Accepted
Price range..Budget
Style..Casual
Cuisine..Italian
Recommended for...Late night

'I love the mortadella panini.'—Wylie Dufresne

CAFÉ MOGADOR

Recommended by
Mario Carbone

Saint Mark's Place
East Village
Manhattan
New York 10009
+1 2126772226
www.cafemogador.com

Opening hours..............7 days for breakfast, lunch and dinner
Reservation policy...Yes
Credit cards..Accepted
Price range..Budget
Style..Casual
Cuisine..Moroccan
Recommended for...Breakfast

CARACAS AREPA BAR

Recommended by
Christina Tosi

93½ East 7th Street
East Village
Manhattan
New York 10009
+1 2125292314
www.caracasarepabar.com

Opening hours................................7 days for lunch and dinner
Reservation policy..No
Credit cards...Accepted but not Diners
Price range..Budget
Style..Casual
Cuisine..Venezuelan
Recommended for..Bargain

CRIF DOGS

Recommended by
Christina Tosi

113 Saint Mark's Place
East Village
Manhattan
New York 10009
+1 2126142728
www.crifdogs.com

Opening hours................................7 days for lunch and dinner
Reservation policy..No
Credit cards..Accepted
Price range..Budget
Style..Casual
Cuisine..Hot Dogs
Recommended for...Late night

DBGB KITCHEN & BAR

Recommended by
Paul Newman

299 Bowery
East Village
Manhattan
New York 10003
+1 2129335300
www.danielnyc.com/dbgb.html

Opening hours................................7 days for lunch and dinner
Reservation policy...Yes
Credit cards..Accepted
Price range..Affordable
Style..Smart casual
Cuisine..French-American
Recommended for.................................Wish I'd opened

'French brasserie meets American tavern. Great food, service, ambiance and value. And the best sausages and beer.'—Paul Newman

EMPELLÓN COCINA

Recommended by
Wylie Dufresne

105 1st Avenue
East Village
Manhattan
New York 10003
+1 2127800999
www.empellon.com/cocina

Opening hours...........2 days for brunch and 7 days for dinner
Reservation policy..Yes
Credit cards...............................Accepted but not Diners
Price range..Affordable
Style...Casual
Cuisine...Modern Mexican
Recommended for................................Worth the travel

'Great Mexican food really well executed.'
—Wylie Dufresne

Wd-50's and Alinea's former pastry chef Alex Stupak
first decided to flex his sweet talent in a totally
different direction in 2011 with the opening of Empellón Taqueria in the West Village. This, the follow-up to
that classy and creative taco joint, opened around a
year later in the East Village, takes even more risks
in its adventurous approach to Mexican food. Forget
about cheap and cheerful carb and dairy-heavy
staples and think fresh and delicate tapas-style small
plates that often make use of unexpected ingredients
– wagyu beef, shitake mushrooms, shigoku oysters
– while still maintaining a Mexican soul.

GRAFFITI

Recommended by
Alfredo Hoz

224 East 10th Street
East Village
Manhattan
New York 10002
+1 2126770695
www.graffitinyc.com

Opening hours..................................6 days for dinner
Reservation policy..Yes
Credit cards..Accepted
Price range...Budget
Style...Casual
Cuisine...Modern American
Recommended for................................Worth the travel

INDOCHINE

Recommended by
Michael Guerrieri

430 Lafayette Street
East Village
Manhattan
New York 10003
+1 2125055111
www.indochinenyc.com

Opening hours.................................7 days for dinner
Reservation policy..Yes
Credit cards..Accepted
Price range..Affordable
Style...Smart casual
Cuisine...French-Vietnamese
Recommended for...High end

IL BUCO ALIMENTARI E VINERIA

Recommended by
Zakary Pelaccio

53 Great Jones Street
East Village
Manhattan
New York 10012
+1 2128372622
www.ilbucovineria.com

Opening hours...........2 days for brunch and 7 days for dinner
Reservation policy..Yes
Credit cards..Accepted
Price range..Affordable
Style...Casual
Cuisine...................................Italian Bar-Bistro-Deli
Recommended for...............................Regular neighbourhood

IPPUDO NY

Recommended by
Andrew Carmellini, Anita Lo

65 4th Avenue
East Village
Manhattan
New York 10003
+1 2123880088
www.ippudony.com

Opening hours.......................7 days for lunch and dinner
Reservation policy...No
Credit cards..Accepted
Price range...Budget
Style...Casual
Cuisine...Japanese
Recommended for...Bargain

KAFANA

Recommended by
Gabrielle Hamilton

116 Avenue C
East Village
Manhattan
New York 10009
+1 2123538000
www.kafananyc.com

Opening hours	2 days for lunch and 7 days for dinner
Reservation policy	Yes
Credit cards	Not accepted
Price range	Budget
Style	Casual
Cuisine	Serbian
Recommended for	Bargain

'Yugoslavian meats and salads, and a wine list made up almost exclusively of Serbian and Croatian labels. Hardly anyone in the room speaks English.'
—Gabrielle Hamilton

KAJITSU

Recommended by
David Chang, Jason Fox

414 East 9th Street
East Village
Manhattan
New York 10003
+1 2122284873
www.kajitsunyc.com

Opening hours	6 days for dinner
Reservation policy	Yes
Credit cards	Accepted
Price range	Expensive
Style	Smart casual
Cuisine	Japanese Vegan
Recommended for	Wish I'd opened

'They serve Shojin temple food, an ancient cuisine developed in Buddhist monasteries - sort of Japanese comfort food. It's all vegetables, but you're not going to miss the meat. It's a thought provoking experience, but the food is also incredibly fun and very delicious. Chef Masato Nishihara is extremely talented, and has created an amazing restaurant.'—David Chang

This evening-only, vegan-friendly, *kaiseki*-serving, East Village Japanese specializes in *shojin ryori*. Brought, in the thirteenth century, by Zen monks across China to Japan, where it was perfected – or rather brought closer to perfection – *shojin ryori* is all about celebrating seasonal vegetables. In twenty-first-century Manhattan this translates to a very Zen, twenty-eight-seat space that's all wood, beige walls and stone floors, with colour and beauty provided by

the tableware and the food itself. The multi-coursed menu changes every month, the only constant being a serving of soba noodles. A very enlightening experience regardless of whether you are vegan or not.

KANOYAMA

Recommended by
Harold Dieterle

175 2nd Avenue
East Village
Manhattan
New York 10003
+1 2127775266
www.kanoyama.com

Opening hours	7 days for dinner
Reservation policy	Yes
Credit cards	Accepted but not Diners
Price range	Affordable
Style	Casual
Cuisine	Japanese
Recommended for	Regular neighbourhood

KYO YA

Recommended by
Takashi Inoue

94 East 7th Street
East Village
Manhattan
New York 10009
+1 2129824140
www.kyoyarestaurant.com

Opening hours	6 days for dinner
Reservation policy	Yes
Credit cards	Accepted
Price range	Affordable
Style	Casual
Cuisine	Japanese
Recommended for	Regular neighbourhood

'A great traditional Japanese restaurant. I always start with the sashimi, then have their delicately fried tempura, which transports me back to Japan.'
—Takashi Inoue

MOMOFUKU KO

163 1st Avenue
East Village
Manhattan
New York 10003
+1 212500831
www.momofuku.com/restaurants/ko

Recommended by
Alberto Chicote, Angela
Hartnett, Corey Lee, Ségué
Lepage, Vicky Ratnani

Opening hours	3 days for lunch and 7 days for dinner
Reservation policy	Yes
Credit cards	Accepted but not Diners
Price range	Expensive
Style	Smart casual
Cuisine	Asian-American
Recommended for	Worth the travel

'Delicious.'—Angela Hartnett

You'll need patience and a computer to register for a Momofuku account to even have a chance of securing a reservation at David Chang's twelve-seat counter. To actually get one you either need luck, or a dedicated team of personal assistants, multiple accounts and more patience. You can book only a week in advance, the seats released online each morning at 10.00 a.m. seemingly gone seconds later. Assuming your luck's in, once you locate the low-key entrance, you'll find no waiters, no printed menu, and your no-choice ten courses (sixteen if you snag a lunch booking) served to you by the chefs behind the counter.

MOMOFUKU NOODLE BAR

171 1st Avenue
East Village
Manhattan
New York 10003
+1 2127777773
www.momofuku.com

Recommended by
Mark Hix, Adam Horton,
Marcus Samuelsson,
Stephen Stryjewski, Michel
Troisgros

Opening hours	7 days for lunch and dinner
Reservation policy	No
Credit cards	Accepted
Price range	Budget
Style	Casual
Cuisine	Asian-American
Recommended for	Wish I'd opened

'I think chef David Chang has revolutionized modern Asian cuisine.'—Adam Horton

MOMOFUKU SSÄM BAR

207 2nd Avenue
East Village
Manhattan
New York 10003
www.momofuku.com/restaurants/ssam-bar

Recommended by
Michael Anthony, John
Besh, Sean Brock, Andreas
Dahlberg, Wylie Dufresne,
Benjamin Greeno

Opening hours	7 days for lunch and dinner
Reservation policy	Yes
Credit cards	Accepted but not Diners
Price range	Affordable
Style	Casual
Cuisine	Asian-American
Recommended for	Wish I'd opened

'I first ate there late one night in 2007 and it changed the way I looked at restaurants.'—Benjamin Greeno

David Chang's follow-up to his noodle bar, opened in 2006, is the restaurant that made him a superstar. Named after the Asian answer to the burrito that was originally to have been the mainstay on the menu, it has evolved to offer a menu that's heavy on meat – particularly pork – and that's not afraid to feature offal – or 'variety meat' as it's more commonly called stateside. At the back is Booker and Dax, a recently opened cocktail bar that offers a short menu of snacks from country hams to Chang's famous pork steamed buns of which everyone still can't seem to get enough.

MOTORINO

349 East 12th Street
East Village
Manhattan
New York 10003
www.motorinopizza.com

Recommended by
Andrew Carmellini

Opening hours	7 days for lunch and dinner
Reservation policy	No
Credit cards	Accepted but not Diners
Price range	Budget
Style	Casual
Cuisine	Pizza
Recommended for	Bargain

PANYA

Recommended by
Masato Shimizu

8 Stuyvesant Street
East Village
Manhattan
New York 10003

Opening hours	7 days from breakfast until late
Reservation policy	No
Credit cards	Accepted
Price range	Budget
Style	Casual
Cuisine	Bakery-Café
Recommended for	Breakfast

PRUNE

Recommended by
Sam Hayward, Francis
Mallmann, Russell Moore

54 East 1st Street
East Village
Manhattan
New York 10003
+1 2126776221
www.prunerestaurant.com

Opening hours	7 days for lunch and dinner
Reservation policy	Yes
Credit cards	Accepted but not Diners
Price range	Affordable
Style	Casual
Cuisine	Modern American
Recommended for	Regular neighbourhood

'Always a fantastic experience. Every plate is as good
as it can possibly be. I'm always amazed by the intense
presonalness of Prune.'—Sam Hayward

VANESSA'S DUMPLINGS

Recommended by
Jesse Schenker

220 East 14th Street
East Village
Manhattan
New York 10003
+1 2126258008

Opening hours	7 days for lunch and dinner
Reservation policy	No
Credit cards	Accepted but not Diners
Price range	Budget
Style	Casual
Cuisine	Chinese
Recommended for	Bargain

VESELKA

Recommended by
Christina Tosi

144 2nd Avenue
East Village
Manhattan
New York 10003
+1 2122289682
www.veselka.com

Opening hours	7 days for 24 hours
Reservation policy	No
Credit cards	Accepted but not Diners
Price range	Budget
Style	Casual
Cuisine	Ukranian-American
Recommended for	Late night

BABBO

Recommended by
Gabriel Rucker

110 Waverly Place
Greenwich Village
Manhattan
New York 10011
+1 2127770303
www.babbonyc.com

Opening hours	7 days for lunch and dinner
Reservation policy	Yes
Credit cards	Accepted
Price range	Affordable
Style	Smart casual
Cuisine	Modern Italian
Recommended for	Worth the travel

MAMOUN'S

Recommended by
Scott Conant

119 MacDougal Street
Greenwich Village
Manhattan
New York 10012
+1 2126748686
www.mamouns.com

Opening hours	7 days for lunch and dinner
Reservation policy	No
Credit cards	Not accepted
Price range	Budget
Style	Casual
Cuisine	Middle Eastern
Recommended for	Bargain

MINETTA TAVERN

113 MacDougal Street
Greenwich Village
Manhattan
New York 10012
+1 2124753850
minettatavernny.com

Recommended by
Govind Armstrong, Mario
Carbone, Harold Dieterle,
Michael Ferraro, Brendan
McGill, Tom Oldroyd, Marcus
Samuelsson

Opening hours	5 days for lunch and 7 days for dinner
Reservation policy	Yes
Credit cards	Accepted
Price range	Expensive
Style	Smart casual
Cuisine	French
Recommended for	Worth the travel

'I could return here over and over again for their pied de porc pané – crisp Berkshire pig's trotter (feet), Dijon mustard, lentils and herb salad.'—Tom Oldroyd

A Greenwich Village fixture since 1937, Keith McNally has breathed new life into the old joint, giving it the same sort of upscale French brasserie polish that served him so well at Balthazar. There was no bouncer on the door back in the day when the Beats hung out here, nor, I imagine, were banquettes trimmed in such crisp crimson leather. But enough of the original tavern's features remain for it to retain its character. Add a menu that delivers gutsy Gallic comfort, such as truffled pork sausage and roasted bone marrow, and it's not hard to see why the retooled Minetta has been such a hit.

MURRAY'S BAGELS

500 Avenue of the Americas
Greenwich Village
Manhattan
New York 10011
+1 2124622830
www.murraysbagels.com

Recommended by
Jesse Schenker

Opening hours	7 days from breakfast until late
Reservation policy	No
Credit cards	Accepted
Price range	Budget
Style	Casual
Cuisine	Bakery-Café
Recommended for	Breakfast

Nostalgic Greenwich bagel shop opened in 1996 by Wall Street escapee Adam Pomerantz. Inspired by memories of the smoked fish filled bagels his father brought home from the Lower East Side, he named it after him. Although Murray's core business is naturally bagels of all sorts, the breakfast menu also includes Irish oatmeal with bananas, raisins and brown sugar. When it comes to their breakfast sandwiches – they boast that their bagels are never toasted and are always 'served fresh from the oven' – they fill them with scrambled eggs and various omelettes, as is the case with the Leo, which somehow manages to gets lox and onions in there too.

OTTO ENOTECA PIZZERIA

1 5th Avenue
Greenwich Village
Manhattan
New York 10003
+1 2129959559
www.ottopizzeria.com

Recommended by
Gabrielle Hamilton

Opening hours	7 days for lunch and dinner
Reservation policy	Yes
Credit cards	Accepted but not Diners
Price range	Budget
Style	Casual
Cuisine	Pizza
Recommended for	Regular neighbourhood

THELEWALA

112 MacDougal Street
Greenwich Village
Manhattan
New York 10012
www.thelewalanyc.com

Recommended by
Daniel Boulud

Opening hours	7 days for lunch and dinner
Reservation policy	No
Credit cards	Accepted but not Diners
Price range	Budget
Style	Casual
Cuisine	Indian
Recommended for	Bargain

L'ARTUSI

Recommended by
Anita Lo

228 West 10th Street
West Village
Manhattan
New York 10014
+1 2122555757
www.lartusi.com

Opening hours	1 day for brunch and 7 days for dinner
Reservation policy	Yes
Credit cards	Accepted
Price range	Affordable
Style	Smart casual
Cuisine	Modern Italian
Recommended for	Regular neighbourhood

BARBUTO

Recommended by
Bruce Bromberg,
Gabrielle Hamilton

775 Washington Street
West Village
Manhattan
New York 10014
+1 2129249700
www.barbutonyc.com

Opening hours	7 days for lunch and dinner
Reservation policy	Yes
Credit cards	Accepted
Price range	Affordable
Style	Smart casual
Cuisine	Italian
Recommended for	Local favourite

'Handles nicely both my children – plain buttered pasta with Parmesan – and me, the grown-up – a negroni.'
—Gabrielle Hamilton

LA BONBONNIERE

Recommended by
Takashi Inoue

28 8th Avenue
West Village
Manhattan
New York 10014
+1 2127419266

Opening hours	7 days for breakfast, lunch and dinner
Reservation policy	No
Credit cards	Not accepted
Price range	Budget
Style	Casual
Cuisine	Diner-Café
Recommended for	Breakfast

BUVETTE

Recommended by
Alexandra Raij

42 Grove Street
West Village
Manhattan
New York 10014
www.ilovebuvette.com

Opening hours	7 days for breakfast, lunch and dinner
Reservation policy	No
Credit cards	Accepted
Price range	Affordable
Style	Casual
Cuisine	French
Recommended for	Breakfast

'If I were meeting a friend for a girly breakfast I'd go to Buvette.'—Alexandra Raij

DADDY-O

Recommended by
Mario Carbone,
Harold Dieterle

44 Bedford Street
West Village
Manhattan
New York 10014
+1 2124148884
www.daddyonyc.com

Opening hours	7 days for breakfast and lunch
Reservation policy	No
Credit cards	Accepted
Price range	Affordable
Style	Casual
Cuisine	Bar-Bistro
Recommended for	Late night

Styled like a classic neighbourhood bar, locals far outnumber the out-of-towners. Jocks come to shout at sports on the big screen and drink beer, others for the cocktails, the bar carrying a sizeable selection of single malts, rum and tequila. The kitchen, open until 4.00 a.m., serves a dependable menu of bar classics. A special mention must go to their sides of tater tots and The Plate – a tribute to Nick Tahou Hots' (Rochester, NY) cult classic Garbage Plate: two red or white hot dogs or two cheeseburgers, topped with hot sauce, mustard and onions, served over homemade fries and macaroni salad.

EN

435 Hudson Street
West Village
Manhattan
New York 10014
+1 2126479196
www.enjb.com

Recommended by
Peter Hoffman

Opening hours................................7 days for lunch and dinner
Reservation policy...Yes
Credit cards..Accepted
Price range...Affordable
Style..Casual
Cuisine..Japanese
Recommended for...High end

'For homemade tofu for family celebration
meals.'—Peter Hoffman

FATTY CRAB

643 Hudson Street
West Village
Manhattan
New York 10014
+1 2123523592
www.fattycrab.com

Recommended by
Robert J.K. Kranenborg

Opening hours................................7 days for lunch and dinner
Reservation policy..No
Credit cards..Accepted
Price range...Affordable
Style..Casual
Cuisine..Malaysian
Recommended for.............................Worth the travel

GRAND SICHUAN

15 7th Avenue South
West Village
Manhattan
New York 10014
+1 2126450222
www.thegrandsichuan.com

Recommended by
Harold Dieterle

Opening hours................................7 days for lunch and dinner
Reservation policy..No
Credit cards..Accepted
Price range...Budget
Style..Casual
Cuisine...Szechuan
Recommended for...Late night

DELL'ANIMA

38 8th Avenue
West Village
Manhattan
New York 10014
+1 2123666633
www.dellanima.com

Recommended by
Anita Lo

Opening hours..........2 days for brunch and 7 days for dinner
Reservation policy...Yes
Credit cards..Accepted
Price range...Affordable
Style..Smart casual
Cuisine..Modern Italian
Recommended for...Late night

'I love to go to Dell'Anima.'—Anita Lo

HAKATA TONTON

61 Grove Street
West Village
Manhattan
New York 10014
+1 2122423699
www.tontonnyc.com

Recommended by
Carlo Mirarchi

Opening hours..6 days for dinner
Reservation policy...Yes
Credit cards..Accepted
Price range...Budget
Style..Casual
Cuisine..Japanese
Recommended for...Late night

JEWEL BAKO

239 East 5th Street
West Village
Manhattan
New York 10003
+1 2129791012

Recommended by
Anita Lo

Opening hours..6 days for dinner
Reservation policy...Yes
Credit cards..Accepted
Price range...Expensive
Style..Smart casual
Cuisine..Japanese
Recommended for...High end

'Have the omakase sushi.'—Anita Lo

JOE

Recommended by
Anita Lo

141 Waverly Place
West Village
Manhattan
New York 10014
www.joetheartofcoffee.com

Opening hours	7 days from breakfast until late
Reservation policy	No
Credit cards	Not accepted
Price range	Budget
Style	Casual
Cuisine	Café
Recommended for	Breakfast

THE LITTLE OWL

Recommended by
Harold Dieterle

90 Bedford Street
West Village
Manhattan
New York 10014
+1 2127414695
www.thelittleowlnyc.com

Opening hours	7 days for lunch and dinner
Reservation policy	Yes
Credit cards	Accepted but not Diners
Price range	Affordable
Style	Casual
Cuisine	American
Recommended for	Regular neighbourhood

LUPA

Recommended by
Harold Dieterle,
Jesse Schenker

175 Thompson Street
West Village
Manhattan
New York 10012
+1 2129825089
www.luparestaurant.com

Opening hours	7 days for lunch and dinner
Reservation policy	Yes
Credit cards	Accepted but not Diners
Price range	Affordable
Style	Casual
Cuisine	Italian
Recommended for	Wish I'd opened

Lupa is a traditional Roman-style *osteria* in the portfolio of dynamic New York restaurant duo Joe Bastianich and Mario Batali (Babbo, Del Posto, etc). As rammed now as it was on its launch in 1999, Lupa is testament to New Yorkers' love affair with real Italian cuisine (and their willingness to queue/line for it). The Lupa kitchen doesn't shy away from 'ordinary' Roman dishes — *bavette cacio e pepe* or spaghetti carbonara, for example — but makes something extraordinary of them. It also cures its own *testa* and *coppa cotta* (the salumi here are superb). Tables are held back for 'walk-ins', so try your luck.

MARY'S FISH CAMP

Recommended by
Karam Sethi

64 Charles Street
West Village
New York 10014
Manhattan
www.marysfishcamp.com

Opening hours	6 days for lunch and dinner
Reservation policy	No
Credit cards	Accepted but not Diners
Price range	Affordable
Style	Casual
Cuisine	Seafood
Recommended for	Worth the travel

'For their lobster rolls, and fried oysters.'—Karam Sethi

THE MEATBALL SHOP

Recommended by
Christina Tosi

64 Greenwich Avenue
West Village
Manhattan
New York 10011
+1 2129827815
www.themeatballshop.com

Opening hours	7 days for lunch and dinner
Reservation policy	No
Credit cards	Accepted
Price range	Affordable
Style	Casual
Cuisine	Italian-American
Recommended for	Late night

MORANDI
Recommended by
Peter Hoffman

211 Waverly Place
West Village
Manhattan
New York 10014
+1 2126277575
www.morandiny.com

Opening hours	7 days for brunch and dinner
Reservation policy	Yes
Credit cards	Accepted but not Diners
Price range	Affordable
Style	Casual
Cuisine	Italian
Recommended for	Breakfast

MOUSTACHE
Recommended by
Anita Lo

90 Bedford Street
West Village
Manhattan
New York 10014
+1 2122292220
www.moustachepitza.com

Opening hours	7 days for lunch and dinner
Reservation policy	No
Credit cards	Not accepted
Price range	Budget
Style	Casual
Cuisine	Middle Eastern
Recommended for	Bargain

PEARL OYSTER BAR
Recommended by
Anita Lo

18 Cornelia Street
West Village
Manhattan
New York 10014
+1 2126918211
www.pearloysterbar.com

Opening hours	5 days for lunch and 6 days for dinner
Reservation policy	No
Credit cards	Accepted
Price range	Affordable
Style	Casual
Cuisine	Seafood
Recommended for	Wish I'd opened

SOTO
Recommended by
Tyson Cole, Alexandra Raij,
Jesse Schenker

357 6th Avenue
West Village
Manhattan
New York 10014
+1 2124143088
www.sotonyc.com

Opening hours	6 days for dinner
Reservation policy	Yes
Credit cards	Accepted but not Diners
Price range	Affordable
Style	Smart casual
Cuisine	Japanese
Recommended for	Regular neighbourhood

'The food is transporting.'—Alexandra Raij

Named after the proprietor, Sotohiro Kosugi, this whitewashed room behind a door with no sign does a modest forty-two covers. A third-generation sushi chef, he performs his craft in front of expectant diners propped up at the blonde wood bar. Together with some exceptional raw fish, delicately cooked dishes also come out from the kitchen in impressive fashion. This is a very serious operation. Tables run in line along the side of the restaurant amid a very stark decor of spotlighting, slats and symbolic red circles. Pleasingly, there is also a lengthy list of speciality sakes.

THE SPOTTED PIG
Recommended by
Anita Lo, Francis Mallmann

314 West 11th Street
West Village
Manhattan
New York 10014
www.thespottedpig.com

Opening hours	7 days for lunch and dinner
Reservation policy	No
Credit cards	Accepted but not Diners
Price range	Affordable
Style	Casual
Cuisine	Bar-Bistro
Recommended for	Late night

REDFARM

529 Hudson Street
West Village
Manhattan
New York 10014
+1 2127929700
www.redfarmnyc.com

Opening hours	2 days for brunch and 7 days for dinner
Reservation policy	No
Credit cards	Accepted but not Diners
Price range	Affordable
Style	Smart casual
Cuisine	Modern Chinese
Recommended for	Worth the travel

TAÏM

222 Waverly Place
West Village
Manhattan
New York 10014
www.taimfalafel.com

Opening hours	7 days for lunch and dinner
Reservation policy	No
Credit cards	Not accepted
Price range	Budget
Style	Casual
Cuisine	Middle Eastern
Recommended for	Bargain

TERTULIA

359 6th Avenue
West Village
Manhattan
New York 10014
+1 6465599909
www.tertulianyc.com

Opening hours	7 days for lunch and dinner
Reservation policy	No
Credit cards	Accepted but not Diners
Price range	Affordable
Style	Smart casual
Cuisine	Bar-Small plates
Recommended for	Worth the travel

The conviviality of the *sidrerías* – local cider houses – in Asturias, northern Spain, was the inspiration for chef Seamus Mullen's West Village 'Spanish gastropub'. Set in raffish surrounds – rough brickwork, distressed wooden tables, a cider barrel behind the bar and an open wood-fired oven – in a former Prohibition-era speakeasy, it's heart-warming stuff, but certainly doesn't lack ambition. Deftly executed tapas classics – tortilla, Ibérican ham croquettes, grilled prawns (shrimp) with garlic and Padrón peppers – are elevated by fine ingredients and judicious flourishes. Mullen stretches his legs with the sharing dishes and seasonal daily specials, chalked up on a blackboard above the kitchen.

USHIWAKAMARU

136 West Houston Street
West Village
Manhattan
New York 10012
+1 2122284181

Opening hours	6 days for dinner
Reservation policy	Yes
Credit cards	Accepted but not Diners
Price range	Affordable
Style	Casual
Cuisine	Japanese
Recommended for	Regular neighbourhood

THE WAVERLY INN

16 Bank Street
West Village
Manhattan
New York 10014
+1 9178281154
www.waverlynyc.com

Opening hours	2 days for brunch and 7 days for dinner
Reservation policy	Yes
Credit cards	Accepted
Price range	Affordable
Style	Smart casual
Cuisine	American
Recommended for	Local favourite

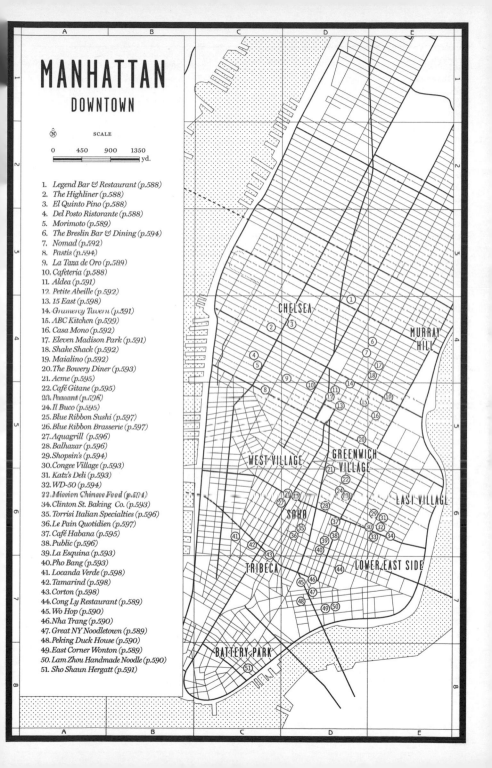

MANHATTAN
DOWNTOWN

N

SCALE

0   450   900   1350 yd.

1. *Legend Bar & Restaurant (p.588)*
2. *The Highliner (p.588)*
3. *El Quinto Pino (p.588)*
4. *Del Posto Ristorante (p.588)*
5. *Morimoto (p.589)*
6. *The Breslin Bar & Dining (p.594)*
7. *Nomad (p.592)*
8. *Pastis (p.594)*
9. *La Taza de Oro (p.589)*
10. *Cafeteria (p.588)*
11. *Aldea (p.591)*
12. *Petite Abeille (p.592)*
13. *15 East (p.598)*
14. *Gramercy Tavern (p.591)*
15. *ABC Kitchen (p.599)*
16. *Casa Mono (p.592)*
17. *Eleven Madison Park (p.591)*
18. *Shake Shack (p.592)*
19. *Maialino (p.592)*
20. *The Bowery Diner (p.593)*
21. *Acme (p.595)*
22. *Café Gitane (p.595)*
23. *Peasant (p.596)*
24. *Il Buco (p.595)*
25. *Blue Ribbon Sushi (p.597)*
26. *Blue Ribbon Brasserie (p.597)*
27. *Aquagrill (p.596)*
28. *Balhazar (p.596)*
29. *Shopsin's (p.594)*
30. *Congee Village (p.593)*
31. *Katz's Deli (p.593)*
32. *WD-50 (p.594)*
33. *Mission Chinese Food (p.594)*
34. *Clinton St. Baking Co. (p.593)*
35. *Torrisi Italian Specialties (p.596)*
36. *Le Pain Quotidien (p.597)*
37. *Café Habana (p.595)*
38. *Public (p.596)*
39. *La Esquina (p.593)*
40. *Pho Bang (p.593)*
41. *Locanda Verde (p.598)*
42. *Tamarind (p.598)*
43. *Corton (p.598)*
44. *Cong Ly Restaurant (p.589)*
45. *Wo Hop (p.590)*
46. *Nha Trang (p.590)*
47. *Great NY Noodletown (p.589)*
48. *Peking Duck House (p.590)*
49. *East Corner Wonton (p.589)*
50. *Lam Zhou Handmade Noodle (p.590)*
51. *Sho Shaun Hergatt (p.591)*

CHELSEA

MURRAY HILL

WEST VILLAGE

GREENWICH VILLAGE

EAST VILLAGE

SOHO

LOWER EAST SIDE

TRIBECA

BATTERY PARK

CAFETERIA

Recommended by
Michael Guerrieri

119 7th Avenue
Chelsea
Manhattan
New York 10010
+1 2124141717
www.cafeteriagroup.com

Opening hours.............7 days for breakfast, lunch and dinner
Reservation policy...Yes
Credit cards..Accepted
Price range..Budget
Style..Casual
Cuisine...Modern American
Recommended for...Late night

'Contemporary comfort food with a twist.'
—Michael Guerrieri

DEL POSTO

Recommended by
Mario Carbone, Gabrielle
Hamilton, Andy Ricker, Ben
Roche, Christina Tosi

85 10th Avenue
Chelsea
Manhattan
New York 10011
+1 2124978090
www.delposto.com

Opening hours.............5 days for lunch and 7 days for dinner
Reservation policy...Yes
Credit cards..Accepted
Price range...Expensive
Style..Smart casual
Cuisine..Modern Italian
Recommended for.......................................High end

'It's the best kept secret in New York, if you ask
me.'—Christina Tosi

Delightfully over the top as ever, Del Posto seems
to be hitting its stride and winning back New Yorkers
years after opening. The polished mahogany and
marble interior, live piano soundtrack and perfectly
poised service pushes deep into occasion dining
territory, pitched more at Wall Street power lunchers
than Meat-packing locals. The food, however, is for
everyone. Don't miss the outstanding pastas –
piquant crab, jalapeño and minced spring onion
(scallion) spaghetti; unctuous lamb ragù and *orec-
chiette* topped with crisp rye crumbs. Be warned, the
bill here comes on heavyweight stationery, but the
$39 (£25) three-course prix fixe is one of Manhat-
tan's best bargains.

EL QUINTO PINO

Recommended by
Daniel Boulud

401 West 24th Street
Chelsea
Manhattan
New York 10001
www.elquintopinonyc.com
+1 2122066900

Opening hours.................................7 days for dinner
Reservation policy...No
Credit cards..Accepted
Price range..Budget
Style..Casual
Cuisine..Tapas
Recommended for...Late night

THE HIGHLINER

Recommended by
Marcus Samuelsson

210 10th Avenue
Chelsea
Manhattan
New York 10011
+1 2122066206
www.thehighlinernyc.com

Opening hours.............7 days for breakfast, lunch and dinner
Reservation policy...Yes
Credit cards..............................Accepted but not Diners
Price range..Affordable
Style..Casual
Cuisine..Diner-Café
Recommended for...Late night

LEGEND BAR & RESTAURANT

Recommended by
Scott Conant

88 7th Avenue
Chelsea
Manhattan
New York 10011
+1 2129291778
www.legendrestaurant88.com

Opening hours................................7 days for lunch and dinner,
Reservation policy...Yes
Credit cards..Accepted
Price range..Budget
Style..Casual
Cuisine.............................Szechuan-Vietnamese
Recommended for...Bargain

MORIMOTO

Recommended by
Ken Oringer

88 10th Avenue
Chelsea
Manhattan
New York 10011
+1 2129898883
www.morimotonyc.com

Opening hours	5 days for lunch and 7 days for dinner
Reservation policy	Yes
Credit cards	Accepted but not Diners
Price range	Expensive
Style	Smart casual
Cuisine	Japanese
Recommended for	High end

'Go for the omakase.'—Ken Oringer

LA TAZA DE ORO

Recommended by
Marcus Samuelsson

96 8th Avenue
Chelsea
Manhattan
New York 10011
+1 2122439946

Opening hours	6 days for breakfast, lunch and dinner
Reservation policy	Yes
Credit cards	Not accepted
Price range	Budget
Style	Casual
Cuisine	Latin American
Recommended for	Bargain

'Love the vibe.'—Marcus Samuelsson

CONG LY RESTAURANT

Recommended by
Alexandra Raij

124 Hester Street
Chinatown
Manhattan
New York 10002

Opening hours	7 days for breakfast, lunch and dinner
Reservation policy	No
Credit cards	Not accepted
Price range	Budget
Style	Casual
Cuisine	Vietnamese
Recommended for	Bargain

'I love Cong Ly for pho.'—Alexandra Raij

EAST CORNER WONTON

Recommended by
Zakary Pelaccio

70 East Broadway
Chinatown
Manhattan
New York 10002
+1 2123439896

Opening hours	7 days for breakfast, lunch and dinner
Reservation policy	No
Credit cards	Not accepted
Price range	Budget
Style	Casual
Cuisine	Chinese
Recommended for	Bargain

GREAT NY NOODLETOWN

Recommended by
Andrew Carmellini, David
Chang, Michael Ferraro,
Zakary Pelaccio,
Alexandra Raij

28 Bowery
Chinatown
Manhattan
New York 10013
www.greatnynoodletown.com

Opening hours	7 days for breakfast, lunch and dinner
Reservation policy	No
Credit cards	Not accepted
Price range	Budget
Style	Casual
Cuisine	Chinese
Recommended for	Late night

'Great NY Noodletown is good night and day.'
—Alexandra Raij

This Chinatown classic delivers on the far from empty promise of its name. It's true that service can be brisk understandable since it's open until 4.00 a.m., making it a popular post-bar crawl, small hours spot for the well oiled and the weary. But the lengthy menu — which covers all the bases from congee to barbeque meats, via various poultry and seafood dishes, to a lengthy list of noodle soups — is good enough to warrant inspection in the cold and sober light of day. Particularly worthy of investigation is their soft-shell crab, in season from around May until about October.

LAM ZHOU HANDMADE NOODLE
Recommended by
Sang-Hoon Degeimbre
144 East Broadway
Chinatown
Manhattan
New York 10002
+1 2125666933

Opening hours	7 days from breakfast until late
Reservation policy	No
Credit cards	Not accepted
Price range	Budget
Style	Casual
Cuisine	Chinese
Recommended for	Bargain

'Fresh noodles and ravioli hand made in front of you for only $4-$6.50 (£2-£4).'—Sang-Hoon Degeimbre

Flushing, Queens, is well known for its northeastern, central and western Chinese food, while Chinatown tends to offer better Cantonese and southern Chinese cuisine. Lam Zhou maintains this trend: a hearty bowl of hand-pulled noodles with beef tendon in a rich, nourishing broth costs just $6.50 (£4). The tiny restaurant is already famous among bloggers. The English menu is shorter than the Chinese and the staff don't all speak English, so bring a Mandarin-speaking friend or plan your order before you arrive. Although Lam Zhou is most famous for its noodles, its dumplings are fluffy and generously filled as well.

NHA TRANG
Recommended by
Hugh Acheson
87 Baxter Street
Chinatown
Manhattan
New York 10013
+1 2122335948
www.nhatrangone.com

Opening hours	7 days for lunch and dinner
Reservation policy	No
Credit cards	Accepted
Price range	Budget
Style	Casual
Cuisine	Vietnamese
Recommended for	Bargain

PEKING DUCK HOUSE
Recommended by
Harold Dieterle, Carlo
Mirarchi, Christina Tosi
28 Mott Street
Chinatown
Manhattan
New York 10013
+1 2122271810
www.pekingduckhousenyc.com

Opening hours	7 days for lunch and dinner
Reservation policy	Yes
Credit cards	Accepted
Price range	Affordable
Style	Casual
Cuisine	Chinese
Recommended for	Regular neighbourhood

'You and your three closest friends can dine on Peking Duck and cheap beer for less than $100 (£60).'—Christina Tosi

Peking Duck House has two Manhattan locations, in Midtown and China Town, both of which hide themselves behind unremarkable facades (and a red curtain). Unlike many restaurants of this type, there are no ducks hanging in the windows like a butcher's shop. Instead, the animals are treated with more respect, prospective diners having to cross the threshold to experience any part of the mallard magic that awaits them. The decor is more clean than comfy but people don't come to scrutinize the red carpet and bleached walls – they flock here for the legendary Peking Duck and house-made pancakes.

WO HOP
Recommended by
Bruce Bromberg
17 Mott Street
Chinatown
Manhattan
New York 10013
+1 2129628617
www.wohopnyc.com

Opening hours	7 days for lunch and dinner
Reservation policy	No
Credit cards	Not accepted
Price range	Budget
Style	Casual
Cuisine	Chinese
Recommended for	Late night

SHO SHAUN HERGATT

Recommended by
Hans Välimäki

40 Broad Street
Financial District
Manhattan
New York 10004
+1 2128093993
www.shoshaunhergatt.com

Opening hours.............5 days for lunch and 6 days for dinner
Reservation policy...Yes
Credit cards...Accepted
Price range...Expensive
Style...Smart casual
Cuisine...French-Asian
Recommended for...Worth the travel

ALDEA

Recommended by
Sean Brock, Scott Conant

31 West 17th Street
Flatiron
Manhattan
New York 10011
+1 2126757223
www.aldearestaurant.com

Opening hours.............5 days for lunch and 6 days for dinner
Reservation policy...Yes
Credit cards...Accepted
Price range...Affordable
Style...Smart casual
Cuisine.......................Modern Portuguese-Spanish
Recommended for...Worth the travel

'It manages to be avant-garde while still being
homey.'—Scott Conant

ELEVEN MADISON PARK

Recommended by
April Bloomfield, Mauro
Colagreco, Eloi Dion, Sergio
Herman, Philip Howard, Tony
Maws, Patrick O'Connell,
Eric Ripert, Emanuele
Scarello, Hans Välimäki

11 Madison Avenue
Flatiron
Manhattan
New York 10010
+1 2128890905
www.elevenmadisonpark.com

Opening hours.............5 days for lunch and 6 days for dinner
Reservation policy...Yes
Credit cards...Accepted
Price range...Expensive
Style...Formal
Cuisine...Modern American
Recommended for...Worth the travel

'I'm a big fan of chef Daniel Humm. When I go to
Eleven Madison, I know I can relax and eat wonderful
food. It's such a treat to eat there.'—April Bloomfield

Doing away with traditional à la carte dining has
brought Eleven Madison Park dazzling accolades that
would make any chef weep. Swiss-born chef-owner
Daniel Humm joined the team in 2006 and has been
widely credited for EMP's ascendancy. Housed in a
theatrical Art Deco space above Madison Square
Park, Humm's confident and contemporary French
cooking is as opulent as that of his high-end Manhattan competitors and has won EMP three Michelin
stars. To encourage dialogue between diner and chef,
there is no conventional menu; instead, a grid of
ingredients from which you pick four, and the kitchen
does the rest. For grander budgets there's also a
bespoke tasting menu.

GRAMERCY TAVERN

Recommended by
Claudio Aprile, Christian
Page, Ben Pollinger

42 East 20th Street
Flatiron
Manhattan
New York 10003
+1 2124770777
www.gramercytavern.com

Opening hours.............5 days for lunch and 7 days for dinner
Reservation policy...Yes
Credit cards...Accepted
Price range...Affordable
Style...Smart casual
Cuisine...Modern American
Recommended for...Wish I'd opened

'They deliver the entire package. The servers don't miss
a beat and the food is always amazing.'
—Claudio Aprile

NOMAD

Recommended by
Scott Conant

Nomad Hotel
1170 Broadway and 28th Street
Flatiron
Manhattan
New York 10001
+1 3474725619
www.thenomadhotel.com

Opening hours	7 days for breakfast, lunch and dinner
Reservation policy	Yes
RCredit cards	Accepted
Price range	Expensive
Style	Smart casual
Cuisine	Small plates
Recommended for	Regular neighbourhood

PETITE ABEILLE

Recommended by
Fernando Trocca

44 West 17th Street
Flatiron
Manhattan
New York 10011
www.petiteabeille.com

Opening hours	7 days for breakfast, lunch and dinner
Reservation policy	No
Credit cards	Accepted
Price range	Affordable
Style	Casual
Cuisine	Belgian
Recommended for	Breakfast

SHAKE SHACK

Recommended by
Jesse Schenker, Ruth Rogers

Madison Square Park
Flatiron
Manhattan
New York 10010
+1 2128896600
www.shakeshack.com

Opening hours	7 days for lunch and dinner
Reservation policy	No
Credit cards	Accepted
Price range	Budget
Style	Casual
Cuisine	Burgers
Recommended for	Bargain

The queue (line) is almost as famous as the food at
the original Madison Square Park branch of super-
restaurateur Danny Meyer's glossy burger chain,
Shake Shack. Local office workers and tourists stand
in line for up to an hour for their ShackBurger — a
juicy made-to-order wonder comprising squidgy bun,
American cheese, hand-formed beef patty and secret
Shack Sauce — with crinkle-cut cheese chips (fries).
Enjoy with an outrageous 'concrete' of hot caramel
and Valrhona chocolate, a freshly squeezed lemonade or a Brooklyn Brewery Shackmeister Ale. Starting with one branch in 2004, Shake Shack now has
fourteen, including outposts in Miami and Dubai.

CASA MONO

Recommended by
Daniel Boulud,
Perfecto Roger

52 Irving Place
Gramercy
Manhattan
New York 10003
+1 2122532773
www.casamononyc.com

Opening hours	7 days for lunch and dinner
Reservation policy	Yes
Credit cards	Accepted but not Diners
Price range	Affordable
Style	Casual
Cuisine	Tapas
Recommended for	Late night

'Tapas and fun!'—Daniel Boulud

MAIALINO

Recommended by
Michael Anthony, April
Bloomfield, Michael Ferraro

Gramercy Park Hotel
2 Lexington Avenue
Gramercy Park
Manhattan
New York 10010
+1 2127772410
www.maialinonyc.com

Opening hours	7 days for breakfast, lunch and dinner
Reservation policy	Yes
Credit cards	Accepted
Price range	Expensive
Style	Smart casual
Cuisine	Italian
Recommended for	Regular neighbourhood

'Excellent pasta and one of the best lamb
chops I've had.'—Michael Ferraro

LA ESQUINA

Recommended by
Daniel Boulud

114 Kenmare Street
Little Italy
Manhattan
New York 10012
+1 6466137100
www.esquinanyc.com

Opening hours	7 days for breakfast, lunch and dinner
Reservation policy	Yes
Credit cards	Accepted
Price range	Budget
Style	Casual
Cuisine	Mexican
Recommended for	Late night

PHO BANG

Recommended by
Peter Hoffman

157 Mott Street
Little Italy
Manhattan
New York 10013
+1 2129663797

Opening hours	7 days from breakfast until late
Reservation policy	Yes
Credit cards	Not accepted
Price range	Budget
Style	Casual
Cuisine	Vietnamese
Recommended for	Bargain

THE BOWERY DINER

Recommended by
Alexandra Raij, Christina Tosi

241 Bowery
Lower East Side
Manhattan
New York 10002
+1 2123880052
www.bowerydiner.com

Opening hours	7 days for 24 hours
Reservation policy	Yes
Credit cards	Accepted but not Diners
Price range	Affordable
Style	Casual
Cuisine	Diner-Cafe
Recommended for	Breakfast

CLINTON STREET BAKING CO.

Recommended by
Takashi Inoue

4 Clinton Street
Lower East Side
Manhattan
New York 10002
+1 6466026263
www.clintonstreetbaking.com

Opening hours	7 days for brunch and 6 days for dinner
Reservation policy	Yes
Credit cards	Accepted
Price range	Budget
Style	Casual
Cuisine	Bakery-Cafe
Recommended for	Breakfast

CONGEE VILLAGE

Recommended by
Bruce Bromberg, Takashi
Inoue, Masato Shimizu

100 Allen Street
Lower East Side
Manhattan
New York 10002
+1 2129411818
www.congeevillagerestaurants.com

Opening hours	7 days for breakfast, lunch and dinner
Reservation policy	Yes
Credit cards	Accepted but not Diners
Price range	Budget
Style	Casual
Cuisine	Chinese
Recommended for	Bargain

KATZ'S DELI

Recommended by
Daniel Boulud, Mario
Carbone, Wylie Dufresne,
Marc Fosh, Carlo Mirarchi,
Eduardo Moreno

205 East Houston Street
Lower East Side
Manhattan
New York 10002
+1 2122542246
www.katzsdelicatessen.com

Opening hours	7 days for breakfast, lunch and dinner
Reservation policy	No
Credit cards	Accepted
Price range	Budget
Style	Casual
Cuisine	Deli-Cafe
Recommended for	Local favourite

'When I'm in New York I love to get up late and get
down to Katz's Deli for a Pastrami on Rye sandwich. It
sets me up for the whole day!'—Marc Fosh

MISSION CHINESE FOOD

Recommended by
Daniel Boulud, Jason Fox,
Carlo Mirarchi,
Christina Tosi

154 Orchard Street
Lower East Side
Manhattan
New York 10002
+1 2125298800
www.missionchinesefood.com

Opening hours.................................6 days for lunch and dinner
Reservation policy...No
Credit cards...Accepted
Price range..Budget
Style..Casual
Cuisine...Modern Chinese
Recommended for................................Regular neighbourhood

'I probably eat there an unhealthy amount.'—Jason Fox

SHOPSIN'S

Recommended by
Marcus Samuelsson

Essex Street Market
120 Essex Street
Lower East Side
Manhattan
New York 10002
+1 2129245160
www.shopsins.com

Opening hours...........................5 days for breakfast and lunch
Reservation policy...No
Credit cards..Not accepted
Price range...Affordable
Style..Casual
Cuisine..Diner-Cafe
Recommended for..Local favourite

WD~50

Recommended by
Andoni Luis Aduriz, Ben
Batterbury, Sean Brock,
David Chang, Julius Jaspers,
Vicky Ratnani

50 Clinton Street
Lower East Side
Manhattan
New York 10002
+1 2124772900
www.wd-50.com

Opening hours..7 days for dinner
Reservation policy..Yes
Credit cards...Accepted
Price range...Expensive
Style..Smart casual
Cuisine..Modern American
Recommended for................................Regular neighbourhood

'Their eggs benedict is delicious and amazing. One of the best dishes in the city.'—David Chang

Wylie Dufresne's wildly creative 'New American' on the Lower East Side opened in 2003 with the backing of fellow chef Jean-Georges Vongerichten, who didn't carve out his own restaurant empire without recognizing talent. Front of house they pull off the trick of making things feel casual, with a room that's laid-back and modern, while keeping the service switched-on and seriously literate. It needs be when you're explaining a menu that's all about quirky combinations and playfully deconstructing beloved American comfort-food classics – whether that's clam chowder, Southern-fried chicken, a lox and cream cheese bagel, or a root beer float.

PASTIS

Recommended by
Daniel Boulud,
Michael Guerrieri

9 9th Avenue
Meatpacking District
Manhattan
New York 10014
+1 2129294844
www.pastisny.com

Opening hours.............7 days for breakfast, lunch and dinner
Reservation policy...Yes
Credit cards...Accepted
Price range...Affordable
Style..Smart casual
Cuisine..French
Recommended for..Late night

THE BRESLIN BAR & DINING ROOM

Recommended by
Harold Dieterle

Ace Hotel
16 West 29th Street
Midtown South Central
Manhattan
New York 10001
+1 2126791939
www.thebreslin.com

Opening hours.............7 days for breakfast, lunch and dinner
Reservation policy...No
Credit cards...Accepted but not Diners
Price range...Affordable
Style..Smart casual
Cuisine..Bar-Bistro
Recommended for..Breakfast

'The Breslin's egg sandwich is a good start to the day.'—Harold Dieterle

Attached to the New York branch of the hipper-than-thou but still heavily branded Ace Hotel group, The Breslin's kitchen is overseen by expat Brit April Bloomfield of The Spotted Pig fame, who is also responsible for The John Dory, the hotel's oyster bar. The Breslin's retro-tavern good looks, quality cocktails and gutsy cooking have won it a loyal following. Particularly for its breakfast and weekend brunch menus, which run from an authentic Full English (although they call their black pudding 'blood sausage') to much more familiar takes on U.S. classics, such as lemon ricotta pancakes, frittatas and fried peanut butter and banana sandwiches.

ACME

Recommended by
Rob Evans

9 Great Jones Street
NoHo
Manhattan
New York 10012
+1 2122032121
www.acmenyc.com

Opening hours	6 days for dinner
Reservation policy	Yes
Reservation email	reservations@acmenyc.com
Credit cards	Accepted
Price range	Affordable
Style	Smart casual
Cuisine	Modern American
Recommended for	Worth the travel

IL BUCO

Recommended by
Hugh Acheson, Francis Mallmann, Zakary Pelaccio, Bruce Sherman, Masato Shimizu

47 Bond Street
NoHo
Manhattan
New York 10012
+1 2125331932
www.ilbuco.com

Opening hours	6 days for lunch and 7 days for dinner
Reservation policy	Yes
Credit cards	Accepted
Price range	Affordable
Style	Smart casual
Cuisine	Italian
Recommended for	Regular neighbourhood

CAFÉ GITANE

Recommended by
Matthew Dillon

242 Mott Street
NoLita
Manhattan
New York 10012
www.cafegitanenyc.com

Opening hours	7 days for dinner
Reservation policy	No
Credit cards	Not accepted
Price range	Budget
Style	Casual
Cuisine	French-North African
Recommended for	Breakfast

CAFÉ HABANA

Recommended by
Anna Hansen

17 Prince Street
NoLita
Manhattan
New York 10012
www.cafehabana.com

Opening hours	7 days for breakfast, lunch and dinner
Reservation policy	No
Credit cards	Accepted
Price range	Budget
Style	Casual
Cuisine	Latin American
Recommended for	Breakfast

'The best corn smothered in mayo and cheese, deep-fried plantain and Cuban sandwich. Great hangover food!'—Anna Hansen

On the corner of Elizabeth and Prince streets is Café Habana, founded by Sean Meenan, an entrepreneur with an affinity for revolution in more ways than one. The café and its siblings are eco-friendly and are inspired by a Mexico City joint where Che and Fidel Castro plotted the Cuban Revolution. An enthusiastic and upbeat atmosphere is matched by a fiesta of flavour across their breakfast menu. All-American morning classics – sunny-side-up eggs, pancakes and coffees – are offered with a touch of Hispanic flair. Think chorizo-spiked omelettes, fried eggs with salsa and variations of tortilla throughout the menu.

PEASANT

Recommended by
David Pasternack

194 Elizabeth Street
NoLita
Manhattan
New York 10012
+1 2129659511
www.peasantnyc.com

Opening hours................................6 days for dinner
Reservation policy...Yes
Credit cards.........................Accepted but not Diners
Price range...Affordable
Style...Smart casual
Cuisine..Italian
Recommended for............................Wish I'd opened

PUBLIC

Recommended by
Miles Kirby

210 Elizabeth Street
NoLita
Manhattan
New York 10012
+1 2123437011
www.public-nyc.com

Opening hours..........2 days for brunch and 7 days for dinner
Reservation policy...Yes
Credit cards.........................Accepted but not Diners
Price range...Affordable
Style...Casual
Cuisine..Modern American
Recommended for...........................Worth the travel

TORRISI ITALIAN SPECIALTIES

Recommended by
David Chang,
Daniel Humm,
Stephen Stryjewski

250 Mulberry Street
NoLita
Manhattan
New York 10012
+1 2129650955
www.torrisinyc.com

Opening hours..............3 days for lunch and 7 days for dinner
Reservation policy..No
Credit cards..Accepted
Price range...Affordable
Style...Casual
Cuisine...Italian-American
Recommended for...........................Local favourite

'It's not just Italian-American food. It's definitely their food and their point of view.'—David Chang

When this tiny twenty-seater in NoLita opened in the summer of 2010, styled as an old school Italian grocers', it operated as a sandwich shop during the day. Now that Rich Torrisi and Mario Carbone (chefs and equal partners in the operation who liked the sound of 'Torrisi' best) have Parm next door (and at Yankee Stadium) doing the retro Italian sandwich thing, Torrisi's open kitchen is given over to a daily changing seven-course set menu and elaborate twenty-course tasting menus. The former takes the traditional Italian structure of antipasto, pasta, meat or fish, followed by dessert.

AQUAGRILL

Recommended by
Marc Fosh

210 Spring Street
Soho
Manhattan
New York 10012
+1 2122740505
www.aquagrill.com

Opening hours................................7 days for lunch and dinner
Reservation policy...Yes
Credit cards..Accepted
Price range...Affordable
Style...Smart casual
Cuisine..Seafood
Recommended for...........................Worth the travel

BALTHAZAR

Recommended by
Daniel Boulud, Mario Carbone,
Christian Domschitz, Michael
Ferraro, Gabrielle Hamilton,
Henry Harris Justin Ip, Luke
Mangan, David Pasternack,
Eric Ripert, Christina Tosi, Hans
Välimäki

80 Spring Street
Soho
Manhattan
New York 10012
+1 2129651414
www.balthazarny.com

Opening hours..............7 days for breakfast, lunch and dinner
Reservation policy...Yes
Credit cards..Accepted
Price range...Affordable
Style...Casual
Cuisine..French
Recommended for............................Breakfast

'I love the café au lait here that's served in a bowl like it is in France.'—Gabrielle Hamilton

Keith McNally is among the most prolific restaurateurs in the Western Hemisphere. In the elegantly distressed warehouse-y district of SoHo, his restaurant Balthazar is a textbook Burgundy banquette-clad brasserie. The attention to detail by which it honours the French model is obsessive. The continuously bustling atmosphere is brought by the hordes of all-day diners who delight over Eggs Benedict and waffles in the morning and steak frites and confit duck in the evening. This is an institution not just within New York City but in the wider world of modern gastronomy.

BLUE RIBBON BRASSERIE

Recommended by
Gastón Acurio, Armand Arnal, Daniel Boulud, Scott Conant, Brad Farmerie, Michael Ferraro, Daniel Humm, Douglas Rodriguez, Jesse Schenker, Keith Silverton, Fernando Trocca

97 Sullivan Street
Soho
Manhattan
New York 10012
+1 2122740404
www.blueribbonrestaurants.com

Opening hours	7 days for dinner
Reservation policy	No
Credit cards	Accepted but not Diners
Price range	Expensive
Style	Casual
Cuisine	American
Recommended for	Late night

'I think that Blue Ribbon sets the standard for late-night dining destinations, serving throngs of guests until 4.00 a.m. I love to go and meet chefs there after work and always get a pile of food to share. Most nights there go into the wee hours and turn into epic events. '—Brad Farmerie

It's easy to forget that the original Soho outpost of what's now an empire — a bakery brand, a Brooklyn bowling alley and a series of sushi bars, including one in Vegas — was once such a game changer. Now branded as the Blue Ribbon Brasserie, when it first opened back in 1992 it became a haven for restaurant industry types by insisting on keeping the same unsocial hours as they did. While the policy of only being able to book for tables of five and more frustrates a few, the seafood heavy menu of classy comfort food is still the business.

BLUE RIBBON SUSHI

Recommended by
Miles Kirby

119 Sullivan Street
Soho
Manhattan
New York 10012
+1 2123430404
www.blueribbonrestaurants.com

Opening hours	7 days for lunch and dinner
Reservation policy	No
Credit cards	Accepted
Price range	Affordable
Style	Casual
Cuisine	Japanese
Recommended for	Late night

A soothing and accomplished Soho presence since 1995, when it opened in a Sullivan Street basement on the same block as the original Blue Ribbon, the quality comfort food-touting restaurant that founded the Bromberg brothers' New York empire back in 1992. Open until the small hours, seven days a week, the lengthy menu — bolstered by daily specials based on whatever Pacific and Atlantic Ocean catches have come in — is overseen by Toshi Ueki. Well into its second decade, it remains, despite the hours it keeps, as fresh as is the fish in its nigiri and one of New York's finest sushi bars.

LE PAIN QUOTIDIEN

Recommended by
Sam Hayward, Eric Ripert, Mara Salles

100 Grand Street
Soho
Manhattan
New York 10013
www.lepainquotidien.us

Opening hours	7 days from breakfast until late
Reservation policy	No
Credit cards	Accepted but not Diners
Price range	Budget
Style	Casual
Cuisine	Bakery-Café
Recommended for	Breakfast

'I know it's a chain, but good viennoiserie, good coffee and a soft-boiled egg is heaven.'—Sam Hayward

CORTON

Recommended by
Sean Brock,
Marc-André Jetté

239 West Broadway
Tribeca
Manhattan
New York 10013
+1 2122192777
www.cortonnyc.com

Opening hours	5 days for dinner
Reservation policy	Yes
Credit cards	Accepted
Price range	Expensive
Style	Smart casual
Cuisine	Modern French
Recommended for	High end

TAMARIND

Recommended by
Vikram Vij

99 Hudson Street
Tribeca
Manhattan
New York 10013
+1 2127759000
www.tamarinde22.com/tribeca

Opening hours	7 days for lunch and dinner
Reservation policy	Yes
Credit cards	Accepted
Price range	Affordable
Style	Smart casual
Cuisine	Indian
Recommended for	Wish I'd opened

LOCANDA VERDE

Recommended by
Ted Anderson, David Chang,
Jun Tanaka

377 Greenwich Street
Tribeca
Manhattan
New York 10013
+1 2129253797
www.locandaverdenyc.com

Opening hours	7 days for breakfast, lunch and dinner
Reservation policy	Yes
Credit cards	Accepted
Price range	Affordable
Style	Smart casual
Cuisine	Italian
Recommended for	Breakfast

'I love the lemon and ricotta pancakes here.'
—David Chang

Styled as a fashionably casual neighbourhood Italian, Locanda Verde rapidly replaced the widely panned and damned Ago in 2009. Attached to The Greenwich Hotel, a luxurious eighty-eight-room operation co-owned by Robert De Niro — Hollywood icon, restaurateur extraordinaire and patron saint of Tribeca's revival — it's an in-demand Downtown breakfast destination. The kitchen is overseen by New York restaurant scene legend Andrew Carmellini (also currently of The Dutch and ex of A Voce and Café Boulud) whose morning menu includes ricotta with truffle honey and burned orange toast; oatmeal with grappa-stewed fruit; and polenta waffles with spiced apples and marsala cream.

15 EAST

Recommended by
Daniel Boulud, Harold
Dieterle, Takashi Inoue

15 East 15th Street
Union Square
Manhattan
New York 10003
+1 2126470015
www.15eastrestaurant.com

Opening hours	5 days for lunch and 6 days for dinner
Reservation policy	Yes
Credit cards	Accepted
Price range	Expensive
Style	Smart casual
Cuisine	Japanese
Recommended for	High end

'My favorite sushi restaurant in the city. I could eat their omakase menu every day. It's probably the highest quality sushi I've found in New York and has a correspondingly high price tag, so on the rare occasions I go it's a treat.'—Takashi Inoue

'Traditional Japanese cuisine with a modern perspective' is the concept behind this restaurant. The sushi bar is overseen by executive chef Masato Shimizu who, having apprenticed under sushi master Rikio Kugo in Tokyo, has collaborated with the owners of 15 East to create what New York Times critic Frank Bruni called 'exemplary work'. Sit at the sushi bar for atmosphere and education — Shimizu is a character — rather than the more grown-up and spacious adjacent dining room. If it's on the menu, try the exquisite chu-toro (a medium-fatty tuna) or the duo of Japanese red and golden eye snapper.

ABC KITCHEN

Recommended by
Ben Pollinger, Masato
Shimizu, Susan Spicer

35 East 18th Street
Union Square
Manhattan
New York 10003
+1 2124755829
www.abckitchennyc.com

Opening hours	7 days for brunch and dinner
Reservation policy	Yes
Credit cards	Accepted
Price range	Affordable
Style	Smart casual
Cuisine	Modern American
Recommended for	Regular neighbourhood

'Dan Kluger serves amazing creative yet simple food.'—Ben Pollinger

A&A BAKE & DOUBLES SHOP

Recommended by
Zakary Pelaccio

481 Nostrand Avenue
Bedford-Stuyvesant
Brooklyn
New York 11216

Opening hours	6 days for breakfast and lunch
Reservation policy	No
Credit cards	Not accepted
Price range	Budget
Style	Casual
Cuisine	Caribbean Bakery-Café
Recommended for	Breakfast

GORILLA COFFEE

Recommended by
Saul G. Bolton

97 5th Avenue
Boerum Hill
Brooklyn
New York 11217
www.gorillacoffee.com

Opening hours	7 days from breakfast until late
Reservation policy	No
Credit cards	Accepted
Price range	Budget
Style	Casual
Cuisine	Café
Recommended for	Breakfast

CHAR NO. 4

Recommended by
Harold Dieterle

196 Smith Street
Carroll Gardens
Brooklyn
New York 11201
+1 7186432106
www.charno4.com

Opening hours	3 days for lunch and 7 days for dinner
Reservation policy	Yes
Credit cards	Accepted
Price range	Affordable
Style	Casual
Cuisine	Bar-Southern American
Recommended for	Regular neighbourhood

Whisky-soaked bar and restaurant in a nineteenth-century Cobble Hill terrace (row) house, Char No. 4 is named after the practice of ageing Bourbon in charred oak barrels. Although American whiskey is their main passion, with an encyclopedic 150 behind the bar and a nine-strong-bottle menu, their love of the honey-hued spirit extends further with another 150 or so whiskies that take in Scotland and Ireland, as well as more esoteric producers such as India and Japan. The scent of the wood-fired smoker, employed by chef Scott Damboise in a menu that majors on meaty Southern-accented comfort, is a fine pairing for the whisky.

LUCALI

Recommended by
Saul G. Bolton,
Mario Carbone

575 Henry Street
Carroll Gardens
Brooklyn
New York 11231
+1 7188584086

Opening hours	6 days for dinner
Reservation policy	No
Credit cards	Not accepted
Price range	Budget
Style	Casual
Cuisine	Pizza
Recommended for	Bargain

'The best pizza.'—Saul G. Bolton

STINKY BKLYN

Recommended by
Saul G. Bolton

215 Smith Street
Cobble Hill
Brooklyn
New York 11201
www.stinkybklyn.com

Opening hours	7 days from breakfast until late
Reservation policy	No
Credit cards	Accepted
Price range	Affordable
Style	Casual
Cuisine	Deli-Cafe
Recommended for	High end

'The best cheese and hams.'—Saul G. Bolton

BROOKLYN FARE

Recommended by
Gastón Acurio, Andrew
Fairlie, Neal Fraser, David
Kinch, Michael Mina, Hans
Välimäki

200 Schermerhorn Street
Downtown
Brooklyn
New York 11201
+1 7182430050
www.brooklynfare.com/chefs-table

Opening hours	5 days for dinner
Reservation policy	Yes
Credit cards	Accepted
Price range	Expensive
Style	Smart casual
Cuisine	Modern American
Recommended for	Wish I'd opened

'Great ingredients, no compromise on quality or technique and a limited amount of covers so the chef is hands on with every client – it's fantastic.'
—David Kinch

The fanfare for Cesar Ramirez's eighteen-seater attached to a Brooklyn neighbourhood grocery store has inevitably brought some changes. They've finally got their liquor licence for one – which means that the previous BYO, no-corkage set-up may go and prices rise for his superb market-driven tasting menus that don't skimp on luxury. Officially known as 'The Chef's Table at Brooklyn Fare', diners sit around a D-shaped stainless-steel counter, while Ramirez and brigade cook in front of them in a spotless state of the art kitchen, gleaming copper pans hung from the ceiling. A second branch in Manhattan is said to be on its way.

TOMMASO

Recommended by
Peter Hoffman

1464 86th Street
Dyker Heights
Brooklyn
New York 11228
+1 7182369883
www.tommasoinbrooklyn.com

Opening hours	7 days for lunch and dinner
Reservation policy	Yes
Credit cards	Accepted
Price range	Budget
Style	Casual
Cuisine	Italian
Recommended for	Local favourite

'World class wines, classic Italian fare with a traditional Brooklyn Italian clientele.'—Peter Hoffman

GRIMALDI'S PIZZERIA

Recommended by
Michael Ferraro

Under the Brooklyn Bridge
1 Front Street
Fulton Ferry
Brooklyn
New York 11201
+1 7188584300
www.grimaldis.com

Opening hours	7 days for lunch and dinner
Reservation policy	No
Credit cards	Not accepted
Price range	Budget
Style	Casual
Cuisine	Pizza
Recommended for	Local favourite

AL DI LÀ TRATTORIA

Recommended by
Saul G. Bolton

248 5th Avenue
Park Slope
Brooklyn
New York 11215
+1 7187834565
www.aldilatrattoria.com

Opening hours	7 days for brunch and dinner
Reservation policy	Yes
Reservation email	info@aldilatrattoria.com
Credit cards	Accepted
Price range	Budget
Style	Smart casual
Cuisine	Italian
Recommended for	Wish I'd opened

CAFÉ STEINHOF

Recommended by
Harold Dieterle

422 7th Avenue
Park Slope
Brooklyn
New York 11215
www.cafesteinhof.com

Opening hours..........6 days for brunch and 7 days for dinner
Reservation policy...No
Credit cards...Accepted but not Diners
Price range...Budget
Style...Casual
Cuisine..Austrian
Recommended for...............................Regular neighbourhood

FRANNY'S

Recommended by
Daniel Humm, Cal Peternell,
Alexandra Raij

295 Flatbush Avenue
Prospect Heights
Brooklyn
New York 11217
+1 7182300221
www.frannysbrooklyn.com

Opening hours..............2 days for lunch and 7 days for dinner
Reservation policy...No
Credit cards.......................Accepted but not AMEX and Diners
Price range...Budget
Style...Casual
Cuisine..Italian
Recommended for...............................Regular neighbourhood

'It's very authentic and everything there is always a
perfect expression of what is promised on the menu. I
like everything about it.'—Alexandra Raij

POK POK NY

Recommended by
Brad Farmerie,
Carlo Mirarchi

127 Columbia Street
Red Hook
Brooklyn
New York 11231
+1 7189239322
www.pokpokny.com

Opening hours...7 days for dinner
Reservation policy...No
Credit cards.....................................Accepted but not AMEX
Price range...Budget
Style...Casual
Cuisine..Thai
Recommended for...............................Regular neighbourhood

'My apartment literally looks over the back garden of
Pok Pok Ny, Andy Ricker's amalgamation of incredible
northern Thai cookery, Portland's free spirit and a bit of
Brooklyn's "anything-goes" mentality. It is seriously
good, mind-alteringly addictive spicy/herbaceous/
gutsy/sweet/sour/salty plates of food. To eat there
once is to spar with temptation, so my wife and I just
give in and go once a week.'—Brad Farmerie

VINEGAR HILL HOUSE

Recommended by
Zakary Pelaccio

72 Hudson Avenue
Vinegar Hill
Brooklyn
New York 11201
+1 7185221018
www.vinegarhillhouse.com

Opening hours..............1 day for brunch and 7 days for dinner
Reservation policy...Yes
Reservation email.....................info@vinegarhillhouse.com
Credit cards...Accepted
Price range...Affordable
Style...Casual
Cuisine...Modern American
Recommended for..Local favourite

THE BROOKLYN STAR

Recommended by
Carlo Mirarchi, Christina Tosi

593 Lorimer Street
Williamsburg
Brooklyn
New York 11211
www.thebrooklynstar.com

Opening hours..........2 days for brunch and 7 days for dinner
Reservation policy...No
Credit cards...Accepted
Price range...Affordable
Style...Casual
Cuisine...American
Recommended for..Late night

DINER

Recommended by
David Taylor

85 Broadway
Williamsburg
Brooklyn
New York 11249
+1 7184863077
dinernyc.com

Opening hours	7 days for lunch and dinner
Reservation policy	No
Credit cards	Accepted
Price range	Affordable
Style	Casual
Cuisine	Modern American
Recommended for	Worth the travel

EGG

Recommended by
Harold Dieterle

135 North 5th Street
Williamsburg
Brooklyn
New York 11211
+1 7183025151
www.pigandegg.com

Opening hours	7 days for breakfast and lunch
Reservation policy	No
Credit cards	Not accepted
Price range	Budget
Style	Casual
Cuisine	Southern American
Recommended for	Breakfast

ISA

Recommended by
Russell Moore, Christian
Page, Zakary Pelaccio

348 Wythe Avenue
Williamsburg
Brooklyn
New York 11211
+1 3476893594
www.isa.gg/isa

Opening hours	2 days for brunch and 7 days for dinner
Reservation policy	Yes
Credit cards	Accepted
Price range	Affordable
Style	Casual
Cuisine	Mediterranean
Recommended for	Worth the travel

PETER LUGER STEAKHOUSE

Recommended by
Daniel Boulud, Michael
Ferraro, Corey Lee, Vicky
Ratnani

178 Broadway
Williamsburg
Brooklyn
New York 11211
+1 7183877400
www.peterluger.com

Opening hours	7 days for lunch and dinner
Reservation policy	Yes
Credit cards	Not accepted
Price range	Expensive
Style	Smart casual
Cuisine	Steakhouse
Recommended for	Local favourite

'Their porterhouse steak is very New York City.'
—Michael Ferraro

There's a brutal simplicity to the menu at Peter
Luger's when it comes to ordering your main course.
Of course you'll find a few other things on the menu
but it's the USDA Prime porterhouse, available for
one, two, three or four, that most diners go for. After
all, lamb chops can be found anywhere. Luger's is
not perfect – the dining room, despite its kitsch
charm, could do with an update – but the steaks, and
for that matter, the extra thick slices (rashers) of
bacon – are to die for.

PIES 'N' THIGHS

Recommended by
Christina Tosi

166 South 4th Street
Williamsburg
Brooklyn
New York 11211
+1 3475296090
www.news.piesnthighs.com

Opening hours	7 days for brunch and dinner
Reservation policy	No
Credit cards	Accepted
Price range	Budget
Style	Casual
Cuisine	Southern American
Recommended for	Wish I'd opened

'It's the ultimate chick restaurant, serving fried chicken
and home-baked goods, run by amazing friends and
chefs.'—Christina Tosi

ROBERTA'S

261 Moore Street
Williamsburg
Brooklyn
New York 11206
www.robertaspizza.com

Opening hours...............7 days for lunch and dinner, until late
Reservation policy...No
Credit cards...Accepted
Price range..Budget
Style...Casual
Cuisine...Italian
Recommended for...Wish I'd opened

'It's this amazing jumble of a radio station meets a farm meets pizzeria meets a bar meets a disco meets a fabulous tasting menu restaurant. There are no rules to the way they do things and that strikes me as the quintessential modern day Brooklyn restaurant.'—Christina Tosi

If when folk describe a place as 'very Brooklyn' you don't quite know what they mean, head to Roberta's in Bushwick for a primer. The breeze-block frontage, concrete floors, tattooed waiting staff and obscure craft beers served in jam jars spell hipster heaven, as does this former garage's predilection for foraged ingredients and crops from its own urban farm. Launched by former musicians in 2008, Roberta's initially offered little more than its amusingly moni-kered, wood-fired pizzas such as Pablo Escarole and WTF, but brilliant, self-taught chef Carlo Mirarchi doesn't just sling dough – his limited-edition tasting menus are now much in demand.

THE SAINT AUSTERE

613 Grand Street
Williamsburg
Brooklyn
New York 11211
+1 7183880012
www.thesaintaustere.com

Opening hours............1 day for brunch and 6 days for dinner
Reservation policy...No
Credit cards......................Accepted but not AMEX and Diners
Price range..Budget
Style...Casual
Cuisine...Tapas
Recommended for...Bargain

CHAO THAI

8503 Whitney Avenue
Flushing
Queens
New York 11373
+1 7184244999

Opening hours..................................7 days for lunch and dinner
Reservation policy...Yes
Credit cards...Not accepted
Price range..Budget
Style...Casual
Cuisine..Thai
Recommended for...Bargain

A modest storefront close to a busy intersection in an unfashionable area of Flushing might sound less than promising. But this tiny café is home to what many claim is some of the best Thai food in New York. There are just sixteen seats, no liquor licence and you'll have to pay cash, but authentically delicious renditions of classics like som tum (shredded green papaya and tomato salad), pad see ew (vegetable stir-fry with flat noodles) and green curry with prawns (shrimp) more than make up for the slight drawbacks. If you can stand the heat, order one of the spicy specials posted on the wall.

HAN JOO

41-06 149th Place
Flushing
Queens
New York 11355

Opening hours..................................7 days for lunch and dinner
Reservation policy...No
Credit cards...Accepted
Price range..Budget
Style...Casual
Cuisine..Korean
Recommended for...Local favourite

SPICY & TASTY

Recommended by
Harold Dieterle

39-07 Prince Street
Flushing
Queens
New York 11354
www.spicyandtasty.com

Opening hours	7 days for lunch and dinner
Reservation policy	No
Credit cards	Not accepted
Price range	Budget
Style	Casual
Cuisine	Szechuan
Recommended for	Regular neighbourhood

Calling your restaurant 'Spicy and Tasty' is perhaps rather presumptuous, although in this case the self-confidence is not misplaced. The authentic Szechuan cuisine has garnered rave reviews from the national press, restaurant guides and food bloggers alike. However, the specialities at this casual and affordable joint in Queens are not for the faint-hearted: intestines in fresh hot pepper reflects the region's love of offal (variety meats) and heat. You'll also find tripe and beef tendon, all accompanied by distinctive and oddly mouth-numbing Szechuan pepper. More familiar dishes, such as lo mein noodles, on the 100-item menu will please the less-adventurous diner.

TONG SAM GYUP GOO EE

Recommended by
Takashi Inoue

162-23 Depot Road
Flushing
Queens
New York 11358
+1 7183594583

Opening hours	7 days for lunch and dinner
Reservation policy	Yes
Credit cards	Accepted
Price range	Budget
Style	Casual
Cuisine	Korean
Recommended for	Local favourite

'I think access to Flushing, Queens, is something that sets New York apart—authentic Korean food, only a train ride away. '—Takashi Inoue

SRIPRAPHAI

Recommended by
Saul G. Bolton

64-13 39th Avenue
Woodside
Queens
New York 11377
www.sripraphairestaurant.com

Opening hours	6 days for lunch and dinner
Reservation policy	No
Credit cards	Not accepted
Price range	Budget
Style	Casual
Cuisine	Thai
Recommended for	Regular neighbourhood

'There is a "Rum Shop" turned restaurant that does the best curries. It throws the idea of location, location, location out the window.'

KHALID MOHAMMED P613

'Sea urchin tostada with pismo clam and avocado on top.'

JAIR TELLEZ P608

'You'll never see corn in the same way again.'

RUSSELL MOORE P611

CENTRAL AMERICA & CARIBBEAN

'AMAZING BASQUE-MEXICAN FOOD. A FANCY RESTAURANT THAT MANAGES SOME HOW TO BE WARM AND KIND.'

JAIR TELLEZ P609

'A true experience and a great take on Mexican cooking.'

MARTIN WISHART P610

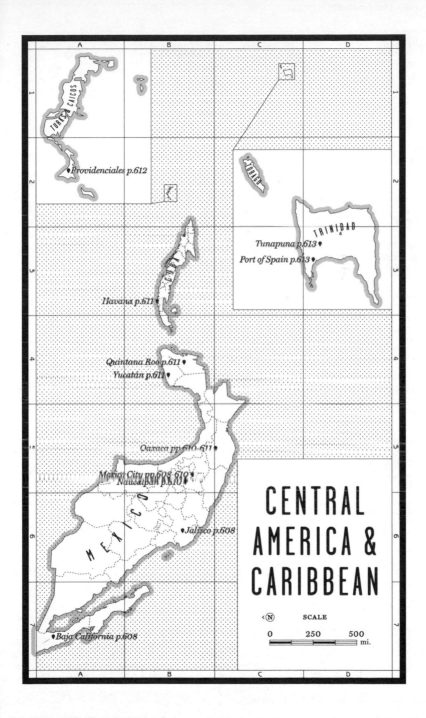

Providenciales p.612

Tunapuna p.613
Port of Spain p.613

Havana p.611

Quintana Roo p.611
Yucatán p.611

Oaxaca pp.610-611

Mexico City pp.608-610
Naucalpan p.609

Jalisco p.608

Baja California p.608

TURKS & CAICOS

TRINIDAD

CUBA

MEXICO

CENTRAL AMERICA & CARIBBEAN

⟨Ⓝ⟩   SCALE

0   250   500
                    mi.

LA GUERRERENSE

Recommended by
Jair Tellez

Primera Avenida & Alvarado
Zona Centro
Ensenada
Baja California 22800
Mexico
+52 6461742214

Opening hours..........................6 days for breakfast and lunch
Reservation policy...No
Credit cards...Not accepted
Price range...Budget
Style...Casual
Cuisine...Seafood
Recommended for...Breakfast

'Go for a sea urchin tostada with pismo clam
and avocado on top or a few *almejas preparadas*,
open pismo clams with cucumber, lime and chilli.'
—Jair Tellez

MUELLE 3

Recommended by
Jair Tellez

Boulevard Teniente Azueta 187
Ensenada 22760
Baja California
Mexico
+52 6461740318
www.muelletres.com

Opening hours..5 days for lunch
Reservation policy...Yes
Credit cards...Accepted
Price range...Budget
Style...Casual
Cuisine...Seafood
Recommended for...Local favourite

'Run by friendly warm people, this is the right place
to eat oysters with nice white wine while looking
at the bay.'—Jair Tellez

MARISCOS RUBEN

Recommended by
Ricardo Zarate

Corner of 8th and Quintana Roo
Tijuana
Baja California
Mexico
Opening hours............7 days for breakfast, lunch and dinner
Reservation policy...No
Credit cards...Not accepted
Price range...Budget
Style...Casual
Cuisine...Seafood
Recommended for...Worth the travel

RED CABBAGE CAFE

Recommended by
Michael Steh

Calle Rivera del Rio 204a
Colonia Remance
Puerto Vallarta
Jalisco
Mexico
+52 3222230411
www.redcabbagepv.com

Opening hours...7 days for dinner
Reservation policy...Yes
Credit cards...Not accepted
Price range...Budget
Style...Casual
Cuisine...Mexican
Recommended for...Worth the travel

ASIAN BAY

Recommended by
Jair Tellez

Avenue Tamaulipas 95
Colonia Condesa
Mexico City 06140
Mexico
+52 5555534582

Opening hours..................................6 days for lunch and dinner
Reservation policy...Yes
Credit cards...Accepted
Price range...Affordable
Style...Casual
Cuisine...Chinese
Recommended for...................................Regular neighbourhood

'Amazingly consistent dishes of dim sum, peking duck
and szechuan pig's ear salad.'—Jair Tellez

LA ESTACIÓN

Recommended by
Enrique Olvera

Calle Saltillo 73
Colonia Condesa
Mexico City 06100
Mexico
+52 5559165644
www.laestacion.mx

Opening hours..................................6 days for lunch and dinner
Reservation policy...Yes
Reservation email.............................contacto@laestacion.mx
Credit cards...Accepted
Price range...Budget
Style...Casual
Cuisine...Tapas
Recommended for...................................Regular neighbourhood

MEROTORO

Recommended by
Thomasina Miers,
Enrique Olvera

Amsterdam 204
Colonia Condesa
Mexico City
Mexico
+52 5555647799
www.merotoro.com

Opening hours	6 days for lunch and dinner
Reservation policy	Yes
Credit cards	Accepted
Price range	Affordable
Style	Casual
Cuisine	Mexican
Recommended for	Worth the travel

PUNTARENA

Recommended by
Alfredo Russo

Avenida Paseo de las Palmas 275
Colonia Condessa
Mexico City 11000
Mexico
+52 5555201723

Opening hours	6 days for lunch and dinner
Reservation policy	Yes
Credit cards	Accepted
Price range	Affordable
Style	Smart casual
Cuisine	Seafood
Recommended for	Worth the travel

FONDA MARGARITA

Recommended by
Jair Tellez

Adolfo Prieto 1364
Plaza Tlacoquemécatl
Colina del Valle
Mexico City 03100
Mexico
www.fondamargarita.com

Opening hours	6 days for breakfast
Reservation policy	No
Credit cards	Not accepted
Price range	Budget
Style	Casual
Cuisine	Mexican
Recommended for	Breakfast

'Everything is cooked on claypots over coals and they have the most amazing scrambled eggs and beans.'
—Jair Tellez

BIKO

Recommended by
Juan Mari & Elena Arzak,
Matias Palomo Reyes,
Jair Tellez

Avenida Masaryk 407
Colonia Polanco
Mexico City 11550
Mexico
+52 5552822064
www.biko.com.mx

Opening hours	6 days for lunch and dinner
Reservation policy	Yes
Credit cards	Accepted
Price range	Expensive
Style	Smart casual
Cuisine	Basque-Mexican
Recommended for	Worth the travel

'Amazing Basque-Mexican food. A fancy restaurant that manages somehow to be warm and friendly.'
—Jair Tellez

Basque–Mexican fusion best describes joint chef-owners Bruno Oteiza and Mikel Alonso's style of cooking, but before you go running for the Sierra Madre Mountains their restaurant Biko is not half as mad as it sounds. Two menus are offered – creative and traditional – meaning that if foie candy floss (cotton candy) isn't your bag you can opt for more obviously Mexican food, albeit with an avant-garde Spanish twist, such as almond-infused pork cheeks with horchata foam or a rib-eye steak served with baby corn and pig's ears. At around £60 ($94) the tasting menu's a snip, but you'll have to negotiate the city's high rollers to get a table.

PUJOL

Recommended by
Matias Palomo Reyes, Daniel
Patterson, Martin Wishart

Francisco Petrarca 254
Colonia Polanco
Mexico City 11570
Mexico
+52 5555453507
www.pujol.com.mx

Opening hours.................................6 days for lunch and dinner
Reservation policy...Yes
Credit cards..Accepted
Price range..Expensive
Style...Smart casual
Cuisine..Modern Mexican
Recommended for..Worth the travel

'A true experience and a great take on
Mexican cooking.'—Martin Wishart

Enrique Olvera's *alta cocina* outpost in the affluent
Polanco district of Mexico City has established him
as one of Mexico's most forward-thinking chefs. He
graduated from the Culinary Institute of New York to
open Pujol in 2000, when he was still only twenty-
four. Inspired by the richness of Mexican street food
and home cooking, Pujol successfully elevates simple
national staples (most notably in a haute take on the
humble taco), champions indigenous ingredients and
artfully uses traditional techniques such as cooking
in clay pots. All of which is delivered with a playful
sense of fun and a pleasing lack of pretention.

TAQUERÍA LOS PARADOS

Recommended by
Jair Tellez

Monterrey 333
Colonia Roma
Mexico City 03650
Mexico
+52 52647138

Opening hours................................7 days for lunch and dinner
Reservation policy...No
Credit cards..Not accepted
Price range..Budget
Style...Casual
Cuisine..Mexican
Recommended for..Late night

TORTAS AL FUEGO

Recommended by
Jair Tellez

Ámsterdam 285
Colina Roma
Mexico City 06100
Mexico

Opening hours.............7 days for breakfast, lunch and dinner
Reservation policy...No
Credit cards..Not accepted
Price range..Budget
Style...Casual
Cuisine..Mexican
Recommended for..Bargain

'Go to this street cart late at night for a *torta de pierna
en adobo* – oven roasted pork.'—Jair Tellez

EL FAROLITO

Recommended by
Enrique Olvera

Avenida de las Fuentes 28
Lomas de Tecamachalco 53950
Naucalpan
Mexico
www.tacoselfarolito.com.mx

Opening hours................................7 days for lunch and dinner
Reservation policy...No
Credit cards..Accepted
Price range..Budget
Style...Casual
Cuisine..Mexican
Recommended for..Late night

ORIGEN

Recommended by
Thomasina Miers

Calle Hidalgo 820
Colina Centro
Oaxaca 68000
Mexico
+52 9515011764
www.origenoaxaca.com

Opening hours..........7 days for brunch and 6 days for dinner
Reservation policy...Yes
Reservation email............reservaciones@origenoaxaca.com
Credit cards..Accepted
Price range..Affordable
Style...Casual
Cuisine..Modern Mexican
Recommended for..Worth the travel

Of the handful of fine-dining restaurants in Oaxaca,
Origen, in the historical heart of the city near the
Basilica of Our Lady of Solitude, is by far the best.
With white walls, high arches, stone floors

and limestone columns, the building is traditionally Mexican, but the brightly coloured furniture and modern art bring it bang up to date. Rodolfo Castellanos does the same with Mexican food, using organic ingredients and contemporary techniques to show just how good Mexican food can be. Here you can have beef carpaccio with Mexican flavours, mole is used with restraint and, even though miles inland, beautifully fresh seafood is served.

ITANONI

Recommended by
Russell Moore, Enrique Olvera

Belisario Domínguez 513
Colonia Reforma
Oaxaca 68050
Mexico
+52 9515139223

Opening hours	7 days for breakfast and lunch
Reservation policy	No
Credit cards	Not accepted
Price range	Budget
Style	Casual
Cuisine	Mexican
Recommended for	Worth the travel

'You'll never see corn in the same way again.'
—Russell Moore

LE CHIQUE

Recommended by
Normand Laprise

Karisma Hotel Azul Sensation Resort
Carretera Federal Cancun
Puerto Morelos
Quintana Roo 77580
Mexico
+52 9988728450
www.karismahotels.com

Opening hours	6 days for dinner
Reservation policy	Yes
Credit cards	Accepted
Price range	Expensive
Style	Smart casual
Cuisine	International
Recommended for	Worth the travel

NÉCTAR

Recommended by
Jair Tellez

412 Avenida 1
Díaz Ordaz
Mérida 97130
Yucatán
Mexico
+52 9999380838
www.nectarmerida.com.mx

Opening hours	6 days for dinner
Reservation policy	Yes
Credit cards	Accepted
Price range	Expensive
Style	Smart casual
Cuisine	Modern Yucatecan
Recommended for	Worth the travel

LA GUARIDA

Recommended by
Jordi Butrón Melero
Douglas Rodriguez

Concordia 418
Gervasio y Escobar
Havana
Cuba
+53 78669047
www.laguarida.com

Opening hours	7 days for lunch and dinner
Reservation policy	Yes
Reservation email	paladar@laguarida.com
Credit cards	Not accepted
Price range	Budget
Style	Casual
Cuisine	Modern Cuban
Recommended for	Worth the travel

La Guarida (The Lair) is well worth the climb up three flights of imposing stairs. Located in a century old crumbling mansion, which was the setting for scenes in popular Cuban film Fresa y Chocolate (Strawberry and Chocolate), walls are plastered with paintings, posters and framed pictures of celebrity visitors. These have included Uma Thurman, Jack Nicholson and Queen Sofía of Spain, whose visit is commemorated by a hanging chair in one of the restaurant's more quirky spaces. Dishes, which delight, are presented on disparate 1950s tableware, and might include papaya lasagne, roast chicken with honey, and, of course, strawberry and chocolate ice cream. Particularly sought-after are the balcony seats.

LAS BRISAS

Neptune Villas
Chalk Sound
Providenciales
Turks & Caicos Islands
British West Indies
+1 6499465306
www.neptunevillastci.com

Opening hours.............6 days for breakfast, lunch and dinner
Reservation policy...Yes
Credit cards...Accepted
Price range...Budget
Style..Casual
Cuisine...Spanish
Recommended for...Breakfast

DA CONCH SHACK

Blue Hills Road
Providenciales
Turks & Caicos Islands
British West Indies
+1 6499468877
www.daconchshack.com

Opening hours...............................7 days for lunch and dinner
Reservation policy...Yes
Credit cards...Accepted
Price range...Budget
Style..Casual
Cuisine..Caribbean
Recommended for...Local favourite

'Simply the best conch salad, cracked conch rice
and peas and coleslaw, served on picnic benches on
the sand in Blue Hills.'—Paul Newman

GARAM MASALA

Regent Village
Grace Bay
Providenciales
Turks & Caicos Islands
British West Indies
+1 6499413292

Opening hours.................................6 days for lunch and dinner
Reservation policy...Yes
Reservation email................................garam-masala@live.in
Credit cards...Accepted
Price range...Budget
Style..Casual
Cuisine...Indian
Recommended for..Late night

'Best naan bread ever.'—Paul Newman

THE RESTAURANT

Amanyara Ámar Resort
Malcolm's Beach
Providenciales
Turks & Caicos Islands
British West Indies
+1 6499418133
www.amanresorts.com

Opening hours...............................7 days for lunch and dinner
Reservation policy...Yes
Credit cards...Accepted
Price range..Expensive
Style...Smart casual
Cuisine...International
Recommended for...High end

YOSHI'S SUSHI BAR

Salt Mills Plaza
Grace Bay Road
Providenciales
Turks & Caicos Islands
British West Indies
+1 6499413374
www.yoshissushi.net

Opening hours.................................6 days for lunch and dinner
Reservation policy...Yes
Credit cards...Accepted
Price range...Budget
Style..Casual
Cuisine...Japanese
Recommended for.............................Regular neighbourhood

'Simple good sushi.'—Paul Newman

THE BREAKFAST SHED

Recommended by
Khalid Mohammed

Wrightson Road
Port of Spain
Trinidad

Opening hours...........................7 days for breakfast and lunch
Reservation policy...No
Credit cards...Not accepted
Price range...Budget
Style..Casual
Cuisine..Creole
Recommended for..Breakfast

'Have the fish broth or the fried fish and bake.'

ME ASIA

Recommended by
Khalid Mohammed

48 Ariapita Avenue
Woodbrook
Port of Spain
Trinidad

Opening hours...............................5 days for lunch and dinner
Reservation policy...No
Credit cards...Not accepted
Price range...Budget
Style..Casual
Cuisine..Chinese
Recommended for...Late night

'Try their noodle soup.'—Khalid Mohammed

WINGS RESTAURANT & BAR

Recommended by
Khalid Mohammed

16 Mohammed Terrace
Tunapuna
Trinidad

Opening hours...6 days for lunch
Reservation policy...No
Credit cards...Not accepted
Price range...Budget
Style..Casual
Cuisine...Caribbean
Recommended for...Local favourite

'A "Rum Shop" turned restaurant that does the best
curries. It throws the idea of location, location, location
out the window.'—Khalid Mohammed

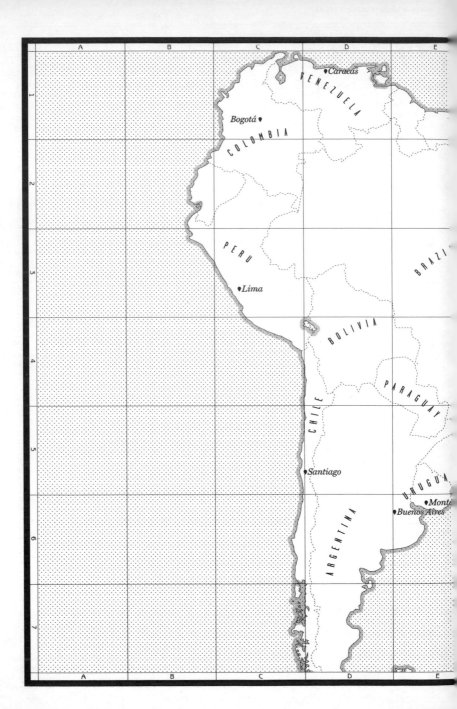

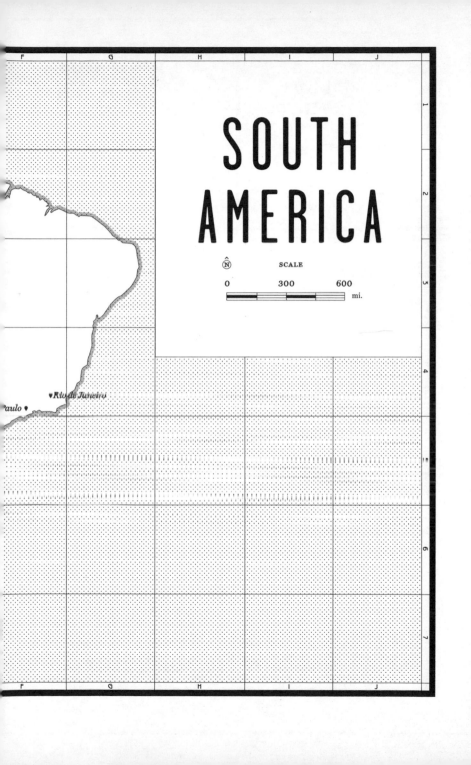

SOUTH
AMERICA

N

SCALE

0   300   600
         mi.

♥ Rio de Janeiro

aulo ♥

'The cuisine is provocative. You might try something that you haven't tried before from the Peruvian Amazonas. I love it!!'

RODOLFO GUZMÁN P621

'FRIED HOT PORK WITH SPRING ONION FLOWERS.'

EDUARDO MORENO P618

SOUTH AMERICA NORTH

'A cebicheria in Barranco that serves just great ceviches. Friendly atmosphere and the location in that part of Lima is just amazing.'

VIRGILIO MARTINEZ P619

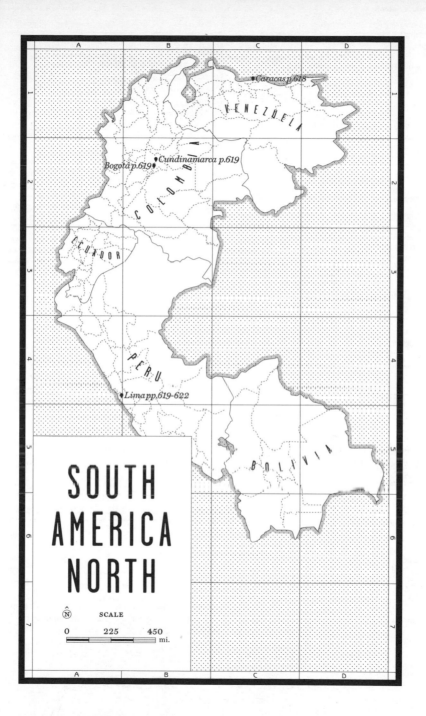

SOUTH
AMERICA
NORTH

SCALE

0   225   450
                 mi.

TROLLY
Recommended by
Eduardo Moreno

Avenida La Guairita
DC Trolly
Caracas
Venezuela

Opening hours.............7 days for breakfast, lunch and dinner
Reservation policy..No
Credit cards...Not accepted
Price range...Budget
Style..Casual
Cuisine..Fast food
Recommended for...Late night

FUGU
Recommended by
Eduardo Moreno

Calle La Trinidad
Las Mercedes
Caracas
Venezuela
+58 2129935647
www.sushifugu.com

Opening hours.............................7 days for lunch and dinner
Reservation policy..No
Credit cards..Accepted
Price range...Affordable
Style..Casual
Cuisine..Japanese
Recommended for.................................Regular neighbourhood

LE GOURMET
Recommended by
Eduardo Moreno

Tamanaco Intercontinental Hotel
Avenida Principal de las Mercedes
Las Mercedes
Caracas
Venezuela
+58 2129097221
www.ichotelsgroup.com

Opening hours.............5 days for lunch and 6 days for dinner
Reservation policy..Yes
Credit cards..Accepted
Price range...Expensive
Style..Formal
Cuisine..French
Recommended for...High end

MOKAMBO
Recommended by
Sumito Estévez

Calle Madrid con Calle Monterray
Las Mercedes
Caracas
Venezuela
+58 2129912577

Opening hours............................7 days for brunch and dinner
Reservation policy..Yes
Credit cards..Accepted
Price range...Affordable
Style..Casual
Cuisine...Mediterranean-Caribbean
Recommended for...Breakfast

ALTO
Recommended by
Sumito Estévez,
Matias Palomo Reyes

Primera Transversal
Los Palos Grandes
Caracas
Venezuela
+58 2122867748

Opening hours.............................6 days for lunch and dinner
Reservation policy..Yes
Credit cards..Accepted
Price range...Expensive
Style...Smart casual
Cuisine..European
Recommended for..Worth the travel

CHINO DE LOS PALOS GRANDES
Recommended by
Eduardo Moreno

3era Avenida con 2da Transversal
Los Palos Grandes
Caracas
Venezuela

Opening hours.............................6 days for lunch and dinner
Reservation policy..No
Credit cards...Not accepted
Price range...Budget
Style..Casual
Cuisine..Chinese
Recommended for...Bargain

'I order fried aubergines (eggplants), potato salad and
fried hot pork with spring onion (scallion) flowers.'
—Eduardo Moreno

EMILIA ROMAGNA

Calle 69a 5-32
Bogotá
Colombia
+57 16089670
www.emiliaromagnarestaurante.com

Opening hours	7 days for lunch and 6 days for dinner
Reservation policy	Yes
Reservation email	camilo@emiliaromagnarestaurante.com
Credit cards	Accepted
Price range	Budget
Style	Casual
Cuisine	Italian
Recommended for	Worth the travel

HARRY SASSON

Carrera 9 75-70
Bogotá
Colombia
+57 13477155
www.harrysasson.com

Opening hours	7 days for lunch and 6 days for dinner
Reservation policy	Yes
Credit cards	Accepted
Price range	Affordable
Style	Smart casual
Cuisine	Asian
Recommended for	Worth the travel

ANDRES CARNE DE RES

Calle 3 11a-56
Chía
Cundinamarca
Colombia
+57 18637880
www.andrescarnederes.com

Opening hours	4 days for lunch and dinner
Reservation policy	Yes
Reservation email	acr@andrescarnederes.com
Credit cards	Not accepted
Price range	Affordable
Style	Casual
Cuisine	Colombian
Recommended for	Wish I'd opened

CANTA RANA

Génova 101
Barranco
Lima 04
Peru
+51 12477274

Opening hours	7 days for lunch and 5 days for dinner
Reservation policy	Yes
Credit cards	Accepted
Price range	Budget
Style	Casual
Cuisine	Seafood
Recommended for	Wish I'd opened

'A *cebicheria* in Barranco that serves just great ceviches. Friendly atmosphere and the location in that part of Lima is just amazing.'—Virgilio Martinez

SALÓN DE LA FELICIDAD

Jiron Paruro 795-799
Barrio Chino
Lima 01
Peru
+51 14264516
www.restaurante-oriental.com

Opening hours	7 days for breakfast, lunch and dinner
Reservation policy	No
Reservation email	reservas@restaurante-oriental.com
Credit cards	Accepted
Price range	Affordable
Style	Casual
Cuisine	Chinese
Recommended for	Breakfast

Lima's *chifas* (Chinese restaurants) date back almost to the start of the Barrio Chino – five-year-old Salón de la Felicidad is brand new in comparison. Rather than trot out the Peruvian–Chinese fusion dishes favoured by their competitors, head chef Luo De Siu Siu Ching's menu is resolutely traditional Cantonese. Dim sum is made to order from 9.00 a.m. onwards and an attached bakery provides sweetly authentic pastries and tarts to a largely Chinese ex-pat crowd. The decor is the usual budget Asian palace theme, and it can get very loud during peak dim sum hours, but it's popular for a reason.

ASTRID & GASTON

Calle Cantuarias 175
Miraflores
Lima 18
+51 12424422
www.astridygaston.com

Opening hours	6 days for lunch and dinner
Reservation policy	Yes
Reservation email	reservas@astridygaston.com
Credit cards	Accepted
Price range	Affordable
Style	Smart casual
Cuisine	Modern Peruvian
Recommended for	Worth the travel

'The new menu is really great.'—Sumito Estévez

FIESTA

Avenida Reducto 1278
Miraflores
Lima 18
Peru
+51 12429009
www.restaurantfiestagourmet.com

Opening hours	6 days for lunch and 5 days for dinner
Reservation policy	Yes
Reservation email	reservas@restaurantfiestagourmet.com
Credit cards	Accepted
Price range	Affordable
Style	Casual
Cuisine	Peruvian
Recommended for	Worth the travel

LA LUCHA

Ólvalo Gutiérrez
Miraflores
Lima 18
Peru
www.lalucha.com.pe

Opening hours	7 days for breakfast, lunch and dinner
Reservation policy	No
Credit cards	Not accepted
Price range	Budget
Style	Casual
Cuisine	Sandwiches
Recommended for	Bargain

'The best sandwiches.'—Fernando Trocca

LA MAR

Avenida La Mar 770
Miraflores
Lima 18
Peru
+51 14213365
www.lamarcebicheria.com

Opening hours	7 days for lunch
Reservation policy	No
Credit cards	Accepted
Price range	Affordable
Style	Casual
Cuisine	Seafood
Recommended for	Worth the travel

MAIDO

Calle San Martin 399
Miraflores
Lima 18
Peru
+51 14442568
www.maido.pe

Opening hours	7 days for lunch and 6 days for dinner
Reservation policy	Yes
Reservation email	reservas@maido.pe
Credit cards	Accepted
Price range	Affordable
Style	Smart casual
Cuisine	Japanese-Peruvian
Recommended for	Regular neighbourhood

EL MERCADO

Hipólito Unanue 203
Miraflores
Lima 18
Peru
+51 12211322
www.rafaelosterling.com

Opening hours	6 days for lunch
Reservation policy	Yes
Reservation email	elmercado@rafaelosterling.com
Credit cards	Accepted
Price range	Affordable
Style	Smart casual
Cuisine	Seafood
Recommended for	Worth the travel

LA RED

Recommended by
Gastón Acurio

Avenida La Mar 391
Miraflores
Lima 18
Peru
+51 14411026
www.lared.com.pe

Opening hours	7 days for lunch
Reservation policy	No
Credit cards	Accepted
Price range	Affordable
Style	Casual
Cuisine	Seafood
Recommended for	Local favourite

Such is the fame and popularity of Lima's *cebicherias* (ceviche restaurants) that their influence is rapidly spreading around the globe – Mexico City, San Francisco and even London now boast their own. But the originals, and many would argue the best, are still to be found along the Avenida La Mar in Miraflores. Opened in 1981, La Red is the oldest on the street and, aside from a recent brief expansion and spruce-up, is still trotting out the same classic dishes (ceviche and *tiradito*, *pulpo a la parrilla*, *arroz con mariscos*) to the same high standards, to the same happy locals.

RODRIGO

Recommended by
Matias Palomo Reyes

Francisco de Paula Camino 231
Miraflores
Lima 10
Peru
+51 14476881
www.restauranterodrigo.com

Opening hours	6 days for lunch and dinner
Reservation policy	Yes
Reservation email	reservas@restauranterodrigo.com
Credit cards	Accepted
Price range	Affordable
Style	Smart casual
Cuisine	European
Recommended for	Worth the travel

LA GRAN FRUTA

Recommended by
Virgilio Martinez

Las Begonias 463
San Isidro
Lima 27
Peru
www.lagranfruta.com.pe

Opening hours	7 days for lunch and 6 days for dinner
Reservation policy	No
Credit cards	Accepted
Price range	Budget
Style	Casual
Cuisine	Cafe
Recommended for	Breakfast

From humble beginnings as an itinerant street cart that hawked its juices around Lima, La Gran Fruta is now a success story, with branches that deliver across the Peruvian capital, including one at the airport. This branch in the city's San Isidro district is arguably the best from which to enjoy its menu of freshly squeezed and blended juices, many made from exotic fruits that you won't find anywhere but South America. Try cherimoya, a variety of custard apple native to the Andes, which tastes like a combination of banana, pineapple and strawberry. Or have an avocado juice with your coffee and well-stuffed Peruvian sandwich.

MALABAR

Recommended by
Rodolfo Guzmán, Matias
Palomo Reyes, Helena Rizzo

Calle Camino Real 101
San Isidro
Lima 27
Peru
+51 14405200
www.malabar.com.pe

Opening hours	6 days for lunch and dinner
Reservation policy	Yes
Credit cards	Accepted
Price range	Affordable
Style	Smart casual
Cuisine	Modern Peruvian
Recommended for	Worth the travel

'Pedro Miguel Schiaffino's cuisine is provocative. You might try something that you haven't tried before from the Peruvian Amazonas. I love it!!'—Rodolfo Guzmán

MARAS

Recommended by
Gastón Acurio

Westin Hotel
Calle Las Begonias 450
San Isidro
Lima 27
Peru
+51 12015023
www.starwoodhotels.com/westin

Opening hours............5 days for lunch and 6 days for dinner
Reservation policy...Yes
Credit cards..Accepted
Price range...Affordable
Style..Smart casual
Cuisine...Modern Peruvian
Recommended for..Worth the travel

Andean ingredients such as sweet potato, sweet
corn and cherimoya get the five-star treatment in
the hands of Rafael Piqueras, a bright star of *novo
andina* cuisine, at Maras in Lima's shiny new Westin
Hotel. Piqueras is fully conversant with cutting-edge
techniques from time spent at elBulli, which here he
applies to the food of his childhood – such as *chupe
de camarones* (prawn/shrimp chowder) and *causa* (a
layered potato dish). Hit the bar first for a Pisco Sour
– Peru's national cocktail – or try it deconstructed in
Piqueras's foie gras with *Pisco* aromas and roasted
mango. Maras's international wine list is excellent.

SANKUAY

Recommended by
Virgilio Martinez

Enrique León García 114
Santa Catalina
La Victoria
Lima 13
Peru
+51 14706217

Opening hours.................................5 days for lunch and dinner
Reservation policy...Yes
Credit cards..Accepted
Price range...Budget
Style..Casual
Cuisine..Seafood
Recommended for...Local favourite

Don't turn up at Sankuay without a reservation. Not
because it's particularly grand – on the contrary, it's
a humble *huarique* (Peruvian slang for a speakeasy
that specializes in a dish or two) – but you just won't
get past the doorman without one. The doorman is
also the waiter and the busboy – in fact the only
other member of staff working alongside the owner-
chef, the Peruvian-Chinese Javier Wong. Nicknamed
Chez Wong, inside it's bare walls, a handful of tables,
a primitive stove and a take-it-or-leave-it two
courses of stunningly simple seafood – one a
ceviche, the other wok-fried.

'THEY HAVE ONE OF THE BEST VIEWS OF RIO AND THEY SERVE GREAT SHRIMP, SIRI AND BEEF PASTÉIS.'
FLÁVIA QUARESMA P630

'Traditional Chilean food: ribs, veal shanks, blood sausages and tongue.'
MATIAS PALOMO REYES P628

'The best bread in Rio and great fruit juices.'
FLÁVIA QUARESMA P629

SOUTH AMERICA SOUTH

'AMAZING PLACE, FLAWLESS BRAZILIAN CUISINE, A PLACE TO DREAM ...'
ROBERTA SUDBRACK P627

'Delicious boteco food. The best Brazilian appetizers and draft beer.'
FLÁVIA QUARESMA P628

'THIS PLACE IS A MUST IN CHILE! IT'S A GREAT SPOT WHERE YOU CAN TRY THE BIGGEST KING CRABS ON EARTH.'
RODOLFO GUZMÁN P642

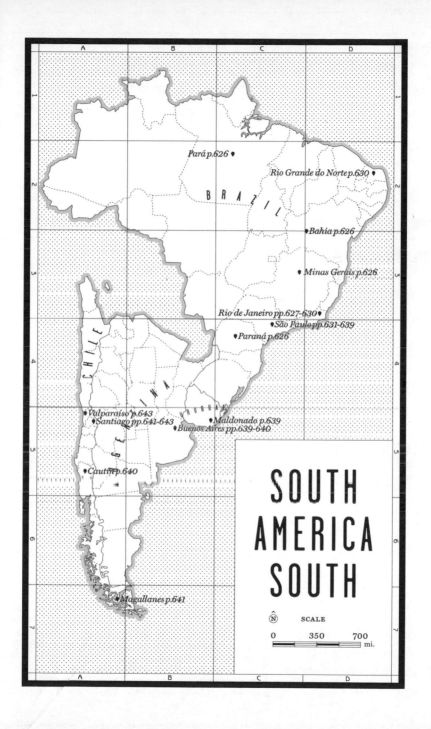

Pará p.626

Rio Grande do Norte p.630

B R A Z I L

Bahia p.626

Minas Gerais p.626

Rio de Janeiro pp.627-630
São Paulo pp.631-639
Paraná p.626

C H I L E

A R G E N T I N A

U R U G U A Y

Valparaíso p.643
Santiago pp.641-643
Buenos Aires pp.639-640
Maldonado p.639

Cautín p.640

Magallanes p.641

SOUTH
AMERICA
SOUTH

N̂   SCALE

0   350   700
mi.

CHEZ BERNARD

Recommended by
Edinho Engel

Rua da Gamboa de Cima 11
Salvador
Bahia 40060-008
Brazil
+55 7133281566
www.chezbernard.com.br

Opening hours..........6 days for lunch and 5 days for dinner
Reservation policy..Yes
Credit cards..Accepted
Price range...Affordable
Style...Smart casual
Cuisine...French
Recommended for..........................Regular neighbourhood

MARIETTA SANDUICHES LEVES

Recommended by
Edinho Engel

Avenida Tancredo Neves 148
Salvador
Bahia 41820-908
Brazil
www.marietta.com.br

Opening hours..........................7 days for brunch and dinner
Reservation policy..No
Credit cards..Accepted
Price range...Budget
Style..Casual
Cuisine...Sandwiches
Recommended for..Bargain

MERCADO CENTRAL

Recommended by
Mara Salles

Avenida Augusto de Lima 744
Belo Horizonte
Minas Gerais 30190-922
Brazil
www.mercadocentral.com.br

Opening hours....7 days for breakfast and 6 days for lunch
Reservation policy..No
Credit cards..Not accepted
Price range...Budget
Style..Casual
Cuisine...Brazilian
Recommended for.................................Local favourite

KITANDA BRASIL

Recommended by
Mara Salles

Rua Antonio Caetano Rosa 217
Gonçalves
Minas Gerais 15051-400
Brazil
+55 3536541417
www.kitanda-quitandasequitutes.blogspot.co.uk

Opening hours................................7 days for lunch and dinner
Reservation policy..Yes
Reservation email............tanearomao@kitandabrasil.com.br
Credit cards..Accepted
Price range...Affordable
Style..Casual
Cuisine...Brazilian
Recommended for...............................Wish I'd opened

REMANSO DO BOSQUE

Recommended by
Helena Rizzo

Avenida Rômulo Maiorana
Marco
Belém
Pará 66095-662
Brazil
+55 9133472829
www.restauranteremanso.com.br

Opening hours.............6 days for lunch and 5 days for dinner
Reservation policy..Yes
Reservation email.......contato@restauranteremanso.com.br
Credit cards..Accepted
Price range...Affordable
Style..Casual
Cuisine...Brazilian
Recommended for...............................Worth the travel

MERCEARIA BRESSER

Recommended by
Edinho Engel

Avenida Sete de Setembro 5831
Batel
Curitiba
Paraná 80240-001
Brazil
+55 4130290880
www.merceariabresser.com.br

Opening hours..7 days for dinner
Reservation policy..Yes
Credit cards..Accepted
Price range...Affordable
Style..Casual
Cuisine..Italian
Recommended for...........................Regular neighbourhood

CERVANTES

Recommended by
Flávia Quaresma

Rua Prado Júnior 335b
Copacabana
Rio de Janeiro 2275-6147
Brazil
www.restaurantecervantes.com.br

Opening hours..6 days for lunch
Reservation policy..No
Reservation email.........................cervantescopa@gmail.com
Credit cards..Accepted
Price range...Budget
Style..Casual
Cuisine...Brazilian
Recommended for...Late night

'They have a great pork shank, cheese and
pineapple sandwich.'—Flávia Quaresma

PÉRGULA

Recommended by
Luis Baena

Copacabana Palace Hotel
Avenida Atlântica 1702
Copacabana
Rio de Janeiro 22021-001
Brazil
+55 2125487070
www.copacabanapalace.com

Opening hours.............7 days for breakfast, lunch and dinner
Reservation policy..Yes
Credit cards..Accepted
Price range...Affordable
Style..Casual
Cuisine...Brazilian
Recommended for..Breakfast

POUSADA DA ALCOBAÇA

Recommended by
Roberta Sudbrack

Rua Agostinho Goulão 298
Correias
Petrópolis
Rio de Janeiro 25730-050
Brazil
+55 2422211240
www.pousadadaalcobaca.com.br

Opening hours.................................7 days for lunch and dinner
Reservation policy..Yes
Credit cards..Accepted
Price range...Affordable
Style..Casual
Cuisine...Brazilian
Recommended for..Local favourite

'Amazing place, flawless Brazilian cuisine, a place
to dream ...'—Roberta Sudbrack

ESPLANADA GRILL

Recommended by
Felipe Bronze

Rua Barão da Torre 600
Ipanema
Rio de Janeiro 22411-002
Brazil
+55 2125122970
www.esplanadagrill.com.br

Opening hours...........................7 days for lunch and dinner
Reservation policy..Yes
Credit cards..Accepted
Price range...Affordable
Style..Smart casual
Cuisine...Brazilian
Recommended for..Local favourite

TEN KAI

Recommended by
Felipe Bronze

Rua Prudente de Moraes 1810
Ipanema
Rio de Janeiro 22420-042
Brazil
+55 2125405100
www.tenkai.com.br

Opening hours..............................7 days for brunch and dinner
Reservation policy..Yes
Credit cards..Accepted
Price range...Affordable
Style..Smart casual
Cuisine...Japanese
Recommended for...........................Regular neighbourhood

Located on the tree-lined Rua Prudente de Morais,
and named after a distinguished Japanese Buddhist
monk, Ten Kai restaurant won immediate plaudits
for its distinctive, nervy interior. This features brutal
concrete panels, hand-painted Japanese characters
and paper lanterns that edge the sushi counter. Chef
San Taro's sashimi and sushi may include seasoned
jellyfish, squid with sea urchin roe and spicy cod
roe, *maguro nutta* (tuna with sweet and sour sauce
with raw quail's egg yolk) and *croc furi*, a Japanese-
style spring roll of salmon tartare with dried
horseradish flakes.

PIZZERIA BRÁZ
Recommended by
Felipe Bronze
Rua Maria Angélica 129
Jardim Botânico
Rio de Janeiro 22470-201
Brazil
+55 2125350687
www.casabraz.com.br

Opening hours	5 days for lunch and 7 days for dinner
Reservation policy	Yes
Credit cards	Accepted
Price range	Affordable
Style	Casual
Cuisine	Pizza
Recommended for	Late night

Heady aromas of oregano, rosemary and garlic suffuse the open room from the sweltering pizzas baking in Pizzaria Bráz's wood-fired brick oven. The bases, made of Brazilian flour, are an important factor in helping ensure what regulars believe are the best pizzas in the world. A popular spot with families, house specialities include Affumicata – the slightly abstract-looking white pizza, which features smoked mozzarella and sage –alongside enduring classics such as the Margherita and Pepperoni. The decor is comfortable and portions generous. Leave space for panettone, the sweet brioche imported – like the olive oil – direct from Italy.

ROBERTA SUDBRACK
Recommended by
Rodrigo Oliveira,
Flávia Quaresma
Rua Lineu Paula Machado 916
Jardim Botânico
Rio de Janeiro 22470-040
Brazil
+55 2138740139
www.robertasudbrack.com.br

Opening hours	1 day for lunch and 5 days for dinner
Reservation policy	Yes
Reservation email	info@robertasudbrack.com.br
Credit cards	Accepted
Price range	Expensive
Style	Smart casual
Cuisine	Modern Brazilian
Recommended for	Worth the travel

'Every three months Roberta chooses a Brazilian ingredient to investigate and study. With her delicate way of cooking she shows its flavour and texture without loosing its authenticity.'—Flávia Quaresma

ESCOLA DO PAO
Recommended by
Felipe Bronze
Rua General Garzon 10
Lagoa
Rio de Janeiro 22470-010
Brazil
www.escoladopao.com.br

Opening hours	2 days for breakfast
Reservation policy	Yes
Reservation email	escoladopao@escoladopao.com.br
Credit cards	Accepted
Price range	Affordable
Style	Casual
Cuisine	Café
Recommended for	Breakfast

FILÉ DE OURO
Recommended by
Flávia Quaresma
Rua Jardim Botânico 731
Lagoa
Rio de Janeiro 2259-2396
Brazil
+55 2122592396

Opening hours	7 days for lunch and dinner
Reservation policy	No
Credit cards	Accepted
Price range	Affordable
Style	Casual
Cuisine	Brazilian
Recommended for	Regular neighbourhood

'Great beef, delicious black beans and crispy chips (fries).'—Flávia Quaresma

CHICO E ALAÍDE
Recommended by
Flávia Quaresma
Rua Dias Ferreira 679
Leblon
Rio de Janeiro 22431-050
Brazil
+55 2125120028
www.chicoealaide.com.br

Opening hours	7 days for lunch and dinner
Reservation policy	Yes
Credit cards	Accepted
Price range	Affordable
Style	Casual
Cuisine	Brazilian Small plates
Recommended for	Local favourite

'Delicious *boteco* food. The best brazilian appetizers and draught beer.'—Flávia Quaresma

OLYMPE

Recommended by
Felipe Bronze, Flávia Quaresma,
Roberta Sudbrack

Rua Custódio Serrão 62
Lagoa
Rio de Janeiro 22470-230
Brazil
+55 2125394542
www.claudetroisgros.com.br

Opening hours	1 day for lunch and 6 days for dinner
Reservation policy	Yes
Credit cards	Accepted
Price range	Expensive
Style	Smart casual
Cuisine	French
Recommended for	High end

BB LANCHES

Recommended by
Felipe Bronze,
Flávia Quaresma

Rua Aristides Espínola 64
Leblon
Rio de Janeiro 22440-050
Brazil
+55 2122941397

Opening hours	7 days for breakfast, lunch and dinner
Reservation policy	No
Credit cards	Not accepted
Price range	Budget
Style	Casual
Cuisine	Sandwiches
Recommended for	Bargain

PADARIA RIO LISBOA

Recommended by
Roberta Sudbrack

Avenue Ataulfo de Paiva 1030
Leblon
Rio de Janeiro 22440-035
Brazil

Opening hours	7 days for breakfast, lunch and dinner
Reservation policy	No
Credit cards	Not accepted
Price range	Budget
Style	Casual
Cuisine	Bakery-Cafe
Recommended for	Breakfast

SUSHI LEBLON

Recommended by
Felipe Bronze

Rua Dias Ferreira 256
Leblon
Rio de Janeiro 22431-050
Brazil
+55 2125127830
www.sushileblon.com

Opening hours	7 days for lunch and dinner
Reservation policy	Yes
Credit cards	Accepted
Price range	Affordable
Style	Smart casual
Cuisine	Japanese
Recommended for	Late night

TALHO CAPIXABA

Recommended by
Flávia Quaresma

Avenida Ataulfo de Paiva 1022
Leblon
Rio de Janeiro 22440-035
Brazil
+55 2125128760
www.talhocapixaba.com.br

Opening hours	7 days from breakfast until late
Reservation policy	No
Credit cards	Accepted
Price range	Budget
Style	Casual
Cuisine	Cafe
Recommended for	Breakfast

'The best bread in Rio and great fruit juices.'
—Flávia Quaresma

ENE

Recommended by
Felipe Bronze

Avenida Prefeito Mendes de Moraes 222
São Conrado
Rio de Janeiro 22610-095
Brazil
+55 2133226561
www.enerestaurante.com.br

Opening hours	3 days for lunch and 6 days for dinner
Reservation policy	Yes
Credit cards	Accepted
Price range	Affordable
Style	Casual
Cuisine	Spanish
Recommended for	Regular neighbourhood

BAR DO MINEIRO

Rua Pascoal Carlos Magno 99
Santa Teresa
Rio de Janeiro 20240-290
Brazil
+55 2122219227

Opening hours	6 days for lunch and dinner
Reservation policy	No
Credit cards	Accepted
Price range	Budget
Style	Casual
Cuisine	Brazilian
Recommended for	Bargain

'Very simple place with great homemade food.'
—Flávia Quaresma

BAR URCA

Rua Cândido Gaffrée 205
Urca
Rio de Janeiro 22291-080
Brazil
+55 2122958744
www.barurca.com.br

Opening hours	7 days for brunch and 6 days for dinner
Reservation policy	Yes
Credit cards	Accepted but not AMEX
Price range	Budget
Style	Casual
Cuisine	Brazilian
Recommended for	Bargain

'They have one of the best views of Rio and they serve great prawns (shrimp), *siri* and beef *pastéis*.'
—Flávia Quaresma

GEPETTO

Estrada Bandeirantes 23417
Vargem Grande
Rio de Janeiro 22783-116
Brazil
+55 2124281100
www.restaurantegepetto.com/br

Opening hours	7 days for lunch and dinner
Reservation policy	Yes
Credit cards	Accepted
Price range	Budget
Style	Casual
Cuisine	Italian-Brazilian
Recommended for	Bargain

O BULE

Avenida Doutor Severino Lopes da Silva 118
Lagoa do Bonfin
Nísia Floresta
Rio Grande do Norte 59164-000
Brazil
+55 8491846653

Opening hours	2 days for lunch and 5 days for dinner
Reservation policy	Yes
Credit cards	Accepted
Price range	Expensive
Style	Smart casual
Cuisine	Modern Brazilian
Recommended for	Worth the travel

KINOSHITA

Recommended by
Matias Palomo Reyes,
Vítor Sobral

Rua Jacques Félix 405
Vila Nova Conceição
Moema
São Paulo 04509-000
Brazil
+55 1138496940
www.restaurantekinoshita.com.br

Opening hours	6 days for lunch and dinner
Reservation policy	Yes
Credit cards	Accepted
Price range	Expensive
Style	Casual
Cuisine	Modern Japanese
Recommended for	Worth the travel

A sleek modernist cube bordered by rounded hedges, Kinoshita provides a sophisticated contrast to the tall, residential buildings of Vila Nova Conceição. It is the domain of chef Tsuyoshi 'Mura' Murakami, who named the restaurant after his émigré father-in-law who launched the original version of Kinoshita. Murakami practises *kappo* cuisine, which combines aromas and textures to extremely sensual effect, 'like poetry,' he says. Such renditions may include cod-fish roe sushi with quail egg; tuna sashimi with foie gras and teriyaki; and sous-vide wild boar grilled with miso. Lucky diners may be offered a green tea bonbon made by Murakami's wife. Kinoshita boasts a sake sommelier and a brave cocktail list, viz. the Midori-wasabi martini.

CASA GARABED

Recommended by
Rodrigo Oliveira

Rua José Margarido 216
Santana
São Paulo 02021-020
Brazil
+55 1129762750
www.casagarabed.com.br

Opening hours	6 days for lunch and dinner
Reservation policy	No
Credit cards	Accepted
Price range	Budget
Style	Casual
Cuisine	Lebanese
Recommended for	Regular neighbourhood

'A family run, garage-like restaurant, opened in the 1940s, that is a temple for Lebanese food. A sixty-year-old wood oven provides the menu's best dishes: *esfiha de bastrmá*, *esfiha fechada de carne*, kebab and more. It's a modest place with amazing food and nice prices.'—Rodrigo Oliveira

'THE BEST JAPANESE IN BRAZIL.'
RODRIGO OLIVEIRA P636

'THIS PLACE SHOWS THE VERY BEST FOOD IN BRAZIL.'
FELIPE BRONZE P636

'One of the best pork leg sandwiches in São Paulo and a very nice bohemian place to go late at night.'
EMMANUEL BASSOLEIL P638

SÃO PAULO

'The best restaurant to go eat and drink in a French surrounding in a fancy street of São Paulo.'
EMMANUEL BASSOLEIL P636

'THE BEST BREAD IN OUR REGION. ORDER THE YUCCA LOAF AND THE PORTUGUESE BREAD WITH FRESH CHEESE.'
RODRIGO OLIVEIRA P635

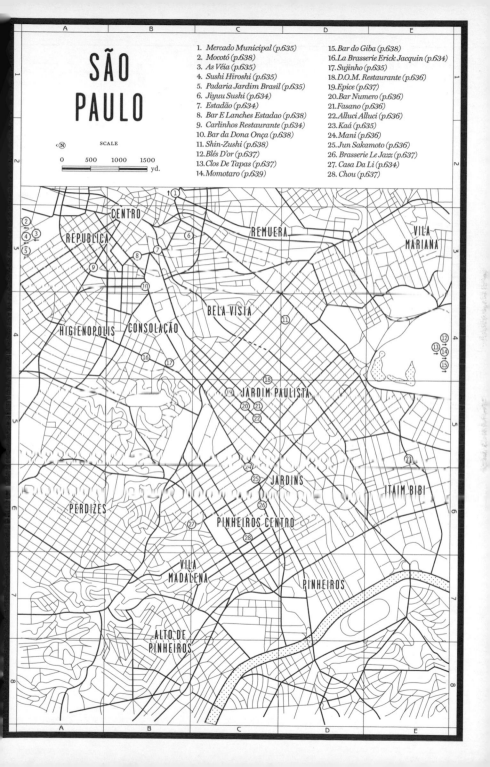

SÃO PAULO

SCALE

0   500   1000   1500 yd.

LA BRASSERIE ERICK JACQUIN

Rua Bahia 683
São Paulo 01244-001
+55 1138265409
www.brasserie.com.br

Opening hours.............7 days for lunch and 6 days for dinner
Reservation policy...Yes
Reservation email....................brasserie@brasserie.com.br
Credit cards...Accepted
Price range..Expensive
Style...Smart casual
Cuisine...French
Recommended for...High end

'An unforgettable experience.'—Emmanuel Bassoleil

CARLINHOS RESTAURANTE

Rua Rio Bonito 1641
São Paulo 03023-000
+55 1133159474
www.carlinhosrestaurante.com.br

Opening hours.......................................6 days for lunch
Reservation policy..Yes
Credit cards...Accepted
Price range..Affordable
Style..Casual
Cuisine..Brazilian
Recommended for..Bargain

'Delicious comfort food.'—Rodrigo Oliveira

CASA DA LI

Rua Aspicuelta 23
São Paulo 05433-010
+55 1138711002
www.casadali.com.br

Opening hours...............................7 days for lunch
Reservation policy...No
Credit cards...Not accepted
Price range...Budget
Style..Casual
Cuisine..Brazilian
Recommended for...Worth the travel

'Frankly amazing. They respect the product, the
preparation and seasonality. A must.'
—Roberta Sudbrack

ESTADÃO

Viaduto Nove de Julho 193
São Paulo 01050-060
www.estadaolanches.com.br

Opening hours.............7 days for breakfast, lunch and dinner
Reservation policy...No
Credit cards...Accepted
Price range...Budget
Style..Casual
Cuisine..Brazilian
Recommended for...Late night

'A popular bar/restaurant open all night, where you
can eat delicious pork sandwiches.'—Mara Salles

A bright bar for the city that never sleeps, 'Bar ESP',
as it is affectionately known by regulars, is open
twenty-four hours. It seems to constantly teem with
a colourful clientele – from ladies of the night to taxi
drivers, politicians and journalists – flocking for the
legendary ham sandwich. The presence of writers is
hardly surprising given that when it was founded, in
1968, the headquarters of São Paulo's daily paper,
O Estado de São Paulo, was a neighbour. Roast pork
hangs in the window ready to be carved, seasoned
and slid into French baguettes. Regulars believe this
institution should be listed...

JIYUU SUSHI

Rua dos Estudantes 166
São Paulo 01505-000
+55 1132081159
www.jiyuusushi.com.br

Opening hours................................6 days for lunch and dinner
Reservation policy..Yes
Credit cards...Accepted
Price range..Affordable
Style..Casual
Cuisine...Japanese
Recommended for...............................Regular neighbourhood

KAÁ

Recommended by
Emmanuel Bassoleil

Avenue Presidente Juscelino
Kubitschek 279
Vila Olimpia
São Paulo 04543-010
+55 1130450043
www.kaarestaurante.com.br

Opening hours............5 days for lunch and 6 days for dinner
Reservation policy..Yes
Reservation email..............contacto@kaarestaurante.com.br
Credit cards...Accepted
Price range...Affordable
Style...Smart casual
Cuisine...International
Recommended for..Wish I'd opened

MERCADO MUNICIPAL

Recommended by
Julien Duboué,
Maria Helena Guimaraes

Rua da Cantareira 306
São Paulo 01024-000
www.mercadomunicipal.com.br

Opening hours.........................7 days for breakfast and lunch
Reservation policy..No
Credit cards..Accepted
Price range...Budget
Style..Casual
Cuisine..Brazilian
Recommended for...Bargain

SUJINHO

Recommended by
Alberto Landgraf,
Mara Salles

Rua da Consolação 2068
São Paulo 013002-001
+55 1132311299
www.sujinho.com.br

Opening hours.........................7 days for lunch and dinner
Reservation policy...Yes
Credit cards..Not accepted
Price range...Budget
Style...Casual
Cuisine...Brazilian
Recommended for...Late night

SUSHI HIROSHI

Recommended by
Rodrigo Oliveira

Rua Cap Manuel Novais 189
São Paulo 02017-030
+55 1129796677

Opening hours................................7 days for lunch and dinner
Reservation policy..Yes
Credit cards...Accepted
Price range..Budget
Style..Casual
Cuisine...Japanese
Recommended for...............................Regular neighbourhood

'The best order is the "exotic menu" that's available if
you sit at the balcony.'—Rodrigo Oliveira

PADARIA JARDIM BRASIL

Recommended by
Rodrigo Oliveira

Avenue Jardim Japão 1298
Jardim Brasil
São Paulo 02221-001
www.padariajardimbrasil.com.br

Opening hours..Opening
Reservation policy..No
Credit cards...Accepted
Price range..Affordable
Style...Casual
Cuisine...Bakery-Café
Recommended for...Breakfast

'The best bread in our region. Order the yucca loaf
and the Portuguese bread with fresh cheese.'
—Rodrigo Oliveira

AC VÉIA

Recommended by
Rodrigo Oliveira

Estrada Santa Inês 3000
Jardim das Samambaias
São Paulo 07600-000
www.velhao.com.br

Opening hours.........7 days for brunch and 2 days for dinner
Reservation policy..No
Credit cards..Not accepted
Price range...Budget
Style...Casual
Cuisine...Brazilian
Recommended for...Local favourite

ALLUCI ALLUCI
Rua Vitório Fasano 35
Jardim Paulista
São Paulo 01414-020
+55 1130861252
www.alucci.com.br

Recommended by
Emmanuel Bassoleil

Opening hours..6 days for dinner
Reservation policy...Yes
Credit cards...Accepted
Price range...Affordable
Style...Casual
Cuisine...International
Recommended for...................................Regular neighbourhood

'The best restaurant to go eat and drink in a French
surrounding in a fancy street of Sao Paulo.'
—Emmanuel Bassoleil

FASANO
Rua Vitório Fasano 88
Jardim Paulista
São Paulo 01414-020
+55 1130624000
www.fasano.com.br

Recommended by
Maria Helena Guimaraes

Opening hours..6 days for dinner
Reservation policy...Yes
Reservation email.........................restaurante@fasano.com.br
Credit cards...Accepted
Price range...Expensive
Style..Smart casual
Cuisine...Italian
Recommended for...High end

JUN SAKAMOTO
Rua Lisboa 55
Jardim Paulista
São Paulo 05413-000
+55 1130886019

Recommended by
Alex Atala, Rodrigo Oliveira

Opening hours..6 days for dinner
Reservation policy...Yes
Credit cards...Accepted
Price range...Affordable
Style...Casual
Cuisine...Japanese
Recommended for...High end

'The best Japanese in Brazil.'—Rodrigo Oliveira

MANI
Rua Joaquim Antunes 210
Jardim Paulista
São Paulo 05415-000
+55 1130854148
www.manimanioca.com.br

Recommended by
Alex Atala, Flávia Quaresma,
Mara Salles

Opening hours.....................6 days for lunch and dinner
Reservation policy...Yes
Credit cards...Accepted
Price range...Affordable
Style...Casual
Cuisine...Spanish-Brazilian
Recommended for...High end

BAR NUMERO
Rua da Consolação 3585
Jardins
São Paulo 01416-001
+55 1130613995
www.barnumero.com.br

Recommended by
Rodrigo Oliveira

Opening hours..5 days for dinner
Reservation policy...Yes
Credit cards...Accepted
Price range...Affordable
Style..Smart casual
Cuisine...Argentinean
Recommended for...Late night

D.O.M. RESTAURANTE
Rua Barão de Capanema 549
Jardins
São Paulo 01411-011
+55 1130880761
www.domrestaurante.com.br

Recommended by
Luis Baena, Andrea Berton,
Felipe Bronze, Maria
Helena Guimaraes, Alberto
Landgraf, Matias Palomo
Reyes, Helena Rizzo,
Michael Wolf

Opening hours.............5 days for lunch and 6 days for dinner
Reservation policy...Yes
Credit cards...Accepted
Price range...Expensive
Style..Smart casual
Cuisine...Modern Brazilian
Recommended for..Worth the travel

'In São Paulo, D.O.M still shows the very best food
in Brazil.'—Felipe Bronze

One-time painter and decorator and punk DJ Alex
Atala has almost single-handedly put experimental,
fine-dining Brazilian cuisine onto the world
stage thanks to an ungodly amount of dedication
and vision. At D.O.M. – *domus optimus maximus*

(home is greatest and best) – Atala has turned scouring the Amazon rainforest for forgotten ingredients into an art form, as well as a pretty solid business model. Thanks to him, Brazilian food is no longer regarded as being merely comforting and unsophisticated but as vibrant, interesting and, at times, downright cool. If you like eating ingredients that are unlikely to have ever left Brazil, D.O.M.'s the place to go.

EPICE

Recommended by
Alex Atala

Rua Haddock Lobo 1002
Jardins Paulista
São Paulo 01414-000
+55 1130620866
www.epicerestaurante.com.br

Opening hours.............6 days for lunch and 5 days for dinner
Reservation policy..Yes
Reservation email...................lara@epicerestaurante.com.br
Credit cards..Accepted
Price range..Expensive
Style...Casual
Cuisine..Brazilian
Recommended for.............................Worth the travel

Epice is a cool haven amid the high-end boutiques of the long, palm-fringed Rua Haddock Lobo and is the relative newcomer of the truly international chef Alberto Landgraf. With Japanese and German blood, Landgraf grew up in Southern Brazil, but learned to cook in London, working alongside Gordon Ramsay and Tom Aikens. The interior is suitably chic and precise, with abundant woods bathed in natural light. Landgraf's food is also finely formed, with the pig the star, viz. the well-regarded crispy pork belly and home-made charcuterie. As the restaurant's name suggests, spice is also a regular component, notably in the dessert of sautéed pear with pain d'épice and pear sorbet.

BLÉS D'OR

Recommended by
Emmanuel Bassoleil

Rua Tuim 653
Moema
São Paulo 04514-103
www.blesdor.com.br

Opening hours.............7 days for breakfast, lunch and dinner
Reservation policy..Yes
Credit cards..Accepted
Price range..Budget
Style...Casual
Cuisine...French
Recommended for.....................................Breakfast

'The quiches and chocolate bread are delicious.'
—Emmanuel Bassoleil

CLOS DE TAPAS

Recommended by
Emmanuel Bassoleil,
Alberto Landgraf

Rio Domingos Fernandes 548
Nova Conceição
São Paulo 0409-011
+55 1130452154
www.closdetapas.com.br

Opening hours.............6 days for lunch and 5 days for dinner
Reservation policy..Yes
Credit cards..Accepted
Price range...'.Affordable
Style...Casual
Cuisine...Brazilian Small plates
Recommended for.............................Worth the travel

'Husband and wife execute creative cuisine with great techniques. '—Emmanuel Bassoleil

BRASSERIE LE JAZZ

Recommended by
Helena Rizzo

Rua dos Pinheiros 254
Pinheiros
São Paulo 05422-012
+55 1123598141
www.lejazz.com.br

Opening hours ....6 days for lunch and 5 days for dinner
Reservation policy..Yes
Credit cards..Accepted
Price range..Affordable
Style...Casual
Cuisine...French
Recommended for.............................Regular neighbourhood

CHOU

Recommended by
Helena Rizzo

Rua Mateus Grou 345
Pinheiros
São Paulo 05415-050
+55 1130836998
www.chou.com.br

Opening hours...5 days for dinner
Reservation policy..Yes
Credit cards..Accepted
Price range..Affordable
Style...Casual
Cuisine..Mediterranean
Recommended for.............................Wish I'd opened

BAR DO GIBA

Avenida Moaci 574
Planalto Paulista
São Paulo 04083-010

Opening hours...............1 day for lunch and 6 days for dinner
Reservation policy..No
Credit cards..Not accepted
Price range...Affordable
Style...Casual
Cuisine..Brazilian
Recommended for...Local favourite

'A simple and great bar to taste nice Brazilian
caipirinhas and snacks.'—Emmanuel Bassoleil

BAR DA DONA ONÇA

Avenida Ipiranga 200
República
São Paulo 01046-010
www.bardadonaonca.com.br

Opening hours...............7 days for lunch and 6 days for dinner
Reservation policy..No
Credit cards..Accepted
Price range...Budget
Style...Casual
Cuisine..Brazilian
Recommended for...Local favourite

SHIN-ZUSHI

Rua Afonso De Freitas 169
Vila Mariana
São Paulo 04006-050
+55 1138898700

Opening hours.............5 days for lunch and 6 days for dinner
Reservation policy...Yes
Credit cards..Accepted
Price range...Affordable
Style...Casual
Cuisine..Japanese
Recommended for...Worth the travel

MOCOTÓ

Avenida Nossa Senhora do
Loreto 1100
Vila Medeiros
São Paulo 02219-001
+55 1129513056
www.mocoto.com.br

Opening hours.............7 days for lunch and 6 days for dinner
Reservation policy..No
Reservation email.............................contato@mocoto.com.br
Credit cards..Accepted
Price range...Budget
Style...Casual
Cuisine..Brazilian
Recommended for...Worth the travel

You will find Mocotó at Vila Medeiros, a traditionally
working-class district of São Paulo. It is run by
Rodrigo Oliveira de Almeida, the son of an émigré
who came to São Paulo seeking his fortune armed
with little more than a couple of shirts, one pair of
trousers (pants) and the shoes on his feet. Dishes
— offered alongside some 350 sturdy *cachacas*
(white rum made from sugar cane) — offer a lighter
version of Northeast Brazil's cuisine. These include
Sarapatel (pork offal/variety meats), *Atolado de Vaca*
(beef stewed with manioc, cherry tomatoes, spring
onions/scallions and olives, served in a pan) and,
only on Sundays, *Paleta de Cordeiro do Velho Chico*
(braised lamb feather blade). *Mocotó* (cow's foot
broth) is the house classic.

MOMOTARO

Recommended by
Emmanuel Bassoleil

Rua Diogo Jácome 591
Vila Nova Conceição
Moema
São Paulo 04512-001
+55 1138425590
www.restaurantemomotaro.com.br

Opening hours	7 days for lunch and dinner
Reservation policy	Yes
Credit cards	Accepted
Price range	Affordable
Style	Casual
Cuisine	Modern Japanese
Recommended for	Bargain

'Incredible, innovative Japanese food.'
—Emmanuel Bassoleil

MARISMO

Recommended by
Julien Duboué

Ruta 10, km 185
Jose Ignacio
Maldonado
Uruguay
+598 424862273

Opening hours	7 days for dinner
Reservation policy	Yes
Credit cards	Not accepted
Price range	Affordable
Style	Casual
Cuisine	Uruguayan
Recommended for	Worth the travel

PARADOR LA HUELLA

Recommended by
Stephen Stryjewski

Playa Brava
Jose Ignacio
Maldonado
Uruguay
+598 44862279
www.paradorlahuella.com

Opening hours	7 days for lunch and dinner
Reservation policy	Yes
Credit cards	Accepted
Price range	Affordable
Style	Casual
Cuisine	Uruguayan
Recommended for	Worth the travel

EL POBRE LUIS

Recommended by
Fernando Trocca

Calle Arribeños 2393
Esquina Blanco Encalada
Belgrano
Buenos Aires C1428APE
Argentina
+54 1147805847

Opening hours	6 days for dinner
Reservation policy	Yes
Credit cards	Accepted
Price range	Affordable
Style	Casual
Cuisine	Steakhouse
Recommended for	Local favourite

'The best sweet bread in the world.'—Fernando Trocca

CASA CRUZ

Recommended by
Matias Palomo Reyes

Calle Uriarte 1658
Palermo Viejo
Buenos Aires C1414DAR
Argentina
+54 1148331112
www.casacruz-restaurant.com

Opening hours	6 days for dinner
Reservation policy	Yes
Reservation email	reservas@casa-cruzrestaurant.com
Credit cards	Accepted
Price range	Expensive
Style	Smart casual
Cuisine	Modern Argentinian
Recommended for	Worth the travel

This is one of the trendiest restaurants in Buenos Aires, popular with the young and beautiful. Beyond the 5-m (16-ft) high brass doors, the large dining room is sleek and romantic, with subtle lighting, a lot of moody black and red, mahogany panelling, comfortable chairs, and wine bottles stacked from floor to ceiling. Chef Germán Martitegui's cooking is classically inspired but has modern accents. Veal comes with crisp potatoes and a green pepper sauce, there's a good mushroom risotto, and king crab is accompanied by pear shavings. But be warned that the wine list includes some rather bold mark-ups.

TEGUI

Calle Costa Rica 5852
Palermo Viejo
Buenos Aires C1414BTJ
Argentina
+54 1152913333
www.tegui.com.ar

Opening hours	5 days for lunch and dinner
Reservation policy	Yes
Reservation email	info@tegui.com.ar
Credit cards	Accepted
Price range	Expensive
Style	Smart casual
Cuisine	Modern Argentinian
Recommended for	Worth the travel

UNIK

Soler 5132
Palermo Viejo
Buenos Aires C1425BXN
Argentina
+54 1147722230
www.unik.pro

Opening hours	5 days for lunch and 6 days for dinner
Reservation policy	Yes
Credit cards	Accepted
Price range	Expensive
Style	Smart casual
Cuisine	Modern Argentinian
Recommended for	Worth the travel

The creation of French Argentine architect Marcelo Joulia, Unik is a bar, restaurant and design hub in the stylish Palermo barrio of Buenos Aires. A mismatched array of carefully selected furniture, such as design classics by Charles Eames, hotchpotch hanging lights and 1970s Formica tables makes for a setting as zeitgeisty as the menu. Appetizers include beef carpaccio with olive oil ice cream and a cold almond gazpacho. Keep room for their speciality main of Patagonian lamb cooked two ways. Finish off with dulce de leche sandwiched between mascarpone macaroons and wash down with one of many wines, including some serious Argentine Malbecs.

CARLITOS LNG

Calle Guido 1962
Recoleta
Buenos Aires C1119AAD
Argentina
+54 1147471025
www.carlitoslng.com.ar

Opening hours	7 days for breakfast, lunch and dinner
Reservation policy	Yes
Credit cards	Accepted
Price range	Budget
Style	Casual
Cuisine	Fast food
Recommended for	Bargain

L'ORANGERIE

Alvear Palace Hotel
Avenida Alvear 1891
Recoleta
Buenos Aires C1129AAA
Argentina
+54 1148082949
www.alvearpalace.com

Opening hours	7 days for breakfast and lunch
Reservation policy	Yes
Reservation email	lorangerie@alvear.com.ar
Credit cards	Accepted
Price range	Expensive
Style	Smart casual
Cuisine	Cafe
Recommended for	Breakfast

'I'll never forget their fine home-made pastries.'
—Alberto Chicote

LA COCINA DE LA ÑAÑA

La Cocina Mapu Iyagl
La ruta Pucón
Curarrehue
Cautín
Chile
+56 987887188

Opening hours	7 days from breakfast until late
Reservation policy	Yes
Reservation email	raykiyen@yahoo.com
Credit cards	Not accepted
Price range	Budget
Style	Casual
Cuisine	Chilean
Recommended for	Local favourite

'Anita Epulef Panguilef cooks for tourists with whatever seasonal ingredients are available. The place it is just amazing, the surroundings and the local produce. It is something that you won't find anywhere else in the world.'—Rodolfo Guzmán

ALTIPLÁNICO HOTEL

Lote E, Sector Hinere
Easter Island 2770000
Chile
+56 322552190
www.altiplanico.cl

Opening hours.............7 days for breakfast, lunch and dinner
Reservation policy...Yes
Reservation email..................centralventas@altiplanico.com
Credit cards...Accepted
Price range..Expensive
Style...Casual
Cuisine...Chilean
Recommended for...Breakfast

'Located in one of the most beautiful and interesting places on earth, it's an amazing experience. They serve *poe*, a kind of native bread that they make with seven different kinds of banana.'—Rodolfo Guzmán

KIOSKO ROCA

Calle Presidente Jullo Roca 875
Punta Arenas
Magallanes 6201065
Chile

Opening hours...........................6 days for breakfast and lunch
Reservation policy..No
Credit cards...Not accepted
Price range..Budget
Style...Casual
Cuisine...Café
Recommended for...Breakfast

EL HOYO

San Vicente 375
Estación Central
Santiago 8370329
Chile
+56 26890339
www.elhoyo.cl

Opening hours...............................6 days for lunch and dinner
Reservation policy...Yes
Credit cards...Accepted
Price range...Budget
Style...Casual
Cuisine...Chilean
Recommended for...Local favourite

'Traditional Chilean food: ribs, veal shanks, black puddings (blood sausages) and tongue.'—Matias Palomo Reyes

LA PIOJERA

Calle Aillavilú 1030
Santiago 8320355
Chile
www.lapiojera.cl

Opening hours...........................6 days for lunch and dinner
Reservation policy..No
Credit cards...Not accepted
Price range...Budget
Style...Casual
Cuisine...Chilean
Recommended for...Local favourite

CAFÉ MELBA

Don Carlos 2898
Local 1, Las Condes
Santiago 7550115
Chile

Opening hours...........................7 days for breakfast and lunch
Reservation policy..No
Credit cards...Accepted
Price range...Budget
Style...Casual
Cuisine...International
Recommended for...Breakfast

FUENTE CHILENA

Avenida Apoquindo 4900
Local 110, Las Condes
Santiago 7560973
Chile
+56 22286756
www.fuentechilena.cl

Opening hours	6 days for lunch and dinner
Reservation policy	Yes
Credit cards	Accepted
Price range	Budget
Style	Casual
Cuisine	Sandwiches
Recommended for	Late night

COQUINARIA

Isidora Goyenechea 3000
Local S-101, Las Condes
Santiago 7550653
Chile
+56 22451958
www.coquinaria.cl

Opening hours	7 days for breakfast, lunch and dinner
Reservation policy	Yes
Credit cards	Accepted
Price range	Affordable
Style	Smart casual
Cuisine	International
Recommended for	Breakfast

LA BAMBA

Avenida Vicuña Mackenna 976
Ñuñoa
Santiago 7750555
Chile

Opening hours	7 days for lunch and dinner
Reservation policy	No
Credit cards	Not accepted
Price range	Budget
Style	Casual
Cuisine	Fast food
Recommended for	Late night

AQUÍ ESTÁ COCO

La Concepción 236
Providencia
Santiago 7500014
Chile
+56 24106200
www.aquiestacoco.cl

Opening hours	6 days for lunch and dinner
Reservation policy	Yes
Credit cards	Accepted
Price range	Affordable
Style	Smart casual
Cuisine	Seafood
Recommended for	Wish I'd opened

'This place is a must in Chile! It's a great spot where you can try the biggest king crabs on earth.'
—Rodolfo Guzmán

DONDE EL GUATÓN

Avenida Manuel Montt 536
Providencia
Santiago 7500664
Chile
+56 29187794
www.dondeelguaton.cl

Opening hours	7 days for lunch and dinner
Reservation policy	No
Credit cards	Not accepted
Price range	Budget
Style	Casual
Cuisine	Sandwiches
Recommended for	Late night

FUENTE ALEMANA

Avenida Pedro de Valdivia Norte 210
Providencia
Santiago 7520254
Chile

Opening hours	6 days for breakfast, lunch and dinner
Reservation policy	No
Credit cards	Not accepted
Price range	Budget
Style	Casual
Cuisine	Sandwiches
Recommended for	Bargain

'This place does the best sandwiches ever.'—Matias Palomo Reyes

LIGURIA MANUEL MONTT

Recommended by
Matias Palomo Reyes

Avenida Providencia 1373
Providencia
Santiago 7500576
Chile
+56 22357914
www.liguria.cl

Opening hours	6 days for lunch and dinner
Reservation policy	No
Credit cards	Accepted
Price range	Budget
Style	Casual
Cuisine	Italian
Recommended for	Late night

CASAMAR

Recommended by
Matias Palomo Reyes

Avenida Padre Hurtado Norte 1480
Vitacura
Santiago 7650191
Chile
+56 29542112
www.restaurantcasamar.cl

Opening hours	7 days for lunch and 6 days for dinner
Reservation policy	Yes
Credit cards	Accepted
Price range	Affordable
Style	Smart casual
Cuisine	Modern Chilean
Recommended for	High end

OSADÍA

Recommended by
Matias Palomo Reyes

Avenida Nueva Costanera 3677
Vitacura
Santiago 7630485
Chile
+56 2065549
www.osadiarestoran.cl

Opening hours	6 days for lunch and dinner
Reservation policy	Yes
Credit cards	Accepted
Price range	Expensive
Style	Smart casual
Cuisine	Modern Chilean
Recommended for	High end

Osadía, which means 'audacity', occupies a beautiful neo-classical building on a quiet street in Vitacura, one of Santiago's more upmarket districts. The decor is cooling and romantic: black and white tiles, high ceilings, the tables spaced far apart. There's also a gorgeous terrace and a garden. The chef Carlo von Mühlenbrock is rather famous, appearing frequently on Chilean TV. His food is high-end but unfussy. A typical menu might be turbot à la plancha, ricotta ravioli with finely chopped aubergine (eggplant) and courgette (zucchini), grilled grouper with mushy peas, followed by perhaps a bitter chocolate terrine with yogurt panna cotta to finish.

AQUÍ JAIME

Recommended by
Rodolfo Guzmán

Avenida Borgoño 21303
Caleta Higuerillas
Concón
Valparaíso 2510866
Chile
+56 322812042
www.aquijaime.cl

Opening hours	7 days for lunch and 5 days for dinner
Reservation policy	Yes
Reservation email	reservas@aquijaime.cl
Credit cards	Accepted
Price range	Budget
Style	Casual
Cuisine	Seafood
Recommended for	Regular neighbourhood

'A very casual restaurant where you can get fresh Chilean seafood, especially *locos*, delicious native sea snails. If you are going there you have to try them. There are no words… they're simply amazing!'
    Rodolfo Guzmán

INDEX BY RESTAURANT

INDEX BY TYPE

REGULAR NEIGHBOURHOOD

WISH I'D OPENED

WORTH THE TRAVEL

Phaidon Press Limited
Regent's Wharf
All Saints Street
London N1 9AP

Phaidon Press Inc.
180 Varick Street
New York, NY 10014

www.phaidon.com

First published in 2013
© 2013 Phaidon Press Limited

ISBN 978 0 7148 6541 6

A CIP catalogue record for this book
is available from the British Library.

As many restaurants are closed Sunday and/or
Monday, and some change their opening hours
in relation to the seasons or close for extended
periods at different times of the year, it is always
advisable to check opening hours before visiting.
All information is correct at the time of going to
print, but is subject to change.

Commissioning Editor: Emilia Terragni
Project Editors: Sophie Hodgkin and Emma Robertson
Production Controller: Laurence Poos

Designed by Kobi Benezri

The publisher would like to thank all the participating
chefs for their generosity, time and insightful
restaurant recommendations; Joe Warwick for his
commitment and enthusiasm; and Hilary Armstrong,
Tania Ballantine, Rosie Birkett, Trish Deseine,
Douglas Blyde, Stefan Chomka, Adam Coghlan, Tim
Glynne-Jones, Corinna Hardgrave, Mina Holland,
Clodagh Kinsella, Anna Longmore, Andy Lynes, Laura
Nickoll, Chris Pople, Gregor Shepherd and Oliver
Thring for their contributions to the book.

Printed in Italy